THE FLAMES
OF ROME

Books by Paul L. Maier

THE FLAMES OF ROME

A DOCUMENTARY NOVEL
BY PAUL L. MAIER

DOUBLEDAY & COMPANY, INC.
GARDEN CITY, NEW YORK
1981

Library of Congress Cataloging in Publication Data

Maier, Paul L
The flames of Rome.

1. Sabinus, Flavius, ca. 8-69—Fiction. 2. Rome—
History—Claudius, 41-54—Fiction. 3. Rome—History
—Nero, 54-68—Fiction. 4. Church history—Primitive
and early church, ca. 30-600—Fiction. I. Title.
PS3563.A382F57 813'.54
ISBN: 0-385-17091-2
Library of Congress Catalog Card Number: 80-2561
Copyright © 1981 by Paul L. Maier
All Rights Reserved
Printed in the United States of America
First Edition

For
Laura and Julie

CONTENTS

CONTENTS

PREFACE

SOME of the most extraordinary, colorful, and tragic events in all of history shook Rome in the score of years following A.D. 47. Claudius and then Nero ruled over that volatile blend of idealism, sensuality, and cruelty which was the Roman Empire. Into such an unlikely setting Christianity made its own quiet—then shocking—entry, and a mortal struggle between the worlds of power and faith began. This is a serious attempt to reconstruct that conflict through portrayal of a Roman family caught up in the clash.

Since the true story of these times is so much more intriguing than the many fictionalized versions, I have not tampered with known facts in retelling it—unlike almost all historical novelists—nor invented characters that could never match the kind who actually lived in this era. The factual undergirding is documented in the Notes, some of which unveil new historical data.

But here as elsewhere in ancient history, yawning gaps in the original sources prevent any telling of the *full* story. I have tried to fill these in by devising a genre which I call the "documentary novel," resorting to fiction for such connective material as well as dramatization, dialogue, and subplot to flesh out the story and bring its characters to life.

To insure accuracy, I adopted these rules: 1) All persons named in the book are historical; no proper name has been invented—if it is not known, it is not given. 2) No portrayal of any personality, description of any event, episode, or even detail contradicts historical fact (unless by author's error). 3) Only where all evidence is lacking is "constructed history," based on probabilities, used to fill in the gaps. Such created segments are clearly identified in the Notes.

These rules in no way curb the drama of these incredible times, and readers should rather gain the added satisfaction of knowing that much of what they are reading actually *did* happen, while the rest could well have happened.

Though several episodes in these pages may seem lurid or jar our sensibilities, all are historical—none is contrived; as authentic fertilizer in the Roman seedbed of Christianity, it would have been dishonest to omit them.

P.L.M.

Western Michigan University
July 18, 1980—the 1916th Anniversary of The Great Fire

BOOK ONE

THE HEARTH

1

SPRING was daubing a drab and hibernating Italy with brush strokes of fertile green. High in the Apennines, the last patches of snow were surrendering to fragrant Mediterranean winds, and the boot-shaped peninsula seemed to quiver in rebirth, as if this year at last—A.D. 47—it would find the energy to give Sicily that great kick it had threatened for ages.

The city of Rome was already in full blossom, at least in mood, because in Roman reckoning this was the anniversary year 800 A.U.C. The Latin initials for *ab urbe condita,* "from the founding of the city," fairly shouted the fact that Rome had stood for eight proud centuries, during which she had spread across her seven hills and mastered all of Italy. Then, as if answering some trumpet call of destiny, she had gone on to conquer the entire Mediterranean world.

Claudius Caesar, Rome's bandy-legged but able emperor, was doing his imperial best to celebrate the anniversary with games, festivals, and religious observances. Once he even climbed up the endless staircase to the Capitoline Temple on his arthritic knees—Rome winced for him at every step—to inform Jupiter of the civic milestone.

Now in his seventh year as emperor—"and my fifty-sixth as a human being," he would quickly add, in a weak drollery that never quite succeeded—Claudius seemed shortchanged by life. A childhood paralysis had left him with a wobbly head, a speech defect, and a halting gait, though his own mother surely exaggerated his motor handicaps when she called him "a monster of a man, begun but never finished by Mother Nature." Some in the Senate would clutch their togas and ape his shambling pace, imploring the gods to loosen the stammering tongue of "Clau-Clau-Claudius." His critics were sure that the three new letters he had added to the alphabet —Ⅎ, Ↄ, and Ⱶ—would not endure (and they were right), and even his love life had become stock comedy on the streets of Rome.

But high above the Forum's laughter in his sprawling palace on the Palatine hill, Claudius Caesar was indulging in the final smile. He knew that a lucid mind lurked underneath his whitish shock of hair. Even his foes had to admit that he had stabilized the Empire after the mad Caligula, and had also added dramatically to its boundaries. Whenever he found himself listening too closely to criticism or gossip, Claudius would amble over to the colossal map of the Empire that covered an entire wall in his office suite and smile at the great island on the northwestern corner, now shaded in with Rome's colors: *Britannia!* He, Claudius the Clown, Lord of the Lurch, Wobblemaster of the World, had conquered Britannia!

It was because of this conquest that T. Flavius Sabinus had to have an audience with the emperor one morning early in May. A smartly dressed lieutenant commander, fresh from the Roman forces in Britain, Sabinus was waved inside the palace and now paced through its marbled corridors to the entrance chamber of Claudius' office suite. A Greek-looking man of slender build rose from his desk, extending a perfumed hand of greeting. "Ah . . . welcome, Flavius Sabinus!" said the second most powerful man in the Roman Empire.

"Greetings, worthy Narcissus!" Sabinus responded, while thinking, *Worthy* indeed—worth, say, 400 million sesterces as secretary of state . . . not bad for an ex-slave. But Sabinus ventured only the obvious query: "Is the emperor expecting me?"

"Indeed. Please follow me."

The aging, imperial huddle of flesh, well insulated in the folds of a plain white toga, sat at a sprawling desk of polished cyprus, squinting at reports from Britain. Looking up at Sabinus, Claudius stared for a moment, as if trying to recall who the tall, well-structured intruder might be. Then he brightened and came to life. "Well, well,

Ca-Commander, you don't seem to have aged any since we fought together in the north country four years ago. Not a trace of gray in that black thatch of hair. Why yu-you're handsome as ever."

"And you, Caesar, are looking admirably fit," Sabinus lied.

"So, y-you're just back from Britannia. Tell me, how's my friend Aulus Plautius? And w-when is he due back in Rome?"

The pleasant sparkle in Claudius' lead-blue eyes made Sabinus overlook the soft slurs and occasional stutters that pock-marked the emperor's speech. He also knew the stammer would fade once their conversation got under way. "The governor general sends you his warmest greetings, Caesar," Sabinus replied, in an officer's baritone. "I was sent ahead to report their arrival plans. At this moment they should be crossing the Alps, which would bring them to Rome about the Ides of June."

"Hmmm. A month from now." Claudius cupped his chin in thought, then turned to his freedman secretary. "Well, Narcissus, how shall we celebrate his return?"

"Ah yes." The secretary frowned slightly, for he had given no real thought to the matter. "Well, perhaps a . . . a state dinner would be appropriate."

Claudius' lips broke into a low smile. "And you, Sabinus? Do you think that would be sufficient?"

Sabinus reddened a bit and replied, "I'm sure the governor general would be honored by such a dinner, although—" He cut himself off.

"Although what?"

"Nothing, Princeps," said Sabinus, using the alternate name for emperor that meant "first citizen."

"Oh, but you had something else in mind," Claudius insisted.

"It's just that—now please understand that Aulus Plautius mentioned nothing of this—but doesn't Rome usually confer a *public* welcome on her conquering generals?"

"It was the *emperor* who conquered Britannia," Narcissus interposed coldly. "And he has already celebrated a triumph for it. Don't be impertinent, Commander."

An ex-slave talking to him of impertinence? Turning angrily to Narcissus, Sabinus spat the syllables out. "*Of course* Caesar conquered Britannia! But have you forgotten who designed the strategy? And who led most of the fighting? And who diplomatically held our forces to the banks of the Thames until Caesar could get up there and take command for the final victory? A victory Aulus Plautius had all but won?"

"Impudence!" Narcissus gasped, turning pale as his bleached tunic.

"*Impudence?*" Sabinus struggled to contain his rage. "Perhaps. But the truth nevertheless."

In an instant, Sabinus regretted his last statements. They were accurate, the gods knew, but they were hardly diplomatic. And talking that way before the person who could adjust one's destiny with the wave of a hand was at least foolhardy. He looked over to Claudius and saw his pinkish complexion turning turgid red. His lips had parted, and a string of drool started dangling from a corner of his mouth. His head was pitching slightly from side to side, the nervous tic that affected him whenever he was under stress.

"I . . . I'm sorry, Princeps," Sabinus apologized. "Our forces were . . . *much* heartened by your arrival in Britain. Forgive me."

Claudius made no reply. The room grew mortally silent. Had he really managed to offend the two most powerful men in the world *that* quickly, Sabinus wondered. Was truth that urgent? Cursed be that foolish tongue of his which had once again responded to mood rather than clear thought.

"Heh-heh-heh-heh."

Sabinus looked up to see Claudius grinning at him, and then chuckling some more in his inimitable cluck. Narcissus, too, appeared startled.

"Heh-heh-heh," Claudius affirmed. "Y-you're right, of course, Sabinus. I wasn't glaring at you at all just now, but at you, Narcissus."

"At *me*, Princeps?"

"Yes, of course. For daring to call Sabinus impudent. He's not impudent . . . no, not at all. *Honest* he is, not impudent."

"But Caesar . . ."

"Silence, Narcissus!" Then Claudius turned to Sabinus and smiled. "By the gods, Commander, that *is* the way it was: Aulus Plautius won Britannia for us. *He* did the work, but *I* got the glory. —Well, no matter. Now I'll share some of that glory, in the name of honesty alone." Pitching himself toward them, he chortled, "Yes, honesty . . . something we need more of around here, eh, Narcissus?"

"What do you propose, Caesar?" Narcissus asked coolly. "You know it dare not be a triumph."

"Oh, don't play the pedant with me, Narcissus!" Claudius huffed, sliding his bony fingers through whitish wisps of hair as he shuttled unsteadily between them. "Yes, I know: only the Caesars celebrate triumphs now. Very well, then. Let it be an ovation."

Sabinus broke into a beaming smile, while Claudius happily winked at him. The coveted *ovatio* was a lavish celebration nearly as impressive as the full-dress triumph.

"But, Caesar," Sabinus demurred, "will the Senate agree?"

Claudius turned to his secretary. "Isn't the Senate in session at the moment, Narcissus?"

"Yes, Princeps."

"Then go over and make the necessary arrangements. Immediately. Sabinus and I will look in there within the hour."

A minor guard of a dozen praetorians escorted Claudius and Sabinus as they walked down the heights of the Palatine and crossed the Forum to the Senate house. The emperor led Sabinus into an alcove that overlooked the Senate chamber, where they could watch the proceedings unobserved to avoid the fuss and formality of an official welcome. Below him, Sabinus saw a quorum of about 300 senators, all wrapped in the voluminous folds of their togas, listening to the presiding consul, who had already opened deliberations on an ovation for Aulus Plautius. In a sonorous Latin that rattled off the semicircular marble benches of the chamber, he called out the prescribed questions.

"*Iustum bellum?*" "Was Plautius waging a just war?"

"*Certe! Certe!*" responded the senators, "Certainly!" There was no opposition.

"*Quinque milia occisi?*" "Were at least 5,000 of the enemy slain in a single battle?"

"*Certe.*"

After further ritual queries, there were cries of "*Divid-e! Divid-e!*" —calls for the usual vote by separation.

The consul held up his hands for order. "All in favor of the ovation for Aulus Plautius move to the right side of the chamber," he directed. "Those opposed, to the left."

Several hundred toga-clad figures rose together, but instead of threading past each other, as on normal votes, they all walked to the right side of the hall.

"Done," Claudius whispered. "And unanimously. So you see, Sabinus, I didn't exactly keep Plautius' role in Britannia a secret."

"I'm delighted, Caesar. In the name of our legions, I thank you."

"A final matter. When did you say Aulus plans to return to Rome?"

"About the Ides of June."

Claudius' eyes had a playful sparkle. "I have a weakness, Sabinus —well, perhaps many weaknesses, but one in particular: surprises. I dote on them. Now, when you return to the governor general, you are to say *nothing* about the ovation. Only the banquet, do you understand? When you reach your last encampment north of Rome, you'll send a messenger to me, and this is how we'll work it out . . ."

As they broke camp at dawn on June 14, Aulus Plautius mustered his troops for a final review. He stood tall as a six-foot Roman javelin and almost as straight. Middle age had grayed his hair, and four northern winters had tautened his skin into a rough canvas which only accentuated his squarish forehead, the wide-set eyes, the determined mouth and chin. Now he mounted his great, bay-colored horse—a souvenir from Britain's Medway—and called over to his lieutenant commander. "Last leg of our journey, Sabinus, thank the blessed Fates! We should reach Rome just after midday, not?"

"Early afternoon. Which will leave us time to freshen up for Claudius' dinner."

"*Bah!* Couldn't you have talked him out of that?"

"Not one for fuss and ceremonial, are you, Governor?" Sabinus grinned. "Are you sure you wouldn't have preferred a parade? Perfect day for it."

"*Sweet Jupiter*, no!" He frowned. Then he gave the order to march.

They clattered onto the Via Flaminia and continued southward. A long column of legionaries followed them on horse and foot, each troop quickening its pace in anticipation of seeing Rome again. By noon they had approached the Tiber River bridge. Aulus Plautius halted his forces on the north bank and stared down at the sluggish yellow-green waters that sloshed around the northwestern edge of Rome. Then he peered at the maroon brick walls of the city itself in the distance and frowned. "Something's wrong, Sabinus. Haven't you noticed?"

"No, Governor. What?"

"The people. There aren't any *people* around!"

"Of course there are." Sabinus pointed to several old men staring at them quizzically from the upper story of a tenement, and a woman nursing her baby behind flapping curtains.

"Don't be foolish. Here we are, just outside the largest city in the world and no people! Something's wrong, Sabinus. Sickness? Plague?"

"I . . . I've no idea." Sabinus was trying his best to share Aulus' frown.

They marched across the bridge and finally reached the massive walls of the city, pierced only by two small arches of light that were the Flaminian Gate. Aulus took the lead in trotting through it, followed by his cavalcade.

An overpowering roar thundered down upon them. Tens of thousands were massed on both sides of the Via Flaminia inside the city, trying to burst through a double line of Praetorian Guards stationed along the roadway as far as they could see. Aulus Plautius' jaw sagged limply at the human forest of swaying arms and the shrill screams of the citizenry.

"It seems we've located a few of the people you were worried about," Sabinus chuckled, enormously relieved that the emperor's little game had succeeded.

"Your work?" Aulus demanded.

Sabinus shook his head and grinned. "Claudius'. It's a formal *ovation*, Governor, and eminently justified, I would add.—Ho there, Vespasian!" Sabinus called to his brother, a fellow commander who was mounted on the other side of Aulus. "Help me with this toga."

Ignoring Aulus' dazed protests and almost pulling him off his mount, the brother officers removed his traveling cape and draped him in the folds of a toga fringed with royal purple, standard dress for one receiving an ovation. Then they pressed a wreath of myrtle onto his graying locks and finally helped him back onto his horse. Raising an arm in stiff salute, Sabinus called out, "Hail, Aulus Plautius, conqueror of Britannia! *Io triumphe!*"

"*IO TRIUMPHE!*" the troops and multitude erupted in colossal unison, and the procession began. A large delegation of senators and magistrates joined the cavalcade, while a corps of flute players started piping. Straight as a spear, the Via Flaminia skewered their way through the shouting masses into the very heart of Rome. Three quarters of the city's million inhabitants were shrieking their appreciation to Aulus Plautius for delivering Britain to them. Incense smoked from every altar, flower garlands sprouted from the shrines, and everywhere the waving arms and endless cheering.

Flanking Aulus on each side a horse's length behind were Sabinus and Vespasian, exchanging grins of relief that their general had finally gotten into the spirit of the day, for at last he was smiling to acknowledge the cheers and waving his myrtle wreath from time to time.

Now they had reached the Roman Forum, a canyon of swarming humanity, reverberating with applause and shouting. The noise was overpowering, and Sabinus had some difficulty controlling his skittish mount, whose ears had flattened in a vain attempt to escape the sound. Suddenly a man dashed out of the crowd, yelling, "Remember, Plautius, you're *only a man!*" Then he shoved a scourge under Aulus' saddle. Vespasian leaned over and clamped the man's arm in a powerful grip.

"Let him go, brother! It's part of the ritual!" Sabinus laughed. "Whenever Romans treat somebody like a god, they also remind him that he's merely brother to a slave—"

"Hence the scourge," Vespasian nodded, sheepishly releasing his grip.

A brisk trumpet flourish plunged the Forum into incongruous silence. Sabinus squinted against the sun, but then his face bloomed with a great smile. Standing in the middle of the Sacred Way was the emperor himself. Claudius was not supposed to have joined them until the end of the procession, but here he was, honoring them even earlier. "*Hail, Caesar!*" cried Aulus, in formal salute.

"Hail, Aulus Plautius!" replied Claudius. "May I have the privilege of accompanying you to the Capitoline?"

"It would be a supreme honor, my comrade-in-arms!"

Just the right touch, Sabinus thought, for it underscored the emperor's role in Britain. Claudius beamed and then looked over to say, "Well done, Flavius Sabinus! A complete surprise, I take it?"

"My own brother here didn't know, Caesar!"

"Splendid. Just splendid!"

They all dismounted as the procession continued on foot. Aulus moved to the left of the emperor to accord him the place of honor. Claudius frowned and pulled him over to his right. "No, friend. Today we honor the conqueror of Britannia!"

Winding past the Senate house, the Sacred Way brought them to the foot of the great staircase up to the Temple of Jupiter Capitoline, the lofty citadel of Rome that was the goal of the cavalcade. Now a thunderous applause rattled down on them from every side.

"Turn around and smile, gentlemen," Claudius advised. "There are times when a person must not be modest. This is one of them."

After thirty ponderous steps up the staircase, Claudius lurched to one side and almost collapsed. "No, no!" he huffed. "Don't try to help me. I'll make it up this accursed mountain." He paused to catch his breath and then commented, "It seems Father Jupiter doesn't hear very well. We have to climb halfway to heaven before he catches our prayers."

Aulus chuckled and said, "You shouldn't have gone to this exertion, Caesar. Meeting us up at the temple would have been honor enough."

"Oh, I'm merely showing our Romans that they still have an ambulatory emperor. There are rumors that I'm a senile old carcass"—he grinned wryly—"and maybe I am. But, by Hades, I'm a walking one."

Finally, with Claudius wheezing and gasping, they reached the very summit of Rome, the ridge of the Capitoline hill on which towered the classic columns of the Temple of Jupiter. The afternoon sun splashed across its searing white marble, constricting Sabinus' eyes to narrow slits as he took in the breathtaking panorama of the city flowing down from them in all directions—the brick and marble, stadiums and temples, streets, parks, and baths that were Rome.

At last the whole procession had filed onto the esplanade in front of the temple. The emperor, now facing them on a lofty dais, nodded to the priest of Jupiter, who would serve as augur. The priest picked up a lamb and gently cradled its head in his left arm. Then he raised a mallet with his right and smashed it down on the animal's skull. The lamb twitched and died instantly. Several other priests slit open its belly, while the augur carefully probed inside to find the liver. For several moments he peered at the crimson viscera, then announced, "*Exta bona!*" "The entrails are favorable." The ceremony could now proceed.

"My fellow Romans," Claudius began, in a surprisingly firm voice. "Let us celebrate again the conquest of Britannia and honor the man who led our legions to victory." And the emperor's address all but conquered Britain again, tracing the invasion from the Channel to the Midlands.

Sabinus, standing at attention, was reliving the campaign when his gaze fell to the right of the dais and he saw a pair of smiling eyes fastened on him from among the official guests. Looking back to Claudius, he found his memory adding brush strokes to form the portrait of an uncommonly attractive girl. His mind was probably playing tricks. He stole a glance at her again, and found that he was wrong. The girl was not pretty at all—she was instead beautiful. Spectacularly so.

Again he stared at her, and felt a stab of chagrin: the girl's eyes were not locked on him after all but on Aulus Plautius, who was standing a half step in front of him. Aulus now stood forward as Claudius read from an official proclamation, engraved on a bronze tablet:

For extraordinary services rendered to
the Senate and the Roman People
in the conquest of Britannia

AULUS PLAUTIUS

was accorded an ovation
in the consulship of Lucius
Vitellius and Claudius Caesar, DCCC A.U.C.

Volleys of acclaim erupted, the sound cascading down the Capitoline, and it was fully five minutes before Aulus could acknowledge the ovation from the dais with a brief response.

Sabinus' eye was wandering again. The girl was still beaming at Aulus, and he noticed her profile for the first time. Too perfectly sculptured, he mused, even the nose. Then came the blunder he would never be allowed to forget. He failed to hear the emperor's final surprise. "Two Roman officers," Claudius was saying, "must also be commended for their wisdom during the Britannic campaign. It happens that they are brothers: T. Flavius Vespasian and T. Flavius Sabinus. Gentlemen, stand forward!"

Vespasian broke rank, presented himself, and saluted. But Sabinus just stood in place, apparently lost in thought.

Dumbfounded, Claudius barked, "Flavius Sabinus, *stand forward!*"

Jolted back to reality, Sabinus complied at once, his face flushing a healthy shade of scarlet. Now the emperor solemnly approached them, hanging triumphal medallions around Vespasian's neck, and then his own, amid general applause.

A pair of white bulls, their horns painted gleaming gold, were now led before Aulus Plautius. Taking out his commander's dagger, he drove it deep into the throats of the pair and slit them. Bellowing in a frenzy, each bull collapsed, gushing dark crimson across the pavement. Then, while the priests completed the sacrifice, Aulus went inside the temple and laid his myrtle wreath at the base of the great statue of Jupiter. For several moments he gazed into the huge stone eyes of Zeus, trying to detect some glint of appreciation for his gift. Smiling at the useless effort, he then turned about and left the temple. With a final fanfare, the ovation was over.

"By all the gods, Sabinus, whatever happened to *you* just now?" Aulus asked, after the ceremonies. "Were my remarks really *that* boring?"

"Certainly not, sir. I was—"

"Great gods! There they are!" Aulus shouted. "My family!" He hurried over to a knot of people gathered to the right of the dais. Sabinus saw him rush into the outspread arms of a stola-draped woman in tears. "Pomponia, Pomponia," he whispered.

"At last you're ours again, my husband," she sighed. "It's been . . . so *many* months."

The surging joy of the moment nearly overcame Aulus. He pulled himself back to arm's length and caressed each gentle curve on Pomponia's face, as if to familiarize himself with old, and loved, territory.

"But where's little Plautia?" he suddenly remembered. "And who is *this* radiant young woman?"

"Yes, who *is* she?" Sabinus almost whispered. It was the face in the crowd that had immobilized him. No mirage that disappeared on approach, the girl, if anything, was even more striking at close range.

"Oh—you know it's me, Father." Plautia blushed. "Have I really changed *that* much?"

"A full metamorphosis!" He beamed, giving his daughter a resounding kiss. "When I left for the North, you were a pudgy little chub of a girl. Now look at you! Why you're almost as lovely as your mother."

An identification at last, Sabinus thought, and he had to agree with the family banter. Pomponia's features, crowned by chestnut tresses, were soft and balanced and not exaggerated in any part, something of a rarity among Roman women who so often just missed beauty by the bend of a nose or the warp of a mouth. Her serene face had blended with her husband's distinguished facial accents to produce the beauty in Plautia, Sabinus calculated, a bubbling, effusive girl of probably sixteen—younger than he had at first supposed and doubtless bravely reaching toward womanhood.

"Oho, there you are, Sabinus," said Aulus. "Poor bachelor—he has no family to welcome him. Well, we have more than enough family for you here." With that he began introducing Sabinus to the numerous Plautii and Pomponii, for all the relatives on both sides had gathered to help celebrate Aulus' great hour. Putting his arm around a broad-shouldered young senator, Aulus said, "Here's the pride of the clan, Sabinus, my nephew—"

"Quintus Plautius Lateranus!" Sabinus exclaimed. "How are you, friend?" He clasped both hands to his shoulders.

"Hello, Sabinus!" Quintus beamed. "You're looking marvelously fit."

"Oh, that's right," said Aulus. "You do know each other."

"*Know* each other?" Sabinus exclaimed. "Just before you dragged me off to Britain with you, I put every sesterce I could scrape together into Quintus' hands to invest. So how did we do, Senator?"

Lateranus' smile faded. "Not as well as I'd hoped, Sabinus." He paused, shuffled, and continued. "The orange groves in Apulia caught a blight. Then our pottery works in Arretium ran out of clay . . . and you know the grain ship we had half of?"

"Yes?"

"Our half sank. We're wiped out."

For exactly two seconds, Lateranus held his look of death. Then the corners of his mouth twitched out of control and he bent over laughing. "Just the opposite, Sabinus! It's all gone better than we schemed." He leaned over to whisper, "What would you say to . . . 150 percent on your funds in four years?"

Sabinus let out a whoop, lifting the stocky Lateranus off his feet. "Oh, put me down, do," Quintus said in an effeminate tone. "Else they may guess why neither of us got married."

Sabinus dropped him like a stone. "*Idiot!*" he laughed.

"Tell me, Quintus," Aulus interposed. "Was Sabinus here telling me the truth about the Senate's vote on my ovation? Wasn't there *any* opposition?"

"No, Uncle. The Fathers hurried over to the right like so many sheep at feeding time."

"You're sure you were actually *in* the Senate that day, and not off somewhere adding another hundred thousand sesterces to your fortune?"

"Uncle Aulus!" Quintus protested with mock surprise. "You know I consider wealth merely secondary to—"

"Women!" Aulus chuckled. "Tell me, young stallion, have you found the girl who will be your wife? Or are you still out wenching around?"

"The latter," Quintus admitted, grinning. "Though one of these days I'll have to submit to the 'happy tedium of marriage.'—But tell me, Uncle, what did you think of the sham out here today?"

"Sham? What do you mean?"

"I mean you should have had a *triumph,* not an ovation. Claudius spends all of sixteen days up in Britain, grabs credit for your victory, and celebrates a triumph, while you spend four years to get an ovation. He wears the laurel wreath, you get myrtle. He rides a chariot, you—"

"Still living in the Rome of a century ago, aren't you, Quintus? Still the diehard republican? You know the rules now. Triumphs go only to the emperor, not his commanders."

"Not back in the Republic."

"Ah, Quintus. If you'd been alive then, you'd also have stabbed Julius Caesar to save the Republic, right?"

"Probably."

"But Caesar *was* stabbed and the Republic still died. These are different times, Senator." He clapped him on the back. "But now get ready for the emperor's dinner, everyone.—Oh, Sabinus." He winked. "See that Quintus doesn't bring any daggers along."

A ruddy golden yolk of sun was just dropping over the hills west of the Tiber when Sabinus arrived at the palace with the other guests of honor. Perfumed fountains were bubbling in the polished marble corridors—a wild balsam fragrance—and a corps of servants glided up to them with great silver trays of exotic appetizers and snow-cooled wines. Sabinus found himself assaulted on all sides by friends he had not seen for months, former colleagues in the Senate, and well-wishers. At last he managed to reach the great dining hall for Claudius' feast, a gastronomic marathon that would feature a roast generously supplied by the two bulls sacrificed that afternoon.

He had nearly taken his place at the principal table when he noticed young Plautia reclining at the place assigned her across from Vespasian. In an instant, his hand was on Vespasian's shoulder. "Sorry, brother," he said, "your place is over there near Caesar."

"I don't think so," Vespasian remonstrated, until he felt pressure building on his clavicle. Then he rose and excused himself, while Sabinus reclined in his place.

Plautia wondered at all the shuffling and stared curiously into Sabinus' large brown eyes. He had a pleasant outdoor face, she thought, tanned from too much exposure to sun and wind, and it matched his lean and well-proportioned frame. Somehow, though, his ringlets of black hair seemed too neatly combed and deserved a good tousling.

"We met earlier this afternoon on the Capitoline," Sabinus began, flinching at his pedestrian comment.

Plautia merely nodded. Then she reached over to finger the gold medallion hanging from his neck. "Is this what Caesar gave you?" she asked. "What in the world are those animals doing?"

"The Roman wolf is biting through the throat of the British lion. Subtle, don't you think?"

"What's on the other side?" She flipped the medallion and said, "Oh, your name's engraved alongside Claudius'. How nice!" Suddenly she looked up at him to ask, "Incidentally, whatever was the matter with you today when Caesar asked you to stand forward?"

Her nearness only added to the impression she was making on him, and he barely restrained himself from saying, "*You* were the cause . . . you incredibly lovely stripling—too young for me even to think about." Instead he said, "I was merely lost in memories of Britannia."

"Your brother, Vespasian . . . he doesn't look at all like you. Why, he's stocky as a wrestler. Is he married?"

"Oh yes. Has two boys, in fact."

"And you're not married? Why?"

"A problem of the right woman appearing.—But tell me, pretty Plautia, what have you been doing these four long years while your father was in Britain?"

It almost seemed as if she had been waiting for him to ask, since she spent the next hour telling him in detail, well beyond the main course of sacred sacrificed bull. Sabinus hardly minded. It gave him a chance to watch the girl without risking the impression that he was staring at her. No girl had a right to be that . . . flawless, he thought, almost nettled at how Nature had likely robbed from others to create this masterpiece. Lustrous, light brown hair, free as a water-fall, flowed around sea-blue eyes, a—thank the Fates—non-aquiline nose, and lips that—

"Could I see you for a moment, Sabinus? If my beauteous cousin will permit?"

Sabinus looked up at Quintus Lateranus. "Of course, Senator. By the way, where have you been keeping yourself all evening?"

"I . . ." He faltered and frowned. "I'll explain in a moment."

Sabinus pushed himself up from that delightfully languid position in which Romans dined and followed Quintus out of the dining hall to a balustrade that overlooked much of central Rome. Lamps had been lit in the city below, and flickering daggers of orange flame were stabbing the evening sky. But Quintus seemed too disturbed to enjoy the view. "Has Claudius been asking for me?" he inquired, with a worried glance.

"No, but I think he's been looking for Messalina."

The very name seemed to raise globules of perspiration on Quintus' brow, and he uttered a soft oath.

"Yes, Senator?" Sabinus laughed.

"Sorry, friend. But you can't believe the . . . the terror I'm in be-cause of"—he quickly looked about—"because of Messalina . . . 'wife of Claudius Caesar' . . . 'empress of Rome' . . . 'Beauty Incar-nate'—but Sensuous Slut!"

"Now really, Quintus, surely you don't believe those wild stories."

"Shhh! Believe? You can't imagine what's happened since you left for Britain, Sabinus. The empress Messalina is . . . simply the most improbable woman in all our history." His brow knitted even more deeply. "And now she's all but demanded that I—how shall I put it gracefully?—well, that I spend the night with her."

Sabinus' jaw dropped. Then he broke out laughing. "The em-press? With you? Ridiculous!"

"No, it's not. And I'm far from the first," he sighed. "Lately, Messalina's been, ah, 'entertaining,'—let's see, her doctor, Valens . . . that Rufus who runs the gladiators' school . . . Mnester, the actor . . . and several of our colleagues in the Senate. Probably half a dozen others, too."

"But that's not possible, Quintus! Claudius . . . doesn't he know? Wouldn't he put them to death if he found out?"

"Of course he would. But no, he doesn't know."

"Beyond belief! Why not?"

"No one dares tell him. Messalina would deny it—Claudius dotes on her and would believe her—and they'd both lash out at the informer. One or two *did* threaten to tell Claudius, but . . . they're no longer with us."

"What happened?"

"Messalina had them condemned to death for treason. Using false testimony, of course."

Sabinus' features grew taut. Finally he asked, "How did you answer Messalina when she . . . issued her invitation?"

"I told her no, because a senator shouldn't aspire to the imperial level, but I'm afraid *that* excuse won't work again. Just now, though, I could tell her it was too dangerous with all the people here for Aulus' celebration."

"Just now?"

"I just came from her," Quintus moaned. "What, in the name of all the Olympian gods, am I supposed to do, Sabinus?"

Indulging a bit of whimsy, Sabinus said, "Well, she *is* very beautiful . . ."

Lateranus merely looked at him with widening eyes.

"Sorry, friend! I shouldn't be joking when you're under such . . . pressure. But here's some quick advice. Get back inside immediately, or Claudius may connect your empty place at his board with Messalina's. We'll talk it over later when we total up all those sesterces you owe me, all right?"

"Right. And thanks, friend."

At last the celebration for Aulus Plautius drew to a close. Twice Claudius had dozed off during the lengthy banquet, and that was the proper sign for guests to depart. Leaving after the emperor's first nap would have been an affront; staying on after the second, equally bad taste. While Aulus was gathering his clan, Claudius roused himself and conducted the guests of honor to the vestibule of the palace. A great cheer arose from crowds still gathered outside, who were waiting to escort Aulus to his mansion on the Esquiline hill. Torches were lit, and the corps of flute players struck up a tune.

"Aha, my Aulus," Claudius crackled, "you won't lose your way home with these guides. But please don't make Duilius' mistake, dear friend." He was looking expectantly at Aulus, for he had just dropped a typical Claudianism: some obscure reference from Rome's lengthy past that would have delighted only another antiquarian like himself.

Aulus surrendered. "You have me, Caesar. What *was* Duilius' mistake?"

Claudius beamed, for he prided himself on knowing every nook and cranny of Roman history. "Doesn't *anyone* know about Duilius?" he asked.

"Back in the First Punic War, wasn't it, Caesar?" Sabinus volunteered. "Duilius was so proud of his victory that for the rest of his life whenever he returned home at night—"

"He had torches and flutes marching in front of him to celebrate," Claudius interrupted, nodding enthusiastically. "Well done, Sabinus!"

"Ah, *vanitas!*" Aulus smiled. "But thank you for today, my friend. You too, Sabinus. Quite a day you planned for me!"

"Good night, Governor." Then, seeing Plautia under the arm of her father, Sabinus looked a last time into the eyes that had bedeviled him but were frustratingly removed from him by time and circumstance. "Good night, Plautia," he said softly.

She smiled. *"Vale,* Commander."

2

VALERIA MESSALINA twisted about on the broad expanse of her bed with half-opened eyes. Ever so slowly, she came to terms with the new day. "Claudius?" she called, in a languid tone. There was no response from the adjoining room. Evidently her husband was up and about his emperor's business. She thought back to the previous night and the brief appearance she had put in at the banquet for Aulus Plautius. By the gods, how such functions bored her!

For that matter, Claudius himself bored her. True, he had seemed a desirable enough prize when she married him eight years ago. But she was only fifteen then and Claudius was a member of the imperial house—the family idiot, to be sure, but an idiot of the Caesars. He had gone on to make her empress, the envy of the world. And for several years she had tried to be a decent wife—the gods knew she had tried—and didn't their little children, Octavia and Britannicus, help prove that?

There was no doubt that Claudius loved her. And why shouldn't he, after two marital failures? His first wife was a real prize, Messalina mused. Urgulanilla! That murderous Amazon was every bit as ugly as her name. Ha! Poor Claudius had to divorce her for reasons of personal safety! And the second was a transparent little fawn—Paetina—whom Claudius never really loved. No, he never knew what love was until *she* stepped into his life and made him supremely happy.

Yet she herself was anything but happy. "Love is the center of a woman's world," she explained to her intimates, "and a husband thirty-three years older than I can't possibly satisfy me." Messalina stood up to dress, smiling at the solution to her plight. She had surely owed it to herself to take lovers, she reasoned, for love was very much like food: its taste and enjoyment depended on its freshness and, above all, on its variety. Let the moralists rage. Let jealous women gossip and bewildered elders shake their heads. She was empress and not to be shackled with the customs binding ordinary women. She would live—and love—to the very summit of her inclinations.

Shrugging off her nightdress, which fell into a circlet of purple around her feet, Messalina glanced down at her generous breasts and exquisitely matured figure of twenty-three years. Was it fair to limit such a view to the dimming eyesight of a doddering wreck of a man older than his fifty-six years? Claudius, that spent satyr, could amuse himself with various palace girls at trysts he supposed were secret, so why shouldn't she have similar privileges? She had incriminating documents on all possible informers in the palace, as they well knew, so her own liaisons were shrouded in a conspiracy of silence.

She rang a chime. Several attendants fluttered in to help her dress. One combed the tresses of her raven-black hair, another took jeweled clasps to fasten a crisp white tunic around her body, and then draped the saffron stola she had selected for the day. Messalina gave her girls only wooden responses, for her thoughts had focused on the events of the night before—and on the person called Quintus Plautius Lateranus, that devilishly attractive rogue who was spurning her love with threadbare excuses. But why did he make them? She knew he found her appealing, and he had no wife to answer to. Obviously, the poor dear was afraid of Claudius. Yes. Yes, that had to be the reason. Well, no great problem.

Messalina emerged from her suite to share a light breakfast with her husband. It was not until he had finished munching his wine-soaked bread and cheese that Claudius finally responded to her careful pouting and asked what was wrong. Messalina's sulk darkened into a scowl. "I don't want to talk about it," she snapped.

"All right, don't then." Claudius shrugged.

"Tell me, Claudius," she suddenly demanded, "is it wrong for an empress to interest herself in financial matters? Investments? That sort of thing?"

Claudius looked puzzled, but before he could reply, Messalina resumed. "Does the name Quintus Lateranus mean anything to you?"

"You mean the young senator? Aulus' nephew?"

"The same. Well, I saw Lateranus at the banquet last night, and since he's making a fortune for himself, I asked him for investment suggestions. And do you know what he replied?"

"What?"

" 'Caesar's wife couldn't possibly be interested in how I collected my few crumbs.' Then he turned and walked off."

"Why, the impudent churl! I'll send and have him flogged."

"No you won't. You can't flog a Roman citizen, not to say a senator. But you should punish him somehow."

Claudius was about to summon a guard when Messalina demurred. "Wait, dear. Let's be more subtle. Why not make the man swallow that fierce pride of his? That's the best humiliation." She brushed a delicately manicured hand across her mouth in thought, then smiled. "I have it. Summon Lateranus to the palace and tell him that an empress should be able to expect common courtesy from a senator. That in the future he must cooperate with *all* my requests, or face some dire consequences."

"All right." Claudius smiled. "I won't mind lecturing that fellow. Why must these young dandies always find success and conceit at the same time?"

"Thanks, dearest." She turned to leave but then stopped. "Oh . . . one more thing, Claudius. Don't deliver a lecture to Lateranus and don't say anything about investments. Be very curt with the man. Say simply, 'Cooperate with her. Do *whatever* she says.' And let it go at that. Above all, don't tolerate *any* back talk from him. A one-minute interview would be too long. The shorter the audience, the more effective the humiliation."

"Fine thinking, carissima.—Guards! Send in a messenger."

The summons from the Palatine renewed the torque of anxiety deep inside Quintus. Certainly he hadn't made a cuckold of Claudius, but what if he'd learned of Messalina's interest in him? Or, more probably, what if she had used that ancient stratagem of the spurned woman and accused him before Claudius of making indecent advances to her? The emperor would never believe him.

Fear, but anger too, tingled inside him as Narcissus opened the door to Claudius' office for his audience. Ominously, the state secretary was staying with them. As witness?

"Oh yes, Lateranus," Claudius gurgled. Then he cleared his throat and resumed. "The empress has informed me about last night. I . . . I wouldn't have thought that the nephew of my comrade Aulus would have been so . . . indiscreet."

Quintus' eyes appeared to bulge. "But what indiscretion, noble Caesar?"

"You were rude in not complying with the empress. Now, Senator, may I advise you that from now on you are to answer any request my Messalina may make of you, and I shall not discuss the c-consequences if you refuse."

Quintus was dumfounded. Quickly shifting his stance to keep his knees from buckling, he asked, "*Any* request?"

Claudius nodded.

"You mean," Quintus swallowed, "even—"

"Yes, yes, yes, man!" Claudius grumbled, without trying to understand Quintus.

"But, Princeps, you—"

"Enough, Senator!" Narcissus interrupted with a glowering glance. "Caesar has spoken. The matter is settled." Impatiently he waved Quintus out of the room.

For one last moment Quintus peered directly into Claudius' eyes, trying to fathom his intentions, but he found nothing which would suggest that his directive had been only a bizarre joke. Then he whipped about and left.

Returning eastward to his mansion on the Caelian, Quintus was baffled and thoroughly alarmed. And he found only one solution to the ridiculous puzzle: Claudius was actually to be taken at face value. He only too clearly meant what he said—the debauched pander! Jaded in his twilight years, Claudius was evidently giving his wife free rein, probably as part of an agreement by which his own privileges were also unlimited. Messalina *had* dropped broad hints that this, in fact, was their arrangement.

He glanced skittishly about the city, now blanketed by the shadows of late afternoon and finally shook his head. After burying the Republic, had Rome really come to this? It certainly explained Messalina's conduct. Why addle one's brain trying to figure out how Claudius could be so dense about his wife? He knew all the time!

Quintus stepped inside his town house. No sooner had he shaken the dust off his toga than two bejeweled arms tenderly wrapped themselves about his waist. Messalina's eyes gleamed and her lips glistened as she pulled him into the shadows of the vestibule and whispered, "Quintus . . . my Quintus."

The change from military to civilian life was exhilarating for Flavius Sabinus. He had not really wanted to leave the Senate for duty in Britain—he was not a soldier at heart, like his brother Vespasian—but military service was obligatory for anyone with political ambitions. He had put in his time. But now everything was falling handsomely into place for him back in Rome. The beast that hounds all men—financial insecurity—had been easily tamed by Quintus' uncanny ability to make sesterces spawn sesterces. As a leisured Roman, then, he had two options: indolence or politics. No contest. The choice had been as inexorable for him as it proved to be for Aulus Plautius.

Both, in fact, were formally welcomed back into the Roman Senate on the same day. The consul designate, Gaius Silius, was presiding over the chamber with another of his bravura performances at the dais. It was said that the golden-tongued Silius could have fended off any of Rome's enemies by syllables alone, not swords.

"You, Aulus Plautius," he exclaimed in peroration, "and you, Flavius Sabinus, we shall no longer style as 'Commanders' but as 'Conscript Fathers,' fellow members of this august body. We forgive you your absence over the past months: something detained you in the north country, we understand." He paused for the laughter he had anticipated, and then concluded, "Resplendent as you appeared in armor on the day of your ovation, the public togas you are now wearing strike us as even more glorious uniforms. You will, of course, be courted fiercely by every political faction in the state— what else would one expect of returned military heroes?—but we wager in advance that you will pursue your own independent strategies. Welcome back, gentlemen! Help us govern Rome!"

Aulus and Sabinus, who were seated front and center on the marble benches, now stood to receive prolonged plaudits from the chamber, and even some rather unsenatorial cheering. When the session was adjourned and senators were filing out into the Forum, Sabinus

felt an arm across his shoulders and heard the same voice, now subdued. "And how is dear Polla? Still up in the hill country north of
Rome?"

"My mother is fine, Gaius. I visited her in Reate last week. And
thank you for the . . . brilliant reception inside just now."

Gaius Silius merely raised his palm by way of acknowledgment.
Then he inquired, "How long has it been since your father died?"

Sabinus winced inwardly while responding, "Six years." His father had been a customs collector in Asia Minor, so exceptionally
honest that the citizens there had actually erected a statue to him
with the inscription, "To AN HONEST TAX COLLECTOR." (It was said
to be the only such statue in the Empire, because this was the only
occasion for one!) Sabinus' father had, in consequence, returned
penniless to Rome, but Gaius Silius' father had befriended him,
lending him the capital necessary to establish a bank in Switzerland.
So when the younger Silius made reference to his father, Sabinus
guessed that he was setting up a mood of obligation for him, even
though the financial debt had been repaid.

He was not mistaken. As they strolled through the Forum toward
the late morning sun, Silius carefully probed into Sabinus' political
views. Sabinus gave guarded responses, trying to fathom the intentions inside that boyishly handsome head next to him. "Gaius Silius
is the only man in Rome who can truly be called beautiful," the
women of Rome agreed.

At a secluded corner of the Forum, Silius stopped, looked about to
make sure no one was near, and then confronted Sabinus directly.
"You may or may not agree with what I shall now tell you, Senator,
but I must ask your word, no, your *oath* of secrecy—absolute secrecy
—in this matter. Your father once told mine, 'If someday we can
repay this favor, command us.' Well, Sabinus, the time has come.
This is the only favor we'll ever seek."

Sabinus nodded. "You have my oath for secrecy, Gaius."

Again Silius looked about and then whispered, "A growing number in the Senate—and elsewhere—are *tired* of the Empire, Sabinus,
disgusted with Claudius' performance, and we aim to restore the
Republic.—Now, before you say anything, hear me out. Yes,
Augustus was necessary as a strong man—he ended the Civil Wars—
but that randy old hypocrite Tiberius fled any statecraft in Rome for
the tangled sexual games he loved to play on Capri. And he was a
saint compared to Caligula—"

"A madman, Gaius," Sabinus interrupted. "No commentary necessary."

"And now this dawdling cripple of a Claudius who runs at the mouth both literally and figuratively, this stuttering simpleton who is making Rome the laughingstock of the world—oh, what a *magnificent* succession of Caesars: a hypocrite, followed by a madman, and then a fool!"

Sabinus was hardly shocked by Silius' language—it was standard fare in republican circles—but he did ask why Silius was singling him out.

"Because of your prestige, Sabinus. Because—*if* you sympathize with us—we want you to approach Vespasian and possibly Aulus Plautius too—but only when the time comes. We already have the night watch on our side, and some of the praetorians. It *can be done,* Sabinus! We can restore the Republic and return real power to the Senate." Silius' eyes were glowing, piercing those of Sabinus for some response.

Sabinus carefully looked across the Forum to the palace on the Palatine. Then he replied evenly, "Claudius is no paragon, Gaius. I'll grant you that. But he's no fool either. I won't be part of his assassination."

"He wouldn't have to be assassinated, Sabinus. Exile would do. He could spend the rest of his life with his beloved scrolls in Spain. Or Egypt. Anywhere."

Slowly, Sabinus nodded. "The matter requires much thought, Gaius. I'll give it that thought. Meanwhile, I *quite* understand your need for secrecy."

It was so studied an understatement that both broke into laughter.

"I will say this," Sabinus added. "It's not the emperor who has made Rome a laughingstock so much as the empress."

"Messalina?" Silius' eyes suddenly flared toward, then avoided, his. "Ah yes, the empress. She . . . ah . . . *is* a problem." Color was suffusing Silius' youngish cheeks, and he asked a final time, "Absolute secrecy? Even if you decide not to join us?"

"You have my word, Gaius."

"I ask you on the bones of our dead fathers, Sabinus."

"I *gave* you my word, Gaius."

They parted, Sabinus returning to the Quirinal hill, where he was staying with Vespasian and his family. Soon he would move into his own newly purchased town house on the Quirinal, now being redecorated. He gave a moment's thought to discussing Silius' conspiracy with his brother—he was *supposed* to contact him eventually—but then he dismissed the idea. Vespasian held secrets like cracked crockery held water. Besides, he knew what his brother's response would be without asking him. Tough, loyal soldier that he was, Vespasian would have headed directly to the Palatine to warn Claudius. Lucky for Silius that Vespasian wasn't wealthy enough to sit in the Senate, because if he had been party to their conversation, Silius' conspiracy would have been pried wide open.

But what of his own attitude? Would nudging Claudius aside be a crime—treason—or patriotism? A healthy Republic, governed by a truly independent Senate in place of the present chamber, always deliberating with one ear cocked toward the Palatine, had to be preferable. But he had many more questions to ask, many more assurances to be pledged before committing himself.

Sabinus was also struck by Silius' strange reaction, his almost telltale response to one word: Messalina. And speaking of Messalina, why hadn't Quintus said anything more about his predicament?

3

OVER THE NEXT MONTHS, Senator T. Flavius Sabinus was indeed wooed by various factions that tugged away at the Roman body politic—and by one in particular. The eyes of the consul designate, Gaius Silius, turned to him embarrassingly often during deliberations, hungry, imploring eyes. At the close of each session, Silius would seek him out to comment cryptically: "The number grows." "Soon now." "Have you decided?" Freighting about conspiracy and treason in his head, yet sworn to secrecy, Sabinus wondered whatever happened to his peace of mind.

Aulus Plautius caught him after adjournment one day and said, "You'll be seeing less of me in the Senate from now on, Sabinus, because I've . . . given in."

"Your memoirs of the campaign in Britain?"

Aulus smiled and nodded.

"*Excellent*, Governor! I've been urging you to get started ever since we returned."

"Which is almost as long as we've been inviting you to dinner at our place, Sabinus. You've declined twice now. 'Courtesy' has been served. But now, barring revolution, catastrophe, or death itself, we'll expect you this coming Saturday evening. Can you make it?"

"Delighted," Sabinus concurred, with a sheepish grin.

The Plautii lived on another of Rome's seven hills, the Esquiline, which loomed up northeast of the Forum. Near the crest of its pine-encrusted slopes stood the Plautius mansion, target of some controversial gossip in Roman society. One of Aulus' rivals in the military wandered through its Doric columns and commented, dourly, "A palace? For a Roman officer?" Yet Caligula once took the same household tour and grumbled, "Oh, it's shelter, Aulus, but why don't you climb out of this hovel and build yourself a *real* home?" But Caligula, of course, was mad.

Sabinus found Aulus' twenty-two rooms at least adequate for a family of three. All of them opened onto one of two large adjoining courtyards: the atrium, nearest the street, and the more richly ornamented inner peristyle. The servants lived upstairs in rooms that also faced the interior courts.

Pomponia's dinner was savory in taste and conversation. Whatever reserve Aulus' wife showed in public seemed to disappear in the privacy of her own home. And daughter Plautia showed no reserve at all. Sabinus felt curiously unnerved, reclining across the table again from this radiant slip of a creature. How old was she, anyway? Whatever age, she was too young for him, and he privately cursed the Fates that had placed them almost a half generation apart.

To make matters worse, Plautia was chattering away about a young girl's favorite topic—herself—and the boys in her life. "Roman girls are terribly sheltered, Senator," she complained. "Why, I can't even go down to the Forum—or anywhere else for that matter—unless Mother or Father comes along."

"Nonsense," Aulus countered. "Any one of the servants would do."

"And marriage will change all that, Plautia," Sabinus laughed. "You'll be spared your chaperones someday when the proper man comes along."

"Someday? I'm old enough for that right now."

"No you aren't, daughter." Pomponia smiled.

"Oh yes I am. I'm sixteen, and three of my friends are sixteen and engaged. One is even married."

"Well, then," said Aulus, in a patronizing tone. "When do we announce your betrothal, Plautia? And what Roman male has Fortune favored?"

"Don't think I haven't had the chance." She pouted. Then she brushed her tawny locks aside, turned toward Sabinus, and said,

"You can't believe how it goes, Senator. The boys my parents want me to like—proper family and all—well, they're a collection of curiosities." She paused as the others laughed. "But the men I like all seem to have a 'hopelessly wrong background,' as Mother puts it. So I suppose I should have become a Vestal Virgin," she sighed. "I could have, you know. When I was ten years old, the high priest invited me to become a novice.—Just think, I could have spent my whole life in sacred spinsterhood!—But Father said no."

"Oh, thank the Fates," Sabinus said to himself.

"I really should have joined the Vestals, I think," she persisted, pouting, and then jabbered on about her sheltered existence and the lot of Roman women in general.

Her comments and bearing tended to cool Sabinus' interest, for they showed the girl to be a flighty adolescent after all, and much too young to take seriously. He almost felt a perverse consolation in learning that, for all her beauty, she was also shallow and immature. Nature had dealt normally with her after all.

Pomponia had been staring curiously at her guest. "You know, Sabinus," she said, "I find that you resemble our nephew Quintus rather *closely*—except for your build. He's heavier than you."

"*Aha!*" Sabinus chuckled. "Now you'll understand why we chose the name we did for our joint business ventures."

"What's that?"

"*Gemini*. The Twin Brothers."

"Who's Castor and who's Pollux?" Aulus laughed.

"We haven't decided yet."

Plautia, who had said nothing for some minutes, now seemed to change tack. "Suppose for a moment, Senator," she said, in a more serious tone, "that you possessed the same mind and talents that you now have . . . but that you had a woman's body. Do you realize how drastically different your life would be? You could never have become consul or commander. Or senator. You could not even vote for one of these offices. You could never serve as juror or judge. The law would treat you almost as a minor. Now, is that fair, I ask you?"

Sabinus was taken by surprise. "Perhaps not," he replied. "But the women of Rome are marvelously free when compared to those of Greece and elsewhere."

"True. But that's like a rich man telling a peasant to be glad he's not a slave," she countered. "Could it be that you men are afraid of us? Wasn't it Cato who said, 'On the day that women are our equals, they will be our masters?'"

Sabinus swore to himself. He had misjudged the girl. She had a mind after all. And a fine one.

A servant entered the dining room, excused himself, and then whispered something into Aulus' ear. The face of the paterfamilias suddenly took on a serious cast, and he rose from the table.

"It's all very confidential," he said, "but Narcissus is here. Alone."

"No aides?" Sabinus asked, for Claudius' state secretary was always accompanied by a train of assistants.

"No one else. He has to see me privately. A *very* urgent matter, he says."

"Time for my exit," said Sabinus, rising from the table to thank his hosts. "Your family suits you well, Governor. Now I know the sacrifice you made to leave them for Britain."

Aulus walked toward his library with a knit brow. He numbered the emperor's secretary among his friends, but he had purposely kept a respectful distance from him. Narcissus was indeed the second most powerful person in the world, and any closer involvement with him meant swimming in waters close to the treacherous vortex of Roman politics.

Narcissus' greeting and apologies for his sudden visit seemed sincere enough. Then the pleasant-looking Greek started frowning as he nervously brushed aside the scented strands of his black hair and tugged at one of his earlobes, pierced from the days of his slavery. "Rome's in desperate danger, Aulus," he said, with a deadly serious cast to his eyes. "Claudius is threatened. We have a situation that's nearly out of control. But I hope your commander's mind can help devise a strategy to save us."

"Sounds like a Parthian puzzle, Narcissus. What do you mean?"

"You've heard the stories about the empress Messalina?"

"Yes, but what does that gossip have to do with your problem?"

"Everything. But first of all, you should know that the 'gossip,' as you call it, is not only accurate, it's really very kind to Messalina. No one's yet compiled a full inventory of her lovers, but I'm trying. We're up to nineteen."

"The wife of a Roman princeps? That's beyond belief!"

"But true, Aulus."

"How do you know, Narcissus? Were you around, taking notes behind a curtain, I suppose?" he chortled.

"I have more than enough proof." Reaching into his tunic, Narcissus extracted a folded piece of papyrus. "Look. Here are only a few of the prominent Romans who . . . have violated the emperor's bed. In alphabetical order. I have written proof on each of them." He handed a list to Aulus:

> Suillius Caesoninus
> Decrius Calpurnianus
> Mnester, the actor
> → Traulus Montanus
> Polybius
> Titius Proculus
> Sulpicius Rufus
> Gaius Silius
> Saufeius Trogus
> Pompeius Urbicus
> Vettius Valens
> Juncus Vergilianus

Aulus studied the names. "Thundering Jove!" he growled. "Senators . . . magistrates . . . prefects. Messalina certainly has aristocratic tastes."

"Not necessarily. Remember, these are only the prominent names. There are many more."

"What's the arrow doing there?"

"I'll explain in a moment. Now, which would you say is the most dangerous name on the list?"

Aulus studied the names again. "Probably that 'rising star' in the Senate, Gaius Silius."

"Exactly. And there lies the danger. Messalina is after more than passion now. She wants power too. We've learned that she has an overwhelming infatuation for Silius. She even wants to marry him and make him emperor in place of Claudius. And Silius *is* consul designate, you know."

"*Emperor?*" Color was draining from Aulus' face. "But I thought Silius had republican sympathies."

"Oh, he does, he does—*when* he's trying to enlist support. And he may have been an honest republican at one point, but now he has loftier goals in mind. Messalina may have corrupted him. Or his own ambitions did. No matter. He now promises to restore the Republic only to build a following."

Aulus' brow wrinkled into a deep frown. What were only the mad flagrancies of an empress-strumpet now seemed to shake the very foundations of Rome. Not that Claudius himself was so indispensable, he knew, but an Empire ruled by a palace whore and that vain and limited Gaius Silius, a pretty youth who spoke too often and too grandiloquently in the Senate, would surely court disaster. He stepped over to his wine cabinet, extracted a bottle of strong, aged Falernian, and poured cups for both of them.

"She can't stop showering gifts on the man," Narcissus continued. "She paid for Silius' new mansion and then hounded his wife out of it. And she's all but moved in herself. She's there day and night. She's moved much of the palace furniture over there too. Ah, but dear Claudius! He never seems to notice anything missing."

"You mean he *still* doesn't suspect? Why haven't you told him?"

"Because I'm very selfish about my life, Aulus. I want to keep it, you see. Was it Homer who said, 'Pity him who brings bad tidings to the powerful'? Everyone in the palace agrees that Claudius must be told, but no one wants to tell him."

"Why not Pallas?" Pallas, also a freedman, was Claudius' other most intimate secretary and in charge of the state treasury, while a third ex-slave, Callistus, supervised all petitions addressed to the emperor.

"I know what you're asking," Narcissus replied. "Claudius . . . is a charioteer drawn by three horses: Pallas, Callistus, and Narcissus. Why doesn't one of them turn about and neigh loudly enough to warn his master? And you're right, of course. But the other two are even more afraid than I, if that's possible. Messalina has threatened that if we inform on her, she'll 'prove us liars,' and have us executed for treason."

"Could she?"

Narcissus thought for several moments. Then he said, "Yes, she probably could. Claudius is still helplessly in love with her, and he'd *much prefer* to believe her innocent than guilty. He loves the children she gave him. Against these odds, an accuser would be courting suicide. And even if Claudius *did* believe us, he'd be furious that he wasn't told earlier, since Messalina's been . . . deceiving him for the last five years." He threw up his hands. "We're all caught . . . caught in a horrible trap."

"So. You'll say nothing, and let Rome pass over to that conceited fool, Silius?"

Narcissus looked down, grabbed his goblet, and drained it. Then he clipped his words. "No, we can't let it go on any longer. That's why I'm here. I need ideas. I need advice. I need support. Let's talk about support first. When the crisis breaks, I'm asking you to use your influence with the officers of the Praetorian Guard to keep them loyal to Claudius. That way Claudius must eventually win—*if* he isn't assassinated first."

"You have my word on that, Narcissus."

"That's a relief." He smiled. "Now for the advice: if you were in my position, Aulus, how would you go about breaking the news to Claudius?"

Aulus slowly twirled the cup in his hands, staring at the crimson inside. Then he tightened his lips and said, "Draw up detailed documentation on Messalina's . . . conduct. Have Pallas and Callistus at your side with corroborative *proofs* of her infidelity. Have witnesses in waiting. Claudius will *have* to believe such evidence."

Narcissus pondered briefly and then nodded. "Yes, that's really the only way."

"But you'll have to hide your plans from Messalina at any cost, or she'll strike first.—But you were going to tell me about the arrow on your list there."

Narcissus winced. "No detail escapes you, does it, Aulus?" He drew in a deep breath and said, "The name of your nephew Quintus Plautius Lateranus belongs in the list at that point. I . . . I'm sorry, friend."

Aulus' features froze in disbelief, only his eyes reflecting the pain. "Are you certain?"

"As it happens, I witnessed the very start of your nephew's involvement. But you'll be glad to know he was duped into it. Didn't he ever tell you what happened?"

"No. Never."

Narcissus then reported the strange interview on the Palatine. When he had finished, Aulus snapped, "Why didn't you warn Quintus then?"

"At the time I had no idea what was involved. Later, when I learned, it was too late. But now I must ask you: does this change your opinion that Messalina should be exposed?"

Aulus' knuckles whitened around the stem of his goblet. "No," he muttered, then more distinctly, "no, of *course* not."

"Honorably spoken. I can only promise that we'll . . . try to keep Lateranus' name out of the affair. But if this fails, he'll certainly have a solid defense: Claudius innocently ordered him to do the very thing for which he will have been accused! I'll testify to that."

"Mmmm. Kind of you, Narcissus."

"Oh, one last thing, Aulus. The moment I leave, you will probably send a warning to your nephew, and I can't blame you for that. But Lateranus does have republican connections, as you know, so I would say *nothing* about Silius and his conspiracy . . ."

"I'd already thought of that, Narcissus."

4

FOURTEEN MILES southwest of Rome, the Tiber River spilled into the Mediterranean at Ostia. This was supposed to be the port of Rome, but the yellow sludge disgorged by the river had silted up the harbor for years. And so the grain ships from Africa and Egypt that kept Rome fed had to stand offshore and unload their vital cargo onto heaving flat-bottom barges that ferried the grain up the Tiber. When Mediterranean storms made chaos of such transfers, the people of Rome went hungry. Several such famines and they would start looking for another emperor, Claudius knew, so he conceived his grand plan of carving out a deep new harbor at Ostia to the north of the old one.

Claudius' engineers told him the scheme was impossible. He quite agreed, but ordered them to go ahead anyway. Their kind had been arguing over the project for some ninety years now—ever since Julius Caesar first dreamed about it—and it was time to move. An army of laborers converged on the area, and a huge basin was slowly dredged out, while breakwaters, built over a base of sunken ships, gradually took shape.

Claudius decided to spend several weeks of Rome's glorious autumn at Ostia, surveying progress on his beloved harbor, and he asked Messalina if she would care to accompany him. She'd love to go along, she said, were it not for indigestion. Kissing her tenderly, the emperor left for the coast with a minor entourage, leaving Narcissus in charge on the Palatine.

Messalina watched her husband's retinue wind its way out of the palace courtyard and then called for a writing tablet. She inscribed only two words on it: "Now, Darling." Sealing the tablet, she summoned her most trusted aide and told him, "Deliver this to Senator Gaius Silius on the Esquiline. Immediately."

Roman financial circles were starting to watch the activities of "The Twin Brothers" with increasing interest. Sabinus and Quintus Lateranus not only bore a curious resemblance to each other, their personalities also matched. They were both outgoing, adventurous sorts, a little bored with the status quo; both were bachelors, both senators, and both, lately, were making a fortune with their joint business ventures. The money men of Rome tried to ape their style, always a step behind them in timing—and profits. Until now, the shrewdest businessman in Rome was supposed to have been Narcissus, the "Sage of the Sesterce," but when the mighty Narcissus conceived his bright idea of buying property near Claudius' harbor works at Ostia, he found that most land titles on both sides of the new basin were already vested in the name of the Twin Brothers.

Lately, though, Quintus seemed more interested in politics than business, and Sabinus almost regretted it, because Quintus, with his republican sympathies, had been trying to draw him into Silius' conspiracy. Shrewd as they were in financial matters, neither of them had any idea that Silius might have higher ambitions for himself.

Because it was midautumn, Gaius Silius' great party would have a harvest motif. Quintus carefully hand-delivered Sabinus' invitation and added, "It's going to be *the* social event of the season, Sabinus, and I'd like to emphasize that it is to be social indeed—not political. So you can bury your qualms about what we're doing and come and have a good time." Sabinus was predictably disinclined, but Quintus could be extremely persuasive.

The Twin Brothers arrived together early on a bright and warm October afternoon. Decorated in a vintage motif, the atrium of Silius' mansion was now a country vineyard, framed by actual vines laden with luscious grapes. Huge wooden vats stood in the peristyle, in which guests were merrily trampling grapes with their bare feet while gulping down wines of every variety. Threading their way between the vines and vats, a corps of stewards bore great silver flagons emblazoned with signs advertising their contents: Setinian or Falernian, hot or cold, sweet or dry, watered or straight.

Several smiling slaves surrounded Sabinus and Quintus, whisked them out of their togas, and presented them with rustic costumes made from animal skins, for this was to be a festival of Bacchus, god of wine and revelry, whose harvest and fertility rites dated back to the dawn of Mediterranean civilization.

"Darling Quintus!" Messalina cooed, as she implanted a lingering kiss on one of the two bucolic figures just entering the atrium-vineyard. "You have forgiven me for my . . . for my friendship with Gaius, haven't you?"

Shaking his head but smiling, Quintus replied, "Don't ask the impossible, my goddess."

"Oh, you did bring him along, didn't you? Welcome, Flavius Sabinus!" She extended her hand, which Sabinus kissed mechanically, too stunned to do anything else.

"Before this is over, you should be able to do better than that, Senator." She smiled coyly.

Sabinus flushed, the color rising as he noticed Messalina's outrageous costume—or lack of it: a narrow band of bleached leather barely covering her breasts, tied to another that wound between her legs and around her waist to form a belt.

"I designed it myself, Sabinus," she beamed. "Excuse me for now, gentlemen. Enjoy yourselves . . . as much as I *know* you will!"

As she turned away, Quintus planted a goblet of cold Setinian into Sabinus' hand and said, "Drink this, friend. And *don't* try to understand the woman."

Mingling with the merry mélange of guests, they chuckled at how the women were adapting to their scanty costumes, also designed by Messalina, which were little more than loose-fitting loincloths and halters of skins bleached to match flesh tones.

The shrill blast of a cornet blanketed the hall with silence. Gaius Silius stood up to greet his guests. "A cordial welcome, my friends! Today we celebrate Italy's bountiful harvest!" He held his cup high.

"But more!" Messalina cried, reclining at his side.

"We also celebrate our Cause, which has nearly triumphed!" Silius exclaimed.

Sabinus leaned over to whisper to Quintus. "So public? Has he gone mad?"

"*Shhhh!*"

"But more! But more!" Messalina was squealing with delight.

Silius stopped, leaned down to place a passionate kiss on Messalina's lips, and then continued, "Ah yes, more indeed! Today, my beloved friends, we also celebrate . . . my marriage . . . to the empress Messalina!"

A sepulchral silence followed. Sabinus inhaled a breath which hung in his lungs and did nothing else. Quintus raised himself from a reclining position to stare at Silius.

"Some here were witnesses to our wedding several days ago," Silius continued, "but we swore them to secrecy so we could surprise you all. This feast, my friends, will go down in Roman annals because it marks a bold and public change in Roman government, not a clandestine assassination. I took only Claudius' wife, not his life! So raise a cheer for the bridal couple!"

Everyone about them jumped up in a frenzy of applause and wild cheering, as Sabinus and Quintus stayed reclining opposite each other at the table. "Madness," Sabinus whispered. "*Madness!*" he now fairly shouted.

"By all the gods," Quintus murmured, still staring at Silius.

"No, no, no, *no!*" a piping voice behind them broke in. "It isn't madness at all." A middle-aged rail of a man reclined next to them.

"Sabinus, this is Vettius Valens," Quintus said softly, still in obvious shock. "He's a physician."

"Not necessary, I know the senator," said Valens. "No, the empress' problem isn't madness at all but *kindunophilia.*"

"Which means?"

"Love of danger. It's the last resort for a jaded soul that has tried all the pleasures life can offer and wearied of them. It was Messalina who arranged—who demanded—this marriage, not Silius. She was tired of deceiving Claudius so easily—night after night, month after month. She's just a . . . a child of excess."

When he got no response, Valens added, "You doubt me? Look, I'm Messalina's doctor, and I've also examined her thoroughly. Many times." He gave a wicked chuckle. "No, her only refuge now is danger itself. She needs it to prod and revive her senses. Messalina needs danger like a party needs wine."

"And Silius?" Quintus wondered.

"Had to go along with her plans. *Had* to. Probably wants to, though, now. The husband of an empress is an emperor, isn't he? Heh-heh."

"But . . . *bigamy?*" Sabinus demanded.

"What else?" Valens shrugged his shoulders. "After adultery, theft, conspiracy, treason, and maybe murder . . . why not bigamy too?"

Sabinus felt ill. Silius' vaunted "return to the Republic" had been only the thinnest tissue of lies, then, a screen of deception to mask his own ambitions. "Let's go, Quintus," he said.

"Wait. Just a little longer. I can't . . . really believe this . . ."

"*Let's go,* I said."

"Just a few minutes longer. I . . . have to think."

Their wine-soaked wits were responsible for their staying on, they later argued. And it was true that, in a more sober state, they would easily have abandoned such a theater of treason. Perhaps, though, the madness of the moment also held them in thrall, infecting them with a curious rage also to taste danger at first hand. In fact, no one was leaving the hall.

From one corner of the room, a company of drummers started tapping a languid beat, answered from the opposite side by other drums. An orchestra of flutists and lyrists, all dressed as satyrs, struck up a sensuous tune. The throbbing rhythms grew in volume. "The Dance of Bacchus!" a herald cried.

One by one, the women got to their feet and started a slow series of bends and whirls, which soon picked up tempo and intensity. The music cast a spell over the guests, luring more of the women into a wilder dance across the artificial hills and dales erected in the great court.

Messalina and Silius lay on a nuptial couch in the center of it all, luxuriating in the success of their party. Breathless from the dance, her hair as disheveled as a genuine bacchante, Messalina screamed with delight and shook the ivy-twined staff of Bacchus. She was cheerfully aware that one of her breasts, its tip carefully painted gold, was now exposed in her torn halter. Silius, with his crown of ivy, was impersonating Bacchus himself. His legs, laced with the buskins of the god of drink, were twitching about in time with the music, and he grasped his bride from time to time in an ecstatic embrace.

The music grew even louder, coaxing echoes throughout the marbled mansion and overcoming everyone's reserve. All the women now joined in near-manic choruses of delirious, frenzied dancing, vaulting about like crazed fawns.

The men could stand it no longer. Stumbling off the couches where they had been reclining, they started chasing the women. A planned delirium broke out, a laughing, shrieking, howling chase throughout the premises. The skin costumes, poorly stitched at the seams, started coming apart as they were meant to. Couples found each other between the hedgerows of the vineyards, in shady glens contrived in the rear garden, in any convenient nook. Several actually embraced while thrashing about in the slimy purple mash inside the wine presses.

Sabinus watched it all with an exotic mixture of disbelief and his own unavoidably rising lust. Quintus had left him for adventures in the vineyards, but some nagging shred of conscience told Sabinus that he should remain an observer at the bacchanal, not a participant. And then a woman dropped down next to him. She was staring at him through the coolest orbs of green he had ever seen, eyes that seemed to pierce and study and smile at him all in the same instant. Her smallish mouth parted into a delightful smirk, as she sat up to comb curly strands of brown hair that had become disheveled from the dance.

"Are you enjoying all this, Flavius Sabinus?" she finally asked, her voice caressing his ears, assaulted as they were by the shrieks about him.

"How d'you know me?" Sabinus slurred even as he tried to speak distinctly.

She reached over to finger the triumphal pendant hanging from his neck. "Only two men in all Rome can wear this," she said. "I was at the ovation."

"You were? Well, forgive me, then, but who're you?"

"You really don't know?" Her green eyes suddenly narrowed a bit.

Sabinus studied her uncommonly pretty face, but then shrugged. "No. No, I don't. Should I?"

"That's not important now," she smiled, leaning over to brush his cheek with her lips and kiss his ear. "This is."

The unexpected tactile shock unleashed the passion that had been building inside him, and he clasped the woman to his chest as she crossed his cheek and mouth with insistent kisses. "Come, Sabinus," she finally whispered. "An olive grove in back. No one's there."

Later he tried to recall exactly what followed—so bizarre was the scene—but it all seemed a wine-hazy, frustrating dream. The woman with the green eyes—*if* he remembered correctly—led him by the hand outside into the grove, where she caressed the pendant off his neck, untied the thongs of his exhausted skin tunic, and began running her hands across his bare chest. What happened next? Was it the fresh outside air cooling him down, or some moral impulse warning him that he must *not* do this with a stranger? Whatever it was, he grabbed her exploring hands and halted them.

Puzzled, she demanded an explanation. Sabinus, searching his wits for some excuse, came up with the worst one any woman can hear: "You . . . you don't appeal to me . . . that way."

He had not meant it, but evidently he'd said it, for his one sure memory from the delirium that afternoon was the woman hissing like a furious feline, lashing out with both her hands and scratching ten painful trails of red down his bare chest. Then she hurried back inside, but not before unleashing a withering curse: "May the Gorgons turn *all* of you into stone, you simpering eunuch!"

Earlier that day, Pallas, the emperor's financial secretary, stormed into Narcissus' quarters in the palace. Pallas had let his dark, scented locks grow long enough to hide his earlobes, pierced when he was a slave boy. Now they trembled with fury as he bellowed at Narcissus, "She's done it! Our palace prostitute has gone and done it. She *got married* to Gaius Silius!"

Narcissus cringed. "She *what?* How do you know?"

"You know my source. He was invited to the ceremony—witnessed the whole thing."

"When did it happen?"

"Last Tuesday. He tried to tell me immediately, but I've been away."

"An official *wedding?* Is she *insane?* Bigamy?"

"Yes. Or automatic divorce from Claudius, depending on which law you follow."

Slumping into a chair, Pallas continued. "To all appearances it was a normal wedding—the witnesses, the vows, the sacrifices. They ate cake on bay leaves. They were constantly kissing and slobbering over each other. Oh, it was a regular marriage, all right, including the wedding night."

"How would you know?" Narcissus asked woodenly, scarcely comprehending the news.

"Well, at the end of the feast, Messalina shooed the guests out of the house because—how did she put it?—oh yes, 'We must pass the night in that freedom which marriage permits.'"

"Unbelievable."

"So now the happy couple are man and wife," Pallas sneered, his grim humor only barely disguising the anxiety they both felt. "Well, what do we do now?"

"There's no option. We have to tell Claudius. At once."

Pallas shook his head. "No. Not now. It's too late. He'd have our heads for not telling him sooner. Gods, he might even accuse us of conspiring in the affair."

Narcissus shot Pallas a chilling stare. "Well, do you want to do that? Make Silius emperor?"

Pallas bristled. "Are you suggesting . . . are you trying to get me to commit treason? Is that it?"

"Calm yourself. I'm just showing you the consequences of not telling Claudius."

Pallas thought for several moments. Then he said, "All right, Narcissus. He has to be told, then . . . But you're his chief of staff— you wear the dagger, not I—so you'll have to tell him. And, by flaming Hercules, leave me out of it." With that he stalked out of the room.

"Coward," Narcissus muttered. "Simple, spineless dastard!"

Not that Pallas' attitude was any real surprise. A leaden certainty had hung over Narcissus that eventually he would have to convey the terrible truth. He rehearsed his strategy and then recalled Aulus' advice some weeks earlier. Yes, he thought, that's it.

Before hurrying off to Ostia, Narcissus sent this message:

Narcissus to Aulus Plautius, greeting! Messalina has just committed public bigamy with Gaius Silius. We are informing Caesar. Urgent that you control the praetorians as planned. Farewell.

It was not Narcissus' visit that surprised the emperor so much as the fact that Calpurnia and Cleopatra, Claudius' own concubines, had made the trip too. "Proceed now, as planned," Narcissus quietly told them. "We will confirm everything."

An anxious, dour look on her face, Calpurnia asked, "Master, may I see you privately? A matter of gravest importance?"

"Certainly, my dear."

While the others waited outside, Calpurnia threw herself on Claudius' knees and began weeping.

"But what is it, child?"

"I . . . I know this will hurt you terribly, Master, but"—she burst into fresh tears—"*someone* has to tell you. You should have been told long ago, but we all wanted to spare you, I suppose. But now you must know the terrible truth."

"What happened, Calpurnia?"

"Your wife, Messalina . . . she's married."

"Aha! Of course she is. Heh-heh. Else how could I be her husband?"

"No, no. Several days ago, she . . . got married to . . . Gaius Silius."

Claudius gave Calpurnia an empty stare. She waited for him to digest the poisonous tidings, but he did not seem to comprehend.

"What do you mean, Calpurnia?" he croaked, then cleared his throat.

"Senator Gaius Silius, the consul-elect, married my lady Valeria Messalina. At his home . . . while you were here in Ostia. There were public vows. And witnesses. They . . . they," she faltered, "they also consummated the marriage." Then she broke into sobbing.

Absentmindedly, Claudius began stroking her head, but the deepening furrows on his brow showed that the news was finally taking some effect.

"*My* Messalina?" he wondered. "The empress?"

"Yes. Oh, my lord, how we tried to—"

"I don't believe it."

"It's public knowledge in Rome, Master . . ."

"She loves me too much to do something like that."

"But, Caesar, there's no question—"

"And I love her too much," he grumbled. "It's not possible."

"Cleopatra!" she cried. "Cleopatra, come in here! Maybe he'll believe you."

The door opened and the other concubine hurried inside, her eyes filling rapidly with tears. Cleopatra nodded and said, "It's all true,

Caesar. The empress and the senator are man and wife. She now has two husbands."

For some moments there was total silence. Finally Cleopatra shouted, "Narcissus! Come in and help us!"

The state secretary entered the room, hunched over with anxiety but prepared to deliver the most carefully rehearsed speech of his life.

"Narcissus," Claudius crackled, coughed, and then continued, "explain these . . . lies about the empress."

"Would that they *were* lies, Caesar. Unfortunately, they're quite true. An official wedding *did* take place: a dowry . . . omens . . . banquet . . . everything."

Claudius glared at the three and then finally exploded, "Thundering Olympian Jupiter! Are you telling me that my own wife married somebody *else*? Without telling me first? Without divorcing me? Bigamy was outlawed seven centuries ago among the Romans!"

"But it happened, Princeps," said Narcissus. "You can confirm it with the praetorian prefect and the chief magistrates. The tragedy is that so much more is involved."

"What else? What possibly else?"

"Silius . . . isn't the first. Actually, he's the last in a series. The empress has been deceiving you for several years, Caesar. We can document perhaps twenty men. There may be more."

Claudius' face became a glowering mask of anger and incredulity. The women, terrified by the hideous transformation, started weeping again.

"Who?" Claudius gargled. "W-who else was involved?" A string of saliva started dangling from his lower lip, and the twitching of his left cheek caused him to wink.

"Here are the names, Caesar," said Narcissus, handing him the list he had shown Aulus, with some additions.

Claudius' hands were trembling, and he had to squint to make out the names. Each one induced a new ripple in the muscles around his eyes. When he laid the list down, he asked, "What does that arrow mean?"

Narcissus winced. He had forgotten to erase the arrow! He groped for some explanation other than the truth in order to spare Aulus, but then gave up the attempt. "The name of Quintus Plautius Lateranus belongs there," Narcissus admitted. "And I make a special point of his case to show that several on the list were involved against their will. Do you recall the interview with Lateranus in which you said, 'Do whatever the empress says'?"

"Yes, but I thought she wanted some . . . business advice."

"She was lying, we found out later. Poor Lateranus thought you were ordering him to commit adultery."

Claudius' face reddened, and his blue-gray eyes sparkled the awful sheen of a wounded animal. He sprang to his feet, grabbed Narcissus by the arms, and bellowed, "If all this is true, why didn't you tell me long before now?"

"For several reasons, Caesar," Narcissus replied, trying to stay composed. "At first, we also knew nothing of the empress' crimes. And when we did learn, we had to be *sure* of her affairs before exposing them. It would have been worse to accuse her if she were innocent." He paused to let Claudius digest the logic, then resumed. "But I will admit, Caesar, we also tried to overlook her infidelities, hoping she would mend her ways. We knew how much you loved her and how this would wound you. Then there were the children, too."

The prime reason for the delay—fear of Messalina—could not be mentioned, since imperial secretaries were expected to risk their very lives for the emperor.

"But her affair with Senator Silius is *far* more dangerous than the others," Narcissus continued. "Her bigamy suggests that she and Silius are planning to depose you and take over the Empire. Our informers tell us of overtures they've made to the legions, members of the Senate, and even the praetorians."

"*What?*" Claudius darkened. He clapped his hands. "*Guards!*" he shouted. "Get me Geta and my whole staff. Bring them here immediately!"

Lucius Geta, the praetorian prefect who always attended the emperor, made a hasty entry, as did other powerful friends of Claudius who had accompanied him to Ostia. Heads lowered and eyes askance, they all confirmed Narcissus' noxious report.

"W-well, wo—, w-what do we do now?"

Narcissus looked over to Geta and asked the questions on which the future of the Roman Empire depended: "Well, Prefect, will the praetorians stay loyal? Or will they support Silius?" The guard commander was somewhat unreliable, Narcissus knew, and he *might* abandon Claudius if he thought Silius could win. Or if he were bribed enough.

Geta flashed a scornful glance at Narcissus, then turned to Claudius and replied, "The Guard will stay loyal, Caesar. But only if you return immediately to the Castra Praetoria and *show* them that you are still in charge of the Empire."

For a moment Claudius did nothing. Then he slowly nodded and said, "Pack up! We return to Rome at once."

The journey back to Rome was fourteen miles of exquisite agony for Narcissus. Besides the emperor and himself, two others were seated in the jogging imperial litter, Claudius' friends Vitellius and Caecina. Both were spineless opportunists, he knew, and could only complicate the crisis. Vitellius had even made a fetish of Messalina's slipper, carrying it inside his tunic and kissing it from time to time! What if they should induce Claudius to spare her? In that case, he himself would surely die, Narcissus knew. Everything now depended on Aulus Plautius keeping the praetorians loyal, since Geta could be leading them into a trap at the Castra Praetoria with his advice.

Claudius suddenly broke down and wept convulsively. The odious revelations about the woman he truly loved had burned through the logical part of his mind and were now searing his emotions. When he partially recovered, his comments were random and distraught. There were long, lugubrious silences. Then he would roll his eyes and babble, almost incoherently, "You *couldn't* have done this to me, my beloved . . . my pet." The next moment he would snarl, "Oh, but a harlot must be paid for her services!" After that he muttered darkly about those who withheld information from the emperor, for whatever reason.

Vitellius became unnerved. He thought the only safety lay in aping the moods of Claudius, and so he wept or threatened in tune with the emperor, wringing his hands extravagantly. Caecina chimed in with slavish echoes.

Later, Claudius did become lucid enough to ask, "Well then, gentlemen, what shall I do about . . . Messalina?" Significantly, he looked first to Narcissus for an answer.

"If it were only a matter of her adulteries, Princeps, you might banish her to an island. But since the empress also conspired to depose you, there is only one punishment for such treason." Even in exile, he knew, Messalina would have her agents try to assassinate him for his disclosure. And what if she were pardoned?

The litter was silent. Several tears slid down the ruddy, wrinkled cheeks of Claudius. "And what would you do, Vitellius?" he groaned. "What if you had the misfortune to preside over such a garden of adultery as Rome?"

Vitellius' hands grappled with one another for an answer. He could have joined Narcissus in recommending death, but what if Claudius should finally forgive Messalina? "Ah, Princeps," he whined. "The gods have put you, rather than us, to such a test, for they know that your superior wisdom will unfailingly choose the proper course."

Narcissus shot Vitellius a loathing glance. "Come, come, worthy Vitellius," he challenged. "Let's hear you more plainly. Clear up those ambiguities, like a good emperor's adviser should."

"I merely hate the taking of any human life. I'm only trying—"

"To be as vague as possible," Narcissus cut him off. "You're a weathervane, Vitellius. A jellyfish! You used to have some backbone —like the time you dismissed Pontius Pilate as governor of Judea— but now—"

"Insolence!" Vitellius cried.

"'And from an ex-slave!' you'll say next," Narcissus mimicked. "But we really have no time for this, gentlemen. I fear, Caesar, that you're underestimating the danger to Rome and to your own life. If this treason isn't punished immediately, you'll lose the Empire."

The distraught Claudius actually began weeping again and cried, "Am I . . . am I still emperor of Rome, Narcissus? Is Silius still my subject?"

Before he could reply, they heard the clatter of horses' hoofs outside the litter. Narcissus looked out and saw that it was several of his aides, fresh from Rome. They whispered something in Narcissus' ear. A gleam of triumph lighting his eyes, Narcissus said, "Tell Caesar. Tell him everything."

The men reported the bacchanal in progress at Silius' residence. As the lurid details unfolded, Claudius' self-pity melted into smoldering rage.

"May I issue the orders in your name, Caesar?" Narcissus inquired.

Claudius nodded emphatically.

"Take a cohort of men, Tribune, and arrest Senator Gaius Silius, the empress Messalina, and all who are at his residence on the Esquiline."

"The empress too?" he asked, with widening eyes.

"The empress too. Take them to the Castra Praetoria and hold them there."

5

SABINUS tied his skin tunic together and returned to Silius' party, but only to find Quintus and then leave the premises as quickly as possible. The nameless woman's fingernails and her seething curse must have overcome the effects of the wine, since he remembered the rest of the day more clearly. Inside, the bacchanal had moderated somewhat, and couples were returning to the tables. Everyone was watching the irrepressible Dr. Vettius Valens scampering atop a large cask. Holding up a crystal goblet, he called out a series of treasonable toasts.

"May our magnificent Messalina mother a new dynasty of emperors!" he cried.

"*Io! Io!*" the guests shouted.

"And may her children be *normal* Romans, not slobbering old satyrs from Hades like Ci-ci-claw-claw-claudy-claudy-Claudius!"

"*Io! Io!*" This time there was laughter and wild cheering too.

"And may our new emperor Gaius rule for many, many years!"

"*Io! Ave Imperator!*" Many of them stood up and took long sips from whatever cup was nearest.

"Silius, you hypocrite traitor, I'll see you in —— first!" Sabinus swore. He looked everywhere for Quintus but could not find him.

Someone shouted a lewd remark about Valens' professional services for the empress, and several young revelers scrambled up the cask, trying to grab the doctor. Valens playfully sprang down from his perch and the girls chased after him. They ran out into the garden, where he escaped by climbing up a tall pine tree—a remarkable achievement for one in his condition. "Oho, what a view!" he shouted.

"What do you see?" the girls called up to him.

"A terrible storm coming from Ostia!"

Everyone knew Claudius was in Ostia at the time, and they roared with laughter at the clever remark. Sabinus, meanwhile, finally located Lateranus sleeping under one of the tables. He pulled him out, slapped some cold water on his face, and said, "Let's go, friend!" Quintus grunted his consent as Sabinus lifted him to his feet, and the two began a swaying exit.

Suddenly they heard a loud banging at the doors of the mansion. Silius was called out to the vestibule. Not a minute later he reappeared with an ashen face and trembling lips, holding up his arms for silence. "Your weather forecast is correct, Valens," he shouted in the awkward stillness. "A storm *is* coming from Ostia! Claudius is on his way to Rome. He knows everything!"

For a moment, nothing happened, and some drunken guests never did get the message. Then a low moan arose, a babbling, hysterical chaos of confusion. People rushing for the door knocked Sabinus off balance, pitching Quintus onto the terrazzo floor of the vestibule, where his head struck the hard marble. Sabinus made a lunge to prevent his friend being trampled, and managed to drag him behind a column. Husbands were snatching their wives, if they could find them, and scrambling off in their party costumes. Tables were overturned in the panic to escape, one of them crashing against the spiggot of a great cask, which now jetted spurts of wine across the marble floor—little help for those fleeing, who slipped and slid across the slick.

When all who were able had left, Sabinus turned to the host for help with Quintus. But Silius ignored him. He was holding Messalina by the shoulders and saying, "Get hold of yourself, carissima. We'll use the other plan. I'm going down to the Forum as though nothing happened, and, remember, you have to get to him *before* he reaches Rome."

"Help me with Quintus, Silius!" Sabinus called again.

"Go to Hades!" Silius barked, hurrying off.

"*You* will for certain, you adulterous reptile!" Sabinus shouted after him. A rage that pulsed down to his fingertips gave Sabinus the strength to hoist Quintus' sturdy frame onto his shoulders and hurry away.

Moments later, a large company of praetorians converged on Silius' place just as the last guests were scattering in every direction. But they had little trouble chasing down and arresting some of them because of their bizarre dress. "Just look for skin-covered savages, reeking with wine!" the tribune ordered his men. When they burst into the house, they found only a besotted few, snoring in drunken slumber. The host and hostess were missing. "Seal up the place as is," the tribune commanded. "No one gets in or out till Caesar arrives."

Messalina and three of her women companions were hastening southward on foot to the Ostian Gate. There they searched desperately for transportation down the Via Ostiensis, but found none. Finally Messalina noticed a tethered mule standing in a park. A cart was harnessed to it, but no one seemed to be attending it at the moment. Rushing over, they untied the beast and scrambled onto the wagon. It was muddy and stank from garden refuse. No matter. Messalina gave the reins a jerk, and the cart clattered out onto the Ostian Way.

They did not have far to ride. About three miles down the road, they saw Claudius' entourage approaching them. Messalina pulled in the reins, but the trotting mule, happy to be free of hauling manure and blissfully unaware that it was approaching the lord of the world, refused to obey. The imperial litter-bearers, in fear of collision, dropped the gilded litter in a swirl of dust and took to the ditches. With all four women tugging at the reins, the mule finally came to a halt, inches from the imperial party.

Narcissus stuck his head outside and flinched. There, incredibly, was Messalina, stained with what appeared to be compost, climbing off the cart and running up to the litter. Eyes tearful but flashing, she cried, "My husband! Listen to me!"

Claudius stared at her, then sullenly turned the other way.

"Everything can be explained, dearest! Listen to the mother of Octavia and Britannicus! You've been listening instead to false rumors."

"False?" Narcissus turned to her with a sneer. "Your public big-amy with Senator Gaius Silius . . . is *that* a false rumor?"

"The marriage was only a sham!" Messalina insisted. "Claudius, you remember the portents threatening 'the husband of Messalina'? I *feigned* marriage with Silius to avert the danger from *you*. I did it to save you."

Claudius turned and looked at her blankly. Then his eyes shifted to Narcissus.

"Here, look at this," she said, thrusting a document into Claudius' hands. "That's your signature, isn't it? This is the contract for the dowry. You signed it with your own hand so that the marriage would *look* legal."

Claudius studied the signature. Then he said, "I . . . I don't remember this. But I must have signed it, I think. It *looks* like my signature."

"Which proves *nothing*, Princeps," Narcissus objected. "You sign dozens of documents each day. She merely slipped this in with the others. It's all a lie, Caesar, an incredibly audacious lie designed to cover her crimes."

"No," Messalina cried. "My husband, you do remember those threatening omens, don't you?"

"Yes . . . I remember your saying something about them."

Narcissus' eyes widened. "If there *were* portents, Caesar, she must have bribed the priests to find them. But did you ever give her per-mission to marry Senator Silius? Even in a sham wedding?"

Claudius' hands teased his silver locks and his forehead wrinkled. Slowly, he shook his head. "I . . . don't think so. Wouldn't I have remembered . . . something like that?"

"Of course you would, Caesar," he rushed on. "And even if you had agreed to a mock wedding, you didn't intend that it be *consum-mated*, did you? If it's documents you need, begin with this stack." He thrust a pile of papers into Claudius' hands.

Painfully, Claudius began reading the testimony. Even that was part of Narcissus' strategy: the emperor's eyes must be drawn away from Messalina. Her unkempt, though still lush, beauty must not continue working its spell on him. The old feeling dared not be rekindled.

Messalina fired a glance of mortal hatred at Narcissus and her lower lip quivered. She flashed about to order guards to arrest the upstart state secretary, until she realized that only her three attendants would follow her orders now.

Narcissus ordered the litter-bearers to continue toward Rome. They bent to their task. Claudius did not interrupt his reading. Messalina protested and cried, but Narcissus called back that she should not disgrace herself further. The four women and their mule stood astride the Ostian Way, watching the litter jog on toward Rome.

Silius' mansion was surrounded by smirking guards who had occupied their time by telling the latest Messalina stories. But when the imperial litter lumbered up they quickly wore faces of sympathetic concern. Narcissus helped Claudius out of the litter and told the two who were still inside, "You'd better join us, gentlemen. We'll need witnesses"—you equivocating dastards, he added, to himself.

At that moment, Aulus Plautius galloped up to the imperial party, dismounted, and saluted.

"Oh . . . Aulus," Claudius moaned. "I'm glad you're here, my friend. Have you heard the terrible news, too?"

"Yes, Princeps. But—"

"What about the Guard, Aulus?" Narcissus interrupted. "What's Geta doing?"

"Good news. Silius *had* sent agents to bribe the praetorians, but when I got there I lectured the men on the subject of treason and its consequences. Geta arrived toward the close of it. Now, I'm sure I didn't influence the prefect"—Aulus smiled—"but he promised us his loyalty and full cooperation. They're all waiting for you over at the Castra Praetoria now."

Narcissus was beaming, while Claudius put his arm around Aulus and hugged him. "You've saved Rome for us, Aulus," he exulted. "You've saved Rome for us. But first there's this . . . matter of evidence here. Join us, friend."

The imperial party inspected the site of the bacchanal, a shambles of wine-smeared floors, scattered food, toppled decorations, and broken furniture. The resinous, fermented odor of drying wine saturated the place, which had all the atmosphere of the inside of a dank barrel. Narcissus, whose agents had briefed him on what to look for, appointed himself as tour guide, identifying which furnishings had come from the palace, and which had been confiscated from the estates of those whose death Messalina had caused. Claudius had to hear a painful running commentary:

"Those murrhine vases used to stand in your atrium, Caesar . . .

"You were wondering about that missing Cupid? Over there . . .

"Oh, here's one of your slave boys. Hello, lad!"

Claudius' emotions churned away from grief and self-pity toward fury and revenge. But it was in the master bedroom that he lost control of himself. There, at the end of the bed, stood a magnificent inlaid table that he had presented Messalina as a wedding gift. Standing on it was a carved, obscene wooden caricature of himself. His face flushed purple and his left cheek quivered as he thundered, "Sh-she will *die* for this! By the Olympian home of the gods, sh-she will die!"

"But first, Princeps, save the Empire," Aulus cautioned.

"Ye-yes indeed! To the camp, everyone!"

By an agile zigzag in and out of the roadways, malls, and alleys of eastern Rome, Sabinus managed to avoid Claudius' troops. Fortunately for his aching shoulder, Quintus' concussion was only minor, and when Sabinus heard him yell, "Put me down. I'm not a blathering baby," he knew all was well. At last they reached the safety of Lateranus' town house on the Caelian, where a cold bath did much to restore their wits.

News arrived that Claudius was on his way to the Castra Praetoria to place Silius and Messalina on trial for treason. Quintus brightened and said, "Into your clothes, Sabinus. We can't miss this: Claudius the Cuckold, quaking up to the rostrum and bawling out to his praetorians, 'Strange, I never noticed that my wife was playing the prostitute these last years—'"

"Much too dangerous, Quintus. What if—"

"None of Claudius' men saw us at Silius' place. And we don't exactly have to stand in the front row over at the Castra . . ."

"No! We should stay out of sight for a while!" Sabinus kept remonstrating all the way over to the Castra Praetoria, for naturally he could not leave his foolish friend in the lurch—nor stifle his own gnawing curiosity.

When they reached the praetorian barracks, the Guard cohorts were all standing at attention before a raised tribunal. Their helmets, each sprouting a curved red plume, flashed gilded silver in the late afternoon sun. Claudius, evidently, had just finished his pathetic confessional, since Narcissus was calling out to the guards: "Do you, then, maintain your allegiance to the emperor?"

"Hail, Caesar! Ave Imperator! Hail, Caesar!" they all shouted.

Brushing a tear from his eye, Claudius addressed the guards, "It was seven years ago that you men first declared me emperor as I stood on this very platform. I'll not forget your loyalty!"

"Let those arrested now be brought before this tribunal," Narcissus announced. "Caesar's assessors—his advisory justices—have taken their places. Let the trials begin."

Sabinus, who was standing next to Quintus in the midst of a large crowd of spectators, whispered, "There's your Uncle Aulus sitting to the right of Claudius."

Lateranus whistled softly. "I guess he's one of the assessors too."

"You still think we should have come?"

Quintus merely chuckled. It was, perhaps, the last time he smiled that day, since they both found the trials unnerving. The very guests they had been partying with just hours earlier were now being sentenced to death. Gaius Silius himself, white as the senatorial toga he was wearing to bely the revels, looked defiantly at Claudius and said, "I am *guilty*, Caesar, guilty of wanting a better emperor for Rome than your silly self. I ask only a quick death."

"And you shall have it," replied Claudius evenly. He turned to his assessors and briefly tallied their response, which was unanimous. He then pronounced sentence of death. Silius was led off to a block set up at the opposite end of the camp courtyard, where he bent over and bared his neck for one great slash of the sword.

Silius' late-blooming courage became contagious, and the other accused also requested a quick execution. Decrius, prefect of the night watch, was very soldierly and professional about it. The tree-climbing Dr. Valens even had a twinkle in his eye as he asked Claudius, "I trust the palace no longer has need for my . . . services?" There was a ripple of laughter from the praetorians.

"Silence!" Narcissus shouted, and the trials and executions ground on. Each time Sabinus and Quintus heard the muffled thud of sword on flesh, they cringed. "Let's get out of here, Quintus," Sabinus whispered.

"No, wait. They're about to try Mnester, the actor."

Mnester surprised everyone by making a spirited defense for himself, pointing his finger at Claudius and telling the imperial face, "You yourself ordered me to do Messalina's bidding, Caesar! Remember your own words: 'Serve the empress in *any* manner'! And she threatened me with death itself if I didn't cooperate."

Quintus shook his head in disbelief. Evidently Messalina hadn't even used a fresh stratagem in seducing him! Claudius, meanwhile, seemed touched by Mnester's appeal, and Aulus flashed him the thumb-up signal for mercy. But then Pallas walked over and advised, "When you are felling so many illustrious Romans, Caesar, will you then pardon an *actor?* And did this mime really sin from compulsion? Or choice?" Like the others, Mnester was sentenced to death. Quintus looked at Sabinus in horror.

Claudius now leaned over and asked Narcissus, "By the way, where's that arrow fellow, anyway?"

Narcissus tried to ignore the question, primed as it was by Mnester's parallel experience.

"The name you didn't have down," Claudius persisted. "Quintus Lateranus, wasn't it?"

"But Caesar, I don't think—"

"Arrest him! Bring him here! He's an adulterer like the rest of them and must also be punished. By very Hades, he must."

Narcissus tried valiantly to dissuade Claudius, but the emperor was clearly losing control of himself. The relentless succession of shocks seemed finally to be macerating his mind, for he now got shakily to his feet and bawled out to the crowd, "One of the culprits is still at large! Do any of you know where the Senator Quintus Plautius Lateranus might be?"

Up on the tribunal, Aulus' mouth sagged open. Down in the crowd, Sabinus, paralyzed by disbelief, barely seemed to notice a figure to the right of him leave his side and make his way up to the tribunal. Quintus stopped in front of the emperor and said simply, "I am here, Caesar."

An excited babble welled up from all sides. What could Quintus possibly do, Sabinus agonized. His defense was not only shopworn by now, but obviously impotent. And yet, as eloquently as he could, Lateranus simply reported his interview with the emperor in detail, calling Narcissus to witness that every word of it was true. Narcissus nodded emphatically. Then Aulus, who had disqualified himself from the bench, stepped forward to testify in his nephew's behalf. He had only begun when Claudius cut him off.

"Enough, dear friend. Rome remains indebted to the conqueror of Britain, and we need no further testimony than your word. It is our decision that Quintus Lateranus will *not* suffer the death penalty."

A commotion broke out among the guards.

"Aha! You're suggesting that Caesar is not fair?" Claudius turned to the praetorians. "That I am pardoning one for the defense ignored in the case of another? You should know, then, that the adultery of the actor took place over many months, in which time he should have learned the truth! That of the senator was brief and almost innocent. Still, he will not go entirely unpunished. Oh no, especially since—I am informed—he was foolish enough to attend the disgusting debauch at Silius' residence."

A low rumble of surprise swept the crowd. Sabinus felt blood rushing to his head.

Turning to the defendant, Claudius said, "Senator Lateranus, you are herewith expelled from the Roman Senate, with loss of all attendant privileges. You may no longer wear the broad purple stripe of the senatorial class. Guards, remove the *ex*-senator from my sight!"

As Quintus was forcibly escorted out of the camp, Claudius called out: "Did anyone else here attend the . . . treasonable 'festivities' at Gaius Silius' residence?"

The noise of the crowd stilled to a hush, although Flavius Sabinus heard a ringing in his ears. Claudius was looking back and forth across the crowd, when he stopped and looked expectantly in his own direction, Sabinus saw, with a sense of despair. Did he have any choice in the matter, or was it all over for him in Roman statecraft? There was the matter of honor, too: should he not step forward and share his friend's fate? Of course he should.

He started to shoulder bystanders out of the way and move forward, but then he stopped. He might also be playing the fool, he realized. Oh, how Lateranus would curse him for stupidity afterward!

But no. Claudius was staring directly at him. There he was, only waiting for him to confess like an honest Roman. The emperor knew, somehow. He would have to make a clean breast of it.

Sabinus threaded his way to the front of the crowd and cried, "Hear me, Caesar—" This was all he managed to say before a brawny arm crossed his face and he tasted the salt of arm flesh pressing into his open mouth. Jerked backward, he saw the horizon dropping below his eyes and then only the deepening purple of twilight overhead. Pinned to the ground by two ponderous figures he had never seen before in his life, Sabinus seemed to hear a voice saying,

"It's the falling sickness, Princeps. Poor fellow . . . excitement always brings it on."

Sabinus tried to get up, but his head was slammed down on the brick courtyard with such force that he saw only pinpoints of gleaming gold in his blackening vision. And then nothing more at all.

Up on the Palatine, Claudius was reclining at dinner—drained of energy, but almost master of himself again. His secretaries were dining with him to celebrate their success in the Silius affair. But for Narcissus, the agony of suspense was far from over: Messalina continued to live, and while she did, the sword was only inches from his own neck. They had just discovered her whereabouts. She had withdrawn to her favorite grove in the Gardens of Lucullus, composing letters of love and appeal to Claudius.

The emperor had dined sparingly and was allowing himself more wine than usual. A messenger arrived with another of Messalina's notes. Claudius read it, folded it up, and tucked it inside his tunic. Now he smiled and ordered more wine. Warmed with its effects, he began reminiscing about happier times he'd had with the empress. Narcissus grew tense, for he knew Claudius better than any of the palace staff, and easily recognized the sensual smile that was mellowing the emperor's face. The evening had descended; the night was bringing its memories. And Claudius was obviously recalling happier nights with Messalina.

"Will someone do something for me?" asked Claudius, the half smile broadening.

"Yes, Princeps?" Narcissus volunteered, casting a worried glance at Pallas.

"Why doesn't someone go and inform that poor creature that she must come back home tomorrow and plead her cause?"

"You . . . you mean Messalina, Caesar?" asked Pallas, losing all color.

"Yes. The empress."

Narcissus' hands grew clammy and he flexed them to regain control. "I . . . Princeps," he said. "I'll do it." With that he left the dining room and hurried to the vestibule of the palace. There he told the officer in charge, "Instructions from the emperor, Tribune: take the centurions who are on duty and their troops and go at once to the Gardens of Lucullus. There you will find the empress Valeria Messalina. Execute her."

The tribune showed no surprise. "We've been expecting *that*." He smirked but then grew serious. "Still, since it *is* the empress, shouldn't we have a signed order from Caesar?"

Narcissus glared. "Almighty Jove, Tribune, hasn't Caesar been plagued enough by that harlot? He wouldn't deign to draw up something so formal as an order. Messalina has simply ceased to exist for him, and if you delay any longer in carrying out these orders, you'll be under arrest for treason."

"All right, all right! Done!—Guards!" He clapped his hands.

"Oh, Tribune," Narcissus added, in afterthought, "if she wants to . . . take her own life rather than having her neck severed, give her the time."

"Certainly." He gave a stiff salute and led his men out of the palace.

"Evodus, go along and see that it's done properly," Narcissus told the youthful staff assistant at his side. "Better yet, get there first and see she doesn't escape. Kill her yourself if she tries."

Evodus nodded, grabbed a dagger from the palace arsenal, and was off into the night.

After the fiasco on the Ostian Way, Messalina finally realized that she had been living in a fool's paradise. When her child's mind finally awoke to the impending disaster, she did what any child would do: she ran to mother. Or rather, she asked her mother to join her at the Gardens of Lucullus, a favorite haunt, where she had been writing her succession of notes to Claudius. Mother Lepida had long since tried to warn Messalina of the catastrophe awaiting her conduct, but the advice was spurned and the two had become estranged. Now it was too late for Lepida to do anything, she thought, but help prepare her daughter for death.

Yet Messalina knew Claudius' weakness, and she was composing messages in the erotic imagery she knew he could not resist. But still there was no reply. An hour passed, then several more, yet no hint of a response from the Palatine.

Then Lepida heard it first—a rustling of men and weapons. "It's all over, dearest," she said. "You couldn't have hoped for mercy—no, not after all that." She burst into tears. "But Messalina"—she suddenly straightened—"let your last act be noble, and people will always remember it: take your own life. Don't wait for the executioner. It's better that way." Weeping, she drew out a stiletto and handed it to her daughter.

Messalina moaned and threw herself to the ground, crying and kicking like a child. At that moment Evodus arrived and saw, to his relief, that Messalina was still inside the grove. He heard the pathetic dialogue: a mother urging an honorable death, a daughter complaining that the ground was cold and damp, then crying, "*Don't* show me that awful dagger!"

And now the tribune arrived with the troops. They cordoned off the area and then burst through the gateway into the gardens. Evodus held a flickering lamp over the two women and said, "It's the one on the ground. Spare the other."

The tribune hovered over Messalina. She looked up, terrified, then started sobbing hysterically. The tribune drew out his sword with a shrill rasp.

"No!" Messalina shrieked. "I'll do it." She grabbed the dagger and pressed its point against her throat, making only a minor cut. Then she tried pushing it into her breast, with no effect.

Evodus sneered, "You've sent a dozen others to their deaths, little bawd. Can't you take the journey yourself?"

"Shut up, Evodus!" the tribune barked. Then, laying his sword on the ground, he bent down to Messalina and said, gently, "Don't worry, Empress. Here, let me see the pretty little handle on that dagger."

While Messalina opened her palm to show him the hilt, the point still aimed at her breast, the tribune struck a sudden blow at the end of the handle, driving the blade deep inside her. She gasped, wild-eyed, tried to clutch at the dagger, and then huddled over in death.

Lepida burst into convulsive sobbing and cradled the body of her daughter in her arms, heedless of the crimson saturating both their garments.

"You all saw it," the tribune commented. "Her hand was on the dagger. The empress died a noble death." He and the guards marched out of the grove.

For some minutes, Lepida rocked Messalina in her arms, shedding bitter tears for the daughter who had just died, and for the Messalina who, in many respects, had died years before. Only the stars now shared the vigil over the body of Rome's beautiful third empress, dead at twenty-four.

Claudius was finishing his dessert when Narcissus returned to the dining room and said, "I was too late, Princeps. The empress Messalina is dead. By her own hand."

Claudius, who by now was well fortified with drink, frowned momentarily. Then he shrugged his shoulders, banged his cup down on the table, and shouted, "More wine!"

The freedman secretaries looked at each other in surprise—and profound relief. Had Claudius meant to condemn her anyway, they wondered. Even after a hearing?

About midnight, a figure stealthily evaded the ring of guards around Silius' mansion and climbed over the garden wall in bright moonlight. Near some olive trees, he dropped down to the grass on all fours and began a frantic search for a missing medallion pendant.

Earlier that evening, Sabinus had awakened in a park just outside the Castra Praetoria, rubbing a painful bump on the back of his head. Someone, obviously, had not wanted him to admit attending the bacchanal. But who? The someone had been dead right, of course, for here he was, a free Roman, albeit a Roman with a substantial headache. Massaging his scalp, Sabinus almost welcomed the pain, for now no one need ever know about his presence at Messalina's bacchanal.

It was only then that he suddenly clutched at his throat to feel for his triumphal pendant. It was missing! The green-eyed girl in the grove . . . he'd forgotten to put it back on! It took several moments for the full implications to splash icy apprehension over him. Claudius was planning to sift out every crumb of evidence at Silius' place, and the large, golden medallion, engraved with his name, which all but shouted his participation in the collective treason, now lay waiting to be found—unless someone had discovered it already.

Combing the grass desperately, Sabinus squinted for something that would reflect the moonlight. Suddenly a guard emerged from the residence and began a leisurely patrol around the perimeter of the grove. Sabinus planted himself against a gnarled old olive tree, and had to make a slow, agonizing full circuit of its trunk to stay out of view. The guard loitered, apparently enjoying the moonlight. But eventually he returned inside. While hiding, Sabinus realized that this, in fact, was the very tree under which he had almost been seduced by the nameless woman. Dropping down again, he probed the entire area, but found nothing.

Someone else must have found the pendant, then. Someone in Rome could now easily prove that he had been part of the tainted, disastrous festivities. Was it the woman who cursed him? Who was she, anyway? And who had assaulted him at the Castra? And what was happening to Rome, that such grotesque actors as Messalina and Silius had commanded center stage? And almost triumphed? *Madness!*

6

AULUS PLAUTIUS was also trying to make sense of it all but could not. Like Rome itself, he was in a patchwork of moods. He could cheer with the common people as they pulled down statues of Messalina and chiseled her name off the monuments. He was relieved that Claudius had triumphed and could abandon the ugly role of cuckold which had threatened to make Rome a laughingstock among the nations of the world. He was naturally elated to hear Narcissus and himself styled as "saviors of Rome."

But he also worried for Rome, that such an imbecilic conspiracy might nearly have succeeded. He was embarrassed by his nephew's role in it, however innocent. He sympathized with the domestic tragedy on the Palatine that had now left little Britannicus and Octavia half orphaned. And above all, he was concerned for Claudius. Unquestionably, the emperor was deeply scarred by the affair. Stories told of him wandering around the palace in bewilderment, asking where Messalina was. He had settled down to a wooden existence, Narcissus reported. He merely sat at his gaming boards with a vacant expression, shooting roll after roll of dice, his tired eyes hardly bothering to count the throw.

One day, Aulus paid a quick visit to the Palatine, hoping to cheer Claudius a bit. And it seemed to be a proper tonic, for the emperor was glad to see his old friend, though he did apologize for having had to expel Lateranus from the Senate. "But you saw the mood of the guards," he added.

"Forget that, Princeps." Aulus smiled. "I thank you for his very life."

But what worried Aulus was the pallor and weariness he found in Claudius, who seemed to have aged five years in as many weeks. It was only when he was invited to go along that afternoon for a visit to the Castra Praetoria that Aulus again caught a glimpse of the old Claudius. For, after reviewing the guards, the emperor seemed to come alive again. A twinkle in his eye, he announced, "I understand there's a new bit of gossip making the rounds in this rumor factory with seven hills. It deals with the silly question, 'Will Claudius take another wife?'"

The praetorians rippled with laughter.

"Oh yes," he continued, "and the answer, supposedly, is: 'Yes, Caesar *will* marry again.' And you should see the candidates being suggested . . . you should hear the names."

The men laughed louder.

"There isn't a hopeful patrician mother in Rome who isn't planning 'a little party for the princeps' so that he can meet her 'lovely' daughter." Claudius said it in an affected way, and the men howled.

"But hear me, my praetorians! Marriage and I just don't get along. I should know—I've tried three times, and that's enough. From now on, it's the bachelor's life for me!"

"*Io Caesar!*" the Guard broke out cheering.

"And if I change my mind—by the sword of Mars, you men can happily kill me!"

Claudius was applauded and cheered all the way to the gate. Aulus thought it a remarkable performance, played by the Claudius of old, who had little trouble establishing rapport with his troops. The emperor would survive.

Aulus was more concerned that the great family name of the Plautii was tarnished by his nephew's disgrace. He also knew that time would erase the smudge, but the aftermath of the affair now led him to spend less time in the Senate and more on his memoirs. Julius Caesar had made his literary reputation with the *Commentaries on the Gallic Wars*. Could he do less for Britain?

Composing had been difficult at first. He would sit for hours in his scroll-lined library, a weather-beaten battle diary at his elbow on the broad worktable strewn with maps and blank rolls of papyrus. Yet only a quarter of a scroll bore any writing. He would stare at the inkwell and tell himself it was merely a matter of scratching black fluid onto papyrus—certainly simpler than slashing a heavy sword to victory in Britain. But each chapter was a special problem child that seemed to require its own nine months to produce. He found his library stuffy and constricting, and he crossed out phrase after phrase that failed to pass muster.

It was a magnificent day in golden autumn, bright, warm, and beautiful, that suggested a solution. Aulus set up a table and chair in the rear garden and carried his writing materials outside. Peering at his cedars and cypresses, he filled his lungs with fresh air and sat down to reach for his quill. Soon the British campaign itself descended on him, and he wrote with ease and relish.

Before the afternoon was over, he had finished a whole chapter. Pomponia read the material at supper and thought it moved nicely. He tried the outdoor scheme again the next day, and the lines continued to flow. "I know this sounds ridiculous," he told Pomponia, "but I conquered Britain in the outside air, so I suppose I'd best write about it there too."

There were some distractions in his garden study. An occasional insect would scuttle out of the way of his pen, and the sun sent shifting spears of blinding light across his pages. A passing bird once splattered his scroll with a preliminary critique. But when a sudden squall drove him back inside one morning, the oppressiveness seemed to return, household noises interfered, and the work ground to a halt.

"Just as well. I have to quit anyway." He threw down his quill. "Claudius wants me to go to Ostia with him."

"How long will you be gone?" Pomponia inquired.

"About a week. He wants me to see the new harbor works."

Just long enough, she thought.

No sooner had he left for Ostia than she called in a Syrian carpenter who had installed some handsomely worked cabinets in their kitchen. She asked him to build a roofed porch facing the garden, where her husband could escape the sun and rain, and still write in the fresh air.

The wizened little Syrian, whose name was Hermes, probed about at the rear of the house. Finally he said, "Happily done, my lady. But may I offer a suggestion?"

"Yes?"

"I'm afraid a porch of any size would mar the appearance of your home. But if you merely want some shelter for your husband, why not a canvas awning? I'd build a floor of crushed stone and gypsum —say here"—he pointed—"arrange supporting ropes over there, and when your husband isn't working, the awning could be rolled back to preserve the beauty of the garden."

Pomponia brightened. "A good plan, Hermes. Excellent in fact. What would it cost?"

The canny Syrian cupped his chin. "Oh . . . I'd estimate no more than, say, seven or eight thousand sesterces."

Pomponia said nothing, and for some moments there was an embarrassing silence. It was simply her method of bargaining. No counter offer. No hint that the sum was too high. Just a patrician silence until the vendor grew worried about losing a sale and offered a lower figure.

"Yes, my lady. It'll come to eight thousand sesterces—*if* we get the canvas from the usual sources who supply the Palatine. But I know a dealer on the Aventine who imports his fabric from Cilicia and sells it for less. If we used his canvas, I could do the job for, say, six thousand."

"Is the quality as good?"

"Frankly, it's better—thicker, more weather resistant—better."

"Done, then. And use the Cilician fabric."

Three days later, when the concrete base had hardened sufficiently, Hermes appeared with a red-haired, bearded fellow who stood a head taller than himself.

"This is Aquila, noble Pomponia, the man who deals in Cilician canvas."

"Peace be with you," Aquila nodded.

"Yes, this Aquila is quite a bird," Hermes punned.* "He's a Jew, and you know we Syrians aren't too friendly with the Jews. But I'd trust this one with my own daughter."

Aquila flashed a brief, indulgent smile, and then went out to pull four large rolls of canvas off a pair of donkeys that were braying im-

* Aquila is "eagle" in Latin.

patiently in front of the house. He stretched the fabric on the ground and began taking measurements. It was largely mohair, which Pomponia had ordered in a rich, Tyrian purple.

"Well, my work's finished, noble mistress," said Hermes. "I'll be back tomorrow and see if this Jew has spoiled what I've done." He clapped Aquila on the shoulders and was off.

For the rest of the morning, Pomponia found excuses to visit the garden and watch her project take on final shape. Aquila was a nimble craftsman, sewing the material into seams that had no bulge or crease. He cheerfully showed her several stitches she had never seen before, and she was pleased enough to invite the tentmaker in to lunch.

He was a slender man, perhaps in his early forties, with a well-clipped russet beard edging the lines of his jaw. A ruddy complexion enhanced the slight Semitic cast to his face. With typical Roman prejudice, Pomponia had at first recoiled a bit when Aquila was introduced as a Jew. Jews were supposed to be canny, clannish traders who had some absurd belief in an invisible god who disdained statues and pork flesh and was never satisfied with the world he was supposed to have created.

Pomponia inquired about Aquila's background—he came from Pontus in Asia Minor—and about his family—he was married to a woman named Priscilla, and they had no children. Finally, she also ventured to ask him about his "Jewishness," as she expressed it, with less tact than candor. But Aquila seemed pleased with the query and gave a spirited explanation of Judaism, setting the lofty, single God of the Jews in stark contrast to the "many immoral deities who clutter up your Greco-Roman myths," as he candidly phrased it. Pomponia might have been offended, but she had abandoned her own belief in the Olympians ever since girlhood.

Then Aquila said something that mystified her, for it seemed to go beyond Judaism—mention of a recent special revelation of the Jewish deity in the form of some victim crucified in Jerusalem. But she could make little sense of it.

Aquila returned to his work on the canvas, and by late afternoon the awning was finished. With pride of craftsmanship, he showed Pomponia how to raise and lower the tarpaulin. Then he bowed respectfully and took his leave.

When Aulus returned, still dusty from his trip, Pomponia happily shoved him into the garden and lowered the awning over his new outdoor study. For a moment he scratched his head at Pomponia's surprise, but then he beamed. Reaching out to the stola flowing off the head and shoulders of the lovely woman standing next to him, he pulled her into his arms and kissed her.

The ominous summons from the Palatine arrived just about the time Flavius Sabinus expected it would: when Narcissus had finally finished investigating the Silius conspiracy. The curt note suggested that Claudius himself would be seeing him. Painfully, he anticipated the emperor's opening statement: "I once hung this medallion personally around your neck, Senator. Why was it found at the house of bigamist traitors?"

Sabinus tried not to look anxious while entering the palace, grateful that no one could see his pounding heart. Not in his wildest fancies did he imagine that his interview with Claudius would have nothing to do with the missing pendant, or that an hour later he would be leaving the palace in an aura of exhilaration as he hurried to share the glad news with Aulus Plautius.

He found his former commander writing in his outdoor study, and before Aulus could even greet him, Sabinus declared, "Claudius has just appointed me Provincial Governor! In Moesia!"

"*Well done*, Sabinus!" Aulus beamed. "Congratulations! Oh, I'll admit, this doesn't come as a complete surprise: there have been inquiries about you from the Palatine. And what could I say but that your experience in Britain easily qualified you for service along the Danube."

"I'm afraid Moesia won't be anything like the challenge we had in Britain."

"Nonsense. One day those Dacians are going to cross the Danube and give Rome a terrible fight, so watch out for them.—By the way, what's been happening to your brother Vespasian lately?"

"He's trying civilian life for a while. Narcissus is grooming him for a public career."

A touch of color now crept into Sabinus' face. "Just wondering . . . I'll . . . be leaving for Moesia very soon. So may I say good-bye also to . . . ah . . . Plautia? And Pomponia too, of course," he hastily added.

The slightest smile played at the corners of Aulus' mouth as he tried to guess the reason for Sabinus' halting performance. "Certainly, Governor!" He grinned. "Pomponia isn't home, but Plautia's here, I think. I'll send her into the peristyle."

Sabinus sauntered toward the bright inner court, trying to reflect a casual air. Several times he nervously flexed his hands, rehearsing what to say to a girl he barely knew. He was sorry he seemed to have made so slight an impression on Plautia during their few contacts, and even sorrier about their age difference.

"Oh, there you are, Senator." Plautia's voice had a lilt that Sabinus found delightful.

"Plautia!" he greeted her, smiling. "I wanted to bid you good-bye before I leave for Moesia."

"Moesia?"

"Yes . . . our province north of Greece."

"Flavius Sabinus, I certainly know where Moesia is," she said, somewhat irritated. "But why are you going so far away?"

"The emperor has just appointed me governor of Moesia."

"He has? Congratulations, Governor!" She beamed. "How long will you be there?"

"That's indefinite. If I'm a poor administrator, Claudius will see I return to Rome soon enough."

"Which means you'll be there for years and years."

He smiled, groping for an appropriate rejoinder, but found nothing. What tied the man's tongue, what converted a hero of the British campaign into an almost simpering adolescent was the exquisite girl standing before him. Here and now he wanted to declare his feelings for her, but that would have been stupid, he realized. His demeanor probably shouted that. He also had a fierce pride and dreaded the thought that Plautia might, after all, have no interest whatever in him. Why should she indeed?

"I didn't think I'd be leaving Rome this soon, little Plautia," he finally said. "And I'm sorry . . . because I will miss you."

She looked at him with a widening stare and said nothing.

His eyes, which had been flitting about in a vain attempt to escape hers, now stopped their dance and focused on her with a new intensity. "I should be coming back to Rome on rare occasions," he said. "May I . . . see you on one of the return trips?"

"Well . . . certainly, Governor."

"Could you call me Sabinus, instead?"

"If you like . . . Sabinus." Color suffused her cheeks.

He studied her features to etch them firmly in memory. Yes, he thought, several more years for nature to add her finishing touches to this creature and she would be something spectacular. Then he leaned over and kissed her on the forehead. "Good-bye, pretty Plautia," he said. "Next time I see you . . . I may not be so brotherly."

Plautia blushed and looked at him with a curious glint in her blue eyes. "*Vale*, Sabinus," she said, smiling. "The gods protect you."

Just as he was leaving, Aulus called him back into the library and closed the door. "I've been meaning to give you this for weeks, Sabinus, but it slipped my mind. Here, hold out your hand." Aulus took the lid off a little box and turned it over onto Sabinus' palm.

"Your medallion, Governor," said Aulus, with a wry grin.

"How did—"

"I found it the day I inspected Silius' place with Claudius. No one else saw it, the Fates be thanked!"

Sabinus turned scarlet and tried to stammer out an explanation, but Aulus stopped him. "Don't bother. Quintus told me about that, ah, party. Not *everything*, I'm sure!" he chuckled. "By the way, you haven't had any headaches from that blow you got over at the Castra, have you?"

"No, but I was going to ask if that was *your* voice telling Claudius that I had the 'falling sickness.' "

Aulus unleashed a broad grin. "Yes—*epilepsia*—I'll confess it. You see, once Quintus was on trial there was no way I could protect him. But when I saw you standing there too, I knew you'd try to play the noble fool, so I sent a couple of my men to . . . dissuade you. They were sorry they overdid it, and they stayed with you till you started coming around. But I saw no reason for you to ruin your career also. Claudius didn't even know it was you: he's nearsighted."

"Thank you, Aulus!—I saw Quintus a short time ago, and he's not at all resentful. In fact, that rascal claims he can use his time better now, supervising sesterces. Quintus *will* pull out of all this, won't he?"

"Someday. I'm sure of it. But do you think you two lads will ever grow up?"

"Possibly." Sabinus smiled sheepishly. "Let's hope the East will be a . . . maturing experience."

7

WOULD Claudius take another wife *anyway?*

Narcissus shuddered viscerally at the prospect. The emperor was almost sixty years old, so why should he be grumbling about "the curse of celibacy" like some young stallion? And yet here he was, padding about alone in the palace, starved for the companionship of a wife, seized by an almost perverse desire to be bothered, even dominated, by one.

"Give me a good marital quarrel instead of this monotony, Narcissus," he wailed. "I'd take even the shouts and threats and tears of Messalina about now. I . . . I actually miss her sharp tongue. I really do! And at night, I miss the *rest* of her, the gods know!"

"But, Princeps, aren't Calpurnia and Cleopatra . . . serving you well?"

"They're docile. They're no challenge. They *have* to perform. But I crave an equal in status. A friend. A companion. An *alter ego*. In a word, a wife."

"But, Sire, your vow to the men of the Praetorian Guard?"

Claudius' smile faded only momentarily. "Surely those lads are lusty enough to understand me. And to forgive me."

"But, Caesar—"

"So open up the palace to some festivities, Narcissus. You, Pallas, and Callistus should think up a list of candida— I mean guests, of course! Heh-heh-heh."

Narcissus dared enter no further objections, even while cringing at Claudius' resolve. Women had been the very bane of his life, and three failures should have been enough for him. The machinery of Roman government was finally stabilized again, thanks to his own efforts, but another empress could upset everything. Cursed be Claudius' incontinence!

Well, he would try to make the best of it. He would get together with the other secretaries and they would all agree on some harmless beauty, shove her at Claudius, go through the ceremonies, and then let the aging bull content himself with a docile heifer which they would keep well tethered. Yes, he resolved, that had to be the solution.

Narcissus spent the next days thinking of candidates to suggest to his colleagues. The loveliest girl in Rome, to his mind, was Aulus Plautius' daughter, who, at seventeen, was more than nubile. She also came from a perfect pro-Claudian family. But when he tried to picture the wrinkled, aging form of Claudius embracing Plautia's fresh beauty, he dropped the idea, shuddering at the sort of Latin Aulus would have used in rejecting the abhorrent prospect!

He thought further. Again and again he lingered at Paetina's name. Claudius' second wife *was* something of a "docile heifer," not very interested in politics. Paetina, yes. He must get his colleagues to accept her as their joint candidate, and then let Claudius rekindle the embers of a past love. He hurried to discuss the scheme with Pallas and Callistus.

A plague on their greedy ambitions! They had candidates of their own, Narcissus was shocked to learn, for whoever sponsored the woman Claudius chose would have enormous leverage with the future empress—and therefore the emperor. Claudius, meanwhile, was roguishly encouraging the competition, enjoying his little game as some compensation for the domestic disaster he had suffered. With all the resolve of warm putty, Claudius inclined first to one girl, then another, depending on his moods. Finally he called his three secretaries into conference and, much as a judge deciding a lawsuit, he actually had them plead their candidates' cases before him.

"Narcissus, you first," Claudius grinned. "As usual."

"As you know, Princeps," he began, a little defensively, "I've been urging you to marry the lovely Aelia Paetina, your second wife, whom you divorced for—"

"Used merchandise," Pallas commented, a contemptuous warp to his mouth.

"Silence, Pallas! To continue: you once loved her, Caesar. Above all, you're used to her. There won't be any unhappy surprises."

Callistus, a fat and squinting Asiatic, interrupted, "Then why did Caesar divorce her if she's such a gem?"

"You recall why, Caesar. It was only 'for trivial offenses.'"

"Ha!" Claudius cackled. "The real reason was because I was infatuated with Messalina at the time."

"So," Narcissus resumed, "it's merely a matter of welcoming back the woman who was your wife. What could be easier?"

"No!" Callistus objected, in his buzzing, abrasive voice. "On that point you're wrong, Narcissus. Your Paetina would be an arrogant hussy. I can hear her now: 'I'm the only woman ever to marry an emperor twice.'—Now, Lollia Paulina, the woman I've been suggesting, would make a magnificent empress, Caesar. She's fairly young and has the desirable patrician background. And, of course"—he smiled—"she's also very wealthy."

"Since when does Caesar need money?" asked Pallas, with lofty eyebrows.

"I mean, she'd not drain the imperial treasury like Messalina. Why, I've seen Lollia at an ordinary dinner party wearing 40 million sesterces' worth of jewels."

"She needed that many to cover all her wrinkles," Pallas sniffed. "Really, Caesar, Lollia is older than our worthy colleague suggests. Isn't it time we talked about a real possibility?"

"Do you really think I should marry the younger Agrippina, Pallas?" asked Claudius, with noticeable interest.

"Who else, Princeps? The blood of the Caesars already flows in her veins. Both the Julian and Claudian houses unite in her."

Narcissus raised his voice. "But she's Caesar's—"

"She's still young and very beautiful," Pallas continued.

"But she's your *own niece*, Caesar!" Narcissus broke in. "Her father Germanicus was *your own brother!*"

"*Must* you tell Caesar who the members of his own family are?" Pallas huffed. "Of course Agrippina is related . . ."

"Related? Why she's—"

"Do spare us information we already know, Narcissus," Pallas yawned.

"But you're all overlooking the obvious impediment to such a marriage! Civilized Romans have a name for unions between uncles and nieces—or brothers and sisters, for that matter. We call it *incest!* An ugly term. And it happens to be grossly illegal."

"A mere detail," said Pallas, with a wave of his hand.

"But it's against our customs."

"Customs can be changed," he snapped. "But to continue, Caesar: Agrippina has royal blood. She was sister to an emperor—your predecessor Caligula—and she has proven fertility: a son who would make a good companion for Britannicus. And since her husband died, she's free to marry again. My point is this: her bloodline alone makes her a very powerful woman. It wouldn't do well to have her marry someone else and transfer the glory of the Caesars to another family."

Claudius was visibly moved by that argument. Though the other two continued extolling their candidates, Claudius kept peering at Pallas, reflecting on his unsettling comments. Finally he stood up and said, "Thank you, gentlemen. I wish I could marry all three girls to keep you happy," he chuckled. "But I suppose bigamy *is* worse than incest. At this moment, I don't know when I'll choose the girl. I may even let my heart decide the matter."

Aulus Plautius had every reason to be satisfied with his own marriage. Pomponia Graecina was the full name of that serene and gracious woman he had married more than a score of years ago, and she was a good wife. Their life patterns had easily coincided, and they had few quarrels. Besides, anyone who had borne the Plautia on whom he doted could do no wrong. At a time when some illustrious ladies were reckoning the year not by the names of the consuls but by those of their changing husbands, Aulus thought his marriage a happy enough exception.

Pomponia did, however, have one curious quirk. A close friend of hers had been forced into suicide by Messalina, who was jealous of her beauty. The fact that Pomponia had not been able to help her friend, along with Aulus' absence in Britain, made her almost despair at the time. Doctors had not been able to dispel the melancholy entirely, and they told Aulus that she had suffered a mental wound or *trauma,* as the Greek physicians called it.

Recently, however, Pomponia seemed to be winning her battle with depression, although she still wore mourning garments on anniversaries and religious holidays. Aulus thought such devotion to her friend's memory excessive and unnatural—it had been six years now —but he was careful not to say anything that might reopen the wound.

His wife, he knew, was a highly sensitive woman. Back in the days of their courtship, one coarse or careless word from him and she would "blush all the hues of Vulcan's forge," as he told his friends. But nowhere did Pomponia's sensitivity show itself so clearly as in her concern for things mystical and mysterious and religious. "When it comes to spirits, my wife has a woman's curiosity and a child's credulity," Aulus claimed.

"Not so," she would object. "I merely want to answer this question for myself: if Jupiter, Apollo, and the other Olympians don't exist, is there anyone else who does? *Are* there gods after all, or are there not? Are there many? Or is there only one?"

Well and good to ask such questions, Aulus thought, but to try and answer them by dabbling in Jewish beliefs was shocking. And yet his Pomponia had actually invited that red-bearded Jew, Aquila, back to their home not to check on the canvas awning but, of all incredible things, to discuss religion! He appreciated the man's talents with needle, thread, and mohair, and certainly his memoirs were going much better in his garden study now that spring had returned. But if only that fellow would control his tongue as well as his fingers. If he succeeded in making a Jewish proselyte out of Pomponia, the Plautii would be scandalized. Pomponia had told him not to worry—she would not convert—but the thought nagged at him all the same.

One day Aulus returned to the Esquiline, barely concealing a smile of satisfaction. "Well, carissima," he told his wife, "you won't be seeing your friend Aquila anymore . . ."

"Oh? Why not?"

"You know those riots the night before last over in the Jewish quarter across the Tiber?"

"Yes . . ."

"Well, they were a religious squabble between two different Jewish groups. It seems your friends can't even agree on their own beliefs." He smiled.

Pomponia looked pensive. "How was Aquila involved?"

"He was a leader of one of the parties. Claudius investigated the affair to see how it began, and it seems the chief culprit was a Jew named Chrestus."

Pomponia seemed startled at the name, but she said nothing.

"Well," Aulus resumed, "Aquila spoke out for this Chrestus and that must have touched off the rioting. Most of Region XIV got involved in that fanatic turmoil. Anyhow, Claudius is now preparing an edict banishing Aquila and the other Jewish leaders from Italy. And don't frown, Pomponia. It could have been much worse for them. At first Claudius was so furious he wanted to banish all Jews from Rome."

"What changed his mind?"

"Well, that would have been impossible because of their numbers. So only the Jewish leaders will be exiled. The rest can stay here, so long as they don't gather in groups larger than twenty."

"But what about their synagogues? Their worship?"

"No more of that. At least, not for the time being."

"So?" Pomponia tried to look unconcerned and said nothing more.

But the moment Aulus returned to his memoirs, she sent her personal messenger over to the Aventine to try to contact Aquila. An hour later he returned with the message undelivered. "He and his wife Priscilla have left Rome," the servant reported. "They're sailing for Greece. Neighbors said they'd probably settle in Corinth so long as Claudius' ban is in effect. They have friends there."

The next day, Aulus was summoned to the Palatine. Claudius had convened a special conference to discuss foreign cults in Rome and what should be done about them. He was furious that they were prospering at a time when the Roman state religion was languishing and the city's many temples stood almost empty.

Aulus feared that Claudius had somehow learned of his wife's interest in Judaism, but he had not. Aulus was there because the emperor had decided to include Druids in his decree banishing the Jewish leaders, and Aulus, with his experience in Britain, was the ranking available authority on Druids.

The conference labored much of the morning and finally submitted to Claudius a document headed by three lists:

ABSOLUTE PROHIBITION

The Druids
Astrologers
Magi
Sorcerers
Noxious cults

RESTRICTIONS

Judaism
The Neo-Pythagoreans
Cybele
Mithraism

SUBSIDY/REHABILITATION

Roman state religion
Public morality

The rest of the document detailed how this program might be implemented.

Claudius studied the recommendations and nodded. Then he turned to Narcissus and asked, "Did you get any more information on that Chrestus fellow who raised the riot in the Trans-Tiber? Have you captured him yet?"

The scented cheeks of Narcissus flushed rosy pink as he slowly cleared his throat and said, "It seems our first information on that was . . . a little faulty, Princeps. Although the riot took place because of Chrestus, he himself did not lead it. In fact, he could not possibly have led it."

"Oh?" Claudius scowled. "Why not?"

"Because he died about sixteen years ago."

For some moments there was silence. Finally Claudius broke it with a touch of ire. "Clarify your own stupid riddle, then, Narcissus. We know that this Chrestus was involved somehow."

"One of the Jews we arrested explained it to us. Chrestus was some prophet in Judea who roused the people. But our governor there, Pontius Pilate, crucified him at Jerusalem—oh, about three years before you recalled Pilate, Vitellius."

Vitellius, Claudius' indecisive litter companion on the awful trip back from Ostia, was sitting adjacent to Narcissus at the conclave. He nodded in recollection, for in his younger days he had served as governor of Syria in the reign of Tiberius.

"Anyway," Narcissus continued, "several days after his crucifixion, the prophet supposedly reappeared from the dead. They
searched his grave—it was empty—so someone must have stolen his
body. And now a sect of Jews believes he's a god or something. But
the other Jews deny it. That's what the riot was all about."

Vitellius stood up and asked, "Princeps, may I go to our imperial
archives for a moment? I want to check something." Claudius nodded, for the archives were just across the Forum from the Palatine.

Just as Vitellius was leaving, a young woman with light brown
hair combed into a vortex of curls whirled into Claudius' office and
planted herself on his lap. Ignoring the men in conference, she nuz-
zled her pretty face against his cheek and then kissed it. "Hello,
Uncle Claudius," she cooed coquettishly. "Are you coming to
lunch?"

Now she deigned to notice the others present. "Who are these
people?" she asked, her limpid eyes of aquamarine flashing in Aulus'
direction.

"They're my advisers, Agrippina." Claudius beamed. "Now you'd
best go and leave us, little darling. I'll be ready for lunch in half an
hour."

"All right, Uncle," she said, stroking him, while pressing a lingering
kiss on his lips.

Aulus looked with shock at Narcissus, who returned a glance of
tired resignation and a sad shrug.

Claudius had reddened perceptibly and coughed. Agrippina giggled and left the room. "Such a sweet niece," said Claudius, as he
returned to the matter at hand.

The emperor now prodded Narcissus for further information
about the bizarre Chrestus story. He told what he knew, which was
admittedly very little, though he did add one significant detail: the
grave had been officially sealed under Pilate's orders, but the seal
was later broken.

Soon Vitellius returned, carrying several sheets of parchment.
"Here it is," he smiled. "An excerpt from Pilate's *acta* for 786
A.U.C."* He handed the copy to Claudius, who read it aloud:

IESVS NAZARENVS, age 36
Galilean teacher, "prophet," and pseudo-Messiah or "Christus."
Case was remanded to the jurisdiction of the tetrarch Herod

---

* A.D. 33. The *acta* or "acts" were official yearly reports sent to Rome by
provincial governors.

Antipas, who waived his authority and returned the defendant for Roman trial. Convicted of capital blasphemy by the Great Sanhedrin, with verdict endorsed by the prefect. Also convicted of constructive treason for claiming to be "King of the Jews." The prosecution: Joseph Caiaphas, high priest, and the Great Sanhedrin. Tried, sentenced, crucified, and died on April 3, A.U.C. 786, in Jerusalem.

When the emperor had finished reading, Vitellius made the obvious comment: "So you see, gentlemen, the prophet's name was Christus, not Chrestus."

"Hmmm," Claudius pondered. "I wonder why Pilate made no mention of that hubbub following the crucifixion. And don't say he was incompetent, Vitellius. I disagree with you on that."

"Shall we summon Pilate and ask him, Princeps?" Pallas ventured. "He's living over in Antium, isn't he?"

"Gentlemen!" Aulus broke in. "What are you suggesting? That a responsible Roman governor should have cluttered his official records with details on every religious fanatic to appear in Palestine? They have a new pseudoprophet crawling out of the desert every other year out there. I could have sent you sheaves of records on the Druids in Britain, but I had more important things to report."

Claudius and the others chuckled. "That's why we always like to have a military man in on these sessions, Aulus. You keep us in line." The emperor grinned. "No, we won't disturb Pilate's retirement. But there is something in this Chrestus—or Christus—story that bothers me: the grave robbery . . . the fact that the culprit's body was stolen. Out of his very grave. That's bad. Impious."

"What . . . do you propose we do about it, Caesar?" Vitellius wondered.

"Perhaps we ought to draw up an edict for Palestine, warning against any form of grave robbery."

"And the penalty?"

"Why death, of course."

Aulus thought the idea unnecessary, if not a little ridiculous, but since the others were nodding their agreement, he did not feel the issue important enough to bother opposing. Soon the conference had drawn up the following edict, with all the circumlocutions so dear to government administrators:

ORDINANCE OF CAESAR: It is my pleasure that graves

and tombs remain undisturbed in perpetuity for those who have made them for the cult of their ancestors, or children, or members of their house. If, however, anyone has information that another has either demolished them, or has in any way extracted the buried, or has maliciously transferred them to other places in order to wrong them, or has broken the sealing or other stones—against such a one I order that a trial be instituted. . . . Let it be absolutely forbidden for any one to disturb them. In case of contravention, I desire that the offender be sentenced to capital punishment on charge of violation of sepulture.†

"Yes," Claudius said as he reread it. "This will do. Narcissus, see that this is inscribed in stone and set up at several places in Palestine. In Jerusalem, of course, and, ah—what was that prophet's name?"

"Chres—Christus?"

"No. The full name. The legal name . . ."

"Oh. Iesus Nazarenus—Jesus of Nazareth."

"Yes. Have another copy set up at Nazareth. Wherever that is."

"In Galilee, Princeps," Vitellius advised.

"All right, all right. In Galilee, then."

When the conference ended, Aulus managed to draw Narcissus off to a corner and ask, "So what does the performance by that brazen little minx inside just now signify?"

Narcissus replied, looking about to make sure they were not overheard, "Only that she's the one. And Pallas—that serpent!—has won the game. Claudius intends to marry the girl."

Aulus was thunderstruck. "But . . . but his vow of celibacy to the Guard?"

"Means nothing.—Oh, this all began innocently enough. Little Agrippina claimed a niece's right to kiss her 'Uncle Claudius' anytime she pleased. And kiss him she certainly did, and we couldn't raise an eyebrow at such tender displays of affection among relatives, after all. When we weren't looking, of course, she did more than kiss. They've been sharing the same . . . quarters for several weeks now."

"But . . . but that's incest! Agrippina is his *own niece.*"

† This ordinance is authentic, and was found at Nazareth in Galilee. For further discussion, see the Notes.

"Obviously," Narcissus agreed. "But worse than all that is the darling little *son* she'll bring to this wedding from a previous marriage. Her Domitius is three, maybe four, years older than Britannicus. So can you imagine the rivalries? Can you see how the palace here is about to turn into another battleground?"

Aulus nodded darkly. "We have to stop this, Narcissus."

"How?"

"Doesn't the Senate have to approve such a marriage?"

"Yes, but Vitellius is introducing a bill of approval in the Senate. Tomorrow morning, in fact."

"Vitellius? That craven toady?"

"Oh, Vitellius is equivocating only when the gusts of politics blow in crosscurrents. Once a prevailing wind is established, that human weathervane snaps quickly into place."

"I haven't attended the Senate since I started my memoirs. But I'll be there tomorrow."

Vitellius had prepared himself well. Yesterday's sycophant was today's orator, Aulus had to admit. With gilded tongue, Vitellius easily convinced the senators that, with all the cares of empire, Claudius truly needed another wife, and that, ideally, such a wife should also be related to the imperial bloodline. His colleagues, in fact, were now rising to heap praises on Agrippina by name, while Aulus himself squirmed uncomfortably on the marble bench. Incredibly, not one voice had raised the obvious impediment to such a marriage. Well, his would.

Standing up in the quieted chamber, Aulus let just a touch of spleen spill into his tone. "Forgive me, Conscript Fathers, for venturing onto a tender issue, but someone must. If Claudius Caesar marries his own niece, why should this not be construed for what it actually is? Incest! And if incest, the Senate and the Roman People must *not* condone something impious in itself, unprecedented in all of our annals, and which would make the emperor, indeed, the Empire itself an object of derision in other lands!"

Aulus glared several moments more at his colleagues, then sat down. A pall of silence descended on the chamber, then a sudden flutter of whispering. Aulus glanced about him and saw more heads nodding than shaking.

"You are correct, Senator," Vitellius stood up to reply. "Such a marriage *would* be something of a novelty among Romans. But it is permitted in other countries. Even here, marriages between cousins were unknown centuries ago, but now they are common. Custom adapts itself to change. Marriage between uncle and niece will cease to be incestuous the moment the Senate so decides."

Pallas, meanwhile, had orchestrated a huge demonstration in front of the palace that was shouting: "CAESAR MUST MARRY!" "CLAUDIUS AND AGRIPPINA!" "*IO CONNUBIUM!*" And soon the figure of the emperor himself could be seen leaning over the balustrade of the palace, waving to the people below. In a short time, Claudius was threading his way through congratulating masses in the Forum to the Senate chamber, where he submissively bowed "to the will of the people." The Fathers had just legalized uncle-niece marriage, against the votes of Aulus Plautius and painfully few others.

Claudius' marriage to Agrippina was feted at a great celebration on the Palatine, to which all of Roman aristocracy was invited. The emperor had never seemed happier. In giving the groom's toast, he bubbled, "The very gods, including the Divine Augustus, owe me a happy marriage." Then he smiled adoringly at his pretty bride, who looked younger than her thirty-four years, and said, "After three . . . false starts, let this one succeed!"

He said it almost as a prayer. The hundreds of guests, wearied by Claudius' marital misadventures, rose from their recumbent positions at the banquet in an honest cheer. But Aulus and Pomponia, who could not disregard the imperial invitation, remained reclining at their table. The bride carefully noticed this. She whispered to Claudius, "Isn't that the man who called us incestuous in the Senate?"

8

PLAUTIA, now a ripening eighteen, had been attracting more and more attention from the patrician young men of Rome. Several eligible but persistent suitors she eluded only with the cunning native to her sex. Her father's younger colleagues in the government made constant visits, and it was obvious that they had more than politics in mind.

Aulus, however, cheerfully endured the callers—Pomponia had to play hostess on such occasions, and this drew her out. Yet for Plautia it often led to friendships that started innocently enough, but then grew serious much too quickly for her liking, and she would break them off. She had outgrown her girlish weakness of falling in love instantly and ardently with every handsome Roman she met. But was she now becoming too discriminating for her own good?

Or did Flavius Sabinus have something to do with it, she wondered. By now he was little more than a pleasant phantom of memory, although every four months a letter from him arrived, usually filled with news of his province. One letter began with a playful parody on the way emperors started their official correspondence:

Titus Flavius Sabinus, never *pontifex maximus*, consul but once, acclaimed *imperator* at no time, governor of Moesia (that he will confess!) to the pulchritudinous Plautia, greeting.

I often wonder when I shall have finished my term of office here so that I can return to the only really civilized city on earth—or so I would have written before news of the emperor's incest. Is it true that on his wedding day, the statue of Virtue fell over on its face in the Forum? Or did its white marble blush into pink granite? We've heard both stories here in the East, but rumors from Rome come to us very much like waters of the Danube: sometimes in a flood, but always heavily freighted with dirt.

I worry about Rome. It controls the world, but does it deserve to? I'm anything but a moralist, little one, so matters must be bad indeed to alarm even me. Yet I keep reminding myself that Roman woman is not Agrippina but Plautia, and that Roman life is truly lived not on the Palatine but the Esquiline . . .

The letter moved on to events in Moesia. It was clear to Plautia that Sabinus enjoyed being governor of the province, but he was not overly impressed with his own importance. "Poor Ovid," he wrote, "because of his delightful (though pornographic) poetry, he was exiled to the very province I now govern—which speaks volumes for the importance of this place!"

Plautia enjoyed his lines and smiled at all the places Sabinus hoped she would, but she looked in vain for any revelations of a personal or intimate tenor. And so she usually replied in kind—except once when she allowed herself to ask when he planned to return to Rome. All she got by way of reply was:

When shall I return? I looked into the terms of several of my predecessors, and I found that one governor of Moesia stayed in office here for *twenty-four* years! Since it's always my policy to excel and exceed, you may expect me to hobble back to Rome a quarter century from now as a three-legged antique: two aging limbs and one cane.

So much for attempts at romance by correspondence. She had better forget Flavius Sabinus, she told herself. But then another letter would arrive from Moesia and she would hurry to share it with her friends.

She had been seeing much of them lately—too much, Pomponia thought—but it was all normal enough. Plautia and several daughters of the senatorial nobility had reached the age when they were finally allowed out into the city for longer periods—accompanied, of course, by a member of the household staff. The girls celebrated their new freedoms by manufacturing opportunities to leave home whenever possible.

Today it was the baths. Plautia and her companions were enjoying themselves at a swimming party in the great pool of the Baths of Agrippa. Since neither sex wore any clothing in the public baths, men and women bathed at different times: women in the morning hours, men in the afternoon and evening. The girls were playing water tag, jumping in and out of the pool like so many merry dolphins.

It was while she was being chased that Plautia darted behind some statuary set in a broad alcove near the center of the pool. To her horror she found several young boys hidden behind the statues, leering at her and the other girls. Shrieking, the girls all scrambled into the arms of attendants, who covered them with towels and shouted at the boys. Nothing daunted, the youths scampered after the girls with screams of laughter, and a pimply lad who seemed to be their leader shouted something lewd to Plautia.

"I know who that one is," one of her friends whispered. "It's Domitius Ahenobarbus."

Enveloped in towels, Plautia was so furious at his remark that she picked up a strigil and threw it at him. The skin-scraper struck Domitius, gashing him in the cheek.

Wiping away the blood, he spluttered, "I know you—you who threw that. You're Senator Plautius' daughter, aren't you?"

Plautia was startled. But because of the circumstances, she was even angrier that he knew who she was. "And what if I am, you vulgar wretch?"

"Well," Domitius smirked, "you've marked me now, little Venus. And I think I'd enjoy returning the compliment one day."

Plautia, now burning with embarrassment and rage, shouted back, "They tell me your name is Domitius 'Bronzebeard,' you beardless, disgusting whelp! Now get out of here and play your children's games elsewhere!"

When Domitius saw several of the bath guards approaching, he and his friends ran off.

"Don't you really know who that is, Plautia?" a friend asked.

"No. And I don't care. I hope I never see his pimply face again."

However unpleasant at the time, it was a small incident, really, and Plautia told her parents about it only after a long lull in the family dinner-table conversation. Aulus looked at Plautia and his mouth tightened. "You say the fellow's name was Domitius? You don't mean Domitius Ahenobarbus, do you?"

"Yes, that's what the girls said his name was. 'Bronzebeard.' That's what Ahenobarbus means, doesn't it?"

Aulus nodded and asked, "What did he look like?"

"Oh, he was about twelve or thirteen, with a thick neck. Light, curly hair. And"—she flinched—"his face was covered with pustules."

Aulus nodded several times. Then he said, "Think now, Plautia. Do you know whose face you really cut?"

"A disgusting weed of a boy with a foul mouth."

Aulus sighed. "Well, my dear, I must compliment you on your aim with that strigil, but I do wish you'd have chosen a different target. Perhaps next time you won't aim at a . . . prince of Rome . . . the son of the new empress?"

Plautia caught her breath, while her father continued. "Yes, Domitius is Agrippina's son by her first marriage. You didn't attend the reception honoring his betrothal. That's why you didn't recognize him."

"*That* blighted little boy is *engaged?*"

"Yes. To Octavia, Claudius' daughter."

Plautia frowned at the implications. "And anyone who marries the emperor's daughter may have hopes for the throne? Even Domitius the Pimple?"

"Exactly. And it's becoming clearer that young Domitius is *the* reason why Agrippina wanted to marry Claudius."

"Didn't she marry him simply to become empress?"

"More than that, evidently. She was sister to one emperor—Caligula—and wanted to be not only the wife of another, but the *mother* of one as well! She's already starting to groom her Domitius for the succession."

"But he's only a child," protested Pomponia, who had been quietly listening.

"Still, everything points to it. You've heard of the philosopher Seneca?"

"Yes." Pomponia nodded. "One of the finest minds in the Empire."

"Well, Agrippina has appointed him personal tutor to Domitius."

"But Claudius' *own son* is Britannicus," Plautia objected. "Surely he'll be next in line for the throne."

"Ordinarily, yes. A son would be preferred to a stepson—son-in-law-to-be like Domitius. But don't forget the age difference. Domitius is *older* than Britannicus—only about three or four years older—but still, older. If anything happened to Claudius, who would be more likely to succeed?"

Slowly Plautia wrinkled her brow and nodded.

"Poor Britannicus," said Pomponia. "I understand the empress is forever humiliating him at the palace."

Aulus shrugged. "Let's hope Claudius is alive ten years from now. Britannicus will be almost twenty—old enough for succession." Then, putting his arm around Plautia, he said with a twinkle, "And let's hope you haven't marked Domitius for life with that strigil."

Some version of this conversation was being repeated in almost every Roman home, for the question of who would succeed Claudius was being gossiped and debated everywhere. Once again Aulus felt a clutch of apprehension. Rumors were cracking off the Palatine and tumbling across the city, forming sinister mosaics on a common theme: Agrippina smashing all hurdles between her son and the succession. Her former rivals fell: the wealthy Lollia was accused of consulting astrologers and forced into suicide. If Claudius' wandering eye chanced to find some patrician lady attractive, Agrippina quickly secured her ruin. If some wealthy Roman had gardens that she coveted, they were confiscated. Or if any doubted her power outside the city of Rome, she merely flaunted it—even to the point of renaming the Rhenish town where she was born "Colonia Agrippinensis."*

Still, Aulus was heartened by Claudius' refusal to formally adopt her Domitius as son, even though Agrippina hinted about it every time she had her husband's ear. One day, however, Aulus returned from the Senate with a wounded look and said, "He's given in, Pomponia. Claudius finally asked the Senate for permission to adopt Domitius."

"And did the Fathers grant it?"

"Of course!" Aulus threw up his hands. "But without my vote, in any case."

* Today, Cologne, Germany. Mercifully, the second name did not survive.

Pomponia pursed her lips and looked down. "So," she sighed, "Caesar now has a stepson, a son-in-law-to-be, and a son—all in one youngster named Domitius."

"Correct, my dear, except for the name. The Senate found 'Domitius' too common for the young prince, so they awarded him an old name from the Claudian *gens*: Nero."

"*Nero?*"

"Yes. It's supposed to denote strength or courage. And, of course, young Domitius has neither." He turned to her with a frown and said, "I fear for young Britannicus now. If only we knew what was happening inside the palace."

Pomponia offered a suggestion. "What about Titus, Sabinus' nephew?"

"Vespasian's son! Yes, he's attending the palace school with Britannicus, isn't he?"

"Yes, and I understand they're great friends. They even eat together. Narcissus managed it all as a favor to Vespasian."

Aulus invited Vespasian's family to dinner, and there was much reminiscent chatter about the British campaign. After the repast, however, Aulus spirited Vespasian and young Titus into the library, where the ten-year-old was treated to a barrage of questions. A bright lad with tousled brown hair and a robust build for his age, Titus supplied answers that confirmed Aulus' darkest suspicions.

This picture emerged. Agrippina was behaving toward Britannicus like the worst sort of stepmother, kindling a loathing in the lad which prompted his ugly comments—all of which were then carefully reported to Claudius. Britannicus was particularly furious that he had to appear on public occasions wearing only a boy's tunic, while Nero stood next to him clad in a toga of manhood although he was only thirteen years old.

"Tell me, Titus," said Aulus, "how does the *emperor* feel toward Britannicus?"

"Well, he *seems* to like him. Though he spends a lot of his time shaking dice, you know."

Aulus flashed a wry grin at Vespasian. "Claudius has just published a *treatise* on gambling!—Now tell me, lad, how does Pallas behave toward Britannicus?"

Titus shook his head. "Pallas hates him, I think. Of course, he and the empress . . . well, maybe I shouldn't say." He blushed.

"Please do, lad," Aulus urged.

Now flushed with color and wishing he had not moved into an area that was new and embarrassing to him, Titus hung his head and said, "Britannicus tells me the empress has been—no, forget it."

"Speak, son," Vespasian insisted.

"Well," Titus drawled, "that the empress has been . . . doing naughty things with Pallas."

Aulus' wide-stretching eyes flashed at those of Vespasian for several moments. Then he said, "I wonder if Narcissus knows all this."

Titus had reported it all accurately enough, and soon he would have a new story to tell. One morning, he and Britannicus were strolling in the central garden on the Palatine when they chanced upon Nero. "Hello, Britannicus," said Nero, with a certain contrived affability, while ignoring Titus.

"Hello, Domitius," Britannicus replied, carefully using his old name.

Seized by anger, Nero spun around and spat out the words, "There no longer exists any Domitius Ahenobarbus, you little cur! Not since my adoption!"

"Oh, excuse me, Tiberius Claudius Germanicus *Nero Caesar,*" Britannicus responded, with sham pomposity. "Do I have it right?"

His eyes burning, Nero stalked inside the palace to tell his mother.

"'Bye, Domitius!" Britannicus called after him, an impish grin rippling across his lips.

Agrippina was up to Claudius' office in a trice. "An urgent matter, dearest," she said breathlessly. "The first dreadful sign of discord in our happy family. Out in the gardens just now—your Britannicus refused to call our Nero by his proper name."

"What did he call him?"

"Domitius."

Claudius dropped a wan smile and said nothing.

"Well, aren't you going to do anything about it? Must decrees of the Senate be undone by a . . . a ten-year-old changeling?"

"Britannicus is *not* a changeling, Agrippina!" He was glaring at her. "And his comment was only a childish remark."

"Oh no. It's more serious than that. Britannicus' tutors *told* him to say that to Nero. And if you don't punish this kind of insubordination in the palace, woe to the Empire!"

Agrippina had lied about the tutors, but it had the desired effect.

Shifting moods in an instant, Claudius stalked angrily into the palace school and dismissed the entire lot of Britannicus' instructors. Later he would replace them with inferior teachers who, to no one's surprise, were partisans of Agrippina. Meanwhile, the philosopher Seneca was giving Nero the best education available in Rome, while Agrippina launched rumors that Britannicus was an epileptic and slowly going insane.

9

AULUS PLAUTIUS threw down his pen in disgust. He had gotten as far as the Thames River in his memoirs of the Britannic War, but seemed unable to cross it. The present was intruding hopelessly into the past. The new plotting on the Palatine was slowly shattering his peace of mind.

Was Claudius sleeping—again? Why didn't Narcissus act? Why didn't he warn the emperor? To be sure, Narcissus had been grateful for the information supplied by Titus, but he had added, ominously, "What can I really do, Aulus? You know I've . . . drained away all my credits."

He had indeed, Aulus reflected, staking his future to that huge, smelly swamp fifty miles east of Rome called the Fucine Lake. Narcissus had had 30,000 men working there for eleven years, tunneling through the limestone of a surrounding mountain so that the stagnant marsh could be drained and thousands of acres of new farmland be cultivated. A grand celebration was planned for the Day-of-the-Draining, Aulus recalled with a grimace, a mock naval battle before half the population of Rome camped on the banks. But he could still hear the ghastly gurgle of an emptying tunnel when less than half the lake had drained away. Narcissus' engineers had not tunneled deeply enough. More excavations were needed, more millions of government funds expended.

Then dawned the glorious Day-of-the-Second-Draining, when Claudius invited them all to a great banquet next to the sluice gates at the outflow. But when the gates were raised, Narcissus' impressive waterfall broke through the substructure and became a hideous tidal wave that nearly drowned Claudius, Agrippina, and the rest of the imperial party, who had to run for their very lives. Aulus himself had barely managed to carry Pomponia to safety.

If there had been any doubt, there was none now: Narcissus had indeed drained away his credits, Aulus mused. Pallas and Agrippina would win, then. And Domitius the Pimple—her darling Nero— would be the next emperor. Aulus shoved his writing desk away from him and stood up. "*No,* by all the Furies of hell, he will *not* be the next emperor!" he bellowed, stalking inside the house. Hearing the commotion, Pomponia rushed over to ask what the trouble was.

"I'm going to see Claudius. I'm going to stare into his blue eyes and shout: 'Wake up, Caesar! Put away those cursed dice of yours and learn what's been happening under your ruddy nose! Your wives are the very bane of the Empire, and each is worse than the last. Your Agrippina is a ruthlessly ambitious vulture: she'll stop at nothing until her Nero sits on the throne, and you are safely across the Styx!'"

"No, Aulus," Pomponia pleaded. "If you intervene at the palace, you endanger your life! Stay away from the Palatine, I beg you."

"Someone *must.* This is no time to abandon Rome!"

Narcissus arranged the audience for a night when Agrippina, Nero, and Pallas were presiding over a festivity in the city and the emperor would be alone. "Thank you, friend," Narcissus greeted Aulus as he arrived at the palace, knowing that his was the one voice in Rome to which Claudius might still pay some heed. They found Claudius in his suite, sitting upright in bed, reviewing some reports from the provinces.

"Greetings, Aulus," said Claudius, laying his material aside. "Sorry you find me like this, but my bowels refuse to do what's expected of them. Oh, the cramps I get!" He struggled toward the edge of his bed to get up.

"No, please stay as you were, Caesar. And don't go, Narcissus. This is something that concerns us all." Aulus took a deep breath, hoped he had searched out the proper language to pry the blinders off Claudius, and then launched into a lengthy, well-documented warning on the activities of Agrippina and Pallas. The phrases were more diplomatic than those he had unleashed at home, but they conveyed the same message.

Claudius listened to it all without betraying any emotion. He merely pushed himself to sit up straighter in bed. When Aulus finished, the emperor stared at him vacantly, lips slightly parted but saying nothing.

Narcissus finally broke the silence. "What Aulus says is true, Caesar. For months the empress has been—"

"Marvelous consistency, Narcissus!" Claudius cut him off. "You called the empress a ruthless plotter before I married her. And now after, as well. I should have your head for that."

"And you *shall have it*, Caesar, if you wish," Narcissus replied. "My only purpose is your well-being and security—"

"Or is it to ruin as many of my marriages as possible? First Messalina. Now Agrippina."

"This is not our intention, Caesar," Aulus interrupted. "We're concerned only for your safety—perhaps even your survival—as well as that of young Britannicus."

"Britannicus?" Claudius scowled.

"Yes. If I may be candid, Princeps, you seem to be denying the young prince his birthright and handing it instead to Nero."

Claudius frowned for several moments. Then he asked, "Why do you think that?"

Patiently and cautiously, Aulus enumerated all the political advantages conferred on Nero over the past months, culminating with the latest: his marriage to Claudius' daughter, Octavia. "Everything points to Nero's succession, Caesar," he concluded. "The empress has arranged all the details, even to making her supporter Afranius Burrus the new praetorian prefect. The Senate seems to think Nero will be the next Caesar. The people assume it. Don't you?"

Claudius pushed his covers aside and got out of bed. Padding across the chamber, he poured himself a cup of wine. Swishing the crimson liquid through his teeth as if to cleanse them, he suddenly looked up at the other two and thundered, *"No!* I don't think Nero will be the next emperor! The next emperor *will be my own flesh and blood, Britannicus!"*

A hush of silence ended when Aulus whispered, "The Father of the gods be thanked."

"I gave Nero those favors to keep peace in the palace," Claudius huffed, "and because Britannicus isn't old enough to receive them yet. In three or four years he will be. I've only been playing for *time,* gentlemen, as well as feigning a little ignorance just now so you'd bare your souls. You two don't know what it's like to live with that domineering woman. She hounds me from one end of the palace to the other. By the very gods, I should have taken your advice and never married the prostitute."

"The . . . prostitute?" ventured Aulus.

"Yes, prostitute. With Pallas, I found out.—Heh-heh-heh. Don't look so surprised, my friends: the old cuckold has his own sources of information."

"Do you . . . intend any action, then, Caesar?" Aulus inquired.

"What do you suggest?"

"Well, clearly you must guard Britannicus very carefully over the next months, and pray that the lad grows up quickly."

"I've already encouraged him to do so," Narcissus said, with a wan smile. Then, pacing the chamber, he unveiled his plan. "With your permission, Caesar, I'll have my men set up a secret surveillance over Britannicus' bedroom at night, as well as your own."

Claudius nodded. "And by day?"

"By day, all who have an audience with you will first be searched for daggers. We used to do this some years ago, so the empress will not suspect."

"Exactly," Aulus interposed. "She and Pallas must not suspect, or they'll take countermeasures. Play the mime. Play for time. But if you discover any plot against Caesar, Narcissus, we'll have to act immediately—with or without the praetorians."

Again Claudius nodded. "Splendid, Aulus. I've always thanked the Fates for your loyalty and friendship."

"And may those blessed Fates measure out a good long thread for the span of your life, Caesar!"

"Oh, they will, they will," Claudius tittered. "After all, I'm only sixty-two. And I really don't plan on leaving the stage for a long time yet. Just to spite the empress, of course!"

One evening at dinner, Claudius and Agrippina were having a disagreement over a minor household matter, and Claudius drank more wine than usual to blot out the nagging voice and presence re-clining next to him at the table. Cup followed cup. Finally, half in-toxicated, he propped himself up on one elbow, opened his mouth, and emitted a resounding, imperial belch.

"Claudius!" Agrippina reprimanded. "The servants might hear."

"Oh s-silence, woman!" he slurred his words. "I thought of intro-ducing a law permitting people to break wind at the table too. . . ."

"Enough, you drunken sot!"

Claudius lay back and gazed at the ornate ceiling of the palace dining room. "Ah me," he sighed. "It's become my destiny to have wives—all of them unchaste. But not *unchastened!*" Then he turned and gave her a long and chilling stare.

Agrippina excused herself and left the room. The look in Clau-dius' eyes thoroughly alarmed her. They had a fearful, deadly ear-nest. Under other circumstances, his pun might have been no more than a cranky comment, but with that look they were a mortal threat. "Unchaste," he had said. Could he possibly know?

The next day she was sure of it. Pallas told her of a scene he had witnessed that morning before breakfast. Claudius had greeted Bri-tannicus and then, as if on impulse, he had walked over to the lad and hugged him. "Then, dear Agrippina, mark well what he said next: 'Soon you'll be a man, my son, and then I'll explain every-thing that's happened. I may have wounded you, Britannicus, but I'll heal that wound. And do you know what, lad? I'm going to give you the toga of manhood a year early: I want the Roman people to have a *genuine* Caesar after me.' "

Agrippina winced and then reported Claudius' comments the night before. "So, this is how matters stand. Young Britannicus is growing older and older. By the month. By the hour."

"And soon, of course, he'll be legally entitled to all the privileges Nero now enjoys," said Pallas.

"If *only* Claudius would . . . *pay nature's debt* and join his ances-tors."

Pallas nodded, but his next thought dared not be put into words. Agrippina, however, felt no such restraint. She looked at her lover and said, slowly, "So, dear Pallas. We no longer have any alterna-tive. Do you understand me?"

Pallas frowned, teased his left earring several times, and finally nodded slowly.

"But what's to be done about Narcissus?" She knew better than to attempt anything with Claudius' loyal secretary fluttering around the palace like a solicitous mother hen, keeping the bodyguard in trim.

"Can't we eliminate him?" Pallas wondered. "No, that would only alert Claudius to our plans." Then he brightened. "I have it! My dear colleague has been complaining about swelling in his joints —obviously gout. Now surely he should go away for a rest cure, don't you think?"

Agrippina smiled. "Where, dear Pallas, do they heal such a dreadful malady?"

"The standard spot is the bubbling sulfur bath at Sinuessa."

"Yes, and Sinuessa happens to be almost as far south as Naples."

"Far enough for our purposes."

"Yes. Yes, indeed. I'll have one of the palace doctors advise Narcissus that he's been working too hard and should go to Sinuessa for his health."

"That's it. Only he must *not* say that the suggestion came from you."

Narcissus' health had indeed been failing, as much a result of his political anxieties as his gout, but affairs seemed stable enough on the Palatine for him to follow the palace doctor's orders. Early in October, he set out for Sinuessa, accompanied by his chief aides, glad for a brief vacation at the salubrious waters of the resort. He sent word to Aulus telling him where he could be reached and when he would return but, inexplicably, the message was never received.

Trying to shorten the life of a Roman emperor was a particularly dangerous venture, Agrippina knew. If he were universally detested, main force could do the job—a committee of assassins clutching daggers and swords. Her dear, crazed brother Caligula had gone that route.

But Claudius presented a special problem. He was far more popular than his predecessor, and Rome would never tolerate his assassination. He would therefore have to die "naturally," an apparent illness, followed by a very real death. Only poison, she and Pallas decided, filled these qualifications.

A woman named Locusta had the greatest reputation in Roman toxicology. To most people, Locusta was merely a legend—a witch and sorceress who never really existed except to frighten disobedient children. Agrippina knew better. Locusta had recently been condemned to death for poisoning—her arts were in considerable demand in the city—but Agrippina had secretly intervened to save her life. At the moment, Locusta was under house arrest in her dwelling near the Palatine, guarded by a tribune who was directly responsible to the empress.

The evening after Narcissus left Rome, Agrippina disguised herself and made her way to Locusta's house. At her knock, a young praetorian opened the door just enough to peer out quizzically.

"It's I, Pollio," she said, lifting her veil.

"Come in, Empress."

"Wait here and see that no one else enters."

Agrippina descended a steep flight of stairs to what looked like the kitchen of a large villa, poorly illuminated by several flickering clay lamps. She almost retched at the strange, acrid odors of the place, so unlike the essences of rose and balsam that were continually sprayed about the palace. As her eyes adjusted to the darkness, she noticed shelves with dozens of ceramic pots, many marked with strange, occult symbols. Glass bottles stood on an adjacent table, filled with liquids and powders of various colors.

At a central work table sat Locusta, a swarthy, corpulent woman clad in a stola that looked yellow, whether from age or the flaming lamplight Agrippina could not tell. Locusta now looked up suspiciously with jaundiced eyes. "Well, what do you want?" she demanded in a rasping voice.

"Do you know who I am?" Agrippina lifted her veil.

Locusta's eyes squinted, then widened in recognition. "You . . . you're the empress?"

"Yes, the one who saved your life. Now it's time to return this favor . . . without asking any questions. Agreed?"

"Agreed. Certainly. Agreed."

"I must have a special poison."

"For what purpose?"

"I thought we agreed you wouldn't ask any questions."

"But Empress, the potion must *fit* the victim," the hag wheezed. "Those jeweled sandals of yours: they were made to fit you, not your husband. So if it's to have proper effect, the poison must be specially prepared for its victim and administered in the proper dosage."

Agrippina was silent, pondering.

"Empress, I owe my life to you, so I swear that nothing of this conversation will ever pass my lips. What is it? Do you want the horses slowed down at the circus so your colors will win? Eh? I've got a beautiful mixture for that. And there's no way to detect it." She grinned proudly. Agrippina noticed that several of her teeth were missing. "And the horses recover again in a day or so.—No? Not horses? So . . . it's more serious. You want somebody's death? Describe her. Or him."

"A human being, about sixty years old."

"Male or female?" Locusta continued, now very businesslike.

Agrippina hesitated, then replied, "Male."

"How tall? How heavy?"

"Five feet and three-quarters. About 180 pounds."

Locusta gave her a startled look, but did not disrupt the inquiry. "Must he die quickly, or of a lingering illness?"

"Yes, that's important. He must *not* die immediately, for then poison would be suspected. But he should lose consciousness and die within several hours."

"I see." Locusta thought for a moment, stained hands tugging at her wrinkled chin. Then she reached over and uncovered a large pot with bright green crystals. "Here . . . four, no, five pinches of this in his wine at supper. The green won't discolor the wine, even though you might think so. Even if he drinks only half the cup, he'll collapse and die by morning."

Agrippina shook her head. "No, it won't do. This man has all his wine tasted first."

"Ah, well, a different carrier, then," Locusta shrugged. "Is his food tasted too?"

"Yes."

"No matter. Food can be separated. What are his favorite dishes?"

Agrippina pressed her lips in thought. "Well, roast boar, mullet, oysters—"

"Does he like mushrooms?"

"Oh . . . yes, of course. He loves mushrooms. But he knows them so well he'd recognize the poisonous kind."

"I don't mean poison mushrooms . . . *edible* mushrooms as hosts for the poison. We merely have to find a toxin that won't interfere with the delicate taste of a mushroom." Locusta glanced into an aged scroll, then took a dusty amphora off a shelf. "Yes," she said, pulling out the cork and smelling it, "this will do. It's a very rare compound: the juice of the Palestinian wild gourd, and it has almost no taste. Take one or two large mushrooms—that should be enough—

cook them, and then let them steep in this essence overnight. But see that he eats at least one of them completely."

"What will happen then?"

"In a minute or two he'll start gasping for air and then faint. Death will follow in three or four hours."

"How do I know it will work?"

Locusta scowled for a moment but then grinned. She dribbled a single drop of the poison onto some wheat in a feed tray. Next she went to a wall stacked with cages, pulled a pigeon out, and stuffed several grains down its squawking throat. "Now watch that bird," she said.

The pigeon pranced around for several minutes. Then its wings flapped out of control, and it flipped over dead.

"It will be slower with Clau—ah—the man involved," said Locusta, her yellow skin turning orange with embarrassment. "Don't worry, Empress," she added hastily, "we *both* have reason enough to keep our lips sealed."

"Thank you, Locusta. I'll see that you're . . . properly rewarded."

Agrippina climbed the stairs, clutching a flask under the folds of her stola. At the doorway she whispered to the guard, "Locusta is not to leave here for the next two days. She's not to receive any visitors. If she tries to escape, kill her."

"As you wish, Empress."

October 12, A.D. 54 had been a good day for Claudius. His engineers at Ostia had given him a glowing report on the harbor works, and already he was thinking of what extraordinary spectacles to schedule for the opening of the port.

Even Agrippina seemed friendlier than usual. She inquired about his health as if genuinely concerned about him. At lunch she chatted about plans for the coming spring and wondered if they might take a trip to Greece. Could they yet make a success of their marriage, Claudius wondered.

That evening the imperial family dined together, including Nero and his Octavia, and Britannicus. Nero was badgering Britannicus in some argument, but Britannicus took it well: someday he, not Nero, would be emperor. The thirteen-year-old seemed less excited over the prospects of ruling a world empire than in having the chance to pull Domitius off his high horse. He still refused to call him Nero.

The first course of Circeian oysters and crab was followed by green beans and a silver platter of steaming mushrooms. The emperor was always served first, and when the lid was raised and he spied his favorite delicacy, he sighed with contentment.

On this particular evening, the eunuch Halotus was on duty as Claudius' butler and taster, for Agrippina had made him party to the plot. Halotus' fingers deftly poked about for several small pieces of mushroom and he put them into his mouth. He nodded and served Claudius.

Claudius was about to pluck several of the large tainted mushrooms when he looked about the table and stopped. "Aha ha!" he chortled. "You all know about Caesar's weakness for mushrooms, don't you? And you expect to see a hungry old man slobber all over them? Eh?" He looked about with a twinkle in his eye. "Well, I can control myself. Here, Halotus, serve the others first."

Halotus stepped back and looked blankly at Agrippina. She had been watching the mushrooms from the corner of her eye and now had to take her hands off the table to disguise their trembling. Nero knew nothing of the plot. What if he—or anyone else—took the wrong mushrooms?

"Just put some on his plate, Halotus," she said. "We know how much he loves them."

Claudius spread his hands over the plate. "The others first. I have spoken."

Agrippina coughed several times and said, "All right. But remember all of you, save the large, choice pieces for Caesar. Here, Halotus, give me just a few." She extended her plate, hoping the others would follow her in letting the butler serve them rather than making the selection themselves. With a silver fork, Halotus skewered several small mushrooms near the edge and put them on her plate.

In agony she watched the platter go round the table. Only four of the largest mushrooms in the center of the dish had been steeped in Locusta's brew, and Agrippina's eyes never left them. They were safe until the platter came around to Nero. A playful gleam in his eyes, Nero slowly opened his fingers and plucked the largest mushroom off the platter. "Haha, Papa!"

The mushroom was saturated with poison. Agrippina felt dizzy.

Then, as playfully, Nero put it back on the platter for Claudius. But what if he should lick his fingers? Agrippina signaled a slave boy who came running over with a bowl of water and carefully washed Nero's hand. Since Romans ate mainly with their fingers, they were regularly washed between courses. No one noticed anything amiss.

When the platter finally returned to Claudius, he dropped a pleasantry about his self-control, and then plucked two of the four large mushrooms for his plate. Agrippina now added to her helping, taking the two remaining poisoned mushrooms so no one else would eat them.

For endless minutes Claudius seemed to eat everything on his plate but the mushrooms. Agrippina was appalled. The same thumb and index finger Claudius had used to take the tainted mushrooms were poking the other delicacies into his mouth. If enough poison had contaminated his fingers, he might sicken before he got to the mushrooms, but that small a dose would hardly kill him.

"Mmmmm," mused Claudius, and then, still munching, "these mushrooms aren't nearly as good as they look."

Agrippina's eyes swooped over to his plate. He was chewing one of the mushrooms! At last he swallowed it and reached for the second, carefully probing it apart with his fingers.

"Hmmmm. Looks all right, but these really have an odd taste. I wonder if they're spoiled."

Agrippina felt a painful throbbing at her temples as her pulse raced madly. Claudius was showing no ill effects whatever. Had he taken some antidote? Had Locusta or the tribune betrayed her?

"Halotus!" Claudius bellowed. "How about the rest of you? Did everything taste all right to you?"

The others looked surprised and nodded. Then they saw Claudius' right arm fall limply from the table and his eyes roll up in their sockets. His face contorted. He coughed once and then slumped back onto the couch, unconscious.

The dinner circle sat up, stupefied. "Poor dear," Agrippina said, "he's probably had too much to drink. But let's be sure. Halotus, summon Xenophon."

Xenophon was the Greek palace physician who had recommended Narcissus' vacation and, of course, was also in on the conspiracy. He came rushing in to examine Claudius. But in a short time he turned around and smiled. "Nothing to be alarmed about. Caesar has simply had an attack of indigestion, along with the effects of the wine, of course. Let's carry him up to bed, Halotus."

"Poor dear," said Agrippina, stroking the silver hair of her stricken husband. "Finish your dinner, all of you."

The emperor of Rome, his face now hideously flushed, groaned as he lay in his bed. Agrippina allowed no one but Pallas, Xenophon, and herself inside the bedroom. The rest of the palace had accepted the doctor's story and saw no reason for concern.

Suddenly, Claudius regained consciousness, looked around with wild eyes, and staggered out of bed to go to the bathroom and surrender his dinner. Then, without saying a word, he crawled back into bed, breathing very deeply but regularly.

A half hour passed. Then another. And another. Now Claudius, belching, propped himself up in bed and said, "The mushrooms . . . spoiled. But I feel better now. Bring me some cold water, Agrippina."

"Certainly, dearest." Outside the bedroom she asked Xenophon, "He *can't* be recovering, can he?"

"I'm afraid he is. He may have thrown up much of the poison. Or purged it."

"By all the infernal gods," she cried, "what shall we do now?" She looked at Pallas, who stood mute and ashen-faced.

"Cursed be the day I agreed to all this," Xenophon muttered. "But we'd better finish what we started. I have another drug here." He inserted a feather into a jar of slimy blue substance and swirled it around. Then he carried it into the bedroom.

"You're doing much better, Princeps," he said. "But we must be certain that all the spoiled food is out of your body. So we'll use this feather to induce nausea, as usual."

Claudius nodded. It was a standard remedy.

While Agrippina held out a bowl, he quickly swabbed Claudius' throat with the undiluted poison. The emperor retched, gagged, and fell unconscious.

"Now it's done," Agrippina whispered.

Xenophon nodded. "It's a very rapid-acting poison."

But by midnight Claudius was still alive. His pulse, after almost stopping, was now beating regularly again, and his breathing seemed almost normal. He stirred and nearly regained consciousness.

"How does he do it?" the doctor whispered, grinding a fist into his palm.

"I'll kill the witch who gave me that poison," Agrippina seethed.

"No. I know that essence of gourd. It's very powerful. It would have killed him if he'd kept it down. Then, too, his body is used to all kinds of excesses. He can probably absorb anything . . . even poisons."

"Well, what can we do? Smother him with pillows? We've got to end this all *now*. Britannicus won't go to sleep. He keeps asking about his father."

"We can't smother him. There's a chance he might waken and cry out. What did you do with Locusta's poison after you steeped the mushrooms in it?"

"I . . . I put it back into the flask."

"Good. Get it. Quickly."

When she returned with the flask, the doctor ordered, "Roll him over." Then he opened his case and took out a strange-looking vessel, which he filled with the fluids remaining in Locusta's flask. Then he applied it to his patient.

Claudius Caesar, fourth emperor of Rome, died fifteen minutes later of a poison enema.

BOOK TWO

THE TINDER

10

"IT'S DONE, Pallas!" Agrippina whispered to her paramour. "Go. At once. Everything must work exactly as planned, or we'll still lose everything."

Pallas embraced her warmly and hurried out of the room. "Understand, everyone," he told his aides, "the emperor is *not* dead. He's seriously ill—a sudden stroke—and Rome must now pray the gods for his swift recovery. All right, then, everyone to his assignment."

News of Claudius' death had to be withheld until transfer of power was safely accomplished. While aides hurried off into the night, Pallas went to the Castra Praetoria to alert the prefect Burrus.

By dawn, the Senate convened in extraordinary session as the consuls led the chamber in supplications to Jupiter. Citizens were gathering in the Forum, shouting vows for the emperor's health. And all the while, the lifeless body of Claudius was being wrapped in blankets as if to warm him. People clustered outside the palace saw a troupe of comic actors rush inside. Claudius had revived, guards said, and was calling for entertainment.

Agrippina went up to the chamber of her private astrologer, who was carefully studying the charts of Claudius and Nero and consulting scrolls.

"Well, Balbillus? When shall it be?"

The astrologer looked up from his figures. "Is Caesar dead?"

Agrippina looked at him suspiciously. "Don't your stars tell you that he is? Yes. Six hours ago."

Balbillus coughed with slight embarrassment and busily adjusted his calculations, drawing new lines and scribbling down occult signs and configurations. Then he frowned and said, "Your son must *not* be declared emperor this morning. Something dire would result."

Agrippina blanched. "What would happen?"

"The stars are not that specific. But it would be calamitous."

"Well, what about this afternoon?"

The astrologer returned to his charts, staring at them with hypnotic detachment. At last he nodded and said, "Yes. Noon or after will be favorable. Very favorable."

Agrippina hurried off to prepare Nero. She had awakened him at early dawn with the news that he was now emperor of Rome. Sleepy and bewildered, he yawned and replied, "Whatever you say, Mother."

Now Pallas had returned with Burrus, and all the heads of Agrippina's party held a final strategy session. The philosopher Seneca, Nero's tutor, started writing down what his ward was to say in his first public address. But Afranius Burrus, the praetorian commander, was the crucial key to empire, and they now asked him the momentous question: "Will your men declare for Nero?"

Burrus brushed a hand through his auburn hair, which had been cropped short in the military manner. Then he massaged his maimed left arm—an old war wound—and nodded.

Just after high noon, October 13, the gates of the palace suddenly burst open and Nero, resplendent in imperial purple, marched out with Burrus at his side. A light rain was falling, and Nero tried to brush the droplets off his cloak, overconscious of his first appearance as Caesar. The elite First Cohort of the Praetorian Guard was standing at attention in front of the palace steps.

Nero and Burrus stopped at the center of the staircase. Slowly, the prefect made his announcement: "Tiberius Claudius Caesar Augustus Germanicus is dead!" The red plume across his helmet seemed to quiver with each syllable of the imperial name. "The end came this morning. A stroke."

A commotion of surprise and sorrow broke out among the praetorians.

"Attention!" Burrus barked. "I have the supreme honor to present to you the new emperor and princeps of the Senate and the Roman People: Tiberius Claudius *Nero Caesar!*"

Some of the praetorians looked startled. Burrus backed off and saluted, "Hail, Caesar!"

"*Hail, Caesar!*" many of the men joined in, but others continued to look perplexed.

"What about Britannicus?" someone shouted.

"Yes, where is Britannicus?" cried another. "Whom did Claudius appoint in his will?"

"Order!" Burrus fumed. "Stop this incredible display! For shame! Now, whoever fails to hail the new emperor will be arrested on the spot for treason!" He scowled several moments more, then turned, slowly extended his right arm, and cried, "Hail, Caesar!"

"*Ave imperator! Long live Nero Caesar!*" came the now unanimous refrain. Burrus' eyes combed through the ranks and saw every arm saluting.

Nero entered a litter and was carried over to the Castra Praetoria. He cursed the rain. He would have preferred riding triumphantly to the camp on horseback, but he could hardly show himself to the praetorians spattered with mud and soaked to the skin. He made a brief speech to the assembled troops, who paid most attention to what he said at the close: "As a reward for your allegiance, I pledge each of you a gift of 15,000 sesterces."

The jubilant roar from the Castra could be heard as far away as the Forum. Nero and his party left for the Senate with the men still shouting, "*Ave imperator!*"

Earlier that morning, Aulus Plautius had thought the sudden summons to the Senate ominous enough. But when Claudius' possibly mortal illness was announced, he had jumped up from his bench and left the chamber. Outside he met one of Pallas' junior aides and asked him where Narcissus was. "Why he's down in Sinuessa," he replied, smirking. "He's taking the baths."

A dozen thoughts raced through Aulus' mind. Why hadn't Narcissus stayed in touch? Was there still time to reach him and make a move for Britannicus? No, hardly enough—unless Claudius were not that seriously ill. Painfully, he returned to the Senate.

Just after noon, the official prayers were interrupted with the bulletin that the emperor was dead. Aulus sank back on his bench and covered his face with his hands. His friend, his comrade-in-arms was no more, and he immediately had very dark thoughts about the circumstances of his illness. At the moment, there were no further details of any kind, but the senators were already gossiping about his successor.

And now young Nero himself was presented to the Senate. The Fathers rose to bestow honor after honor on the prince, and soon it was official: the Senate solemnly declared the blondish-haired youth emperor of Rome. One of the senators even stood up and said fawningly, "I propose that our beloved new princeps also be awarded the title *pater patriae!*"

Immediately Nero was on his feet. "Father of the Fatherland?" he protested. "No, my elders in government. My seventeen years do not justify so esteemed a title. I must refuse."

The chamber broke into deafening applause, and Seneca, off to one side, beamed his approval. Squinting and blinking a bit because he was nearsighted, Nero now delivered a eulogy for Claudius, and the Senate formally decreed divine honors to the dead emperor.

During Nero's address, Pallas had been sitting in a gallery behind him, watching the faces of the senators and jotting down names on a slip of papyrus. He recorded those who seemed less than pleased with the succession, and he underlined the names of the only two Fathers who had given no external sign whatever that they approved of Nero. They were the Stoic senator Thrasea Paetus and Aulus Plautius. Not once that afternoon had either man applauded or even smiled.

Nero returned to the palace after the most dizzying day of his life. At dawn the sleepy teenager had learned of Claudius' death. By dusk all Rome had acclaimed him emperor. Agrippina was waiting for him at the portal, radiant and triumphant. Nero saw her at the head of the stairs and he paused to smile adoringly at the woman who had made it all possible.

Just then, a tribune of the palace guard came up to ask him what the watchword for that night would be.

"*Mater optima!*" he said. "The best of mothers!"

Meanwhile, alone in his bedroom, an inconsolable Britannicus was weeping bitter tears at the loss of a father—and an empire.

The next morning, the palace awoke to the smell of smoke. It seemed to be coming from Claudius' office. Rushing in with several guards, Agrippina found Narcissus burning all of Claudius' secret documents in a brazier. Haggard from a furious ride back to Rome, Narcissus had a tired smile as he watched the last papers turn to ash. "There," he sighed. "I've kept faith with you, Claudius. Until the end."

"It's the end, all right," Agrippina seethed. "Guards! Throw this . . . filthy wretch into the dungeon. The deepest and rankest cell you can find!"

Less than an hour after Narcissus was dragged off, Pallas visited him in the subterranean prison on the Palatine. "You knew it was suicide coming back here, Narcissus," he said. "Why did you do it?"

"Loyalty, Pallas. You wouldn't understand the concept."

Pallas unleashed a scowl at his rival and said, "Well, your situation's hopeless, you arrogant fool. So you might as well use this." He threw him a dagger and left.

"I'll just borrow it, Pallas," he called. "You'll need it again some-day . . . because of the usurper you created!"

Not since that of the great Augustus had Rome witnessed such a funeral. Aulus led the senatorial pallbearers carrying the body of Claudius in solemn procession down to a Forum crowded with Romans. Young Nero ascended the rostrum and delivered what even Aulus had to admit was a brilliant address, promising wisdom, moderation, and clemency as the hallmarks of his future administration. Seneca must have written every word of it, Aulus assumed.

The funeral procession continued northward to the Campus Martius, halting before a tall pyramid of stacked logs which had been saturated with spices and sprinkled with incense. Aulus and the pallbearers carefully hoisted the bier onto the apex of the pyre. Nero was then handed a torch. Averting his face, he touched the kindling of cypress boughs which had been threaded between the logs, and the pyre quickly ignited in a great blaze.

Aulus and his colleagues waited in respectful silence until the pyramid collapsed in a shower of sparks but left before the embers were quenched with wine and Claudius' ashes collected for his urn inside the Augustan Mausoleum. While returning to the city, Aulus was astonished to find Nero's tutor-adviser Seneca falling in line at his side. The philosopher was a man of short stature and spare build, but his deep-set, penetrating eyes and well-chiseled nose lent dignity to what otherwise would have been an unattractive face. Turning to

Aulus, he asked in an amiable tone, "May I presume to accompany the conqueror of Britain?"

"You are welcome, Annaeus Seneca."

"Tell me, Senator. How did the princeps' remarks in the Forum strike you?"

Aulus frowned. "Moderation? Clemency?" he challenged. "Then why did Narcissus have to die?"

Seneca flushed. "Believe me when I tell you that Nero was furious when he heard the news. He would have pardoned him. It was Agrippina and Pallas who drove him to suicide."

Aulus said nothing. His mood was as smoldering as the embers he had just left. For a moment he thought of demanding from Seneca the full details of Claudius' death, but then he decided that this was neither the time nor place for such a discussion.

"But again, Senator, what did you think of the new Caesar's address?" Seneca persisted.

"A fine performance, certainly. I only hope he'll be able to do exactly as he promises."

"I too. But why are you smiling, if I may ask?"

"Nothing, really. I just happened to think that the new emperor must be precocious indeed to have written such a speech at his age."

"Oh, he is, he is . . . though I think he *may* have had a little assistance." He smiled. "Sometime, Aulus—if I may call you that—let us meet to exchange views on Rome's future. May we?"

"Of course."

So, Aulus thought, as he watched Seneca rejoin the imperial party, the new government was losing no time in trying to conciliate possible opposition. But Seneca's singling him out also proved what he had already suspected: in the new administration, Aulus Plautius was a marked man.

One afternoon, late that fall, a strange figure appeared at the door of the Plautius residence, demanding to see the master of the house. When Aulus appeared, he saw a scalp full of dark hair bent low toward him in the posture of a suppliant and a hand thrust out with a note in its open palm:

I cannot speak. My tongue was cut out by Rome's enemies in the East. I have no employment, but would like to add myself as client to this noble household, and receive the patronage I deserve from so famous a family as the Plautii.

Aulus was startled and asked, "Who are you?" before he recalled that the man could not talk. The figure only grunted in a miserable baritone.

"Enough *obsequium!*" Aulus snapped. "Hold your head up, man!"

The stranger lifted his head and unleashed a broad smile, exposing the perfect teeth of which the Flavii were so proud. "Hello, Governor!" he said, in perfect Latin.

"Flavius Sabinus, you *scoundrel!*" Aulus bellowed. Then he shouted for Pomponia and Plautia. Sabinus had just returned to Rome after resigning his governorship in Moesia, for when an emperor died, all magistrates tendered their resignations. He was now sweeping back into their lives with the exuberance of a Mediterranean gale, breaking up the gloom that had overshadowed the Plautii.

Inevitably, he and Aulus took a long excursion into the new political climate of Rome—until Plautia could stand it no longer and all but snatched Sabinus away from her delighted parents and pulled him out into the peristyle. Now that they were alone at last, he flashed a great smile and asked, "Have I aged much, pretty Plautia?"

"Yes, you have. You look about a week older than when you left for Moesia."

"Five years ago?" Sabinus laughed. "It's not fair, then. I'm the same, but you—you're astonishingly different."

"How I've grown? That sort of thing?"

Sabinus shook his head and grinned. "It's not a question of growth. The term is transformation. Alas, the lovely little slip of a girl I left is no more." He said it with mock grief.

"Disappointed, Sabinus?"

He looked at Plautia carefully. Her now-mature beauty made him almost uncomfortable, for nature had added several soft finishing touches to the girl that both surprised and delighted him. Her perfect nose had not been spoiled by time, her once-thin lips had fleshed out into a handsome, patrician mouth, and her blue eyes had more sparkle than he ever remembered.

"Disappointed?" he finally replied. "With a woman of . . . incredible charm?"

"You shouldn't say that to me." Her cheeks were flushing. "At least, not so directly. And besides, I've a score to settle with you, and how can I do that when you're saying such nice things?"

"What's wrong?"

"Well," she bit her lip. "Let's put it this way: why didn't you bring your wife along on this visit?"

"My wife?"

"Yes, and your children too, for that matter?"

Sabinus looked at her uncomprehendingly. "But I'm not married."

"Pity!" Plautia smiled. "Because I am."

"You? Married?"

"Yes, didn't Father tell you? I'm just visiting here today."

He looked at her blankly. "Who? When?"

"Last fall. After all, Sabinus, I was becoming an old woman. I was twenty-one at the time—twenty-two now."

"Who? Why didn't you mention it in a letter?"

"I . . . think you know him. What's the matter, Sabinus? You wouldn't be disappointed now, would you?"

He put his hands to her shoulders and pressed them. "Enough of this! Whom did you marry?"

"Marcus Otho."

Sabinus stepped back. "Marcus Salvius Otho?"

She nodded, avoiding his eyes.

"But that wild dandy is still a bachelor! I know it for a fact!"

"Hades!" She stamped her foot. "He's my age, but I picked the wrong name!"

Sabinus shook with a hearty laugh and hugged her. *"Vixen!"* he cried.

"But that's the point, Sabinus." She pouted. "I could easily *have* fallen in love and gotten married during the five years you were away—for all you cared."

"But I *did* care, Plautia . . ."

"Then why didn't you visit me on your trips back to Rome?"

"I did."

"Once. Hurriedly."

"But I got back to Rome only once. I thought I'd return more often, but Moesia was *quite* a chore. And my letters certainly showed I was . . . well, concerned about you."

"Did they? Oh, I appreciated hearing from you, Sabinus. But there was never anything really personal in your lines. And you were away for so *long*."

"I'm afraid that's the political side of me, Plautia. I hate to express feelings in words. But you're right, you know. I really was presuming to find you here—still unmarried. And it has been a long time."

"A *very* long time." She frowned, but then brightened. "I suppose I do understand, though. Men in government have very full lives. Time passes rapidly. But we gir—ah—women think about other things."

"Maybe I'm still presuming too much, Plautia, but I forgot to ask you. You've never said anything about it in your letters—but *is* there someone in your life? Or have your parents arranged anything?"

"I'd love to tease you some more and parade a whole list of names—"

"Aha! Then, at least, there would be safety in numbers."

"And don't for a moment think there haven't been suitors around."

"More than were buzzing around Penelope as she waited for Ulysses, I'll wager!"

"Oh stop it, Sabinus, I'm serious, and—what are you looking for?"

"Where do you keep it?"

"What?"

"Your loom, of course. Remember, Penelope promised to marry when she'd woven a shroud, but each night she unraveled the day's work?"

"*Monster!*" Plautia shouted, playfully pommeling his broad chest with her smallish fists. Then she broke into childish laughter. He *had* changed after all, she thought. He was ever so much surer of himself than when he had left for Moesia. Five years of issuing commands as governor of a province had finally made a man of that shy semisuitor who had first shown up on the Esquiline, eyes askance and foot in mouth.

"Tell me about Moesia, Sabinus," she said.

"You must see it with me some time, Plautia, its lush, rolling hills, heavily wooded at places. A greenish river called the Danube rims it to the north . . ." The description lasted until the dinner hour, after which Aulus and Pomponia retired early, leaving Sabinus and Plautia alone.

In bed, Pomponia heard the chatter and laughter as well as the intriguing silences, and she smiled, remembering the days when Aulus had wooed her—and had won so easily. Would that distinguished-looking Sabinus try to steal their only daughter from them? For Plautia's sake, she hoped so. For herself, she dreaded the day.

It was the small hours of the morning when Plautia finally saw Sabinus to the door. Hours earlier, they had easily fallen into each other's arms, kissing and embracing with an intensity that astonished them. He leaned over to brush her cheek with his lips one more time. Her skin—soft, resilient, tingling—inflamed him as much now as their first rapturous kiss earlier in the evening. And when his lips met hers a final time, their very souls seemed to flow together.

Tradition ruled that it was the wrong time to fall in love. Romances, like nature, usually blossomed in spring. But the wind and rain of that Roman winter found Sabinus and Plautia glowing with a deepening attachment that easily took command of their lives. They seemed to see everything with a new intensity because joy had added a fresh dimension to life. The marble columns of Rome's public buildings never seemed so majestic, the art in the Forum never so impressive. Nature herself, though she lay in mourning for spring, seemed bursting with color for the lovers. Patches of lead blue in the cloud-flecked skies overhead became living azure, and even the pines shed their drab for a brilliant wintergreen. The very air they breathed seemed to acquire, for the first time, a special aura of its own, so that something so common as breathing itself had meaning for them.

So magnificent was love, Plautia told her parents. But it was also demanding. Love possessed one. The image of Sabinus was always there, whether or not the man himself was. Everything in her day— every plan, hope, detail—seemed related to him. Her life now had a new set of values: things were no longer good or bad in themselves; they had meaning only to the extent that they brought him to her or took him away.

Sabinus had resumed his seat in the Senate, and this filled much of his day, wrenching his thoughts away from the Esquiline and Plautia. But he could never really put her out of mind, and he found every excuse to visit her as often as possible. He was intrigued —no, astounded—by life's happy surprise called love, and he now regretted the years he had spent apart from Plautia.

As they watched the relationship ripen, Aulus and Pomponia found it difficult to conceal their enthusiasm, though they had the good sense not to flaunt their approval. Pomponia's parents had favored Aulus' courtship too eagerly—and almost ruined it in the process.

Sabinus was listening carefully to what Annaeus Seneca had to tell him in the privacy of his suite at the palace. For some minutes the philosopher confided—in muted tones—the tragic circumstances of Claudius' death, but swore that he had no part in it. His mood brightened, however, as he paraded out for Sabinus the great hopes he had for Nero's regime. Then he gave abrupt focus to their conversation.

"The emperor and I have studied your record in Moesia, Sabinus. Frankly, we're impressed." Touching the tips of his fingers together, he asked, "Do you suppose you could tear yourself away from the Senate long enough to do a job for us?"

"What is it, Seneca?"

"We'd like to appoint you *curator census Gallici*, supervisor of the census in Gaul. For once we need an accurate count there, Sabinus. Everything depends on it—taxation, the military, representation in the Senate. You can take a staff along with you, of course."

Sabinus was disappointed. After a governorship, this hardly seemed a promotion, and the thought of leaving Plautia at this point was painful. "How long would I be gone?" he finally responded.

"Shouldn't take more than a year. Probably less. But let me add this, Sabinus: Caesar and I feel you're capable of *much* more in Roman government, of course. Do a good job for us up in Gaul, and we'll take you into the administration here in Rome—if you're willing."

Sabinus was too diplomatic to press Seneca for details on the last interesting point, so he exhaled a long breath and asked, "May I think about it for a day or two?"

"Certainly.—By the way, I have no idea how the empress mother knew you were coming here, but she's asked that you see her before leaving the palace."

"Agrippina? But I've never even met her—thank the gods! What could she possibly want of me?"

Seneca shrugged. "Here's her note: 'I should like to see Flavius Sabinus immediately after your interview today, Annaeus Seneca.' So I'd best show you the way."

Seneca escorted Sabinus up a staircase and across a hall. Then he pointed to a doorway and excused himself.

A servant girl admitted Sabinus into a lavish waiting room, and then withdrew. Several minutes later, Agrippina appeared, wearing a robe of spun silver, a light smile on her lips. Sabinus looked at the cascades of dark curls and burning green eyes. Glints of recognition started piecing themselves together in his memory. Then he gasped. It was . . . yes, it unmistakably was the woman he had spurned at Messalina's bacchanal!

Several moments more she let him suffer, and then said, "So, Sabinus, you *do* recognize me, don't you? That's the first compliment you've ever paid me, since it *has* been some years . . ."

"I . . . *you* are the empress Agrippina?"

"That's rather lame, Senator. But, then, I always did have the advantage of knowing who you were, rather than vice versa." Then she flashed an almost malicious smile. "Well, Sabinus, it seems the Gorgons didn't turn you into stone after all." She broke into a low, mischievous chuckle.

Sabinus was struggling for composure. He thought he had banished from memory the hissing voice that had once called him a simpering eunuch, but here it was again, belonging to the most powerful woman on earth, who had become empress-mother over the bodies of her victims and the poisoned flesh of her husband.

"Nothing to say, Sabinus?"

He was struggling for something as simple as a coherent sentence. "I . . . I was drunk then, Empress," he finally managed. "So was everyone else."

"I wasn't," she said, giving no quarter. "How did you put it that day? 'You don't appeal to me . . . not that way.'" Now her voice shifted to a lower register. "No one has *ever* told me that, Sabinus. Ever. Before or since."

"I dare say not." Desperately, he tried to shift their excruciating conversation. "You are surely to be congratulated for achieving the very—"

"No need for that, Sabinus. No garlands. No politics. No obvious comments." She stepped over toward him, eyes fixed on his as they flaunted her superiority and his helplessness, flashing green versus constricting brown. "Did I leave any scars?" she finally asked, stroking the front of his tunic.

"No, Empress."

"Too bad. I wanted to mark you for life, I think." Now she reached out to pull his head down to hers, giving him a long kiss with penetrating tongue. Then she did something that had never before happened to him. No woman had ever taken off her robe in his sight. Roman women didn't do such things. But Agrippina was never detained by such minor restraints as custom, Sabinus realized, while trying to tear his eyes away from Agrippina's remarkably supple figure as she plunged into a milk bath at the corner of her bedroom.

"I'd best be leaving, Emp—"

"Come over here, Sabinus," she commanded. "Don't worry: I'll stay submerged if you're prudish." She ran her fingers along the skin of his forearm and said, "You're very rough, Sabinus. A bath would do you good, too. Join me?"

Sabinus jerked his arm away and moved out of range. "I'll be going now, Empress," he said in a strained tone, turning to leave.

She wore a dark smile. "I'll be seeing more of you, Sabinus. *Much* more."

On the way out of the palace he stopped again at Seneca's office and told the philosopher, "I've just made my decision, noble Seneca. I accept the post of *curator census Gallici,* but under one condition."

"Which is . . . ?"

"That I leave for Gaul as soon as humanly possible."

The wise Seneca pondered only a moment or two before replying, "Of course, Senator, of course. So much the better!" Then he smiled and shook his hand.

Sabinus went directly to the Plautii. He decided not to mention a word about Agrippina for fear it would frighten the family. Aulus supported his decision on Gaul, intrigued by Seneca's closing comments.

Telling Plautia, however, proved an ordeal. She had grown too accustomed to having him near her to even consider his leaving Rome once again. She immediately conjured up for herself another five-year absence and ran off to her room crying. Vainly he stood outside her door, protesting that it would merely be a matter of months. Finally he tried the door. She had barred it.

"Be reasonable and let me explain, Plautia," he pleaded.

"Go away," she cried, between sobs.

"But Plautia. It won't be that long—"

"Good. *Leave then!* Go off to Gaul! Go off to Hades, for all I care!"

"Please, darling . . ."

"And don't come back. *Ever!*"

It had been quite a childish performance, Plautia decided the next day, something that could have been expected from a thirteen-year-old, not a woman of her maturity. She should not have carried on so. Flaunting custom, she decided to go over to his town house on the Quirinal and apologize personally.

At the same time, though, she would announce the end of their romance. His decision showed all too clearly that he was much less serious about their relationship than she had imagined. She was always presuming too much. He could so easily have declined the post in Gaul and continued in the Senate. Even if Seneca had exerted pressure, he might have pleaded his five long years away from Rome, or even told Seneca about herself. No, Sabinus was plainly a bachelor sort who really wanted to stay single—probably for the rest of his life. She was a temporary infatuation—nothing more. But she would redeem herself.

When a servant answered at Sabinus' place, she carefully avoided going inside, asking only that he summon his master. Sabinus appeared, but she cut off his greeting with a brisk apology for her tears the night before.

"You darling girl," he soothed. "There's no reason for you to—"

"I'm not finished yet, Sabinus." Then she proceeded to unload all the thoughts that had been tormenting her on the way over to the Quirinal, embellishing them as her ire—and voice—rose.

Finally she reached under her palla, pulled out a jeweled bracelet and necklace Sabinus had recently given her, slapped them into his hand, and said, "It's best for us not to see each other again, Sabinus."

For a moment he looked thunderstruck. Then, slowly, he nodded in sad resignation. "I suppose you're right, little Plautia. Our wonderful romance is . . . is over, it seems"—he stopped just long enough to be effective—"but our *marriage* should be just as wonderful, shouldn't it?" Instantly he was smiling. "Now, I leave for Gaul in two weeks and return in about ten months. We can either be married before I leave and you come along with me to Gaul, or we get engaged now and married the moment I return. Which do you prefer, *carissima mea?*"

She merely stood there, dumfounded.

Sabinus had a radiant flame in his eye.

"You . . ." she faltered, "you're just saying that because . . . you'll think I forced—"

"Darling, darling Plautia." He threw his arms around her and pressed her to himself. Then he lavished kisses on her forehead and cheeks and lips. "Don't you *know* how much I love you? Didn't you realize I would have come to carry you off had you said no?"

Hot tears flowed down her cheeks and she smothered her face in the folds of his tunic.

Neighbors, who had been watching the argument from windows on both sides of the street, now burst into applause and cheering. Sabinus and Plautia broke off their embrace and laughed ecstatically.

They hurried over to the Plautii with their joyous announcement. Mother Pomponia wept for happiness, and Aulus could at last tell Sabinus how very much he had hoped exactly that would happen. However everyone—even Plautia—agreed that a proper patrician wedding would take months to prepare, though if they worked quickly, they could at least manage the formal betrothal before Sabinus left for Gaul.

In a matter of hours they had drawn up a lengthy guest list and dispatched messengers to deliver the sealed invitations. Two weeks' notice was a little brief, though quite acceptable. There was some debate on whether the new emperor should be invited, but Aulus would not have it, and Plautia worried lest Nero remember her aim with a strigil. Sabinus roared with laughter at the story. As a courtesy to the palace, however, Seneca was invited.

On the day of the betrothal, a parade of litters invaded the secluded lane on the Esquiline, depositing a throng of guests at Aulus' mansion. At the appointed hour, Flavius Sabinus walked out to the center of the atrium, his stocky brother Vespasian standing at his side.

The chattering crowd stilled to a hush when Aulus entered the hall, his daughter on his arm, followed by a serene and stately Pomponia. Solemnly they walked to the center of the atrium and saluted the Flavian brothers.

With a broad, confident smile, Sabinus then asked Aulus, in the legal formula, "*Spondesne Plautiam, tuam filiam mihi uxorem dari?* Do you solemnly promise to give me Plautia, your daughter, as wife?"

After a slight pause, for due dramatic effect, Aulus replied, "*Di bene vortant! Spondeo.* The gods bring luck! I betroth her."

"*Di bene vortant!*" Sabinus replied.

Even though Plautia had said absolutely nothing, they were now legally engaged, and the atrium broke into cheering and applause. Sabinus tenderly kissed Plautia, his *sponsa* or betrothed, and presented her with several traditional gifts: a jeweled comb and other toilet articles, and a gold ring which he carefully placed on the third finger of her left hand. A nerve or sinew ran directly from this finger to her heart, so they all believed. Plautia, in turn, gave Sabinus a golden stationery kit, whose purpose was at least obvious.

The formalities were over, and festivities followed, lasting well into the night. Everyone had to agree: it had been a very proper betrothal in the best traditions.

When all their friends had left, Aulus congratulated Pomponia on how well she had managed the affair, embracing her happily. It was just the kind of tonic she had needed, he thought, for her moodiness had disappeared in the excitement of preparation. At the celebration, in fact, Pomponia had been so rarely effusive in a circle of confidantes that she had expressed herself quite candidly about the empress mother. "These delicacies are more 'reliable' than Agrippina's," she said, in urging food on her guests.

How was she to know that one of the senators' wives, whom she thought a friend, was a very aspiring sort who was on intimate terms with Agrippina? The next morning, the empress mother learned everything that was said at the reception to which neither she nor her son had been invited. She was more than interested.

At the same moment, Sabinus was saying a very tender farewell on the Esquiline, cradling the cheeks of his beloved between his large, strong hands.

Plautia looked up at him and murmured some poetry:

> Whenever I see you—
> sound is silenced and
> my tongue falters;
> thin fire steals through my limbs;
> an inner roar shrouds my ears
> and darkness my eyes.

"Catullus." He smiled.

"But he was translating Sappho. It's how a *woman* feels . . ."

"It's how *I* feel," he objected. "A short time now, darling. A very short time. Meanwhile, you prepare the best wedding ever." He caught the lithe, willowy figure in his arms and trembled at the touch of her body and the delicious tickle of her warm, pliant lips.

"Please take care of yourself, *mea vita*. If anything happened to you, I . . . I couldn't go on living."

11

ANNAEUS SENECA had a villa just south of Rome, where he retreated each evening after a busy day at the palace. He had invited Aulus here for dinner and the long-promised chat. After a wholesome repast, the host invited his guest into the library, which was stacked from floor to ceiling with a diamond-shaped latticework of wooden pigeonholes, projecting thousands of scrolls. They were grouped into the main sectors of Mediterranean culture, with "Greece" by far the largest category. Three lemonwood tables were covered with open scrolls, while the fourth, with inkstand, contained pages of papyrus on which Seneca had been working.

"It's a treatise on clemency I'm writing for Nero," he explained to Aulus. Then he showed him some of his rare scrolls, including an Aristotle autograph of his *Metaphysics.* "Do feel free to use this collection at any time, Aulus, even when I'm not here."

"That is most kind of you, Seneca."

"But let us move to the present, my friend. Now, shall we start with the assumption that, having been close to the Divine Claudius, you're—shall we say—not too enthusiastic about the new regime?"

Credit the man for candor, Aulus thought, and then replied, carefully, "It's really too early to judge, isn't it?"

"Well, then, let me ask, how did you regard the circumstances of Claudius' death?"

"As a profound disgrace to the state. As the disgusting, premeditated murder that it was." Despite precautions, details of the poisoning had seeped down from the Palatine.

"Good, I agree. And don't raise your eyebrows, Aulus. You may not believe this, but I had nothing to do with Claudius' death. True, Pallas and Agrippina tried to entangle me, but I absolutely avoided any involvement."

"I see." Aulus darkened. "Then why didn't you warn Claudius? Like a good citizen?"

Seneca frowned. "Put yourself in my place, Aulus. Claudius banishes you from Rome for eight years—ninety-six months on that dreadful island of Corsica."

"But was your exile justified, Seneca? *Did* you . . . commit adultery with Caligula's sister Julia?" The question had passed his lips before, on second thought, he would not have uttered it.

His face coloring, Seneca replied, "You know it was Messalina who made the charge, Aulus. Need I say more?"

In fact, yes, thought Aulus, but he let it pass while Seneca continued. "Some people like to play the hermit, but not I. For a person who *must* have intellectual exchange, Corsica was a living death. None of my letters to Claudius did any good. Gods, he didn't pardon me even after Messalina's death! It was Agrippina who secured my recall. Can you really think I'd then betray her to favor him?"

"Probably not," Aulus had to agree. "But did you and your brother really have to cackle that loudly when Claudius died?"

Seneca looked surprised. "Which brother do you mean?"

"Gallio."

"Oh." Seneca smiled. "You mean his remark about Claudius being dragged up to heaven by a hook?"

"Yes, a hook—just like they use to drag criminals' bodies down to the Tiber."

"Oh, just a bit of satire.—In any case, we have more important things to discuss. Now, I know you've every reason to be suspicious of the new government. All we're asking is that you give us a chance."

Aulus nodded, now a little amazed at his candor with Seneca, who was one of the most powerful men in Rome. But he would have retracted nothing. Aulus Plautius hated hypocrisy, worshiped honesty, and feared no man.

"Now, Aulus, do you remember what Plato once said about the ideal government? 'Until philosophers are kings, or kings and princes have the spirit of philosophy . . . only then will the state behold the light of day.' Well, we *may* have a chance to test his theory here in Rome. Perhaps Nero is that prince."

"And you the philosopher?" Aulus smiled.

"Well," Seneca chuckled, "don't we have a unique opportunity to create an enlightened government for Rome? Nero's a fine pupil so far. He's young and quite pliable. He can easily be molded for the good—if *only* we can win out over Agrippina and Pallas."

"What . . . do you mean?" Aulus was obviously surprised.

"This shows the confidence I'm placing in you, despite your . . . critical comments, Aulus. But reveal this to no one: a *fierce* household struggle is raging in the palace over who will control Nero. It's Burrus and I against Agrippina and her minion Pallas."

"But Agrippina recalled you from exile . . ."

"I know. And I suppose I should be obligated to her for a whole lifetime. But I place the welfare of Rome higher than this personal debt. You see, Agrippina has no intention of letting Nero rule Rome —at least not without her. Ever since his password that first day— 'the best of mothers'—she's acted as if she were empress in fact as well as title. A month ago we had a scene that could have made us the laughingstock of the world. Some envoys from Armenia were paying a state visit to the palace. Nero was sitting on his throne when his mother suddenly appeared and tried to climb up the dais to sit on a throne beside him."

"As *co-regent?*"

"So what could we do? I told Nero to stand up and 'greet' his mother. He caught on immediately and did so—he's quite bright, you know—and then he led her out of the hall, returning alone. The Armenians saw only a son's courtesy."

"Well, I hope you succeed in your campaign against her, Seneca. And you *must* guard poor Britannicus from any evil plots. His position is quite precarious, you realize."

"I know. We will."

During a lull, Aulus, somewhat puzzled, asked, "Why are you . . . kind enough to tell me all this, Seneca?"

"In other words, why this visit?"

"Yes. Surely Aulus Plautius can't be that important to you."

"Oh, but he is. You have enormous influence in the Senate, Aulus, and the public has not forgotten about Britain. You'll also be father-in-law to a man we'll soon need in our administration. Now, if I hadn't told you where we're aiming the new regime, you might have assumed that Burrus and I were merely Agrippina's creatures and have influenced your colleagues to work against us. Now you know the truth. Mind you, Burrus and I aren't asking you to *campaign* for our policies in the Senate. Not at all. We're only asking for a little time to try to bend Nero for the better. It *is* worth a try, isn't it?"

Aulus softened, smiled, and nodded. "All right, Seneca. Much luck in your noble experiment. And do tell Burrus I knew he'd make the right decision, ultimately."

"Oh . . . I almost forgot to give you this, Aulus." Seneca walked to his writing desk and pulled a document out of the drawer. "And I want you to know you'd have received this even if you'd sworn to fight us to the death."

"What is it?"

"Another token of Nero's clemency. Go ahead. Open it."

Aulus took a knife and slit the imperial seals on the document Seneca handed him and read the following:

Nero Caesar, son of the deified Claudius, great-grandson of Tiberius, great-great-grandson of the deified Augustus, *pontifex maximus,* consul, holding the tribunician power for the first year, acclaimed *imperator,* to the Senate and the Roman People, greeting.

By agreement with the censor and to further our expressed policy of clemency, we herewith restore

QUINTUS PLAUTIUS LATERANUS

to his full rights and prerogatives as Conscript Father in the Roman Senate. Given the Calends of February, A.U.C. 808.

"Will you see that your nephew receives this?"

"Happily done!" Aulus beamed. "And the timing is superb: Quintus is finally getting married. Three weeks from today. Thank you, Seneca. Thank you *very* much indeed!"

"Oho! Don't thank me," he said with a twinkle. "Thank Nero's clemency, remember?"

"True. And may the gods guide your efforts to . . . Platonize Rome."

Later Aulus thought about their frank exchange and shook his head in amazement at that extraordinary phenomenon who was Annaeus Seneca. Born in Spain, he had come to Rome and quickly won fame as a Stoic philosopher, until disaster struck and he was forced into exile. But now, as Nero's tutor and adviser, Seneca virtually ruled the Empire, for his pupil was too busy growing up to be bothered with government and merely signed the documents Seneca prepared for him. Burrus, as prefect of the Praetorian Guard, was equally powerful, Aulus knew, but he represented the brawn more than the brain of the new government, and he was quite content to let Seneca chart Rome's course. When not tending the government, the versatile philosopher penned a stream of satires, tragedies, and treatises that were being read from the Nile to the Rhine.

However much Aulus had wanted to despise young Nero, he had to admit that the lad was making all the proper decisions, due, undoubtedly, to Seneca's promptings. Rich sycophants begged Nero to let them cast statues of him in gold and silver, but he refused. Toadies in the Senate suggested that the new year begin with December, when Nero was born, not January. He vetoed the proposal. And when Burrus once asked him to sign orders for the execution of a condemned criminal, the seventeen-year-old Caesar looked up and said, "How I wish I had never learned to write!"

Perfect freedom of speech and pen were again permitted—Seneca saw to that—and Rome's provinces prospered as never before as a result of Nero's strategy of peace. "The Empire is large enough for now," he said. "Let's consolidate what we have. That should be enough of a task."

Aulus saw Nero in the Senate rather frequently, a deferent, respectful youth who was even trying to learn all the Fathers by name. When he heard that several worthy senators were resigning because of financial reverses, he supplied them a subsidy so Rome would not lose the benefit of their advice. Aulus thought it all too good to be true. He caught Seneca after one of the sessions of the Senate and told him, "The Palatine *is* becoming Plato's Academy indeed. Bravo!"

Northward, in Gaul, where he hurried to complete the census, Sabinus received a scroll with two different handwritings: one, an effusive love letter from the girl he missed more than he thought possible; the other, from a future father-in-law who seemed to be changing his politics. "Despite its violent beginning," Aulus wrote, "Nero's principate may yet be the best since that of Augustus himself. It's Seneca's work. I've misjudged the man, I think. I only hope he continues to shape the emperor . . ."

Just when Pomponia seemed to be improving, she suffered a relapse. Aulus fretted over what to do. Not that his wife was getting moody again—preparations for Plautia's wedding kept her much too busy for that. It was religion, once again. Not only had that fanatic Jewish tentmaker Aquila returned to Rome, he had even dared to show his ruddy face on the Esquiline, ostensibly to see if the garden canopy was in good repair.

Such a pretext! The real purpose of his visit was apparent when Pomponia spoke excitedly about what had happened to Aquila and his Priscilla in the meantime. During their temporary exile in Corinth, they had met another Jewish tentmaker named Paulus. And this fellow, evidently, was a leader of sorts in that Jewish sect called the Christiani.

Aulus was appalled to hear Pomponia tell their daughter wild tales about that Chrestus or Christus who had started it all, and of the tentmaker who was spreading the stories. It seems Paulus had so impressed Aquila and his wife that they had invited him to live with them while they were in Corinth.

Aulus thought of a solution. He would pry his wife free of this foreign cult by proving some discrepancy or falsehood in Aquila's bizarre stories. It was easy in the case of the founder himself: rising from the dead was so obviously a fairy tale it required no further thought.

"I don't know why you're so hostile about the Christians," Pomponia complained. "They teach morality. They help people. They believe in one supreme God who created everything. And that he sent a . . . an extension of himself into the world—Jesus, the Christ —who lived and died and rose again to save all mankind. They believe he forgives their errors and helps them also find life after death. They tell others about this 'good news,' as they call it, and they've organized congregations to do this. They offer hope and love—"

"*Bah!*" Aulus snorted. "If they get started here like the other foreign cults, they'll soon be a menace to Rome."

"Oh no." Pomponia laughed. "In fact, there's already been a . . . a 'test case,' I think you call it. Paulus was tried before one of our governors, and he was declared *not* guilty."

"When did this happen? Where? What governor?"

"In Corinth . . . oh . . . about two or three years ago."

"Who was the governor, I asked."

"Don't get so excited, dear," she soothed. "You can ask Aquila all about the trial. He was there."

"I don't want to talk to him. Or see him. You tell me. Who was the governor?"

"I'm not sure. I think his name was Gallus . . ."

"Gallus?"

"Or Gallio . . ."

"Not Junius Gallio—Seneca's older brother? The 'wit' who said Claudius was 'hooked up to heaven'?"

"That *could* be the one . . ."

"Gallio *was* governor of Greece about that time." A shallow smile lit Aulus' face. "The next time I see Gallio in the Senate, I think I'll have a word with him."

There it was, that providential flaw that would expose Aquila's story for the hoax it was. Roman governors were far too busy to bother with zealot preachers. Then Aulus frowned. It was ominous how religious fanatics like Aquila so often fastened themselves, leechlike, to wives of the wealthy. He might have to introduce protective legislation.

Aulus knew L. Junius Gallio only casually. Originally he had shared his brother Seneca's family name "Annaeus," but changed it when he was adopted by the wealthy Gallio family. Since his brother now virtually ruled Rome, Gallio had never been more popular, and he was not at all surprised when Aulus detained him one day as they were leaving the Senate chamber, probably to seek a favor.

"I've an odd question for you, Senator," Aulus led off. "Several years ago, when you were governor in Corinth, did the case of a Jewish tentmaker named Paulus ever cross your tribunal?"

"A Jewish *tentmaker,* you say?" Gallio smiled. Then he shook his head. "No, I don't think so. The proconsul of Greece has more important things to do than keep the canvas merchants honest."

"Just as I thought," Aulus frowned. "I was merely trying to trace down a story I'd heard. But it's not important."

"What story?"

"Oh . . . this Paulus was supposed to be leader of a Jewish sect called the Christiani."

"Yes, now I remember," Gallio nodded. "Sorry, Aulus, but the climate in Greece didn't agree with me. I got malaria over there and I've been trying to forget the year I put in at Corinth. It was a rabbi or teacher named Paul. I didn't know he was a tentmaker too. Smallish build? Big nose?"

"I don't know, Gallio. I've never seen him."

"Well, it was nothing much. Some of the Jews in town brought him to my court and accused him of—what was it?—teachings about their god contrary to Jewish law. Something like that."

"How did Paul defend himself?"

"He didn't. I threw the case out of court. I told the accusers I wasn't about to decide the fine points of their religious law. Besides, this Paul was a Roman citizen."

"He was?"

"Yes. And how *could* I decide it, Aulus? The Jews themselves were divided about Paul's teaching. Yes, I recall it now. Some in their synagogue believed the same way Paul did. Others didn't. Anyhow, I washed my hands of the case."

"Hmmmm. Just like Pontius Pilate. Does that name mean anything to you?"

"Pilate? Of course. Although I must confess I've lost track of what he's doing now."

"It's not important, and thanks for the details, Gallio."

"I hardly think I was any help. *Vale,* Aulus."

It had been a blind effort. It did not disprove Aquila's story, as he had hoped, but it was far from the "test case" that Pomponia was claiming. Evidently Paul had never even opened his mouth to defend himself. It was probably little more than the Chrestus riot in Rome transferred to Corinth.

Why did his wife get involved in these matters?

12

AGRIPPINA looked out across Rome from the veranda of her bedroom suite in a mood of limitless superiority. Romans had fallen into a ridiculous habit, she mused, assuming that their rulers must be males. Hatshepsut and Cleopatra certainly proved that the Egyptians were wiser than that. Some of the greatest rulers in far-off Mesopotamia were queens. But now at last, she swore, future ages would speak with awe about Agrippina of Rome: the sister, the wife, and the mother of emperors, to be sure, but also empress in her own right with supreme power as her son's co-regent. She had seen to it that *two* thrones stood in the palace reception hall, and her image was engraved on imperial coinage next to Nero's.

Who could challenge her? That vile Narcissus was dead, Callistus was dismissed, and her dear Pallas controlled the treasury, as always. Seneca and Burrus were her creatures, and Nero would live the rest of his life in debt to her—docile, faithful, obedient—the doting son who owed her absolutely everything. Agrippina of Rome—the first woman to rule the greatest empire in history.

Tears welled up in her eyes. A sweep of her arm sent the breakfast crystal flying across the veranda and smashing onto the courtyard below. Then she parted her teeth and screamed, *"Why,* by the very fiends of Hades, is it all coming apart?" Her authority was being undermined insidiously, she knew, her power eroded. There was that disgraceful day with the Armenian ambassadors. She saw Seneca whisper to Nero and prevent her assuming her rightful place next to him. Burrus was slighting her. And recently, even Nero was showing her a certain coolness and independence. By the gods, even a colorless sparrow like that Plautius woman could ridicule her in public!

Pallas, who had heard her scream, came running in to see what was the matter. With smoldering epithets, Agrippina quite candidly told him.

"It's all the work of Seneca and Burrus," Pallas confided. "From morning to night, they're telling Nero: 'Be your own man' . . . 'You're old enough to make decisions for yourself' . . . 'Caesar isn't a mother's boy, is he?'—that sort of thing."

"The treacherous ingrates!" she fumed. "I made both those men. Seneca was rotting on Corsica and Burrus was a maimed nobody. And this is the thanks I get for it."

"They're swine, certainly." Pallas brushed his lengthy strands of hair aside to scratch one of his pierced earlobes.

"Only you've stayed loyal, darling Pallas." She kissed his cheek. "Well, how shall we stop them?" Her green eyes flashed in appeal.

"I've been thinking about that. You'll have to do one of two extremely different things to restore your control over Nero, and I can't for the life of me tell you which is the better course," he fretted. "Either you reassert yourself as a strict mother—cow the wayward son into submission—or, quite the opposite, you become his partner and confidante rather than mother. In either case, you have to win him back. Then Seneca and Burrus will be powerless."

"So. The flavoring must be sour or sweet."

"Anything, I think, would be better than ignoring the situation . . . letting it all crumble away."

"Yes, it can't go on like this. All right, I'll wait for the proper moment and then show him he still has a mother to deal with. Don't worry, dear Pallas, we won before"—she caressed his cheek—"and we'll win again. And when we do, there are a few other scores I have to settle." Her thoughts drifted over to the Esquiline.

Nero was not very happy with his wife, Octavia. Even though the sixteen-year-old girl was starting to show some of the beauty of her mother, Messalina, Nero had never fallen in love with her and complained about her complexion. Their marriage had been arranged. It was totally political. Worse than that, their politics didn't agree. Torn between loyalties to her brother, Britannicus, and her husband, Octavia tried desperately to avoid taking sides in the murky rivalries swirling about her. But soon she and Nero were sleeping in separate bedrooms and spending as little time together as possible.

One day Nero stalked into her quarters and found a dark-haired girl in charge of the domestics there. Her profile had a classic cut to it, and when she turned to Nero and smiled a greeting, he was momentarily stunned. Olive-skinned and with hair cascading freely down her back, she was so very striking that Nero lost his composure.

"Who . . ." His voice had an unnatural, squeaky sound. He swallowed and tried again. "Who are you?"

"My name is Acte, Caesar. Claudia Acte."

"By the very gods! Some relative I haven't heard about?"

"Oh no," she laughed, revealing her small, perfect teeth. "Quite the opposite. I was a slave until the Divine Claudius freed me. I adopted his name in gratitude."

"A freedwoman, eh? I find a trace of Greek in your Latin. Where are you from?"

"You have a good ear, Caesar. I was born in Ionia."

"Doesn't Acte mean 'the place where waves break'?" Seneca's Greek lessons were serving him well.

"The beach, the seashore. That's right."

"Perfect name for you. What's more beautiful than the coastlands?"

Acte blushed and replied, "Don't forget, *acte* also means 'bruised grain.'"

"Aha! A bit of wit behind that Aphrodite's face of yours. But why haven't I seen you before?"

"There are hundreds of us in the palace, Master. I worked in the kitchen until my mistress Octavia placed me in charge of her personal staff."

"*Hades!* The kitchen? Did we hide an Olympian goddess in the *kitchen?*"

She laughed and continued with her chores as Nero followed her about, asking details of her Greek heritage. Seneca's tutelage had instilled in him a vast appreciation of Rome's debt to Greece, and

Nero was smitten not only by Acte's beauty but her Hellenism as well. The combination was overpowering.

Heedless of whether Octavia or anyone else knew, much less approved, Nero mooned about the palace, setting up trysts with his beloved. At first perplexed but then flattered by the emperor's attention, Acte soon returned his affection but was clever enough to withhold the ultimate gift. Nero was frustrated, then maddened, and finally so captivated that he decided to divorce Octavia and marry Acte. He was utterly serious. Brimming with surprise and joy, she agreed.

Nero was heady with elation. He hurried over to Seneca's office suite and shared the glad news with his tutor and Burrus, who was conferring with Seneca at the time. Burrus darkened and said, brusquely, "You're planning to *what?!*"

Seneca quickly covered for him. "I think news like this can't wait, Caesar. Hurry and tell your dear mother immediately!"

Nero whipped about and ran upstairs. It took Burrus exactly five seconds to comprehend. Now he knew why they called Seneca a genius.

Agrippina had at first dismissed Nero's infatuation with Acte as a temporary madness. But the illness lingered, and with Nero's announcement, it had become full-blown insanity. Yes, now was the time, she decided. "You say you want to *marry* Acte, my son?" she asked, trembling to control herself.

"Yes, Mother. I love her deeply. So very deeply."

"More than you love me, Nero?"

"Well," he mumbled, "not more, dear Mother. It's a . . . a different sort of love, isn't it?"

"Well," she huffed, reddening with fury, "I will not have a *freed-woman* as a *rival!*" she shouted, just inches from his ears. "The empress mother of Rome will *not* have a *slave girl* as a daughter-in-law!"

"Sweet Jupiter, will you lower your voice, Mother! I'm almost deaf!"

"And you must be *blind* as well to want such a marriage! I've overlooked your colossal ingratitude so far, Nero, listening to the Spanish Tongue and the Praetorian Cripple instead of your mother."

"Who?"

"Seneca and Burrus, young fool, who else? Now Pallas and I forgive your many discourtesies . . . above all, your failure to realize that you wouldn't be Caesar today *if it weren't for me!*" She fairly spat the words, as Nero cringed.

"But, Mother, I—"

"Hear me out! Do you know what you'd be today if it weren't for me? A worthless wreck . . . like your ridiculous father, the first Domitius Bronzebeard. He took one look at your horoscope the day you were born and laughed like a hyena. It was a horrible forecast! And why shouldn't it have been? The only thing he ever did for Rome was to aim at a child on the Appian Way and run him over."

"When did that—"

"Oh yes, he also gouged out someone's eye in the Forum. And he slept with his own sister, your Aunt Lepida."

"You never told me *that*, Mother."

"I wanted to spare you, my son."

"What . . . what did the horoscope predict?"

Agrippina blanched. "I . . . can't tell you that, Nero. Not now. Someday, perhaps. But this is the point: despite what the stars said, I planned night and day to change all that. Your father died when you were only three, and then came years of persecution by the Imperial Harlot."

"Messalina?" Nero always had to be sure of her terms. Agrippina had her own names for everyone.

"Yes, yes, yes. And when she died, why, dear son, do you suppose I wanted to marry Claudius?"

"Why? Well, I know you didn't really love him, Mother. You just wanted to become empress."

"No!" she cried, with mock shock. "I did it all for *you*, my son. So that *you* would succeed Claudius. So that *you* would become emperor one day."

It was time for her to pause and let several tears trickle down her cheeks. Even Seneca would have approved that dramatic touch. But Nero was not entirely taken in by his mother's performance.

"Yes, dear Mother, I appreciate all you've done for me. I've expressed my gratitude a dozen times to the Senate, to Rome, and to you. But what does all this have to do with my forthcoming marriage to . . . my darling Acte?"

"*Dolt!*" she shrieked, again losing control of herself. "*Don't you see?*"

He was cowering, trying to protect his ears. "Gods! Softer, Mother!"

"If you divorce Octavia and marry Acte, you'll ruin everything! The only reason you were accepted as emperor was not that artificial business of Claudius adopting you as son, but the fact that you married Julio-Claudian blood in his daughter Octavia. The imperial line really continues through *her*, not you. Divorce her and you'll have to give back her dowry: the Empire. Marry Acte and Rome will be so scandalized by a Caesar being seduced by a slave girl that—"

"Freedwoman."

"—that you'd have a revolt on your hands. Think about it, my son. And isn't it time you started listening to your mother again?"

Nero sulked for some moments. Then he threw up his arms and said, "I think I'll give it all up: I'll marry Acte, and we'll sail off to Rhodes for the rest of our lives."

For a moment Agrippina glared again. Then she stroked his cheek and said, "No you won't, dear son."

Nero was deeply troubled. He found his mother's performance abusive, but there was some logic to her comments about a marriage with Acte. Yet in moments when it seemed their wedding could not take place after all, Acte became an even loftier object of his love by her very unattainability. In hopeless confusion he sought out his mentor Seneca.

In contrast to the scene with Agrippina, his conversation with Seneca was conciliatory, subdued, friendly. The philosopher had to admit that marriage with Acte would indeed be a false step "at this time." But then he continued, "Tell me in candor, Caesar. If Acte hadn't appeared in your life, couldn't you perhaps have returned to your love for Octavia?"

"I never loved her. Never at all. I rather loathe her, in fact. They forced us to marry, you know."

"Yes, yes. But a divorce just wouldn't do right now—for reasons of state."

"So everyone tells me."

"Yet you truly love Acte?"

"By the Goddess of Love herself, I adore her."

"Well, then. Why not take Acte as your mistress?"

Nero looked startled. "Will . . . will she?"

"Yes." Seneca smiled. "Burrus and I had a long talk with her, explaining why marriage just was not possible for the present. But that you loved her more than any wife and that she should . . . ah . . . cooperate. And I know she will."

Nero's eyes gleamed with gratitude and he threw his arms about his teacher.

"You two must be very discreet, of course," Seneca warned. "And we've worked that out too. Annaeus Serenus, my relative, will quite publicly pretend to be in love with Acte. Any notes you want to send her, any gifts you want to give her will all come 'from Serenus,' you understand. You may also use his home for your trysts." For this help, Seneca knew his enemies would call him a pander, but, given a lusty young emperor whose passion would not be bridled, it was better to let him indulge in an affair with a harmless freedwoman than risk worse scandals with some of the powerful and ambitious women of Rome.

Nero was beaming with joy. "In all the Empire, only two men have my interests at heart, beloved teacher: you and Burrus. I shall not forget that."

Seneca smiled, then had a sudden thought and replied, "No, Princeps. There are *three*, at the very least!"

"Who's the third?"

"Flavius Sabinus, who is taking the Gallic census."

"Sabinus? Oh yes. Tall man. Good build?"

Seneca nodded and said, "Well, he's achieving a masterstroke for you up in Gaul."

"How?"

"By lowering the Roman tribute."

"Lowering?" Nero was frowning.

"And yet our tax income from Gaul will almost double!"

"But how is that possible?"

"Well, Sabinus replaced our fiscal 'experts' up there with a Gaul who studied in Rome—Julius Vindex. And Vindex convinced his countrymen that Sabinus was right with his slogan: '*If everyone registers, everyone pays less tribute!*'" Seneca started chuckling, and then continued, "Ah, Princeps, it certainly worked. There are far more Gauls up there than Rome ever knew!"

Nero was smiling. "Good for Sabinus! A masterstroke indeed!" Then he returned to his favorite theme. "And thank you for helping me . . . with my beloved Acte."

Pallas had to break the news to Agrippina that they had been completely thwarted by Seneca, who was now higher than ever in Nero's favor. "I think it's time you tried the opposite approach," he said. "I only wish I would have had the foresight to suggest it the first time."

"If the Spanish snake hadn't come slithering in as procurer, I would have succeeded. But you could be right, Pallas. Maybe it *is* time for honey."

One evening, after the rest of the imperial party had left the dinner table, Agrippina sat pensively looking at her son until Nero asked what was wrong.

"*Mea maxima culpa,*" she sighed. "My greatest error was to regard you as my son and apply what I thought was a mother's proper discipline. But . . . you're so much more than that, my darling Nero. You're young, but you are no longer anyone's son. You are father to the whole Empire. I'm no longer your mother, just a humble subject, and I shouldn't have been so strict with you."

"You'll always be my mother, Mother." He winced, knowing Seneca would have disapproved his syntax.

"No. Nero is emperor. Nero must decide his life from now on. And please forget my ill-timed remarks and harsh words. I've wept over them. Repeatedly. But what caused our quarrel, beloved? Was it Acte? Well, if you love her, then I love her too."

"You . . . do?"

"Oh yes. She *is* a magnificent, charming girl, and there's really no need for you to have to go sneaking off for your trys—ah—appointments with the lovely Acte. You might be seen. No, indeed. Why don't you simply meet in my suite instead?"

"W-where?"

"In my rooms. And anytime, dear one. Just drop a hint, and I'll be gone. Don't look so surprised, my son. Why shouldn't you be permitted these indulgences? You're burning with the flames of life and you need Acte. And besides, Caesar can do anything he pleases."

"That's very generous of you, Mother."

"Now come with me. I'll show you how to lock the door."

Astounded at the change which had come over his mother, Nero found himself being led up to her lavish quarters, where she showed him a concealed latch. Then she turned to him and said, "I know you, my son. You're thinking that your mother isn't capable of so complete a change of heart. But she is. Let this prove it."

Agrippina walked over to her desk and took out a piece of parchment. "Here, dearest," she said. "This document lists my personal funds in the palace treasury . . . and grants you access to all of them."

Nero looked at the totals and his eyes bulged. "By Hercules, Mother. This is almost as much as we have in the imperial treasury!"

"I know. I inherited much. And Claudius was quite lavish with his gifts to me."

"Well, this is amazingly generous of you, dear Mother. But I won't touch your funds. I have quite enough."

"No, dear one. What's mine is yours."

As they left the suite, Agrippina clasped Nero in an almost passionate embrace.

Over the next days, Nero was puzzled. The change in his mother seemed too good to be true. He decided to test the promised arrangement regarding her room and found his mother happily compliant. Though Acte was almost quivering with fright, he led her triumphantly into Agrippina's suite. Everyone had vanished. Inside there was merely candlelight and a gift of perfume for Acte.

Nero reported the change to Seneca. The philosopher was careful not to dash his hopes, but he did urge him to be wary. "Aesop said it first," he added. " 'Appearances are deceptive.' " Seneca, of course, had a reason for saying that, Nero realized, for he saw clearly enough the battle lines being drawn in the palace. But what if his tutor were wrong? Agrippina was, after all, his own mother, and seemed to have recognized her proper role at last. Yes, he decided, he must do his own part to repair their relationship.

One day he inspected the imperial wardrobe, selected a jeweled turquoise robe from India, and sent it to his mother as a gift. He also told one of his aides to go near her quarters and report her reaction, but to stay out of sight. He wanted to know every joyous comment she made. Surprises were such fun.

The aide returned fifteen minutes later, a lugubrious warp on his face. "Pallas was there at the time," he reported, "and perhaps the Lady Agrippina was only . . . trying to impress him."

"Let me draw the conclusions. What did she say?"

"I'm . . . sorry to report this, Caesar, but . . . I can only tell you what I heard. She said, 'Oho, will you look at *this*, Pallas? Nero thinks he's furnishing my wardrobe—with a single, ridiculous dress!

What about the others in his collection? They're probably for that silly little strumpet, Acte! Such a son! He's only sharing with me one scrap of what I gave him in the first place.'"

Nero was livid. He began trembling, and his lips moved to form several words without succeeding. Finally he stammered, "Fa-Father Zeus knows it was done in good faith! And then this! What did Pallas say?"

"Something like: 'Behold what Nero gives in return for an Empire: one robe.'"

"That does it. Fetch Seneca."

Several hours later, Pallas was summoned to appear before Nero. With his heart throbbing, but determined not to betray a trace of emotion, Nero looked up at his finance minister and said, "Antonius Pallas, I thank you for your services to the Divine Claudius, and to me. However, that service is at an end as of this moment. You have two days in which to remove yourself, and all your effects, from the palace."

Pallas seemed less surprised than Nero thought he would be. "Very well, Caesar"—he bowed—"as you request, so shall it be."

"You didn't ask the reason for this decision, but I shall tell you anyway: you betrayed your loyalty to me by sharing my mother's terrible arrogance this morning. Do you understand?"

Pallas nodded.

"And don't alter any of the state accounts in the next two days, Pallas. At the moment, my agents are sealing all your records."

"Perfectly understandable, Caesar. But you'll find all my accounts with the state in balance." He bowed and left the room.

Nero sat and waited for the approaching storm. He knew it would break within a half hour, and he was not disappointed. Agrippina came roaring in with the fury of a Mediterranean tempest. "Why?" she screamed, her mouth quivering, her face drained of all color.

Nero did not retreat. "Do you and Pallas deny receiving my gift with disgusting arrogance? Don't lie. You were overheard."

"You . . . you would actually dismiss the man who helped make you emperor—because of a *robe?*"

"That was only a tiny token of his insolence and your hypocrisy, Mother. You've both been wearing masks of deceit, conspiring against the best interests of the government—"

"Nero!"

"It's true, and I could say so much more besides. A few people in this vast establishment are loyal to their emperor and they've reported on your incredible conduct, Mother. Your effusive new display of 'maternal love' is sinister, and I saw through it at once. So what are you *really* planning, Mother? Do you want to send me the way of Claudius?" He looked at her with burning eyes. "Well, I don't like mushrooms that much."

"That *won't be necessary!*" she cried. "We'll just send you back to the slums where you belong. At last Claudius will have a *legitimate* successor to replace you!"

"Who?"

"*His own son,* you dunce!" She spat out the words.

"Britannicus?" Nero scowled.

"Yes, Britannicus! He's the *true* heir, not you. He's *worthy* of the Empire. You're obviously not!"

"Careful, Agrippina."

"Aha! You no longer call me Mother. Well, that's fine," she seethed, "because I'd hate to claim you. You'd embarrass anyone."

"Be careful, I said!" Nero was tingling with anger.

"What are you, anyway? Merely an adopted prince, while Britannicus is genuine. The blood of the Caesars pulses through his veins. And what runs through yours? The fluid of the Bronzebeards. That's why you can commit these outrages against your own mother . . . the mother who gave you empire."

"Oh spare me that refrain, Mother. Please do."

"*Ingrate!*" she shrieked. "Get out of the palace! You have no business here!"

"Have you lost your mind?" Nero gritted his teeth.

"I don't care what happens to me: let the whole world learn about the dark deeds in this dreadful house—the poisoning . . . everything. One thing they'll have to give me credit for: Britannicus lives. I'll take him to the Castra Praetoria and we'll let the guards decide. There your cripple, Burrus, and your exile, Seneca, can plead your shabby cause . . . using a maimed arm and a pedant's tongue to claim the government of the world! Ha! But the daughter of the hero Germanicus will present her case. And she will be heard."

"You're dreaming, Mother."

"Dreaming, am I?" she raved, trying to strike Nero while he nimbly dodged the blow. Then she tilted her head upward and cried out in a quavering voice: "Hear me, Divine Claudius! You will be vindicated, finally vindicated, when I put your own son on the throne.

By the shades of all my victims in Hades, I *will do* this!" Her emerald eyes flashed a frightful intensity.

"Get out, Mother! And stay out of my sight!" Nero hissed.

His first impulse was to run and tell Seneca what had happened. But then he checked himself. He really must stop bothering his tutor for advice on every step and start acting like a Caesar. He was shaken, tense, and very frightened, but he was Caesar.

Britannicus in his place? The threat tingled endlessly in the very marrow of his bones. He had always loathed his stepbrother, but recently that fourteen-year-old whelp had been growing obscenely fast. In no time he would assume the toga of manhood. Worse yet, the sullen little ox still had a large following of witless Romans who would support him in a challenge for the throne.

In the days following, Nero cringed to see his mother making a great fuss over Britannicus. But then he learned that she was also smuggling regular messages to the Castra Praetoria, and had even entertained some tribunes of the Guard the previous night at a private reception in her quarters. Smashing a fist onto his desk, he called to an aide, "Summon Julius Pollio!"

Must he spend the rest of his days in a lingering clutch of apprehension? Must he wait for his mother or Britannicus or the praetorians to strike first? Of course not, he told himself. He was emperor. An emperor must sometimes act above the law. Yes, this crisis he would solve himself, and how proud Seneca would be that he had finally learned to take matters into his own hands. He grabbed a wax tablet and began writing.

"Greetings, Tribune," said Nero as Pollio entered. "One of the wisest things I did on my accession was to remove you from service to the empress mother. Now, you still have a woman named Locusta in your custody?"

"Yes, Princeps."

"Bring her this sealed message. Tell her you received it from the hand of Caesar himself. And you're to tell *no* one of your mission. Your very life depends on it."

"Of course, Caesar." He saluted and was off.

When the vial of poison arrived, Nero handed it to one of Britannicus' tutors and told him, "Empty this into the prince's wine. At bedtime, of course, when there's no taster around."

A loyal agent of the emperor, the tutor complied without question.

That night, Britannicus drank the wine and promptly felt ill. But he suffered only a harmless diarrhea and so passed the drug.

Nero told Pollio to bring Locusta before him. When she arrived, he stared at the disheveled hag for several moments and then bellowed, "What were you two trying to do? Make a fool of Caesar? I ordered poison and you gave me a laxative. Your 'victim' is purged and healthier than ever!" He crossed her cheeks with stinging slaps.

Wincing with pain, Locusta said, "Blue vitriol is *no* cathartic, Caesar. But sometimes it acts slowly. I only wanted the death to seem like illness so you wouldn't be accused of a crime."

"Bah! It's likely that I'm afraid of the Julian law against poisoners! I condemn you to death, Locusta. And you, Pollio, will follow her if you can't—"

"Forgive me, Caesar!" Locusta had fallen on her knees before him. "Give me another chance! The next preparation will be a rapid poison which cannot fail. It will cut the victim down like a dagger's steel."

"So you say. But I won't take your word any more, Locusta." He cupped his mottled chin with a hand and then looked up. "Unless you're ready to bring your drugs and prepare the poison here in the palace so we can test it first?"

"Happily done, Master!"

"All right, then. But wear a veil, and don't be seen by anyone. Pollio, help her with her things and set everything up in the room next to my quarters. Here—I'll show you."

Several hours later, Locusta and her baggage arrived. Nero helped them set up the equipment, and, like some apprentice wizard, he watched her heating and stirring the ingredients. When Locusta said the potion was ready, Nero hurried out to fetch a kid that he had tethered inside his bedroom and led the animal in. With the undiscriminating appetite for which their kind are famous, the young goat obediently lapped up the poison and fell over on its side. But it lingered on an agonizing hour before its heart finally stopped beating.

"Like a dagger's steel, Locusta?" Nero grumbled. "It's not strong enough."

"Don't worry, Caesar. We'll distill it several times more."

The stench that rose from the brewing mixture made Nero gag and he stumbled out of the room. Soon he was back, carrying a young pig under his arm. "Are you ready?"

Locusta nodded. They threw some mash on the floor and dripped the poison over it. The pig ambled over, snorted a bit, and began eating the mash. Suddenly it stopped munching, squealed twice, and fell over dead.

"Good," said Nero. "And the poison is colorless too." He took the remaining potion and carried it himself down to the palace kitchen. Then he prepared for dinner.

It was customary for the younger princes to sit with their companions at a separate table in the imperial dining room, while their elders reclined as they ate at the main table. Britannicus was still assigned the children's table, and this evening he was surrounded by other noble youths, including Sabinus' nephew Titus, sitting at his right. Britannicus and Titus had remained close friends at the palace school, always choosing the same sides during Palatine sporting contests.

It was a chilly night, and hot wine was served early in the meal. A butler poured a cup for Britannicus, one of his attendants tasted it, and then passed it on to the prince. "Careful, Master," he warned. "It's good, but it's hot."

Britannicus sipped it, gingerly, then spat it out on the mosaic floor. "Yeccch! Was this piped up from Hades? Burns your mouth. *Water!*"

Another servant hurried over with a silver flagon and poured in some cold water to chill the wine. Nero watched his stepbrother out of the corner of his eye, for the water was saturated with Locusta's poison. Britannicus was cramming a crust of bread into his mouth. Now he paused to take a drink of wine. Several sips and he started sliding down his chair and then collapsed onto the floor, coughing and gasping.

Titus jumped down to assist his friend, and there was commotion at both tables. Nero turned on his side to see what the trouble was. "Oh . . . that," he snickered. "Poor Britannicus has epilepsy. He's had it from birth. Don't worry, the lad will regain his senses soon. Guards! Carry the young prince up to his room."

Titus tried to feel Britannicus' heart. It was fluttering irregularly. Then his gasping stopped entirely, and his skin turned livid. His eyes popped open, unblinking, the pupils fiercely dilated. He was dead.

Titus stood up and made a lunge for Britannicus' cup before the servant who had poured the water could remove it. Snatching a sip from it, he let the tainted wine swish about in his mouth for several moments before spitting it out. There was an unmistakable after-taste, and he quickly rinsed his mouth from another cup.

Agrippina and Octavia were watching the scene with mounting horror as it dawned on them that Britannicus had been poisoned. Octavia assumed the frozen mask with which she had had to hide her emotions for months, but Agrippina had great difficulty disguis-ing her terror, and her hands began trembling uncontrollably. She forced herself to look at Nero. He was staring at her with a dark glint in his slate-blue eyes, as if to say, "Well, you can't threaten me with Britannicus any longer, can you, dear Mother? What's next?" There was even a challenge in his expression that shouted what remained unsaid, "And as to murder: like mother, like son."

After a brief, shocked silence, they all left the table, each bearing a different personal burden. Octavia cried herself to sleep: she had not had so much as a last embrace from her brother. Agrippina won-dered, in horror, how to deal with the son she had brought into the world.

Seneca, profoundly shocked at what his pupil had done, held a hasty conference with Burrus. "The first real decision he made on his own," he said, "and look what he did!"

Burrus shook his head and said, "I always told you Nero had great potential for good—or evil."

And yet Seneca was surprised to find another part of his mind al-ready hard at work, searching for some shreds of justification for Nero's conduct. There was, after all, his mother's wretched example and her threats . . . fratricide was a familiar evil in royal houses . . . Britannicus' comments *had* been quite careless . . . and any joint rule of Rome was impossible: emperorship knew no partner-ship.

Still, it was hardly enough justification. And would he have to go on apologizing for Nero? Or could he still salvage the good qualities in the young prince?

Britannicus' funeral was indecently hasty. The palace announced his death at midnight, and the rites were held the following dawn. Just as the procession was about to begin, Nero looked at the dead Britannicus and gasped. The body was hideously livid from the ac-tion of the poison, a virtual advertisement of his murder. Nero or-dered the skin hastily rubbed with whitish gypsum to cover the evi-dence, and the procession set out. But as they wound their way through crowds of mourners in the Forum, a cloudburst suddenly descended, drenching the lifeless face of Britannicus. Romans recoiled in horror at the sight: a rivulet of chalky water was dripping from the bier, and the ghostly white face and arms of Britannicus were turning a bloated, angry purple. The rumors that had spread through the city were no longer whispered.

Aulus Plautius could not attend the funeral because of the emergency at Vespasian's house on the Quirinal. After Britannicus' poisoning, Titus had slipped away from the palace and made his way across Rome in a gathering delirium, stopping at fountain after fountain in a vain attempt to rinse his mouth of that dreadful, clinging aftertaste. He had absorbed enough poison merely tasting his friend's cup to make him dangerously ill, though he did manage to stagger up to his threshold before collapsing.

When Aulus arrived in the morning, he found doctors hovering over the prostrate youth, who was breathing with some difficulty and seemed to have a slight spasm in his lips. Yet Titus was playing the soldier as only a fourteen-year-old can play it, telling everyone he'd be fine in a short time.

"But *why* did you have to taste it?" Vespasian asked his son again and again, his brow knotted with anxiety. "Anyone would have known it was poison . . ."

"I . . . don't know, Father. I felt . . . I owed it to Britannicus."

"What did it taste like?" Aulus wondered.

"Not very much like wine." Titus made a wry grin. "More like . . . like peach blossoms. Or almonds . . . bitter almonds."

Aulus exchanged a dark glance with Vespasian and the doctors, for this was the most deadly toxin they knew of.

"Don't worry, lad." One of the doctors chucked him under the chin. "If it hasn't gotten you so far, you're safe."

But it would be six months before Titus finally recovered from the last stubborn symptoms of Locusta's brew.

Aulus left the house, wondering darkly about Nero. His early prejudice against the prince seemed justified after all. He wondered, now, why he had spent some of his prime years in that cold and foggy island to the north. Was it to foist on the Britons a "superior culture" that was all but worm-eaten by intrigue and murder on the Palatine? The Roman Republic didn't work, and now the Empire seemed to be failing. What was left?

He would gladly have blamed Jupiter and his clan for what was happening—*if* he thought for an instant they really existed. At times he gave serious thought to emigration, a happy self-imposed exile with Pomponia, perhaps to some Greek island where he would not have to feel embarrassed for his government, and where he could think and write in peace.

13

IN RECENT MONTHS, Plautia seemed to exist for but two reasons: exchanging tender letters with Sabinus in Gaul, and preparing for their wedding. Under other circumstances, the dreadful news from the Palatine would have distressed her as much as it did her father, but she had too many glorious prospects now to be concerned with anything more than Sabinus' safe return.

His brother Vespasian visited them with his ailing Titus to give a more complete account of events at Britannicus' table. But Plautia could only ignore the tragic politics and embrace Vespasian as "darling Sabinus' closest relative." Aulus frowned at the display, but Vespasian for once relaxed his tense features and treated his face to a warm smile.

Even Pomponia seemed to have solved her religious problems, and Aulus thanked the elaborate wedding preparations for that. The Plautii would have only one chance to host a nuptial celebration, and they planned to make the very most of it. The guest list would be lengthier this time, and again the nagging query posed itself: should Nero and Agrippina be invited? Yes, Aulus' closest friends advised, it would be a diplomatic gesture that could do much for Sabinus' career, not to mention the fact that Nero had reinstated Quintus Lateranus.

Aulus listened to all the arguments and then brushed them off: "*Two* poisoners in the house? I wouldn't feel safe at my own daughter's wedding!" No amount of coaxing would change his mind, though he did concede to letting Seneca and Burrus be invited to represent the Palatine. If Nero were offended, they would claim: "The wedding was too modest to expect a Caesar to attend, and the invitation would only suggest that a gift was desired."

Sabinus had promised to finish his Gallic census early in October, but the Ides of that month had arrived, and Plautia still had no definite date for his return. Nor had she heard from him in several weeks, and the wedding was set for mid November. Another week passed without word. A nub of anxiety began gnawing at Plautia, which she tried to suppress in the rush of wedding preparations.

That night—she could not tell when it was—she woke to the sharp crack of a breaking roof tile, followed by a thud in the hallway outside her bedroom. Several floorboards creaked. Lighting an oil lamp at her bedside, she saw, to her horror, that the latch on the door to her room was turning. She tried to scream but fear muted her cry to a hollow gasp.

Slowly the door opened, and in the orange flicker of light she saw the face of Flavius Sabinus. Squealing with delight, she rushed into his arms, and they kissed each other ravenously, trying to make up in moments of rapture the months of separation. At last they managed bits of dialogue, exquisitely broken by further embraces.

"Forgive me for waking you like this, my darling . . ."

"Ohhh, I'm glad you did . . ."

"I rode the final stretch without stopping. Hoped to arrive earlier . . ."

"No matter, my love. But how did you ever get in?"

"I climbed a tree . . . along a branch over the wall . . . and came in through the court. I didn't want to wake the whole household."

"You're here. You're actually here, my darling."

They snuggled together on her bed, kissing and caressing each other again hungrily. Love, the sublime attractor of minds and personalities was rapidly being joined by passion, the flaming blender of bodies. Love and passion was a combination that only the gods could have devised, they thought, but their fullest expression had to be reserved for marriage, Plautia still insisted, even on that night of nights.

"*Please*, my darling!" he implored, with an urgency she had never heard before. "We'll be married in *such* a short time."

"Soon we'll be one, dear Sabinus. Let's try . . . try to be patient. But do hold me close." He took her in his arms. How very gentle and understanding he was at her refusal, she thought, as she placed herself as close to him as was possible, every part of her body tingling to be in touch with his.

However far in advance they had been preparing for the wedding, the final week proved frantic for the Plautii. While Pomponia laid in vast supplies of food and drink, Aulus was running about the house, developing strategies and issuing commands as if he were at the Thames, not the Tiber. Jabbering servants started a final cleansing of the whole mansion, which now fairly sprouted with flowers, garlands, and greenery. Somehow, the Plautii survived their own preparations.

At dawn on her wedding day, Plautia heard the trumpets from the Castra Praetoria saluting the sunrise. Usually they awakened her, but not today. The first pale tinges of pink filtering into her room had sent her springing out of bed to begin the intricate process of arranging her hair into the traditional six locks of a bride. Soon Pomponia was there with breakfast and a mother's solicitude to help her dress.

Now the whole house was rumbling with activity. Aulus, the last fold of his toga carefully adjusted, was supervising last-minute decorations in his domain. Pomponia was running between Plautia's room and the kitchen, which now resembled the commissary of a Roman legion. "At least thirty more bottles of Setinian from the wine cellar," she ordered. "And fetch more of the pickled squid."

Aulus kept darting outside to look at the sky. There were comforting traditions about rain being a good omen on a wedding day, but he preferred that sort of clear day which was its own happy portent. A cold morning haze lurked overhead, but it was the kind that would burn off by noon, when the guests were expected.

Late in the morning, the litters began arriving, large gilded conveyances swinging their way up the slopes of the Esquiline on the shoulders of hard-breathing slaves. Running footmen surrounded each litter, insulating it from the next in what was becoming a colorful procession. Senators and their wives stepping out of the litters flashed an almost immodest display of purple and jewels and gold.

Some veterans of the war in Britain from the lower ranks of Roman society had also been invited and were now climbing the Esquiline in their best clothes.

The groom arrived and stood next to his attendant, Vespasian. Sabinus was dressed, like Aulus, in a white woolen toga bleached to special brilliance by processing with fuller's chalk. It was the garb of hosts, bridegrooms, and those running for public office (the *candidati* or "white-dressed"). Later they would change to gala dinner costumes, which some of the ultrafashionable senators were wearing in various tones of saffron, azure, and amethyst—still no match for the women, who quite outdid the men in the color and dazzle of their garments.

Plautia, in contrast, was dressed almost simply. When Sabinus saw her enter the crowded atrium from the opposite side, she was crowned with a flower garland and wore the traditional ivory tunic, shoes of white leather stitched with pearls, and a gauzy silken veil the color of fire.

The groom's business partner, Quintus Lateranus, was serving as augur. With a wink at the bridal pair, he grandly uncovered a coop of sacred chickens and fed them some meal—the Senate's method of discovering the day's portents. The chicks, of course, had been carefully starved and now pecked away with gusto. A half smile on his face, Lateranus announced, "*Omina . . . bona!* The omens are favorable!"

"*Bene! Bene!*" shouted the guests, for the ceremony could now begin.

Plautia's matron of honor—her cousin Quintus' wife—led her up to Sabinus, who had moved to the center of the atrium. Plautia thrust her right hand out from under the flame-colored veil and placed it into Sabinus'. Smiling broadly and in a resonant voice, Sabinus looked into her eyes and asked, "Will you be my *materfamilias?*"

"*Certe.*"

Then Plautia asked him, in her lilting tone, "Will you be my *paterfamilias?*"

"*Certe.*"

The guests were pleased. The personal wedding vow had been selected. The traditional "Where you are Gaius, there am I Gaia" always sounded so stilted.

The bridal pair, now joined by Aulus and Pomponia, advanced to a small altar at the center of the hall. The four united in placing a cake of coarse bread on the altar, uttering brief prayers to Jupiter, Juno, and several rural gods—all except Pomponia, who helped place the bread but then bowed her head and said nothing.

"The gods bring luck!" cried Aulus.

"*Feliciter! Feliciter!*" the guests immediately responded, for the two were now man and wife.

A phalanx of relatives and friends converged on the bridal pair and escorted them into the peristyle, where the wedding banquet would be served. Polla, the wiry little mother of Sabinus and Vespasian, was entranced with Plautia. She had never met her before, because Polla hated to leave her beloved Reate in the picturesque Sabine hill country, and she cordially disliked Rome. Now she threw her bony arms about Plautia and thanked her for relieving the Flavii of years of anxiety over "my wayward bachelor of a son who shunned marriage like the very plague." Then she added wistfully, "If only my husband could have lived to see this day."

Vespasian proudly introduced his wife, Flavia, to everyone and presented their children: Titus, who had finally recovered from Locusta's poison, and a younger brother and sister, Domitian and Domitilla.

Everyone reclined at tables flanking that of the bridal party, as a corps of servants brought the appetizers: fresh oysters, crab, sauced egg, and greens, all served on glittering silver platters from which guests hungrily plucked the food with their fingers. Eight courses followed, for this was to be more than a wedding banquet. It would also serve as clan feast, gala, and gastronome's delight, and it would last the rest of the day.

Seneca and Burrus not only came, but they seemed to enjoy themselves enormously. Just before the ceremonies, they had had a few words with Sabinus. No one could hear what was said, but Sabinus' face was cut by a vast grin and he had shaken their hands enthusiastically. They were now reclining with the wedding party at the head table, befitting their imperial rank.

Next to the bridal pair was the other member of the Twin Brothers enterprises and his wife. The bride forbade Sabinus and Quintus to talk business, and they complied for at least five full minutes. After that, there was no stopping them. Using coded signs so as not to flaunt sums before the guests, Quintus signaled the bonanzas he had achieved in Sabinus' absence. "We sold our grain ship for a much larger one," he said, "over 140 feet long—stole it really—and we've registered it in Alexandria."

"Egypt? Why not a port in Italy?"

"Tax advantages."

"Need I have asked?" Sabinus made a wry face. "What's the name of the ship?"

"It had been the *Isis*. Now it's the . . . *Twin Brothers*."

"Need I have asked?" Sabinus repeated, and broke out laughing.

"We did have one reverse, though. We had to sell the pottery works at Arretium. Took a small loss on it."

"Loss? That doesn't sound like you, Quintus."

"Be glad we're out. They're making the same ceramics in Gaul now, undercutting the whole Roman market. The fellow we sold the factory to has to close down, sorry to say."

"Quintus, you have better timing than the Fates themselves. What did you do with the proceeds?"

Lateranus had been waiting half the afternoon for Sabinus to ask. Unleashing a great smile, he asked, "I trust you like what you're drinking?"

"The wine? Naturally, it's Falernian. Oh . . . you mean—"

"Exactly! Vineyards too: five hundred acres down in Campania." Quintus caught the arm of a servant and showed Sabinus a wine bottle labeled GEMINI, with a figure of Castor shaking Pollux's hand. The Twin Brothers, it seems, were now in the wine business, too. Sabinus shook his head in disbelief.

When the feast had reached its final course of pastry and almonds, a towering wedding cake was sliced and served to guests on traditional bay leaves. Sabinus leaned over to his bride and said, softly, "I have *quite* a surprise for you . . ."

"What this time, darling *husband*?"

"It's rather . . . important."

"Tell me."

He leaned over to whisper something to her, but nibbled at her earlobe instead.

"Stop it. And tell me, Sabinus."

"No. You'll find out shortly."

Now it was time for toasts and speeches, the first given by Aulus Plautius in one of his rarest moods. Then he introduced Annaeus Seneca. The philosopher, whose stock in trade was words—spoken, written, whispered, implied—delighted the guests with a witty performance. At the close, he slit the seals on a document from the palace. There were a few indrawn breaths, and Aulus' smile faded.

Seneca read Nero's message of congratulations to the bridal couple and regrets that business detained him in the palace—Aulus was squirming uncomfortably—and he had special praise for the bride's beauty:

Once, if I recall correctly, I lauded her loveliness perhaps too highly, but a tiny mark on my cheek has cautioned me to mind my manners the better. Forgive my youth, fair Plautia!

The head table broke into a roar of laughter, while the other guests could only smile. Clearly, it was something esoteric. Then Seneca read on:

Fortune smiles on you, Flavius Sabinus, and so do the Senate and the Roman People. You won triumphal regalia for your valor in the Britannic campaign under an illustrious father-in-law. You were the finest governor Moesia ever had, and for the first time Gaul has had an honest census. Because of your distinguished qualifications, I have appointed you to the high office of *praefectus urbi*, your inauguration to take place this coming January.

Seneca could hardly be heard as he finished Nero's letter, for all the guests were scrambling to their feet in applause and wild cheering. As *praefectus urbi* or prefect of the city, Sabinus would be lord mayor of Rome, the highest office to which a senator could aspire. The post held enormous prestige, and, in terms of actual power, the new ranking in the Roman Empire would be: Nero, Seneca/Burrus, and Sabinus, in that order.

Plautia kissed him proudly, and the other Plautii and Flavii pommeled his back in congratulations, while his little mother had tears in her eyes. Vespasian cuffed him playfully on the shoulder and said, "I always knew you were the man of destiny in our family."

"No, Vespasian," he bantered. "It's just that you crested too early." The brothers had been having a lively political rivalry, and at one time Vespasian was clearly ahead as Sabinus' superior in Britain.

"*Pompa! Pompa!*" someone yelled. The other guests took up the cry, calling for the customary procession to escort the bride to her new home. By now it was dark and a band of veteran comrades, serving as torchbearers, lit firebrands until the vestibule was flaming with a ruddy glow.

"Music!" Aulus called, and a dozen flute-players began piping.

Guests fell into line behind the bridal party and streamed out of the house to join a procession westward across central Rome to the Quirinal. The parading revelers broke into traditional wedding songs as they marched under flickering torchlight, while bystanders at the roadsides shouted cheers honoring the god of marriage: "Talasse! *Io* Talasse!"

Sabinus' town house was ablaze with light as the cavalcade arrived, his domestics standing at attention to greet their new *domina*. To avoid any chance stumble—a dreadful omen—Sabinus gently lifted Plautia over the threshold. Then he placed a cup of water and a glowing firebrand into her hands, symbols of life together. She now produced three silver coins. One she gave her husband in token of the dowry; another she put on an altar in the atrium for the household spirits of her new home; and the third she threw back into the street for the spirits of the roadway.

"The consummation," Plautia's matron of honor now whispered, with a coy smile. She led the bridal couple to the marriage chamber and carefully shut them inside. Guests serenaded them with a final nuptial song, and then took their leave. The wedding was over at last.

It had been an exhausting day—and one they would remember forever. Gathering his bride into his arms, Sabinus bent down to her lips and kissed them with tender passion. "Plautia, *my* Plautia," he whispered, while untying her ivory tunic.

"I love you, *mea vita.*"

"*O summa voluptas!*"

She started breathing heavily and heard a distant roar in her ears. She held onto him even more tightly, hoping in that way to halt the warm and delicious waves of desire that were gently eroding her will. But that very gesture merely inflamed her further, and she could only float out with the roaring tide of their love. She cried softly with ecstasy, and then sobbed with relief and a gladness she had never known before.

Sabinus was engulfed in an exquisite flood of rapture. He thought that if he died the next instant, his whole life would have been lived to the full. The radiant creature who had invaded his senses ever since that day on the Capitoline but seemed so unattainable a dream for so long was part of him now. He slipped off the bed and onto his knees to worship his very goddess of love, pressing his burning cheek against her hand, kissing the ring he had slipped on her finger. No man anywhere, he swore, was happier, luckier, or more in love than he. Or ever had been. Or ever would be.

14

THEIR LOVE was a very private thing, yet it became public soon enough. A popular senator—soon to be city prefect—marrying the daughter of a war hero tickled the people's fancy. Clusters of Romans started gathering in front of their house in hopes of seeing the bride and groom come or go. Their appearances in the city drew plaudits, and the remaining weeks of the year were filled with dinner parties and social engagements in their honor.

The joy of their life together was more than they had dared imagine. Love was rich and various, all-consuming yet all-renewing, and now total too. "Somehow, it's different every time," Plautia would sigh with wonderment.

"Yes. Exactly. Each . . . encounter is unique," he agreed. "I don't see how that's possible, my darling."

To learn his new responsibilities, Sabinus had to spend considerable time at Rome's municipal headquarters, which stood just across the Forum from the Palatine. Saturnus, the retiring mayor of Rome, proved quite cooperative in grooming Sabinus for the post, though he also gave the impression that Rome would never be quite the same after he retired.

"Coming back to you after a day's work is like a shivering man plunging into a warm, bubbling pool," Sabinus murmured, as he brushed aside Plautia's chestnut tresses to kiss her neck. "I know, the analogy isn't very graceful, but the feeling's cozy."

"Sabinus, there's something I want to ask you about your new position," she said, with a slight frown.

"I think I already know what it is."

She hesitated. "About Nero?"

He nodded. "I think you want to know if I'll be working closely with him?"

"Yes, that's it."

In fact, it was the unexpressed question on the minds of all the Plautii and Flavii, the slight shadow edging their bright happiness. It was the reason why Aulus, after congratulating his son-in-law on the new post, had also seen fit to add, with a knowing glance, "You must be very careful."

"It's a legitimate question, carissima," Sabinus conceded. "And the answer is yes and no. Yes, I'll be closely available to Nero if he wants me, just across the Forum from his palace. And if any major decisions have to be made about the city, he, Seneca, and I will have to discuss them. But no, I won't be in daily contact with him. The headquarters of the Empire and of the city are entirely separate, and if I keep things running smoothly in Rome, he'll have little reason to look in."

"Oh, Sabinus"—she frowned—"why did you have to . . . get involved?"

"Why does anyone choose a career in politics, Plautia? High stakes are always involved. I suppose I should say, 'I do it for Rome,' and, believe it or not, that's a large part of the answer. Seneca and Burrus are trying something very noble for the state: to see if Nero can still be groomed as an ideal ruler. And I want to be part of it."

"Is that the whole reason?"

He smiled and shook his head. "No, I'll admit it. I also like . . . the excitement of public life."

On New Year's Day of A.D. 56, Flavius Sabinus was sworn into office. Nero gave a glittering palace dinner in his honor, to which much of the senatorial aristocracy was invited. The dining room held sentimental memories for the newlyweds—they had their first conversations here—but this time Plautia tasted every morsel of food suspiciously, although, actress that she proved to be, she seemed to be having a wonderful time.

Sabinus was combing the crowd of guests for familiar faces when suddenly he felt his stomach tighten. Agrippina had stationed herself as if to have an unobstructed view of the new city prefect and his bride. He had never revealed to the Plautii Agrippina's ominous interest in him and only hoped that the empress had forgotten him entirely during his absence in Gaul.

During the feast, Sabinus carefully avoided looking at Agrippina except for stealthy side glances. But now all his apprehensions were richly confirmed. Not some times, but *every* time, the flaming fluorescence of Agrippina's green eyes were locked onto him with a studied intensity. She could not have been eating much, because her lips seemed continually pursed together in a taunting grimace. He hoped Plautia would not notice the sight, but he was wrong. During a lull, she leaned over and whispered, "That harpy wants you in her claws, Sabinus. She's been consuming you instead of her food."

In the melange of conversation following the banquet, while some of the younger senators were clustering about his wife, Sabinus saw Agrippina advance toward him, smile, and say, briskly, "Congratulations, Prefect! May I have a word with you privately . . . in the alcove over there?"

She turned and walked toward it, assuming that he would follow, mayor of Rome or not. Sabinus thought seriously of ignoring her. Let Agrippina talk to the walls instead, he thought. Let her hear, for the first time, her own imperious, demanding tones and get as disgusted by them as everyone else.

One does not, however, create a crisis at one's own inaugural banquet, Sabinus decided, as he followed her. Predictably, Agrippina had the first word.

"I'll be brief, Sabinus, but you must weigh my words carefully.— No, don't look away.—After your little 'escape' up to Gaul, I *could* have arranged for your . . . sudden illness, shall we say? Yes, Sabinus, even in faraway Gaul. But I didn't. Do you know why?"

Sabinus hated even to think of asking.

"Because I knew then—and I know now—that you and I will share love, Sabinus. If not now, then shortly. No one has *ever* refused me, and what—"

"Empress," Sabinus cut her off. "I'm *married,* and very happily so."

"And what does that prove?" She laughed. "Oh, your bride is a tender little dove—I'll grant you that—but what I'm offering is a rich and *mature* relationship, with untold possibilities. You'll *not* be able to refuse that." She stroked his cheek with a cool hand. "Nor would you want to."

She turned to leave, but he decided to say it now, whatever the consequences. "Empress, this cannot—this *will not*—take place. Not now. Not ever. I love my wife very much."

Her mood chilled instantly. Grasping his wrist so tightly that her fingernails imprinted his flesh, she said, in a very low voice, "What if there will be no wife to love, Sabinus? Or no Sabinus to love her?"

One flash of fear rippled through him, but then anger took its place. "I *don't* like being threatened, Empress," he sliced out the syllables, "and I am not without resources. Threaten me again, and I'll lay the matter before the emperor, Seneca, and Burrus."

"I won't *threaten* you again, Sabinus," she seethed. "I'll *act*."

Sabinus turned about and walked away.

"By the infernal powers, Sabinus, I'll *destroy* you! First those you love. And then you!"

In the weeks that followed, Sabinus mentioned nothing of the scene to Plautia, since she was a more exuberant worrier than he. In fact, he found himself guilty of "moral lying" when she inquired about Agrippina from time to time. He did, though, have a confidential discussion with his chef on matters of security, since Agrippina usually felled her victims by poison. "Don't worry, Prefect," the rotund Sicilian told him, "I'll personally taste everything before it gets to your table."

"But that wouldn't serve you well if it *were* poison," Sabinus objected.

"Bah!" he scoffed, patting his paunch. "I can absorb anything. What would kill other people only gives me indigestion!"

Sabinus did not have much time for worry. The inaugural glitter faded soon enough as he came to terms with his awesome responsibilities. As city prefect, he had to maintain the general good order of Rome with four Urban Cohorts of a thousand troops each under his command. These police were billeted in the Castra Urbana at the north of Rome.

But as an entirely civil, not military, official, Sabinus went to work each day dressed in a regular toga, draped over a tunic banded with the broad purple stripe of the senatorial class. His sprawling suite of offices was composed of a secretariat, a tribunal where he sat in judgment, and the municipal archives. His titular rank was Clarissimus, "most illustrious," and an honor guard of six lictors officially preceded him on the streets of Rome.

His range of responsibilities was almost too wide, Sabinus soon concluded. In his first months of office, he had to deal with traffic problems, scheduling the public games, supervising trade associations, curbing the rising price of food, and dozens of other administrative functions. He was also chief justice of Rome, and while minor cases were heard in lower courts, all important trials arising in the city, particularly those involving capital punishment, were referred to Sabinus and his assessors.

Fortunately, he was assisted by a prefect of the grain supply, and a prefect of the *vigiles*, seven thousand troops who acted as night police and firemen. Several commissions also helped him supervise the streets, the aqueducts, the sewers, and maintain the public buildings and monuments.

Anxious to master his duties quickly, Sabinus was spending long hours at city headquarters, and Plautia voiced her concern. "It's only a matter of learning the office," he assured her. "Once I've figured it out, I'll delegate all my responsibilities and spend my days up here in amorous ease with you."

It was only a pleasantry, he knew, for solving the problems in a metropolis of over a million people continued to consume massive amounts of his time. He was forever having to make instant decisions or immediate rulings. Eventually, though, he discovered the bureaucratic redundancies and petty empire-building of city magistrates and ruthlessly curbed it. His whole staff was put on notice to find ways of making the municipal administration more efficient.

In several months, the effort succeeded, and the improvements were noticed even on the Palatine. Nero wrote Sabinus a note of appreciation for the new directions in city government. But apart from this—and mercifully, Plautia thought—there had been little contact with the emperor.

Early that summer, a crime wave struck across Rome. A large gang, operating only at night, was breaking into shops and causing riots in taverns and brothels. Sometimes there was only horseplay—people stopped in the street and tossed in a blanket—but at other times, they were assaulted and robbed. Anyone who resisted was beaten, or even stabbed to death and dropped into the nearest sewer. Not one of the culprits had been caught.

Sabinus debated the problem with Serenus, the go-between in Nero's romance with Acte, who was now prefect of the night watch. "If your *vigiles* can't seem to catch any of them," Sabinus said, with bite, "can't they at least describe them? From reports of victims?"

"We're trying," Serenus sighed, scratching a scalp full of black curly hair. "The victims say they look like slaves."

"Slaves? That's ominous," Sabinus replied, with a Roman's memory of the Spartacus revolt.

"But that doesn't mean they *are* slaves. They could be disguised. Last week we found a wig lying on the street after one of the brawls."

"Any other clues?"

"Nothing yet. But we're committing most of our men to patrol the streets at night."

"We may have to call in the Urban Cohorts as well. Good luck, Serenus."

With a sickening regularity in the next days, Sabinus had to pin reports of fresh assaults onto his large map of Rome. Here a girl ravished, there a boy molested, a couple beaten and robbed. But Serenus' latest report was alarming: when his men were closing in on a gang of ruffians, the previous night, they were suddenly attacked by what seemed an unidentified *military* force.

"That does it," Sabinus told Serenus. "We commit the Urban Cohorts too." Just then, his secretary came in and said, "Senator Julius Montanus is here, Clarissimus. He urgently requests a conference."

"All right, send him in. Let's confer each day from now on, Serenus. *Vale.*"

Montanus, a sturdily built young senator, stepped in just as Serenus left.

"How are you, Montanus?" Sabinus smiled. "Lately I find myself wishing I'd never left you people in the Senate. But what's that gash over your eye? Haven't been fighting with your beautiful wife, now, have you?"

"Not fighting *with* her, friend. *For* her. Gods, what a *horrible* mess I'm in."

"Sit down and tell me about it."

"Maybe I should go into exile immediately," he muttered wearily, as he sank down on the proffered couch. "The Father of the gods knows my life isn't worth very much now."

"What happened? From the beginning."

"It was last night. My wife and I were returning from a banquet with some friends when we were attacked by a gang of thugs on the Via Lata. Well, we gave back what we got, and it . . . was a pretty good fight. But while we were brawling, I heard my wife scream. One of the ruffians—he had a thick neck and spindly legs—was dragging off my wife. I caught up with them and pounded his ugly face bloody. I . . . I really mauled him, I think. Anyway, with one of my punches his . . . his hair seemed to slip off—it was a wig!—and in the torchlight I saw his real hair. It was blondish, and . . . oh, sweet Mother of the gods . . . you know who it was."

"No, I don't. Who was it?"

"Nero."

Sabinus' head jerked backward. "How do you know it was Nero, Montanus?"

The senator looked up in surprise. "Don't I know what Caesar looks like?"

"The light wasn't good. There are a million people in Rome—a few must look like Nero."

"Don't you think I've thought of that? But how many of those few also talk like Nero? Have his pot belly? His pock-marked face? His bull neck? Oh, it was Nero all right. I also recognized several of his friends, I think . . . Otho for sure."

Sabinus felt his pulse quicken, and asked, "What happened then?"

"As soon as I recognized him, I held back, of course. And then they all ran off, hooting and yelling and laughing."

"Assuming for the moment that it *was* Nero, what do you plan to do now?"

"That's why I'm here. I figured only the 'Lord Mayor of Rome' would have the answer to that riddle," the senator said, with a grim smile.

"Does Nero know you? And did he seem to know it was you?"

"No question. I heard one of them mutter 'Montanus' as they left."

"All right, now the big question: did Nero *know that you knew* it was he? Think carefully."

"I'm not sure. I . . . I don't think so. I didn't mention his name. I just quit beating him when his wig fell off and I saw his face in the torchlight. Right after that, they all ran off."

"All right, then. The matter's solved."

"What should I do?"

"Nothing."

"Nothing?"

"Absolutely nothing. If Nero *were* out on that mad escapade, he should have had sense enough to realize that any Roman would defend his wife. It would have to be part of their crude game to expect blows in return."

"Shouldn't I apologize? What if he did think I recognized him?"

"That's just the point, man: by not apologizing, you show you didn't know it was Nero. If you do, you admit that you beat up the lord of the world, and *that* he couldn't stand. And if your attacker were *not* Nero, you'd make new trouble for yourself."

Montanus thought for some moments. "Maybe you're right, Sabinus," he said slowly. "I . . . I appreciate the help, friend."

In a kind of haze, Montanus left the office, but in a moment he was back. "You keep saying 'if it really were Nero.' Do you still doubt it?"

"I'm afraid I do, Montanus. It's really rather preposterous, isn't it? The richest man in the world stealing? The most powerful person getting bruised and beaten?"

"He's young, Sabinus. He does it for excitement. And if you don't believe me, I suggest you try to see him today or tomorrow. If his face isn't worse than mine, you can thank the palace physicians for that."

"That *would* be proof." Sabinus smiled. "But relax, Senator. *Vale.*"

Sabinus tried to get back to his work, but he was too preoccupied by the visit from Montanus. If Nero and his comrades *were* behind the string of disorders in the city, it would easily explain why they were rescued by unidentified guards. He got up from his desk, hurried across the Forum, and climbed several colonnaded staircases to Burrus' office at the base of the palace, where he found the praetorian prefect at his desk.

"Hello, colleague," Sabinus said hurriedly. "Sorry to bother you, but have you seen Caesar today?"

"No, Sabinus. He's not seeing anyone right now. Says he isn't feeling well, I understand."

"This is important. Can you think of some excuse to see him—even for a moment? I just want you to tell me what his face looks like today."

Burrus cocked his head askew. "What his *face* looks like?"

"Trust me, friend. I'll wait here and explain the moment you return."

"Well . . . all right. I'll have him sign several of these documents for Egypt."

Burrus left his office and returned some fifteen minutes later. "Well, how did *you* know anything was wrong with him? By Neptune's soggy beard, he's a mess, he is . . . eyes all purple and black, welts across his forehead . . . puffy cheeks."

The color drained from Sabinus' face. "Did Nero offer any explanation?"

"Mumbled something about an accident while running his horses . . ."

"Did he, Burrus? *Did* he work out with his horses yesterday?"

Slowly Burrus shook his head. "I don't think so."

"And what does Caesar do with his evenings lately?"

When this brought no response, Sabinus snapped, "Well, I'll tell you then." And he launched into a furious recitation on the cause of Rome's recent crime wave.

Burrus interrupted him several times, suggesting he lower his voice, but finally he nodded in agreement. "All right . . . yes, we know all about it, Sabinus. Gods, he even tries to sell the loot to our palace staff! Seneca and I have been trying to stop him, but he has his own tight circle of revelers. All right, I'll see Seneca and we'll *have* to figure some way to put a halt to it."

"*Immediately*, I trust?"

"Yes, Sabinus." Then he added, "All in confidence, Prefect?"

"How else?" Sabinus shrugged his shoulders.

Rumors spread through Rome that Nero and his roistering companions were, in fact, behind the recent disorders in the city, and the fact that they were beyond arrest gave criminal elements in Rome an ingenious idea. Turning their own gangs loose on the city, they gave warning shouts of "Caesar! Caesar!" if any of the night watch tried to arrest them, leaving the police puzzled about whether to give chase or not.

But what destroyed Sabinus' patience was a very tragic bit of news: Julius Montanus, unable to stand the uncertainty, had dispatched a letter to the palace anyway, apologizing for the "accident" and craving the emperor's pardon. Nero, who had thought Montanus' blows normal enough, now read the letter with surprise and remarked, "So! He *knew* he was striking Nero, did he?" Then he issued orders. Montanus committed suicide.

Sabinus slumped down in his chair at the report, strangling an ink well until his knuckles whitened. "*Why* didn't poor Montanus keep his head?" he muttered to himself. But the more appropriate query then posed itself: what had become of Rome when a senator had to apologize to a felon for defending his own wife? And then had to take his own life for his pains?

Sabinus immediately ordered his Urban Cohorts into the streets, and soon Rome was crawling with so many troops it resembled a captured city. Next, although they outranked him, he summoned Seneca and Burrus down to a conference at city headquarters. They were not offended, for here they could converse in the kind of privacy denied them up on the Palatine.

Embarrassed and almost despairing, Seneca threw up his hands and admitted, "It's all we can do to *try* to control him, Sabinus. He now knows, unfortunately, that he's lord of the world. And all his young friends are filling his ears with slogans like, 'Is Nero a slave to Burrus and Seneca? Show them who's master of Rome!'—that sort of thing, and, for the moment, he's taking their advice. But I don't think we've lost him. He's going through a period of his life in which he craves adventure and danger."

"Granted," said Sabinus. "But meanwhile, Rome's being torn apart by street gangs. We're in the worst crisis since the 'municipal wars' of Cicero's time."

"I know. We'll have to act now. I'll tell Nero that criminal gangs are copying his escapades, and it just *has* to stop. I think he'll listen."

"All right," Sabinus replied, "but if he doesn't take your advice, I want you, Burrus, to send an agent to follow Nero's retinue at night and alert us where they're headed. We'll have police ready and waiting."

"Good," said Seneca. "And when these nightly exploits get less rewarding for Caesar, he'll soon tire of them. Meanwhile, I'll try to deepen his interest in literature and the arts. If that fails, there's always sports, the races—*anything* to get his mind off this . . . this pillage."

The strategy eventually succeeded. After several run-ins with Sabinus' police, Nero grew weary of his mad lust for nocturnal adventure and abandoned the escapades. In the meantime, Sabinus had restored order in the city. Rome was civilized once again.

15

AULUS' MEMOIRS of the campaign in Britain—the project forever interrupted by Rome's political turbulence—were finally completed. Finding a publisher was simple enough. Several had even
approached Aulus, though everyone knew the manuscript would
finally go to Atticus House. The firm had been founded by T. Pomponius Atticus, Cicero's close friend, who happened to be Pomponia's great-grandfather, and her relatives were still in charge.

The publishers invited the Plautii to pay them a visit on the great
day when production of the book began. The author and his wife
were there, as were Sabinus and Plautia. "They're already beyond
your introduction," the director told them. "And I also have a happy
surprise for you, Senator. Atticus House will publish . . . *one hundred* copies in the first edition."

"That many?" Aulus seemed staggered by the news.

"How will you ever sell them all?" Pomponia wondered, until she
saw her husband glaring at her.

"Oh, we're not worried." The director smiled. "Of course, the Britannic War was fourteen years ago, and we do wish we'd had the
manuscript earlier. But the name Aulus Plautius is still revered in
Rome. Here we are. Step inside, please."

A hundred scribes were seated at rows of oblong tables, writing on rolls of papyrus coiled at both ends. At the front of the hall on a raised dais sat a reader with Aulus' manuscript. Aulus heard his own words being enunciated loudly in a monotonous but precise voice, while the corps of scribes busily copied it all down word for word. Hands were occasionally raised when scribes wanted to know the spelling of a difficult British name or term.

The director walked over to the nearest scribe and showed Aulus the quality of the papyrus he had chosen. "It's *hieratica*, Senator, Egypt's very best."

Several weeks later, the publisher personally delivered four sets of author's scrolls at the Plautius residence. Each book comprised three scrolls, wrapped in a parchment cover marked with the author's name and the title *De bello Britannico* (*On the Britannic War*) in large red letters.

Smiling, and with the immense pride of new authorship, Aulus carefully unrolled the first scroll and showed his wife the dedication:

> For my magnificent
> Pomponia Graecina,
> *sine qua non*

She had known nothing about it. Several great tears filled her eyes, and she pulled Aulus' leathery cheek down to her lips.

Over the next weeks, enough colleagues in the Senate stopped Aulus to comment on passages of his work to assure him that his lines were circulating in fact. But it was on such a day that a shattering blow struck the Plautii.

Aulus would never purge himself of the bitter, corrosive memory of that morning in the Senate. The consul had just called for new business, when chubby little Cossutianus Capito stood up to deliver a prepared statement. Capito was a minor senator known for disreputable dealings, and one of the most feared informers in Rome. Stretching out his right arm, he began in a shrill, piping voice, "I regret to detain you, Conscript Fathers, with a charge against the family of a colleague, but the matter must be made public if we are to maintain the sanctity of Rome and her gods. I herewith accuse the Lady Pomponia Graecina, wife of our illustrious Aulus Plautius, of practicing a dangerous and alien superstition."

A hubbub arose in the august chamber. Aulus, who sat bolt upright at Pomponia's name, clutched the cold marble slab on which he was sitting and stared at the accuser. Capito continued in his strident, abrasive tone.

"The Lady Pomponia has become a devotee of a weird and noxious cult, somewhat related to Judaism but quite different from it. The cult has been illegal at Rome ever since the Divine Claudius expelled its members eight years ago after the Trans-Tiber riots."

Immediately Thrasea Paetus was on his feet to interrupt. "The *Senate* decides whether a cult is legal or illegal at Rome, and I know of no senatorial decrees on this matter." Gray-haired and mid-sized, Thrasea was the most independent, fearless, and candid member of the Senate, the non-compromiser among colleagues, many of whom were toadies. He continued in a cool, contained tone, "What is the name of this cult, Senator Capito?"

"I wish I knew! Like Hercules slaying the hydra, it comes up in many new places with as many new names. First its members were called 'Followers of the Way,' then 'Nazarenes,' and now, as I understand it, the term is 'Christiani.' "

Aulus' palms were clammy and his mood equally divided between anger and embarrassment. Half the Senate was glancing in his direction. But his nephew Quintus Lateranus loyally hurried over to sit beside him.

"The Lady Pomponia," Capito continued, "in order to worship with this cult—and who knows for what other, perhaps illicit, purposes?—makes secret visits by night to the house of a Jewish Christianus named Aquila on the Aventine, and—"

"You *dare* impugn the honor of Senator Plautius' wife?" Lateranus stood up and shouted in a rage.

A great commotion arose, and the consul rapped for order. Then he recognized Thrasea. Fixing an icy glare at the smallish accuser, Thrasea measured his words. "It is not enough that our unworthy colleague has seen fit to invent edicts of the Senate—for whatever tawdry purposes of personal aggrandizement. He must also try to besmirch one of the great families of Rome, particularly the wife of the man to whom the Empire remains in debt. Since it is now a question of her good name and family honor, I move that we follow the ancient custom and refer this case to her own family tribunal. In this way, our ears need not be assaulted by what will doubtless prove to be a worthless and self-serving accusation."

"*Euge! Euge!*" the shouts rang out. "Well said! So be it!"

Capito tried to reply. "But this is a matter of grave—"

"*Order!*" the consul cried. "There is support for Senator Paetus' suggestion, and we shall vote on it." He glared at the accuser. Then he announced, "All those in favor of committing this charge to the family tribunal of Senator Aulus Plautius, move to the right. Those opposed, to the left."

The vote was a magnificent demonstration of support for Aulus: 320 in his favor, 24 opposed. Immediately he asked for the floor. In a remarkably steady voice for one whose emotions were churning, he said, "Thank you, my colleagues. But I must assure you that, in conducting this trial, I shall set before me the example of the first Brutus, who judged and condemned his own sons when he found them guilty. I shall also request that one of the clerks of the Senate record the entire proceedings and make them available to you. And you are all welcome at the hearing, which I shall conduct tomorrow morning."

"*Euge! Euge!*"

When they left the Senate chamber, Aulus and Quintus headed directly for city headquarters. Five minutes later, three men were seen crossing the Forum and climbing the familiar route up to the Palatine.

Seneca and Burrus seemed as disturbed as Aulus. "First of all, you should know that Nero had nothing to do with this," Seneca advised, "and we just found out who did. Can you guess?"

"No," Aulus snapped.

"The empress mother."

"Agrippina?"

"Yes, she's calling it a 'patriotic gesture' to expose one who might corrupt the state with a new religion. Probably she also has something against your Pomponia—what, we don't know. At any rate, she's been having her followed."

Sabinus seemed to hear a voice saying, "First those you love . . . and then you." He interrupted the dialogue, "Gentlemen, I hadn't wanted to trouble any of you with my personal problems, but the time has come." He went on to reveal the threats Agrippina had made at his inaugural banquet. All four looked at him with astonishment.

"But the important thing is this," Seneca commented. "Nero,

evidently, isn't interested in the matter. So don't let him be, Aulus. The 'domestic tribunal' idea is superb."

"Thrasea has a great mind," Burrus observed. "So simply acquit Pomponia and have done with it, my friend."

"Not so fast," Aulus responded. "If Pomponia *is* guilty, I'm not going to dismiss the case."

Seneca looked at him curiously and then smiled. "You know, Aulus, you *are* one of the last of the old Romans . . . you and Thrasea. I really think you *would* condemn her."

"But who are these Christiani anyway?" Sabinus wondered.

Burrus and Seneca shrugged their shoulders. Aulus related what he knew about the Christians, and since Aquila figured so prominently in his report, Quintus said, "I'll go over to the Aventine and question him. That will help me in preparing the defense."

"*You'll* defend her?" Aulus asked.

"Could I do less for my favorite aunt?"

Aulus spent the rest of the day summoning relatives and witnesses, and preparing for the trial. That evening he had a long talk with Pomponia. Some of the accusation was substantially true, and both knew it. In recent months, Pomponia *had* made frequent trips to Aquila's, for a congregation of the Christians assembled there each Sunday night. No, she had not formally joined them through a certain washing rite of theirs, but she had not kept her interest in them secret from Aulus. For his part, he had tried to dissuade her by every means short of outright quarantine, but Pomponia was a free woman and could come and go as she pleased.

Before falling asleep that night, Pomponia reached over to touch her husband's arm. "Are you sorry you married me, Aulus?" she asked. There was a silence longer than she had feared before Aulus managed a quiet "No."

"That's not very convincing," she sighed. "Though I can't really blame you. I . . . I never wanted any of this to happen. *Why* can't I believe as I wish? Quietly? In my own way?"

"You could have, I suppose, if it hadn't become public knowledge."

"Rome has dozens of different religions, hundreds of philosophies. Why should they be so concerned about the Christians?"

"It's not that so much, Pomponia. It's Agrippina and her vendetta against us. Besides Sabinus rejecting her, she learned about your remark at the betrothal: 'These delicacies are more reliable than Agrippina's.' Somehow, it got out."

"Well, why not explain that to the Senate, then?"

"Ha!" Aulus huffed. "Attack the emperor's mother in public? Besides which, your . . . beliefs are now a matter that must be decided in court, whatever motives were behind the suit."

She was silent for several moments. Then she said, quietly, "I know you, my love. You *could* find me guilty, couldn't you?"

"If the evidence warrants it."

"What would the punishment be?"

"Probably none, *if* you rejected this superstition immediately." He said it with obvious animus.

"I don't believe I could do that, Aulus."

"Then I'd probably have to stand by Claudius' precedent in the case of illegal religions."

"What's that?"

"Exile from Rome."

There was another silence. "So? You'd exile your own wife?" she finally asked.

"I'd *have* to, Pomponia. There would be no other way. No other honorable way. Can't you see that *I'll* be on trial tomorrow too? As judge?"

Turning away from him in bed, she let the dreadful impasse finally register on her emotions. She started crying very quietly, hoping he would not notice.

Aulus reached over to stroke her hair. "Don't worry, carissima," he said. "I'd join you . . . wherever I had to send you. It might even be the excuse I need to leave Nero's cesspool."

Before falling asleep, Aulus suddenly realized the extreme irony of it all: the Christians *were* going to have a test case for themselves anyway, and right under his own Roman's nose! Thrice-cursed the day that cursed tentmaker ever set foot in his house!

By midmorning, their atrium was filled with solemn-faced relatives and friends who were milling about nervously and conversing in muted tones. Thrasea and a number of senatorial colleagues were there, as well as all Plautii who could be reached in time, for the honor of the family name required it. Sabinus and Plautia had arrived earlier, while the prosecution, represented by Cossutianus Capito and several of his aides, stood off in a corner by themselves.

Capito was furious that the trial had been remanded to Aulus' family tribunal—a legal throwback to Republican Rome—and he would not have bothered pursuing the case further had the empress mother not insisted on it. Aulus' natural bias in favor of his own wife would at least be tempered by the Senate's interest in his impartiality, Capito knew, for the clerk of the Senate was there to record the proceedings word for word.

Pomponia now appeared, clad in the customary dark mourning garments of one about to face trial. The excited babble stilled to a sympathetic hush as she walked through the atrium into the peristyle, followed by the whole assembly.

At the center of the hall, Aulus sat down on an ivory curule or judge's chair, a memento of his own consulship. His wife took a seat directly in front of him. To her right was Quintus Lateranus to conduct the defense. To her left, a suspicious-looking Capito took his place, along with his aides, while the assembly seated itself through the rest of the mansion.

Aulus looked up and said, "At the request of the defendant, this court will dispense with the taking of omens at this time"—a sudden mumble vibrated through the hall—"because as judge I took them earlier this morning, and I assure you they were quite favorable." Sabinus thought he detected a low smile on Aulus' face.

Then, turning to the prosecution, he said, "Yesterday in the Senate, you brought two charges against the defendant. In essence, they were: first, that she is a follower of the Christian cult, which may be illegal in Rome; and second, that she may have gone to the house of one Aquila for immoral purposes."

Capito stood up at once. "If it please the court, I should like to withdraw the second charge entirely. It was . . . totally unwarranted."

"I shall allow you to withdraw it only upon your apology for an unnecessary and malicious blunder, for which I could hold you personally liable."

Capito looked down and made what he hoped was a suitably abject apology. He had meant only that some of the Christian practices were immoral, he said.

"That will be determined in the course of this hearing," said Aulus. "Proceed with your accusation."

Capito began deliberately. "I shall attempt to prove, by the testimony of several witnesses, that the defendant did indeed frequent the house of one Aquila on the Aventine hill for purposes of cultic worship, and that this sect of the Christiani so-called is illegal, subversive to the state, and a foreign superstition of the worst kind."

Lateranus stood up. "If the honored judge will permit, the defense would like to simplify this hearing by agreeing to one of the charges: Pomponia Graecina *did* in fact visit the house of a couple named Aquila and Priscilla on the Aventine for purposes of Christian worship."

The peristyle broke into a low rumble of surprise.

"Order!" Aulus called out. Then, looking at his wife, he asked, "Pomponia Graecina: *did* you frequent the house of Aquila, as charged?"

"I did," she replied, her eyes fixed on the tessellated floor over which she had walked so many times.

"Was the cult of the Christiani practiced at this house while you were there?"

"Yes . . ."

"Are you a member of this cult?" Aulus continued.

"Well . . . no. No, I am not."

"But do you share their beliefs? Their practices?" Capito interposed.

There was a tomblike silence while everyone cocked an ear to hear her reply. Pomponia said nothing for some moments. Then she admitted, "Yes. I do."

Again the undulating ripple of surprise, as relative nudged relative and stole glances at the city prefect and his wife sitting just behind the accused.

"Very well, then," said Aulus. "It remains for this hearing to determine whether the Christians practice a *religio licita*—a legally accepted religion—or not. If they do, the defendant is not guilty. If not, she has committed a crime. Do you accept this as the remaining purpose of this hearing, Senator Capito?"

"Yes. Yes indeed."

"And do you, Senator Lateranus?"

"Well, not quite, honored Judge. What would happen, for example, if it could be demonstrated that the Christians, while not yet possessing the status of *religio licita*, might still cherish harmless beliefs and practices not at all dangerous to the state so that they could be accorded legal status in the future? In that case, it would be morally wrong to condemn the defendant."

Aulus pondered the objection for a moment, but then replied, "That would be for a future senatorial hearing to decide. But in any case, the defendant would be guilty of practicing an illegal religion in the present."

The boyish, handsome features of Lateranus lifted in surprise. Sabinus turned to Plautia and whispered, "He's making the first ruling against his own wife!" Pomponia raised her eyes to explore those of her husband.

Turning to the prosecution, Aulus asked, "What evidence do you have to support your charge?"

Capito stood up to corroborate his indictment, and it was clear that this time he was much better prepared than in the Senate. Beginning with the "Chrestus" riots in the Trans-Tiber, he showed how Claudius had banished the Christian leaders and added his rescript against grave robbery, the hoax on which the new cult was building itself. The fact that the Christians had returned in the meantime was due to the generous oversight of the new government, but such laxity must no longer continue.

"This is a very dangerous cult," Capito argued, his high pitch escalating in excitement. "Their secret assemblies witness a nauseous rite in which they eat the body and drink the blood of their god—not really, of course. Like the Druids, they probably get their ingredients from people whom they kidnap and then sacrifice." He paused and noted with satisfaction the look of horror on everyone's face. "But I've heard another and even worse report: they set a large, oblong wheat cake before their initiates and tell them to carve it up. They do, but the cake screams! For inside is a little sleeping baby . . . who is then murdered . . . drained . . . and eaten."

"All this is a *lie!*" Pomponia shouted, rising from her chair. "A horrendous *falsehood!*"

"You'll have your chance to testify later," Aulus admonished her. "The prosecution may continue."

"Some of their rites are more enjoyable, I understand," Capito said with a leer. "The men and women meet for a very special kind of worship. They enter a room, where only one lamp is burning . . . on the floor in the middle of the chamber. Then they select one another in the flickering light, sometimes even brother and sister. Finally a little dog is let loose in the chamber, and it dashes for a bone that is tied to the lamp, toppling it over. The room is plunged into darkness. Aha! And then—"

"Disgusting *fabrications!*" Pomponia cried, against a background of astonished whispering.

"All right, all right. Let me spare you any of their other lurid rites. Their beliefs are equally revolting to civilized Romans, for they hate the world and the people in it. It's not good enough for them, and they look forward to a . . . a mythical paradise at the end of life. Their faith centers on a convicted criminal who was crucified by one of our governors. They seek to overthrow the state. They despise the emperor. They practice sorcery. They reject the gods of the Senate and the Roman People. For this reason, and many more, this is a most dangerous and vicious cult that will destroy Rome if it is not halted now . . . today . . . at this very tribunal."

Then, looking at Aulus, he concluded, "Some have thought me a fool to prosecute this case, honored Judge, before one so closely related to the defendant. I replied, 'You do not know Aulus Plautius. This is a man who puts Rome first in his mind, in his heart, and in his judgment.' Relying on your patriotism and sense of justice, I rest my indictment."

Aulus found the final flattery especially galling, because it raised again the tender issue of his impartiality. "The prosecution," he announced, "has made many charges, some of them new. But I must ask again: what *evidence,* apart from rumor and hearsay, do you have that the Christians believe and practice all these things?"

"Oh, this is very simple." Turning to the defendant, Capito asked, "Lady Pomponia . . . *do* you believe in that Christus who was crucified as a criminal by our governor of Judea?"

"Yes, but—"

"And you do *not* believe in Father Jupiter, Mother Juno, Minerva, the divine Venus, and the other Olympian gods and goddesses, do you?"

"No . . ."

"And in your solemn rites, do you not claim to eat the body and drink the blood of your founder?"

"Well, yes, but this is—"

"And aren't little children also involved in your worship?"

"Certainly, but not in the way that—"

"By her own admission, then, the Christians believe substantially as I've indicated, even though I don't claim to have every detail accurate. And here is the rest of the evidence: written depositions

from my infor— ah—aides who witnessed the defendant's presence at
the house of Aquila."

Aulus took the testimony in hand and thumbed through it. "Before this hearing can continue," he announced, "I must have the opportunity of reading the depositions. This court is adjourned for two
hours."

When the hearing resumed, Aulus handed the documents to the
clerk of the Senate and said, "Let these be entered in the record of
this hearing. But I must inform the prosecution that a great amount
of rumor is included in these lines, not hard fact. They prove little
more than the defendant's presence at meetings where there were
readings and prayers and hymns. And the consumption of a little
bread and wine."

"But this is such a *new* cult," Capito protested. "It's difficult to
get decent information about it."

"Which is exactly what we must have. Perhaps the defense can
supply it. Senator Lateranus?"

Quintus stood up and made a flowery little introduction that
achieved little more than loosening his vocal cords. But when he
focused on the charges, he became more effective. That Claudius
had dismissed the leaders in *both* factions of the "Chrestus" riots
proved nothing, he argued, because Jewish leaders had also been exiled, and Judaism was certainly a legal religion. Labeling the claims
of human sacrifice "an absurd misunderstanding," Quintus did his
best to disentangle the rites of what the Christians called "commun-
ion" and "baptism."

"Children are involved," he said, "but only to receive a sacred
washing, *not* to give their blood! And those ridiculous rumors about
indecencies in dark rooms probably grew out of their practice of
greeting each other with a simple kiss as a 'brother' or 'sister' in their
faith. Really now, that's rather harmless, isn't it, Senator Capito?
Only a filthy mind would draw worse conclusions."

Capito flashed him an ugly scowl. Sabinus whispered to Plautia,
"Don't worry, dear. My twin seems to have matters well in hand."

"It's true that the Christians reject the gods of the state," Quintus
conceded. "But again, this doesn't make them guilty of practicing an
illegal cult. The Jews also reject the Olympian deities, yet Rome, in
its tolerance and maturity, permits such diversity in matters of religion. In fact, this is one of the glories of the Empire.

"But far more serious are the charges that Christians hate the state, seek to overthrow it, and despise the emperor. I call to witness the husband and wife known as Aquila and Priscilla."

Immediately all heads craned to get a glimpse of the pair who were most responsible for getting the clan into legal difficulty. What they saw disappointed them: a simply dressed couple who stepped before Aulus' tribunal and seemed not at all threatened by the possible hostility about them. Priscilla was a composed, dark-haired woman of middle age with soft, cream-colored skin and nut-brown eyes. She was clutching a scroll under her arm.

Aulus gave them both a look of ill-disguised scorn. This was the pair that had caused the present family torture.

"Are you both Christians?" Lateranus asked them.

"Yes," each replied.

"But aren't you Jews too?"

"Yes," replied Aquila. "The two are not exclusive."

"This is a point to which we must return. But for now, give us a brief summary of what you Christians believe. Perhaps your wife might do this, since the defendant is also a woman."

Priscilla explained her beliefs in simple, direct language, but her mention of some salvation concept with its promise of a resurrection after death was difficult for the hearers to understand. Then Quintus questioned Aquila about the Christians' attitude toward the Roman state. His reply was in such marked contrast to Capito's charges that the prosecutor leaped to his feet, objecting, "How do we know he's telling the truth? Suddenly, these cultists seem to have become patriots!"

Lateranus frowned. "If you call his veracity into question, does the name Paul of Tarsus mean anything to you?"

"Yes, he seems to be the chief troublemaker in this sect. He goes from place to place in Greece and Asia, trying to make Christians of the whole Greek world."

"Then Paul of Tarsus would speak with some authority for this sect?" Quintus asked.

"Yes. Why do you ask?"

"Aquila, please read several excerpts from the letter that your people in Rome just received from this same Paul of Tarsus."

"But it's written in Greek, Senator," he replied.

"No problem. Most of us here are educated enough to understand Greek. I'll translate for the rest."

Priscilla handed the scroll to Aquila, opening it to a marked section. He began reading from the thirteenth chapter:

Let everyone be subject to the governing authorities. . . . Pay them your obligations, taxes to whom taxes are due, tribute to whom tribute, respect to whom respect is due, honor to whom honor.

Owe no one anything except to love one another, for he who loves his neighbor has fulfilled the law. The commandments, "You shall not commit adultery, You shall not kill, You shall not steal, You shall not covet" and many other commandments are all summed up in this sentence: "You shall love your neighbor as yourself". . . .

"Thank you, Aquila," said Quintus. Then he gave a loose translation in Latin and commented, "Now it seems, Senator Capito, that the official teachings of this sect are quite the opposite of what you have suggested."

"That still doesn't make it a legal religion," Capito objected, taking his cue from Aulus' ruling.

"We shall now deal with that issue. In your friend Paul's letter, Aquila, there was reference to various 'commandments.' Are these not the same as the famous Ten Commandments of the Jews?"

"Yes. Certainly."

"Do you regard yourself as a Jew? I mean, not only in origin, but in belief?"

"Yes . . . but there are various kinds of Jews, of course."

"Precisely. And your friend, Paul of Tarsus. Is he a Jew?"

"Yes."

"And Jesus, the founder of your sect. Was he a Jew?"

"Yes."

"And his followers in Judea—Jewish?"

"Yes, mostly."

"But Gentiles may also become Christiani?"

"Oh, yes. The faith is open to everyone."

"At this moment among your Christians, are there more Jews or Gentiles?"

"Jews."

"Thank you, Aquila. You may be seated." Quintus now turned to the defendant and said, "Lady Pomponia, the questions I shall now

address to you are very important. Please consider them carefully before answering. The first is this: do you believe in one God, the God
of the Jews?"

Pomponia replied, "Yes, I do."

"Do you believe in the Ten Commandments of the Jews?"

"Yes."

"Do you believe that the Scriptures of the Jews are their God's
revelation?"

"Yes."

"Well, then, distinguished Judge, Senator Capito, honored
friends and relatives, we must come to the quite obvious conclusion
which has been implicit all along: the Christiani are merely a sect
within Judaism—no more, no less—and as such they are indeed
members of a *religio licita*, which is protected by our Law of Associations."

Excited murmuring broke out. Capito was on his feet, objecting,
"If they're all Jews, how come they rioted against each other in the
Trans-Tiber?"

"Everyone knows the Jews have many factions. I understand
there are Pharisees who believe in a resurrection and Sadducees who
do not. Yet they're both good Jews. There are Essenes and Christians. There are Greek Jews, Egyptian Jews, Roman Jews. Their
customs differ but they all believe in one God and his commandments. That's what makes them Jews."

Capito countered by insisting that the Christians had a different
enough faith to be a wholly different cult. Quintus rebutted by asking what was more basic than belief or non-belief in an afterlife, and
yet no one doubted that Pharisees and Sadducees were both Jews.
Clearly, he had been well schooled by Aquila.

Both prosecution and defense delivered their summations. Finally
Lateranus concluded, "Since the defendant seems to believe everything the Jews believe—so what if it is *more* than they believe in the
case of the prophet Jesus—and since the founder, the first followers,
the present leaders, and most of the members of this faction were or
are Jews, it *is* a Jewish sect, pure and simple. Therefore the Lady
Pomponia is *not* guilty of practicing a foreign superstition, as
charged, but a legal religion, recognized by Rome and protected by
our Law of Associations. We rest our case."

Aulus adjourned the hearing while he pondered his decision. Sabinus badly wanted to talk to him as he walked for some minutes alone out in his garden, but he thought better of it. He had nothing but the profoundest sympathy for the turmoil that had to be boiling inside Aulus' mind. Whatever his decision, Quintus had done extremely well, Sabinus thought, and he told him so.

Presently, Aulus stepped back inside. After a final check of depositions and a brief conference with the Senate clerk, he again mounted his tribunal. For several moments he glanced down at his wife with a sad expression, so sad, in fact, that it frightened the Plautii. At last, he announced, "I must pass this judgment with keen personal disappointment that *any* member of our senatorial order—the fact that she is my wife is incidental—should have become converted to Judaism in any form. But by participating in the rites of the Christian sect of Judaism, the defendant has not exceeded the bounds of what is legal. I therefore find the defendant, Pomponia Graecina, not guilty."

Plautia ran over to her mother and twined her arms about her neck, crying with relief. Sabinus walked over to Quintus and fairly pounded his shoulders. Aulus would later congratulate Lateranus on his defense strategy, but for the moment he had to continue pursuing a neutral posture. He was moved, though, when Thrasea Paetus walked over, shook his hand with a broad smile, but said absolutely nothing. Aulus did not feel in a mood to be congratulated.

Capito, meanwhile, had hurried over to Aquila, barking the question, "Is your conscience entirely clear, *worthy* tentmaker?"

"Yes. Why do you ask?"

"Taking refuge under the protective blanket of Judaism? Are you Christians *really* Jews?"

"Yes, in all the senses brought out in the trial. In fact, we call ourselves 'the true Israel.' And we hope and pray that all Jews will become one with us."

"Hmmmm. I wonder what the Jewish leaders in the Trans-Tiber would have to say about that."

Before Aquila could reply, Capito and his aides took their leave in something of a huff. But the Plautii, of course, were obliged to host their vast clan for dinner.

When Aulus returned to the Senate the next day, only a few made the error of congratulating him on his conduct of the trial. Most of his friends—those who really knew the man—simply treated him as if nothing had happened, for, in their opinion, nothing had.

Aulus hoped they were right, but he was not entirely convinced. He felt that he could never share his wife's new religious interests, and the fact that she believed something which he did not bothered him more than he cared to admit.

16

"WE NEED a closer link between the city and the Empire," Seneca told Sabinus during a chat at municipal headquarters. "So Burrus and I want you to attend our conferences with Nero each Friday in the palace. Caesar admires you, and your presence would do much to help our cause."

Sabinus listed a half-dozen reasons why he did not especially favor the idea, but Seneca brushed them aside in the name of Duty. Duty was deity in Rome. The sure way to bend any Roman statesman to your cause was to invoke that quasi-magical term Duty.

Sabinus now met with the emperor, Seneca, and Burrus around a black marble table in Nero's office suite each Friday morning. This was the council of state that governed the city and the world—*urbem et orbem.* More casually, Sabinus called it his weekly "Date with Fate," for the decisions made by that foursome usually produced repercussions across the entire Mediterranean.

Seeing Nero regularly, and at close range, Sabinus was pleased to note some maturity, finally some improvement in the young emperor's approach and bearing. The way he reacted to the aftermath of Pomponia's trial, for example, was almost heartening. No sooner had Sabinus arrived one Friday than Nero told him wryly, "The Lord Mayor of Rome may be delighted to learn that Cossutianus

Capito, who prosecuted his mother-in-law, has just been indicted by the Senate for extortion, and I've given him a week to get out of Italy."

Sabinus' smile was so enthusiastic that it brought chuckles from the other three. Seneca went on to explain, "Last year, you'll recall, Capito was governor of Cilicia?"

"Yes . . ."

"Well, our good friend Thrasea Paetus helped a delegation of Cilicians indict him for extortion. Thrasea did such a noble job of it that Capito didn't even try to defend himself. He simply threw up his pudgy hands and waddled out of the Senate."

Nero looked at Sabinus and frowned. "I ought to be embarrassed about all this, you know, since it was my own mother who egged Capito on in that suit against dear Pomponia."

"Oh?" Sabinus responded, as if it were fresh news. He looked with some concern to Seneca and Burrus.

"But then"—Nero cleared his throat—"it's not the first time that Mother and I have disagreed on something." Nero's smile broke the tension and gave Sabinus some relief from his gnawing concern about Agrippina and her threats. Perhaps this major reverse would keep the harpy at bay.

Seneca's tutoring, his calculated gamble might yet pay off, Sabinus reflected. The twenty-year-old Nero was now expressing himself well at their council meetings, while classical culture seemed to have taught him restraint. When the four approved plans for a new amphitheater in Rome, Nero humanely decreed that no combat there be carried to the death. Greek games, which were bloodless athletic contests, had inspired him.

When Sabinus returned home that Friday, he told Plautia of the favorable signs in Nero. "Is it possible?" she responded. "Can we really hope that it will still work out, Sabinus? That violence and murder in the palace are all history now?"

That evening, Nero had dinner with his close friend and comrade-in-escapade, Marcus Otho, a fashionable young dandy who had become the emperor's alter ego. Of medium size, like Nero, Otho was slightly bowlegged and splayfooted, but he had a woman's concern for the rest of his appearance. He depilated his body and drenched his feet in scent. No one, not even Nero, knew that he wore a well-fashioned hairpiece.

When they had finished supper, Nero suggested an evening fling, but Otho begged off with a simple, "I have to get home."

"What is it, friend?" Nero frowned. "Nothing's come between us, has it?"

"Perish the very thought, Caesar," Otho apologized. "It's just that—"

"Lately I almost have to *order* you to join us for a night on the town. And the women we find—you take no interest in them. What's the matter with you, man?"

"The simplest reason in the world," Otho chuckled. "I'm in love."

"Good for you," Nero smiled. "Who?"

"Poppaea Sabina, of course."

"But that's your own wife, Otho."

"It *is* a little unique, isn't it?" He smirked. "But that girl's making me . . . deliriously happy. She eclipses everyone. She's—well, Poppaea is the most serenely beautiful creature in all Rome. No, in all the Empire."

"Rather extravagant claim, isn't it? Of course, I've never seen the girl without that veil of hers."

"She still wears it whenever she goes out in public. Has to, in fact."

"Why?"

"She'd disrupt the city if people saw her. Too striking. Too extraordinary."

"Enough of that, Otho!" Nero laughed. "It's sweet and old-fashioned for a man to be proud of his wife, but let's not carry it too far."

"No, that girl is Venus herself. And she has a mind too—enough wit to keep a philosopher on tenterhooks. After we . . . after our embraces, it's actually fun just to *talk* with Poppaea."

"I know. That's the way it is with Acte."

Otho made no comment, for comparisons were decidedly not in order here. But he was telling himself, "No contest." Then he smiled and rose from the table.

"Where are you going? Home?"

"Of course. And forgive me, good friend"—Otho sighed extravagantly—"I'm returning to that treasure for which all men pray . . . but which I possess."

"Come now, Otho! You sound like a slave auctioneer. Or a pander."

"Or a supremely happy husband. You'd agree if you saw her, Caesar."

"Well, let me see her then. Bring her to dinner here . . . to make up for my missing your wedding."

Otho thought for a moment, then nodded. "Why not?"

"When? Is tomorrow night all right?"

"Should be fine."

"But fair warning: I'll give you my candid opinion—privately, of course—and you mustn't take anything amiss. We'll still be friends?"

"Always!" Otho smiled.

The next afternoon, Nero ordered a private dinner for three and waited for Otho and his wife with rising interest. He had spent an abnormal amount of time getting himself dressed and groomed, and was now redolent of his favorite Arabian perfume. He glanced into a large mirror and tried, for the first time, to look at himself objectively. As an emperor he had no limitations, of course. But as a man? His height? Average. His appearance? A few detestable spots and pimples still marked his skin, but they were well covered this evening. His darkening blond hair, set in rows of curls, his deep blue eyes, and handsome features more than compensated for his skin problems, he thought.

Nero was satisfied. And no one would have dared complete his physical description, at least not to his face. But his perfumes never quite disguised his problems with body odor. His features were effeminate rather than handsome. His eyes were a weak slate blue—hardly the royal blue he imagined. And a thick, squat neck, protuberant belly, and spindly legs completed the bodily ensemble of the man behind the emperor.

Finally Otho and Poppaea were announced, and Nero rose to greet them. Poppaea was wearing a thin aquamarine stola, with gilded jewelry to set off tresses of the same golden amber hue. Her hair, the blondest Nero had ever seen, was combed back and fastened. But everything below her eyes was covered with a gossamer veil. Ridiculous conceit!

Said Nero, "Forgive me, fair Poppaea, for not having asked you to the palace before this."

"Caesar needs beg no one's forgiveness"—she smiled—"simply because he is Caesar."

Nero admitted to himself that the vain thing did have beautiful skin and entrancing greenish-blue eyes. And she knew it. More the pity.

A butler brought in a flagon of wine and three jeweled cups. "A bit of Falernian to whet the appetite?" Nero asked, chuckling inwardly at what would follow: the little minx would have to remove her precious veil to drink the wine.

Poppaea shook her head. "I'd prefer mine with dinner. I want to relish every moment of the evening, Caesar, and I fear your Falernian would dull me a bit."

Nero looked at her lamely, trying to control his impulse to reach over and tear her precious veil to shreds. Poppaea, evidently, was fully aware of the impression she was making on him if those laughing eyes were any indication. Presently, they all reclined for dinner.

Nero never saw her take the veil off, but when next he looked at Poppaea, she had removed it and was smiling at him with lips parted slightly to reveal teeth of flawless white. The rest of her face easily fulfilled what was promised by the forehead and eyes. Poppaea *was* striking. In fact, she was a masterpiece, Nero thought, as he took in her exquisitely chiseled features. Small wonder Otho was so dazzled, the lucky fellow. And she proved an extraordinarily good conversationalist at dinner as well.

Later on, when they prepared to leave for the evening, Otho pulled Nero aside to gauge his reactions. "Well—what do you think?" he probed.

"Love to twist your nose a bit"—Nero grinned—"but . . . forget it. Yes, she *is* a splendid girl. And what's more, you don't deserve her, you scoundrel."

"I know," Otho sighed. "But I'll try to make the best of it."

Poppaea's thanks seemed warm and very genuine, and again her fascinating eyes seemed to pierce into Nero's soul. Was he imagining a slight extra pressure in her handclasp as she said good-bye?

He must *not* play the fool, Nero solemnly decided after they left, giving way to a hasty infatuation like some smitten schoolboy . . . embarrassing . . . not fair to Acte . . . or Otho, for that matter . . . He certainly mustn't fall in *love* with the girl, for what if she were really aiming for power? . . . Or maybe she only wanted the satisfaction of turning a Caesar's head . . . Or maybe she wasn't interested in the least. But *such* a striking creature!

The next morning, a courier delivered a note in small, cursive lettering:

Poppaea Sabina to Nero Caesar, greeting. Last night was a delight, thanks to you, though I do apologize for my coy performance with the veil. (Will I ever reach maturity?) I am, however, old enough to set a good table, and Otho and I would like to invite you to dinner a week from today, if Caesar will not find a visit here demeaning. Farewell.

"I have to wait a whole *week?*" Nero moaned, until he realized that the messenger was still standing there, waiting for a reply. "Tell your mistress that I'll be delighted to come."

After a week in which he maundered in distraction about the palace, Nero arrived at Otho's house on the appointed evening. Poppaea greeted him heartily, her hypnotic eyes burrowing into him once again. She was dressed in a diaphanous saffron house tunic that set her figure off to much better advantage than the smothering folds of a stola.

"Where's Otho?" Nero wondered, gazing for a moment at the entrancing twin hillocks of yellow gauze that crowned Poppaea's chest.

"I have another apology to make," she said, with a sly little smile. "I should have sent a message, but it was getting too close to dinner. Otho, unfortunately, has urgent business down in Antium and won't be back till late tonight. But I hope you'll still have dinner with me?"

Through a light, tasty supper of five courses, Nero barely noticed what he was eating, for Poppaea's animated dialogue ranged over many subjects, betraying a quick and versatile intellect. Like himself, she was a restless soul, trying to break free of the ordinary, the expected, and the customary. She was entranced with art and drama. She toyed with astrology. She was fascinated by the eastern cults, and even admitted to a certain admiration for Judaism. No, she was not a proselyte, but the idea of believing in one supreme deity seemed appealing to her.

Nero agreed, but then, he was so captivated by the alluring girl he would have agreed to anything. Radiating her sensual charm all the while, Poppaea seemed even more beautiful than during her visit to the Palatine, probably because her honeyed strands of hair were not tied back but cascaded over the edge of the couch, glistening in the soft amber glow from the solitary candelabra on the table.

They had finished dinner, and the servants had retired. But they were still reclining at the table. Nero edged closer to Poppaea, his heart throbbing, and he brushed her cheek with a kiss. She turned the other way for a moment or two. But then, holding out both her arms, she slowly pressed her lips to his forehead, cheeks, and mouth, until he was groaning with anticipation. Her approach had been emboldened by the messenger's detailed report of Nero's reaction to her invitation.

"No, Nero," she said, suddenly holding him off. "First you have to know the whole truth about me."

"It can wait," he said in a husky voice.

"No. Else you'll think the worse of me later—a shameless girl who gives herself lightly."

"I won't. I promise."

"What I'm trying to tell you is this: my love for you isn't something sudden. I've seen you on many public occasions, and—I know it sounds impossible—but I . . . I think I fell in love with you even at a distance. I told myself it was madness, and I tried to forget you. But now, Nero, you must hear this confession: do you know why I married Otho?"

"Well, he's a grand and very handsome fellow . . . probably my closest friend."

"Yes—that second reason."

"What?"

"Simply *because* he was your closest friend, I knew someday I'd get to meet you. It's madness, isn't it? Sometimes I hate myself for using Otho that way. But . . . what choice does a woman have when she's so . . . *completely* in love?"

Nero had broken into a rapturous smile. "Darling, darling Poppaea," he whispered, touring her cheeks with burning kisses. "I had no idea. These are . . . the most wonderful words I've ever heard."

"You won't think badly of me?"

He shook his head emphatically.

She parted her lips and let him kiss her deeply. "This really is a . . . a culmination of a long romance, then, isn't it?" she whispered.

"Sweet Venus, how I love you," Nero crooned. Then he moved closer to her, kissing and caressing her until they were both smoldering with flames of desire. Moaning with quiet ecstasy, they embraced with reckless, heedless passion.

Nero had never known such joy. Sex he had sampled, almost to satiety. Love he had ventured with Acte. But Poppaea brought him the most intense blend of the two he had ever known. From that moment on, she would have to be part of his life, Nero vowed.

The problem of Otho posed itself immediately, of course. Nero was ashamed of himself for taking the wife of his best friend as mistress, but everything was now subordinated to his love for Poppaea. Otho, meanwhile, was trembling with outrage, cursing the day he had so stupidly boasted of Poppaea in front of the man he had thought his friend. However, there was little he could do now but play the bitter role of cuckold. Perhaps Nero would tire of her. Or she of him.

It was not to be. Nero grew hopelessly enthralled with Poppaea, but she complained that their love was hardly being expressed on an honorable level. "It . . . simply can't go on this way, Nero," she told him one night. "I come from too noble a family to be anyone's mistress, even Caesar's. Otho can't tolerate it any longer, of course. And sometimes I think we live better than you do here on the Palatine."

"How do you mean?" he scowled.

"I mean, Otho and I live as husband and wife. It *is* rather normal, isn't it? But you keep your own wife in a closet while you're enslaved to a slave—or an ex-slave, at any rate. Yes, I know you continue to see Acte. I suppose I'm jealous of every moment someone else spends in your arms, Nero."

"I despise Octavia. And I love you *far* more than Acte, *carissima optima*."

"Well, as I said, it just . . . can't go on this way. Much as I love you, I'd sooner be wife to Otho than mistress to Nero."

Nero lost control of himself. He slammed his fist on a table of fretted ivory, cracking it neatly in half. Then he fired a salvo of abuse at Poppaea, followed by remorseful weeping. She let him vent a maelstrom of emotions without saying a word. Then, preparing to leave, she placed a good-bye kiss on the bared imperial neck, slumped over in dejection. Nero suddenly looked up and asked the question she had waited so long to hear: "You said you'd rather be Otho's wife than Nero's mistress, Poppaea. But what if you were to be . . . Nero's *wife*?"

She uttered a cry of joy and kissed him exuberantly. It would all be a lengthy process, he admitted, and he could promise no dates or schedule, but he would not rest until she were empress. Meanwhile, no matter where her husband was sent, she was to remain in Rome with him. Happily, she agreed.

Nero appointed Otho to the high post of governor of Lusitania.* For all intents and purposes, it was at the end of the world. Sadly, Otho packed his things, closed that chapter in his life entitled "Poppaea," and sailed to the far west. For the next decade, Lusitanians would find him a surprisingly able and honest governor. Apparently, he had left all his flaws of character back in Rome.

Just after Nero left at the close of one of their Friday conferences, Sabinus huddled with Seneca and Burrus for strategy. Poppaea was a powerful new force that had to be taken into account in the delicate balance of Roman statecraft. All three wondered anxiously to what extent ambition was fueling the fires of her love for Nero. Seneca had more information on her background, and he confided, "Poppaea is a less political girl than, say, Agrippina, but if Nero is determined to marry her, there could be danger."

"*Could* she become empress?" Sabinus asked. "I mean, is there legal precedent?"

"That's the problem we *didn't* have with Acte," Seneca responded. "As a freedwoman, Acte could never have aspired. But Poppaea is a daughter of the nobility. If Nero divorces Octavia, he certainly could raise Poppaea to the throne."

Burrus was shaking his head. "But if he divorces the daughter of Claudius, he severs his claim to empire," the praetorian commander warned. "The people won't stand for it. At least my praetorians won't."

An aide entered the room, whispered a long message into Seneca's ear, and then withdrew. The philosopher's brow knitted with concern. "We have a *major* problem, gentlemen. You know, of course, that Caesar moved his mother out of the palace some months ago into her own town house, but lately they seem to have become reconciled. Agrippina spent last night at the palace, and this noon she's having a private lunch with Nero."

"So?"

* Today called Portugal.

"You also know that she's *seething* over his affair with Poppaea—she's always been jealous of anyone coming between herself and Nero. Well, the palace maid who attended her this morning reported that while she was preening herself in front of a mirror, Agrippina talked to her reflected image and said, 'I'll never let that blond harlot have you, my son. I'll *get you myself*, first.'"

"What in the world is *that* supposed to mean?" Sabinus wondered.

"I have no idea. But to me it sounds threatening. Very threatening."

Burrus, in charge of palace security, suddenly came to life. "All right. I'll have the usual taster on duty in case she tries poison. And I'll also hide inside the observation cubicle in the dining room."

"What's that?" Sabinus asked.

"Claudius had it installed during one of his paranoid periods," Seneca explained. "It hasn't been used since. Nero doesn't even know it exists."

"Come to think of it," Burrus added, "if any infamy were attempted, I'd need witnesses. You both had better join me."

It was easily the most boring hour Sabinus had ever spent. He, Seneca, and Burrus were ensconced in a small closet peering into the palace dining room through a long slit cut into the wall. Nothing unusual transpired at the luncheon, other than that Nero was drinking more than usual. In fact, he was half intoxicated by now, and waved the taster out of the room. Burrus tensed at that point. Since Agrippina had been drinking hardly anything, her befuddled son was now more vulnerable than ever.

Three pairs of eyes watched as Agrippina moved closer to Nero. Burrus was breathing heavily, his hand clasped on the dagger at his side. Agrippina now removed her stola until only a sheer tunic of briefest dimensions hugged the still-lush contours of her body. Nero turned to look at her. For a moment, his eyes widened in surprise, but then his thick, wine-stained lips curled into a smile. She snuggled over next to him as they reclined at the table and took him in her arms in a motherly sort of way. But her maternal caresses suddenly grew wanton as she lavished kisses on his ears, and her fingers started probing forbidden regions. The drunken Nero began breathing heavily and reciprocating.

"By all the Olympian *gods!*" Sabinus whispered. "So *that's* how she's going to 'get him'!" He felt physically ill and nauseous.

Seneca had already hurried out of the closet in a quiet panic. Several minutes later he pushed Acte into the dining room; she rushed over to Nero and fell in a huddle at his feet, weeping and clutching at his knees. "*No*, Master!" she cried. "Not *that* crime . . . not incest! Rumors are already circulating about you and your mother."

"Wha' rumors?" Nero sat up.

"About what your mother just tried to do. I'll tell you this: the praetorians will *never* follow a Caesar guilty of . . . of such an outrage!" Then she shook with sobs.

Agrippina quickly refastened her tunic, beaming waves of cordial hatred at Acte. Then she rolled off her couch and flew out of the room in a rage.

Nero stroked Acte in consolation and tried to get up. But he was tipsy and lurched to one side. She had to help him out of the dining room.

As they left the closet, Sabinus debated whether or not to tell Plautia of the revolting scene. Was she old enough, or would she even understand the shabby story? Before leaving the palace, he asked Seneca what would happen if Poppaea learned, but the philosopher gave his shoulders a sad and vacant shrug.

The answer came later that day. Poppaea stormed into Nero's suite and fulminated, "And how is our darling Oedipus this evening?"

"I was drunk, Poppaea," he growled.

"Talk about my rivals!" she hissed. "I used to think a slave-girl was bad. Now, by all the gods, it's a *mother* too! Of course, incest's an old habit with her, and dear Uncle Claudius wasn't the first. How old was she when her brother Caligula first seduced her? Twelve?"

"I told you I didn't know what I was doing. And if it's any consolation to you, I . . . I'll never forgive Mother for *this*."

"Oh yes you will! Just like all the other times. She threatens you, and you forgive her. She plots against you, and you forgive her. She defames you behind your back, steals from you, intrigues against you. And now, to cap it all off, she tries to seduce you too." Poppaea ranted on, knowing that she had to break the power of Agrippina forever if she were to marry Nero. Never again would there be an opportunity like this.

"Trust me, my darling," said Nero softly. "Leave it to me."

Nero banned his mother from the Palatine. Then he had friends start harassing her with petty lawsuits to keep her on the defensive. When she took a trip down to her country estates, he praised her for courting repose, implying that she would do well to stay away from Rome permanently.

But the steel-nerved, resilient woman had as much foolhardy courage as an army of the opposite sex, as much stamina as a troop of gladiators. She returned to Rome and tried to rebuild her power base once again through secret interviews with key members of the nobility and the military. She amassed a treasury, and, putting a brave front on it all, she told Nero quite scorchingly what she thought of him and his lawsuits. Rumors also surfaced that she was bypassing the Praetorian Guard and establishing touch directly with the legions.

So it was that Nero pondered a final solution to his maternal problems. He did first weigh other alternatives. Banishment from Rome and Italy? Perhaps. But, knowing his mother, she would be busily plotting, whatever her Mediterranean island of exile. Imprisonment? Never. It would not look proper for an empress mother, and she would attract public sympathy behind bars. There were, then, no other alternatives, Nero decided.

But one. He wrote Locusta at the toxicology academy he had set up for her, and received several samples of their latest research. But he finally decided against poison. His mother now knew nearly as much as Locusta, and had been adding antidotes to her diet for months. Were there other ways of inducing the necessarily "accidental" death? Should he discuss it with his council of state? No, this was Caesar's business.

One evening in early spring, Sabinus was returning from a pleasant stroll across the Quirinal with Plautia when a figure accosted him from behind some shrubbery near their door.

"*Who* in the—" Sabinus was startled. "Oh, it's you, Hermes."

"Ssshhh! Forgive me, Clarissimus," whispered the face in the shadows, "but I have to see you on a *very* urgent matter. Privately."

"Inside then. The library."

Plautia recognized him as the Syrian contractor who had helped build her father's outdoor study. Sabinus had been impressed with the little Syrian and taken him into the city engineering staff.

"Why so secret?" Sabinus asked the raven-haired Levantine once they were alone inside. "Are you being followed?"

"I hope not, but I didn't want any witnesses to my being here. Now, Clarissimus, do you remember when Caesar wanted some carpenters from our staff and you sent me over to the Palatine in charge of a detail?"

"Yes . . ."

"Well, we didn't stay at the palace. We were sent to Agrippina's house instead. She was off to one of her country places, and while she was gone, we were ordered to—oh, gods, why am I telling you this?"

"Go on, Hermes."

"We were ordered to install a . . . a collapsible ceiling in her bedroom."

"A *what?*"

"A collapsible ceiling. At the pull of a lever, huge concrete panels will dislodge and drop down on her bed—"

"Sweet Jupiter! Heavy enough to kill her?"

"Yes. Yes of course."

"Did you actually do it?"

Slowly he nodded. "We had to. Nero's personal orders."

"Is the ceiling . . . operative now?"

"We finished it this afternoon. Before we left, Nero himself came over to test the mechanism. Only we propped up the panels so they wouldn't fall out and cause a mess. It'll work, all right. Then he looked the four of us in the eye and threatened us with death if we told anyone a word about it. Plus a big reward if it works as planned."

Sabinus sank back into a chair, a fist supporting his large, square chin. For some moments he said nothing. Then he asked, "Why did you come here and tell *me* all this, Hermes?"

"I . . . I didn't know what to do. I really despise the empress mother, you know, but I couldn't just . . . let her die like that. Oh Hades, I might just as well admit it, Prefect: I think I'm becoming a Christian—that Aquila is *quite* persuasive, you know—and we're supposed to love our enemies."

"You too?" Sabinus smiled. "I thought that sect was just for mothers-in-law." Then he frowned. "Well, thanks Hermes," he said sardonically. "Now you've placed the matter squarely in my hands while you're free of it. By the way, when is Agrippina supposed to return?"

"Tomorrow afternoon."

"Oh, splendid." Sabinus shook his head. Then he saw Hermes to the door and advised, "Say nothing. Do nothing. We never saw each other tonight, right?"

"Right." Hermes slipped out furtively.

Let Agrippina die, Sabinus thought, and all her vile threats with her. She aims to destroy us . . . A faulty ceiling would finally free us all. She tried to ruin Aulus and Pomponia. Let her die. She's a cancer on the body politic. Besides, anyone warning her would endanger his own life. Yes, let the overambitious, murderous, incestuous harpy die.

He went to bed. Plautia was sleeping, fortunately, so he did not have to answer a fusillade of questions. But sleep did not come to him, and he tossed about for several hours. Finally he got up and went to the lavatory. It was there that the idea occurred to him. "Yes," he said to himself, "she must use the privy."

Before returning to bed, he wrote a note in small block lettering but carefully left it unsigned.

The litter ride back to Rome had exhausted Agrippina, and she was now preparing to retire early. On the table near her bed stood a stack of correspondence that had accumulated while she was gone. She would glance through it tomorrow.

She shut her eyes and was nearly asleep when her mind's eye looked again at the pile of mail and saw something unusual. She sat up in bed and stared at it, a small scroll tagged with purple. She broke the wax seal that strangely bore no monogram, and read the note. Cringing with disbelief, she jumped out of bed and climbed onto a chair for a closer look at the ceiling. She noticed the telltale alterations—a series of parallel cracks between panels of fresh plaster —and was horrified. Obviously, the unsigned warning did not come from a crank. Almost helpless as her nerves caught fire, she did exactly as the note suggested. She made a pallet on the floor of her adjoining lavatory and tried to sleep on it.

In the dead of night, a thundering clatter shook the house. By the light of a half moon streaming in through the windows, Agrippina saw the jagged scene of devastation that had been her bedroom. Her bed itself was smashed beyond recognition, and a powdery substance had coated everything. Coughing from the plaster dust, she climbed over the wreckage and hurried into the hall to see if she could catch anyone who might have tripped the mechanism. But she saw no one until her whole household staff came running to assist her. She was about to announce that one of them had just tried to murder her, but she shrewdly checked herself. Otherwise Nero would know she knew, and her life would be snuffed out. "A terrible accident!" she cried. "Luckily, I was out in the lavatory at the time."

What should she do now? Driven by the fiercest hatreds for her "monster son," Agrippina spent the next days deciding whether to try to poison Nero, or cast herself on the mercy of the Senate and implore the Fathers for asylum. Or should she flee north to the legions?

Sabinus, with the rest of Rome, publicly marveled at Agrippina's luck in avoiding catastrophe. Privately, he hoped Nero was having second thoughts about murdering his own mother. Should he tell Seneca and Burrus of his role in the matter? Under any other circumstances, yes. But it was just possible that one or the other had condoned the matricide.

Nero was beside himself with fury and yet fright at the failure of his collapsible ceiling. He was not sure whether to believe his mother's explanation of her escape or not. If she suspected him, his own life was in danger, and in any case he must act at once, and successfully. His every morsel of food now twice tasted, he conspired with the one man who hated his mother as much as he did, Anicetus, commander of the Roman fleet. Anicetus had been Nero's boyhood tutor, and his violent quarrels with Agrippina had left wounds that only festered with age.

"What's simpler than an accident at sea, Princeps?" Anicetus suggested. "At a play the other day, there was a ship on stage with a hull that opened up to let out some wild animals and then snapped shut again. We could adapt the idea to . . . eject a beast of another kind."

Nero pondered the plan for several moments, then smiled. "Why not, Anicetus? But nothing at Ostia—too near Rome."

"Here's what I had in mind. You're going down to Baiae for the Feast of Minerva, aren't you?"

"Yes, we'll spend about a week down there." Then he grinned. "Of course, you . . . scheming son of a satyr."

"So. Now, of course, you must do everything possible to stage a 'reconciliation' with your mother and invite her along."

"And no one will outdo me in shedding filial tears after the accident." Nero spread his arms. "There will be temples and shrines in her honor."

While Anicetus went down to the Bay of Naples and devised a collapsible ship, Nero carefully reversed tack and started begging his mother's forgiveness for the dark thoughts that had been brewing in his mind. At first Agrippina was extremely suspicious, but some of the lines in his almost pathetic letters had a ring of truth about them:

. . . Of course, you've done your part too, Mama, in nourishing our quarrels. You can be quite a formidable antagonist! But children should bear with the irritability of their parents and be first to show a spirit of forgiveness. . . .

A hypocrite would have been only apologetic, she thought. Besides, rumors trickled down from the Palatine that Nero truly wanted a reconciliation. And then his cordial note arrived, inviting her to spend the holidays with him down at Baiae. "The family should be together at the Feast of Minerva," he added, in a pious touch. It *had* to be true then, she thought. Reconciliation!

The Gulf of Baiae, the most northwesterly inlet in the great outspread arms of the Bay of Naples, was a favorite resort of the emperors and a fashionable watering place for Roman nobility. Agrippina and her escorts sailed down the Mediterranean coast to Baiae in mid-March of 59. Exuding smiles and cordiality, Nero met them at the dock and escorted her up to a country villa where she and her party would stay. The villa lay on the coastline north of Baiae and was separated from it by a cove of water several miles wide.

The following evening, Agrippina and her attendants sailed across the cove for a great feast of reconciliation at Nero's villa. Again he stood at the wharf with widespread arms, and was gallantly helping her up the steep path leading to his villa when they heard a splintering crash from below. Turning about, they saw that a ship had rammed into Agrippina's galley as it was docked, damaging its stern. Nero was furious. "Is that you, Anicetus?" he shouted.

"I'm afraid it is, Caesar. Forgive our clumsiness!" he wailed. "We'll start repairs immediately."

"You'd better, you blundering idiot! Unless you want to see a new fleet commander here!—Come, Mother."

Nero's banquet disarmed any remaining doubts. Only those members of the imperial party who were friendly to Agrippina had been invited, and she herself reclined at the place of honor. In high spirits, Nero bubbled, "This merely symbolizes your return to highest favor, dear Mother. And I have some happy news for you: your beautiful profile will soon be next to mine again on our coinage."

Agrippina was exuberant. Her spirits surged. But she had never seen Nero so unmatched in his moods. One minute he would chatter playfully and poke fun like a boy; the next he seemed overcome with an air of constraint, as if his thoughts were miles distant. Most of all he wanted to talk about the past.

In the middle of the feast, he seemed to have remembered something, for he leaned over to whisper, "One thing we've never cleared up, dear Mother. You once told me that when I was born, astrologers made some sort of dreadful prediction about me. What was it?"

Surprised by the query, Agrippina shook her head. "No, darling son. This isn't the time to talk about anything like that."

"Oh, but it is, Mother, it is." It was time indeed to ferret out any secrets. "In a true reconciliation, nothing is concealed."

She frowned and hesitated. "Well, if you insist," she gave in. "Yes, maybe it *is* a good time. Let it be a token of my great love for you. It was Balbillus who cast your horoscope and said, 'Your son will be emperor one day, but he will also . . . kill his mother.' "

Nero, who was swallowing an olive, choked on it and coughed violently. Then he cleared his throat and asked, "Is that it, Mother? Anything else?"

"Yes . . . my reply to him. I said, 'Let him kill me, then, *provided he is emperor!*' "

Nero flushed. "Such . . . great love, dear Mother. But what a ridiculous horoscope. Astrologers *are* a pack of deceivers and scoundrels!" He grabbed a cup of wine and drained it, hoping Agrippina would not notice his sweat and agitation.

About midnight, after the feast, Nero escorted her down to the dock. It was a magnificently warm night for early spring, with thousands of stars hanging in the heavens. The sea was calm, barely ruffled by a fragrant, pine-scented breeze that seemed to be blowing up from Capri.

At the dock, an apologetic Anicetus greeted them. "I'm sorry, Caesar. It'll take another day's work to repair the galley."

"Dunce! Why didn't you ever learn to sail?" Then he softened. "Well, no great problem. Here, Mother, use one of my ships. Do you suppose you can sail this one without smashing it, Anicetus?"

The fleet commander merely hung his head in shame. Nero then bade his mother good-bye with a lingering embrace, straining her to his breast and kissing her eyes and hands. "Strength and good health to you, Mother," he said. "For you I live, and because of you I rule."

"Good-bye, dearest son," she said, slurring her words a bit from the quantities of wine she had consumed. A male aide helped her onto the ship, while a girl attendant, Acerronia, followed. Anicetus and his crew now cast off as mother and son continued waving good-bye to each other across a widening strip of water.

Agrippina went below to stretch out on a couch inside the cabin, while Acerronia jabbered joyfully at her feet about the glories of reconciliation. Ten minutes later, Gallus, the male aide, stepped inside to check on the comfort of the empress mother. Someone topside yelled, *"Now!"* Instantly, heavy lead ingots crashed down upon them from the cabin ceiling. Gallus' head and shoulders were crushed, and he died instantly. But the women were saved by the high oaken sides of the couch which were too solid to give way and held up their share of lead bars.

"Pull the *other* lever!" Anicetus barked. It was supposed to open the hull.

"Won't budge!" someone else shouted and then swore. The hull panel, which had opened easily in dry dock, was held shut by subsurface water pressure.

"Capsize the cursed ship, then!" the commander yelled. "Everybody to the starboard rail! Then to portside! Get her rocking!"

But now Anicetus paid his price for secrecy. Only the officers had been alerted to the true purpose of the voyage. The crew, who thought their commander had suddenly gone mad, resisted all efforts to capsize. When the officers ran to one rail, they dashed to the other, stabilizing the roll.

"No, idiots! Help us *sink* it!" Anicetus shouted, as he and the officers plummeted over toward the crew, who just as quickly threaded through them to the opposite side. Sounds of confusion and cursing filled the night air.

Agrippina, meanwhile, managed to salvage a plan of action from her soggy senses. Creeping out of the cabin, she slipped quietly over the side of the ship into the water. At the same time, Acerronia stumbled onto the deck shouting, "Help me! Help the empress mother!" Swimming away from the ship, Agrippina watched in horror as officers clubbed her attendant to death with oars, her crumpling tunic yellow orange in the ship's running lights.

Was Acerronia trying to save herself or cover her escape, Agrippina wondered, as she swam farther away from the ship toward lights on shore. She felt a stab of pain in her right shoulder—somewhere in the melee, evidently, she had been wounded after all. She counted one hundred breast strokes and was starting to weaken when a flotilla of small oyster boats returning to shore glided past her. She screamed for help. They hove to and pulled her out of the water. When the dumfounded oystermen learned that they had rescued the empress mother of Rome, they reverently delivered her to the villa on shore—miserable, enraged, exhausted, but alive.

First she must dress her wound and sleep, Agrippina thought. Then she would decide how to outwit the murderous beast she had spawned and save her life.

Two men had been watching the ship in distress out on the gulf. One of them, Nero, stood on a hill by his villa until he heard the shouts and screams. Then he smiled and went back inside.

The other was a ship's passenger, who was watching the scene from the portside gunwales of a large Alexandrian merchantman named *The Twin Brothers,* for its figureheads were Castor and Pollux, carved to bear an uncanny resemblance to Sabinus and Quintus Lateranus. The vessel was approaching the great harbor of Puteoli after wintering in Malta. The passenger, a short, slightly built Jew, had stayed up to see the ship glide into the Bay of Naples, and he now heard the shouting and screaming, apparently from the small vessel with running lights a mile or so to the west. Peering into the night, his balding gray locks and pointed beard ruffled by the breeze, the Jew alerted a Roman centurion on board, but when

the soldier peered out to see what was wrong, the shouting had
ceased, and everything seemed normal. The centurion seemed to be
a friend of the Jew. In fact, however, he was his imperial guard,
conducting him to Rome for trial before Caesar. And the Jew was
named Paul of Tarsus.†

† Lest this be deemed too great a coincidence, please see the Notes.

17

SLEEP PROVED IMPOSSIBLE for Agrippina. Her mind was painfully alert, searching feverishly for a way out of mortal danger. First she must escape imminent assassination. Later she would flee to the Senate chamber in Rome and denounce Nero for the monster he was. Nero, of course, would now be learning that she may have survived. If he thought she knew it was attempted murder, he would be forced to kill her. He *must*, therefore, be led to believe that she thought it all an accident, like the other times.

"Agermus!" she called to her freedman. "Go to Caesar—immediately—and deliver this message, exactly as I word it. Tell him: 'By heaven's favor, O Caesar, the empress mother—no, *your* mother—has escaped a terrible accident. She knows you'll want to come over and inquire after her health, but she begs you to put this off, since she's well and needs nothing so much as a little sleep.' . . . Yes, that's it. Can you remember it?"

"Certainly, mistress."

Nero had been waiting nervously in the dead of night for Anicetus' return. When he did appear, the fleet commander was a little defensive. "We think she's dead, Caesar," he said. "Her attendants are dead for sure—we saw to that—and she was clubbed too and must have drowned afterward. That would be *some* swim!"

"Sweet Neptune!" Nero wailed. "You don't know my mother! What happened out there?"

Anicetus was giving a detailed report when a guard raced in from the beach and cried, "Caesar! Some oystermen found the empress mother out in the gulf, swimming for her life. They rescued her. You'll be glad to know she's back in her villa with a slight wound, but nothing serious."

Nero threw his hands over his face and cried, "Oh . . . gods!" while slowly collapsing onto a couch. The guard thought it a touching display of filial affection and withdrew.

"She's . . . she's immortal, I suppose," Nero whimpered. "That woman . . . just won't die! By all the flames of Hades . . . how *do* we help her across the Styx? *How,* Anicetus?"

The fleet commander said nothing.

"Oh, but we're dead men, we are. She'll be here in a moment, breathing fire. She'll kill me. She'll take over Rome."

"I doubt that, Caesar," Anicetus said. "Why don't you summon Seneca and Burrus for some . . . ah . . . advice in—?"

"Yes, yes, *yes!* Get them. Get them at once!"

Both men had been part of the imperial entourage spending the holidays at Baiae, but they had not attended the reconciliation banquet and were not informed about the collapsible ship. It took Nero some embarrassed minutes to explain to them why he had plotted his mother's death, and why the attempt had failed.

"Does she know it wasn't an accident?" Seneca asked, with an anxious frown shared by Burrus.

"She couldn't *help* but know," Anicetus muttered, staring at his sandals to avoid meeting anyone's eyes.

"Oh yes. Mother's very bright about plots . . . especially on her own life," Nero groaned. "But you two are here to tell me how to save my life, because"—he faltered, with the look of a cornered, maddened animal—"because she'll get us all otherwise. She probably has messengers going at this moment to the Senate. She'll do anything. She'll arm the slaves. She'll get the Guard to defect. O immortal gods!" He broke down and cried. "What should we do?"

Seneca looked down to the mosaic floor and said nothing.

Burrus shifted uneasily from one foot to the other, rubbing his stubbed arm but saying nothing, though he was trying to catch Seneca's eye.

"Help me!" Nero finally howled. "You're my advisers, aren't you?"

"Give us a moment, Princeps," Seneca snapped. "This is all very sudden for us." Then he paced about the room, chin in hand, thinking of all the alternative courses of action. His Stoic conscience told him he must try to save Agrippina, enemy that she was. "What if we were to arrest your mother and send her into exile?" he asked.

"Impossible!" Nero cried. "After this, she'll not rest until she kills me. And you too. The whole Empire isn't big enough for both of us. You ought to know that."

There was another alternative, Seneca thought to himself. If Agrippina were not crushed, Nero might indeed perish. Rome would be rid of its tempestuous and unpredictable young emperor. Yet that alternative was equally grim, or worse: Agrippina triumphant and reigning as empress? His own life would be snuffed out shortly after Nero's. No, at this point in the incredibly bungled state of affairs—and despite any philosophical principles—Agrippina would have to go . . . if, indeed, she could still be caught. Looking up at Burrus, Seneca asked, "Well . . . who gets the fatal order, then? The guards?"

Burrus shook his head. "Not the praetorians. They're pledged to protect the whole family of the Caesars." Then he looked over to the fleet commander and said, "No, let Anicetus finish what he set out to do. The army respectfully defers to the navy."

Nero looked up and nodded. Anicetus bowed and left the room. He had a reputation to clear.

A guard entered with news that Agermus had arrived with a message from his mother. Nero's eyes darted to Seneca for advice, but then snapped back again. He was Caesar. After his emotional and childish performance he and he alone must decide what to do next. "Bring him in," Nero commanded.

Agermus was ushered in and he delivered Agrippina's statement almost word for word. For an instant Nero wondered if his mother really did think it was all an accident. He could still recall Anicetus and halt her murder. He would not be accused of matricide. But . . . oh, gods, he quailed inwardly, what if it were just another of her stratagems to save her life now for revenge later? He must make an instant decision. Self-preservation. Yes, for an emperor, self-preservation always came first. His mother had to die. To justify his action in Rome, he must now frame her for an attempt on his life.

Nero instantly pulled out a dagger and threw it at Agermus' feet. Then he shouted, *"Guards! Guards!"* until several praetorians came rushing in. "Arrest this man for treason! Agrippina sent him to assassinate me! See the dagger? Clap him in irons!"

Meanwhile, news had spread about the empress mother's injury from shipwreck, and the beach about her villa was now ablaze with the flickering torches of concerned coastal folk and groaning with prayers for her recovery. But suddenly an armed company of marines wedged through the crowds, trotted up to the villa and surrounded it. Anicetus drew his cordon a bit tighter, then broke through the entrance and marched to the master bedroom. Kicking the door open, he saw Agrippina lying in bed, being tended by a terrified slave girl.

Agrippina stared at Anicetus and his marines in terror. But, preserving her dignity, she said calmly, "If you've come to visit a sick woman, take back word that I'm recovering."

Anicetus said nothing. He merely gazed at her in contempt.

"But if you're here to . . . to commit a crime, the blood will be on *your* hands. My son couldn't possibly have ordered you to murder his own mother."

Armed marines surrounded her bed. "Now?" the captain asked. Anicetus nodded.

The captain raised his club slowly, then brought it down on her head.

Stunned with a flood of intense pain, Agrippina saw another marine drawing out his sword. She opened her mouth but no words came out. Drawing on her powerful will one last time, she finally screamed, "Strike here!" and uncovered her abdomen. "Strike my womb, for it bore Nero!"

The sword came down repeatedly. The green of her eyes assumed a last, fearful fluorescence and then faded in death.

Nero had to see for himself that his mother was truly dead. He went to her villa, and then had her body carried outside on a couch and cremated in a mean and hasty funeral.

Returning to Baiae, he slowly began to absorb the enormity of his deed. Befuddled by events, terrified by sounds and shadows, he wandered about the villa, dreading the dawn and yet waiting impa-

tiently for it. Haunted by the scene of his crime, he left Baiae for
Naples several days later.

When he had finally gathered his wits, he dictated a letter to the
Senate, telling how Agrippina's chronic plotting had finally led to
her suicide when the assassination she had planned for him failed.
Seneca edited the letter, appending a list of her crimes ever since
Claudius' time.

But the true story of Agrippina's death followed, by word of
mouth, hard on the heels of the official story. Romans had little trouble deciding which to believe, and a fresh rash of graffiti on the
theme of matricide was daubed on the walls of Rome.

Sabinus was not particularly shocked by the news from the Bay of
Naples, since he guessed it was only a matter of time before Nero
would strike again. But it was sad, he thought, that someone's death
should spell relief for himself; yet relief he felt, in every fiber of his
being. He wondered how Aulus was reacting to the news.

At the other side of the Forum, Nero's explanatory letter was
being read aloud in the Senate. The Fathers showed disgust with
Seneca for having added his rhetorical flourishes to such a message—
no one believed the dagger story—and yet they knew their actions
would be reported to Nero in detail. So they took the easy, docile,
obsequious course and vied with one another to introduce decrees
declaring Agrippina's birthday inauspicious in the calendar and
offering thanksgiving for Nero's deliverance.

Aulus Plautius had suffered directly at Agrippina's hands, but the
sham unfolding in the marbled chamber nauseated him. He stood
up and walked out of the Senate, joined by his friend Thrasea
Paetus, who had taken the same route. Aulus asked him with a wry
smile, "Why didn't you express yourself inside on Nero's letter?"

"I couldn't say what I would. I wouldn't say what I could."

Aulus nodded. "Do you think we'll get into trouble?"

"Nero can kill me, Aulus. But he can't harm me."

Aulus smiled and said, "It would take Seneca a whole treatise on
Stoicism to say the same thing. Soon I'll have to have a talk with my
son-in-law. I really wonder if Sabinus wants to . . . stay in this regime."

On that fateful night in the Bay of Naples, Paul of Tarsus had
disembarked at Puteoli, where he was met by a small group of Chris-

tians. They urged the great missionary to spend a little time with them in the port city. Paul turned to his guard and asked, "Would it cause you any problems, Julius? Delaying our trip to Rome for several days?" His voice had an unexpected depth and resonance for one with so slender a build.

The ebony-haired centurion, dressed smartly in the uniform of the Augustan Cohort, shook his head. "Sorry, Paul. That's just not possible. Military regulations." But then he burst out laughing. "On the other hand, we're merely five months overdue anyway, so what's another week! Yes, take a week. Long enough?"

"Certainly. And thank you, Julius."

"Besides, the emperor's mother just died, so the road to Rome must be clogged with traffic. We'll do better to avoid it."

When they set out a week later, spring had fully splashed across the Italian countryside. The hills were lush green, and the breezes fragrant from the legion of wildflowers standing sentinel along the roadsides. Now Paul and his traveling companion, a Gentile physician named Lucanus, easily forgot the terrors of their voyage from Palestine, which had ended in shipwreck on the coast of Malta, winter there, and transfer to the ship that had brought them to Puteoli.

They traveled up the Appian Way to a halting place called Three Taverns on the thirty-third milestone from Rome. A large cluster of people seemed to have gathered at the village crossroads here. Suddenly someone shouted, "There they are!" and a couple rushed out into the roadway and into Paul's arms. The apostle's eyes filled with tears as he cried, "Priscilla! Aquila!"

"Seven years, Paul," said Aquila. "It's been seven *years* since we were in Greece together!" His face blooming with a great smile, Aquila proudly introduced Paul and Lucanus—or Luke, the more affectionate form his friends preferred—to the welcoming delegation of Roman Christians.

"My brothers and sisters," said Paul, beaming, "most of you I know only by the names I wrote at the close of my letter to the church in Rome. But seeing you gives me courage, for, as you know, I must stand before Caesar." Then he introduced his guard to them. "And my case has begun very well indeed, for I'm in the custody of a distinguished centurion. Julius, meet the Christians of Rome."

"Oh, but there are many more," said Aquila.

"I should think so." Paul smiled. "I'd hoped that you would have had Caesar himself converted by now!"

They all laughed, relieved to find Paul a very human sort, not that larger-than-life saint of God who seemed to command a prestige in the church second only to that of Jesus himself. Luke they also found impressive, though in a different way. He stood a head taller than Paul, and his dark brownish hair and cultured beard, clipped close to the edge of his jaw line, set off a very Hellenic visage in contrast to the Semitic cast of Paul's face, fringed by its gray and pointy beard.

Together they traveled the final leg of their journey, and the black stones of the Via Appia seemed to have a destination at last. In the distance lay Rome, her red brick walls pierced from all directions by gracefully arched aqueducts, a vast, living hub for the network of roads that seemed to be breathing in and exhaling traffic at the same time. It was the greatest city even the much-traveled Paul had ever seen, and, as with any tourist, his eyes widened to gather its wonders.

Julius led them across town to the Castra Praetoria, where he turned Paul and several other prisoners over to the camp commandant.

"Here are the documents of indictment on these men," Julius told the commandant. "They're to stay in irons until their punishment is decided. But this one here—his name's Paul of Tarsus—he gets free custody."

"Free custody?" the commandant asked, arching his eyebrows. "Why?"

"He's a Roman citizen. He's waiting for Nero to hear his case."

"He appealed to Caesar?"

"I did," Paul interrupted.

The commandant shrugged his shoulders. "Must be important. You'll have to have a guard anyway, Paul of Tarsus, since you're not from Rome."

"I understand."

"Ah, Commandant." Julius drew him aside. "If possible, I'd like every courtesy extended to this prisoner. We've just been through a voyage that . . . was designed in hell. And, by all the Furies, if it weren't for this Paul, we'd be at the bottom of the Mediterranean. Besides, I think he's innocent."

"That's for Caesar to decide . . . *if* he hears the case." Then, turning to Paul, the commandant said, "If you can manage to find lodging near here, we'll send over a praetorian each day to . . . ah

. . . to keep you company. Rome pays for the guard, but you'll have to rent the house. Do you have the funds?"

"Yes. But will my friends be able to visit me?"

"Why not? And you'll be able to get out too, if your guard doesn't mind. But he has to be with you at all times, and you can't leave the city."

Aquila and Priscilla found a house for him on the Viminal hill near the Castra Praetoria. Aquila's congregation helped Paul and Luke get settled, and they brought them furnishings and enough food supplies to last for several months. Soon they were more comfortable than they had dared hope, despite the constant presence of a guard.

Aquila gave them a full report on the progress of the Faith in Rome, including a word-for-word account of the trial of Pomponia Graecina. Paul strained to catch every syllable.

"But now I wonder if what we did was justified," Aquila fretted, "staking our defense to Judaism. Was it honest? Letting our fellow Jews protect us?"

"You're a Jew," Paul replied. "I'm a Jew. And if our faith isn't the fulfillment of Judaism, it's nothing." He paused several moments, then resumed. "You know the pattern I've followed in all of my missionary journeys: 'to the Jew first and only then to the Gentile.' The same holds for Rome."

Several days later, Paul invited the leaders of the Roman synagogues to a reception at his house, where they had a free and lively discussion on any topic they chose, for they were alternating between Hebrew and Aramaic, while the bored guard—to whom Paul was attached by a long chain—knew only Latin.

"Brothers," said Paul, "I did nothing against the customs of our fathers, and yet I was delivered into Roman custody. Two governors of Judea examined me, and both wanted to set me free. But some of our brothers objected, and I was forced to appeal to Caesar to save my life. Hence my trip here. I wanted to see you and talk with you, since it's because of the hope of Israel that I'm bound with this chain."

When Paul had finished explaining his view of the "hope of Israel," one of the rabbis stood up and said, "I haven't received any letters from Judea about you, Paul. Has anyone else?" There was no response. "But you're an interesting man, Paul of Tarsus. A Pharisee, aren't you?"

Paul nodded. "Yes, from the Tribe of Benjamin. I studied under Gamaliel."

"And yet you're clearly one of the Nazarenes. That sect, of course, is being spoken against everywhere. But we'll still encourage our brothers to give you a hearing. Shall we set a date, gentlemen?"

True to their word, the rabbis appeared two weeks later with a large number of members from their synagogues. "Now I know why you insisted on a house with an atrium and peristyle," Aquila commented to Paul.

The meeting lasted a whole day. In the morning, Paul expounded his view that Christianity was fulfilled Judaism—that Jesus was the Messiah predicted in Hebrew Scriptures. In the afternoon, there was much debate over this claim. Some were convinced and, in fact, later joined the Christians. But the majority were not.

"It's the great *Shema*, Paul," said one of the rabbis. "Your elevation of Jesus challenges it: *Shema yisroel, adonai elohainu adonai echad.*"

"True," Paul agreed. "Hear, O Israel: the Lord our God, the Lord *is* one!"

"Not two."

Paul then tried to explain why Christians had no quarrel with that Scripture. But later it seemed clear to him that he would have to carry his message also to the Gentiles of Rome.

Flavius Sabinus virtually ruled Rome in the months following Agrippina's murder, since Seneca and Burrus were staying near Naples with Nero, who was afraid to show his face in Rome. The city enjoyed a calm and pleasant summer under Sabinus, because Nero, always the chief troublemaker in town, was absent.

Sabinus' docket was crowded with the usual trials, some petty, others serious. There was one case of considerable interest that struck close to the family, but he could not adjudicate it since his was the wrong court. It concerned the recently arrived Jew, Paul of Tarsus. Sabinus remembered the name from Pomponia's trial, and in fact it was she who brought the case to his attention.

As a favor to her, Sabinus had Paul come down to city headquarters to see if he could assist in his defense. But ten minutes' discussion with the man convinced him that it was a religious case, so he arranged for Paul to meet with him at Aulus Plautius' place, "since the senator is a better judge than I in such matters," he said with a wry smile.

Aulus winced when he learned of Sabinus' comment. But Pomponia seemed so enthusiastic at the prospect of meeting Paul that he could not deny her. Plautia was also visiting her parents the evening the manacled apostle and his guard arrived on the Esquiline.

Sabinus turned to the guard and asked, "Do you have the key to his chain with you?"

"Yes . . ."

"Unlock him, then. I'll be surety for him."

"But . . . this isn't permitted."

"When the city prefect tells you to do something," Sabinus growled, "you'll *do* it! Immediately!"

"All right, Prefect. Sorry." He dropped the chain from Paul's wrist.

"That's fine. Now leave us and go get something to drink in the kitchen."

They moved into the peristyle and sat down. Sabinus began. "You should know, Paul, that our interest in your case stems only from our love for Pomponia here, who wants us to help you in any way we can. Now suppose you tell us . . . well, yes, your whole story."

It proved to be an extraordinary saga, consuming much of the afternoon. Paul started with his young days as a persecutor of the Christians in Jerusalem, and then told of his conversion on the Damascus road, his various missionary travels, the circumstances of his arrest in Jerusalem, his appeal to Caesar, and finally the shipwreck voyage to Rome.

When they learned that Paul had sailed the final leg of his voyage from Malta on *The Twin Brothers*, everyone exploded with surprise at this stunning coincidence, especially Sabinus. The apostle was puzzled until Sabinus explained the nature of Twin Brothers Enterprises.

Paul smiled to himself, wondering whether this "coincidence" had a higher purpose. Throughout his presentation, his hosts reacted in different ways to his story. The women were held spellbound. Aulus too thought it a remarkable tale—and told with sincerity—but he still wondered how this slight, balding, bandy-legged Jew could have had such an influence among members of the new sect. Sabinus merely jotted down notes from time to time, trying to frame his suggestions for legal procedure.

As Paul finished his story, he added, "One comment at the Castra Praetoria I didn't understand. The commandant said something about '*if* the emperor hears' my case. Surely he will, won't he?"

"That's just the point," Sabinus replied. "It's by no means definite *where* your hearing will take place. Not many appeal directly to Caesar. Claudius, of course, always heard such appeals personally—"

"And zealously, too," Aulus interposed. "Poor man. He had so many cases that lawyers sometimes found him nodding at the tribunal. Then they'd suddenly shout, '*If Caesar agrees . . .*' He'd wake with a start and continue listening."

"But since Nero was so young when he acceded," Sabinus explained, "he usually delegated appeals to senatorial friends and confirmed their verdicts afterward. Generally, he still does."

"What about the prefect of the Praetorian Guard?" Paul inquired.

"Burrus? Sometimes he'll take a case for Nero, but usually he serves only as one of the assessors—advisers—in the imperial court." Then Sabinus smiled. "And of course, if only you'd committed your 'crime' here in Rome, Paul, can you guess who would have judged you?"

"You?"

"Yes indeed. And you'd be a free man by now." Then he shook his head. "But you're on record as appealing to Caesar, so he—or Seneca and Burrus—will decide if he hears your case or someone else."

"When will they decide this?" Paul wondered.

"After the prosecution registers its formal charges."

"The prosecution? From Jerusalem?"

"Oh yes. Under Roman law, no trial can take place until a plaintiff lodges his indictment."

"But aren't the *literae dimissoriae* enough?"

"No. The documents of indictment simply show basis for imprisonment while awaiting trial."

"But what if the prosecution doesn't choose to make so long a trip here?"

"That's a sticky point. And I must confess that our law code doesn't really allow for such a situation. This hardly ever happens, you see. The burden of our law is to *compel* a plaintiff to carry through his charges to public trial, and to penalize him if he does not. But there's no provision for freeing the accused in the meantime."

"But that's . . . unfair." Paul frowned.

"It certainly is," Pomponia interposed.

Paul had bitter memories of his two-year imprisonment in Caesarea, and he had hoped his case would be resolved quickly in Rome. He also feared that, having failed to secure a conviction in Palestine, his prosecutors might not bother making the lengthy trip to Rome.

"Of course, if your prosecution doesn't appear, we'll do what we can to compel some kind of hearing," Sabinus said. "But tell me, Paul: *why* did you ever appeal to Caesar? Once you did, you got yourself inextricably enmeshed in our Roman legal machine."

"I *had* to appeal. After your governor, Felix, heard my case in Caesarea, he wanted me to bribe him for my freedom, but I wouldn't do that."

"Felix, the brother of Pallas?" Aulus inquired.

"Yes."

"Of course!" said Aulus, with a smirk. "Any brother of our retired Pallas would want money."

"Then Festus, the next governor, was trying to conciliate the prosecution, so he suggested sending me back to Jerusalem for trial. Since that would have meant certain death, I appealed to Caesar. And I later realized that God had intended me to do exactly this, so that I might preach the Faith here in Rome also."

"Yes, yes. But—well, for obvious reasons, please keep our next remarks utterly confidential. Why do you seem so eager to have the . . . the present Caesar hear your case? He's still quite young. He'll hardly understand the religious depths in the matter. He's unpredictable, and—we all hate to admit it—he's also quite dangerous."

"It's not that I'm so *eager* to stand before Caesar, Prefect. It's just that I *know* I'll be facing him, regardless of—"

"How do you know that?" asked Sabinus.

"During our terrible voyage, when all hands had abandoned hope, I had a vision or dream during the night of the worst storm. A messenger of God spoke to me and said, 'Don't be afraid, Paul. You must stand before Caesar. And God has granted you all those who sail with you.' And, as you know, not one of the 276 lives was lost."

Sabinus smiled. "Do you *really* think you had a message . . . from your god, Paul?"

"Yes. I do. It was such a vision on the road to Damascus that transformed my life a quarter-century ago."

Sabinus looked at the intensity in Paul's bluish-gray eyes—and shook his head in wonder.

18

IN SEPTEMBER, Nero hesitantly returned to Rome. But his flatterers were right: he need not have stayed away for fear of the people. Privately they might call him "matricide" and now also "coward," but a dead Agrippina was no basis for revolution. His return to the city, in fact, was greeted by more enthusiasm than even his lickspittles had promised.

For the first time in his life, the twenty-one-year-old emperor felt truly free. "At last I can do whatever I like," he told himself. "Great Jupiter, I can even kill my mother and they cheer me!" Now he could fly into Poppaea's arms without worrying about whether Agrippina were looking on from some palace balcony.

As a man of age, he could also do with less advice from Seneca and Burrus. "It doesn't suit the emperor of Rome to be seen racing horses," they had told him. But Nero craved the excitement of standing in a lurching chariot, grasping the reins behind four snorting steeds while careening around a curve of the circus. Now he would simply do it. Seneca and Burrus gave up any hope of restraining him, but Sabinus saved the day with his suggestion: have Nero manage his horses out of public view across the Tiber in the Vatican valley, where there was a hippodrome that Caligula had begun but never finished. Nero was pleased with the idea and spent several hours here each day running his horses.

Busy as he was with other pursuits, Nero started absenting himself from the Friday councils of state, which gave the other three remarkable privacy in their conferences. Seneca's morale was drooping. "All I can do is try to cushion Rome from the worst shocks," he told Sabinus and Burrus. "Last week, the idiot palace astrologer had his planets mixed up and told Nero some ugly portents lay in his path. The charlatan also told him he could escape if he diverted the impending evil onto others. So he actually prepared a long list of victims until I looked over his shoulder and said, 'Forget the astrologers, Caesar—they're deceiving fools—and no matter how many people you cut down, you could never kill your successor.'"

"Bravo, Seneca!" Sabinus smiled. "What did he say?"

"He agreed, thank the Fates, and crumpled up his list."

"Why not throw that star-gazing fraud out of the palace?"

"I'd love to, but Poppaea wouldn't have it.—At other times, my friends, the crime is committed *before* I can stop it. You know Nero's aunt, Lepida, who was sick in bed with constipation before she died? When Nero visited her, she stroked the fuzz on his cheeks and said, 'As soon as I receive your first shavings as a man, I'll gladly die.' Nero turns around and tells her doctors to give her so much laxative she'd never need any more."

"But why?" Sabinus asked, in anger.

"So he could seize her properties now rather than later. Lepida was *very* rich. No, Nero has other plans for that golden gristle on his face. He wants to shave it off at a great public festival he's originating—the Juvenalia. Everybody is to help celebrate Nero's manhood in a huge ceremony. We're all going on stage, it seems."

"You *are* joking, Seneca," Sabinus countered.

"I wish I were. Here. These invitations are just going out to all the patrician families of Rome."

Sabinus read the parchment and his skin tingled. The last two sentences he read aloud: "Act, sing, dance, do a mime—anything that will set off your skills to best advantage. But you *must* attend, even if only to sing in the choruses." He paused and looked up. "That's ridiculous. No, it's disgusting. Our nobility won't walk on stage—the plebes would hoot us out of the theater."

"We know that," said Burrus in a tired voice that broke his long silence. "But what can we do?"

High on the Esquiline, Aulus Plautius read the imperial invitation, crumpled it in disgust, and threw it away. "It's obvious what Nero's doing," he told Pomponia. "He desperately wants to go on stage himself. But Seneca tells him—and correctly—that as emperor he simply can't."

"So if members of the nobility perform first," Pomponia commented, "the precedent will have been set. What shall we do, Aulus?"

"Nothing."

"Couldn't we take a trip to the south and say we didn't receive the invitation in time?"

"We'll do nothing."

Sabinus and Plautia wished they could have taken the same course, but Nero insisted that they join him in the imperial box at the festival. Sabinus agreed, but only on condition that they not be expected to perform. Nero concurred, although he was not especially pleased at the diffidence of his city prefect.

The marine theater of Augustus, just across the Tiber, was packed for Nero's command performance. Sabinus and Plautia were seated in the center orchestra with the imperial party, and at high noon cornets blasted out an opening fanfare. Slowly, dramatically, Nero stood up and faced the expectant crowd.

A slave solemnly daubed his jaw and cheeks with oil. Nero then reached for his razor. Its handle was of gold, studded with precious gems, and he held it up for all to see. Looking into a small hand mirror, he gingerly severed the amber-red stubble that had erupted along the lines of his jaw and chin. Another slave carefully held a towel under the emperor to catch any severed hairs and to receive the precious wipings from his blade. When his cheeks were suitably smooth, Nero gathered the shavings and placed them inside a small golden globe, which he now held up triumphantly. "To Jupiter Capitoline!" he shouted. Applause flowed down the tiers of the theater, and the Juvenalia could now begin.

A herald walked out onto center stage. "Look who it is!" Sabinus nudged Plautia. "It's Gallio, Seneca's brother—the one who set Paul free in Corinth." Sabinus winked at Seneca. The philosopher returned a wan smile and a slow shake of the head.

Gallio now announced grandly, "Only the highest quality of entertainment will grace this occasion. Therefore, our performances today will be given exclusively by families of Roman nobility."

He went on to announce each family act, the great names from Rome's past re-echoing across the theater, followed by their amateurish performances. Some played the flute or sang to the lyre. Others, acutely embarrassed, tried to dance in mimes or give exhibitions of prowess in hunting, although several of the performers showed hidden talent and even seemed to be enjoying themselves.

"See, Sabinus," Nero leaned over and smirked. "There's a bit of the mime in every one of us, and it was left to me to bring it out. So maybe next time you won't be so . . . condescending about my arrangements."

Sabinus saw, even felt, Nero's smile fading into a chilling stare. Plautia reached for her husband's hand.

After several more performances, Sabinus looked over to see if Nero were still relishing his spectacle, but he had disappeared. Then Gallio stood up to declare, "Caesar has often told us, 'Hidden talent counts for nothing.' Nor does he exempt himself from his own advice. Although Rome is 812 years old, and never in her history has the chief of state deigned to give a public performance, Caesar loves you too much to be shackled by past traditions."

A droning buzz of excitement in the crowd almost drowned out Gallio's climax: "Fellow Romans, our last performance today will be given by . . . Nero Caesar himself, singing his own verses!"

Happily washed by waves of applause cascading down on him from the galleries, Nero walked to the center of the stage, clad in the simple tunic of a lyre-player. Holding up his hands for silence, he nervously bent over his instrument, tuning it with care. He gave each string a final, testing twang, looking into the wings for a signal from Terpnus, his music tutor and the leading lyrist in Rome.

When Terpnus nodded his approval, Nero smiled and called out, "My lords, of your kindness, lend me your ears," the performer's traditional opening. "First I shall sing a poem I composed about Cybele's lover, entitled *Attis*, and then a . . . a more rousing piece of mine called *The Bacchantes*."

The thousands stilled to a hollow hush. Nero strummed several notes and then began singing. But his throaty bass was muffled, hesitant, indistinct. "Louder!" Terpnus advised in a shouted whisper. "More body!"

The instructions confused Nero, and his playing and singing became unsynchronized. Laughter and then even hissing broke out in various pockets of the audience. Sabinus glanced at Plautia, who had thrust a hand over her open mouth. Seneca was cringing in a hot pool of embarrassment. Nero stopped, started over, and finally blended music and lyrics.

After finishing his breathy *Attis,* he launched with more spirit into *The Bacchantes* and gave a better performance. When it ended, the Augustiani, Nero's hired claque, rose as one man in wild jubilation and cheering. Soon the entire crowd learned the proper way to receive an imperial recital, and joined in the acclaim.

In his exhilaration, Nero invited the imperial party and all the Augustiani to an evening feast, and it was midnight before Sabinus and Plautia returned to the Quirinal.

"Well, what did you think of Nero's music?" she asked, as they were preparing for bed, since he had dropped no comment whatever.

"I think Nero's voice would improve remarkably if he shared the fate of the Attis he sang about."

"Oh? What was that?"

"Attis was castrated."

The next morning, Nero summoned Terpnus for a frank critique of his performance. The master lyrist came into the emperor's suite and found him on the floor, almost suffocating under two massive sheets of lead strapped across his chest.

"Don't overdo it, Caesar!" Terpnus warned. "I told you *one* lead plate would be quite enough to build up your wind."

"Well, how can I develop—aahh—my diaphragm otherwise?"

"Have you been purging yourself as I instructed?"

"Aahh—yes, enemas each time I eat too much."

"And disgorging?"

"Oh yes—aahh—always the feather."

"Have you been eating fruit? Apples? Anything else harmful to your voice?"

Nero shook his head. Then he looked up at Terpnus and asked, "Huuhh—how did I do last night?"

"Rather splendidly, Caesar, considering . . ."

"What?"

"That you have a rather weak and husky voice, dear boy. But it's improving . . . improving remarkably. So let's consider last night's performance something of a dress rehearsal. With patience, you'll soon be able to give your first concert. Oh, and you'll also have to work on your poetry if you want to use your own material." With that, Terpnus patted Nero's cheek and whisked himself off.

Nero doggedly continued his labored breathing for a half hour more. Then he unstrapped the lead plates and called for Seneca.

"Now don't complain about last night," Nero said, as soon as the philosopher came into view. "Terpnus said I did just splendidly."

"He's . . . a better judge than I in such matters."

"Yes he is." Nero frowned. "But I have some good news for you, Seneca. I think I *will* take your advice about broadening myself. You see, I don't want to be known only as a lyrist or an actor. I want to write more verse. I want to try painting and sculpture. Even philosophy."

Seneca could scarcely believe his ears, but he quickly organized a working circle of poets that met regularly with Nero on the Palatine. The emperor spent many hours on some of his verses, but when Seneca saw the polished versions, he was impressed. He was also certain that Nero had assistance, until one day he saw his worksheets. Unquestionably, the poems were his own—so heavily had the early drafts been crisscrossed with lines and arrows, and the wording erased. Nero also encouraged philosophers to come debate with Seneca after palace banquets, and he actually seemed to enjoy the intellectual wrangling that took place.

Might Nero choose the better path after all, Seneca wondered.

Late that spring, Pomponia had a slight edge to her voice as she reminded her son-in-law that Paul of Tarsus had been in Rome a year now, with prospects of his trial no nearer than when he arrived. But Sabinus had not been idle. Months before, he had given Burrus a full briefing on Paul and wondered if he could devise a legal means of quashing the case, since the prosecution still had not appeared.

As a favor to Sabinus, Burrus promised to do what he could. He laid the matter before Nero, though without mentioning the special interest of the Plautii. Had he chosen the wrong time, Burrus wondered, or was the emperor suddenly trying to play the legal purist? For Nero merely replied, "We'll wait for the prosecution to arrive in this case."

To help soften Paul's disappointment, Sabinus personally took him word of Nero's decision. While approaching Paul's lodging on the Viminal, he heard the missionary's voice through the open windows, apparently dictating some correspondence:

> . . . I want you to know, brothers, that what has happened to me has really served to advance the gospel, for it has become known throughout the whole Praetorian Guard and elsewhere that my imprisonment is for Christ. . . .

Poor man, Sabinus thought. As if the praetorians really cared about him! Here he was, trying to convert detention into some kind of success.

Sabinus knocked on the door. Inside, Paul and Luke welcomed him happily and then introduced a young, slender Greek with soft features named Timothy, who was sitting at a desk, taking Paul's dictation.

When Sabinus reported Nero's decision, Paul seemed not in the least dismayed. "I had no idea free custody would be this favorable," the apostle confessed. "I'm able to teach unhindered. Anyone who wishes to see me, can. And many, many come. Luke and I have a busy correspondence with our congregations in Greece and Asia. And the church here in Rome is *growing*, Prefect, more than we dreamed. Your dear mother-in-law finally asked to be baptized. Several of my guards are now converts, and they're carrying the 'good news,' as we call it, to comrades at the Castra Praetoria. Even in Caesar's household there are enough Christians for them to hold their own worship in the palace."

"There *are?*"

"Oh yes, especially among the group of servants who once belonged to Narcissus."

"Does . . . Caesar know about this? I don't believe he'd take kindly to news of Christians increasing their numbers in Rome."

"Why?"

"Paul . . . you just don't understand Caesar. If you did, you might even hope the prosecution would never arrive."

"I'd be glad enough to have things go on this way indefinitely." Paul smiled. "But I will, of course, have to stand before Caesar eventually."

"I don't know. We'll try to quash your case somehow."

"No, Prefect," Paul remonstrated, tugging more slack into his chain. "You must *not* try to do that, much as I appreciate your good will. I *must* stand before Caesar."

"Why? Oh, that vision of yours?"

"Yes, and—"

"I'm finally beginning to understand you, Paul of Tarsus. You really *want* Caesar to hear your case so that you can convince him to rule Christianity a legitimate religion. Pomponia's hearing was not enough to determine this. Your trial will be?"

"I don't know, my friend. There *is* some wisdom in what you say. But I'm merely heeding the words told us by the Christ: 'You will be dragged before governors and *kings* for my sake, to bear testimony before them and the Gentiles.'"

Several days later, Sabinus realized that he would no longer be in any position to give Paul official help. He read it several times before really believing it—that curt note just delivered from the Palatine. It bore Nero's official seal, but the rest of the message seemed hasty and informal. He read:

Nero Caesar, *Princeps et Imperator,* to T. Flavius Sabinus, greeting. I hope you are in good health. I also am well.

Rome has appreciated your performance as city prefect for the past five years. But I have decided to terminate your services as of July 1. Your successor will be L. Pedanius Secundus. I trust you will show him every courtesy in helping him learn the responsibilities of your office. Farewell.

Later in the day, Seneca and Burrus paid a visit to city headquarters to explain. "Obviously, we had nothing to do with it, Sabinus, but here's the reason," Burrus led off. "Or, there really are two reasons. One, Nero was angry about your attitude at the Juvenalia—which was ours too, of course, though we concealed it better." He smiled wryly. "The other reason is—well, do you know that Sicilian who sells Nero his racehorses?"

"Tigellinus?"

"Yes. He and Nero are getting *very* friendly, and he doesn't seem to like you."

"Small wonder!" Sabinus smirked. "I once saw him rubbing Nero with . . . with *boar's dung!* He said it was 'a charm against injury,' so I called him a simpering, superstitious fool. To his face!"

Burrus and Seneca chuckled briefly, then returned to their task of consoling Sabinus over the loss of his position. By now, however, his mood had changed abruptly, and he was smiling. "Enough, gentlemen!" he said. "Will you believe that I was nearly at the point of resigning anyway? And that the longer I dwell on Nero's note the happier I become?"

Seneca, who was only momentarily surprised, nodded slowly and sighed, "How many times have I said almost the same thing, Burrus?"

"And I, too. Well, you're the lucky one, Sabinus: now you're *able* to quit. But we'll miss you . . . more than we can say."

When Sabinus told Plautia about his dismissal, she looked at him for several moments in shock before screaming with delight and throwing her arms about him. "I'm so *very* happy, Sabinus," she cried, "so relieved, so—"

"That's hardly the way to talk to someone who's just lost his job!" he trifled.

"Oh, *good riddance* to that awful job! Think of it, darling: now we can get away from *him*. That fearful, flabby face of his and those puffy eyes won't be leering at us any more."

His smile quickly faded. "But what am I supposed to do with my life now, Plautia?"

She drew back and looked at him curiously. "Your income? Money's not the problem, is it, Sabinus?"

"Hardly," he laughed. "The Twin Brothers are doing *ridiculously* well, thanks to your cousin Quintus and his Midas touch!"

"Well, you could always take a more active role in the partnership."

"Perhaps. But I think the Senate would be more challenging . . ."

"Don't, Sabinus. Don't resume your seat there."

"Why not?"

"Please, darling, can't you stay clear of *all* politics? I . . . I might as well tell you. For months, now, I've wondered if I shouldn't have married some pleasant, unassuming man rather than someone so much in the public eye. I'm *weary* of all the anxieties. Yes, Sabinus. At this point, I'd prefer being a . . . a milkmaid somewhere in Apulia, as far away from Rome as I could manage." She paused and smiled. "But only if *you* were the peasant down there beside me." Then she pulled his face down to hers and kissed it.

Over the next weeks, Sabinus patiently groomed Pedanius in the tasks of city administration and found him capable enough. The wealthy senator was slightly embarrassed by his role as successor, though he could hardly disguise his pleasure at reaching the summit of senatorial privilege.

Without fanfare on the first of July, Flavius Sabinus quietly retired from office. He even declined Nero's offer of a farewell dinner, fearing that he might also supply the entertainment. Happily, he would now be able to see much more of Plautia. And appropriately, for she was gloriously pregnant.

"Congratulations on your timing, carissima mea," he said, stroking her hair upon learning the news. "You let us have a five-year honeymoon before starting the family."

"Disappointed, my darling?"

"Yes . . . I have to wait several months yet until I hold our son in my arms."

"You're sure of that, aren't you?"

"Of course."

Several weeks before the birth, Mother Pomponia moved into their Quirinal residence. Aulus made the traditional protests at losing a wife, but, all things considered, the aging new bachelor managed rather well on the Esquiline—with a corps of servants to assist him.

It was in the hottest part of August that Plautia chose to deliver. At the first symptoms, Sabinus nervously summoned the doctor. It was not an easy labor in that stifling, fervid atmosphere. Fretting and anxious, Sabinus had servants continually fanning Plautia, but Pomponia, sensing the time had come, finally ordered him out of the room. Not long afterward, Sabinus heard the cries, vaulted inside the door, and stared at the infant—a flushed pink, scrawny, dark-fuzzed, bawling bundle. "It's . . . it is a boy, isn't it?"

"What do you think?" Pomponia laughed.

Sabinus roared his approval, then hurried to the bedside. Pale and perspiring heavily, Plautia could still manage a serene smile as Sabinus covered her face with adoring kisses. Then he ran out into the atrium, cupped his hand in the central fountain and sent water splashing across the floor. "I have a son!" he shouted. An oversize laurel wreath was hung on his door, announcing the glad news to the neighborhood.

When Grandfather Aulus arrived, Pomponia made him promise to keep the exultant new father out of the bedroom. The men sat down to compose a list of those who should be notified of the birth and the grand *lustratio* nine days later.

Babies were unnamed the first eight days, lest they die and carry off a precious family name with them. But then the *lustratio,* or naming-day, arrived, and Sabinus' house was thronged with a merry mélange of guests. At noon, a nurse walked into the hall, cradling the infant and bowing to all the guests. She then approached the new father himself and gently laid the baby at his feet.

Solemnly, Sabinus bent over and lifted his tiny son off the floor. The guests burst into applause and cheering, for the act of "lifting up" declared the baby legitimate, a member of the Flavian gens, and entitled to all the protection of Roman law.

Sabinus formally announced, "Let the child be called Titus Flavius Sabinus!" Such a name was fully expected for a firstborn, though later they would start calling the baby Flavius to avoid the confusion of two Sabinuses in one house.

Relatives came forward and strung cords about the infant's neck with little metal toys attached: tiny dolls, animals, and tools, all designed to rattle and amuse the baby. Sabinus himself added a golden amulet which little Flavius would wear until the day he grew up and donned the toga of manhood.

The fall, winter, and spring that followed were months of pure discovery for Sabinus and Plautia. In that magnificent recapitulation of the life process called rearing a child, they watched their baby shed his blotchy infant features and look more like the human species. Their exuberant love—serene yet exciting, mature yet ever-fresh —now seemed to find a more profound basis for itself. Perhaps fame or wealth or power or adventure was not really the *summum bonum* in life, but this: the love of a man and a woman, the begetting of a child.

Pedanius was giving an adequate performance as city prefect, although members of his staff wished, a little wistfully, that Sabinus were back at his post. "Pedanius doesn't have your touch," they told him. "There's no group approach to problems, and he even has trouble in his own house, we understand." Sabinus appreciated their loyalty, but he was careful not to criticize his successor. New magistrates had a difficult enough time, he well knew.

No longer bound by the daily responsibilities of office, Sabinus took Plautia on a trip away from Rome. They both needed the change, and they were also searching out "the most pleasant spot in Italy" to build their country villa, a refuge from the noise and congestion of Rome. They visited Capri and the Bay of Naples. They were shown luxurious properties along the west Mediterranean coast of Italy. But the section that finally lured them was the picturesque, olive-groved Apennine foothills near Tibur (later, Tivoli), an enchanting resort area fifteen miles east of Rome. The place bubbled with hot springs and crystal fountains, and was shaded by fragrant groves full of exotic flowers and wildlife.

The captivating countryside seemed to return Sabinus to boyhood, and he romped up and down the hills and valleys at Tibur with tireless exuberance, as he had years earlier up in the Sabine country. He and Plautia bought acreage and selected the site for their villa, which lay very near Horace's fabled Sabine farm. Sabinus drew up his own plans, and presented them to his builder—who but Hermes? The Syrian later claimed he lost all his profits commuting each day from Rome with his detail of carpenters. He also admitted that building the villa was the most delightful project he had ever undertaken. The only engineering problem he encountered was the overzealous ex-Lord Mayor of Rome, hovering about to supervise the driving of each nail in the structure.

Late in the fall of A.D. 61, the villa was finished. Set into the brow of a hill, its peristyle overlooked a lush valley at Tibur on one side, and a trellised garden covering a sloping hillside on the other. Plautia wanted to move into the place permanently. They were to spend some of the happiest hours of their marriage here. They could not know that others would shortly spend some of their saddest.

19

"IT'S BEEN OVER TWO YEARS, Burrus," Sabinus told the praetorian commander. "I think Paul of Tarsus has waited long enough. The prosecution just hasn't arrived. I doubt they ever will."

"Why not?" Burrus frowned. "Any idea?"

"Paul tells me it was the chief priests at Jerusalem who indicted him—specifically, the high priest Ananias. But he's been deposed. So why should he, or anyone else, bother making the trip here merely to accuse one man who no longer troubles them?"

Burrus nodded.

"In any case, there seems to be no prosecution against Paul. But what happens to him, then? Is he to grow old and die under house arrest?"

Burrus scratched his russet scalp for several moments. Then he said, "All right. I'll press Nero to open the case. And I'll suggest that he follow Claudius' precedent: if the prosecution failed to appear, Claudius would dismiss the suit."

"Thanks, Burrus." Sabinus squeezed his shoulder in gratitude.

"Ah, Sabinus . . . what's your special interest in this case? You wouldn't be . . . turning Christian, would you?"

"Hardly!" Sabinus laughed. "It's my mother-in-law. Dear Pomponia's been hounding me. Though I will admit that Paul's a good and harmless sort."

Later that day, Sabinus sent Paul a message with the promising news. The apostle read it with a broadening smile. "At last, my brothers!" he cried. "My case will soon go before Caesar! And it looks favorable."

They cheered and embraced Paul.

"And Luke," he said, "this part involves you. Flavius Sabinus suggests we prepare in writing our version of what happened at Jerusalem in case it's needed. An excellent idea, I think. But why not begin it earlier? Yes, perhaps with my appearance before Gallio in Corinth."

"The first time you faced a Roman judge?"

"Exactly." Paul smiled.

"I'll cast an outline of the material today."

The next morning, Sabinus found Burrus at his door. "I'm sorry, friend," he said, "but Nero won't quash the case. He insists on hearing it personally."

"But who will serve as prosecution?"

"I don't know. He may just use the documents of indictment from the two governors of Judea: Felix and Festus."

"Felix *is* in Rome, isn't he? Maybe we should summon him as a witness."

Burrus shook his head emphatically. "I don't think I would. Felix finished his term in disgrace. In fact, Nero was wondering where to banish him when Pallas suddenly crawled out of retirement and worked his magic once again. He pleaded in his brother's behalf and Nero gave in."

"Ha! Using Felix *would* be a misstep, then. But tell me this, Burrus: would it prejudice Paul's case if *I* conducted his defense? After all, Nero dismissed me from office . . ."

"I wonder . . . No, I don't think so. Nero's not too happy with Pedanius. I recently heard him say that he lost a good man in you."

"Then he's forgotten about my . . . opinion of his recitals?"

"Let's hope so." Burrus smiled.

In November of 61, Paul of Tarsus was summoned to the Palatine. His close companion-secretary, Luke, accompanied him, as did, of course, the guard to whom he was chained. Luke was carrying a new scroll, his record of Paul's activities ever since the days in Corinth.

Inside the palace, Sabinus met them, also carrying a sheaf of scrolls. His eyes were narrow with concern. "I've some bad news for you, Paul," he said. "Caesar's going to make a case of this anyway, and a certain Ofonius Tigellinus will serve as your prosecutor. Have you heard the name?"

"No."

"Well, he's something new on the political scene here. Not a very happy record. He's a Sicilian who took his first step in politics . . . into Agrippina's bed. Then he was exiled to Greece, where he turned fishmonger to stay alive. Claudius let him return only if he promised to stay out of sight, so Tigellinus bred racehorses in southern Italy. That's how he came to Caesar's attention, and now they're close friends."

"Don't worry, Senator," Paul reassured Sabinus. "My life is not in Caesar's hands. If I have further work to do, God will deliver me and I'll surely be acquitted. If not—if my task is finished—I'll gladly depart to be with Christ, which is far better."

Sabinus shook his head. "I can't believe your serenity, Paul. But you'd better make a strong defense for yourself. If you don't—if you're passive as that Jesus of Nazareth was, you'll surely be condemned."

"He was determined to die for us, as part of God's plan. But certainly I'll testify in my defense."

By now they had reached the forest of columns that was the imperial hall of justice, refulgent in the rays of the morning sun. Overlooking the Forum, the hall was lined with precious red marble from Egypt and domed in blue-glazed tile spangled with golden stars to represent the sky. At the far end was the imperial tribunal, where toga-clad figures were slipping into benches on both sides of the emperor's dais.

"The men filing in behind the tribunal will act as Caesar's assessors—assistant judges," Sabinus explained to Paul. "See, there's Annaeus Seneca. And Burrus. And the other three are senators."

"Are there always five assessors?"

"Oh no. There may be as many as twenty for important cases. Ah —excuse me, but—"

"I understand." Paul smiled and took his place in front of the dais, Sabinus at his side.

At last, Nero himself entered the chamber, followed by a tall, middle-aged man with broad shoulders and tanned, swarthy skin whom Sabinus identified as Tigellinus. But Paul stared far more curiously at the blond-haired young man in the amethystine toga who ruled the world. Everyone rose to salute the emperor as he seated himself in an ivory magistrate's chair on the raised dais. Bidding the court be seated, Nero leaned over to converse with his colleagues on either side of him. Then he glanced at the prisoner in chains before him, clearly less than impressed by what he saw.

"Are *you* Paul of Tarsus?" he asked, with obvious emphasis.

"I am, Caesar."

"And you claim to be a Roman citizen?"

"I *am* a Roman citizen, Caesar."

"Can you prove it? How did you get it, by purchase?"

"No. I was born a citizen. My father was awarded citizenship by the governor of Cilicia for his services to the city of Tarsus. My name is on the censor's list in Tarsus and may be checked by any of your agents in the East. Certainly I would not have dared appeal to you unless my citizenship could be attested."

"All right," Nero nodded. "This court is now in session in the case of . . . ah"—he snapped his fingers and a secretary came running with an inscribed tablet—"in the case of Ananias, former high priest of Jerusalem, versus Paul of Tarsus. I understand that Ofonius Tigellinus will serve as prosecutor, and T. Flavius Sabinus will conduct the defense. Is that correct?"

Heads nodded. And no eyebrows were raised at two prominent Romans pleading the case of an obscure Jew, for similar instances were common.

Nero opened, "If this were a civil case on appeal from the provinces, I, like my divine predecessors, would have delegated it to a senator of consular rank. But since it involves a criminal charge, I've decided to hear it personally. However, I must regret, my colleagues" —he turned to the assessors—"that a regular prosecution did not appear. Still, lest it be said that Caesar awarded a case by default, Tigellinus has kindly consented to serve as prosecutor. You may proceed." Nero nodded to his tall friend, who now arose.

"Noble Caesar, honored assessors," Tigellinus began, in a deep voice. "I have informed myself on this case from various sources, including these documents of indictment compiled by our governors in Judea, Felix and Festus."

"Ah . . . pardon me, Tigellinus," Nero interrupted. "Would you show me those scrolls for a moment?"

Tigellinus handed the documents to Nero, who unrolled them and then became irritated. "I've never in my life seen an uglier pair of scrolls! The papyrus is stained. The ink runs. They're wrinkled and smell too, musty as a sewer! What's the matter with our governors . . . sending in something as disgraceful as this?"

"True, Caesar." Tigellinus smiled. "But the documents were saturated with seawater, I understand, in a shipwreck off Malta. Is that correct?"

Sabinus and Paul nodded.

"Oh," said Nero. "Continue, then."

"It was before Felix in Caesarea that the Jewish high priest and his colleagues indicted the defendant on three charges. We herewith reiterate these charges as our own formal indictment: first, that this Paul is a pestilent agitator, who is causing disturbances among Jews throughout the Empire; second, that he is a ringleader of the sect of the Nazarenes—"

"What in the world is that?" Nero frowned.

"In Rome we call them Christiani, Caesar."

"Oh . . . them. Yes, I've heard of them. Continue."

"And third, that Paul tried to desecrate the temple in Jerusalem. Indeed, he was seized in the very act. Now, as to—"

"*Were* these the charges, Paul of Tarsus?" Nero again interposed.

"Yes, they were, Caesar."

"Continue."

"As to the first charge, there is no question but that disorder and rioting erupt wherever this agitator goes. He has undertaken three long journeys in Asia and Greece to gain adherents for the Christian sect, and just as sickness follows exposure to the plague, so violence follows this man. He was driven out of Antioch, attacked in Iconium, and stoned in Lystra. Then he carried the disease to Europe! He enraged the merchants in Philippi, raised turmoil in Thessalonica, and set off a riot among the Jews of Corinth and the silversmiths of Ephesus. He created his *final* uproar, thank the Fates, in Jerusalem, where he was arrested."

Nero's eyes were widening on the defendant. "This *one man* did all these things?" he asked.

"Yes, and much more, Princeps. The Empire hasn't had such a treasonable troublemaker since Spartacus himself!"

"What proof do you have for this charge?" asked Nero, in the standard formula.

"If Caesar pleases, I thought I would expand on the other two charges first, and then present the proofs."

"No, no, no. I like to exhaust each charge—hearing both the accusation and defense on it individually—before moving on to the next."

"An excellent procedure, Caesar"—Tigellinus bowed—"and one our courts would do well to follow. Very well, then. I have here depositions from Asia and Greece testifying to these riots." He handed them to Nero.

The emperor studied the documents for some minutes. Then he passed them on to his assessors. "Continue."

"I call as witness Senator Lucius Junius Gallio, the brother of our esteemed Annaeus Seneca."

Gallio, whose presence had been desired by both sides in the case, rose to take his place before the tribunal. He looked at the defendant a little curiously, then nodded. Paul, in turn, smiled a greeting at his former judge.

"Senator Gallio," said Tigellinus, "you were proconsul of Achaia in the city of Corinth?"

"I was. Ten years ago."

"Have you ever seen the defendant before?"

"Yes. Some of the Corinthian Jews indicted him before my tribunal."

"Could you tell us what happened?"

Gallio reported the case as best he could remember, admitting that there had been a riot. But he defended his decision in dismissing the suit: "Obviously, it was an internal matter concerning the Jewish religion."

"Not so obviously, Senator," said Tigellinus. "But we shall discuss that point later on. However, this testimony proves, noble Caesar, that the defendant is in fact an agitator who touched off rioting in Corinth. And the depositions from our magistrates elsewhere prove the same for the other cities. I rest my evidence on the first charge."

"As well you might," commented Nero. "This is a serious business. *Very* serious indeed! I had no idea a man so small could cause so much trouble."

Sabinus winced at this display of partiality, which was adverse to Roman legal procedure. Clearly, Nero was not very practiced at the bar. Yet he was glad that Tigellinus had raised this charge first, for, by all odds, Paul was most vulnerable on this point.

Nero conferred with his assessors. Then he looked at Sabinus and said, "We will now hear the defense on the first charge."

Sabinus stood up and said, "The prosecution has ably listed the altercations that sometimes arose when the defendant taught the beliefs of the Christiani, although comparing him to the bloody rebel Spartacus was both inept and false. More than anything else, Caesar, we are dealing here with the Eastern—not Roman—mind. We in the West are a tolerant, practical people who are not swept up into such furious partisanship for or against a new philosophy or religion. But the Greeks, as you know, will wrangle endlessly in the Athenian agora and even come to blows over some minor point in logic. But when they discuss religion and the gods—well, we all know what happened to Socrates."

"Oh, I don't know about that," Nero broke in. "We in Rome also debate philosophy, and I saw one of Seneca's opponents once leap for his throat after he'd nicely cut his arguments to shreds," Nero chuckled. "Eh, Seneca?"

The philosopher smiled and nodded.

Nero was swallowing his bait, Sabinus grinned to himself, or at least seemed to be mellowing a bit. He resumed, "Now as different as the Greek genius is—or seems to be—from the Roman, so the Jewish mind is *much* different again. To the Jew, statecraft is not important. Neither is the military. Nor is philosophy, or art, or sculpture, or science. Only *one thing* has ultimate significance for the Jew, and that is his religion, his belief in one God. He will hold to this with a furious tenacity that dare not be tampered with."

"But your defendant *did* tamper with it," Tigellinus exclaimed, "and so caused—"

"Please don't interrupt." Sabinus scowled and then continued, "Now the Jew has another trait: call it his 'priceless individuality' if you please. He is quick and bright, and he has his own opinions about everything—especially religion. We all know the expression: 'Two Jews, three opinions.' So it's not surprising that when a very religious people is also very opinionated, disturbances are *bound* to result. The defendant, therefore, is merely the latest teacher to cause what is almost normal controversy within Judaism."

"But Gentiles rioted too—"

"Only when Paul's teaching rubbed against some vested interest.

In Ephesus, it was the silversmiths, who feared that worshiping an invisible god would halt sales of their little silver statuettes of Diana."

Seneca began chuckling at this point, but he stopped when Nero turned to him with raised eyebrows.

"I now call the accused himself as witness for the defense," Sabinus announced.

Paul, who had been listening to the trial with extreme interest, almost as if it concerned someone else, now stood up.

"Would you care to add anything to what has been said so far?" Sabinus inquired.

"Yes, I would. First this. In every city we visited, we made it a practice to teach *both* the Jews and the Gentiles as well, for faith in the Christ is not limited to one or the other. Everyone is welcome."

"Aha!" Tigellinus stood up. "That proves, then, that the Christians are *not* a sect of Judaism: Jews do not wish to make converts of Gentiles. Christians do."

"It proves nothing of the sort," Sabinus rejoined. "And you are misinformed, Tigellinus, for Jews certainly *do* make converts among Greeks and Romans."

"I'm afraid they do," Nero smirked ruefully. "Even my . . . or, ah . . . the Lady Poppaea is interested in them. Though she's not a proselyte. They call her a 'god-fearer' . . . whatever that means. But let the defendant continue."

"I would also like to emphasize that I have never incited anyone to riot anywhere. And I have never been judged guilty of anything before any tribunal—Judean, Greek, or Roman—and I would beg this court to remember that fact."

"Well said, Paul," commented Sabinus. "Would you care to cross-examine the witness, Tigellinus?"

"I would. In essence, the defense argues that Jews are prone to factionalism, and this is only more of the same. What, then, are the other factions among the Jews?"

"Some are Sadducees, who do not believe in a resurrection," Paul replied. "Others are Pharisees, like me, who do. Again—"

"You're a Pharisee too?"

"Yes. To continue, a third Jewish sect is that of the Essenes who lead an ascetic life near the Asphalt Lake in Judea. A fourth would be the nationalistic Zealot party. A fifth is—"

"But none of these factions quarrel among themselves or cause the sort of rioting that follows your preaching."

"On the contrary. Sometimes it's much worse, with bloodshed too." Paul frowned and cited several recent examples.

"So, then, are you really claiming that you Christians are merely a Jewish sect? Tell me honestly, Paul." Tigellinus stared directly into the apostle's eyes.

"No, not 'merely a Jewish sect,'" Paul replied. "The Faith considers itself the *fulfillment* of Judaism because it centers in the Christ or Messiah foretold in the Hebrew Scriptures."

"I see. But isn't it possible that the Christians and the Jews will *separate* from one another in the future, since they seem to be at such odds?"

"Yes," Paul sighed. "I regret that this *is* possible, though it's not the ideal we seek."

"Indeed. Has this separation not already taken place?" Tigellinus probed, a gleam in his eye.

"Yes. It has in certain places. Some of the synagogues have become Christian. Many have not."

"So! We've proven, then, noble Caesar, that the Christians are *separate* and *distinct* from the Jews, so they dare not claim legitimacy by hiding behind our generous laws favoring the Jews! I have no further questions for the witness."

"Then you may continue, Senator," said Nero.

Sabinus was nettled. "The prosecution must *not* vault over to unwarranted conclusions," he said. "The fact that Jews and Christians may now be separating or will separate in the future proves, in fact, that they were *not* separated in the past, when Paul did his preaching! Indeed, the founder was Jewish and so were his twelve closest associates. So is much of the membership. The chief Christian in the city of Rome—this Aquila sitting over there with the red beard," he pointed, "is Jewish. The defendant is Jewish. So if this is not a Jewish quarrel, what is? And such religious debate *is* permitted to Jews under our Law of Associations. The defense rests on the first charge."

Nero conferred with his assessors for several minutes. Then he looked to Tigellinus and said, "We are ready to hear the second charge."

"The next accusation against Paul of Tarsus," said Tigellinus, "is that he is a leader of the sect of the Nazarenes or Christians. Now this charge is so obvious that—"

"If it please the court," Sabinus interrupted, "the defense agrees that Paul of Tarsus *is* a leader of the Christians. But we wonder why this is called a 'charge'?"

"Because the sect is illegal: Christians are not protected by the Law of Associations."

"The sect is legal," Sabinus rejoined. "Christians, as Jews, *are* so protected."

"I see we're back to that point again. But let me go on to sketch some of the crimes perpetrated by this cult, patient Caesar, and you'll see why Christians cannot be tolerated in the Empire." Tigellinus then opened his bag of vicious rumors about Christians and sorted out the lurid contents.

"Objection!" Sabinus cried. "I let the prosecution speak on to see if the ridiculous lies about the Christians would actually be used in this court. We're after truth here, not fantasy. These are tired old calumnies, Caesar, and they have no more basis in fact than the shopworn tale of Augustus' wife smearing poison on his figs to make herself a widow. Do you recall the trial of Pomponia Graecina four years ago?"

"Yes, but not the details," Nero replied. "She also was accused of being a Christian, wasn't she?"

"Yes, and her case is so relevant to the present charges that I've taken the liberty of preparing copies of the Senate's transcript of that hearing for you and your assessors."

"Do you really think it would be germane, Senator? This trial of a wife by her own husband?"

"It would, Caesar. And it would save us all much time in the present case." At that point, Sabinus noticed Tigellinus giving him a particularly malicious frown.

"Well, we've sat long enough this morning anyway." Nero yawned. "We'll adjourn court until tomorrow morning at the same time. Meanwhile, my colleagues, we can all read what happened to dear Pomponia," he added, with a wry smile.

Before leaving, Sabinus reviewed strategy with Paul and Luke, and then returned to the Quirinal, where he related everything to Plautia. Certainly the most difficult part of the trial was past, and Nero had taken it in rare good humor. With his new boon companion as prosecutor, however, this proved nothing.

Then he recalled something. There was a *reason* for Tigellinus' scowl over the transcripts of Pomponia's trial. Yes indeed! It was Tigellinus' *own son-in-law,* Cossutianus Capito, who had served as bungling prosecutor at Pomponia's hearing! Unquestionably, Sabinus sighed, he—and the Christians—now had a powerful enemy.

The next morning, Nero opened deliberations by commenting, "We have read the transcript of Pomponia Graecina's trial. And I must say, *some* of the things for which the Christians are accused would make them quite an intriguing sect indeed." He paused to leer at his assessors.

"Now as I see it," Nero continued, "we have three alternatives in this case. One, to regard the Christians as a sect of Judaism and therefore protected by law; two, to regard them as different from Judaism, but harmless enough to be similarly protected; and three, to regard them as a noxious sect which must be eliminated. The defendant would be declared not guilty if either of the first two were established, but guilty if the third were. Is this a proper summary?"

While Tigellinus hesitated, Sabinus nodded his agreement, delighted that Nero had been fair enough to consider the middle alternative.

"But before this can be done," Nero continued, "we must have more information about the defendant." He stared at Paul for what seemed like a long time, then asked, *"Why* have you decided to dedicate your life to spreading this new message?"

"It was a direct commission, Caesar. To me it was as clear and definite as your assigning a governor to some overseas province."

"Who commissioned you?"

"I'll be happy to explain. Originally, I was hostile to the Christians. I even traveled to Damascus to arrest any I found there and return them in chains to Jerusalem for trial. But just as I approached Damascus, an intense light from heaven overcame me and I fell to the ground. I heard a voice saying, 'Saul'—for that was my former name—'Saul, Saul, why do you persecute me?' I replied, 'Who are you, Lord?' And the voice said, *'I am Jesus, whom you are persecuting. But rise and enter the city, and you will be told what you are to do.'*

"The men who were traveling with me stood speechless, hearing the voice but seeing nothing. Then I stood up and opened my eyes, but all was darkness. I was blind. I had to be led into Damascus by hand. For three days I was in that condition, but then a leader of the Christians came to the place where I was staying and said to me, 'Brother Saul, Jesus who appeared to you on the road has sent me to restore your sight.' He put his hands on me, and . . . I could *see* again! Then he baptized me and said, 'The Lord told me that you are his chosen instrument to carry his name before the Jews and the Gentiles and the rulers.' Then, after months of intense study, I came to see that Jesus is indeed the promised Messiah, and that one day I would stand before even you, Caesar, to testify that there is only one God, who created this world, and that he saved it through Jesus the Christ, and that one day he will also judge it."

Nero shifted uneasily in his ivory chair, while Seneca, Burrus, and the other assessors were staring uncomprehendingly at Paul. Any reference to the supernatural was something ominous and uncomfortable to superstitious Romans.

But Tigellinus started laughing. "Really, Caesar, are we to take such weird tales seriously? This Paul must be a fanatic. Or mentally unbalanced. Only wild men conjure up such visions for themselves."

"I call Paul's associate, Lucanus, as witness," said Sabinus.

When Luke had been identified, Sabinus asked him, "Besides serving as the defendant's secretary and—as I see from your record—historian, do you have another profession?"

"Yes. I am a physician."

"Did the defendant ever manifest symptoms of mental illness?"

"No."

"Or of the falling sickness—*epilepsia?*"

"No."

"What is his medical condition, then?"

"Fine, except for some squinting, due to nearsightedness."

"Bah!" Tigellinus huffed. "Anyone who has to have a personal physician traveling with him must be quite sick indeed."

Luke smiled. "I wasn't accompanying Paul in that capacity. And I will swear to the fact of his health."

Nero was beginning to lose patience. "Enough! Let's finish with this. Sweet Jupiter, why are religious matters always so complicated and mysterious? That's why I'm not a religious man myself." He turned to Paul. "But continue. What did you do after that . . . weird vision of yours?"

Paul resumed with an account of his missionary journeys, with some emphasis on his hearing before Gallio in Corinth. At that point, Sabinus called Gallio as witness, and he repeated his testimony, adding, however, that Paul had not seemed a seditious sort, and that his opponents had caused the confrontation.

"All right," said Nero. "We're ready to hear the final charge."

Tigellinus stood up and said, "The third charge is that the defendant desecrated the Holy Temple in Jerusalem by bringing a Gentile inside its sacred limits. Surrounding the Jewish temple, noble Caesar, are thirteen columns, each of which bears the following inscription:

Let no Gentile enter within the balustrade and enclosure surrounding the sanctuary. Whoever is caught will be personally responsible for his consequent death.

As you know, Rome has granted Jews the privilege of administering the death penalty in *this instance alone*. The defendant, then, is worthy of death."

"And the proof for this charge?"

"The trial documents show that he was arrested in the very act."

"The defense?"

Sabinus was smiling. "I'm happy to say, Caesar, that this is the easiest charge of all to disprove, for no Gentile was ever involved. Again I call the defendant to witness. Please tell us what happened that day, Paul."

"I went up to the temple with four other Jewish Christians to perform a vow. But several of my opponents who had previously seen me *outside* the temple with a Gentile Christian named Trophimus now assumed that he was one of the four who were with me inside, but this was false. It was this misunderstanding that led to my arrest."

"And the evidence for this defense?" Nero asked Sabinus.

"Depositions from the four Jews and from Trophimus were laid before both Felix and Festus, as their documents indicate." He handed a copy to Nero.

Scanning the material, Nero passed it on to his assessors and said, "Now hear me, gentlemen. I'm getting very *tired* of all this . . . it's much too quibbling for my bones. In fact, I *despise* all religious cults because they take normal men and women and turn them into fanatics. I don't believe *any* of them!—Oh, once I had some faith in the Syrian Magna Mater, but I finally uri—ah—relieved myself on her image too.—So, gentlemen, we really must finish this. Please deliver your summations, and I pray you: *keep them brief*."

Tigellinus now delivered a brilliant summary of the charges against Paul. The man *could* do more than breed horses after all, Sabinus admitted to himself. When a quarter hour had passed, he closed ominously: "If the defendant had caused only one or two disturbances, we might overlook them. But we have here a long and ugly list of civil disruptions, and if 'no slander is without some foundation,' imagine what a structure of evil is building from his efforts. What this man preaches is *not* Judaism—mark my words, it will become separate from Judaism—and it must *not be given a legal basis* in the Empire. I ask you, noble Caesar and distinguished assessors, do we really want a new and noxious eastern cult in Rome? Do we need another Isis and Osiris, a new Magna Mater, a fresh Cybele or Mithras, an occult astrology that gives its leaders a sunstroke? Or, for that matter, a different and more poisonous Judaism? Don't we have enough trouble with these religions that compete against the gods of the state? Because *if* you release this man, you will be giving his religion legal precedent in Rome. In the name of the gods who made Rome great, I plead that you take on to yourselves the courage of our ancestors and *condemn* this man! To death! I rest my case."

"Bravo, Tigellinus!" Nero stood up to applaud his friend. "Well spoken! Well spoken indeed!" The emperor's clients and friends took their cue and began shouting similar approval from the sides of the hall.

Sabinus cringed at this display, trying to maintain an inner calm in the face of Nero's blatant partiality. He noticed that Seneca's face was as rosy as he had ever seen it.

Now he stood up to deliver his summation, first refuting Tigellinus' "specious suggestions" that Christians were eastern cultists with a gore-saturated worship like Cybele. Had Pomponia Graecina become some raving devotee? Then he concluded:

"There is no question but that Paul of Tarsus is innocent of all charges brought against him. Perhaps Senator Gallio here was the wisest of all: he saw that it was merely a religious dispute, and so he dismissed the case. And at every Roman tribunal since that time, Paul was, or would have been, acquitted. In Philippi the magistrates apologized to him. In Judea, Felix knew he was innocent but wanted a bribe for his release. On Cyprus our proconsul Sergius Paulus befriended him, and on Malta he healed the father of Publius, our governor there, as he has many others. The centurion Julius who accompanied him testified to his great assistance during their shipwreck. Here in Rome he has lived for two years, doing nothing more or less than what he had done in the ten years previous: telling people about what he calls 'the good news.' And there have *not* been any riots.

"Finally, I would ask you to remember that the greatness of Rome lies in her tolerance of many diverse opinions. Rome has learned what Athens forgot at the trial of Socrates: that ideas are, and must remain, *free*. I beg the court not to reverse what has become our glorious tradition. If the defendant had truly sought the overthrow of Roman government, as a senator and former magistrate, I would never have undertaken his defense. But, as you know, Paul of Tarsus has advised his Christians that they are to pray for you, Caesar, and obey the imperial government. The defense rests."

Pockets of applause arose as Sabinus returned to his seat.

"Very well," said Nero, holding up his hands for silence. "My assessors and I will retire to prepare our verdict."

While they withdrew to an anteroom of the great hall of justice, a knot of excited people surrounded Sabinus. "You were *marvelous*, darling!" Plautia said adoringly.

"When did *you* get here? I thought you were—"

"Back home? I couldn't stay away. Mother and Father would have been here too, but she's preparing a celebration for Paul tonight."

"A *celebration*? That's what I call faith."

"Your lovely wife was escorted, partner, and I had the privilege," said Quintus Lateranus. "Not a bad job, Sabinus. You could have been a pleader."

"Well . . . there was this proven defense strategy some amateur used at Pomponia's trial . . ."

"I know, I know," he laughed.

Minutes passed as they waited for the verdict. Then a half hour. A wisp of apprehension tingled inside Sabinus. He had hoped for a quick and favorable decision. He saw that Tigellinus, on the other hand, seemed to have no concerns whatever. And why need he have had any? He had conducted the prosecution as a favor to Nero and without the presence of plaintiffs.

Sabinus tried to assess the assessors. He *hoped* Seneca and Burrus were in his camp, but he could not be entirely sure, especially if

Seneca had taken a philosophical dislike to Paul. And the other three were very questionable. Two of the senators were ominous: known parasites of Nero and Tigellinus. The third was honest, but his old-school republicanism might, like crusty old Cato's, be opposed to importing any more "foreign superstitions."

Almost an hour had elapsed, and now everyone was concerned. The lively conversations in the hall had muted into strained and whispered comments. Sabinus looked for Paul, and noticed that he and the guard had wandered off to a corner. The apostle seemed completely lost in thought—or was it prayer?—as he paced back and forth with his eyes closed, his manacled wrist rubbing against his free hand.

Nero and his assessors reappeared at last, and solemnly reseated themselves. When all was quiet, Nero declared: "I need not tell you that this has been a *very* difficult case for us to decide. And first I must commend Ofonius Tigellinus for undertaking the prosecution. In view of the circumstances, he has done magnificently. And it was also generous of you, Flavius Sabinus, to devote your time to the defense. Because of both your efforts, I wish it were possible for this court to decide here and now the legal status of the Christians. If this were the Senate, and if the Fathers were minded to deal with such religious intricacies, and if all plaintiffs were present—if, if, if . . . there are too many ifs in this case—but *if* all these conditions had been met, then a senatorial court might well have decided to legalize or proscribe the religion of the Christiani.

"This court, with its limited evidence, is clearly unable to do that. However, the case of one, Paul of Tarsus, must certainly be resolved, and we shall resolve it. But his condemnation or acquittal must *not* be regarded as setting a precedent in any sense for other Christians, in view of the difficulties cited. Is this understood?"

Tigellinus nodded, but Sabinus looked disturbed. Paul seemed particularly crestfallen and was on the point of trying to say something.

Nero cut him off. "I would remind the defense that this is the unanimous opinion of the assessors, and the best you can expect for now. It may even work to your advantage—if Paul is condemned, the Christians of Rome need not follow him."

Sabinus looked up and said, "Certainly, Caesar. We accept this decision . . . and, of course, the verdict, whatever it may be."

"Very well, then. We will vote in the Augustan manner. Each

assessor has received the usual three voting tablets, marked with an *A* for *absolvo*, *C* for *condemno*, and *NL* for *non liquet*."* Then, turning to each side of him, Nero said, "I will cast my vote only after totaling yours, my colleagues, since I intend to abide by the will of the majority. Leave your tablets face down in front of you. When your decision is reached, place the appropriate tablet into the voting urn."

Seneca was the first to rise. He walked purposefully to the urn in front of Nero and dropped his tablet inside. Following him, Burrus did the same, and the three senators after him.

Nero now carefully retrieved each tablet. He reached into the urn, picked one out and announced, for the benefit of the court secretary, "*Condemno*."

Perspiration broke out on Sabinus' forehead.

Nero plucked out a second tablet. "*Condemno*," he declared.

A jab of anxiety pierced Sabinus' stomach. One more condemnation and Paul could not possibly be acquitted. He looked over at Tigellinus and saw a triumphant smile breaking across his face. Paul seemed strangely passive, though his intense eyes never left Nero.

"*Absolvo*," said Nero, holding up the third tablet.

Again his hand reached into the urn and withdrew another tablet. "*Absolvo*," he announced.

The entire hall now held its breath for the final, tie-breaking tablet. Even Paul straightened a bit and moved ahead in his seat.

Nero pulled it out, and his forehead wrinkled with disgust as he let the words drip out of his mouth: "*Non liquet!*"

For some moments, a mortal silence hung over the hall of justice. The five assessors—their number intentionally odd—had still managed an even split.

"So, as always, Caesar must make the ultimate decision," Nero almost whimpered. "And this is one I'd hoped not to have to make." He looked at Tigellinus and saw a smile that all but shouted, "I know how you'll vote, *amicus meus*." Then he glanced at Seneca and saw eyes pleading for clemency. There was no question of how Seneca had voted: a philosopher, secular or religious, must always fight for freedom of expression.

Then Nero looked at Paul, who had stopped squinting and now

---

* "Not proven," the equivalent of abstention.

gazed at him with a penetrating serenity. Nero heard himself say, "The prisoner will rise to receive the verdict."

He stared at the manacled figure for several seconds more, and then started constricting the back of his palate for the hard C sound of *condemno*. But he stopped abruptly and murmured, "*Absolvo*."

"What was that?" the clerk inquired.

Nero cleared his throat and repeated, in a strange voice, "*Absolvo*."

A shocked silence was cut by cheering as friends joyfully surrounded Sabinus and Paul. But Paul and Nero continued looking at each other almost hypnotically, the apostle's smile of gratitude finally breaking the spell. Later Tigellinus would ask his friend what had happened and why he decided as he did, but would get no clear reply.

Nero now came out of his trance and held up his hands for silence. "Guards, remove the chains from the prisoner. But I must remind the court again that *no precedent whatever* has been set for the toleration of Christians in the Roman Empire. This movement is on probation . . . at best." Then his eyes shifted back to Paul, and he clipped his words. "We Romans don't wish to become Christians, Paul of Tarsus. For the time being it seems you are not leading a seditious movement, but you would do well to leave our city and stop your preaching here."

"I do indeed plan to leave Rome, Caesar."

"Very well, then. This court is adjourned."

Paul's first sensation was a left wrist that was cool and free—that joint which had been encased in metal, warmed by his perspiration, for more than two years. The next was a chorus of congratulations. Gallio grasped his hand to remark, with a chuckle, "I *told* them they should simply have followed my precedent in Corinth." But it was Gallio's brother Seneca who surprised Paul by stepping down from the dais to come over and greet him.

"I'm somewhat intrigued by your beliefs," said Seneca, "what little I could learn of them from this trial. Perhaps we could discuss them before you leave Rome."

"Indeed. And I've been much impressed with your treatises, esteemed Seneca. Of all the 'pagan philosophies,' as we call them, none approaches Christianity more closely than your Stoicism. You believe in a supreme god—and so do we. You stress the equality of all men, be they slave or emperor—so do we. And your famous statement, 'Treat those below you as you would be treated by those above you' is quite similar to something Jesus taught us."

"Amazing." Seneca looked incredulous. "And where will you travel after Rome?"

"Eventually I'll pay another visit to our new congregations in Greece. But first I plan a brief trip to Spain. I've always hoped to travel that far west, and our teaching must be heard in all the world —so the Christ said."

"By all means, *do* get to Spain. Iberia's a very different country, but very beautiful. And please greet the good people in my home town of Corduba."

Pomponia's faith had not been misplaced. That evening, she gave a victory celebration for Paul. Their door had been crossed with palm leaves to salute the legal triumph, and even Aulus shared the gladness because of the way his wife brimmed with joy at Paul's release. The apostle publicly thanked God—and Sabinus—for their efforts in his behalf. He also told them that Simon Peter, the leader of the apostles, would soon be arriving in Rome, and he hoped they would give him as warm a reception as he had enjoyed.

"But for now," he said, a little wistfully, "my mission in Rome has ended, and the Lord clearly has other work for me to do. Perhaps we shall never see each other again. Perhaps we shall—I hope so. Meanwhile, farewell and thank you, my beloved friends." Then he raised his hands for the blessing: "The grace of our Lord Jesus Christ, the love of God the Father, and the fellowship of the Holy Spirit abide with you all."

"Amen," they responded.

Late that night, back at their lodging on the Viminal, Paul paced the floor restlessly. Luke asked him what was the matter.

"If only mine *had* been a . . . what they call a 'test case,' " said Paul. "I was so certain that my appeal to Caesar would result in a decision favoring the Faith, not Paul of Tarsus. It would have made everything so much easier for us . . . everywhere in the Empire."

"Perhaps the Faith isn't supposed to grow so easily," Luke observed. "Didn't Jesus say, 'If they persecuted me, they will also persecute you'? Maybe it must grow through hardship and challenge."

"And pain. And blood. And persecution." Paul nodded. "And not merely, as now, through quarreling and division and schism. Whenever our powerful friends ask about our progress, we smile and say the cause grows mightily. And it has. But oh, the *inner* troubles!" he sighed. "The factions, the bickering over how much of the Hebrew law still applies, the party spirit, the loveless strife—it's *not* supposed to happen among us, but it does. Jewish Christians and Gentile Christians suspicious of each other, the orthodox versus the freer-minded, the Greek faithful versus the Roman faithful, jealousies, disputes, resentments, mistrust."

He turned to Luke with a smile. "I'm sorry that your record of our travels didn't get presented in court. They're very well written, Luke. I wonder if they would have made the difference."

"I doubt that. Nero was getting impatient with all the depositions as it was."

"But your work isn't in vain. The church will need a record of her early years. Why not take your document and add to it? Tell the whole story—long before Gallio. Start with the birth of the church. Tell about Peter. Tell how I began as a persecutor. Tell about poor Stephen, and carry the story forward. Perhaps you might even call it the 'History' or, no . . . the '*Acta* of the Apostles.' "

"How far shall I carry it?"

"Up to the present, of course."

"But I broke off with this statement . . . here"—he reached for the scroll—"I'll show it to you." He unrolled the document to the final lines:

> . . . And Paul lived in Rome two whole years at his own expense, and welcomed all who came to him, preaching the kingdom of God and teaching about the Lord Jesus Christ quite openly and unhindered.

"Fine. End with that."

"But your trial? Your release?"

"If Caesar had declared the faith legitimate, it would have made a glorious ending to your record. But he did not. That only I was spared is disappointing, and I don't want you to close on such a personal note. Christ is important, not Paul."

"What about your ministry from now on—the work in Spain? Or the East?"

"Perhaps a separate scroll, Luke—if God permits. But the most important part of the story will already have been told."

BOOK THREE

THE BLAZE

20

ROME woke to the horrifying news on a morning in late summer. It jolted Nero out of bed and sent the Conscript Fathers scurrying into their togas for an emergency meeting of the Senate. Pedanius Secundus, Sabinus' successor as city prefect, had been murdered by one of his own slaves. Caught soon after the act, the slave admitted his motive: Pedanius had agreed to sell him his freedom for a certain price but then refused when the sum was handed him. It was too much for the slave, who lost his head and stabbed Pedanius to death in his bedroom.

But what made this murder so unprecedented an outrage was the ghastly law the Senate had passed to keep Rome's growing army of slaves terrified into proper submission: if any Roman citizen were murdered by one of his slaves, the law required that *all* slaves in his household ("living under the same roof") were to be dragged off to execution. It was hoped that the law would be totally preventative: to save their lives and families, slaves would certainly alert their masters to any word of conspiracy in their ranks.

Now, however, the law would have a grisly test. Pedanius presided over one of the largest household staffs in Rome, as well as the corps of slaves attached to city headquarters. In the eyes of the law, *both* groups of slaves were implicated—the murderer also served in the urban administration—and they numbered no fewer than four hundred men, women, and children.

News that four hundred would have to die for the crime of one horrified the people of Rome—and many inside the Senate, too, where the session was stormy and raucous. Opinions, epithets, threats ricocheted off the marble walls.

"Four hundred didn't kill Pedanius! *One* did!" cried Quintus Lateranus. "What about the innocent women and children? Think of your own!"

"Repeal the barbaric law!" shouted another. "Are we savages? *Four hundred* for one?"

Finally the presiding consul waved his arms in desperation and recognized Senator Gaius Cassius, one of the most respected legal minds in the Empire. The Fathers waited expectantly, hoping he would inject some sanity into the terrible impasse.

Slowly the aging senator rose, faced the chamber, and said, "Your outcry, my colleagues, is a tribute to your humanity, and I sympathize with it. We must, however, face realities. A former governor, a senator, and city prefect has been murdered in his own home by the treachery of his slaves. Each of those slaves knew the penalty, but not one warned his master. You claim it's not fair that all should die? By all means, then, vote impunity! But henceforth don't think your rank or your purple-banded tunics will protect you from similar stabbings. Not when the prefect of Rome has fallen! Not when 399 were unable to protect one!

" 'Only one hand plunged the dagger,' you say. And true it is. But did the murderer decide to kill his master without dropping a threatening word or hint to anyone? Could he pass the night watch, open the doors of the bedroom, carry in a dagger, and then stab Pedanius without *anyone* knowing it? A crime has many advance symptoms. Unless our slaves tell us those symptoms, we're all dead men."

Senator Cassius paused for a moment, letting the Fathers digest his words. Then he concluded: "Will some innocent lives be lost? Of course they will! Yet when one of our cohorts shows cowardice on the field of battle, don't we decimate? Don't we seize every tenth man in the ranks and club him to death, including some innocent brave ones? Shall we then spare slaves if we don't spare freeborn Romans? In every great precedent, there is some injustice, which, though it injures the individual, works to public advantage. Therefore, my colleagues, you *must* decree the death penalty . . . to all!"

The chamber rattled with loud applause. Senators still calling for lenience appeared disorganized. Some, like Quintus, were too numbed by the implications of the case to find the proper eloquence for a firm rebuttal to Cassius. In the civic emergency, only the narrow mind of that legalist had prepared itself.

The consul called for a vote. "All those in favor of condemning to death the private and public slaves of Pedanius Secundus—in numbers about four hundred—pass to the right. Those opposed, to the left."

A dramatic reshuffling took place, and it was several minutes before senators stopped bumping into each other as they made their emphatic move to one side of the chamber or the other. The consul studied the line of demarkation and announced, "To me, it looks as if there is a majority for execution."

"Take the count! *Take the count!*" the lenient faction called out.

For the next half hour, the clerk of the Senate did a roll call of the Fathers. Then he added his columns and handed the results to the consul, who announced, "The vote is 188 in favor of execution, 158 against. The motion for the extreme penalty is upheld."

The cheers of the majority were suddenly drowned out by an angry chorus of shouts outside the Senate house. The walls of the chamber started clattering with what sounded like hail, and the consul hurried outside to investigate. A vast, threatening mob of Romans had surrounded the building, shrieking, "*Clementia! Misericordia!* Mercy!" They were pelting the walls of the Senate house with stones and shaking firebrands to underscore their threat: they would burn the place to the ground if all but the murderer were not released.

Inside, the Fathers quavered in fear, knowing that several times in the past century, the Senate house had indeed been burnt to ashes by such a mob and rebuilt at great expense.

"*Clementia!*" the shouting grew into a crescendo. "*Quadringenti pro uno?* Four hundred for one?"

Now there was an even greater tumult as thousands of praetorians wedged through the throng to permit Nero to enter the Senate. The senators stood and cheered when the emperor stepped inside the chamber. Clearly, he would not have been there unless enough praetorians were outside to protect him—and them.

Stalking over to the presiding consul, Nero asked him what the

Senate had decided about Pedanius' murder. He nodded, and then addressed the chamber.

"You have decided well, my colleagues. The ancient precedent is proper, and such a dastardly crime will never be repeated after the example we set today. I am ordering the entire Praetorian Guard to line both sides of the route along which the condemned will be taken to execution. The people will not prevent them."

The chamber applauded until a sycophant stood up and said, "I go farther, noble Caesar. I propose that all *freedmen* of the deceased Pedanius also be condemned, at least to exile."

"*Veto!*" said Nero. "This is excessive. Our law, which mercy has not tempered, must not now be aggravated by unnecessary cruelty."

The emperor was cheered for his clemency. The crowd was dispersed by force, and a majority of the senators went home to a comfortable dinner in good conscience.

But an enraged populace pommeled the praetorians lining the streets along which Pedanius' slaves were dragged. Yet they could not break through, and the terrified four hundred were finally herded inside the courtyard of the Castra Praetoria. Only the guards could now hear the pathetic pleading of aged men and women, the crying of boys and girls, or see the furious hatred in the eyes of the younger slaves. The sole culprit was crucified in a spot overlooking the chopping block. While he gazed down in horror, his fellow slaves were made to bend over the block, one by one. Arms tired quickly. Blades dulled. Ears deafened at all the screaming and shrieking and moaning. A growing stench filled the air, and tribunes had to bark at their men to get them to pile the bodies into carts, heads into separate tubs, and trundle them off.

Self-respecting Romans were horrified. Where in the Senate, some asked, was the voice of Thrasea Paetus? Or of Aulus Plautius? Of Flavius Sabinus? Many, patricians and plebes alike, were calling it Rome's darkest hour. They could not know that a blacker night was approaching.

Sabinus and Plautia were entertaining her parents at their new villa in Tibur. Most of their neighbors had returned to Rome in early fall, but they were so entranced by the natural beauty of the area that they planned to stay on for several more weeks, and they finally prevailed upon Aulus and Pomponia to pay them a visit. Aulus needed the change. He had been putting in long hours, advising Nero on how to put down the massive revolt in Britain under Queen Boudicca.

Then, on that morning they would not easily forget, a praetorian courier galloped up to their villa with an urgent note for Sabinus. It bore only four lines:

Afranius Burrus and Annaeus Seneca to Flavius Sabinus, greeting. Urgent that you return to Rome immediately and come to the palace. The messenger will inform you of the tragic news. Farewell.

The spoken tidings were a relentless succession of shocks. Sabinus had to hear that his successor had been murdered and four hundred lives sacrificed in retribution. Aulus collapsed onto a couch and held his head in his hands. Sabinus' knuckles whitened as he fired furious questions at the courier, his ire boiling over when he realized that some of his former trusted slaves at Rome's city headquarters had also been executed.

A fast horseback ride of about an hour brought Sabinus to the vestibule of the palace. Seneca and Burrus, who were waiting for him, whisked him into an anteroom and asked if he had learned everything.

"That Rome is drunk on the blood of innocent slaves? Yes," he seethed. "That some of my ablest men in the city prefecture were cut down? Yes . . . yes . . . that too!"

"A *horrible* business," said Seneca. "I've always taught that slaves are our equals. It's the Stoic creed. But we had nothing to do with it, Sabinus. You must be sure of that first of all."

"Of *course* you didn't, Seneca!" snapped Sabinus. "Any time anything goes wrong in the state, you and Burrus are *never* responsible!"

"Look, Sabinus," Burrus shot back with ire, "you can save your sarcasm. The *Senate* condemned the slaves, and without consulting the Palatine. Nero only confirmed their judgment. I'm sorry he did— he asked neither of us. As far as my men were concerned, it was a nauseating, disgusting mess."

"To come to the point, Sabinus," said Seneca. "Rome very desperately needs a city prefect. Immediately. The people are muttering. Rebellion's in the air. We need a firm hand at the helm as soon as possible. Nero asked us this morning whom we would recommend. Naturally we suggested you. He actually brightened and asked whether we thought you would accept after the way he dismissed you. We told him we'd ask you."

"You mean he *really* wants me back as city prefect?"

"Yes. Enthusiastically."

Sabinus thought for several moments. Then he replied, "My answer is no. Emphatically."

Seneca and Burrus stared at him blankly. To refuse high public office was almost unheard of, and, in the present case, at least unexpected.

"Now, Sabinus . . ."

Sabinus did not want to hear a discourse from Seneca. "Haven't I served the state? In the magistracies here at Rome? In Britain? In Moesia? In Gaul? In the Senate? As city prefect for five long years?"

"Yes. You have. Admirably."

"And will you believe me if I tell you that I've enjoyed the past months *immensely?*"

"Yes, I believe it," Seneca replied. "But what's the *real* reason, Sabinus? I know you better than to think you'd shun high office for any of those reasons. Politics is in your very blood."

Sabinus brushed a shock of black hair up from his forehead. Then he looked the philosopher in the eye and said, "You're right, of course. And the answer is I will *not* serve under an amateur esthete masquerading as emperor—a poor recitalist, but an excellent fratricide, matricide, tyrant, and, above all, voluptuary. And now a mass murderer too!"

"*Sshhh*, Sabinus!" Burrus cautioned. "Merciful Minerva . . . what if he should hear? On some days Nero rules well enough and makes the right decisions . . ."

"Don't tell me you're still trying to train a 'philosopher-king,' Seneca?"

Slowly Seneca shook his head, a little wistfully.

"Well, you aren't going to quarrel with my reasoning, then, are you?"

Seneca paced the chamber twice. "Yes, Sabinus," he finally said. "Yes, I will quarrel with it. If you love Rome, I think you should accept precisely *because* of what you say about Caesar. If we had an able emperor, our city prefect could be mediocre without much harm to the state. But quite the opposite is the case. Burrus and I are fighting a losing battle, Sabinus, and we need help. We need help desperately. I'll put it to you squarely: if you refuse the post, Nero will probably fall back on his untried, horsy friend Tigellinus, who knows nothing about administration. If he takes the office instead of you, Burrus and I will simply resign and go into retirement."

"No," said Sabinus. "You mustn't. You . . . you can't do that."

"We can. And we will," Burrus affirmed, a strange hoarseness in his voice that Sabinus had never heard before. "My health is failing. And why should you be permitted the luxury of avoiding high office and not we?"

They had won the argument, of course. It took Sabinus several more quiet moments and then he conceded. Seneca and Burrus grasped his hand and shook it. The trio then walked up to the imperial suite.

Nero seemed effusively friendly, though he avoided Sabinus' eye while he managed some unlikely excuse for having dismissed him a year earlier. Then he offered him his old office.

Sabinus' reply was curt and direct. "First I must register my indignation, my outrage at the execution of the four hundred slaves, Caesar. In view of this attitude, do you want to change your mind about offering me the prefecture?"

Nero shook his head, saying quietly, "I only endorsed what the Senate had already decided."

"You could also have vetoed it, Caesar."

Seneca and Burrus were alarmed by his bluntness, but the emperor merely replied, "Perhaps."

"If I accept," Sabinus resumed, "may I have a free hand in administering the city henceforth?"

Again the jaws of Seneca and Burrus dropped slightly, but Nero only nodded.

Sabinus formally accepted. Then he hurried down to his old offices across the Forum and assumed charge of Rome once again. His former staff was delighted to have him back in command. The next day, he addressed his four police cohorts in the Castra Urbana to the north of Rome. In words that would be repeated across the city, he bitterly denounced the Senate majority for condemning the four hundred, and promised to use the office of city prefect to assist relatives of the victims. He also freed all slaves still attached to the city prefecture so that if he himself were assassinated, they might not be punished.

One week with Flavius Sabinus at the helm, and Rome had regained her composure. The people even held a long torchlight parade to hail his return to power. Plautia stood by his side on the Quirinal, watching people file by for a whole hour, shouting their appreciation. She had never been prouder of her husband. And never more concerned.

With the new year, A.D. 62, Sabinus' natural optimism was tempered by the severe illness of Afranius Burrus. The voice of the praetorian commander was little more than a raspy grunt, and an interior swelling in his throat was slowly suffocating him. Palace doctors pronounced the cancer incurable. Still, Sabinus was shocked when a courier from the palace told him the crusty old soldier was already *in extremis*.

Hurrying across to the Palatine, Sabinus was met in the vestibule by Seneca, who whispered, "Caesar is ready to appoint Tigellinus as Burrus' successor."

"*Gods*, no!"

"Well, you could see it coming. The scoundrel's already commander of the night watch."

"We've got to block him."

When they reached Burrus' bedside, Nero was asking him solicitously, "How are you, dear friend?"

With great effort, Burrus managed a husky whisper, "*I*, at any rate, am well." Then he turned his face to the wall. An exquisite insult, Sabinus thought, a declaration of independence on his very deathbed. Nero merely lowered his head and walked over to a corner of the room.

Sabinus bent over his friend and received a victorious smile. Burrus was then seized with a fit of coughing. The tumor blocked the return air flow and he started turning bluish-purple. Sabinus yelled for the doctors, who tried to force a breathing tube down his throat. But Afranius Burrus had ceased his struggle in death.

Sabinus, Seneca, and Nero paid solemn respects to the old commander and left the room. It was Nero who spoke first. "Well, gentlemen, whom do you recommend as Burrus' successor? Sorry to bring this up so soon after his death, but . . ."

They said nothing at first, too shaken by the passing of their friend. But Sabinus seemed to hear Burrus' gravel voice upbraiding them, "Open your mouths, you simple ninnies, and block that scheming swine Tigellinus."

"Faenius Rufus is your man, Caesar," Sabinus quietly advised.

"Hmmm. The prefect of the grain supply?"

"He'd be an excellent choice," Sabinus replied. "Rufus has kept Rome well fed, and he's run the office without profit to himself—"

"A rare enough accomplishment," Seneca added.

"You wouldn't want to command the praetorians yourself, would you, Sabinus?"

"I thank you for your confidence, Caesar. But no—I don't want to return to the military."

Nero pondered several moments more. "Well," he finally said, "Rufus it is, then." Flashing a curious grin at Sabinus, he added, "You see, Prefect . . . I'm not so uncooperative, am I?"

Sabinus returned him an uncomfortable smile and then left. At the door of the palace, he told Seneca, "Well, we won that round, friend. We should be able to build a new triumvirate with Rufus, not?"

"I . . . hope so," Seneca said, a little dejectedly.

Seneca wished he could share Sabinus' optimism, but he could not. On the way to his suburban villa that night, the philosopher sensed it for the first time. Then he pondered it, and finally spoke the word to himself: the *conversio*. Yes, he reflected, the *conversio* had probably come, that remarkable Latin word which meant "turning point," or "change of fortune."

Providence had favored him enormously: wealth, power, fame, wit—his beautiful wife Paulina—nothing more to be desired. How delightful to be a Stoic and accept all such pleasant "inevitabilities." But the Stoic creed cut both ways. Had he been a slave, dying in torment, he would have been obliged to bring the same affirmative response to whatever Providence had provided for him. Well, the *conversio* in his life had come. His very bones told him it had. He would now learn whether he were a genuine Stoic or a fraud.

Seneca's prescience was richly, if ominously, validated in the next weeks. He saw his influence over Nero eroding rapidly. The death of Burrus shook his position, and he watched in revulsion as the reptile from Sicily slithered snugly into Nero's favor. Tigellinus became Nero's companion in vice, the agent who arranged—and shared—his most intimate debauches. Gratefully, Nero soon promoted him to the very summit. Suspicious of Rufus as sole prefect, Nero now made a dual post of it, appointing Tigellinus as co-prefect of the Praetorian Guard.

Sniffing victory in his precipitous rise to power, Tigellinus and his coterie began a studied campaign to undermine Seneca's waning influence. At first there were merely slurring asides. If wealth were the topic of discussion at the palace, someone would observe, "Seneca's so rich he's a kingdom unto himself." If Nero were delighted with some new touch he had added to the palace gardens, the inevitable comment followed, "Almost as lavish as Seneca's parks."

Once, when Nero had finished a new composition on the lyre, Tigellinus responded, "Magnificent, Caesar!" Then, shaking his head mournfully, he added, "I can't understand why others . . . disparage your voice."

"Who does?" Nero finally responded.

"Seneca, for one. But only in private, of course." Tigellinus smirked. "I'll tell you this, Caesar: I'm sick and tired of that critic. *He alone* claims to be eloquent. He alone knows what diversions are right or wrong for his emperor. Nothing is thought brilliant except what *Seneca* has composed. That pedant is perverting our leaders into some kind of cult centering on himself."

Nero darkened and pursed his lips.

"Maybe I spoke out of turn, Caesar, but I'll merely add this. Do you know what the man on the street is saying about you? 'Surely Caesar's boyhood is over,' they're saying. 'Can't he get along without that old hypocrite tutor of his?'"

"They are?"

"Yes, and I agree with them. Why not look to your divine ancestors for any further instruction? Not the Spaniard."

What Tigellinus reported was true only of the smart young voluptuaries in Rome with whom Nero was intimate. Seneca still had enough close friends in the palace to report to him everything that was being said behind his back. He hoped Nero would consider the source of these comments in evaluating them.

Unfortunately, it seemed he did not, for Nero now sought him out less and less for advice and began limiting their social contacts, while he and Tigellinus became inseparable. It was the end, then, Seneca sadly realized, for it would now be impossible to salvage Nero's career. Besides, he was a ripe sixty-six years old. There was no other course . . . no other course at all. He would resign.

Arranging a private conference with Nero, he respectfully asked his permission to retire, pleading ill health and the desire to devote himself full-time to writing and philosophy. Nero was eminently of age now, he argued, and he himself would remain grateful for the rest of his life for the emperor's many favors.

Nero urged that his tutor stay on, but his plea sounded routine and hollow—something a student would *have* to say out of respect to an old teacher. The two exchanged a stiff embrace, and Seneca started vacating his office suite at the palace. Altering his way of life dramatically, he retired to his country villa and seldom appeared in Rome. The philosopher had only one regret at retiring from public life: since Rufus, the praetorian co-prefect, was being ruthlessly eclipsed by Tigellinus, there was now only *one* man of principle left in power. Flavius Sabinus now had to bear the burden alone.

The ominous change of climate on the Palatine blanketed Rome with clouds of foreboding. Over on the Quirinal, Plautia could feel it simply by watching new furrows deepen on her husband's brow each day when he returned from city headquarters, muttering something decidedly unpleasant about Tigellinus. Sabinus knew that a fateful turning point had come in the imperial government with Seneca's retirement, but he could not imagine that political murder would come into fashion again so quickly.

It was after one of the Friday councils of state that Nero called Tigellinus, Rufus, and himself into his office. "I want you to see what just arrived, my friends," he said, with a twinkle. "Until today, I feared only two human beings on this earth. But no longer, thanks to Tigellinus." Standing on a table adjacent to his desk were two large jugs of creamy Egyptian alabaster. Reaching into one of them, Nero pulled a human head out of preservative brine, holding it by the hair.

Sabinus shook at the knees and nearly fainted.

"Sulla here was mailed to us from Marseilles," said Nero. "He was descended from the great dictator of the same name, and might have raised Gaul against us. But I wonder. Look at his premature gray hair." He dropped the head back into the brine with a hollow splash.

Rufus had blanched. Sabinus noticed Tigellinus smirking at him, and for that reason alone he swore he would maintain his composure.

Nero reached into the other jug, extracting another head. "This is Rubellius Plautus, of course, fresh from Ephesus. A short while ago, there was as much Julian blood flowing inside his head as in mine.

He might have raised Asia against us. But why did I ever fear a man with such a nose?"

Nero dismissed the council and sent a letter to the Senate, claiming that both men had endangered the state. Fearing for their own heads, the Fathers decreed a thanksgiving, and, at least tardily, they also expelled Sulla and Rubellius from the Senate.

With all his imperial rivals dead, Nero found no reason to maintain his loveless marriage with Octavia. No longer was she his key to empire. Dear Poppaea had been so patient about their own postponed marriage. To be sure, she had hounded him about it from time to time, but she had not withheld her favors in the meantime. Now, finally, he could make his beloved empress of Rome.

On what basis could he divorce Octavia? Tigellinus tried to torture Octavia's slave girls into accusing her of adultery, but one of them actually spat in his face.

Rather than press the adultery charge, Nero divorced Octavia on the grounds of barrenness—though everyone in Rome knew why the empress had not conceived. Twelve days later, amid much official rejoicing, he formally and finally married Poppaea Sabina.

"You will go down in legend, my empress," Nero cooed as he embraced her in their first legitimate night together. "People will forget Helen of Troy . . . for Poppaea of Rome."

"How *long* . . . I've waited for this evening," she whispered.

"Yes, love," he soothed, fingering the strands of her shimmering golden hair. "But now, my goddess, I'll worship your happiness."

The deposed Octavia, however, remained extremely popular at Rome. Some underground rumor now surfaced that Nero regretted his latest marriage and planned to reinstate Octavia as empress. An excited throng, delirious with joy, toppled statues of Poppaea in the Forum and thanked the gods for restoring Claudius' daughter. Then they threaded their way up into the palace grounds to cheer the emperor's decision and thank him personally. "Come out, Caesar!" they shouted.

Nero came out—in a furious lather, and only long enough to order his praetorians to beat down all treasonable demonstrations in behalf of the divorced—yes, irrevocably divorced—Octavia.

Terrified by the demonstration and worried lest Nero be swayed by the people, Poppaea flung herself at his knees. "I'm not some

. . . some *rival*, fighting for your hand in marriage," she sobbed. "I thought we were already married, Nero."

"We are, my darling. We are," he consoled.

"No." She ignored him. "What I'm fighting for . . . is my life itself. Octavia and her followers—they want my head. *They're* the ones who stirred up the people." She broke into a flood of tears.

"I'll protect you, my goddess."

"Do you know what the people might do, Nero? They might find Octavia a new husband. And then he—not you—will be Caesar."

Her logic was studded with flaws, but the sure and proven way to bring out the worst in Nero was to alarm him, Poppaea knew. And alarmed he certainly was. She could tell it by the way he began tapping his left thumb while pondering a course of action—always a sure sign.

"This time we'll have to make the charge of adultery stick," he finally said. "And it will have to be *treasonable* adultery too. But with whom?"

He thought of various friends who owed him favors, but none could really serve the purpose. A tightening cramp of apprehension reminded him of another time when he had felt the same way. Yes. When he was trying to decide how to eliminate his mother. Anicetus!

Nero sent for the fleet commander, and detailed the reasons why he had to "confess" to adultery with Octavia. Anicetus was startled and reluctant. "But why me?" he wondered.

"That's the treason part of it: she involved you because you both planned to raise a rebellion against me with the fleet."

"Oh, *fine*," Anicetus muttered sarcastically. "And what will happen to *me* because of all these 'crimes'?"

"First, I'll present you with a considerable fortune, Anicetus. And, of course, I'll see to it that your 'punishment' is nothing more than sailing away to some delightful retreat. Though publicly, we'll call it exile, of course."

"And if I refuse?"

Nero was taken aback and glared at Anicetus.

"I mean, this *is* rather dangerous, you know."

"Well, I consider the Empire at stake," said Nero loftily. "If you refuse, I'll . . . well, put it this way: you'll have outlived your usefulness to me."

"Clear enough." Anicetus smirked grimly. "When do I testify?"

"Tomorrow. Today I've just 'discovered' this horrible plot. I'll summon a judicial council in the morning."

The tragic comedy was acted out in due course. Nero and his assessors were duly horrified by Anicetus' "confessions," which were even more lurid than Nero had suggested. The adulterous treason was then announced to the general public. The fleet commander was banished to Sardinia, where he lived out an opulent life, basking in the Mediterranean sun amid luxuries of every kind.

Octavia was exiled to Pandateria, a little island near the Bay of Naples. The modest girl was only twenty, yet she was now irrevocably doomed in her pathetic prison. For memories she could look back on her years with an adulterous mother who had been executed, a father and a brother who had been poisoned, and a husband who hated and maligned her.

And would now kill her too. The orders came a few days after her arrival on the island.

"No!" she screamed. "I'm no longer Caesar's wife! Just his sister! I'm no threat to anyone!"

After some preliminary atrocities, she was thrown into a hot bath and scalded to death.

The Romans who had once shouted in behalf of Octavia were now hushed with horror. The only sounds heard were those of a few parasites offering up public thanksgiving to the gods in the temples of Rome.

21

SABINUS decided that he could no longer work under a man who murdered wives and played with severed heads. He drafted a letter of resignation and then showed it to Aulus Plautius on the Esquiline.

"It's excellent," his aging father-in-law said, in the seclusion of his library. "But now you must crumple it up and throw it away."

"Why? Too dangerous to resign now?"

"Much too dangerous. Nero would take it personally. And more than that. With Seneca and Burrus gone, someone with conscience must stay in the administration."

Sabinus looked about to make sure no servant overheard. Then he leaned over to whisper, "Have you heard any of the . . . ah . . . talk about . . . assassination?"

Aulus nodded. "Quintus has dropped several hints, but I've tried to discourage his involvement. Too premature. Too disastrously dangerous."

"Who's mainly involved? In rumors you've heard?"

"Two groups, it seems. The Stoics—principally Thrasea, Seneca, and their friends—are now philosophically against Nero, though I don't know if they'd go as far as assassination. It's the other group that may: Quintus and a small circle of republican senators and equestrians, but I have no details."

Sabinus frowned. "It may have to come to that—if things get any worse."

Aulus' hands wrestled with each other. "Maybe our problems are deeper than Nero, Sabinus. I recall moments of despair under Claudius also, when he was too blind to see what his wives and freedmen were doing to him—and the Empire. *Ergo*, maybe our whole system of government is wrong. Maybe no individual should ever be given the powers of a Caesar."

"Are you saying that Quintus and his group are right, then? Save the body of the state by cutting away its putrid member?"

"Perhaps. But it may not be that simple. What would happen if Nero were assassinated, and the Republic were restored—and Rome *still* didn't return to her former health? I mean, her condition was hardly better in the late Republic. Maybe a rot exists at the very *core* of Rome—in our moral fiber. I don't think we have many real Romans left, Sabinus. There's you, there's Thrasea, Lateranus and his group, a few in the Senate with the courage to speak out when necessary. But otherwise our government is riddled with time-servers and sycophants, toadies and flatterers, parasites, leeches—all of them Nero's lickspittles, heaping slavish praise on him to his face while shaking their servile heads in dismay behind his back."

Sabinus stood up and walked over to a window that looked out across a stand of pines. Then he turned and said, "Much of what you say is true, Father, but—I don't mean this disrespectfully—but it seems I've heard some of this before. Didn't Scipio find his Rome demoralized too? Didn't Cato? And Augustus after him? Weren't they all trying to revive the 'old virtues' in their days? I wonder if each new generation inevitably suffers by comparison with the old."

Ignoring the last, Aulus observed, "Augustus thought our state religion could restore morality to Rome, but he was wrong. No intelligent Roman can actually believe in that menagerie of gods the Greeks freighted to us." Then he shifted his stance and smiled. "Now don't laugh, Sabinus, but there are times when I wish everyone in Rome had the ethical standards of my Pomponia's beliefs. Because those Christians give a person a *reason* for trying to live the good life. And they certainly avoid the excesses that are making Rome stink in the nostrils of the world. But here's my point: I wonder if we could *use* a few of their beliefs to try to . . . rebuild our civic morality. Anything, I think, would be better than that feast of hypocrisy we call our state religion."

"Well, it's clear that Rome does need *some* source of inspiration, Father, something to motivate it for the better—I'll grant you that. *True* leadership from the Palatine would help. If only Nero had filled one quarter of the hopes Seneca had for him—"

"We all had those hopes."

"By the way, *one* of Nero's crimes I think you'll forgive: old Pallas just died, and it's clear that Nero gave nature a hand."

"Poison?"

"Locusta's best. Nero wanted his enormous wealth."

With a faint smile, Aulus remarked, "I only hope the spirit of Narcissus has been duly informed." Then he resumed a frown of concern. "What does Nero think of *you*, Sabinus?"

"I don't know. At times he can be quite friendly."

"Well, he should be. You're taking good care of Rome. That leaves him free to tend the Empire . . . *or* practice his singing."

"In fact, I think he wants to conciliate us Flavii. I was going to let Vespasian tell you, but I'm sure he won't mind: my brother's been appointed governor of Africa."

"Wonderful!" Aulus beamed. "So, Vespasian's really going to do something with his life?"

"I hope so," Sabinus sighed. "He's just been treading water here, getting deeper into debt. But at times I feel sorry for him: his wife's sudden illness and death . . ."

Aulus nodded, then brightened. "By the way, how's that magnificent girl you spirited away from me?"

"Plautia? Any day now, Grandfather!"

Their second child was a masterpiece of timing. Just as the great end-of-the-year festival was getting under way, Plautia provided Sabinus with a tiny, warm Saturnalia present whom they named Flavius Clemens.

Sabinus looked down into the tortoise-shell cradle and beamed with joy at the wiggling infant, a pink ball of baby fat with chubby cheeks and light hair. Two *boys*? Could any Roman father be happier? He lavished kisses of adoration on Plautia, as if she and she alone had made it all possible.

Plautia had had a much easier delivery this time, and seemed to glow with happiness. "So much for the men in this family," she said. "Next time, a girl?"

"It can be arranged," he replied, with a confident grin.

The palace was looking forward to similar joy. Nothing was more important to Nero than an heir to the throne, and he carefully conveyed the pregnant Poppaea to his seashore villa at Antium. He had been born there, and so the future emperor of Rome must also be born there. Late in January of 63, Poppaea gave birth to—a girl. It was one of the only circumstances in the Empire that even Caesar could not control.

But his disappointment easily mellowed into joy—a gladness which was only fleeting, because in May the infant fell sick of a fever and died. Nero plunged into a grieving despondency that lasted for months. He would not be consoled, even when the Senate decreed the baby instant deification, a temple, and a priesthood.

It was not cares of state which finally snatched him from despair but his career as an artist. He was twenty-six, the last vestiges of puberty were safely past, and his now-reliable bass voice had sung through several test recitals in the theater at Naples. Should he give concerts also in Rome? Was the city finally ready to appreciate good music? Perhaps. But only if the people really wanted to hear him.

Tigellinus saw to that. A crowd gathered outside the palace, pleading that Caesar's "celestial voice" be heard at the Neronia festival.

Nero threw up his hands in sweet surrender, and on the great day of the festival, he cast his own lot into the urn with the rest of the contestants. It was Sabinus himself who now had to shake the lots and announce Nero's turn: "Number Four." To his disgust, Sabinus, as city prefect, had been drafted into serving on the committee of judges for the event, along with Gallio and Gaius Petronius, Nero's adviser in matters of taste.

During the first three performances in the jammed theater, Sabinus toyed with the thought of disqualifying Nero for all the noise he was making, tuning his instrument, clearing his throat, hawking, and even spitting resoundingly. When the emperor's turn came, something of a parade trooped out onto stage. Tigellinus and Rufus both carried his lyre, followed by a cohort of friends, apparently to keep Caesar from feeling lonesome on the vast stage.

When Nero had taken his place, a herald announced, "Our beloved Caesar will favor us with a rendition of . . . *Niobe*."

"Great Hercules, not *Niobe!*" Petronius whispered to Sabinus, adding an exquisite curse, for this was an endlessly long opera about Apollo slaying twelve children, and Nero was singing the entire work.

Secretly, Petronius was also the emperor's shrewdest critic, and Sabinus' only amusement that afternoon was to read some of the comments he jotted down from time to time:

> Contracts his throat . . . squeezes his singing into a raucous buzzing . . . a hollow, grating sound . . . a few tones are gentler and therefore passable. . . . But his respiration is short, his breath never sufficient . . . hopeless.

It was late afternoon when Nero finally finished the last stanza of *Niobe*. While his claque was applauding, the three judges huddled in strategy. "It's too late for anyone else to perform," said Gallio. "So let's simply give Nero first prize and be done with it."

"*Never!*" huffed Sabinus. "What do you say, Petronius?"

"I'll give him first prize . . . for making a jackass of himself!"

"Well, what'll we do?" Gallio worried.

Sabinus stood up and announced, "Since there is hardly time for the other contestants to perform, no prize can possibly be awarded. Learn from the way Caesar accepts this verdict the measure of his obvious fairness! *Vale*, Citizens!"

Tigellinus glared at Sabinus, his mouth forming unheard epithets. Yet Nero seemed to be smiling. *Niobe*, in fact, had been part of his defensive strategy. Its very length was supposed to crowd out anyone else who might have snatched first place from him.

Later, on the Quirinal, Plautia called her husband's conduct "foolhardy."

"But honest, my love," Sabinus replied, a little smile on his lips.

Rome's nobility found Nero's theatrics beneath contempt, particularly since he was now also stagestruck to the point of donning masks and acting in operatic tragedies. His favorite role was *Canace in Childbirth*, where his grunting and groaning as if in difficult labor caused several women in the audience to faint.

Thrasea's circle of Stoics was beginning to doubt Nero's sanity, while others, like Aulus Plautius, wondered if it might not be a case of someone finding his true calling. "He can't govern," Aulus observed, "but he can play the mime."

"Or try to," Sabinus agreed, adding wryly, "no man is ever a complete failure. He can always serve as a horrible example!"

Was it the word failure that prompted Aulus to ask, "By the way, how's Vespasian doing lately?"

Sabinus had a long, sad answer to give, for his brother had returned penniless from his year governing the province of Africa. He had even been pelted with turnips while trying to put down a riot near Carthage. True, Vespasian had been honest in his administration there—his low level of finances was proof of that—but now his credit was gone, and the expense of setting up housekeeping again in Rome was too much for him.

"I need a . . . a very substantial loan," he told Sabinus, soon after his return.

"Again?"

Vespasian nodded his broad and balding head. "Something on the order of . . . a couple hundred thousand sesterces."

Sabinus' eyes widened.

"But this time I'm mortgaging my property to you as collateral."

"Not necessary, Vespasian."

"I *insist*, Sabinus!" he snapped. "Jupiter knows it's embarrassing enough to have to come to you again like this. Let me salvage *some* scrap of personal honor."

"All right. If you insist. But I'll never foreclose. Now tell me, what're you going to do to support yourself?"

Vespasian lowered his head and shook it. "I . . . I don't know, Sabinus. For now, I'm going to . . . deal in mules. It's the only thing open . . ."

"*Great gods!* My brother a *mule-trader?*" Sabinus was on the verge of saying, but he checked himself. Instead, he put his arm around Vespasian and said, "Carry on, old fellow. Let me know whenever I can be of any help."

Later, Sabinus thought about Vespasian's continuing run of vicious luck. His only real success in life had come in Britain, and even earlier when he served as street commissioner, Caligula had personally pelted him with mud from the gutter as reminder to keep the streets clean. *Why* did everything Vespasian touched crumble to ashes, Sabinus wondered. Would his fortunes *ever* turn?

High on the Esquiline, Pomponia was happily aloof from Roman politics. Whatever Nero did or did not do left her quite uninterested, unless it affected Sabinus and Plautia, since her life now centered in the growing Christian movement in Rome. A happy day for her was a visit from Aquila, especially when he brought along one of Paul's latest letters. The apostle had returned from Spain and was now on a round of pastoral visits in the eastern Mediterranean.

That spring, Pomponia was excited by news of Simon Peter's arrival in Rome. Jesus' prime disciple had just taken up lodging in the house of John Mark on the Viminal. Mark had joined Paul's circle in Rome, and stayed on in a dwelling near Paul's when the apostle and Luke left the city. Here he had begun writing the gospel that would one day bear his name. What Luke was to Paul, Mark now became for Peter—colleague, secretary, fellow missionary, and chronicler.

The first Sunday evening after Peter's arrival, Pomponia joined a throng of Roman Christians who crowded into Aquila's house on the Aventine to see and hear, even touch, the man who for more than three years had been Jesus' closest associate. Pomponia knew she would be easily impressed by this human link with the Christ. But the burly, hulking figure of Simon Peter would have been impressive in any case. After Aquila's glad introduction, Peter stood up to address the crowd, which had stilled to a hush broken only by the crackle of the pine torches illuminating the hall.

The tall, muscular frame of the man seemed almost necessary to support that full and strong head of his, covered with short, curly gray hair matched by a similar beard. His skin was leather-tough, browned by the sun of seventy summers. "The Fisherman," they called him, and his brawny arms and hands made him look the role. Pomponia thought it interesting that in the famous story of the huge draft of fish, it was the nets that finally gave out, not Peter's arms in hauling in the catch. So this was the man who pulled out his sword and thought to fight off, singlehandedly, the police arresting Jesus! Well, he looked the Samson type. And yet there was also a certain kindliness in his features that contrasted starkly with the man's build, a warm glint in his brown eyes and a gentle set to his mouth.

With deep, sonorous tones to match his appearance, Peter congratulated the Roman church on its growth and vitality. "Such numbers! Such fervent faith! And there are several thousands more like you in other congregations across Rome, I understand. We are especially proud of the church in Rome, because it was founded, not by us apostles, but by you lay men and women who returned from Jerusalem on that first Christian Pentecost. Some of your faces I recall seeing there thirty-one years ago, for you were among the first converts after my address.

"It was you, then, who were the seed of Christianity here in Rome, and now you've grown into a sturdy tree of faith. Some of you are Jews, some are Gentiles, but all are one in Christ. Some come from the nobility," he said, looking at Pomponia in her patrician stola, "while others are soldiers or servants or slaves. But all *are* one in Christ."

Peter then told of his days with Jesus, but it was clear that the people had not heard enough. They begged for more. And so the apostle continued every Sunday evening that spring, telling a new chapter about that luminous life which, he predicted, would one day change all of history.

June A.D. 64 was awash with social engagements for Sabinus and Plautia. Restraint had been thrown to the winds at a string of lavish parties given by the patricians of Rome. There were eighteen-course dinners with live birds flying out of the roast at a touch of the carving knife, and garish menu oddities like braised flamingo tongues, purée of pheasant brain, or sow's udder. Plautia quickly learned never to ask what she was eating, and usually picked through such delicacies like a sated sparrow.

Yet the feast and garden party given by Nero himself would easily outdo anything that Rome had ever seen. Plautia refused to attend until Sabinus pointed out that rejecting *this* particular invitation would be undiplomatic, if not dangerous.

The banquet, set for midafternoon, was held at a magnificent wooded park in western Rome called Agrippa's Pond. Guests were directed onto a huge pleasure barge, paneled in ivory with gold trim, on which long banquet tables stood ready. Tigellinus, who was directing the extravaganza, assigned places to each—the nearer to Nero and Poppaea, of course, the greater the honor. To Plautia's dismay, she and Sabinus were not only at the head table, but rather close to the emperor.

Tigellinus now clapped his hands three times. The barge cast off slowly, drawn by several smaller boats rowed by a corps of pretty young boys in gilded loincloths, their cheeks rouged to resemble

Cupids. Some were plucking at golden citharas fashioned in the shape of Cupid's bows, while others chirped greetings to the guests.

Sabinus squinted at them and scowled. "I think they're catamites," he whispered to Plautia.

"What's a catamite?" she asked.

Sabinus gave a low chuckle. "Better you don't know."

When they reached the center of the pond, the Cupids quit rowing and drew their craft alongside the imperial barge, where the rarest delicacies were now served along with exquisite vintages to wash them down. The gold-rimmed palace china was all but hidden by the small glassworks of Phoenician crystal surrounding each place setting. Plautia had to watch the empress out of the corner of her eye to see which glass was used for what purpose, and she was forever nudging her husband to identify the exotic white, amber, and red wines and spirits.

A cornet sounded and one of the groves at the edge of the pond quivered to life with strains of sensuous music and a troupe of dancing girls. The forest nymphs were wearing silver sandals but nothing else. Sabinus questioned Nero's taste—no emperor but Caligula had treated a mixed company to such a show.

The other guests, however, started applauding, but no one so loudly as Nero. "Nearer!" he yelled to the Cupids. "Row nearer!"

Poppaea nudged him under the table with a jeweled sandal, but it had no effect.

"Where did you ever find them, Tigellinus?" Nero exulted. "They're beautiful!"

"They're the finest pros— ah—'women of pleasure' in Rome." Then he added, with a tone of pride normally used for vastly different situations, "I chose them myself."

"Aha! What taste!" Nero beamed.

"What taste indeed," Plautia muttered, perhaps too loudly, for Tigellinus now stared at her with a growing smirk.

The dancing nymphs, incredibly libertine, gave even more of themselves as the imperial barge touched the shore of their grove. The girls swarmed onto the deck, fluttering among the guests with coy smiles and giggling each time a sated patrician finger tried to poke them. Then, just when it seemed several of the younger men might make nuisances of themselves so early in the party, Tigellinus gave the signal to cast off while the nymphs scampered back into their grove to continue the show.

"Oh, *must* we leave all this?" Nero wailed.

"Wait, Princeps. There's more to come," Tigellinus promised.

There was more food, of course, and much more to drink. In the darkening twilight Sabinus and Plautia were the only nearly sober ones left at what had all the marks of turning into an imperial bacchanal. For Tigellinus now stood up and announced, "Several of you are asking, 'Where are the *favors* at this banquet?'"

He glanced about and there was much good-natured nodding of heads.

"Well, I'll tell you. From Caesar you anticipate only the ultimate favors—not flowers or jewels or turbans, but this," he extended his arm in a vast circular sweep, "all around this lake—something to delight every taste. Look to the eastern shore, where you boarded the barge: do you see all those purple lanterns burning? Well, purple marks nobility, and those lanterns will show you where women of high rank are waiting impatiently to favor you in tents and arbors."

There was much oohing and aahing, but, incredibly, no one doubted Tigellinus. In the jaded aristocracy of Rome, he had had no trouble finding eager participants.

"There on the south shore," he pointed, "behind the flickering pink lanterns, you'll find groves for those whose taste runs to virgins —young virgins, that is." He flashed a wicked grin.

"Splendid, splendid, Tigellinus!" Nero cackled. "Better than I thought possible."

"Ah . . . will they . . . will they really permit us?" a leering old senator inquired. "What if they . . . resist?"

"No problem," Tigellinus chuckled. "The girls will comply, I assure you. My men are on guard in every grove."

"My prefect thinks of everything," Nero snorted. Then he sniffed the evening air and exclaimed, "Gods, that smells wonderful, Tigellinus! What is it? Incense?"

"Well, incense of a special kind, Caesar. It's an aphrodisiac. We have braziers burning it around the entire pond."

The guests roared with delight, though Plautia was becoming ill as the unbelievable proportions of Tigellinus' scheme unfolded.

"Now some of you seemed attracted to our dancing nymphs on the opposite shore," Tigellinus laughed, with studied understatement. "Well, they're through dancing now, and they're waiting for you with . . . specialties of every kind. Look for the green lanterns.—Now, this barge will continue circling the shore all night, so you can board and disembark at will. And don't forget, there's *much* more to eat and drink."

"*Well!*" Poppaea finally huffed. "You seem to have taken care of all the *men*, Tigellinus! But what are we *women* supposed to do in the meantime?"

"Anything, Empress!" he replied grandly. "Men are waiting on shore too. I've chosen only my handsomest guards to surround the pond. Or, if your taste runs to our Cupids here, help yourself."

Soon it was all happening exactly as Tigellinus had indicated. While lascivious music and ribald song filled the night—and enough drink to keep anyone from fully realizing what was happening—the barge began its series of slow sweeps around the pond. The banquet revelers, men and women, giggled and clucked as they scampered ashore, made their selections, and then disappeared with their tittering favors into some shadowy glade. From the eastern strand came some shouts of embarrassed recognition and delighted surprise. On the south shore, there were a few problems—screams from the unwilling and several curses—but Tigellinus' men soon had the situation well in hand. And from the professional far grove, there were sounds and scenes that beggared all description.

Reeking with wine, Nero stumbled onto shore hand in hand with Pythagoras, the most beautiful of the catamite Cupids. Poppaea, who was tipsy, raised her golden head when Nero left and scowled contemptuously. But then a·dark smile tugged at her crimson lips, and she rolled over to Sabinus, twining her arms about him and whispering, "With me, darling Sabinus! I think I've been in love with you for months."

Stunned, Sabinus tried to disentangle himself and snapped, "*No*, Empress!"

"But you *must*, my love," she murmured, while fondling him, "your empress *commands* it."

"Impossible!" Sabinus hissed. Then, using any excuse that came to mind, he said, "Never! Not with my wife here!"

"Ooohhh," she cooed, languidly, while covering his face and neck with kisses. "But isn't Tigellinus taking care of her?"

Sabinus flashed about. To his horror, Plautia was gone!

"*Where?*" Sabinus demanded. "Where did they go?"

Poppaea let a smug pout warp her lovely face and whined, "Why should I tell you . . . and spoil everything?"

Sabinus had in mind to strangle the truth out of her until he recalled that she was empress of Rome. Instead, he clutched the soft, imperial shoulders in his hands and started squeezing them until Poppaea winced and finally shouted in pain, "Stop it! Back over there!" she pointed westward.

It was a dark section of the lakeshore, between the pink and green lanterns. Sabinus' eyes combed the darkness. Squinting, he thought he saw a tall, stalking white tunic carrying something kicking. He sloshed his way onto shore and ran after them. It *was* Plautia, and she was screaming for help.

"Put her down!" Sabinus yelled.

"Who gives orders to the praetorian prefect?" Tigellinus turned his head and growled.

"The city prefect, you filthy fishmonger!" He made a lunge for Tigellinus' shoulders and pulled him over backward. Plautia's fall was cushioned by Tigellinus' chest, knocking the wind out of him. While he lay gasping for breath, she struggled free of him and rushed sobbing into Sabinus' arms.

"Are you all right, little darling?"

She nodded, her face wet with tears. "He . . . he put his hand over my mouth. Didn't you hear me scream?"

"No. Did he do anything else? I'll kill him if he did. Here and now."

She shook her head. "No, no."

"All right. Let's get out of here."

They started walking out of the grove, but just before they left the beach, Sabinus felt a sandy, wet hand clawing the nape of his neck. A voice grumbled, "As I indicated, you Sabine scum, it's your wife I want." Whirling about, he saw the leering face of Tigellinus.

He had no time to block Tigellinus' jab to his stomach, which doubled him over in pain. A swift uppercut followed, but Sabinus managed to dodge to one side so it only grazed him. Tigellinus had swung so hard that he threw himself off balance, easily tripping over Sabinus' hand clutching at his sandals. The two rolled over and over in the sand, pommeling one another while Plautia looked on in terror. She was going to scream for help but suddenly realized that any help would probably kill Sabinus, since only praetorians were guarding the park. Mercifully, there was enough music and noise to cover the grunts of the struggling men.

It was no contest. Sabinus was younger and had the advantage of being comparatively sober, too. When he saw he was losing, Tigellinus screamed a coward's call for help, and that instant Sabinus realized his mortal danger from the praetorians. Taking careful aim at Tigellinus' chin, he staggered him with an enormous, sweeping blow from his right fist, the knuckles tearing into his lower cheek. Tigellinus dropped over backward and lay very still on the wet sands. Sabinus flashed about to see if any praetorians had seen them, but apparently they were preoccupied with other pursuits.

"Did you . . . did you *kill* him?" Plautia whimpered.

"I hope so!"

"Sabinus!"

"No. He's breathing. Let's go."

It took Nero a day or two to get over the aftereffects of his garden party, but he certainly looked better for the ordeal than did Tigellinus. Puffy-faced and blotched with purple bruises, Tigellinus would tell no one what had happened to him. "If it's a woman you were with, she must have been *quite* the Amazon!" Nero taunted.

A few days later, as a kind of after-party, Nero summoned several of the principal merrymakers—not including Sabinus—to his "wedding with Pythagoras." He had been so taken with the pretty youth that he now played bride, donning a flaming red veil and reciting the marriage formulas. His friends formally witnessed the ceremony, a dowry was announced, wedding torches were lit, and Pythagoras led his imperial bride to the nuptial couch in the palace.

Seething with rage at the grotesque news, Poppaea called Nero names he had no idea she knew.

"It was only in fun," he lamely tried to fib. "I mean, we were only *acting*."

Poppaea was not convinced. Neither was Rome. After the city rocked with reports of the great orgy at Agrippa's Pond—one of the few events that could never be exaggerated—it was fully prepared to believe anything about Nero.

The following Sunday evening on the Aventine, Simon Peter altered his series of addresses to the Christians. That night he talked less about Palestine and more about Rome. Gone was the benign expression. His massive features had firmed into a look of prophetic fury while his eyes blazed with wrath.

"Has Rome become Babylon?" he thundered. "Has the capital of the world degenerated into a new Sodom on the Tiber? Certainly

Sodom's vices are being practiced here! And what happened to Sodom? What befell Gomorrah? The *fire of the Lord* swept down on those cities, and his anger consumed them in brimstone. And it may take flames to purify Rome!" Like an angry lion, his right hand was pawing the air as he scored the city's vices.

Finally, his face softened, and the kindly eyes of The Fisherman sparkled once again as he said, "But the Lord was ready to spare Sodom and Gomorrah if only a few righteous people lived there. May he spare Rome . . . because of you, my beloved."

22

THE WEATHER was very hot and very dry that July. No rain had fallen for weeks, and Rome seemed to shimmer in the parching heat. The colors of the city had dulled to drab and brown. The grasses in the parks and gardens had turned straw yellow. Only the pointing cypresses and the flat-topped umbrella pines offered any green, but even that seemed sick and wilted and thirsty.

Those with country villas had fled the city. The emperor, whose flab could no longer endure the stifling atmosphere, was off to his seaside villa at Antium. Sabinus planned to whisk his family off to Tibur in a short time. But Romans of the lower classes had to stay in town and suffer, waiting for breezes that never came, searching the deep blue skies for puffy rain clouds or even a heavy haze to filter the blistering tyrant sun. But there was nothing, just an impossible succession of clear, burning days that buckled paving stones in the streets and softened the tarry pitch that held them together into a gooey mess.

Finally, on July 18, the air began stirring. Breezes gathered and became a wind. But when the wind started blowing in force, all Rome groaned, for it was a hot blast from the southeast—a mid-summer sirocco that was born in the deserts of Libya and seemed to gather strength as it shot up the Italian peninsula to smother an already sizzling Rome with a suffocating blanket of thermal air.

The night brought no relief. An inflated, rust-colored moon was floating upward in the eastern sky—it was full that evening—but its brilliance only seemed to add warmth to the hot night.

Just east of the Circus Maximus, in a flat area between the Palatine and Caelian hills, stood a ramshackle collection of squalid huts and shops. It was one of the foreign quarters of the city, and a colony of Greek and Syrian traders lived here, selling their wares in the daytime, and retiring to living quarters in the back of their shops at night.

Hermes the contractor lived here too, although Sabinus had urged him often enough to move into better quarters. But it was a matter of convenience for Hermes. Living here, he could keep an eye on his lumber yard and his oil depot too, for recently the canny little city engineer had branched out into the oil business as well. Romans needed olive oil for everything from soap to lamp fuel, and Hermes was making a killing in the commodity.

On that broiling night, however, he wished he had taken Sabinus' advice and been living high on one of Rome's hills rather than sweating to death in that miserable valley. He stalked into the kitchen and found a source of additional heat—the charcoal stove on which his wife had cooked their supper of beans and boar's flesh. Uttering a choice curse in Aramaic, Hermes flung open the door of the stove, scraped the live coals onto a small shovel, and flung them out of his back window.

Under any other circumstances, the coals would have glowed down to ash and gone out. But these fell onto some woodchips, which curled, blackened, and began smoldering. A lazy spiral of smoke twisted upward, looking like a thread of silver in the moonlight. A blast of the sirocco struck, and the wood shavings burst into flame. Yet another quick gust blew them out again.

The chips continued smoldering away until a steady, building wind fanned them back into open flame. Now all the shavings were kindled, and flickering tongues of fire licked onto some boards stacked against the back of the house. Before the pile was half burned through, it had passed the blaze onto the wooden siding of the structure itself, and soon the back of the house was a quivering sheet of flame.

Hermes was preparing for bed when he saw the ugly orange glow and shouted his sleeping wife awake. Dashing outside, he tried desperately to beat out the flames. But several helpless swats with a cloak told him it was too late for that. He must now save what he could.

He and his wife emptied their closets of clothes and jewelry and threw them into the street on the north, screaming for help with each new trip to the window. Finally, when neighbors responded, he yelled, "The vats! Roll the oil vats outside!"

They crashed into his depot and feverishly began tugging at the great earthenware jugs filled with olive oil. Rolling them along their bottom edges, they trundled several of the vats to safety. Then two who found themselves tugging at the same jug from different directions cracked the huge vessel, and oil poured out of the cleft, cascading across the floor toward the living quarters, which were now belching flames through the partition wall into the shop itself.

The sirocco was the giant bellows that provided the final swell of air, and the oil suddenly ignited in a great flash. Flames soared into the night sky, using Hermes' entire premises as their wick. In a trice, houses on both sides caught fire, and their screaming and cursing residents watched their life's possessions blaze away. Playing with the fire like some bright new bauble it had discovered in the darkness, the sirocco sent the flames surging west, then northwest, then north, and back again. They leaped from house to house, and soon the whole block was ablaze on both sides of the street.

Seeing the spreading smudge of orange from their station on the Aventine, the *vigiles* (night watch–firemen) from Region XII trumpeted a fire call and then hurried over to the blaze, where they were soon joined by colleagues from neighboring Region II. In an instant the vigiles saw the mortal danger. They had no hope of saving the immediately surrounding blocks, but they would try to contain the inferno by creating firebreaks ahead of the flames in a line running north from the Circus Maximus, then due eastward to the Caelian.

Rousting sleeping families out of bed, they began demolishing their homes before their drowsy, then dumfounded eyes. Water from a nearby aqueduct was diverted into declivities between the Palatine and Caelian, and, with any luck, they would hold the holocaust to "Hut City"—no great loss, thought the firemen, since the place was a stinking slum anyway. The wind seemed to be abating, and they dared to hope for success.

But again the slumbering sirocco came to life. Shops with paint and other combustibles hissed and sputtered and sizzled. There were muffled explosions and sharp, cracking sounds, each catapulting some still-burning substance into the air, which was wafted upward in the fierce heat. Then the southeast wind took control of the flaming ash and pelted it northwestward in great arcs far beyond the firebreak. Some of the ash blew out. Some did not, and wherever it fell, tinder-dry structures gave it shelter and nourishment.

The Circus Maximus was next to go, not the lower tiers of stone seats surrounding the vast hippodrome, but the rickety super-structure of wooden boards that hovered around the stadium, increasing its seating capacity by 100,000. Several blobs of flaming cinders landed on the northern tier, and soon it was a crackling pyre of reddish-orange, its seats perfectly spaced to provide the flames all the air they required. Since the great hippodrome lay along the same axis as the wind, the hungry blaze leaped voraciously from row to row, gallery to gallery.

Along the entire northern edge of the Circus lay the Palatine and Nero's palace. With mounting, almost hypnotic horror, the palace staff watched the vigiles trying to contain the fire at the base of the Palatine. All seven cohorts of the night watch had now been alerted, and they were desperately ringing the imperial hill, trying to smother the flaming ash raining down on it. Palace slaves were scurrying over the grounds with jugs, splashing water onto the orange blotches that lit up the hillside and steaming them back into darkness. They were coughing and choking in the smoky stench and perspiring in a stifling night suddenly grown drastically warmer.

Nero had just put the finishing touches on what he called the Domus Transitoria, a great new wing of his palace that extended eastward, connecting the Palatine with the Esquiline. Now, almost as if the flames had been ordered to attack precisely this structure, they joined to converge on the Transitoria, for it was the last barrier between them and the valley leading into the Forum. All four stories of the new wing became a thundering, blazing inferno, consuming Nero's works of art, his library, wardrobe, museum, his dozen different lyres and costumes—in fine, everything that had made the man the artist. The palace staff now fled northward for their lives, since the hot breath of the sirocco bloomed the flames into an infernal tour of the Caelian and the Palatine, igniting the rest of Nero's palace as well.

Beyond the Palatine lay the Forum, but the conflagration paid scant respect to its antiquity. The Via Sacra—the world's central street—became a river of fire, hissing and spilling flame into Rome's most ancient monuments, scorching the marble and turning the white travertine into heaps of charred rock. The Vestal Virgins ran screaming from their quarters because the Temple of Vesta, where Rome's sacred fire was kept burning, was now its own gargantuan flame. As of that point, it was the worst disaster the city of Rome had suffered in five centuries, and it was far from over.

On the Quirinal, earlier that evening, Sabinus and Plautia had been preparing for bed when she noticed it first. Standing at their bedroom window for a wisp of fresh air before retiring she looked to the south and saw the Palatine encrusted in a halo of shimmering apricot.

"Come here and look, Sabinus!" she said. "Look at the palace. Isn't that the strangest light you ever saw? It couldn't be fire—there are no flames . . ."

"By all the gods!" Sabinus whispered. "There must be a flaming hell on the other side!"

Jumping into his tunic, he dispatched one of his aides northward. "Alert all Urban Cohorts to converge on city headquarters and meet me there." Then he rushed down to his offices, where the grim-faced commander of the night watch told him, "Started east of the Circus Maximus. Half of Regions III, X, and XI are gone. The Domus Transitoria is going now. You may be next here."

"How did it start?"

"Who knows?"

"Are all your vigiles on duty?"

"Yes. By now. They're trying to build another firebreak behind the Domus along this line." He traced his hand along the great city map hanging in Sabinus' office.

"Too close to the fire. You won't get everything torn down in time with the wind blowing the way it is. Let's let nature help us out: why not the valley between the Caelian and Esquiline farther north? Here."

The commander of the vigiles nodded. "You're probably right. But where are your men, Prefect?"

"They're on their way. Do you want them to help fight the fire or stay on security?"

"Why not have about a thousand help us clear your Esquiline valley line? But you'd better keep the other three thousand on police duty. We already have reports of looting."

"Has anyone alerted the emperor?"

"Ten minutes ago we sent a rider out to Antium."

"All right. Let's set the other firebreak immediately north of the Forum—here." Sabinus pointed. "We should be able to save the rest of central Rome."

"Right. But aren't your headquarters dangerously close to the Forum?"

"Yes, we may not be able to save all this. But I'm not hauling out our documents until we're in imminent danger."

By now the Urban Cohorts had arrived, and Sabinus went out to give them their orders. Then he hurried eastward with the company assigned to clear the firebreak at the base of the Esquiline. If the blaze broke through here, the house of Aulus and Pomponia would be in mortal danger.

Several hours later, about 4 A.M., he and his men had toppled most of the structures likely to transmit the flames when Nero and Tigellinus suddenly appeared, their mounts frothing after a frantic ride up from Antium. Nero, who had been giving a recital when he was alerted, had not even had time to change from his costume as a cithara player. Sabinus gave them a full briefing on the fire.

Tigellinus smirked as he spat out the words, "Can't you manage the city while we're away, Prefect? You've *really* let things get out of hand this time!"

"I expected that from you, Tigellinus." Sabinus glowered. "But instead of making asinine comments, why don't you order your praetorians out to help us?"

"Yes, yes, yes, Tigellinus—*do* get the praetorians!" Nero wailed. "But first, both of you, let's see it all from Maecenas' Gardens."

The gardens lay several hundred feet farther up the Esquiline, and a terrace there provided an ideal vantage point from which to survey Rome and lay strategy for containing the fire. Reining their horses to a halt after the steep uphill ride, the three dismounted to look at the smoldering city. The eastern skies were beginning to flush with the first delicate coral of dawn, but they stared only at the ghastly sight before them. Other Romans were also streaming to that spot, first in curiosity at reports about "some fire in south Rome," then in horror at what the panorama actually showed them. The great valley of the Circus Maximus lay in a million embers, while the Caelian and Palatine were belching up gigantic wriggling cones of flame from a vast, crackling sea of fire. Every time some structure collapsed, a huge column of flame shot upward for several moments, spattering the sky with clouds of luminous gold dust.

Nero broke down and wept. "Sweet goddess Roma!" he wailed. "My new palace? My old palace?" His face was contorted with shock and grief. "Will you look at the Palatine, gentlemen? Only *my* property is burning! Augustus' mansion still stands. So does Tiberius' palace. But my Transitoria is a cinder! All my apartments . . . gone! My treasures, my Greek statues . . . my trophies . . . library . . . wardrobe. Even my buskins!" Each item recalled seemed to strike new torture into Nero.

Sabinus tried to say something, but Nero held up his hand for silence. Now he walked to the balustrade of the terrace and peered at the spectacle before him. The flames, even though they were ruining him, had a terrible beauty of their own. The artist in him was touched deeply by the sight, and he started singing a mournful dirge of his own composition, *The Capture of Troy*. Only Priam's great city had suffered the disaster Rome was now enduring. Verse after verse poured out from Nero's quaking voice as he gestured across his city in tears.

Sabinus struggled to contain his impatience, though he realized Nero must have his moments now or his emotions might overcome him later. Some of the bystanders were moved by the emperor's performance. Others thought it undignified and unnecessary, and they would tell others what they had seen.

Sabinus would not see his wife again for five days. Getting what little sleep he could on a makeshift bed at city headquarters, he was on duty day and night in the crisis. Drawn with worry, Plautia kept watching the flames from the Quirinal but getting reports that her husband, as well as her parents, were safe. In the daytime, the view seemed the most ominous: great belching clouds of angry gray smoke polluting the air, rising from areas that had become scorched and ugly black. At night the scene was more disastrously beautiful as the flickering line of a thousand separate islands of fire seemed to advance northward in a vast arc. Little Flavius stared with childish fascination at the marvel, happily ignorant of the multiplied thousands of personal horrors being perpetrated by the holocaust.

But his father saw it all firsthand. Sabinus and his police were working with the vigiles, trying to copy their techniques. Like the firemen, Sabinus divided his cohorts into siphoners, who tapped the nearest aqueducts for water; blanketeers, who smothered flames with blankets soaked in water and vinegar; and netmen, who, with outstretched mattresses and nets, cushioned the fall of those jumping from windows. But in a catastrophe of this magnitude, even the disciplined firemen were having little success with such procedures.

If fire touched one house in a poor district, the whole block was lost, for homes on those narrow, crooked lanes were built onto one another to save the expense of building a fourth wall. Worse still was the fate of those caught in the upper stories of the many flimsy tenements in Rome.

Sabinus saw and smelled and heard it all: the screams of terrified men and women as the five or six stories of a tenement collapsed in a vast shower of golden sparks . . . the pleading cackle of those too old and decrepit to escape the flames . . . lost children shrieking for their parents . . . men carrying their household possessions awkwardly before them, jostling and shoving one another . . . others, in agony at failing to rescue their families, plunging into the flames to end it all . . . mothers hurrying their children from place to place in a mad flight from the crackling, whirling thunder of the blaze . . . hordes of the homeless occupying every foot of ground in whatever parks and open fields they could find, and then being beaten off by those who got there first.

As in all disasters, Sabinus saw the conflagration bringing out the worst—and the best—in people. Some became clawing animals, looting and thieving or seizing firebrands and adding insanely to the chaos. Bands of gladiators, drunk with wine plundered from burning taverns, roamed the city for new pillage. Slaves, freed by the catastrophe, were chattering in Greek, African, and Asiatic dialects, some vengefully ravaging the mansions that had held them captive. Other citizens heroically found strength to rescue the helpless while disregarding reports that their own homes were on fire. Mortally burned without knowing it, some kept battling the flames until they collapsed.

Strangely, it was not the searing heat that bothered Sabinus the most but the smells—the pungent, acrid odor of smoke, fumes, smoggy haze, and more smoke—that stinking pall hanging over the city, almost darkening the sun and turning day into night. Sometimes the smell was pleasant: if a tall, aged pine went up in flames and the wind blew right, his nostrils could relax. But moments later came the stench of scorching animal or human flesh and he would gag again. From time to time he tried to spit out the taste of soot and ash in his mouth, but in minutes it was back.

He met with Nero, Tigellinus, and the commander of the vigiles twice a day to discuss strategy, and the emperor surprised him by plunging boldly into relief efforts. He threw open to the homeless hordes the great public buildings, temples, and basilicas in the Campus Martius. He set up shelters and food stations in the parks of Rome and converted his gardens in the Trans-Tiber into a vast tent city. Ordering massive supplies of grain from government storage bins in Ostia and neighboring towns, he reduced the price of wheat to three sesterces a peck. No one, he swore, would go hungry.

The firebreak at the base of the Esquiline was holding. After demolition of all structures there, the eager flames met only bare ground and open sky. Sabinus dared to hope that the worst was over. On the morning of the sixth day, with the rest of Rome out of danger, the vigiles finally advanced into fire-gutted areas and extinguished the last remaining embers.

Sabinus staggered home and fell, exhausted, into the arms of Plautia. He slept straight through the next sixteen hours.

"Sabinus!"

He felt Plautia's hand tugging at his shoulder. Cracking his eyelids, he saw her bending over him, her eyes clouded with fear. "Someone from the vigiles is here," she was saying. "It's urgent. Something about fire breaking out again."

Sabinus was instantly awake. "Impossible! Send him in."

The courier marched into Sabinus' bedroom and gave a stiff salute. "Pardon the intrusion, Clarissimus," he said, "but fire's broken out again. It's raging out of control in the Campus Martius."

"*What?* When did it break out?" Icy disbelief clutched at Sabinus.

"About . . . two hours ago, we think. All the monuments there are in danger."

"How did *this* one start?" A feeling of nauseous dread was now suffusing him.

"We've no idea."

Fastening the last strap on his sandals, Sabinus caught Plautia about the waist for a hasty kiss. "This one's closer to us, carissima. It could be more dangerous. So if a strong west wind develops, you must leave the house. Take the children and servants over to your parents' place on the Esquiline. It'll be safe there."

"All right. But be *careful,* Sabinus!"

While he hurried off to the blaze, she stood in the doorway of their home, clenching a fist over her mouth.

Again the vigiles were sweating at their task when Sabinus and his police arrived, but this time he saw that he would have a problem with morale too. The firemen were losing heart: six days of fighting the ghastly inferno now seemed to be in vain, and the men were muttering darkly about a general curse hovering over the city— that Rome must inevitably go the way of Atlantis and Troy and Carthage.

"We can't fight the gods, Prefect," one of them moaned.

"Oh, to Hades with the gods!" Sabinus bellowed.

Several looked aghast at his impiety, but he pressed the point. "Did any of you see Vulcan hobbling about, putting Rome to the torch? He should have been involved, after all: he's the god of fire."

No one would admit to it.

Though it seemed a ridiculous time to deal in pleasantries, Sabinus could now build on the low chuckle of the vigiles. "No, men, don't blame this on the gods. So far, they're the biggest losers in this blaze: about forty of their temples are now in ashes! But we should have an easier time containing this fire. So man the siphons, vigiles! My police will use the Via Lata to set up a firebreak to the east!"

But the perverse sirocco, which had died down, suddenly came back to life and blew a sizable section of northwestern Rome into another raging furnace. This time, some valuable monuments, theaters, and aged temples were charred and ruined, while pleasure arcades in the gardens were seared into blackened wasteland.

Mercifully, however, there was less contagion in the new outbreak, and Sabinus found much less loss of life—none of the roiling scenes of human horror that would never erase themselves from his memory. Soon the sirocco exhaled the last of its baleful breath, and the second conflagration could be stamped out in three days.

Fully drained of all his energy reserves, Sabinus could barely see as he peered across Rome for the last time, searching for any lingering pockets of flame. But the holocaust was finally over. Only some random columns of smoke filtering up harmlessly from blackened acreage told the end of nine days of terror. Dizzy and bewildered from extreme fatigue, Sabinus could not later recall that it was his aides who finally had to carry him home to the Quirinal, where he collapsed and slept as one dead.

Plautia looked at the sooty, deep-breathing figure of her husband and—for some reason—thanked her mother's God for his safe return.

It was a note from the emperor that finally roused him two days later. Nero wanted a written estimate of the total damage Rome had sustained. It was to be delivered to him at his temporary quarters in the Servilian Gardens on the Aventine.

After an ugly week of trudging through the ashes and wreckage to interview survivors, Sabinus and his staff drew up a map of the city showing the fire-damaged areas [see back endpaper] and a table of losses, and presented them to Nero.

REGIONS HEAVILY OR COMPLETELY DESTROYED

III	Isis et Serapis
X	Palatium
XI	Circus Maximus

REGIONS PARTIALLY DESTROYED

II	Caelimontium
IV	Templum Pacis
VII	Via Lata
VIII	Forum Romanum
IX	Circus Flaminius
XII	Piscina Publica
XIII	Aventinus

REGIONS UNTOUCHED

I	Porta Capena
V	Esquiline
VI	Alta Semita
XIV	Trans Tiberim

PRIVATE MANSIONS DESTROYED

132

TENEMENTS DESTROYED

Over 4,000 units

Injured: Not available   *Dead:* Not available

"The last two figures will have to be determined in the next weeks," Sabinus explained to Nero.

"But what these figures *don't* show are the irreplaceables," Nero mused. "Romulus' temple, Numa's palace, Vesta's sanctuary . . ."

"Not to mention the archives."

"And my statues—Greek originals. Now we have only copies of those masterpieces." Then he stopped and smoothed his brow. "But we must look to the future, gentlemen. We must rebuild Rome. And we'll *not* rebuild her helter-skelter as our ancestors did after the Gauls burned the city. No, no! We'll have broader streets—"

"And straighter, I trust?" Sabinus smiled.

"Yes, straighter. We'll require open spaces between buildings and limit the number of stories in them."

"What about all the masses of rubbish from the fire?" Tigellinus inquired.

"I'll pay for clearing it away," Nero volunteered. "But where will we put it all?"

Sabinus pondered a moment, then suggested, "Why not have the grain barges return down the Tiber loaded with ashes and dump them in the marshes around Ostia? They're trying to raise that land anyway, aren't they?"

Nero smiled. "Inspired, Sabinus. Inspired."

"And I think your greatest problem now, Caesar, will be to lift the mood of the people in the devastated districts. They're crushed with this loss. They may not have the heart to rebuild."

"What do you advise, Prefect?" Tigellinus sniffed. "Shall Caesar buy them new homes while you massage their spirits?"

Coolly ignoring Tigellinus' inanity, Sabinus made a proposal. "Why not offer something like a bounty to owners of ruined property? If they rebuild within a specified time, they can claim the reward."

"Hmmm," Nero pondered. "Sounds reasonable, provided the bounty isn't too high."

"Proportion it to the loss sustained."

"All right, Sabinus. They're good suggestions. All of them. We'll incorporate them in our edict."

Nero did what he had promised. He also led Rome in publicly appeasing the gods so that the disaster would not be repeated, offering solemn prayers to Vulcan. At the same time, a somber parade of

Roman matrons trooped up to the Capitoline, which had been spared the flames, and humbly implored Juno to cool her anger, bathing her statue with water from the Mediterranean and holding all-night vigils in her honor.

As wife of the city prefect, Plautia was expected to join Poppaea in leading the women of Rome in these sacred duties, but she would not.

"It's all hypocrisy," she told her husband. "Not one of those women seriously thinks Juno is cocking an ear to their prayers. Or has the necessary existence to do so."

Sabinus, who let Plautia make her own decision in the matter, had to smile at her resolve. He recalled his own exclamation during the great blaze: to Hades with the gods indeed!

23

THE CEREMONIES OVER, Nero plunged into rebuilding a palace for himself. But where? The black wastes of the Palatine were haunted with bad memories, and the Fates seemed to frown on that hill. Severus and Celer, the emperor's master architects who were directing the rebuilding of Rome, pointed out the obvious spot: the great valley below the Esquiline, where everything had been demolished to serve as the massive firebreak.

Nero and Tigellinus hurried over to the site with Severus and Celer, and soon they were captivated by the prospects of a great new palace in that setting. Eyes blazing with faraway visions of future grandeur, Nero suggested its dimensions. The men caught their breath. Nero was stepping off an area of some 130 acres, larger than both Forums.

"Now listen carefully"—Nero beamed—"here's what I have in mind: the four of us are looking at the portals of the new palace . . . say about there." He pointed.* "Inside the vestibule, we ought to have something to symbolize the place. But what?"

Tigellinus picked up the cue. He knew Nero's dream had been to have a gigantic statue of himself erected, so he quickly responded,

* To a place where the Colosseum would later stand, itself named for Nero's colossus.

"Your colossus must stand there, Caesar. In truly heroic dimension."

"You really think so, Tigellinus?" Nero grinned. "Well, that might be appropriate. How . . . large should the statue be, do you suppose?"

"I said a *colossus*, Caesar, not a statue. Let it be at least, say, twenty times your size."

Severus was frowning. "But that would be well over one hundred feet high! And the vestibule housing it would have to be higher still."

"Aren't you and Celer capable of designing something like this?" Tigellinus sniffed.

"Of course, but if the palace stands that high it will also have to be extremely long to keep the proportions in balance."

"Oh, I intend it to be long," said Nero, in a matter-of-fact tone. "I had in mind a great hall of columns forming one axis of the building, running from here to . . . say, that great oak over there at the end of the valley."

Severus' eyes boggled. "But that's almost a mile away!"

"Of course it is!" Tigellinus growled. "We're planning a genuine palace here—not one of those hovels on the Palatine."

"But with this difference," Nero added. "Anyone can throw up *huge* structures. What I want is a *great* structure. Caesar is not merely emperor. Caesar is also an artist, and his residence must reflect that fact. Now, follow me. Here's what I have in mind . . ."

He took them on a tour of his future abode, his arms busy as he pointed out the prospective gardens, lakes, and even fields stocked with game that would surround the palace. Splashing fountains and groves with statuary were to set off separate pools for fresh water, seawater, and even sulfur baths piped in from the hot springs at Tibur.

The architects finally caught Nero's spirit. Several weeks later, they presented him preliminary sketches that were as breathtaking as they were lavish. They also had several surprises they knew would delight his fancy: a grand dining room in which a domed ceiling with sun and stars would revolve to symbolize the day and night skies. The halls would be covered with so much gold and jeweled inlays that they suggested a name for their project: the Domus Aurea.

"The 'golden house'?" Nero mused. "Yes. Yes, I like that very much. Build it, gentlemen."

Severus and Celer laid their plans on Sabinus' desk at city head-quarters. He studied them for several minutes as every muscle in his body seemed to tauten. Walking over to the great wall map of Rome, he moved his left hand over a massive arc of Rome to the west and north. "Here, gentlemen," he said, his voice exuding sarcasm, "here are several sections of the city that you *haven't* reserved for your new palace. Otherwise, you'll have most of Rome!"

"We know, we know," Severus huffed. "But we didn't come here to listen to caustic comments, Prefect—we're just following orders, after all. We *are* here to ask for work crews for the new palace."

"Every last city crew and all private contractors are at work rebuilding Rome."

"Yes, but Nero has to have a place to live too," Celer observed. "We're authorized to take over your crews if you won't cooperate."

Sabinus struggled to contain his fury. He searched for theoretical options and alternatives, but found none in fact. "I want you both to know," he finally said, "that the people of Rome will know *exactly* why the work crews are being diverted."

"Fine," said Severus, shrugging his shoulders. "Now, here's what we'll require . . ."

As many thousands of laborers who had been toiling to rebuild the city were suddenly shifted to the vast project along the Esquiline, Romans frowned and began grumbling. The rumblings grew louder as they saw the incredible dimensions of Nero's new palace and its financing through forced contributions from all over the Empire "for rebuilding Rome." Was it an accident that six great landowners in Africa were suddenly executed on trumped-up charges and their vast estates—virtually half the province—confiscated by the emperor?

The Golden House only served as capstone to an ugly arch of rumor that had been building across Rome ever since the great fire. People were whispering it to their neighbors. Graffiti were shouting it from the walls. Homeless thousands were shaking their fists and screaming it. And Nero's enemies were trying to prove it: as a climax to all his other crimes, *Nero himself* had set fire to Rome!

But why? Finally it was obvious, they thought: to clear out the slums at minimal expense; to be given glory for founding a new city, probably to be renamed Neropolis; and, above all, to seize vast acreage in the very heart of Rome for his Golden House. These were the main motives. And there were others: Priam and Troy were immortalized by their fiery, disastrous end. Nero too wanted to go down in legend, and so created his own catastrophe.

And the proof? Look where buildings were demolished for the firebreak. And the scene of Nero surveying his burning city from the Esquiline terrace had been embellished from mouth to mouth in the retelling. In place of tears, he now wore a dark smile. Instead of merely singing his dirge, he now plucked rapturously at his lyre, nearly salivating over the flames.

"Nero played while Rome burned!" The obvious, angry slogan had arisen shortly after the flames were extinguished. Sabinus, who wanted to be fair, tried to scotch the rumor. "Nonsense!" he countered publicly. "People *always* blame the person in power at times of catastrophe."

But then the colored reports, the misinterpretations, the rumors started saturating the city at a time when Romans were prone to look for culprits and incendiaries. A plebe who had lost his wife and baby on the Caelian stood up in the tent city and shouted, "My cousin works in the palace. She told me that at one of Nero's dinner parties, someone quoted a line from Euripides: 'When I am dead, may fire consume the earth.' But Nero replied, '*No! Rather while I live!*'"

But the greatest fuel for the rumors flowed from the efforts of the firefighters themselves. People saw them demolishing buildings or setting counter fires, and the police were even helping them. Hence it must all have been done at Caesar's orders!

Nero had heard the first rumors while the smoke was still curling up from the blanket of ashes that was south-central Rome, yet he had passed them off as idle gossip. But with the Golden House project, the angry mutters became open shouts. Now the city was rumbling with furious demonstrations as a hundred thousand accusing fingers seemed to rise from the rubble and point toward him.

The graffiti of Rome used to be simple and obvious, merely taunting Nero for matricide. But now there were fresh themes:

> A House of Gold is swallowing Rome!
> Let's flee to Veii and make it our home!
> But the palace—it grows so much faster than hell,
> That soon it'll gobble up Veii as well.

and:

Who set Rome on fire?
The man we must admire
  For killing his wife, and taking the life
  Of mother and brother and so many others
While plucking his damnable lyre.

Nero made no effort to find the authors of such graffiti—a hopeless quest in any case—but he grew alarmed when people no longer spoke of Caesar, but of "The Incendiary" or "The Arsonist-Matricide." Verging on panic, he called a conference at his temporary residence of all heads of government, including his council of state.

Sabinus had forebodings about the imperial conclave. Nero was always at his worst when threatened. All his crimes had been committed when he felt threatened. But now there was a new complication—the voice of the people—for Nero was extremely sensitive about his popularity. With the people against him too, Nero would doubtless be cowardly, suspicious, volatile, and ready to clutch at any convenient solution.

Sabinus was not disappointed. Nero was all this and more. His ruddy face had blanched with a clammy pallor, and it seemed to have fattened over the past months, for the outlines of a double chin were unmistakable and his bull neck was never more ponderous. The sensuous lips now seemed thick enough to touch his nose, Sabinus thought, or were his nostrils stretching down to guard his mouth from overeating?

Nero quickly sounded the keynote of the conference. "I've gathered you all, my colleagues—and even my beloved Poppaea here—to help me decide what to do about the terrible slanders circulating in the city. The people are holding meetings in the streets. They're demanding that I be burnt in the 'troublesome tunic'! Great Vulcan, the incredible injustice! I—who suffered most from the fire—am accused of setting it! Everything I valued is now ashes, and they want to say I made Rome a blazing hell!"

His pudgy hands, sprouting coarse amber hairs, were busy smoothing his tiers of curls at the back of his head or tugging at the purple silk handkerchief about his throat—Terpnus ordered such protection for the "celestial voice." Nero then recounted his losses once again, a list Sabinus had heard so many times before he could recite it from memory.

"Has anyone discovered the *true* cause of the conflagration?" Petronius inquired.

Nero looked to Sabinus and said, "Perhaps our city prefect can enlighten us."

In fact, Sabinus knew exactly what had caused the outbreak. Long before the embers had glowed down, a guilt-ridden Hermes had confessed his accident to Sabinus. Realizing Hermes' life was at stake, Sabinus had sworn him to silence. So now he replied, "As far as we can determine, it was merely an accidental house fire in an oil dealer's shop east of the Circus that set it all off. The sirocco took over, and that was that."

"But *I* get the blame," Nero moaned. "I who was thirty-five miles away at the time. *I* sent incendiaries into the city . . . at the time of a full moon, no less! Fiery Vulcan! In that case, why didn't I get placards painted to advertise the scheme: 'These Flames Courtesy of Nero Caesar'."

"And how you bungled it, Caesar," Tigellinus continued in the same irony. "You were after the Esquiline property, but you destroyed a third of the city before getting the flames that far!"

"Including everything I owned. So I repeat, my friends, what shall we do?"

Silence filled the chamber until Tigellinus asked, "Why don't we find the *real* culprits?"

"The real culprits?" Nero stared at him blankly. "But there aren't any. The fire was accidental."

"I know, I know. But, you see, the people *want* culprits . . . they *want* to believe it was caused by arsonists. So let's supply them."

"You mean, pin the blame on some innocent people?" Petronius asked.

"Yes, innocent of this, but . . . guilty of something else. We could find some criminals—perhaps even some foreign elements we don't like—and indict them to clear Caesar."

"Hmmmm," Nero reflected. "The plan has possibilities . . ."

"Utterly and morally wrong, Caesar," Sabinus countered. "The criminals would confess they'd been put up to this, and you'd be worse off than ever. The only solution is to tell the truth about how the fire started."

"But we've *tried* to do that, Sabinus," grumbled Tigellinus, "and the people just won't believe it."

"Hear me out. Let's circulate a full explanation of the causes of the fire—sworn testimony from survivors on the street where it started—and then add a list of Caesar's own great losses and many relief efforts afterward, and people *must* believe his innocence."

"I'd support that," said Petronius. Several other heads nodded, but Nero seemed less than impressed.

"Disgusting!" he pouted. "It's disgusting that I have to prove my innocence—as though somehow *I* were on trial. If we publish such a statement, Sabinus, it will look as if I'm on the defensive in this matter."

"With all respect, Caesar, you *are*," said Sabinus. "However unjustifiably, the people of Rome have put you on the defensive and you must answer them, clear yourself, and tell the true story. Publish the facts. They'll believe them."

Again there were some moments of silence. Finally Tigellinus said, "You don't understand the people of Rome, Prefect. The common man is a sensation-seeker. That's why feeding him is not enough: we must dazzle his eyes as well as fill his belly. Circuses must follow bread. Now, what does the public *prefer* to believe? That the great fire started by accident—as fires most often do—or by design? The people have already opted for the latter. They always prefer the sensational to the actual. If we try to prove it was an accident, they'll never believe it now. They'll say we're only covering up the truth, and the murmuring will continue as long as Nero rules. Conspiracies will multiply. Assassinations will be attempted."

Nero tightened his eyes and looked visibly alarmed as Tigellinus, who knew his emperor's weaknesses so well, continued. "That's why we *must* protect Caesar by clearing him completely. And the only way to do that is to give the people the victims they want. So I suggest we decide on some gang of 'incendiaries,' indict them, 'prove' their guilt, and then give them a very dramatic execution before the people in one of the great hippodromes. We'll burn . . . we'll torture . . . we'll crucify them while our citizens watch it all. Those who lost their loved ones will finally drink the sweet nectar of revenge as they watch the agonies of the 'arsonists,' and they'll quit blaming their innocent emperor."

"But . . . it's . . . *wrong*, Tigellinus!" Sabinus objected. "Unjust! Immoral! A show, a farce. It could cause complications of the worst kind. Rome's never—"

"Who says what's right or wrong? Are you putting the lives of some wretched criminals ahead of Caesar's own?"

Unhappily, Tigellinus' plan seemed to gain support among some of the advisers, and soon Nero was openly praising it. "The people *do* have to have a show after all this misery," he said. "Imagine how happy it would make them! And that point about getting their vengeance while watching the guilty suffer—it's true, you know. People *are* like that. Yes. Yes indeed! That's the solution, my colleagues. Let's do it."

Sabinus entered an even stronger protest, this time calling on the memory of Nero's ancestors who had governed in justice and equity. But Nero grumbled, "Oh, shut up, Sabinus. You're not much help here. If you can't sing a new song, why don't you leave?"

His ire rising, Sabinus got up to leave the room.

"No, wait!" Nero ordered. "Stay. As city prefect, you'll have to be in on these plans, of course.—Now, Tigellinus, who will the victims be?"

"I don't know." The praetorian prefect shrugged. "The idea just occurred to me. We'll have to think about it."

"Well, how many should there be?"

"Not just a few, Caesar. This must be a spectacle. We'll have to fill the arena of one of the hippodromes with a whole crowd of arsonists."

"Yes, yes. Perhaps several dozen, at least."

"More like several hundred, I should think." Tigellinus smirked. "The greater the number of victims, the greater the feeling of revenge among the people."

"Gods, what sage advice, Tigellinus!" Nero smiled. "Do you see, my friends, why I chose this man as praetorian prefect? Now, where can we round up a gang of criminals this size?"

"Or foreigners . . . cultists . . . any group in society that we despise."

"The followers of Isis and Osiris?" Gallio ventured. "After all, fires raged through their Region III."

"Which means they're innocent," Tigellinus objected. "They'd hardly destroy their own area of the city. Let's look at sections *not* touched by the fire."

Nero called for the city map that Sabinus had shaded in to show the burned-out districts. Spreading it out on their conference table, they studied it for some moments. Suddenly Nero exclaimed, "Do you see what I see, gentlemen? There are only four regions absolutely untouched by fire. Of these, we can eliminate Regions V and

VI, since only the wealthy live on the Esquiline and the Quirinal, not cultists and foreigners. That leaves only Regions I and XIV."

"What are you getting at?" asked Petronius.

"Simply this: what foreign group has settled heavily in both Region I, the Porta Capena, and XIV, the Trans-Tiber?"

"Why . . . the Jews, of course." Tigellinus brightened.

"The Jews. Exactly." Nero smiled. "We have to clean them out of Rome from time to time, but they always manage to come back. *The Jews* set fire to Rome!"

Sabinus was shaking his head in despair, and Poppaea too was frowning. "But there are too many Jews for your purposes." She spoke for the first time. "There must be 30,000 in Rome alone."

"We'd merely ask them for several hundred," Nero replied. "Most of our citizens don't like them anyway. They'd be perfect scapegoats."

"No," Poppaea said, quietly but firmly. "If you'd kill a hundred, the people would go after all the others too and kill many thousands. It would be a horrible blood bath. The Jews are innocent . . . they're loyal. They intercede for you in their synagogues, Nero. You can't do this to them."

"Not even to save your husband, Empress?"

"Don't you *dare* to put it that way, Tigellinus!" she hissed. "Whatever you decide, gentlemen, it will *not* be the Jews."

Silence again dominated the room. Suddenly Sabinus' heart began pulsing in a wild cadence, and he fought to keep his face from reddening and betraying what had just occurred to him. In the horror of the moment, he prayed the great Father of the Gods that Tigellinus was not thinking of the same possibility. He stole a quick glance at him, then looked away again, but his horror was richly confirmed: Tigellinus had been staring at him with a slowly broadening smile. He waited several moments longer to let Sabinus suffer before saying, "Well, Caesar. Search no further. We've found our arsonists."

"Who?"

"Who?" Tigellinus grinned as the full implications became clearer to him. "Simply that special brand of Jews who are not Jews at all, as Sabinus helped me prove in the trial of one, Paul of Tarsus, three years ago. I lost that case, you'll recall. But I think I'll win this one."

"Oh . . . you mean the Christians," Nero replied.

Tigellinus nodded slowly and said, "Exactly. The Christians."

For several moments they all paused to ponder the possibility.

"By the immortal gods, that's *good*, Tigellinus," Nero finally commented. "Excellent . . . in fact, a *superb* suggestion. Our people hate the Christians as much as the Jews, and there are far fewer Christians. They'll suspect them more. They're a weird group anyway. They could so easily have done it."

"Their main congregation is on the Aventine," Tigellinus added. "And the Aventine was almost untouched by the fire."

Sabinus was queasy at the horrendous turn the conference had taken. Hundreds of innocent lives were now hanging on his ability to turn the dreadful decision the conclave seemed to be pondering. By now, of course, he had become *persona non grata* in that discussion, but he would never be able to live with himself unless he made the supreme effort.

"My colleagues," Sabinus began slowly. "I'd like to expand on the very eloquent objection raised by the Empress Poppaea. She was absolutely right in suggesting that our people will not be content with the punishment of a few. They will indeed go after the many. Now, there are more than a few hundred Christians in Rome. By now there are thousands—"

"Oh, he's thinking of his dear mother-in-law, of course." Tigellinus smirked. "Don't worry, Sabinus. We won't touch Pomponia."

"Entirely apart from Pomponia," Sabinus continued, "people of every rank in Rome are now Christians. It's an innocent religion, Tigellinus. Some of your own praetorians are Christians—and the better for it. Some of your own household slaves are Christians, Caesar."

"They *are?*" Nero darkened.

Instantly, Sabinus knew it had been poor timing for that particular argument, since it could feed Nero's suspicions. He resumed as best he could. "They pray for you, Caesar. They're good citizens. And they would never admit to the falsehood that they set fire to Rome."

"They would under torture," Tigellinus huffed.

Ignoring the comment, Sabinus argued, "If you blame the Christians, the hundred innocents you gather in the arena won't be the only victims. The people will seek out the rest and cause a general slaughter. I plead with you, my friends, by all the gods and goddesses we honor, that you choose another group, if choose you must—convicted criminals, perhaps."

"No. Criminals can't be trusted," Tigellinus sneered. "They might expose us—wasn't that your original argument, Sabinus?—and besides, I don't trust the Christians anyway. If they *are* growing here in Rome as you say, then they're a dangerous and subversive element—a state within a state. And maybe they *do* commit those atrocities mentioned at Paul's trial: they meet at night, like a pack of sorcerers and magicians—"

"And the point is that people *think* they do all these things." Nero smiled. "If they murder babies and despise our gods, they might easily have hated Rome enough to burn it too."

"By the gods!" Tigellinus suddenly exclaimed. "I hadn't thought of it until this moment! I've had two of my praetorians attending their meetings on the Aventine to spy out their teachings. Now, their *other* major leader recently arrived in Rome—a Galilean fisherman named Simon, I think it was. Yes, Simon Peter. And what, do you suppose, he told his people just after our . . . magnificent party at Agrippa's Pond?"

"What?"

"I don't recall the exact words, but it went something like this. He told about some cities in Palestine being destroyed by fire, and then he said, 'It may take fire to purify Rome also'—or something like that."

Nero's eyes widened. Then he smiled. "It's settled, then. The Christians set fire to Rome."

"No!" Sabinus interjected. "That was only a figure of speech—a simple coincidence. It means nothing. Certainly Peter never advised arson. Christians are law-abiding—they don't set fires—they rather—"

"Oh, shut up!" Nero bellowed. "At this point I don't care in the least if they do or don't set fires. Again you're missing the point: it's now a question of this government *surviving* or not. Are you too dense to see that?"

"I only know this," Sabinus shot back, a volatile mixture of fury and also anxiety welling up inside him. "Arson is a capital offense. And such crimes in Rome are tried before the *city prefect*. I promise you that in trying the Christians, I'll judge them individually—not as a group—and I'll convict *none* of them because the fire was an *accident*. We know where it broke out."

Sabinus knew it was a desperate statement—no one talked to Caesar like that—but it might cause Nero and the conclave to rethink their decision.

Nero merely turned to Sabinus and gave him an elaborate frown. Then he opened his thick lips and muttered contemptuously, "Do you *really* think we'd wait while you processed your Christians one by one, Sabinus? Releasing all? Convicting none? Embarrassing us—turning us into liars as well as arsonists? *Forget that!* Do you take us for *fools*, Sabinus? *Eh?* You're treading on *very* dangerous ground, Prefect!" He fixed his menacing stare several moments longer, and then commented, "No, we can't use someone as spineless as you in this operation.—What alternatives do we have, Tigellinus?"

"Simple enough, Caesar." He smiled, touching the tips of his fingers together. "My praetorians will take care of it. We're the government police anyway, and we'll use our channels to find out who the Christians are and arrest them. I'll judge them myself of course."

"Excellent! Round them up and bring them into the Circus. No, we can't use the Circus Maximus! Let's use the stadium where I race my horses . . . over in the Vatican Gardens across the Tiber. Great Jupiter! *You* again, Sabinus? What do you want?"

"I . . . I feel it only proper to submit my resignation as city prefect, Caesar. I find this one of the worst and most degrading solutions imaginable. Under these circumstances, obviously, you can't want me to continue in your administration."

Nero's lips quivered, as the veins on his neck were distending. "Let Caesar do his own deciding, will you?" His filmy blue eyes, narrowing in rage, glared into him for several moments. Then he muttered. "Yes, I *should* let you resign. I should *fire* you for that matter! Or *worse!* But I haven't time to look around for a new city perfect just now. You will therefore *not* resign, Flavius Sabinus! You will continue in office for as long as I wish it. Do you hear me?"

24

BARELY COMPREHENDING THE HORROR about to unfold,
Sabinus hurried over to the Esquiline to alert Aulus and Pomponia.
He had failed to avert disaster. Now he could merely warn of its ap-
proach.

Aulus recoiled at Sabinus' dreadful report, while Pomponia broke
down and wept. "What . . . whatever should we do?" she asked, between sobs.

"Make a list of all the Christians you want notified. No time for
them all. Dispatch your most trusted servants at once to warn them.
Aquila, Priscilla, and certainly Peter and the other leaders should go
into hiding at once."

"But where?"

"Anywhere. Not here, though. Tigellinus will probably search
this house first. Oh yes, he promised not to touch you, Pomponia,
but I'd never rest on his word. Your Christians, though, should get
out of the city—*at once*—before it's too late. Better yet, I'll hurry over
to the Aventine myself and warn Aquila. Meanwhile, go to Peter—
now—since he's staying near the Castra Praetoria. If necessary, hide
him at our villa in Tibur."

With that he rushed out across Rome, much of which was still lit-
tered and scorched from the great fire, and hurried up the slopes of

the Aventine. Huffing for breath, Sabinus rapped furiously on the door of Aquila's chapel. There was no answer.

Finally the door opened. Priscilla beamed and said, "What an honor, Prefect! Peace be with you."

"Where's Aquila? Get him if he's here, Priscilla! *Hurry!*"

She called her husband. The moment he appeared, Sabinus announced the mortal danger. "I feared, I feared," Aquila said. "I had the feeling someday it would happen. Jesus said, 'If they persecuted me, they will also persecute you.' What should we do, Prefect? Is there any hope?"

"Not if the praetorians catch you. Warn your nearest Christians to flee Rome if they can. Hide if they can't. Each must relay the message."

"When will they come to arrest us?"

"*Imminently.* You must leave here at once!"

"But . . . but we can't just—"

"I almost forgot. You don't have any list of believers here, do you, Aquila? Any records of who your Christians are?"

"Yes, certainly . . ."

"Gods, man! *Burn* them. Now! At once! Show me where they are."

As they stepped into Aquila's office, there was an ominous clack, *Clack,* CLACK, *CLACK* of approaching troops. "*Cohort . . . halt!*" a tribune shouted. "*Surround this house!*" There was a banging on the door.

Priscilla gasped. The door came crashing open and troops marched inside. Alongside the tribune was Tigellinus himself, who rasped, "Where's your husband?"

Priscilla, horrified, said nothing. They combed the house and easily found the office, but it was empty. Tigellinus looked out its open window, then crawled through it into the back garden.

"So, Sabinus," he laughed. "What are you two doing back here?"

"Just warning a few innocents that a slaughterer is coming."

"I'd say the city prefect is consorting with the enemies of Caesar. That's treason, you know."

"Only by your warped definitions, Tigellinus."

"So bold, Sabinus? At a time when I have a few scores to settle with you? At a time when this house is filled with my men? Why don't I simply arrest you here and now for high treason?"

"I'll tell you why: because Nero doesn't want to take on the whole senatorial class at the moment, does he? The plebes already accuse him for the fire. If the patricians join them too because of your bungling . . ."

He let Tigellinus draw the conclusion. He had to play for time, and in any case he could be of more use to the victimized Christians as prefect than as fellow victim.

Tigellinus gave him a long, supercilious stare. Then his eyes shifted. "Your name's Aquila?"

"It is."

"You are a Christianus, Aquila?"

"Yes. I am."

"You and your wife are under arrest."

"For what reason?"

"Don't you know?" Tigellinus smirked. "For burning Rome, of course. You're an arsonist, Aquila. Learn the term well, for you'll have to confess it."

"I will not confess to something I did not do."

"Oh yes you will. Let's go."

They returned inside. Sabinus tried to say something comforting to Aquila and Priscilla, and then left. He had not gone far when Tigellinus yelled down to him from the chapel: "That's *very* interesting reading material you buried next to the roses, Sabinus!"

Sabinus winced as if he had been skewered with a spear. They had not had time to burn the membership list, hastily burying it instead! Now hundreds would die. His second, horrendous failure that day plunged Sabinus into black despondency. Knowing Tigellinus' methods, however, he would probably have ferreted out the information anyway. At least Aquila and his wife would now be spared torture . . . a small consolation. A pathetic people, the Christians—believing in a god who obviously was unable to save them. Was he so much better, Sabinus wondered, believing in a state that was unable to save innocent citizens?

He groped for alternatives. Should he try to counter Nero at the summit of power? He could ask the consuls to convene an emergency meeting of the Senate, where he could present Hermes, expose the plot against the Christians, and paint Nero and Tigellinus for the cowardly liars they were. Nero's reputation with the Fathers would reach a new low and he might even be deposed, while the innocents would be spared.

Dreaming. That's all it was, he knew. Even if the senators

believed him, would they be courageous enough to stand against Nero? And even if they were transformed into 500 Thraseas and finally rose from their marble benches to depose the emperor, Tigellinus would merely order the 10,000 men of the Praetorian Guard to advance on the Senate. Against this force, Sabinus could field only the 4,000 in his Urban Cohorts, and it was doubtful that they would fight a civil war against these odds. The 7,000 vigiles would doubtless side with Nero—they had been accused of doing a miserable job in containing the flames and were also looking for scapegoats. If only the legions were prepared to revolt. But they could never be reached in time.

So there was no hope. Tigellinus' terrible scheme would become reality: Nero would rescue himself with the blood of others.

Tigellinus' praetorians functioned with ruthless efficiency. They began by purging any in their own cohorts who were Christians, and they were shocked to find twenty-six who admitted to being converts. These were tortured until one of them finally broke and identified the other congregations in Rome besides Aquila's. Praetorian squads were immediately dispatched to these locations and the premises impounded. Where membership lists were not found, members were. And they were tortured until they divulged the names of others. Many revealed nothing at all, even though the flames of a candle were played along the bare soles of their feet. Then there were the terrified marginal members who, to save themselves, exposed others.

In a short time, several hundred Christians were imprisoned at the Castra Praetoria—the camp had not seen such a throng since the 400 slaves of Pedanius were executed—and they were still arriving by the dozens. Nor was Nero's own palace staff exempt. Nothing shocked him more than to learn that some slave whom he trusted implicitly turned out to be a Christian. Rome was harboring what evidently was a larger conspiracy than he or Tigellinus had imagined, for he was beginning to believe his own story. But Simon Peter, the ringleader, was still at large.

With Nero's permission, Tigellinus now published the following edict:

NERO CAESAR to the SENATE AND THE ROMAN PEOPLE, Greeting! By the favor of the gods, the arsonists who burned our beloved city have finally been identified and are now being arrested. They are a criminal cult of foreign misanthropes known as Nazarenes or Christiani. (Their name comes from Christus, a felon who was crucified in Judea by one of our governors.)

If you know of any such Christians, report them at once to any member of the vigiles or the Praetorian Guard. They are now being tried at the Castra Praetoria, and will be publicly executed at special games in the Vatican Circus beginning Monday next. You are all invited to witness their punishment. Thanks be to the gods!

The notice was posted throughout the city, and Tigellinus was overwhelmed with the success of his scheme. The Roman people, always fickle, easily transferred their hatreds from Nero to that cult of little-known fanatics who had tried to infiltrate the city with their silly belief about a dead criminal being some kind of god.

The trials at the Castra Praetoria were abnormal exercises in justice. Brought in groups before his tribunal, the Christians were judged by Tigellinus through his power of *coercitio,* a magistrate's authority to enforce public order at his own discretion. Everyone denied the charge of arson, but "witnesses" were found who testified that they had seen the second and the fourth person in each front row with a firebrand in his hand on the night of the outbreak. Tigellinus then asked if they were Christians, and this, in fact, soon became the fundamental charge. For as Christians they were guilty of what he called *odium humani generis*—hatred of the human race —for they sought its violent destruction by means of fire, conspiracy, vice, and treason. The *odium* charge was also the standard indictment against the poisoners and magicians of Rome—a happy association, Tigellinus thought.

Such a high proportion of those arrested actually confessed to being Christians that Tigellinus released all who denied such belief. He would have more than enough victims for the Circus. He wondered why many more did not try to save themselves by feigning unbelief. Did it have something to do with their fanatic faith? Or maybe they had no idea what sort of punishment awaited them. In any case, he was careful to condemn each group without specifying punishment. He wanted obedient, docile sheep marched out to the slaughter.

"We were able to reach most of our church leaders before the praetorians arrived," Pomponia told Sabinus over on the Esquiline.

"Did they flee? Or are they in hiding?"

"At first they didn't want to hide at all. Mark and Luke insisted that they ought to suffer with the other Roman Christians. But Peter ordered them to go into hiding. 'Apart from God himself,' he said, 'the future of the Faith lies in your hands, my brothers. You must survive to finish writing your gospels.'"

"Where are they hiding, then?"

Pomponia looked down and said, "At your villa in Tibur, Sabinus. I'm sorry. I just didn't know where else to send them."

So, then, he reflected, he was now harboring fugitives wanted by the state. And even though not a Christian, he could easily share their fate if discovered. "It's all right," he finally told Pomponia. "I'll go out to see if I can help them."

Sabinus reached Tibur after a short, hard ride. Peter and about twenty others were huddled in the atrium of his villa, looking anxiously at the doorway. Their tense, frightened faces melted in smiles when they saw him.

For the next hour, Sabinus reported on conditions in Rome and debated their best course of action. The question to which Peter returned again and again was whether the persecution would be limited to Rome, or extend throughout the Empire. Sabinus thought it would remain local, though with Nero, anything was possible.

"In any case, we must alert Christians everywhere, especially in the East. Silvanus"—Peter turned to a recently arrived friend who had also accompanied Paul on some of his journeys—"I'll dictate a letter for you, and you must carry it to Greece and Asia."

The silver-haired amanuensis, who looked like someone's benevolent uncle, went for his pen and some sheets of papyrus.

"But what if Silvanus is arrested?" asked Sabinus. "All roads out of Rome are being searched."

"I hadn't thought of that."

"I'll write out a safe-conduct pass for him," Sabinus decided. "Who else will be leaving? Give me the names, and I'll prepare passes. Luckily, I thought to bring my seal along."

Peter and the elders made a quick decision as to who should flee and who stay. Then he handed Sabinus a list of names.

"I don't see your name here, Peter. They want you more than anyone else."

"I must stay . . . to help our Roman brothers and sisters in this terrible hour."

Instantly the elders were clustering about the big fisherman, pleading with him to flee "for the sake of the church at large."

"No, no. I *must* stay," he repeated.

"You must—and you will—go," insisted Linus, one of the elders.

Finally, Peter gave in, asking, "Will you take care of the flock while I'm gone?"

Linus nodded, solemnly.

"Very well, then," said Peter. "Kindly prepare a pass for me also, good Prefect. But Silvanus must leave ahead of us—as soon as possible, in fact."

"I can take him over the back roads around Rome to a point on the Appian Way well below the city," Sabinus volunteered.

"That is gracious of you, Prefect."

While Sabinus sat down and wrote out the documents, impressing each with his city prefect's seal, Peter started dictating to Silvanus and quickly came to the point of his letter. "Rejoice in your salvation," he said, "though now for a little while you may have to suffer various trials. . . ."

From time to time, Sabinus listened to snatches of the dictation:

. . . Be subject for the Lord's sake to every human institution, whether it be to the emperor as supreme, or to governors as sent by him. . . . Honor all men. Love the brotherhood. Fear God. Honor the emperor.

"*Why?*" Sabinus interrupted. "Excuse me, Peter, but how can you say something like that—after what Nero is doing to your Christians?"

"Because it's what Jesus would say. He told us, 'Love your enemies . . . pray for those who despitefully use you and *persecute* you.' And isn't it important that Christians be known for these qualities? Aren't we charged with hating humanity and dishonoring Caesar?"

"I suppose you're right." Sabinus shrugged, returning to his documents. When he had finished the list, he shuddered a bit thinking of what would happen if any of the leaders were arrested and his pass seized, impressed as it was with the city prefect's seal. Now Peter was concluding:

. . . After you have suffered a little while, the God of all grace
will himself restore, establish, and strengthen you. To him be
dominion for ever and ever. Amen. . . . The church that is at
Babylon sends you greetings, and so does my son Mark.

"Babylon?" Sabinus inquired.

"Yes." Peter smiled. "It's our name for Rome."

"Good name!" Then Sabinus bade them all good-bye and led Silvanus safely to the Appian Way, where they parted. "Better avoid
Naples," he advised. "Go on to Brundisium and take a ship from
there."

BOOK FOUR

THE HOLOCAUST

25

THE HIPPODROME in Nero's Vatican Gardens with its lofty central obelisk was first built by the emperor Caligula. It was he who had barged the huge granite spire from Egypt and set it upright on the *spina* of the stadium, a spinelike platform in the center of the racecourse. But it was Nero who embellished the place, for here he had raced horse and chariot for the first time, to the plaudits of an adoring claque. It was here that suspicions of his putting Rome to the torch would finally be purged. The Senate and all heads of state were invited—the language had more the flavor of "commanded"—to attend, while the people of Rome were promised a spectacle they would never forget.

The last Monday in October dawned bright and clear. An autumn rain had washed the air the night before, and the day gave promise of being warm, perhaps even hot. Bridges across the Tiber were swarming with plebes and patricians alike heading for the Vatican hippodrome. In a short time, all 60,000 seats in the stadium were filled, but Tigellinus had erected extra galleries to accommodate the crowd. By midmorning, however, it was obvious that all places, even for standing room, had been taken, with thousands outside still shouting for admission and pounding on closed gates.

Tigellinus had his praetorians shower them with tokens and announce, "Tomorrow we will have exactly the same games as today! Only half the Christians will be executed today. Present these tokens tomorrow and you will be seated first."

Nero, meanwhile, stepped out of his litter, clad in a rich new amethystine toga, generously accented with gold trim. He took his place in the imperial box, which was situated in the middle base of the south tier so that he would not have to face the sun. Poppaea joined him, resplendent in a chlamys of spun silver that flashed with a brilliance approaching that of the diamond strands about her delicate pink neck. Tigellinus, Rufus, and other emperor's friends also filed into the imperial box, while senators were taking their seats in a large reserved area just behind them.

Directly opposite Nero, in the center of the north tier, was the box of the city prefect, the second most distinguished area here and in the other stadiums of Rome. Nero squinted across the hippodrome to Sabinus' box and frowned. It was empty.

"He'll come, won't he, Tigellinus?"

"After your note 'requiring the presence of the city prefect in view of the large crowd'? Of course he'll come."

"Are your . . . prisoners under control?"

"They're in the stables at the west end. A strange group . . . they're actually singing—hymns of some sort."

"Have you caught their leader yet? That fisherman?"

"Simon Peter? No. Not yet. We will."

"Well now," Nero toyed, "a fishmonger should be able to find a fisherman, don't you think, Tigellinus? Aha! Ahahaha!"

Tigellinus ignored the comment. Then he said, "Sabinus is just arriving" and pointed.

Nero squinted across the stadium through a large concave emerald that he used to correct his myopic vision. "Yes, there's his pretty wife, too. *And* her parents. But the rank effrontery," he wailed. "Her mother's dressed in *mourning* clothes!"

"Nothing new. She often wears them, I understand. Are you ready, Princeps?"

Nero stood up, held out a white napkin for some moments to build the dramatic effect and then dropped it, as if starting a horse race.

A cohort of praetorian trumpeters marched onto the central spina and blasted out a brassy fanfare, repeating the flourish at each corner of the obelisk. Then a tribune, known for his booming bass voice, cupped his hands around his mouth and announced: *"Welcome, O Senate! . . . Welcome, O People . . . of Rome!"* The hesitation between phrases was necessary to give echoes time to spend themselves in the vast hippodrome. *"We have . . . taken the omens . . . and they . . . are favorable!"*

A lusty cheer arose from the stands, sending all birds in the area fluttering off in fright. Then cries of *"Pompa! Pompa!"* welled up from the massed thousands.

"Very well!" the herald boomed. *"You shall have . . . your pompa!"* He flung his arms to the west. *"The procession . . . of those . . . who set fire . . . to Rome!"*

Waves of deafening applause cascaded down into the arena, as the praetorian trumpet corps blasted out the flourish of victory. Doors sprang open at the western end of the stadium and the Christian victims were marched out between files of praetorians. Even though they were distant, Sabinus had little trouble identifying the couple leading the column of Christians. Unmistakably, it was Aquila and Priscilla. They were followed by a motley cavalcade of people of every sort—aging matrons, young men in their prime, terrified children, slaves, an occasional praetorian marching along in what was left of his uniform, derided by his former comrades.

The galleries were howling with hatred. A thousand fingers were raised in obscene gestures, ten thousand fists shook at the procession, as if dripping off the finally-to-be-avenged fury at the fiery loss of a wife, a baby, a friend, a house with all its possessions. *"Arsonists!"* many hissed.

"Anarchists!" *"Madmen!"* others cried.

"Fools!" *"Atheists!"*

"Incendiaries!" *"Dregs!"*

"These shouts are even sweeter music than what I hear from my lyre." Nero smiled, as he leaned back contentedly on his couch. "They'd been calling *me* those names, Tigellinus. You've done *well*, my friend. Very well indeed!"

"Thank you, Caesar. Your happiness . . . your security are my only concerns."

Directly opposite them, Aquila and Priscilla were now marching past Sabinus' box. Just behind them were their friends Hermes and his wife. Incredibly, the man accidentally responsible for burning Rome was arrested as a Christian, not an arsonist. Sabinus looked at the four, and his eyes misted. Pomponia began sobbing and made the sign of the cross over her friends. But the red thatch and russet beard of Aquila stood tall and determined as he returned the sign of the cross, and Priscilla even managed a farewell smile. Poor Hermes, though, seemed in a trance.

Finally the procession of the condemned had wound its way around the racecourse and returned to the stables. Again there was a blistering trumpet fanfare. When the final notes had reverberated and died, the herald bellowed out, *"And now . . . the venatio!"*

For the great "wild beast hunt," ten of the sturdiest Christians—men in their burly prime—were thrust into the arena. At the opposite end, iron gates were drawn up, rasping and creaking, as six Libyan lions padded suspiciously out of their cages. They sniffed the air and grunted several times, their slitted yellow eyes squinting at the unaccustomed brightness of the arena. They seemed unconcerned by all the people, for the masses were sitting dead still and holding their breath as the lions started prowling suspiciously about the arena.

The ten victims, who had just finished praying, stood in a circle, naked but for loincloths. Several looked about for anything that would serve as a club, but they found nothing. They were supposed to "hunt" the beasts barehanded.

The lions, which had been cruelly starved, approached the circle stealthily, stopped and sniffed, but then padded by it again on their slow lope around the racecourse. Now they were below Nero's box. He leaned over to the beasts, pointed to the victims, and cried, "There! Over there, my friends! Food!"

One of the lions stopped, walked over majestically toward the imperial party, opened its massive mouth, and emitted a great, guttural roar in Nero's face. There was snickering from the senatorial section behind the emperor, and Petronius whispered to Quintus Lateranus, "Bravo, lion! Only you can address Caesar so frankly."

Nero leaned over to Tigellinus and said, "Get those cursed beasts to attack, will you?"

Tigellinus stood up and brought his flattened right hand down in a perpendicular arc onto his left open palm—the signal to cut. A band of praetorians rushed out at the circle of Christians and crisscrossed their skins with knife cuts so that the lions could see and smell blood. Some hissing actually boiled up from the galleries, since this was an unusual gesture and quite unsportsmanlike.

Now the lead lion raised his head and again sniffed the air, this time heading back toward the Christians with a low, graceful lope. The others followed and soon they halted in a pack to stalk the ten. Several began growling with anticipation, scratching the ground with great, tawny paws. The other lions answered with menacing snorts, panting as their manes rose.

One of the Christian men, who had a strong, baritone voice, now cupped his hands around his mouth and yelled to the crowd, "We're innocent! We did *not* set fire to Rome! *Falsely convicted!*"

The massed thousands answered with a vast booing. The matter was settled. They were certainly guilty, and it was normal for criminals to shout their innocence. Besides, if they were innocent after all, there would be no show.

The booing startled the lions, and it was nothing more than one of the Christians turning about suddenly that set off the pack. Rumbling a fearful roar, they attacked the circle with great leaps, their open jaws salivating with anticipation and their huge jagged teeth tearing into human flesh. The agonized screams of the victims set the spectators on the edge of their seats, the women whimpering with horror, feigned or real, and clutching at their husbands who were sitting rod-straight as they stared at the ghastly sight, trying to affect an air of cool detachment.

Since the lions had singled out two of the bloodiest victims for their first attack, the other men pommeled their tawny hides and beat them off. The largest of the ten actually charged one of the beasts and knocked him off his feet. Another smashed the snout of a lioness so forcefully that the dumfounded animal backed off dizzily and was out of the fight for some moments.

But whenever the pack retreated, it returned to attack again and again. The lacerations and bites were draining blood from the men, and soon six of them were sprawled on the ground, dying or dead, while the remaining four still fought on hopelessly. A smaller lioness planted her teeth into the ribs of one of the fallen victims and dragged him off to the other side of the arena so that she could dine in peace. The largest of the men, the last to fall, seized an interim to make the sign of the cross over his fallen comrades, and he knelt down in prayer before he, too, was struck down.

Sitting on their haunches in pools of gore, the six beasts voraciously tore away at their prey until the area lay strewn with bones. The wind was from the west, and it carried the sickly odor of blood across the lower tiers of seats in the arena. Women made faces and lunged for their vials of perfume, dabbing several drops under each nostril.

Nero reached for his emerald looking glass and peered across the stadium at Sabinus' box. He saw the two men sitting motionless in their seats, but Plautia seemed to be cradling her mother's head in the folds of her stola.

Again the trumpets sounded and the herald announced, "And now . . . a typical meeting . . . of the Christians!"

Men, women, and even children—about forty in all—were brought to the center of the hippodrome and made to sit down on the spina in rows resembling a congregation. Before them stood one of the prominent preachers in the Christian community, the upper half of his body fitted into the costume of an ass. At a signal from Tigellinus, a praetorian squad tore the clothes off the congregation and tied the members together in indecent postures to dramatize the familiar slander against the Christians. The galleries quaked with peals of laughter. But the victims were crying "Pro Christo!" to one another. "For Christ." Then the praetorians dashed back to the sidelines, because someone had given the signal for the dogs prematurely.

From the eastern end of the stadium a frenzied chorus of yelping and snarling was heard as more than a hundred wild dogs came dashing down the hippodrome and vaulting atop the spina. Like all the animals used that day, they had been starved to build a voracious hunger. But unlike the lions, the hounds attacked immediately, for they had been goaded and prodded to fury in their cages, and made to smell great hocks of raw meat. The crazed canines ran riot through the "congregation," lacerating, tearing, devouring until at last they had their fill and almost meekly waddled out of the stadium with bloated stomachs.

The four who were sitting in the box of the city prefect huddled in horror. Aulus was muttering to himself, defining Nero in terms he had not used since his military days, while Pomponia, who had been pleading to her God, was now moaning in despair. Mercifully, her sight was heavily blurred by her own tears. Plautia was bearing up, but she was pale and frozen in disbelief. Sabinus didn't know why he had let her come. This was a sight only for those who enjoyed wallowing in brutality. But the women had insisted on coming out of some very dubious sense of loyalty to the persecuted victims.

Sabinus was not really that surprised by the inhumanity of it all:

a regime that took four hundred lives for one could quite easily prepare the pitiless panorama of pain unfolding in the arena. But he was utterly nauseated at the reactions of his fellow Romans: presumably civilized men and women, gloating over the grisly horror below. If they were moved by pure vengeance against people they believed truly guilty of arson he could understand it, and doubtless it did explain the delight of some in the vast hippodrome. But what about gladiatorial games, where Romans cheered themselves equally hoarse over the deaths of people who had not wronged them? Was brutality part of the Roman personality, he wondered, and if so, could one justifiably speak of Roman "civilization" in any genuine sense?

Now a figure costumed as Mercury glided out into the arena, waving a wand of red-hot iron. Gracefully, he danced among the bodies of the slain Christians, touching each corpse with his poker to see if it moved. Several did. With a circular swing of his wand, Mercury signaled a band of colleagues, dressed like Pluto, who sallied forth with little mallets and clubbed to death all who were still breathing. Next a squad of arena slaves, costumed like demons of the underworld, swarmed onto the spina, dragging the dead off by their feet and raking over the pools of blood. Meanwhile, a chorus of boys clad like Cupids ran about, scattering rose petals and flowers and spraying perfumes.

A fresh round of trumpets. A new announcement: *"Another meeting . . . of the Christians . . . a more accurate scene!"*

A new congregation was paraded out, and the crowd howled with laughter at what they saw: the victims were all sewed up inside animal skins. The men were standing African leopards. The women, covered with hogshide, were trying to peer through the eye sockets of hollowed-out pig heads, while their children were dressed in dog skins. This time a pack of yapping Iberian hounds came bounding down the stadium, halting to sniff at the strange beings on the spina. A child shrieked, and the hounds then attacked with hungry rage, as if angry at the sham perpetrated on them. The shrill screams of children made many of the women spectators cower on their benches, while men with some shred of conscience were starting to question Tigellinus' taste.

Inside the stables at the western end of the hippodrome, meanwhile, hundreds of Christians were living out their last minutes in prayers and hymns. But leaning against a manger at the far end, one man was moaning uncontrollably.

"My fault! My *wretched* fault!" Hermes groaned again and again, kneading his hands into one another. "My own idiotic, hellish, foolish fault!"

"Nonsense, Hermes. It was an accident," Aquila consoled. "How could you ever know—"

"*My coals did it!*" the little Syrian suddenly stood up and shouted. "My simpering stove was *made in hell! It set fire to Rome!*" He yelled for the guards and bellowed out in a manic rage, "*I'm* the arsonist! *I'm* the killer! *I'm* killing all these people!"

He started raving, and Aquila reached out and slapped his cheeks several times. "Sit down, Hermes!" he commanded. "Compose yourself! Play the man!"

Hermes collapsed and started sobbing uncontrollably. Some minutes later, he looked up and remarked, coolly, "All right. I'm . . . back in control of myself, Aquila. Sorry about the scene." Then he added, with quiet determination, "But I'm going to do it."

"Do what?"

"I'll speak to the chief centurion and tell him I have life-and-death information for the emperor. Then, when he brings me to Nero, I'll tell him that I, alone, set fire to Rome. And I'll tell him how. Then he must release everyone else."

Aquila smiled at Hermes' naïveté. "That would be useless, dear friend. Nero must have his show. In fact, he'd either laugh in your face, or justify himself with a great announcement to the crowd. Can't you hear it now? 'Lest some of you doubt that Christians *did* set fire to Rome, here's the chief arsonist himself, confessing it all!' No, Hermes, don't give him that satisfaction."

"I don't know, Aquila. I think I must."

Out in the hippodrome, a detail of praetorians began dropping tall posts into holes that had been dug earlier along the circumference of the arena. Then they laid a *patibulum* or crossbeam at the foot of each to prepare for crucifixion.

"*The founder . . . of the Christians . . . died this way,*" the herald shouted. "*So should . . . all their leaders!*"

The captured clergy and elders of the Roman congregations were now paraded out into the arena. To the astonishment of the multitude, they were all singing a triumphant hymn, "*Christus regnat.*"

Then each was led away to a separate cross. Tigellinus leaned over to Nero and said, "See that one with the red hair just below us, getting his wrists nailed onto the crossbeam?"

"Yes . . ."

"His name's Aquila, one of their chief leaders. You may recall him from the trial of that Paul of Tarsus."

With a stinging jerk, two men hoisted up the crossbeam with its victim attached, stepped onto little wooden platforms on each side of the post, and lifted the crossbeam over and onto it, resting it snugly in its mortise. They took another spike, drove it first through a broad wooden washer, and then pinned both feet to the cross. Moving on to the next of the condemned, they repeated the process. With grim efficiency, the praetorians managed to crucify the forty leaders in just fifteen minutes.

"I'd say it was a record, Caesar," Tigellinus admitted proudly.

"And now they have the proper vantage point from which to watch the rest of the games. A touch of genius, Tigellinus! There's art in your planning." Nero lolled backward on his couch, staring with fascination at the bloody panorama before him while clutching a silk handkerchief to his mouth and neck to protect his voice from drafts. Glancing over at Poppaea, he wondered why she was so quiet.

On the opposite side of the stadium, a perspiring and trembling Plautia could no longer look at the appalling spectacle. She heard a quiet sigh and turned to see her mother blanch and faint across Aulus' lap, a lifeless heap of mourning garments.

"Enough, Father. Enough," Sabinus said. "You take the women home. They've seen too much already. *Far* too much. I'll stay on until the end."

Plautia made a feeble objection, but the aging senator, almost as sick as the women, nodded in resignation. Several of Sabinus' aides helped them out of the hippodrome and back to the Esquiline.

Now alone in his box and numb with revulsion, Sabinus felt one consistent emotion: a mounting, throbbing hatred for Nero and Tigellinus. Yes, Lateranus and his circle had the only real solution after all: assassination—the excision of two putrid members from the race of Roman man. But if only it had happened *before* all these useless deaths! He also felt stabs of self-recrimination: why hadn't he been able to divert all this that day in the imperial conclave? He, the chief officer of the city of Rome . . . as helpless before the tyrant as the lowest beggar.

His thoughts were punctuated by another flourish from the trumpets. *"Now let's teach . . . these Christians . . . our true national religion!"* the herald cried.

A burst of applause and cheering broke into the announcement, as strange-looking contrivances were wheeled out into the arena. Everyone knew the time had come for scenes from Greco-Roman mythology, always a popular feature.

"Ixion!" the herald shouted. *"Ixion, father of the Centaurs . . . tried to seduce Juno . . . whereupon Jupiter . . . bound him to a wheel . . . which turns forever down in Hades!"*

Now young men, by twos, were selected from the remaining victims and fastened onto opposite sides of iron wheels. While slaves worked gears that slowly turned the disks, the praetorians set fire to combustibles beneath each wheel. When these blazed up, there was just enough reprieve on the upper portions of each revolution to keep the victims from fainting so that they could experience the sensation of roasting to death above the flames.

"Daedalus and Icarus!" the herald cried. *"Their wings of wax . . . melted in the sun!"* Much whistling arose, for this act promised to be spectacular. This time the victims, always a man and a boy with flimsy cardboard wings pinned to their tunics, were attached by hooks to a rope pulley running to the top of Caligula's obelisk. Each time they would be hauled up almost to the top of the spire, where the hooks would open, dashing them to the ground. Several victims grabbed hold of the ropes when the hooks opened, but this only made more fun for the crowd, since the praetorians would wait until the victim was doing a mad hand-over-hand in trying to lower himself and then tug the rope back up again until he finally dropped from exhaustion.

Nero now nudged Tigellinus. "It looks as if your friend may be dying there."

Tigellinus peered at the cross directly in front of them. Then he shouted, "Don't die yet, Aquila! We have a final surprise for you!" Then he signaled the herald.

"A special treat!" he announced. *"Priscilla . . . wife of the leader of the Christians . . . as Dirce!"* Spectators drew in their breath. They knew that Dirce, Queen of Thebes, had been strapped to the horns of a wild bull for persecuting the mother of Castor and Pol-

lux. As a further refinement of cruelty, the herald added that Priscilla's husband Aquila was watching from his cross in front of the imperial box.

Sabinus grasped the railing before him. He felt nauseous. He had not known that Aquila, on the opposite side of the stadium, had already been crucified.

Several minutes later, a great white bull charged into the arena, desperately shaking its head to try to get rid of the naked woman tied tightly across its neck and horns. The bull charged wildly down the hippodrome until it came to Nero's box, where praetorians waved some brightly colored blankets to distract the beast and bring it to a halt. Wife and husband exchanged a final, meaningful glance. Then, completely maddened at the heavy load across its horns, the bull lowered its massive head and charged directly into the wall below Nero, killing its victim instantly. The figure on the nearest cross groaned deeply, shook, and then hung lifeless.

Aides told Sabinus what had happened—his view had been blocked by the spina—and he could only lower his head in rage, grief, and utter helplessness.

By now it was late in the afternoon and the shadows were lengthening. Tigellinus conferred with Nero, then dispatched new instructions to the herald.

"By now," he shouted, "you must all . . . be rather hungry!"

There was much head-nodding but also laughter, since many had quite understandably lost their appetites.

"Caesar has provided . . . dinner for all of you . . . in the gardens outside . . . The food and drink . . . will cost you nothing . . . if"—he paused—"if you return . . . after supper . . . for the climax . . . of these games!"

An enthusiastic roar thundered up from the massed thousands. Cries of "HAIL CAESAR!" and "GRATIAS, IMPERATOR!" ricocheted throughout the vast stadium.

Tigellinus turned to Nero and said, "I do believe your old popularity has returned, Princeps."

"Thanks to you, dearest friend," Nero fawned, then winked, "and the Christians! Come, precious Poppaea. A real feast is waiting for us, I understand."

Sabinus walked about in the Vatican Gardens, watching the plebes gulp down great quantities of food and wine, wondering how people who had just witnessed the gruesome, torturous deaths of almost 250 people could manage to find such an appetite. He carefully avoided the imperial table in the gardens, unsure if he could resist the burning impulse to haul out his prefect's dagger and plunge it into Nero—and Tigellinus, too, if he could possibly manage. He was starting to lose all hope for that species known as *homo Romanus* until, in the clusters of senators who had finished eating, he started overhearing some surprising comments, even from Nero's friends and leeches.

"He's overdoing it," said one.

"Any more and he'll make heroes of these Christians . . ."

"That woman tied on the horns of the bull . . . too cruel."

At an outer edge of the garden, Sabinus came upon a small group of republican senators clustered around Quintus Lateranus. When Sabinus appeared, they suddenly quit talking and looked up a little apprehensively. "It's all right," said Sabinus. "I'm one of you now."

Quintus smiled. "I knew you'd be, Sabinus. But for the moment, you should be one with us in spirit only, not in plans."

"Why?"

"Because you're too important as city prefect. We may need someone who is absolutely untainted by association with the likes of us." He smiled.

"All right, then. But you must let me know when the time is ripe."

"We will. And Sabinus, much as you may feel like it, don't even *think* of resigning as city prefect. Under *any* circumstances. Do you understand me?"

"Yes. I think I do." Then Sabinus added with a wry smile, "Besides, Nero won't let me resign."

While walking off, Sabinus took stock of the faces he saw huddled about Quintus. Senator Piso he recognized, as well as Senator Scaevinus and the poet Lucan, Seneca's nephew. And yes, it had to be—at the far end—the olive-tan face and balding scalp of Faenius Rufus, the *other* prefect of the Praetorian Guard! This would be no minor conspiracy.

A blistering trumpet on the upper rim of the stadium summoned everyone back inside. There was grumbling and jostling as people tried to find their places again. Many tripped in the darkness. Some were angry that others had taken their lower seats and they now had to climb higher.

Again they were trumpeted to silence, and the familiar voice of the herald boomed out: *"You are asking . . . why you returned . . . when you can see nothing?"*

A rumble of affirmatives showed that the people did indeed have the problem in mind.

"People of Rome! . . . Is there . . . a more appropriate . . . punishment for arson . . . than being burned alive?"

There was a shivering blast of cornets as pinpoints of flame began fanning out across the blackened hippodrome. They were praetorians clutching torches, over a hundred of them, racing into the arena until they formed a huge, oblong horseshoe of fire. Then, when Nero himself called out a *"Now!"* the praetorians touched their torches to the posts before them, and a hundred pillars of flame flickered into life and soon bathed the entire stadium in a bright orange glow. The people rose in a standing ovation for the spectacle.

But the posts came alive, and began crying out in piercing human screams of agony. They were Christians, each chained to the top of a post and wearing the *tunica molesta*, the notorious "troublesome tunic"—a shirt that had been heavily saturated in nitrates, sulfur, and pitch. The posts had also been steeped in a resin and oil mixture, and now served as gigantic wicks to illuminate the darkness. Most victims quickly crisped in the scorching, unbearable heat, choked on the smoke, and mercifully lapsed into unconsciousness and death. A few struggled with their chains before they succumbed, uttering prayers until the flames reached them. Their blackened bodies would continue carbonizing down to ash, for the posts would flame on for some three hours.

Nero was so impressed that tears of joy gathered in the corners of his eyes and trickled along the sides of that ruddy, bulbous ridge that was his nose. "Such art, Tigellinus!" he sighed. "Such beautiful, beautiful candles!"

Another trumpet. Another silence. Another announcement. *"Thanks, Christians . . . for enlightening us!"* The laughter was not as much as the herald had hoped. *"And now . . . Hercules in Flames! . . . But this time . . . we'll have the Danaides . . . put out his pyre!"*

The galleries laughed uproariously, for the fifty daughters of the Argive King Danaus were condemned to pouring water into a container down in Hades that was full of holes. Fifty men were now chained down onto separate pyres before the eyes of their terrified wives, and the pyres were ignited.

"Quick!" the praetorians urged the women. "Save your husbands! Take these buckets and bring water from the fountain over there."

The women grabbed the buckets and filled them. But each pail had been riddled with holes, draining all but a worthless splash.

High above the blazing scene, lofty and detached, stood the statues of the gods of Rome, each resting on a column that plunged down to the spina on both sides of the obelisk. From time to time Sabinus pulled his eyes away from the horror and looked up at this pillared pantheon. He almost thought he saw the great head of Jupiter smiling and winking at Vulcan in the glimmering scarlet of the flames, while the statues of the nymphs clustered about them were wearing gleeful grins.

The blazing panorama was too much for Nero. The flickering beauty of the flames and the sensational scenes he had witnessed that day made him, in a monstrously perverted fashion, almost jealous of the Christians. They, not he, had trodden the boards that day. They had put on the outstanding, if painful, spectacles. The actor in him was offended. He craved the eyes and plaudits of the people too.

Leaning over, he whispered something to Tigellinus. In a moment, the prefect had vaulted over the balustrade and was running down to the stables. Meanwhile, Nero, under cover of darkness but before the gaping eyes of Poppaea, crawled out of his purple toga and exposed the tunic he had been wearing that day. It was the garb of a charioteer in the colors of the green faction!

Tigellinus and several aides soon returned along the racecourse, leading a team of four horses hitched to Nero's golden chariot. Almost ecstatically happy, the emperor descended from his box, climbed aboard his quadriga, and took the reins.

The herald now announced: "As the final . . . presentation tonight . . . Caesar himself . . . will display his prowess . . . as charioteer! . . . Hail Caesar!" he saluted.

"HAIL CAESAR!" the crowd replied, their arms similarly extended.

Giving his snorting steeds a whack, Nero drove them in a furious run around the hippodrome, sweeping into turns he knew so well at dangerous speeds and cutting corners with abandon. Certainly he was showing off, he chuckled. But, then, he had so much to show off . . . such versatile talent. He whipped his horses to a frenzied lather, while careening about the course in a mad race with his own shadow. He arched backward as he stood in the lurching chariot, reins bunched in one hand, for that was the most graceful stance of the charioteer. The wind was in his face, the adoring people of Rome around him, and the flickering human lamps showed him the track. Some turns he took on one wheel. Several times he skidded and almost fell out of the cab. But each time, he always managed to regain his balance. For he led a charmed life.

Slowly, the people threaded their way out of the stadium. Some were debating when they had begun to sicken of the spectacle. Was it the poor woman tied to the horns of the bull? Was it when the wind changed and the nauseating stench of the human torches blanketed the galleries, those sickly-sweet whiffs of grilled flesh? Or was it the idiotically parading emperor himself, displaying his wheeled toy like some overindulged child and providing an incongruous close to what had been, after all, a monstrously grim spectacle?

Others started wondering about the Christian victims. They had only Nero's word that they were the arsonists. Had they really been destroyed for the public good? Or was it to glut one man's cruelty? Or to cover his cowardice? Or to hide his guilt?

That night, Sabinus returned to the stadium with one of his Urban Cohorts. They searched the smelly heap of bodies outside the western end of the hippodrome for any survivors, but they found none. Mercury, Pluto, and the demons had done their work with ruthless Roman efficiency. Sabinus and his men gave the victims a mass burial. And he was armed with a proper excuse if Nero protested that gesture: the city prefect was responsible for the public health of Rome.

26

IN THE DEAD OF NIGHT came an urgent rapping at Sabinus'
door. An hour earlier, he had returned, exhausted, from the Vatican
hippodrome and his eyes only half opened when his steward said,
"I'm sorry to bother you, Clarissimus, but a man and a woman are
waiting in the atrium to see you on an urgent matter."

Sabinus threw a robe about his night tunic and sleepily padded
out into the hall. Then he stopped in his tracks and bristled with
utter shock. There stood Aquila and Priscilla!

"Forgive us, Prefect," Aquila apologized, "but—"

"*Gods!*" Sabinus exclaimed. "But you . . . you headed the procession . . . the cross . . . the horns of the bull!"

"Let me explain . . ."

"Wait a moment." He ran out of the atrium and returned, dragging in Plautia who was only half awake. But one glance at the
pair and her eyes and mouth shot open simultaneously. "You . . .
both of you . . . how . . . a resurrection?" she stammered.

"No, Lady Plautia." Aquila smiled. "But I must hasten to explain."

"By all means!" Sabinus could scarcely believe his eyes.

"After I had conducted a final worship for our people in the stables at the hippodrome, a centurion called for Priscilla and me, and

we knew our hour had come. The officer was a secret member of our congregation who thought he could do more for us by *not* revealing his Christianity. Imagine our shock when we came to the main gates of the stables and the guard on duty merely saluted and let all three of us pass outside!

"Our centurion explained that the guard owed him a personal favor, and that a couple in prison who look very much like Priscilla and me would assume our names in case Tigellinus issued special orders regarding us. Priscilla and I thanked him, but we were on the point of returning to die with our people when he said, 'Your elders knew you'd never save yourselves, but they decided that you *must* escape to tell the story of the great Roman martyrdom.' He said the Christians were thrilled with the prospects of delivering us—it would make their last hours happier—and finally we agreed . . . We've been in hiding since then. But now we must know: what happened in the stadium after we left?"

While Plautia prepared refreshments, Sabinus reported the brutal events of the afternoon and evening. It was a corrosive experience for him, watching the horror burrowing into their lives, but when he finally had to tell about the cross and the horns of the bull, Priscilla broke into convulsive sobbing, while Aquila seemed on the verge of black despair.

As Plautia brought in food and wine, tears were glistening in Aquila's eyes. "We're . . . we're going back," he said. "We can't go free . . . not after what they've been through."

"Yes, we must bring comfort to our brothers and sisters still in prison," Priscilla added. "And then gladly share their martyrdom."

Sabinus disagreed. "Nothing would demoralize your friends more than to see you captured again after all their planning. *Don't* disappoint them."

Aquila slowly shook his head.

"Peter himself said the leaders must survive," Sabinus argued, "and there's no time for further delay. I hope you understand, Aquila, I will physically prevent your returning."

The couple looked startled, but saw only determination in Sabinus' eyes as he continued, "Now, you'll sleep here till morning. Then I'll give you money and whatever else you'll need, and my men will see you out of Rome. I'll write out a pass that will carry you to the East. Where will you go?"

For several moments they said nothing. Finally Aquila nodded and said, "Corinth. Yes, we'll go to Corinth again, and then try to rejoin Paul."

"Give him our fond greetings when you see him next," said Plautia.

"Prefect," said Aquila. "Thank you for trying so hard to avert this disaster, and thank you for your help now. Give our special farewell to beloved Pomponia and her husband."

About the time that Aquila and Priscilla were traveling safely down the Appian Way, Nero's games were beginning once again. Another capacity crowd had jammed into the stadium. While thousands of previous spectators were surfeited and had no stomach to return, their reports merely inflamed the dregs of Rome to besiege the entrances to the stadium from early morning.

The senatorial section behind Nero, however, was pockmarked with empty places, and he was on the point of suggesting that Tigellinus take a roll call of the Conscript Fathers. But he became too intrigued by the opening events, in which a pack of German bears was let loose on the procession of the condemned even before they had returned to the stables. There was a screaming stampede for the exit.

"Ah!" Nero smiled. "That was a new twist, Tigellinus!" Then, his emerald looking glass raised to his better eye, Nero noticed that the box of the city prefect was occupied once again.

Over the protests of all in the family, Pomponia had insisted on returning that day. "When my fellow Christians are dying," she insisted, "I should be at their side—at least to witness their triumph over death." Aulus and Sabinus found her last phrase incomprehensible, but they knew Pomponia would probably be worse off if she stayed at home.

Early in the again grisly afternoon, one of his aides came running over to Sabinus' box. "Quick, Prefect. Come with me. It's urgent."

Sabinus followed him out one of the exits and down to the sprawling stables where the remaining prisoners were being guarded. There he was met by a smirking Tigellinus. "Aha, Sabinus! I wanted you to be the first to know." He grinned. "Guess whom we have here? . . . Well, we finally found your fisherman after all. I trust you know Simon Peter?"

"Yes, I know him," Sabinus replied, as calmly as he could, though his heart was pounding. Depending on how Peter had been arrested, he himself might never leave the stadium alive. Yet he had to gamble that Tigellinus knew nothing of the pass he had supplied Peter, so he said, "Why don't you return to your butchery out there, Tigellinus, like the vulture you are?"

"Certainly, certainly." Tigellinus smiled. "Good friends are always allowed a parting visit." Then he left them.

"Where did they find you, Peter?"

"They didn't find me. I returned to Rome of my own accord."

Sabinus' jaw dropped. "Are you mad?"

"Jesus didn't escape when he saw the police coming into Gethsemane Garden. A servant is not above his master. Should I have tried to escape what awaited me in Nero's gardens?"

"Yes. You should have. For the future of your cause."

"The Faith is well seeded across the Mediterranean now, good Prefect. And I *know* the Master wants me to stay here in Rome."

"How do you know that?"

"Once, after his resurrection, He told me, 'When you are old, Peter, you will stretch out your arms and be bound fast, and be borne where you don't wish to go.' I'm old now. My mission is accomplished."

"The cross? Did he mean crucifixion?"

Peter nodded. "And in case I doubted that this was the time, let me tell you this: I was indeed taking the route you suggested—the one avoiding Rome—when I seemed to see Jesus in my mind's eye. He looked as he did on the way to his own cross, so I asked him, '*Maran, la'an att azel?*'"

"What does that mean?"

"'*Quo vadis, Domine?* Where are you going, Lord?'—It's Aramaic, the language we always used in Palestine.—And then he seemed to reply, 'I am going to Rome, to be crucified again.'"

"And such a *vision* brought you back to this inferno?"

"No, far more than that, Sabinus." Peter smiled. "I *must* share these sufferings of my people, also as a witness for the future. Though he doesn't know it, Caesar is accomplishing much today for the church."

More of that Christian logical nonsense, Sabinus thought. That faith loved to deal in paradoxes: enemies are loved, the first is last—the last is first, death brings life, defeat is triumph.

"I do have a bit of happy news for you, Peter," he suddenly

recalled. "Aquila and Priscilla were able to escape. They'll be joining Paul in Greece."

"The Lord God be praised." The apostle beamed.

"But is there . . . anything I can do for you, Peter?"

"Yes. I've left documents and instructions for the church inside
that large blue vase on your desk at Tibur. Please see that the surviving elders get them. And bid good-bye for me to your wonderful
family, especially dear Pomponia, and accept the thanks of all Christians for what you've done for us, Prefect."

"So little." Sabinus shook his head. "So pathetically, painfully little." He looked a last time into the leonine but kindly face of the
apostle and said, "Good-bye, Simon Peter."

"God bless you, Sabinus. Tell everyone *not* to weep for me, because my death is only the portal to a triumphant eternity with
Christ."

With that, several praetorians stepped over to take Peter down the
hall and thrust him into prison. Sabinus could hear the glad shouts
of joyful recognition mingled with moans that the apostle had been
arrested. But in several moments, all was quiet as Peter addressed
comforting and yet, Sabinus thought, victorious and bracing words
to his fellow prisoners.

By the time he returned to his seat, the grand announcement was
being made: *"The Galilean fisherman . . . the leader of these criminals . . . is now in chains . . . in this very stadium!"*

A great oohing and aahing welled up from the multitude.

"His name . . . is Simon Peter," the herald continued. *"He
stands . . . before the emperor."*

Amid thunderous waves of applause, Nero propped himself up
from his couch, grabbed his emerald, and studied Peter. "A big
enough fellow," he commented. "Otherwise unimpressive. How do
you plan to kill him, Tigellinus?"

"Crucifixion, of course." The commander smiled. "It seems so . . .
fitting."

"Did you torture him for additional information about the Christians?"

"Yes. A little. But he said nothing more than prayers to his god.
Besides, we really don't need any more victims, do we, Princeps?"

Nero smirked and then broke out laughing. "No, I suppose not.
How many will have died by the end of the day?"

"Total? Over the last two days? Between six and seven hundred."

"Well, that should just about rid us of the pestilence."

"Yes. We'll never hear of 'Christians' again!"

In the arena sands below the imperial box, Peter, clad only in a loincloth, was told to lie down so that his hands could be fastened to a crossbeam. "Would you do me a favor, Tribune?" he asked the officer in charge of the execution detail. "Crucify me head downward instead of the regular way."

"Why?"

"I'm not worthy to suffer in the same way Jesus the Christ did."

The tribune looked at him and smiled. "Sorry, old man. It just isn't possible to do it that way. Oh, it's *possible*, I suppose, but it's not very practical. You see, the crossbeam is mortised onto the *top* of the post there."

Peter nodded in resignation. They spiked his wrists to the ends of the crossbeam and hoisted him up to face the south, the sun, and the imperial box. Nero's courtiers vied with each other in shouting crude mockeries at Peter, but he ignored them. Apparently, even hanging on the cross, he seemed in an attitude of prayer.

The grotesque events continued throughout the afternoon. Ixion's wheel turned again, dogs tore into new groups of Christians gathered at the foot of Peter's cross, and victims dropped around him from the top of the obelisk. Each new group of condemned first looked to the apostle before undergoing their torture, and he made the sign of the cross over them with his head, as if imparting a final blessing.

Again it was too much for Pomponia. But this time, instead of fainting, she stood up in the city prefect's box, turned about, and held up her hands for silence.

"What kind of Romans are you?" she screamed. "Cheering while innocent people are dying? While children are strangled and women roasted? What kind of . . . *monsters* have you become?"

Aulus was startled and embarrassed over the scene his wife was creating. He rose to whisk her out of the stadium and take her home, until the force of what she was saying suddenly registered with him and he sat back down.

"Can you *really* believe that these innocent victims set fire to Rome?" she continued. "Look at me! Do *I* look like an arsonist? Because I'm a Christian too! Go on, then. Kill *me* too! And cheer like the bloodthirsty *beasts* you've all become!"

A swath of humanity in the north tier of the stadium within earshot had stilled to a hush, an almost guilty silence. Pomponia sat down, buried her face in her hands, and shook with sobbing. Sabinus summoned guards from an Urban Cohort and gave Aulus and Pomponia protected escort out of the stadium.

"I've never been prouder of your mother," Sabinus told Plautia.

"Nor I," she replied. Then she broke down and wept. "But why, Sabinus? Why? *Why?*"

Hermes had just been crucified opposite them. Sabinus feared that he might still try to confess his role in the great fire, but the little contractor was clearly a changed man. Peter had had some words with Hermes just before his own crucifixion, and now, far from losing control over himself, the Syrian, for all his pain, was actually regaling the multitudes with a long recitation of Nero's outrages, including details on the collapsible ceiling he had ordered for his mother's bedroom.

The sensational disclosures easily won him the sympathy of the crowd, and some discernible mood of pity was building also among people in the south tier. Nero and Tigellinus had overdone it again that day, and even the hardened, brutal mind can endure only so much horror. People began leaving the hippodrome in droves, and some of the more outrageous spectacles were starting to draw hissing and boos.

Meanwhile, the serenity of Peter's last hours was also affecting spectators. Late in the day, with his strength ebbing and his arms in agony, Peter looked at Nero, the senators, and magistrates during a lull in the executions and called out in a surprisingly loud voice for one presumed to be almost dead, *"We forgive you, Caesar!* We are all *innocent* victims. But still we pray for you. And forgive you."

Much of the tier quieted abruptly to hear the extraordinary statement.

Nero blanched and his lips twitched with ire. "I don't *need* your forgiveness, fisherman," he sneered.

"Oh, but you *do,* Caesar! The one sovereign God, who is above all, will judge you for all your crimes if you don't repent."

"What crimes, wretch?" Nero's naturally ruddy countenance now flushed to a deep crimson.

"Too many to list, Caesar. You know them. The whole Empire knows them. There is no form of murder you have not committed, no depravity or vice in which you have not . . . wallowed. You have stolen from Romans of every class. Your Senate sits there behind you now, cringing in terror before your tyranny. You are a *stench* in the nostrils of the world, Caesar!"

A muscle in Nero's left jowl twitched involuntarily and he nearly lost control of his bowels. Seething as he snorted for breath, Nero finally stammered, "Shall I have your tongue cut out, you prattling cultist criminal?"

"The truth will triumph no matter what you do, Caesar! Your rule is temporary . . . passing . . . a shadow. But the kingdom of God is eternal."

Petronius, who was sitting just behind Nero, was deeply impressed with Peter but shook his head in embarrassment at Nero's attempts to match wits with him. Tigellinus, meanwhile, whispered that it was beneath the emperor's dignity to continue any conversation with a condemned criminal, while Poppaea was tugging at her husband.

But Nero ignored them and cried, "Oho! *You* can make such lofty claims, fanatic fisherman? What have *you* accomplished in that miserable life of yours besides deluding a superstitious rabble into arson and treason? And now death too?"

"As for these innocent victims, you've only sent them to be with our Lord in paradise. For that . . . we even thank you."

"Oh, *shut up*, you . . . you maddened misanthrope!"

"A misanthrope hates mankind, Caesar. We Christians *love* humanity. Even you."

"Gods!" Nero whined petulantly. "The trumpets, Tigellinus. Have them blow some flourishes so we don't have to listen to this babble."

But the last hour of the afternoon made Nero increasingly uncomfortable. From time to time his eyes darted back to the cross on which Peter was hanging, and each time the apostle's eyes seemed to be riveted on him. Peter, however, was thinking back to the days in Galilee when someone had come up to him while he was casting fishing nets and said, "Follow me," and how he had done just that—down to the present moment.

But soon the superstitious Nero was so uncomfortable that he told Tigellinus, "Kill him."

When Peter saw a tribune approaching with a thrusting spear, he closed his eyes and said, "Blessed Lord, to be like you, even in this!

Receive my spirit." The tribune thrust his javelin deep into Peter's side. The apostle quivered once and then died. His head fell, but his eyes opened in death, and they were again focused directly on the emperor, for the pupils had snapped up toward the eyelids. But Nero was looking elsewhere.

Some minutes later, however, he glanced back at Peter's body and saw the unblinking eyes staring at him. "By the Furies!" Nero shrieked. "Get him off that cross, Tigellinus. Get him off!"

"What's the matter, Nero?" Poppaea inquired.

"I don't know," he said, cold beads of perspiration erupting on his forehead. "Haven't you . . . had enough of this, my dear?"

"Yes. Hours and hours ago."

"So have I. How many more prisoners are left for this evening, Tigellinus?"

"About a hundred or so."

"Well, you can burn them without me. We're going."

"Certainly, Caesar."

Just as he was climbing into the imperial litter, Nero leaned out and asked, "What sort of victims are left for tonight?"

"Men, mainly."

"Are they sturdy? Full grown?"

"Most of them."

"Then why don't you stop it all now? We can use them as slaves in building my Golden House."

"An excellent plan, Princeps." Tigellinus bowed, a perfect weathercock to Nero's wishes.

That evening, under the red-amber glow of their torches, Sabinus and his Urban Cohorts buried the second pile of bodies in a mass grave within a nearby cemetery, which lay along the Via Cornelia on the sides of the Vatican hill. He personally searched for the tall, burly frame of Simon Peter and found it rather easily. Did he imagine it, or was the horror playing tricks with his mind? But it seemed that the rugged features of the apostle had softened into a serene and slumbering face of peace. Sabinus washed Peter's body and reverently buried it in a separate tomb in the cemetery.

"May you enjoy that 'triumphant eternity' with your Christ, Simon Peter," said Sabinus, trying to mirror the apostle's words as a kind of oral epitaph. He himself could not really fathom the faith of the Christians. Jesus told his followers to turn the other cheek to enemies. And Peter had made his suicidal return into Rome to do just that. But he himself swore, on Peter's grave, that he would instead turn Nero's cheeks for him—round and round until that bloated bull neck of his was twisted and throttled in death.

27

IT WAS A CHILL, RAINY NIGHT in March of 65 that Quintus Lateranus and Faenius Rufus climbed the Quirinal for a secret conference with Sabinus. Plautia was whisked out of the library and told to keep all servants out of earshot.

"The time's come to tell you the names and the plans, Sabinus," Quintus confided. "Since Rufus here is one of us, we have *great* hopes for success."

"I should think so." Sabinus smiled.

"Tigellinus, of course, also commands the praetorians, but he's spent so much time on the Palatine he's lost touch with the troops. Rufus, here, sees them every day. Besides, two of the leaders in our plot come from the ranks of his officers . . ."

Sabinus' eyes widened. "Who?"

"Subrius Flavus and Sulpicius Asper."

"Aha! A praetorian tribune and centurion, no less."

"Poor Flavus is really champing at the bit," Rufus chuckled, while scratching his balding scalp. "Twice now he almost did Nero in. Once during the fire he came up behind him with a hand on his sword, and the other time he was going to garrotte him with a lyre string while he was performing."

"Why didn't he?"

"For the same reason that Nero continues to breathe today," Quintus replied. "Everyone wants Nero dead. But everyone wants to live on after the great deed!"

Sabinus smiled. "That's the 'sticking point' in any conspiracy. But proceed."

"Well, among the senators, the leaders are Piso, Scaevinus, and Quintianus."

"Yes, I saw them with you in the Vatican gardens."

"Now, we're all agreed that Nero must go. Beyond that, there's some division among us as to whether to replace him with another emperor or restore the Republic. Some want Piso as emperor *pro tempore*. Some are talking of Seneca. But for now, Piso will hold it all together and the takeover will be announced in his name."

"Why Piso?" Sabinus wondered. "Oh, he's a tall and handsome sort—"

"He's eloquent . . . comes from high nobility. Why do you ask?"

"Oh, nothing," Sabinus hesitated. "It's just that . . . do you really think he has the *character* to see it through? Piso seems to me more the pleasure-loving, passive sort. Lacking in firmness . . ."

"Right. My feelings too." Rufus was nodding. "But those very qualities may be a blessing when we want to replace Piso with the man we all finally decide on. Maybe Seneca. Maybe you, for that matter, Sabinus."

"Oh, please!" Sabinus held up his hands.

"Not unlikely," said Quintus, looking at him seriously. "Your name has been mentioned several times. But to continue: Seneca knows what we're doing and approves . . . tacitly, of course. He's a close friend of Piso, as you know, but he wants no part in the actual assassination."

"Can't blame him," said Sabinus. "Nero suspects him anyway."

"But his nephew Lucan, the poet, is heavily involved with us. Nero's jealous of his poetry and won't let him publish." Rufus smirked.

"Well, Lucan's also very republican in his themes," Sabinus commented.

"Anyway, those are the leading names," Lateranus explained, "and there are more." He went on to mention a dozen prominent equestrians, while Rufus identified six more of his officers who were party to the plot.

Sabinus was appalled. "But you have *more* than enough now. Each new member only adds to the risk of exposure."

"I don't think so," Quintus objected. "*Sixty* were in on the conspiracy against Julius Caesar."

"But they hadn't been plotting as long as you have. In fact, it's almost miraculous that your conspiracy hasn't been exposed already."

"Well, we're getting ready to strike," said Rufus. "That's why we're here."

"Oh, let's tell him the whole truth, Rufus. The fact is, we *have* to strike now, Sabinus, because the plot *was* almost exposed a week ago."

"Yes, that accursed woman just couldn't wait!" Rufus snapped. "Always hounding us for action."

"A *woman* is in on the conspiracy?" asked Sabinus.

"Her name's Epicharis," Lateranus admitted. "She's . . . quite a charming freedwoman—the mistress of Seneca's brother Mela. She tried to get the navy behind our plot by going down to Baiae and calling on Proculus to—"

"Our fleet captain?"

"Yes, he had some grudge against Nero. So she played on his wounded feelings and on his vanity—he'd go down in history, and so forth—if only he and his sailors would kill Nero during one of his vacations down there."

"Anyhow, Proculus turned the tables on the simple fool," Rufus sneered. "He went and told Nero the whole story."

"*Sweet Jupiter!*" Sabinus cried. "It's all over then!"

"Wait." Rufus continued. "The idiot captain forgot to ask Epicharis for the names of the other conspirators."

"So, when Nero summoned her, she put on quite a performance," Quintus interposed, "laughing away any thought of a conspiracy. It was only a lovers' spat, she explained. She had decided to end her affair with Proculus, and this was his way of repaying her."

"What did Proculus say?"

"Well, he's not entirely bright, you know. He just stood there with his arms hanging down, lamely insisting it was all the truth, but the dolt didn't have a scrap of evidence to support him, and there were no witnesses to their conversation."

"So Nero *believed* her?"

"We think so. At least he discharged her into loose custody. What's the latest from Baiae, Rufus?"

"My agents say he's making a few inquiries, but he's learned nothing at all. He doesn't have one name."

"Well, you'll obviously have to strike at once, then," Sabinus sighed. He put his fingers together in thought, then parted them. "Piso often entertains Nero at his villa in Baiae, doesn't he? Why not simply invite Nero to dinner there and do the job?"

"Exactly our thoughts, Sabinus. But we just had a meeting of all the conspirators at Piso's place, and he vetoed the scheme. For a host to murder a guest within his own home would be a sacrilege against the household deities, Piso claims. So we plan to do it here in Rome . . . at the Festival of Ceres on April 12. Nero always attends the opening games at the Circus, and so he'll finally be outside his villa and we can get at him. Now, I'm to make the first move. You know the passageway that leads to the imperial box in the north tier of the Circus Maximus?"

"Yes . . ."

"Well, at the end of the passage, I'll fall down at Nero's feet, as if begging him for some special favor. Now, I'm a fairly husky fellow, and I plan to reach out, grab Nero's knees and tackle him, pinning him to the ground while the others stab him to death. Scaevinus has reserved the privilege of striking the first blow. Then Rufus and the others will finish him off."

"You see, there'll be an interesting coincidence." Rufus smiled. "Most of my men in on the plot will happen to be Nero's guard that day."

Sabinus cupped his chin and paced about the library. Finally he smiled. "The plan has a simplicity about it that's excellent. It should work. Very well indeed. The key, of course, is Rufus and the bodyguard nearest the emperor. Scaevinus and the others will have to place their blows well lest some guards not in the plot try to save Nero."

"We'll control the others," said Rufus.

"So then." Sabinus grinned. "You're really going through with it, are you? And you a consul-designate, Quintus. My, my!" he trifled. Then he grew serious again. "All right, then. Where do I fit into the scheme?"

"At first we wanted you to send one of your Urban Cohorts into the area to support us," Quintus replied, "but that might get Nero suspicious. Besides, we won't need them. Your job comes *after* the assassination, Sabinus. Have only a small component of your police patrolling the city that day. Keep most of them in the Castra Urbana. The moment Nero's dead, we'll signal you from the Palatine by torches—the roof of the Tiberian palace. You'll immediately have your men stand for assembly. Make a careful speech, listing Nero's crimes, then announce his death, have your men swear allegiance to Piso's provisional government, and then send *all* your cohorts into the city—"

"To keep order at a very critical time." Sabinus nodded. "Yes. Good. Easily done. And I'm glad you've thought about what should happen *after* the assassination. Most conspiracies fondly imagine everything will solve itself once the tyrant's dead."

"It never happens." Quintus smiled grimly. "You can ask Brutus and Cassius about that!"

"In fact, I have only one worry about your plans, my dear plotting friends: I wish *tomorrow* were the beginning of the Festival of Ceres, not two weeks from now. All conspiracies have one great enemy . . ."

"What's that?"

"Time."

On the evening of April 11, Senator Flavius Scaevinus was returning to his mansion on the Esquiline. He had spent the afternoon with an equestrian friend named Natalis, and the two had rehearsed final details of the assassination. They had even practiced stabbing daggers through various thicknesses of cloth into a chunk of beef, seeing how much force was required to make a lethal penetration. Scaevinus looked anxiously at the sky overhead but then smiled at its limpid deepening purple. Hardly a cloud cluttered the horizon. Soon the stars would appear. Surely it would not rain in the morning, and the games for Ceres would take place as scheduled. And, if any just gods controlled the destiny of Rome, this would be Nero's last night.

His flabby frame had a certain vigor that evening, Scaevinus thought. Let his wife and friends tease him about his corpulence and various excesses. After tomorrow they would laugh no longer. They would learn that his was the mind that had first conceived the great strike for freedom—he had kindled the original flames under Piso and welcomed Lateranus into the plot—and soon all Rome would know that his blade had been the first to taste Nero's blood. Yet for now he must control himself. Though fidgety and nervous to the gut, he must register serenity and composure. But if only his heart would stop its reckless throbbing!

No sooner had he arrived home than his wife asked why he had ordered so elaborate a dinner for the household that evening.

"All will become clear later," he replied, with a twinkle. "Now, come to our suite, my dear. I've something to show you."

He opened a drawer and took out several documents. "It's my will. I leave everything to you, my darling." Then he called, "Milichus!"

His freedman aide appeared moments later.

"Here . . . witness my signing this." Scaevinus sat down and wrote his name with a flourish. Milichus then added his, and the senator sealed the documents.

"Why are you doing this?" his wife asked, with rising concern.

"I just want you to know you're always first in my thoughts." Scaevinus expected to survive the violence on the morrow, but this gesture would add to the heroism and drama of it all, he thought. Now he stood up, walked over to a trunk, and took out a sheathed dagger. Fondling the weapon, he slowly withdrew the blade from its scabbard and examined it.

"Family heirloom, Milichus." He smiled. "I consecrated it in the Temple of Safety up in Ferentinum. But it's old . . . and very blunt. Take it downstairs and sharpen it on the whetstone till its edge glitters."

The dinner that night was more of a banquet, with all its ostentatious food and drink. But through it all Scaevinus seemed moody. One moment he was obviously deep in thought, the next he was affecting a cheerfulness that was all too contrived. His comments were random and disconnected, and he drank more wine than usual. At the close of the dinner, he startled the household by awarding freedom to his favorite slaves.

Milichus thought this conduct all rather strange, but not as weird as the final orders he received from Scaevinus that night: "Prepare a pile of bandages for me, Milichus. And ligatures. And styptics for stanching blood." The senator was about to add, "And please don't ask me why," but found it unnecessary. He had given Milichus his freedom. For that he must never question his former master.

But questions were indeed churning through the freedman's mind as he assembled the first-aid supplies. Scaevinus' behavior pointed clearly to some mortal crisis the next day, and he had overheard enough comments from the senator in the last months to guess who might be the intended victim of a plot. He placed the sharpened dagger and the pile of bandages in front of Scaevinus' bedroom door and retired for the night.

But Milichus could not sleep. Turning toward his wife, who also was awake now, he voiced his thoughts about Scaevinus' mysterious conduct that day. "What does it all add up to?" he asked finally.

It took her only an instant to reply, "He'll try to assassinate Caesar some time tomorrow."

"That's it, of course. Now, help me solve this second riddle . . . I must *not* betray Scaevinus: he gave me my freedom and I must protect my patron out of gratitude. Yet I *must* betray Scaevinus: for if the plot miscarries—and from all those bandages, he doesn't seem too optimistic!—then I'm a dead man. It was I who sharpened the blade that will have been used in an attempt to murder Caesar. It was I who will have failed to warn him. Now, solve the riddle for me, dearest."

She thought for some moments, and then replied, "You forgot to add that Caesar would reward you handsomely for alerting him. He might even take you into the government for saving his life."

"Oh . . . I doubt that last."

"You must preserve yourself in any case. If Scaevinus was fool enough to perform as he did this evening, how do you know the other servants here aren't thinking exactly the same things we are? And if any one of them gets to Nero first, you *are* a dead man, Milichus: you prepared the bandages and yet you didn't warn him."

Milichus turned over in bed and said nothing for some moments. Then he whispered, "We'll steal out and go at daybreak."

Suddenly he vaulted out of bed and tiptoed down to the doorway of the master bedroom. Thank the Fates! The dagger was still there. Carefully he picked it up and stole back to his quarters. "We'll need this as evidence," he said.

28

BECAUSE the Golden House was not yet completed, Nero was still residing at his temporary quarters in the Servilian Gardens at the south of Rome. It was here that the lanky Milichus and his tiny wife arrived with the first roseate glimmer of dawn. The gates to the palatial villa were locked, and they pounded on the grating. Finally a sleepy gatekeeper stumbled out of his shack, stared at the improbable couple, and demanded, "What—by the Forge of Vulcan—do *you* want?"

"Let us in. We have *urgent* information for the emperor!"

"Don't we all? Go back home. You must be daft."

"But it concerns his personal safety!" Milichus persisted.

"You'll be concerned about your *own* safety if you don't clear out. You must be a pair of imbeciles, coming here at this hour!"

"Let . . . us . . . in, I say!" Milichus hissed. "Caesar's in danger! He must be warned! If anything happens to him, we'll accuse *you* of preventing us."

The gatekeeper cocked his head and smiled. "You have any idea how often we get warnings like this? And what are you doing with that dagger? Maybe *you're* the ones who are endangering Caesar."

"Do you want us to scream for the guards?" Milichus' wife chimed in. "We will, you know." Milichus gave her a swift pinch in the back, for it suddenly occurred to him that maybe they had already said too much. What if the guards were in on the plot too?

"Take 'em to Epaphroditus," a voice called from inside the gatehouse.

Presently another porter stepped out, the gate creaked open, and the pair was escorted into a vestibule of the rambling villa where they awaited Nero's freedman secretary.

Epaphroditus took his time about coming out to see them. First he ate a leisurely breakfast. Then the stocky, swarthy little Greek poked a pomaded head into the anteroom off the vestibule where they were waiting and inquired, "Are you two the bearers of the 'urgent information'?"

"We are . . . yes," said Milichus.

"Let's have it," Epaphroditus yawned.

When Milichus started listing the symptoms of conspiracy that he knew and the rumors he had heard in recent weeks, the sneer on Epaphroditus' face gave way to a look of alarm. "That's enough," he said. "Follow me. But I'll take that dagger, if you don't mind."

They were led up to Nero's suite. Several guards searched them at the doorway, and then they were admitted. Nero was lounging in his night clothes, eating a hearty breakfast.

"Sorry to disturb you, Caesar," said Epaphroditus, "but this sounds rather serious. Quite serious indeed . . . a plot against your life."

Nero scowled, threw down the piece of honeyed bread that he was munching, and wiped his mouth. "Who are they?" he demanded. "And who's involved?"

"My name is Milichus, Caesar. I'm a freedman of Senator Flavius Scaevinus. And this is my wife."

"Scaevinus' freedman, you say? Who wants to kill me? Tell me everything you know."

Milichus was detailing every strange gesture of Scaevinus the previous evening when Nero interrupted him. "If what you say is true, it certainly looks as though he was up to no good. But how do you know I was to be the victim? Did he say I was?"

"Certainly not. And he mentioned nothing of any assassination, of course. But my master has been critical of you, Caesar, very critical. He also belongs to a circle of senators who bitterly oppose you. And he has no other enemies. What would you have concluded? And why did he ask me to sharpen the dagger there which he endowed with religious significance if he had merely planned to use it for common purposes?"

"Let me see it," Nero said to Epaphroditus. Then he fingered the keen edge of the blade and winced.

"And lest you think this any idle accusation," Milichus resumed, "I suggest that you summon the senator himself. I'll be happy to repeat my charges in his presence." Such a confrontation was inevitable, of course, but Milichus' suggesting it served to strengthen his case, he thought.

"*Guards!*" Nero called. Several praetorians marched into the chamber and saluted. "How many of you are on duty at the moment?"

"The usual cohort, Caesar."

"Double the number. And take fifty men and go immediately to arrest Senator Flavius Scaevinus and bring him to me. Hurry! And send Tigellinus in here."

The guards saluted and left the chamber. In the interval, Nero sat lost in thought, staring at the yellowing morning outside while tapping the side of the dagger blade against his open left palm.

When Tigellinus arrived, Nero pointed the dagger at Milichus and said, "Repeat your story for the praetorian commander here."

Tigellinus listened to the tale with a dark, constricting frown until a sparkling glint took command of his eyes. He knew that soon, again, he would be playing his favorite role of high inquisitor.

Milichus had just finished retelling his story when Scaevinus himself arrived, flanked by columns of guards. As the senator saw Milichus, his eyes narrowed momentarily with horror and rage.

"Come in, Senator, come in," said Nero, still flipping the dagger blade across his hand. Then he stopped and held it up. "Have you ever seen this before?"

Scaevinus hesitated some moments while flushing fiercely. Then he regained his composure and said simply, "Why yes, Caesar. It looks like my dagger."

"Why did you ask Milichus to sharpen it?"

"The blade was getting blunt and rusty. It's an old heirloom from my ancestors and I keep it in my bedroom. My *ex-slave* here must have stolen it." He shot Milichus a glance of deadly hatred. "Why do you ask, Caesar? Why was I brought here?"

"Suppose we let your freedman tell us. Milichus?"

For the fourth time that morning, Milichus began his story, this time giving the fullest version he had yet offered, his wife adding details from time to time. All the while, Nero kept his dull blue eyes riveted on Scaevinus to see how he was taking the disclosure. When it was finished, Nero asked him, "What's the matter, Senator? You don't look very well. Not at all."

"For obvious reasons." Scaevinus now scowled fiercely. "Wouldn't you be ill, Caesar, if suddenly you heard Tigellinus here tell a pack of lies about you? This is an idiot's attempt at the great game of playing informer, but what a stupid and threadbare case you've presented, Milichus! You steal my dagger, sharpen it, and call it 'evidence.' You make a great affair of my preparing a will. *Great gods!* Must the implications be ominous when a person merely plays the role of paterfamilias? I adjust my will from time to time, Caesar. It means nothing more than that we live in uncertain times. Just last year, my place was almost destroyed in the great fire."

"All right." Nero nodded. "But what about your . . . strange timing in awarding freedom to your slaves?"

"Strange timing? May I respectfully remind all of you what today is? The beginning of the great Festival of Ceres! What more appropriate time than to honor the goddess of grain who sustains us all?— Well, I will admit another motive also, Caesar: my fortune isn't what it was. My creditors are pressing. I don't know if my will will hold. Better to give my favorites the liberty they deserve than have my creditors foreclose and take them over as slaves. Yes," he laughed, "maybe it was a bit of sharp dealing. But really, Caesar, you do understand, don't you?"

Nero smiled. "I'd have done the same thing, Scaevinus. But the lavish dinner?"

"That's the stupidest charge of all," the obese senator chuckled. "To this jealous ingrate I suppose it looked lavish enough. He still prefers his slave's beans and garlic. But I *always* dine that way"—he patted his paunch—"as you do yourself, Caesar. We're epicures. We love good food. Our tongues find it succulent even while our ears hear the hungry carpings of our critics."

"True enough," Nero tittered, looking down at his own swelling girth. "But what about all those bandages and ligatures, Senator?"

"You'll remember that was where my face was turning various colors during Milichus' servile slanders. The bandages, you see, are a bald and stark and total *lie!* I gave Milichus no such orders. His slave's mind tells him, 'Now if I cut up pieces of cloth, I'll claim they're bandages and use them as evidence.' He's taking us all for fools, Caesar. What would it prove if he delivered a whole cartload of medical supplies to you? Nothing more than my dagger there."

"That's true, of course. All right, the final charge is that Milichus overheard you and other senators making critical remarks of me."

"What sort of remarks?"

" 'The actor will soon go off his stage' . . . 'This lyrist must also give recitals for Father Hades' . . . that sort of thing."

"Lies. And in bad taste, too. You can tell a slave invented something so obvious as that. Oh, I'll admit to occasional criticisms, Princeps. I once called your verses . . . well . . . inferior. And in a group of senators, too."

"You *did?*" Nero frowned.

"Yes." Scaevinus nodded. "I said they were worthy of a Virgil . . . or a Horace . . . or even Homer, for that matter, but not of you, Caesar. You could exceed them all."

"Oh." Nero smiled, relaxing once again. "Then you didn't say my singing could 'harmonize only with the howling of Cerberus' three heads'?"

"Is *that* what he told you?" Scaevinus grinned, knowing, of course, that he had indeed said that very thing. "What a twisted mind in that knave! No, Caesar, if you take the lies of a villainous freedman over the word of a senator, things have come to a sorry pass. Milichus is a wildly ambitious wretch. He thought I should have given him a minor fortune along with his manumission. I did give him his freedom, and this is how he repays me: with a cock-and-bull story he thinks will earn him great rewards from you."

Nero slowly turned to the freedman. "Everything Senator Scaevinus has said suits the facts, Milichus. Do you have any other evidence, any *proof* for your charges? Anyone who can bear out what you say? Or infer?"

"The other servants saw what I saw yesterday."

"That's not proof, Milichus." Nero shook his head. "We get many rumors here. If we believed them all, we'd go insane. We have to have proof."

Milichus was agitated and now perspiring. He looked down and slowly shook his head. "I have nothing else. I . . . I was only trying to do the right thing and protect you, Caesar."

"You mean you were only trying to reap a fast fortune, Milichus," said Scaevinus. "I trust you'll punish him, Caesar. Otherwise, once this story gets out, every slave will be accusing every master in Rome. They've tried such tactics before."

"Have you any idea what the penalties for false accusation are, Milichus?" Nero was frowning.

But Milichus was not listening. His wife was whispering something into his ear. Suddenly he brightened and said, "Yes . . . yes indeed, Caesar. We *do* have what may be additional evidence. Before returning home yesterday, the senator had a long conference with Antonius Natalis. Now both Natalis and my master are on very close terms with Senator Piso, and Piso is the name we keep hearing in whispers. Why not question them too?"

Nero turned to Scaevinus and asked, "*Did* you see Natalis yesterday, Senator?"

"Well . . . yes . . . but it was only to discuss—"

"*Guards!* Take fifty men to the house of Antonius Natalis and bring him here immediately!"

Tigellinus leaned over and whispered to Nero, "This may be the chink in the affair. You have a golden opportunity to question them separately."

"I know, I know," Nero sniffed. "Now, Scaevinus, please continue. Tell me *exactly* what you and Natalis discussed yesterday afternoon."

"Ah . . . it was nothing of any secret or extraordinary nature"— Scaevinus chuckled—"the Festival of Ceres . . . the games . . . that sort of thing."

"How long was he gone, Milichus?"

"Most of the afternoon."

"Come, come, Senator. You'll have to do better than that." He was staring at him with crinkle-eyed suspicion.

"No, that was it, Caesar. We were planning a . . . a party for some of our friends in connection with the festival. That . . . and travel plans for the summer. Really, it was as simple as that."

"On what day is the party to be?" Tigellinus interjected.

"Ah . . . the last day of the festival."

"Who is giving it?"

"Well . . . it's at my place."

"I see," Tigellinus continued. "And where do you plan to travel for the summer?"

"Well, I was thinking of . . . ah . . . Greece."

"And Natalis?"

"He was speaking of Egypt."

"Very well. We'll see."

Natalis arrived a half hour later. When he saw his friend Scaevinus standing there also, his eyes tightened with apprehension.

"Natalis," said Nero, again beginning in a kindly tone, "what did you and Senator Scaevinus discuss yesterday afternoon?"

"I . . . I don't understand."

"I believe I was speaking plainly, Natalis." Nero scowled.

"Go ahead and tell him," said Scaevinus jovially. "Tell him about the party we were planning for the festival, Natalis."

"*Shut up*, Scaevinus!" Nero glowered furiously. "One more word or sign from you and I'll hail you up for high treason! Is that clear?"

Scaevinus nodded his perspiring head.

"Go ahead, Natalis. And look only at me."

"Ah . . ." he hesitated, "just as the senator said. We discussed a party. A party . . . yes . . . for the Festival of Ceres."

"When had you planned to give the party?" Tigellinus inquired.

Natalis hesitated. "Oh . . . soon. On the Ides. In the middle of the festival."

"I see," said Nero, without registering emotion. "And who is giving it? Where will it be?"

"At my place," said Natalis.

"And what else did you and the senator discuss?"

"Ah . . . we talked over . . . ah . . . property . . . investments . . . that sort of thing."

"A final question, Natalis. Were you and the senator planning any trips away from Rome this summer?"

"Uhh . . . no. We both plan to stay in town."

"*Guards!*" Nero shouted. Several praetorians advanced.

"Chain these men immediately! You're both under arrest for high treason and criminal conspiracy!"

Tigellinus barked several other commands at his tribunes: "Tell Rufus to march five praetorian cohorts over here at once and surround the entire villa! And bring torture equipment. All guards' liberties are revoked as of this moment. Do a security check throughout the villa!" Then he whispered something to one of the guards and finally added audibly, "Have the executioner erect his platform in the rear of the garden."

"And go out to the games, someone, and tell them I won't be attending today," Nero added, with a trace of regret in his voice.

"What shall we do with these men?" a tribune asked.

"Nothing. We're not through with them yet," said Tigellinus. "May I take over the inquiry, Caesar?"

"Certainly, Tigellinus."

"Now, gentlemen. You're lying about your conversation yesterday. We've proved that. Are either of you prepared—now, immediately—to reveal this entire conspiracy?"

Natalis looked down, but Scaevinus made the final effort. He raised a shackled hand and said, "What conspiracy, Prefect? It was only—"

"*No more lies!*" Tigellinus shouted. "We're finished with lies, Scaevinus. Only the truth. Only the truth from now on. We'll reward honesty with lenience."

Neither made any response.

"All right, then, the alternative is this: Caesar's life is at stake, so we'll stop at nothing to ferret out the facts." He paused, letting his face assume a vicious grin. "Do you recall how the Christians were tortured to death, gentlemen? I can assure you that their punishment will seem a merry romp around the gardens compared to what's in store for you if you don't tell us—immediately—all the plans, and all the names."

Neither said anything. Both were looking down at the floor. A guard signaled Tigellinus. He nodded. "Throw them on the floor and remove their sandals," he ordered. Suddenly Natalis and Scaevinus found themselves pinioned, while a guard brought Tigellinus a sword that had been heated over coals until it glowed.

"This," said Tigellinus, holding up the red-orange blade, "is only a little appetizer in the feast that awaits you, gentlemen. The main courses are on their way over here from the Castra Praetoria . . . a very delicious menu indeed," he said, with relish, "the scourge, pincers to claw your flesh, red-hot plates applied to your—well, you'll see. Honor of rank, Senator. We'll try the equestrian first."

Slowly Tigellinus approached Natalis' bare feet with the glowing blade. Natalis tried to take the searing pain stoically, until the tender arch of his foot began baking and he screamed at agonies he could not believe that painful. "*O immortal gods!*" he shrieked. "Stop it! I'll tell you."

"Everything?" Tigellinus inquired, not moving the blade.

"Yes. *Everything!*"

"All right." He pulled the sword away. "Take Scaevinus into the next room. We'll want it all corroborated separately."

As the senator was dragged off, Natalis actually assumed the offensive. "What you want is quick, solid information so that you can save Caesar, correct?"

"Precisely."

"And if I'd stall or tell you half-truths and not expose the whole conspiracy, you might not be able to save Caesar even now. So here's my bargain: I'll tell you everything I know—quickly and honestly—and you will grant me impunity."

"I can't promise that," said Tigellinus.

"I can," said Nero, now desperate for his own safety. "I pledge it, Natalis. Now tell us what you know."

Natalis was playing a reckless game, selfishly saving himself certainly, but also trying to limit the extent of the punishments. He would claim to reveal all the conspirators but would not do so in fact. He told of the plot at the entrance to the Circus, but did not mention Rufus or the praetorians. Yes, Piso was to be the new emperor. Quintus Lateranus was part of the plot too. And Seneca.

Nero's mouth dropped but then slowly twisted into a smile. At last he had the evidence he needed to put away his tutorial gadfly.

After the disclosures, Natalis was taken out of the chamber and Scaevinus brought in. Now, of course, it was simple to loosen the senator's tongue. Tigellinus simply led off with what Natalis had told him, suggesting that he merely wanted Scaevinus' corroboration. With everything in the open, Scaevinus saw no reason to remain silent, and he admitted other names in the conspiracy.

Within several hours, these, in turn, were summoned to the Servilian Gardens, confronted with the evidence, and falsely promised impunity for further information. With astonishing speed, Tigellinus had most of the names by nightfall, though no one had yet named Rufus, Sabinus, or the praetorian officers.

"That woman!" Nero suddenly remembered. "Get her out of custody and bring her here, Tigellinus."

"Epicharis! Of course! She's part of it, then. And a woman will never be able to take torture."

The guards brought the girl before Tigellinus, but she would admit nothing. He showed her the rack in the basement of the villa, where the torture equipment had been set up. She scorned it.

A leer on his face, Tigellinus ordered her stripped and then strapped to the instrument. He had her lashed with a scourge while he paraded the known names before the prostrate form now swelling with contusions. "We know they're all involved in your plot. But who else? Talk, woman!"

Epicharis said only, "It's all untrue. They're innocent."

"You half-witted incompetents," Tigellinus taunted the torturers, "you're letting a *woman* get the best of you!"

Now they wound the gears of the rack. Her limbs slowly stretched until her left arm popped out of joint. Epicharis shrieked and lost consciousness. When she came to, Tigellinus said, "That was only one joint. Three more to go. Who are the other plotters?"

"No one," she mumbled, after which she was stretched again until both her legs were dislocated. Then they threw the mercifully unconscious form into prison for the night. The next morning, while being carried back to the torture chamber in a chair, she managed to slip off her breast-band, hook it over the back of the chair as a noose, and strangle herself.

Epicharis would quickly find her way into Roman legend, the woman and ex-slave who did not betray others under the most intense agonies, while freeborn men, untouched by torture, were hastening to betray friends and relatives in a mad effort to save themselves. Seneca's nephew Lucan, the poet, had even named his own mother as a conspirator, though no one took him seriously.

Nero, meanwhile, was horrified at the lengthening list of conspirators. What he had imagined as merely a private grudge of several in the nobility was blooming into a broad and devastatingly dangerous plot against his life. Tigellinus surrounded him with a triple guard of only his trusted minions, while he garrisoned the walls of Rome with praetorian cohorts, occupying even the coastlands and river banks. Until the plot was fully exposed, they had no idea if attack from the outside were imminent. Nero placed special confidence in his German cavalry, foreigners who were paid by—and trusted—him alone.

Earlier on the day set for Nero's assassination, while Sabinus waited for the signal from the Palatine and could not know the plot was miscarrying, Quintus Lateranus hurried down to the Forum to bring Piso news of Scaevinus' arrest.

"We now have only one option left," Quintus told Piso. "We must dash to the Castra Praetoria and have Rufus and his men declare for you. Then we march back here with the entire Guard. You'll mount the rostrum and win over the people. Sabinus will fall in with his Urban Cohorts. Then it'll be Rome versus the praetorians on duty protecting Nero. We'll win!"

"I . . . I don't like it, Quintus. Too risky."

"*Risky?!* With Scaevinus and Natalis probably revealing the whole plot, naming you as Nero's successor? What other course is there?"

"I . . . don't know. How do you know they'll talk?"

"Torture. Neither of them is man enough to take it."

Still Piso said nothing.

"Look, we're all destroyed if we don't act, Senator. It's our one and only hope," Quintus pleaded. "You'll see: Nero *has* to collapse. By all the gods, if competing lyre-players terrify him, how about rebellious praetorians!"

But Lateranus could see from the perspiration on Piso's pallid face that he was losing all nerve. Hesitantly, Piso stopped a passing plebe and asked him, "You . . . what would you say if Piso became your next emperor?"

The commoner looked up at him and wrinkled his brow. "Piso? Who's Piso?"

A defeated look on his face, Piso said, "See, Quintus . . ."

"That proves *nothing!* We must act!"

"I . . . I'm going home now, Quintus. I'm . . . sorry. Very sorry. You'd better do the same."

While Lateranus stood gaping, Piso walked back to his town house and wrote out his will. It was riddled with loathsome but necessary flattery for Nero, necessary because he wished his wife spared. Then he heard the sounds of troops surrounding his house. Looking out, he saw that they were all young praetorian recruits. So! Nero didn't trust his veterans—as well he might not!

Piso hurried inside his bedroom, propped up his legs and trunk on the bed with pillows, and let his head and arms dangle over the side. Then he nodded to a servant, who carefully slashed the arteries in both arms from the wrists upward.

Quintus had just stepped inside his mansion on the Caelian and kissed his wife when the place was suddenly surrounded by praetorians. The tribune Statius entered and announced, solemnly, "Quintus Plautius Lateranus, I have here the order for your immediate execution, signed by the emperor."

It all seemed miserably unreal to Quintus, that the sweet adventure called life should end because Fate seemed blind to the proper course of Roman statecraft.

"May I choose my own death?" he asked the tribune. "It *is* traditional, you know."

"Sorry, Senator. My orders are immediate execution by the sword. I'm also ordered to take possession of this house in the name of Caesar."

"I understand. But my wife and children are to be spared, certainly. They have no idea what this is all about."

"I have no orders concerning them. I assume they'll be untouched."

"Very well, then. May I . . . bid my children good-bye?"

Statius, shaken by emotion and almost breaking into tears, said, "I . . . I'm sorry, Senator. Caesar said, 'Drag him off to the Sessorium the moment you set foot in his house!' It's too long already. My men could report it . . ."

Quintus gave his sobbing, almost hysterical wife a tender kiss and said, "Tell the children how much I loved them—and you, carissima. Some day, too, tell them . . . what I tried to do for the state."

In all her agony, she still managed to nod her quivering head.

"And tell that twin brother of mine to look after you. *And* the cause!—He'll understand." Then he let Statius and his guards drag him off to the Sessorium, a place just outside the Esquiline Gate reserved for the execution of slaves. The tribune himself, trembling and threatening again to give way to tears, whispered to Quintus as he bent over the block, "Thanks, noble friend. I'll imagine it's Nero under me when I swing."

Saying not a word, Quintus stretched his neck across the block.

That night, Statius wept the bitter tears he was holding back. He himself had been a prime conspirator, but Lateranus had maintained a resolute silence about it. The noblest of the plotters was dead.

Sabinus, meanwhile, had been keeping his cohorts on alert inside the Castra Urbana, while waiting anxiously for the fire signal from the roof of Tiberius' palace. A flaming torch was to be waved back and forth three times if Nero were killed, but ten times if he were only wounded or the plot miscarried—the signal to be repeated twice for accuracy.

Sabinus' eyes strained as he watched the Palatine minute after minute, but he saw only the clear cerulean of an April sky atop the palace. Nero had been expected to enter the Circus Maximus at mid-morning, but it was now an hour later than that and still there was no signal.

Another hour passed. His nerves tingled. His armpits dampened. How much better to have been at the Circus waiting for Nero than linger, safely but helplessly, in an agony of anticipation. Again his eyes flashed toward the palace, but, other than one fleecy cloud blooming up on the southern horizon, there was nothing.

Suddenly, the jangling rhythmic thud of marching men filled the eastern end of the Forum. He looked and saw praetorian cohorts marching south around the Palatine. This was *not* part of the plan! One . . . two . . . three cohorts. Going where? The Circus Maximus? Now there were *four* cohorts.

Still no signal. Something must have gone desperately wrong if they forgot even to signal the plot's failure. Sabinus climbed down from his pinnacle, canceled the alert at the Castra Urbana, and committed the normal number of police cohorts to the streets of Rome.

When he returned to city headquarters, Rufus' closest aide, the tribune Flavus, was waiting for him, ashen-faced and trembling, his great mound of blond hair disheveled from haste. He reported the whole story of the plot's exposure to that moment, culminating in the latest word: Piso's suicide, Lateranus' execution.

Rippling with horror, Sabinus staggered backward and slumped into a chair. His face was pebbled with perspiration and blotching with anger, dread, and despair. He felt nauseous as his heart galloped recklessly.

"That histrionic idiot!" he finally muttered.

"Who?" Flavus inquired.

"Scaevinus." He spat the name out as if it were a piece of wormy apple. He wanted to pommel the flabby body of the ostentatious and theatrical Scaevinus until it was a battered heap, for it was his showy stupidity that would now rain more deaths on Rome. But the maelstrom of moods ripping through him seemed to change by the moment. Now grief eclipsed vengeance: cousin Quintus Lateranus was no more. That lovable rascal with the blazing sense of humor who had also made him rich was *dead!* The Twin Brothers had been cut apart. There would be no more financial triumphs for the Gemini. Castor . . . or Pollux—they never did decide which was which —had gone to the gods. How would he ever tell Plautia?

"Tell me, Tribune," he asked Flavus, "is your commander . . . planning anything further . . . so far as Nero's health is concerned?"

Flavus caught the meaning perfectly. "No, Prefect, quite on the contrary. Rufus never even *heard* of the plot now. By philandering Jupiter, if *only I'd* had sense enough to stab that swine when I had the chance! But I've got to leave now, Prefect. They want me over at the Servilian Gardens."

"*Vale*, Flavus." Then Sabinus added, "If you ever find yourself in such a position again, thrust, my man, thrust!"

"I will, Prefect. I'll try hard to find that black heart of his beneath all the lard! *Vale.*"

Sabinus left shortly after him for the Quirinal. His roiling thoughts had difficulty finding any mooring. Now he was even beginning to hate the gods of Rome. He had never believed in them since childhood, of course, but now he resurrected them only long enough to hate them cordially. Jupiter and his crew had let Rome burn herself to ashes, and later they had not intervened while hundreds of innocents were slaughtered. And now they had spared a murderous tyrant with disastrous consequences. No, the gods didn't exist. Gods like that didn't deserve to exist. For that matter, the god of the Christians—milder and more logical as he seemed—was also, evidently, powerless before some higher, impersonal force. Perhaps Fate?

No sooner had Sabinus stepped inside their house than Plautia rushed up to him, sobbing, as she twined her arms around him, burying her face in the folds of his toga. She had learned the tragic news about her favorite cousin in a cruel fashion: Quintus' widow and children, beside themselves with grief, had arrived on the Quirinal earlier to beg shelter.

Aides were arriving hourly with reports that other conspirators were being rounded up. His own prospects heavily shrouded in black, Sabinus quickly wrote out his last will and testament and prepared himself for the end as best he could. He went over all the alternatives with a weeping Plautia. Flight from Italy? It was too

late for that. Turn state's evidence to save himself? Unthinkable.
Revolution? Earlier, perhaps, but now it was no longer possible.

Actually, the only very slender hope of emerging from the disaster
intact was to pursue "business as usual." When his affairs were arranged, Sabinus gave Plautia a long, tender, and meaningful kiss.
Then he hurried back to city headquarters.

Columns of manacled prisoners were arriving at the gates of
Nero's villa and the trials had begun—brief, emergency affairs which
assumed all defendants guilty until proven innocent. Nero sat behind a judiciary table, flanked by his assessors: Tigellinus, a senator
named Nerva, and Rufus, who was flooded with conflicting emotional currents. He tried desperately to mask his own role as a leader
of the plot by fiercely browbeating his fellow conspirators, praying
all the while that they would be gentlemen enough not to expose
him.

Finally the flaxen-haired Flavus, who was standing at Rufus' side,
could stand it no longer. "Thrust, my man, thrust!" Sabinus had advised. Nudging Rufus, he gave him a wide-eyed look while his hand
went to the hilt of his sword. Rufus caught the message: "Shall I
kill the tyrant here and now? Can you control the praetorians in this
place?"

Rufus thought for an instant, almost breaking under the strain of
history waiting for his decision. Rome's destiny would be altered by
a movement of his head one way or the other. His heart pounded
and his body bathed itself in sweat. In a crisis, take the safest course
—the old rule. He shook his head at Flavus. The tribune's hand
dropped away from his sword. Nero would live on.

Retirement had been kind to Annaeus Seneca. He had been traveling in southern Italy with his beloved Paulina and penning his
finest Stoic treatises, the *Moral Letters*. But on the very day set for
Nero's assassination, he had returned to his villa just four miles
south of Rome.

Now he was reclining with his wife and two friends at dinner,
trying to take in stride news that the conspiracy had failed. He himself should have provided leadership in the plot, Seneca sadly realized. Then it might not have come to grief.

Halfway through their simple dinner, they heard the clatter of
troops surrounding the villa. A tribune burst inside and announced

the charges against the aging philosopher. One last play in the game of life, Seneca thought. He rose serenely and responded to all the charges against himself with a witty defense.

Leaving his cordon of guards, the tribune returned to Nero with the message. The emperor asked him, "Did it seem as if Seneca was . . . preparing to take his own life?"

"Not really. At least I saw no . . . sadness in his words or looks."

"Then go back and announce the sentence of death to him, Tribune. Only him. No one else."

When the tribune returned with his fatal message, Seneca's wife Paulina broke into tears, and their two friends joined her.

"Why should this surprise you, dearest friends?" the philosopher frowned. "Everyone knows about Nero's cruelty. After murdering a brother, a mother, and a wife, what's left but the destruction of a guardian and a tutor? But enough of tears," he huffed. "Where are the maxims of our philosophy? If Stoicism teaches anything, it tells us how to meet misfortune."

Then he turned to his wife and embraced her tenderly. "Don't mourn, lovely Paulina. Well . . . only a little while for appearance's sake. Console yourself with virtue."

"I . . . I've decided to die with you, dearest."

"I won't have it, Paulina." He stroked her hair.

"I must."

"Noble, but unnecessary."

"I have *resolved* it, Annaeus. We will not be separated in death."

Seneca looked into her eyes. They were cool and firm with determination. "So?" he whispered. "Do you really prefer the glory of dying too?"

The tiny mouth of the handsome woman smiled serenely and she nodded.

"I won't begrudge your setting so noble an example, precious Paulina. May your courage in death outshine mine"—he smiled—"and win eternal praise."

Together they drew a knife across their wrists. Then he kissed Paulina good-bye, and bade her retire to the bedroom lest they weaken at seeing each other suffer. Unbeknown to Seneca, the praetorians would check her bleeding—against her will—and bandage her arms. She would live on.

As his life drained away, Seneca called in a secretary and dictated his final thoughts for posterity. "See that the city prefect, Flavius

Sabinus, gets this and all my other manuscripts," he told him. Then he added, wistfully, "Nero and Sabinus were my two greatest hopes in life. *One* succeeded, the Fates be thanked!"

Now he asked his physician for poison hemlock—Socrates' last drink—but even that had little effect, for his spare and aging body failed to absorb the drug. Finally, he ordered himself carried into an overheated bath.

"My offering to Jove the Deliverer!" were his last words. Suffocating in the steam, the sixty-nine-year-old Seneca collapsed and died.

Nero's tribunal ground on relentlessly. It was during a second, intensive questioning of Scaevinus that Rufus overplayed his role as inquisitor, browbeating Scaevinus mercilessly. Finally the perspiring senator had enough of Rufus' dual role as accomplice and yet judge. "Oh, that's enough play-acting, Rufus!" he sneered. "No one knows more about the plot than *you* do! Show your gratitude to so 'good' a prince! Go ahead and tell him, Rufus. Tell him *everything!*"

Blanching with terror, Rufus tried to stammer out a denial, but he was a military man, not an actor.

Nero's heart almost stopped in horror. Vaulting up from his chair, he ran over to Tigellinus and clutched him like a frightened child. "Sweet goddess Roma!" he bawled. "Not the man who's been sitting next to me at the tribunal! My own bodyguard! *Gods!*" He cringed.

"*Guards!*" yelled Tigellinus. "Seize the Prefect Rufus and bind him fast. Triple sets of fetters!" Then, turning to Nero, he said, "Maybe now, Caesar, you'll realize that my suspicions of this . . . reptile were not ill-founded."

"Here I thought you were only jealous of someone sharing your rank, Tigellinus," Nero whimpered. "Who *else* among the praetorians is involved?"

In a short time they had discovered them. Flavus and Asper gave a much better performance than the cowering Rufus. When they were hauled up before Nero, the tawny-haired Flavus objected, "Me? Do you really think a rough army type like myself would associate with this . . . ladylike Scaevinus and his fairy friends?"

But when pressed, the tribune made a glorious confession of his whole role in the plot. "Yes, Caesar, three different times I planned to kill you: once, when you were holding a long and very sour note on stage . . . the second, during the great fire . . . and then here at your tribunal."

"Why, Flavus?" asked Nero, his mouth quivering.

"Because you preferred playing butcher, or buffoon, or pervert to emperor."

Nero clutched at the arms of his chair and clenched his teeth. "And you, Asper?" he finally managed. "Why did *you* try to murder me?"

The centurion replied coolly, "It was the only way I could really *help* you, Caesar."

A great vein swelled up across Nero's forehead, and his face darkened to a turgid purple. He opened his mouth several times to say something, but brought up only frothy grunts. Finally he signaled the guards by swinging a flat, trembling hand across his own neck in the "cut" gesture. Both men were dragged off into the garden and decapitated.

Then it was Rufus' turn, later Lucan's, then Scaevinus'. The final total stood at nineteen deaths, twelve senators exiled, and four praetorians degraded in rank.

So much for punishments. As for rewards, the freedman Milichus was lavished with gifts and the term Soter ("Savior") was added to his name. Nero awarded triumphal honors to Tigellinus and other officers who had helped expose the plot. Honors should also have been due the city prefect for keeping Rome secure at a critical time, but Nero did not single Sabinus out for any special award. Tigellinus, in fact, had fondly hoped that someone would raise Sabinus' name in connection with the plot. But Sabinus' only bridges to the conspiracy had been Lateranus, Rufus, and Flavus. They had not exposed him, and all three were dead. Amid the fountains of blood that had splashed across Rome's governing circles, he had survived.

But Sabinus was not particularly grateful to Destiny for that survival. The inner logic of existence was fading in Rome, he thought. The man who should have died did not. Instead, hundreds of slaves and hundreds of Christian victims had been tortured and killed. And now, too, patriots like Quintus, philosophers like Seneca, and a circle of Roman statesmen had been cut down. *Madness!*

Time, high time, to do something about that madness. Sabinus stalked out of city headquarters and crossed into the Forum. It was twilight, and the place was largely deserted. Wandering among the monuments and columns that were the very heart of the city and the Empire, Sabinus felt almost tangibly the judgment of Rome's glorious past against her murky present. Each pillar seemed to issue its separate challenge to him. He and his bystanding friends had wrung their hands while gazing with alarm for too many months, no, years, now, and even those who had just acted should have done so earlier —and successfully. A true tyrant can never be cut down too soon. But past was past.

Now he was standing before the great marble columns of the Temple of Castor and Pollux, wedged into the southern base of the Palatine. Inevitably he thought of Quintus and his last message through his wife: "Tell that twin brother of mine . . . to look after the cause. He'll understand." Yes, he understood well enough.

Climbing up the steps of the deserted temple, he paused before the magnificent bronze statues of the Gemini, and his eyes filled with tears as he recalled several of his escapades with Quintus. Then it suddenly occurred to him: for centuries, Rome had regarded Castor and Pollux as guardians of her liberty. Vengeance now buried grief.

"All right," he finally resolved out loud, "enough of Flavius Sabinus the passive protagonist. Everyone else has failed, but I shall succeed. I *will* overthrow Nero. I will do it legally or illegally . . . peacefully or violently. But the tyrant must be toppled. And if he resists in the slightest"—he paused and almost reverently drew out his prefect's dagger—"then this must assist me. I swear by my ancestors and for my children, I must then kill him. For the Senate, for the people, for Rome, I *must kill Nero*."

29

IT WAS A LATE AFTERNOON in May when Pomponia jumped down from her litter and rapped on the door of her daughter's house on the Quirinal.

"Paul is back in Rome," she told Sabinus, "Paul of Tarsus."

"What? He couldn't have come back at a worse time. Where's he now?"

"At the Castra Praetoria. He was arrested."

"I . . . I'm sorry, Mother." Sabinus shook his head. "I doubt if we can save him this time. You know why."

"I know, Sabinus. Just . . . do what you can."

Sabinus went over to the Castra and peered into the darkness of the dungeon, trying to locate the apostle, when he heard the rattle of chains.

"Prefect," a familiar voice from the shadows called out. "How *very* kind of you to come." Paul was walking toward him from a corner of the prison, carrying part of his chain so it would not make so much noise. Sabinus saw that unmistakable wiry face looming out of the darkness, and the pointed, prying gray beard.

"Hello, Paul. Despite all this you look well. Are they giving you enough to eat?"

"Not always so tasty, but always enough." Paul smiled.

"What happened? Why were you arrested again?"

"It was in Ephesus. At one time I thought I'd never return there—and the way matters developed, perhaps I shouldn't have! But the church in Ephesus is so important for all of Asia that we couldn't tolerate what was happening."

"Persecution?"

"No, the Christians there were being perverted by a false teacher named Alexander. Alexander the Coppersmith. He used to be a Christian, but he got caught up in Gnostic philosophy. Then he tried to subvert other Christians there, so Timothy, Luke, and I had to step in. The Ephesian church finally excluded him from membership. It's an unhappy story, Prefect. Alexander grew so resentful that he formally indicted me before the Roman governor of Asia."

"And again you invoked your Roman citizenship to appeal to Caesar?"

"I'm not sure that would have been so wise." Paul smiled. "No. The governor himself sent us both to Rome, Alexander to repeat his charges here. You see, he knew Caesar had persecuted the Christians, and he wasn't clear on their present legal status in the Empire. So he wanted to make no decision one way or the other."

"When does your hearing take place?"

"It already has."

"What! When?"

"Shortly after my arrival six weeks ago."

"Why didn't you let us know about it, Paul? I'm not sure we could have done much . . . but we could have tried."

"At the time, I was allowed no contacts outside the prison. But even so I wouldn't have bothered you."

"Why not?"

"Because my time has come, Sabinus. And you were all . . . concerned about the recent crisis here in Rome."

"Well, what happened at your hearing? Who served as judge?"

"Nymphidius Sabinus."

"The new praetorian co-prefect? Rufus' successor?"

"Yes. Caesar and Tigellinus didn't want to be bothered with my case again, so they turned it over to Nymphidius and several assessors. They wanted to 'give him judicial experience,' so I'm told." Paul smiled.

"What happened? How did they decide?"

"Well, Alexander the Coppersmith did his worst, painting me as a seditionist, a rabble-rouser, but above all, as an arsonist. He thought he was being shrewd with that charge, since Nero himself tormented us for that. So he said, 'This man is guilty of complicity with those who burnt your city.'"

"Who defended you?"

"No one. Several witnesses I'd hoped to summon all deserted me. May it not be held against them.—But the Lord stood by me, and I showed the judges how ludicrous it was to believe that I, in faraway Ephesus, had touched off the flames that consumed Rome. A fuse almost 900 miles long?"

Sabinus chuckled. "He didn't absolve you, then?"

"No," Paul said wistfully. "Not enough *A* tablets this time! The vote was *NL* . . . 'not proven.' So my trial is postponed for further evidence."

"Any idea when the next hearing will be?"

"No."

Sabinus nodded. "They'll probably get Alexander to drop the arson charge and focus instead on your being the leader of an illegal sect. And ever since the persecution, this has been impossible to refute, Paul. I'll tell you candidly: your fate is beyond any of the courts. It's all in Nero's hands, now. Oh—'and God's', I'm sure you'd add."

"You're learning, friend." Paul smiled.

"I doubt that." He shook his head. "I'm far from a Christian, Paul." Then, leaning close to the grating so no one else could hear, he asked, "How can anyone believe in a supreme god who lets Nero live on while Peter and hundreds of your Christians died—horrible deaths?"

Paul looked about cautiously, then whispered, "You can't imagine how many of our members were *not* seized! We're also finding a new attitude toward Christians in Rome—'pity' or 'sympathy' would be too strong a word—but we feel it, Sabinus. Romans are embarrassed at what Nero did to us. It was all *too* violent, *too* horrible. Luke is back in Rome again, and he reports inquiries about the Faith *because* of the persecution—good pagan Romans wondering how people could die with that sort of courage and conviction."

"Still, I'd advise you all to be very careful, Paul. By the way, how are our friends Aquila and Priscilla?"

"Fine. They're guiding the church in Ephesus now. We'll need their strength when Alexander returns. They want to be remembered to you, of course. They owe their very lives to you."

"I admire your conviction, Paul. You don't think of yourself, only of your 'future church.' Well, I'll make whatever discreet inquiries I can about your case, but I'm afraid there will be . . . so little to promise. Send Luke over from time to time. He can be our contact."

Paul clasped Sabinus' shoulder through the bars and smiled his gratitude.

The Neronia festival was approaching once again. The thought of Caesar returning to the stage, always a disgrace to the state, particularly irked the Fathers in view of the political funerals that year. But Thrasea Paetus found a deft solution. He stood up in the Senate and said, "I propose that we award Caesar the victory in advance of the games—he will surely win anyway—and now he need not even compete."

"*Euge! Euge!*" the senators agreed, and then voted it into law.

Nero was less than pleased with the news. "I *don't need* any special favors—least of all from the Senate," he pouted. "I'll win my honors by merit alone."

Eagerly he returned to the stage, this time shod with high-soled buskins to improve his stature. In bowing to the opening applause, Nero was delighted to note that Sabinus was not only sitting in the city prefect's box adjacent to that of Poppaea but had brought along his brother Vespasian. Now, costumed in rags and fetters, Nero launched into a spirited rendition of *The Frenzy of Hercules*.

Sabinus rippled with repugnance at Nero's theatrics but coolly masked it, for he was attending, not as spectator, but as hunter, stalking his prey. He now wanted to observe every last trait, each mannerism of his quarry so he could learn where Nero was vulnerable and attack successfully where others had failed.

Nero was now pleading so plaintively for help in *Frenzy* that a young praetorian, standing on guard in the wings, actually rushed on stage to assist him. "No, no, you fool!" Nero snapped. "It's just an act."

Sabinus was trying to smother his laughter when he heard a woman's voice near him wondering out loud, "By all the gods, when will he *ever* shut up and sit down?" The voice belonged to Poppaea, who was trying to cover her yawn with a hand. The empress, who seemed to have put on weight, looked dreadfully bored.

During the rest of the warm afternoon, Nero returned to his lyre and launched into another of his interminable epics. Praetorians were guarding all exits so that no one could leave, although several plebes jumped down from the stands rather than listen any longer. Vespasian, who could never sit longer than a quarter hour without nodding, was having a terrible time staying awake. An occasional jab from Sabinus' elbow was enough to return him to the land of the conscious, but later Sabinus also got sleepy and had all he could do to keep himself awake. But Vespasian's eyes snapped shut and his head dropped. It was one of Nero's aides who now hovered over the dozing Vespasian and gave him ringing slaps across the cheeks.

"Vespasian here was *sleeping!*" he huffed to Sabinus. "A grievous insult to Caesar!"

"Nothing of the sort," Sabinus quickly covered. "My brother always concentrates better with his eyes shut. Don't *you* think Caesar's singing should get the most dedicated hearing?"

The aide scowled and ambled off. Vespasian leaned over and whispered, "Thanks, brother. You're always getting me out of trouble, aren't you?"

After his concert, Nero also watched several races and finally made a tardy return to the palace-villa at night. He received an expected scolding from Poppaea that hardly seemed to faze him, for he had assumed his most imperial pout and was indulging the role of a wronged princeling.

Finally Poppaea ventured the obvious query. "All right, Nero. Out with it. What's the matter? *I'm* the one who should be furious with you . . . coming home as late as this."

After several more moments of studied sulking, he replied, "Each time I've returned from one of my concerts, you've told me how *well* I did. This time you said nothing. You even left before I finished. You even acted . . . well, *bored* during my singing. I saw you! I always watch you from the corner of my eye."

"I wasn't feeling very well. Have you forgotten I'm pregnant again?" she sighed. "And . . . I'll admit it: I *was* bored, Nero."

"You were . . . *what?*" He looked as if his soul had been lacerated.

"Bored, Nero. Yes, bored to death . . . and more than a little offended."

"Why, Poppaea?" he asked in a high, gulping voice.

"Because it was *too long,* for one thing. You acted *all morning.* You sang *all afternoon . . .*"

"But . . . but the epics *are* that long."

"Then maybe they shouldn't be sung at all. Especially by you."

"Why you . . . you uncultured little sow."

"Listen, you pompous, bloated bag of wind, I'm only doing this for your own good! *Somebody* has to tell you, Nero! Some of your performances are barely acceptable. A few are even acceptable. Others, like today's, are *terrible!*"

Nero was cut to the quick. He groped for words and finally found them. "Why, you ungrateful little trollop: you went from man to man until I found you and made something of you. But your ears and your mind—they're clearly beyond any help!"

"You can talk to me like that? At a time when I'm carrying your child?"

"Whose child is it really, Poppaea? Tell me true?"

"*Monster!*" she shrieked, giving him a stinging slap across the cheek. "Worthless, would-be artist who *kills* rather than creates! You're a *disgrace,* Nero! A disgrace to the whole Empire!"

Quivering with rage, Nero drew back his right foot and gave Poppaea a hard, painful kick in the abdomen. Shoved off balance, she fell to the floor, striking her head on the marble pavement. Her eyes snapped shut. She lay motionless, huddled under a green silk house robe.

Nero quickly hovered over her. "Oh, my precious Poppaea!" he cried. "Talk to me! Are you hurt, carissima? I'm sorry . . . sorry . . . *sorry,* darling! Speak to me! Poppaea?"

She made no stir. In a frenzy, Nero summoned the palace doctors. They examined the prostrate empress and then carried her up to bed. Nero sat at her bedside in anguish.

In the early morning hours, she regained partial consciousness, but then she suffered a miscarriage. Attending physicians tried desperately to halt the hemorrhaging that followed. They were not successful.

By noon, Nero's beloved Poppaea Sabina, empress of Rome, was dead.

Sabinus had never particularly admired Poppaea, but he now regretted her death because it threw Rome into turmoil and severely complicated the plot he was formulating against Nero. The emperor canceled their weekly conferences and spent weeks moaning about the palace, calling for Poppaea to return from the dead and forgive him. He would sit for hours in her bedroom, staring blankly at the walls, playing with items that used to delight her. Fearing for the emperor's sanity, Tigellinus tried hard to shake him out of his grief. He eventually resorted to a trusty device that had worked so well before: scaring Caesar.

It worked again. Nero's extravagant grief turned into a paranoid vengeance against the "conspiracies" swirling about him, most of them merely products of Tigellinus' depraved imagination. Sabinus felt a second wave of terror strike across Rome, which, in many ways, was more terrifying than the first. In the ruddy wake of the Pisonian conspiracy, the blood list had been drawn up quickly and the executions carried out with ruthless efficiency. But this time it was different: no one could tell whom Nero and Tigellinus would strike—or when—or how—or really why. People like himself were targets of the current purge, Sabinus quickly saw, and if he understood Tigellinus correctly, the man would not rest until he had sipped the nectar of revenge over his own prostrate body. A good hater, Tigellinus was nothing if not relentless, and it was astonishing that he had not yet been able to link him with the original plot against Nero.

Suspected republicans, rivals, critics—types who might plot against Nero in the future—were rounded up and mercilessly dispatched. The two brothers of the dead Seneca were indicted. Mela was accused of sharing his son Lucan's role in the plot. In fact he was innocent, but he saw no alternative to suicide. The same "guilt by relation" felled the eloquent Gallio, tidings that stunned and saddened Paul in prison, who would outlive his judge in Corinth.

Thrasea Paetus was giving a garden party for a few of his friends and had invited the aging Aulus and Pomponia to attend. They were listening to the discourses of a visiting philosopher when a messenger hurried into the grove with ugly tidings: under enormous pressure from Nero, the Senate had just condemned to death its one courageous voice, the most incorruptible of the Fathers, Thrasea Paetus.

Aulus stood up from the table. In a quaking voice, he cried, "May all the spirits of *hell* fatten on Nero's bloated body . . . first his voice, to halt its ghastly grunting. May the Furies—"

"Aulus, my friend," Thrasea cheerfully interrupted, "everyone knew the trail of death would finally wind to this door. After all, I have the honor of having been Nero's earliest and most implacable enemy. And for years on end. The wonder is that I've survived this long."

Then, a smile of serenity on his face, Thrasea hustled his guests out of the grove lest they be incriminated by contact with him. But Aulus refused to leave him, sending Pomponia back to the Esquiline. When the praetorian officer arrived to announce sentence of death, Thrasea took out a knife and neatly slit both of his wrists. "A libation to Jove the Deliverer!" he cried, turning to the soldier. "Mark this well, young man: you've been born into times when it's advisable to steel the spirit with examples of courage."

Aulus and the praetorian helped Thrasea onto his deathbed. Tears rolling down his leathery cheeks, Aulus told the officer to wait outside. Then he whispered into the ear of his dying friend, "Sabinus *will* destroy Nero, Thrasea. He will. Believe it. I know his plan."

"Then I can die a happy man," Thrasea replied, still smiling. "Nero can kill me . . . but he can't harm me."

Had he been a bachelor with no attachments, Sabinus would long ago have plunged his prefect's dagger deep into Nero during any of their conferences. He and Tigellinus were the only armed men allowed in Nero's presence, and he would gladly have sacrificed himself for the state. But he could not demand that his wife and children and their aging parents make the same sacrifice, for Tigellinus' vengeance would surely seek them out. And so he was trying to work out a plan that would spare his family.

It was hard enough sustaining Plautia's spirits through the agony of uncertainty. She was crushed by news of her "Uncle" Thrasea's suicide, and worried incessantly about her husband as the circle of deaths seemed to constrict around him. Her one comfort was the tenderness he showed in their habit of standing together on the roof terrace each day after supper, watching the evening sun drop over the Vatican Gardens across the Tiber. He would stand behind her, his arms locked deliciously about her waist, and whisper in her ear, simply, "One more day, my love."

They had been given another twenty-four hours together. She would nod her dark curls appreciatively and try to pull his arms even tighter about her lissome body. She had never before thought of time as a gift. But with a maturing love—was it actually being intensified by all the danger?—each extra day or week was its own consolation.

Petronius, the imperial arbiter in matters of taste, had invited them to a banquet at his country villa, promising that neither Nero nor Tigellinus nor any of their minions would be present. He wanted only to help break the somber mood hovering over Rome, the invitation insisted.

Sabinus and Plautia both needed the change and were enjoying themselves immensely at the lavish feast, the first time they had laughed or smiled in weeks. As the dessert wines were being served, Petronius leaned over and said, "I almost succeeded in bringing Caesar a little culture, Sabinus. He actually read—and even half understood—my *Satyricon*."

"Why do you say 'almost succeeded'? Nero calls nothing witty or elegant unless you first tell him it is."

Petronius frowned abruptly. "It's that brutish clod Tigellinus. He was afraid I was winning Nero away from him—and I was!—so he bribed a slave to swear I was a ringleader in Piso's conspiracy." Then he shrugged his shoulders and smiled. "Well, I'm leaving tonight, Sabinus. This all is just a friendly farewell."

Before Sabinus could even respond, Petronius had gotten to his feet and raised his hands for silence. "You all know, my friends, how much Caesar has envied my collection of murrhine vases," he said. "I might modestly add that they *are* the finest grouping in the Empire, and worth an entire wing of Caesar's . . . ostentatious new palace."

He clapped his hands twice. Servants filed out of the kitchen, each lifting one of the priceless urns out of Petronius' museum case. A slight nod from the host, and all vases were hurled onto the tessellated floor of the dining hall, shattering into a thousand fragments. To the astonished, indrawn breath of his guests, Petronius continued, "Now the sweaty hands of Caesar will never caress their cold porcelain. Let this symbolize the larger purpose of our *final* dinner together, my dearest friends."

In just moments, Petronius conveyed the grotesque news that the rest of the banquet would be not a grisly deathwatch but the happiest of wakes. "And *please* no remonstrances or sympathies or tears. Seneca left the stage philosophizing"—he grinned—"but for me no serious discussions on the immortality of the soul, if you please. And certainly no philosophy."

There was silence in the hall until Sabinus ventured, "What then, Petronius?"

"Why, bawdy tales, of course," he chuckled. "Light poetry." He lifted a silver razor and made small incisions in his wrists "for a deliciously gradual departure." Then he reclined again to hold his crimsoning arms out of view below the table.

"And now some frivolous verses," he challenged.

Guests told some, he others. From time to time he bound up his wrists to stop the bleeding and win time for several more stories. However unlikely the scheme would have seemed, Petronius was actually bringing it off with verve and style, Sabinus thought, sadly.

Now the host called in two secretaries to record his will. "One copy goes to the Vestal Virgins," he directed. "The other is for Nero." Then he read aloud the codicil he had just added to the will:

I know, Caesar, that many of your victims hope to save a little property for their families by leaving bequests for you and your tasteless leech, Tigellinus. But in this document you shall find only what you deserve, to wit:

I. *A Critique of Your Artistry*

You have sought this for many months, and I am now happy to supply it. Let history judge your other crimes, Caesar, your endless slaughter of relatives and friends and statesmen. I shall not even mention your novelty in devising a new and unprecedented outrage: *double* uxoricide. No, as a parting favor, I shall reveal only your master atrocity, which is this: that you have the brazen effrontery to imagine that your throaty warble should be called singing, and that your caterwauling on the lyre and your sins on the cithara pass, in any sense, for art. An offense to the ears? Certainly! An abrasive test for the nerves? That too. But art? Never! In the name of the Muses, we crave your silence, as we also ask that hopeless laughingstock of the actor in you to take his *final* bow.

II. *A Private Inventory*

Since your recollection of friendships is so very short, you may forget some of your depravities as well, and what would

Nero be without his vices? The following table, however, should refresh your memory. You may be shocked that I should have known about these novel gymnastics of yours, but this makes me all the happier . . .

What followed was a long listing of three columns, each headed, respectively: "Names . . . Dates . . . Specialties, Preferences, Novelties."

Against gales of laughter, Petronius signed the documents and sealed each with his signet ring, which he then crushed to forestall any future forgery. Now he reopened his bandages, bidding farewell to Sabinus, a very pale Plautia, and his other guests.

Nero read Petronius' will the next afternoon. Mortified that his private revels were such public knowledge, he fell into such a rage that he lost control of his bodily functions. Vainly, Terpnus pleaded with him to "spare the celestial voice."

By evening, however, Nero had calmed down. "Well, Tigellinus," he sighed, "with the deaths of Thrasea and Petronius, I feel truly *free* for the first time. All my enemies are now dead or banished. I can breathe again. I no longer have to worry—thanks to you, dear fellow."

For Tigellinus this was unhappy ebullience, since his power rested on manipulating Nero through fear. "I . . . I hope you're right, Princeps," he said.

"What do you mean 'hope'?"

"Oh . . . nothing, really."

"Tell me, Tigellinus. Is there anyone *else*?"

There was. Someone Tigellinus hated more than he could believe. Someone he would indict when a full case could be built against him. But for now he merely replied, "Several people bear careful watching, Caesar. Your city prefect, for one."

"Sabinus? He *seems* all right. I see he's finally attending all the public functions. My concerts, too."

"If you call 'attending' sitting there drowsy and put upon. At your last performance, his brother even fell asleep."

"Ohhhh," Nero winced. "Do you suppose we should indict them?"

"Not yet. Vespasian's innocent, at any rate. He's just an unartistic ox who may yet be useful to us in the army. Sabinus is the one to watch—I *still* think he plotted with the Piso group. He recommended Rufus to us, don't forget, and he was so very friendly with the Christians. *And"*—he smirked—"I just learned that he and his wife attended that treasonable banquet at Petronius' place."

Nero's eyebrows arched. "So? Shall we arrest him then, Tigellinus?"

"Soon, I would think. Let me get a little more evidence first.— Now, Caesar, before I leave, here's a list of cases awaiting your pleasure."

Nero scanned the schedule of trials pending. His eyes narrowed when he came to "Alexander the Coppersmith *versus* Paul of Tarsus."

"Paul of Tarsus . . . Paul of Tarsus? Oh, is that the little Christian fellow—all eyes, hook nose? Aha ha! The case you lost to Sabinus?"

"The same," Tigellinus sneered. Then he reminded Nero about the first hearing of Paul's second trial.

"Why is he still alive?"

"He was stupidly prosecuted on a charge of arson, and Nymphidius got a *non liquet* result."

"Well, I won't see *him* again. I warned him not to come back, didn't I? And we can't let him off—not when all his followers died. Simply reconvene your special tribunal at the Castra, Tigellinus, and condemn him for being one of those treasonable haters-of-mankind. Yes, crucify him, just like that . . . ah . . . what was his name? That fisherman?"

"Peter? Simon Peter?"

"Yes, Peter."

"That's not possible in this case, Princeps."

"And why not?"

"Paul's a Roman citizen. Peter was not."

"Very well, then, the sword."

Luke was able to alert Paul's close friends only after his death sentence, so quickly and without warning had Tigellinus struck. They had all they could do to arrive at the Castra Praetoria in time to accompany the apostle on his final journey. Pomponia was there—red-eyed and mournful—and so were Sabinus and Plautia, though Aulus was confined to the Esquiline with a respiratory illness.

Tigellinus had offered Paul his choice of sites for the execution, "just so long as it's outside the city walls."

Paul chose to die and be buried near the concentration of Christians on the Aventine, so he replied, "Beyond the Ostian Gate."

"All the way across Rome?" Tigellinus scowled. "Which would give you extra time with your friends, wouldn't it, Paul? Very well, then, the Ostian Gate.—Tribune," he called, "you're in charge of the execution. Take only a small detail. I don't think these sheep will give you any trouble." With a haughty smirk, Tigellinus bade them good-bye and left the Castra. Sabinus was merely grateful that Paul's final hour was not besmirched by the presence of Ofonius Tigellinus.

Young Timothy, Mark, Luke, and other elders were waiting outside the Castra and now joined the small, grieving company that wound its way southwestward across Rome. As Tigellinus had surmised, Paul used the time to good effect in giving final directives to the elders of the Roman church. Now they passed under the red brick arches of the Ostian Gate and continued a mile down the Via Ostiensis in order to avoid curiosity-seekers who might be alarmed at the execution of a Roman citizen. Finally they reached a green and level spot, surrounded by low, rolling hills, called Aquae Salviae, "Waters of Sage."

While the tribune and his men carefully set up a chopping block beneath a pine tree, Paul took leave of his friends. He commended the church to God, promising, "This is only the beginning of a cause that will one day be far greater than the Empire. We are *not* ashes, we are embers. Glowing in the Spirit, we shall rekindle the Faith so that Christ *will* triumph!"

Then he gave Pomponia and Plautia parting kisses. Plautia whispered something to him and a great smile bloomed across his face. Finally, he extended a firm hand of gratitude to Sabinus.

For the last time, Sabinus looked into the cool serenity of the apostle's eyes, and then glanced down in remorse. Once again, the chief magistrate of Rome could not prevent the execution of an innocent.

The tribune indicated that all was now ready.

"The time of my departure has come, beloved friends." Paul's face was wreathed in a peaceful smile. "As I once wrote you, Timothy, I have fought the good fight. I have finished the race. I have kept the Faith. And now the prize is waiting for me . . . the crown of righteousness which the Lord, that perfect judge, will award to me on that great day. And not to me only, but to you as well . . . and all who await his coming. Peace be with you all."

Then, bending over the block, he prayed, "Into your hands, O Lord, I commend my spirit."

The tribune raised his sharpened sword with both hands and brought it down in one clean sweep.

Pomponia, Plautia, and several others burst into tears. But Luke consoled them all with the assurance of the resurrection in which Christians confidently believed.

Sabinus had the execution detail help them bury Paul under an oak in a small parcel of wooded property nearby that The Twin Brothers owned. The much-traveled Paul of Tarsus had come to rest at last, buried, appropriately, near the side of a highway.

On the quiet trip back to Rome, Sabinus asked Plautia, "What did you whisper to him? What made him so happy?"

"I told him that I believed. That I was going to become a Christian too."

BOOK FIVE

THE EMBERS

30

PLAUTIA'S CONVERSION should not have surprised him, Sabinus told himself, but it did all the same. She had inherited her mother's sensitivity, and Roman women had always been more religious than their men. And yet in a happy marriage, such as theirs, everything was to be shared. But could he ever really share Plautia's Christianity? He doubted it.

For one thing, it was all so . . . un-Roman—something imported from the East, like Judaism. That there should be one god, not many, was easy to believe, he thought. In fact, it was intellectually satisfying to pin one's worship to a supreme deity, a better-than-Jupiter sort who was in final control of the universe. Yes, the Jews did well to be monotheistic, and it was not surprising that some members of the Roman nobility had become proselytes to Judaism. Even the learned Varro confessed his belief in the one great Soul of the Universe who could also be identified as the god of the Jews, he wrote. And Seneca seemed to share the belief. And Vergil. And Cicero.

But to go beyond this and claim that the one god extended himself into human form in the person of Jesus was difficult to accept. True, it was more rational that the deity should appear as a *man* rather than the various disguises Jupiter assumed when he chose to visit the world—like a snow-white bull or a lusty, rutting eagle. But suppose for a moment that the deity did exist and was sophisticated enough to embrace humanity intimately in the form of a man. Wouldn't he really have brought it off differently?

The Jesus figure, in that case, would not have been born in obscure circumstances at a tiny corner of the Empire far across the Mediterranean, but in the center of the world—in Athens or Rome. And he surely wouldn't have selected twelve uncultured, uneducated types as his disciples. A Paul of Tarsus, perhaps, and a Peter, but the others would have been ranking intellects of the day like Aristotle or leaders like Alexander—*if* the message were to take root in the Greek East. Inevitably, then, like all things Greek, the movement would filter westward into Rome. Here, in the hub of the Empire, the Jesus phenomenon and his disciples would set up their school and convince the Senate, the philosophers, and the masses. From Rome, in turn, the message would reach out to all the world. And if the deity were still suicidally minded—if he insisted on sacrificing the Jesus figure in a crucifixion—then Rome could serve as platform for that too. And wouldn't the cross show up far more prominently on the summit of the Capitoline ("The Place of the Head") than on that small ridge outside of Jerusalem called Golgotha ("The Place of the Skull")?

It was a quarrel between his two boys that pulled Sabinus out of his reverie. But before it all broke into separate shreds and dissolved, he was struck by one thought: even though it had not happened in the artless and obvious manner he had projected, the *result was the same.* The message had indeed reached Rome from the Greek East, and it was beginning to spread out from the capital.

Plautia was happy with the way Sabinus had accepted her new convictions. If he had uttered one critical word on the way home from Paul's burial, she would have collapsed, she felt. But he had maintained a wise, mature silence. And in the days following, while he had not applauded her resolve—that, she knew, would have been hypocrisy—he seemed to have understood it. Mother Pomponia, of course, was radiant at the news. For her it was the perfect antidote to grief in the days following Paul's execution.

She had no choice but to decide as she did, Plautia thought. The gods of Rome were sleeping, or dead, or had never existed—to let the city endure what it had. There was also the problem of focus: *whom* to worship. The pious Roman was supposed to juggle his loyalties between several dozen gods, goddesses, spirits, shades, demigods, and heroes. And dead emperors too! Against such a confusing mélange, the story of a one true God had come almost as an exuberant relief, and the reports that Paul and Peter told about the Christ carried their own indescribable authority and conviction.

But would her faith make any difference to their marriage, she wondered. That she could never have endured, for her joy with Sabinus was something sacred in itself—a kind of religion of its own. But her husband seemed to be adapting rather well to the circumstances. In fact, once when she asked him about it, he laughed and said, "Don't worry, darling. I think it's much more dignified to see you bowing your head in prayer from time to time than poking around a sheep's liver for clues to tomorrow."

His wan smile was broadening as he announced, quite pompously, "You know, I've just discovered the key to the moral problem of the Roman Empire . . ."

"What is it?"

"Romans have been getting their omens from animals for so long that they're starting to behave like them too. Have I told you the latest from the palace?"

Nero still sorely missed his beloved Poppaea. Remorsefully, he remembered that she had remained faithful to him, despite his numerous extramarital affairs. One afternoon at twilight, Tigellinus unveiled a surprise for him. A figure entered his suite dressed in one of Poppaea's favorite costumes—her gossamer turquoise tunic—and redolent with her favorite perfume. Nero stared as the girl came closer, and he clutched a handkerchief to his throat. There, beneath that transparent veil she frequently wore, was—*impossibly*—his beloved herself!

"Poppaea?" Nero asked hoarsely. "Goddess? Poppaea?" His knees shook and he nearly fainted. "My . . . my darling Poppaea?"

Tigellinus reached over and removed the veil. Nero staggered to his knees and clutched at his heart. "*Great Olympian gods!*" he shouted. "It *is* Poppaea! S-s-*say* something, dearest! H-have you forgiven me for what I did?"

"Relax, Caesar. No, it's not Poppaea." Tigellinus reached over and removed the blond wig the figure was wearing. "It's little Sporus. Growing up, isn't he?"

"You . . . you mean . . ."

"Remember that beautiful freedman's boy you once said looked so much like Poppaea? Well, he certainly does . . . more like her every day, in fact."

"By the gods, Sporus! You . . . you *are* so much like her."

The youth blushed prettily and gave Nero a coy smile.

Though no one outside Rome could really believe it, Nero actually started courting Sporus and soon fell in love with him. Several weeks later, he asked the boy to marry him.

Sporus did have an objection, though not the obvious one: "You're already *wife* to Pythagoras, Caesar," he pouted.

"But I'll be your *husband*, Sporus," Nero crooned, caressing his cheek.

Happily, Nero assigned Sporus a regular dowry, wrote up a nuptial contract, and later he publicly celebrated his wedding to the catamite, Tigellinus giving the veiled bride away. Guests even prayed that children would be born from such a union.

When Sabinus learned of it, he told Plautia, "Well, our palace pervert has finally exhibited *all* his talents. No other combinations are possible, I think."

Plautia, who barely understood such things, replied, "If only Nero's father had had a *wife* like Sporus!"

"Excellent, my dear!" Sabinus laughed.

One morning, as he walked into city headquarters, Sabinus found a huge graffito painted in ugly red lettering on the wall near the entrance:

THE FOES OF CAESAR *ALL* LIE DEAD?
AND HAS SABINUS NOTHING TO DREAD
FOR PLOTTING WITH PISO? CUT OFF HIS HEAD!

The shock bristled even the smallest hairs on his neck. But he heard his own voice calmly telling a custodian, "Whitewash this garbage off the wall."

He tried to forget about the incident. But later in the day he was summoned to the palace, his first conference with Nero in some time. Sabinus found the emperor strangely agitated, more like a suspicious, frightened canine ready to leap at him. Gingerly, Sabinus avoided touching on anything Nero might construe as a bone, while avoiding a defensive posture lest he seize on it as some proof of guilt. Once again, the frozen mask of normality.

After some banal platitudes, Nero brought him up short. "What if it *were* true, Sabinus?" he asked.

"What, Caesar?"

"That you *were* one of Piso's men? That . . . that you actually *would* have taken my life? You were friends with all the conspirators—Petronius, Seneca, Gallio. Quintus Lateranus *was* your relative and business partner. You recommended the traitor Rufus to us. And on the day set for the assassination, just *why* were your Urban Cohorts on alert? No, don't look away, Sabinus, look me in the eye!" And the imperial eyes were glistening with a new ferocity.

Sabinus fought to contain the icy flux within him so the climate at the surface would remain unchanged. "The cohorts?" he replied. "They were on alert for one very obvious reason, Caesar: to control any disorders at the Feast of Ceres. And I recommended Rufus purely because of his record in the grain supply." Then he tried a desperate gamble by seizing the offensive. "If you're trying to be humorous, Princeps, I consider it in *very* bad taste. You raised me to highest office in Rome twice, so my loyalty should be obvious. Can you find any fault with my record? Any at all?"

"I . . . I always thought you were reliable, Sabinus. But no one else seems to think so."

"By that you mean . . . Tigellinus, I suppose?"

Nero turned away. "Tigellinus and I will be leaving for Greece in early September—the games, the concert tour are finally confirmed. Now, my freedman Helius will be in charge here while we're gone. You'll be minding Rome while he minds the Empire." Then, facing Sabinus directly again, he lowered his voice. "Helius will be watching you, Sabinus, *watching* you. Closely. He wonders, for example— and so do I—why you daubed a coat of whitewash on your prefecture with . . . such embarrassing haste."

Sabinus' throat went dry, but he did not stammer his reply beyond a quick, inaudible gulp. "Perhaps Helius should be more concerned at finding the liars who defaced city property than in the maintenance of those properties."

"That's all, Sabinus." Nero frowned, waving him off.

He was already out of the imperial offices when he heard Nero call after him, "Oh, Prefect, I thought you'd like to know: your brother Vespasian will be accompanying us to Greece as military aide. His son Titus, too."

"I'm delighted to hear that, Caesar."

While returning to city headquarters, Sabinus pondered both the news and its timing. Put baldly, if not unfairly, *why* had Nero chosen a mule-trader as military aide? Coincidence? More than that, it suddenly seemed clear. Nero and Tigellinus were serving him plain notice: "Don't try anything while we're gone, Sabinus. We have your brother and nephew as hostages."

Curse the Fates who were presiding over the insane course of Roman destiny! He had indeed planned to make his move against Nero while he was in Greece. It would have been the perfect time for it. But now his blundering brother was along as hostage. Unless—. He must have a talk with Vespasian immediately.

Ever since he convinced himself that he was an artist, Nero had been planning his concert tour of Greece, for only the aesthetic Hellenes could truly appreciate genius in a commoner or an emperor —to them it made no difference. Now, in the fall of 66, he set sail with a great chorus of Augustiani and a virtual army of entertainment laden with lyres, citharas, masks, costumes, and buskins.

Curious Greeks craned their necks to see the lord of the world as he disembarked in the land he so admired. By now his paunch had grown, his pustules had never really cleared, and his slender legs seemed more spindling than ever. But, as a kind of compensation, he had let his darkening blond locks grow long, and they now hung down his back in cascades of curls.

Nero had ordered that all the Greek festivals be held during his visit—something sacrilegious and unprecedented—and he carefully enrolled himself in each of the contests, performing from his repertory as tragic actor, reciter of his own poems, lyrist, and charioteer. The judges were very discerning, he thought: in every contest, they declared him the victor! He won everything there was to win at Olympia, Corinth, Delphi, and elsewhere—a grand total of 1,808 trophies and prizes.

Once, though, he nearly made a false step, as Vespasian wrote Sabinus. During a chariot race at Olympia, Nero tried to handle a ten-horse team, but careened out of his cab and was nearly killed. For several moments, everyone had the unparalleled spectacle of seeing the Roman emperor rolling over the sands of the hippodrome. Judges halted the race until Nero, skinned and bruised, could be loaded back onto his chariot. When he had completed the laps he had missed and several more for good measure, the judges ordered the race resumed, but Nero was unable to hold out and gave up before the end. The victor? Nero, of course! Whereupon he lavished Roman citizenship and a million sesterces on the judges.

The Greeks were no fools. If the emperor wanted to play, they would play too—and win immense concessions in the process. Early the next year, Nero proclaimed at least local self-government for the Greeks.

In Rome, meanwhile, a courier delivered another letter from Greece to the Quirinal. "It's from Vespasian!" Sabinus called to Plautia. Then he slit the heavy wax seals and began reading aloud to her:

T. Flavius Vespasian to T. Flavius Sabinus, greeting.—You will not believe the incredible changes in my life, dear brother! At first my prospects were typically terrible. I began by offending Caesar at Eleusis. He was about to participate in the Mysteries there when the herald, as usual, warned "all the wicked and godless" to flee before ceremonies began. Nero got so frightened he refused to participate! And that's when he saw me shaking with laughter.—Then, during another of Caesar's concerts here, I—you will surely be disgusted with me—I fell asleep again. This time Nero went into a rage. "I never want to see your ugly face again!" he cried, and expelled me from the imperial party.

"But where shall I go?" I asked Phoebus, his freedman. "Go to Hades!" he shouted. So I went—not really to Hades—but into exile at a little cottage near Corinth. I'd be there today but for the Jewish revolt in Palestine.

The rebellion there is getting much worse: our forces have been driven out of Jerusalem and most of Judea. Since there's no other general around, Nero was forced to use me, and I've now been appointed supreme commander in charge of 60,000 troops to put down the revolt. You wouldn't believe the praise and flattery Nero is heaping on me, now that he has need of me!—I am just leaving Corinth, and my Titus will join me with

a legion from Egypt. Farewell from "the liberated hostages."
Good hunting!—Given the Ides of February, A.U.C. 820.

Sabinus put the letter down and broke out laughing for joy. "The
vicissitudes of Fortune!" He beamed. "From commander to mule-
trader and back to commander again. *Good* for Vespasian!"

"He should be able to carry his own weight from now on." Plautia smiled. "Did he ever repay the money you loaned him?"

"Part of it. But he's a good risk now." Sabinus grinned. "Though
I can't say the same for Nero." His jaw was clenching with determination and his eyes stared off over the top of her head for several
moments. "Good hunting *indeed!* At last," he whispered, then
louder, "Yes, *at last!* It's not just that Vespasian's no longer a hostage
—he's now one of the strongest men in the Empire! *At last,* carissima! Our great hour has *finally* come."

Minutes later, Sabinus paced about his office in a cadence that
sounded to him like the drumroll of destiny. One last time he
searched out and dissected the alternatives he had been mulling
every day over the past months. Actually, there were only three—just
three ways to topple a Roman emperor. *One:* assassination. But ever
since the Pisonian conspiracy, Nero was more closely guarded than
ever. *Two:* revolt of the Praetorian Guard. But with Tigellinus and
Nymphidius as co-commanders, that was clearly impossible. *Three:*
revolution by the provincial legions. If enough commanders could be
persuaded, it was also the most formidable way to dethrone a Caesar.

It *had* to be the legions, Sabinus reflected. Commanders across the
Empire were furious at the fate of General Corbulo, who had gen-
erated miracles for Rome on the eastern front. Suspecting a conspiracy, Nero had summoned Corbulo and two commanders from Germany to a conference in Greece, where he had all three commit
suicide. That, in fact, was why only Vespasian was available to put
down the Jewish revolt, Sabinus now realized. The commanders
were murmuring indeed. They were also tired of the Praetorian
Guard deciding when to make and unmake emperors. They were
tired, too, of trying to maintain discipline in the troops at a time
when their commander-in-chief was an actor, recitalist, multimur-
derer, and pederast. *The legions!* His brother now suddenly controlled the East. He must therefore win over the commanders of the
West.

"Vindex," he whispered to himself. What had his protégé in Gaul at the time of the census said in his last letter: "If ever I can serve you, Sabinus, command me: I owe my entire career to you!" And Vindex, one of Nero's most caustic secret critics, was now Governor General of Gaul! Time to contact Vindex!

Sabinus paced his office several minutes more to formulate all the arguments. Then he sat down at his desk to write out the most important letter of his life, a solemn call to revolution in the name of saving Rome. He also suggested that Governor Galba of Spain and Otho of Lusitania—Poppaea's former husband—would doubtless make common cause with Vindex, tearing the whole West from Nero's grasp.

Imprisoning the message in a cocoon of canvas and sealing wax, he called in his most trusted aide, hung the message around his neck, and gave him a secret briefing. At the end of it, he said, "Leave at once. And remember, no one but *Vindex himself* sees this. If he agrees, you then visit Galba and Otho to coordinate it all."

Nero staged his triumphant return to Rome in January of 68. A portion of the city wall was breached so that he could ride through it in his chariot, a traditional gesture permitted Olympic victors. Rome was decked with garlands, blazing with lights, reeking with incense and perfume. Nero himself was clad in purple and gold, and crowned with the Olympic victor's wreath of wild olive. All the trophies he had won were paraded through the city, along with signs identifying them, and then put on permanent display in his rambling—and now cluttered—private quarters.

"I understand I have Helius to thank for this fine reception, not you, Sabinus," said Nero, in their first encounter after his return. They were wandering through the nearly completed Golden House, a lavish labyrinth of gilded, pearled corridors with ceilings of fretted ivory. Sabinus took his cue from their surroundings and lied, "It was more a division of labor, Princeps. Helius took care of your reception. I thought it best to keep our city crews busy with this." He spread his arms.

Nero seemed satisfied for the moment. He walked to a corner of the dining room and pulled a lever. Ceiling panels opened to let flower petals flutter down on them while hidden jets sprayed perfume. Then he peered out of a window. The new palace was surrounded by a countryside of lakes, woods, and vineyards—all in the very heart of Rome.

"Good," Nero finally commented. "Now I can begin to live like a human being."

The guttural voice of Ofonius Tigellinus intruded. "Caesar and I have been discussing your record, Prefect. And your sympathies. We quite agree that . . . you are not to leave the city of Rome until further notice."

"I take my orders only from Caesar, Tigellinus. Not you." Sabinus struggled to remain calm. "Am I under some indictment, Princeps?"

Nero looked away nervously. "No, Sabinus," he said quietly. "But . . . do stay in Rome."

For the next weeks, Sabinus lived in a clutch of suspense. His courier had returned from Gaul and Iberia with a strong but secret positive response from the governors there, and Vindex had been particularly enthusiastic. But no further word had arrived from the West. All the while, his own Quirinal mansion was being put on continual surveillance by a series of poorly disguised praetorian agents skulking near the place, who were doubtless reporting everything they saw directly to Tigellinus. After bumping into them several times, Sabinus ordered an equally continuous guard at his place from the Urban Cohorts to show Tigellinus that he would not, under any circumstances, be intimidated.

Well and good at the surface. But how disguise the gnawing dread that was devouring the happiness of each day and converting the life experience into a lingering nightmare for himself, Plautia, and her parents on the Esquiline?

Early in March, she did brighten his life by presenting him their first daughter, a tiny infant with remarkably long raven hair, whom they named Plautilla, "Little Plautia," a glad interim in all the stress. But even while dandling the very apple of his eye, Sabinus could not help but wonder what kind of world it was into which they had brought another human life.

Just a week after Plautilla's naming day, her grandfather Aulus hurried into city headquarters with tears in his eyes. "Get them out of here!" he commanded, as Sabinus dismissed several urban secretaries. Only then did he notice that they were tears of excitement and joy.

"It's *happening*, Sabinus!" he exulted. "We *just* got word in the Senate! Vindex has issued a formal proclamation, calling on imperial armies everywhere to rise in revolt against Nero! He has one hundred thousand troops massed in Gaul for revolution!"

Sabinus let out a whoop of joy. "What about Galba and Otho? Any word?"

"That's just the point." Aulus caught his breath. "They're *joining* the revolution! Galba's Spain, Otho's Lusitania, and Vindex's Gaul—the *whole west* is demanding that Nero abdicate!"

Sabinus' open palm went crashing down onto his desk. "At last!" he exclaimed. "*At last!* How is the Senate reacting?"

"I've never seen such . . . private joy in the Fathers' faces. Because of the praetorians, of course, they can't do anything at the moment."

"I'll write Vespasian at once," Sabinus decided, "even though he could hardly break off the Jewish War to advance on Rome!"

At that moment, Nero was down in Naples watching wrestling contests. It was shortly after lunch when Tigellinus ran almost frantically into the arena with the ominous news from Gaul. Nero merely leaped down from his seat to join in tussling with the wrestlers. Eight more days he idled in Naples, and it was only when Vindex issued another taunt against "Bronzebeard the Bad Lyre-Player" that he was finally stung and wrote the Senate "to take care of the Gallic matter."

More ominous messages finally sent him in a huff to Rome. He set a price of ten million sesterces on the head of Vindex, but Vindex offered even more for Nero's: "Anyone bringing me that buffoon's head can have mine in return," he vowed. Sabinus, now moving in a delirium of joy, knew he meant it. Vindex was a patriot.

Several days later, when Galba's revolt was also confirmed, Nero kicked over his breakfast table. Then he tore his robe, beat his brow, and carefully fainted onto a bed, where he lay prostrate for an hour. Then he roused himself and officially declared Galba a public enemy, confiscating all his property in Rome. In turn, Galba declared Nero a public enemy and seized all his property in Spain. Auctions were held in both places, and Galba came off far the richer from the proceeds.

Still Nero refused to appear in the Senate. One night, instead, he summoned the leading senators, Sabinus, and all his prefects to a conference at his villa. Carefully masking his elation at the revolt, Sabinus was planning to give Nero all the wrong advice. He was amazed at how badly Nero was degenerating physically. A red face and blondish hair still marked the man, but now his sly, suspicious eyes peered out at him between bulges of oily flesh that had puffed up his face. He was a heap of bloated fat, poorly concealed under the costliest garments. Old at thirty, Nero conducted the conference as if he were oblivious of events outside Rome.

Then, with a wave of his handkerchief, he suddenly broke off the conclave. "Come with me, gentlemen." He smiled. "I've something to show you." He led them into a hall where some lofty and strange-looking contrivances were standing—pipes, vertical and horizontal, and keyboards of some kind. "They've just arrived from Alexandria," he effused.

"What . . . are they, Princeps?" Sabinus wondered.

"Hydraulic water organs, silly! The wind pressure for the pipes is kept constant by these columns of water," he pointed. "Here, I'll show you how they sound." He clapped his hands. "That's so the slaves will start pumping."

Like a child with a tantalizing new toy, Nero began tooting away at the largest organ, covering his ears at the chirping, high notes and bringing the most out of the instrument's booming bass. "How's *that*, my friends?" he exulted.

"Superb, Caesar," said Tigellinus, in a rising flush of embarrassment. "Now about Vindex and the—"

"I've discovered how to get even lower notes from it." He beamed and went on to lecture on the theory of water organs, demonstrating various note combinations on the instruments. "I plan to have these set up in the theater and give a concert soon—all, of course, with the kind permission of Vindex." He winked.

Sabinus left the impromptu recital with a lighter heart than he had known in months. Apparently, it would all go easier than he had feared, and he was angry with himself for not having launched the revolution earlier. Nero had clearly lost touch with reality. He was tottering and must soon fall. If only Rome could be spared further bloodshed in that collapse.

He must now keep Nero off balance, Sabinus resolved, also because of what this did to Tigellinus. He could still see the perplexed and wounded look in Tigellinus' eyes during Nero's organ recital. Hurrying over to his agent on the Caelian, who was now supervising Twin Brothers Enterprises, he asked him, "Do we still supply Nero's wine?"

"That we do, Prefect." He smiled. "Caesar drinks as much Gemini brand in various vintages as all others combined."

"Excellent! Now tell me this: is there any way you can double the alcoholic content in bottles you supply him? Or increase it in some way?"

"We've been trying to distill stronger wines, but our only success is with the grapes from Mount Etna. Wine from them is almost twice as powerful. But why would—"

"Don't ask. Make another delivery to Nero's villa and replace Gemini bottles already in his wine-cellar with the stronger stuff. Soon as you can, all right?"

"Certainly, Prefect."

Sabinus hurried off with a low smile. Nero's lethargy after meals would be even longer now, his wits more addled than ever. His wine consumption had been on the steady increase as it was.

Only military force could now put down the rebellions, Nero finally realized, and he prepared a legion to invade Gaul. Crush Vindex, and Galba and Otho would have to sue for peace. Tigellinus was working out the strategy with his praetorian officers' staff when one of the tribunes complained that massive funds from the war chest were being diverted at Nero's orders.

Storming over to the imperial villa, Tigellinus found Nero in his cups, still reclining languidly at lunch although it was late afternoon. He was, however, able to account for the missing funds. They were for a train of wagons that would carry his concubines and theatrical instruments to Gaul. "It needn't actually come to bloodshed," he told Tigellinus. "No, not at all. I'll simply stand in front of Vindex's forces and . . . and do nothing more than weep. The troops will be so touched at the sight of their emperor in tears that they'll stop their rebellion. And then I'll give a concert in honor of the glorious victory." Nero was smiling. And he was serious.

Tigellinus stared uncomprehendingly.

Sabinus, meanwhile, was trying to coordinate the revolution through a mass of secret correspondence with Vindex and the other legionary commanders. He urged a general invasion of Italy by the western legions, his brother to join from the East once the Jewish rebellion had been quelled. Everything now depended on the attitude of Rome's seven legions along the Rhine River, which had not yet joined the revolt, even though Sabinus had pleaded with them to do so.

Early in May, his personal aide arrived with the latest message from Gaul. "I have . . . *extremely* bad news, Clarissimus. You . . . you'd best sit down for this."

"What happened?" Sabinus tensed.

"Verginius Rufus, commander of our Rhine legions, finally made his decision. He . . . stayed loyal to Nero and attacked Vindex's forces in eastern Gaul. Defeated them. Badly. He killed about 20,000."

"What about Vindex himself?"

"Committed suicide just after the battle."

Sabinus sank slowly into his chair, clutching a roll of cheek flesh in his fingers until the skin was tawny white. "Vindex . . . Vindex," he muttered, in a daze. "Oh, *brave* and *faithful* Verginius! Such a loyal soldier!" Tears welled up in his eyes. "Stupid, stinking *dullard,* Verginius! Blasted *dolt!* Helping that murderous voluptuary out of the grave in which he belongs."

For some moments his hands covered his face. Finally, he asked, "And Galba . . . Otho . . . what'll they ever do now?"

"They're in a fiercely bad position, of course. But what *can* they do, Prefect? Retract the nasty things they've said about Nero? Apologize for treason?"

"They *might,* believe it or not. Because Nero's under pressure, he's in a *very* forgiving mood lately. I've *got* to steel them up. It's our only chance."

He sat down at his desk, lost in thought for some minutes, and then carefully wrote this note:

Sabinus to Galba, *Salve!* Forget the code. This message gets through or the cause collapses. Despite poor Vindex, *you and Otho must continue the revolution!* Nero remains very much off balance. At the moment, he's more worried about rival actors catching the public fancy—"taking advantage of Caesar's busy days," he puts it—than in saving the Empire. Exactly four weeks from today, I am mobilizing the Urban Cohorts and the Praetorian Guard in your behalf. My aide will supply all the details. *Start marching,* Galba! Given the Nones of May, A.U.C. 821.

The aide was awestruck. "The Praetorians? But . . . but with Tigellinus, they'd never—"

"Leave that to me. Now, here's my plan . . ."

In the days following, Sabinus kept his ears to the ground. A true revolution could never succeed without the people, he knew, and he wondered how the plebes were taking the current crisis. The common people were always more amused than terrified by Nero. He had purged none of their ranks but treated them instead to a series of sensational shows. Yet even the plebes were starting to murmur, Sabinus found, and in not very muted tones. They were hungry. Nero had mishandled the wheat supply. One day, though, news reached Rome that a grain fleet was sailing into the harbor at Ostia, and thousands of plebes hurried over to the port to help unload the cargo. All of it turned out to be *sand* for the Vatican hippodrome! Already surly, the people's mood now curdled.

Good, Sabinus concluded. Now was the time. Months ago he had abandoned the comparative luxury of merely treading water in the vicious whirlpool of Roman politics for direct involvement against Nero. But others, not he, had taken the prime risks. No longer. The time had come at last for direct exposure, whatever the hazards. Nero had to be overthrown—immediately. The Western legions were taking far too much time. If the Rhine legions marched south, or if Nero recovered his wits in the interim, he might yet survive.

Sabinus made his move. On the night of June 1, long after Plautia and the household had gone to bed, he held a clandestine encounter at his place with only one man, who had arrived without escort. A broad-shouldered hulk with hair no lighter than ebony, the man was Nymphidius Sabinus, co-commander of the Praetorian Guard, the judge who had presided at the first hearing of Paul's second trial.

"So," said Sabinus, as he escorted him into his library and carefully shut the door. "The civil and the military heads of Rome finally meet in private."

"And we're both named Sabinus." Nymphidius smiled, showing a row of milk-colored teeth. But this was the extent of any pleasantries, for his muddy visage tautened again and his eyes narrowed suspiciously.

"First of all, Prefect," Sabinus began, "where is your colleague Tigellinus these days?"

"Why do you ask?" Nymphidius inquired, with a frown.

Sabinus bit his lip. Nymphidius was not giving an inch, at least not at the start. It might all be more difficult than he had imagined. How did two conspirators—or one conspirator and one candidate—ever get into serious dialogue without tipping their hands? What were Cassius' opening words to Brutus?

"Very well, I'll be more direct: who *really* controls the Praetorian Guard now, Nymphidius? You or Tigellinus?"

"We're both in charge. What do you mean?"

"A simple question. Why are you being so evasive?"

"I'm just wondering what you're driving at . . . why you called me here . . . why you insisted on all this secrecy."

"If you knew me better, my friend, you wouldn't have to ask such questions. And if you've gained your impressions of me through Tigellinus, you must know I'm a scheming traitor who ought to be eliminated." He paused briefly, then resumed. "But I'm only a Roman, Nymphidius, a Roman who would still like to pride himself on that designation years from now. And so I'll be candid, whatever the risks." He paused, pondered the syllables that would forever change his life, and then spoke them: "The time has come . . . to depose Nero."

Sabinus carefully studied the praetorian commander for a reaction. A sudden look of shock or horror on the man's face could seal his own doom. But Nymphidius merely crinkled his eyes.

"Go on," he said.

"I'll tell you how I'd *much* prefer to see Nero deposed: an edict of the Senate, pure and simple, with your praetorians following their lead. But I'm not sure the Fathers would make such a decision without cocking their ears in the direction of the Castra Praetoria. The Guard made both Claudius and Nero."

"Aren't some of the legions marching against Nero?" Nymphidius asked, with a smirk.

"And it's taking them a blessed long time to get here. But they *will* get to Rome—eventually. And then what will your praetorians do? Fight for that murdering actor and parricide, poisoner and pervert? Will you really drench Rome with more blood? Or do the sane thing and abandon him for Galba?"

For several moments, Nymphidius studied his sandals. Then he said, "Galba's no prize."

"Of course he isn't! But next to Nero, he'll look like Romulus himself. And he also has the advantage of being seventy-three years old: he can't make that many mistakes before he dies. But Nero must go in any case. And *now*. Otherwise the state's lost."

Nymphidius scratched his scruffy cheek for some moments. Finally he said, "So—you want me to get the Guard to declare for Galba?"

"The moment you do"—Sabinus nodded—"I'll introduce a motion in the Senate to depose Nero. It will pass, I can assure you, because my Urban Cohorts will also be declaring for Galba. Your praetorians will make it unanimous."

Suddenly Nymphidius gave him a vicious scowl and dripped the words out of his mouth like sour wine: "You're committing treason, Prefect . . . outright, treacherous *treason!* Tigellinus has been looking for an excuse to sever your head, and it's obvious why." He walked over and held his face just inches from Sabinus. "I could expose you in twenty minutes and you'd never see dawn. In fact, why don't I do just that?"

"I could physically prevent your leaving this house, Nymphidius," Sabinus answered coolly, staring back at the commander without blinking.

"Your servants? You think I'm afraid of them?"

"I was referring to *myself*, Prefect! I once gave Tigellinus a battered face. I seem to do well against praetorian prefects." He glared at him for several moments, and if one board in the floor had creaked it might have come to blows. Then Sabinus said, "But I won't try anything so obvious this time, because I'd have to kill you to keep you quiet. And I'm no murderer."

"You wouldn't get that far, Sabinus," he sneered. "So, then, what happens when I tell Nero?"

Sabinus hesitated, but then the words poured out. "Civil War, Nymphidius. I'll order my Urban Cohorts to join the legions against you and the praetorians."

"Ha! We'll win. We'll smash your police."

"I'd never give you the chance to shed more blood here in Rome, Prefect. My cohorts are on alert to march out of the city the moment I give the order. We'll establish contact with Galba's forces in north Italy."

"Oh, I'm impressed," said Nymphidius sardonically. "But the Rhine legions are loyal. With them we can beat your friends Galba and Otho."

Sabinus shook his head. "Discontent is brewing also in the Rhine legions, I understand. But if not, think, dear Nymphidius, *think:* where else does Rome have legions?"

A gathering frown suddenly shaded the face of the praetorian commander. "The East," he muttered. "Your brother, Vespasian . . . would he really march on Rome?"

"I believe he could provide the . . . necessary honor guard," Sabinus admitted, with a wan smile. "Of course, that would delay things a bit. But meanwhile, there would be no police to keep order in the city, and your praetorians would have their hands full trying to keep the lid on a rebellious lot of citizens who hate Nero almost as much as I do."

"You . . . you'd actually do that, wouldn't you, Sabinus?"

"My troops are armed and ready."

Instantly Nymphidius' face bloomed into a great smile as he reached over to clasp Sabinus' shoulder. "I'm with you, Prefect! I'm *with you!* For the last couple of weeks I've been looking for an excuse to drop my allegiance to that . . . blundering buffoon of a Caesar. But I *had to be sure* of your politics. *And* your determination. Nero's agents are *everywhere* lately."

Slowly Sabinus sank onto a couch and wiped his brow. "*You* should be on the stage, Nymphidius, not Nero. What a front! Excuse me a moment . . ."

Presently, Sabinus reappeared with a wine flask and poured out two generous goblets for them.

"Now, as I was asking," Sabinus continued, smiling with profound relief, "who commands the Guard? You, or the elusive Tigellinus?"

"We don't even know where Tigellinus *is* for sure," Nymphidius chuckled. "He simply abandoned Nero: couldn't stand the way he was facing the crises . . ."

"When?" Sabinus could hardly believe the good news.

"Two days ago was the last anyone saw him. And Tigellinus *is* a master coward, you know. Just like the proverbial rat scampering off a foundering galley, he's left Rome."

"What's the mood of the praetorians? *Will* they sack Nero and declare for Galba?"

"Yes—*if* I promise them enough of a gift from Galba. But it's Nero's German bodyguard I'm worried about. They have a deadly loyalty . . ."

"The Germans?" Sabinus paced the room in thought. Then he stopped and smiled. "Let's simply get rid of them."

"How?"

"Wasn't Nero planning a trip to Egypt?"

"Yes—he wanted to give concerts there, but now he's sailing there for his own safety."

"All right. Why not have him send the Germans on ahead? To 'check security in Alexandria and welcome him on arrival.'"

Nymphidius nodded emphatically. "Yes. Yes indeed. He'll do it too, if I suggest it."

"When does he plan to sail?"

"June 9 or 10."

"All right, then. Here's the schedule: the German bodyguard goes off at once. Then, on June 8, I'll enter the Senate and ask it to depose Nero. Aulus Plautius, my father-in-law, will support my motion with news that your praetorians are deciding the same way. Meanwhile, my Urban Cohorts will have declared for Galba, and we'll all march over to the Castra Praetoria and help you convince the Guard, if necessary." Sabinus' eyes were blazing. "Well, what do you think of it, Nymphidius?"

He smiled and reached out to clasp Sabinus' hand. "It has to succeed—*if* we stay in close touch."

"Twice a day from now on. Let me know when the Germans have sailed."

"Right."

Now Sabinus grasped his cup and held it high. "*Roma resurgens!*" he toasted.

Nymphidius nodded. "To Rome—rising again!"

31

AT LAST Nero grasped that he was in serious circumstances, and he cast about for help. But Tigellinus had deserted him—the scoundrel was rumored to be somewhere in southern Italy—and only his palace staff was left. But if he kept his wits, his charmed destiny would see him through once again, Nero reasoned, toying with a string of amber worry-beads. His aides were already in Ostia preparing escape ships, for if he could but reach Egypt, he would support himself there as a lyre-player, if necessary. "This little talent of ours will afford us daily bread," he claimed. He did, however, procure a vial of greenish poison from the witch Locusta in case his escape plan miscarried, hiding it inside a golden box in the bedroom of the villa where he was still residing.

Maybe, though, escape wasn't necessary after all. Hurrying into his office, he rehearsed a plan with his private secretary. "I'll dress in black, Epaphroditus, walk into the Forum, and mount the rostrum. There I'll beg the people to forgive me for any past offenses. I'll even fall on my knees if necessary . . ."

The rotund little secretary looked up at him and replied, "Do you *really* think you could soften their hearts in such a way, Caesar?"

"I think so. Why not? But if they won't have me back, I'll ask for something less . . . say . . . the prefecture of Egypt. Or maybe the kingship of Jerusalem?"

Epaphroditus shook his pudgy cheeks in dismay. "The people are hungry, Caesar. They're angry. They might even tear you to pieces before you reached the rostrum."

"Gods!" Nero whimpered. "What . . . what can I do, Epaphroditus?"

"I don't know, Caesar. It was foolish of you to send your German bodyguard on to Egypt, I think."

"But Nymphidius advised me to . . ."

"Yes, and I wonder why. Any word from Ostia yet on the escape ships?"

"No." Nero's pout now faded into a smile. "But I know I'll get through all this: when I was in Greece, the Oracle at Delphi told me, '*Watch out for the seventy-third year!*' Bah! I'm only thirty. I still have a long life ahead of me."

The freedman looked up at him. "Princeps, did it ever occur to you that Galba . . . is seventy-three years old?"

Horror gripped Nero as he stalked out into the Servilian Gardens and paced their wooded lanes, plotting desperately. Returning to his villa about midnight, he summoned the palace guard. No one replied. All the remaining praetorians had left. He yelled for anybody who was there to show himself. Epaphroditus and several freedmen appeared. "But where are my friends?" Nero wailed pathetically, and then went from door to door in the palatial villa to find them. The rooms were empty.

In a panic, Nero fled to his bedroom, which he found in shocking disorder. While he was out roaming the gardens, even his valets had deserted him, taking all his valuables, including the golden box with the poison. Nero collapsed onto his bed, pressing his head between his hands. "They could have *had* the box," he cried, tears streaming down his face, "but I needed the poison."

Now he darted up from his bed and ran out of the villa.

"Where are you going?" Epaphroditus called.

"To fling myself into the Tiber!" he replied, "—iber," "—iber," re-echoing through the cavernous halls.

In a short time, though, he was back. "I need some place to hide while I plan my escape," said Nero, with a new determination. "Where can I go?"

Phaon, another of his freedmen, replied, "I have a villa in the northeastern suburbs. It's between the Via Nomentana and the Via Salaria . . . near the fourth milestone."

"Good, Phaon, brilliant. We'll go there . . ."

Barefoot and dressed only in a tunic, Nero put on a faded cloak, covering the lower part of his face with a handkerchief, then mounted a horse and rode out into the night. Epaphroditus, Phaon, and the catamite Sporus accompanied him on other mounts. Their route led them dangerously close to the Castra Praetoria, near enough for Nero to hear shouts of "Victory to Galba!" and "Nero has warbled his last!" Everything was happening exactly as Sabinus had scheduled.

The dark early hours of June 9 were awesome to the horsemen. Flashes of lightning in the distance and rumbles were heralding an approaching storm, but nothing terrified Nero so much as comments of late-drinking roisterers who were making their way home: "Who're they?" one asked. "Prob'ly after Nero."

At the outskirts of Rome, they rode through some low hills until they came to a bypath leading to Phaon's villa. Here they turned their horses loose and made their way on foot through bushes, brambles, and reeds. Just behind the villa was a sand pit, where Phaon whispered to Nero, "Hide here until I can dismiss my household staff tomorrow morning."

"Oh no," Nero objected. "I'm not going underground while I'm still alive."

"Sshhh, Caesar!" Phaon warned. "All right, then. We'll dig a secret entrance into the basement. Help me, brothers."

All helped except Nero, who walked over to a water hole nearby where he scooped up the water and drank it from his hands. "So this is Nero's snow-cooled, distilled water," he remarked grimly. Then he sat down and pulled the briars out of his cloak.

When the passage tunnel was ready, Nero crawled on all fours into the villa and lay down on an old couch in a small, empty slave's room. His companions brought him coarse bread and water. In whispers, they now plotted Nero's escape.

"Well and good to declare him a public enemy," Sabinus told a predawn meeting of his officers, "but where is the man himself? He's escaped so many times before."

Quickly mustering two companies of mounted police, he rode to the villa in the Servilian Gardens where Nero was last reported. Bursting through the main entrance, they clattered inside.

"In the name of the Senate and the Roman People," Sabinus called out, "I have orders to arrest Lucius Domitius Ahenobarbus, formerly Nero Caesar!"

Only echoes replied.

"Search the place," Sabinus commanded. "Bring me anyone you find."

The police fanned out into the villa. Minutes later they came back with a gardener and two kitchen servants.

"Is this *all* you could find? Out of a staff of hundreds?" Turning to the three, Sabinus asked, "Where's Nero?"

The women shrugged their shoulders.

"Do you know?" he asked the gardener.

The man slowly shook his head, avoiding Sabinus' eyes.

Sabinus grabbed him by the shoulders and held him tight. "Where is Caesar?"

The gardener cleared his throat and said, "He was always kind to me . . ."

"But he was a monster to hundreds of others. Your last chance, or I'm arresting you for high treason."

Sadly, the man nodded. "Late last night . . . on horseback. Epaphroditus, Phaon . . . I couldn't see the fourth."

"Did they say where they were going?"

"No. Well . . . one of them did mention the Via Salaria . . ."

Sabinus studied the floor for several moments. "Phaon's villa." He suddenly brightened.

"One contingency we must admit, Caesar," Phaon whispered in the basement of his villa. "May the gods forbid, but you *may* be found here . . ."

"In which case I must . . . die first. Yes, let's . . . get all that ready. Why not here . . . in the floor?"

"What, Caesar?"

"My grave," Nero said, trembling. "Dig it to the proportions of my body. And Phaon, do you have any pieces of marble around? Find something. The earth alone . . . seems so common. And Sporus dear, do fetch some water and some wood."

"Why? Oh . . . to . . . ." Then he broke into tears.

"Yes, water to anoint the body," Nero said in a hollow tone, warped by dread. "And fire to consume it after you've put it . . . down there. But remember, there's to be *no* mutilation of the body. The"—he broke down and wept—"the head must not be severed from the body." He could not bring himself to say "my head."

He tried to get some sleep during the early morning hours, but he started at every sound—a dog barking, a twig breaking in the wind, the rustle of a bush. With the first light of dawn, a courier delivered a message to Phaon.

Nero snatched the dispatch out of Phaon's hands and read it. It was a public notice from the Senate:

WANTED FOR ARREST

LUCIUS DOMITIUS AHENOBARBUS

formerly *Nero Caesar*, whom the Senate has declared a public enemy. He shall be punished in the ancient fashion. Anyone knowing his whereabouts must report them immediately to the nearest magistrate.

"What's that? Punishment 'in the ancient fashion'?" Nero groaned.

No one seemed ready to tell him, and Nero grew angry.

"All right," said Epaphroditus. "The criminal—or rather, the victim," he corrected himself, "is stripped naked, his neck is chained inside a V-shaped yoke, and he is marched through the city . . ."

"And? And then?"

"Then he is beaten to death with rods, and his body is thrown down into the Tiber."

"*Great Jupiter*, no!" Nero cried, and now began shedding tears in earnest. He reached down to his belt for two daggers he had carried with him from the villa, trying the point and the edge of each. "This one," he said. "But only if necessary."

Then he gingerly tested the size of his basement grave by crawling into it. Whimpering a bit, he then climbed back out and pleaded, "Why won't anyone say anything? Sporus? Little Sporus, sing a lament for me, my dear. Or cry a little, will you?"

Sporus lowered his pretty head and tried.

"I have it." Nero smiled. "Maybe one of you could set me an example by . . . taking your own life ahead of me." He held out his hand and eagerly offered one of his daggers. But no one seemed ready to accept his suggestion.

"For shame, Nero," he frowned, chastising himself. "This doesn't become you . . . doesn't become you at all. *Courage,* man!"

He walked to a corner of the basement and stared at the stone and mortar for several moments. Then he whipped about and said, "I wonder if we aren't giving up too easily, my friends." He had a glint in his eyes, which started twitching with excitement. Fresh energy seemed to suffuse him as he paced the basement in thought, his dark blond curls swinging with every step as he cocked his head low and tightened the muscles in his bull neck for an attempted charge out of the constricting corral of Fate.

"Yes." He smiled. "Yes, there *is* a way. We'll stay under cover during the daylight hours. Then tonight, we steal out, head eastward across the Apennines, and go down the coast to Brundisium. There we'll get a ship and—*what's that?*" he suddenly cried, blanching with terror.

Horses' hoofs were thundering to a crescendo outside. Phaon darted upstairs to investigate. Nero quavered, whispering a line from the *Iliad:* "Hark! The hoofs of galloping horses strike my ear!"

Phaon returned, crying, "Urban Cohorts, Caesar! They've come to arrest you."

His face white, his forehead wet with sweat, Nero turned to his secretary and pleaded, "H-help me, Epaphroditus . . . if it's necessary." Clutching a dagger, he brought it up to his throat and said, "*Qualis artifex pereo!* What an artist dies in me!"

Then he plunged the point into his throat, avoiding his voice box. But the blade had entered only an inch. Nero's wild, agonized eyes told Epaphroditus what he had to do. He gave the dagger a penetrating thrust several inches deeper into Nero's thick neck and then moved it from side to side, widening the wound. Soon Nero collapsed at his feet, and the floor of the basement was washed in a warm tide of imperial blood.

There was a loud pounding at the door upstairs. Brushing aside the domestic who answered it, Sabinus and his centurions stormed inside, calling out the arrest notice. A groan from the basement broke the silence, and they rushed downstairs—to a pathetic sight. Nero, his eyes pink with tears and burning with pain, was clutching the end of a dagger buried in a flowing belt of red girdling his neck.

Sabinus was staggered. He had come to the villa, saturated with vengeance—the spirits of dead friends and hundreds of victims driving him on. His one great dream over the past months—no, years—

had been to load Nero with chains and present him triumphantly to the Senate, or happily slash a sword through his squat, ugly neck if he resisted in the slightest.

But the gasping, kicking victim below him wrenched out a measure of pity. Hurrying to Nero's side, he ordered a centurion to try to stanch the bleeding by putting a cloak next to the wound. Nero looked up at him. "Too late, Sabinus," he gurgled. "This . . . is loyalty."

A final gasp and kick and he stopped breathing, his eyes gaping open in their sockets. Sabinus and the others shuddered at the sight. The thirty-year-old ruler of the world—the last of the Julio-Claudian Caesars—was truly dead.

Shaking his head in persistent disbelief, Sabinus gave Epaphroditus and his friends custody of the remains. Then he left.

Nero's body was taken back to Rome, laid out in white robes embroidered with gold, and quickly cremated lest it be mutilated by the people. His two nurses from childhood carried an urn full of his ashes to the family mausoleum of the Domitii on the summit of the Pincian hill at the north of Rome and deposited them in a sarcophagus of porphyry. There was only one other mourner at the simple interment: the woman who had remained faithful to Nero despite his multiple marriages and tangled perversions—his first great love, the beautiful Greek freedwoman Acte.

32

SABINUS returned to Rome at a furious gallop and called the Senate into extraordinary session within the hour. He also sent special word to Plautia and her parents to come to the chamber at once and witness the great scene.

By midmorning, nearly all Conscript Fathers were in their places, filling the chamber with a buzzing drone of anxious dialogue. The presiding consul stood up and announced, "Our distinguished city prefect, Titus Flavius Sabinus, has urgent news for us. I will only add that for years now, Clarissimus, you have been the one rock of stability in the . . . earthquake around us. The Senate and the Roman People are . . . profoundly grateful."

The Fathers started applauding enthusiastically and even rose in unanimous support of the consul's opinion.

Moved by the sight, Sabinus hurried to the dais with a great smile and motioned the senators to be seated. "Thank you, my colleagues!" he responded, to an instant hush. "My gratitude is that brief because the extraordinary news cannot be denied you any longer. You are, of course, wondering about the former emperor. Last night, he fled from Rome with three aides. At dawn today, we found them hiding at the house of his freedman Phaon northeast of the city.

Honorably judging himself, Nero took a dagger to his throat, and died—not quite three hours ago."

A deathly hush hung in the chamber for several moments. Then it was shattered by a general uproar—a shouting, applauding near-hysteria of jubilation—the final release to years of searing frustration for the Fathers, of enforced hypocrisy and clutching anxiety. Up in the gallery, Pomponia clasped Plautia to herself in exhilaration, staring through her tears at Aulus, who was beaming up at them from below.

It was fully ten minutes before Sabinus could continue. Even then there were still pockets of applause and shouts of "Sabinus for emperor!" "Sabinus Caesar!" "Our new princeps!" Holding up his hands for silence, Sabinus unleashed a broad smile but shook his head. He went on to supply details of Nero's last hours and then answered as many of their questions as he could before dismissing them. "The people of Rome have a right to hear the happy news also. Let each of you be a herald of joy."

In minutes, the city of Rome was erupting in a symphony of rejoicing, each class providing a glad orchestration of its own. The oppressive pall of fear that had smothered the people was dissolved at last. The rich were talking to the poor, commoners were embracing slaves, and even the crime rate dropped. A sense of civic joy was everywhere.

Sabinus and Plautia finally celebrated spring that second week in June, calling their friends up to the Quirinal for a lavish festivity in honor of freedom. The aging Aulus happily brought Pomponia over in the brightest costume she had worn in years. One of the first things he did was to lead a toast in memory of his friend Thrasea Paetus, his nephew Quintus Lateranus, "and all the many victims." The entire company arose in solemn remembrance.

Sabinus, who had aged markedly in the last months, bowed his gray-streaked head, relieved that it was still attached. He thought of how the irrepressible Quintus would have relished the present moment, and his eyes misted at memories of the twin brother. He also wondered if any other age had witnessed so extraordinary a clash of good and evil, so grotesque a collision of violence and depravity with idealism and love.

Plautia played the role of serene and happy hostess at the party, still lovely and suffused with the bloom of youth. When his friends were bantering Sabinus for keeping a child bride on the premises, Plautia loyally proved her age by calling in their eldest and showing him off to the guests. Young Flavius was now almost eight years old, and, with his tousled brown locks, he seemed the very image of his father—in younger days.

Not to be outdone, little Clemens scampered into the atrium as well. His hair was still a childish flaxen yellow, bleached by the hot spring sunshine of Rome. He was aping all the movements of his older brother and showing off to his heart's content until Plautia whisked them both out of the room. Off near the center fountain sat Aulus, his eyes burning with all the grandfatherly delight the old soldier-senator could muster. If only Plautia had brought out baby Plautilla too, his bliss would have been complete.

Pomponia looked at Aulus and breathed a prayer of gratitude to her God. Never had she been happier about her husband. After almost twenty years of scoffing at her beliefs, Aulus was now becoming intrigued by the extraordinary hopes which animated her faith. It had occurred to him one day earlier that spring as he was sitting in his garden study: no other philosophy, no other religious system had such definite plans for people after they died. The concept of a higher existence was appealing enough for one, like himself, who would soon find out if anything lay behind—and beyond—this life. Now he was sure that the Christians could not, as he had earlier supposed, merely be *used* as moral props for Rome, because what they believed had to have a validity of its own, or it was nothing.

Soon the men had withdrawn into the peristyle, where the conversation turned to the new emperor, Servius Galba. Several younger senators in the group voiced qualms about Galba. "Yes, he comes from an old senatorial family," said one of them, "but power has corrupted more than one good citizen in that position. I say let's have done with it all."

"Yes, end the Empire!" a colleague responded. "Restore the Republic!"

"One thing at a time, gentlemen." Sabinus smiled. "Nero's gone, and that's most of the battle."

"Seriously now, Sabinus," one of the older senators remarked, "quite a number of us think that *you* are easily the most qualified man in all Rome to wear the purple."

"Yes indeed," another agreed. "Augustus would—"

"No, no, no, good friends," Sabinus laughed. "Haven't I put in my time? Besides, my brother Vespasian is the one who now controls almost half the Roman legions."

The tall figure with Greek dark hair was late in arriving, and he excused himself for that. Pomponia and Plautia ran to the vestibule and welcomed him with outstretched arms. Sabinus, too, gripped the hand of Luke enthusiastically.

"The Beast is dead, thanks be to God!" said Luke, with a warm smile. "And to your efforts, Prefect! Nero tried to exterminate us . . . but failed. And now the embers of the Faith that Paul spoke about are indeed rekindling into flame. Someday all nations will be brightened with their glow!" Luke's eyes blazed with a distant look, as if peering over their heads centuries into the future.

"What are you carrying under your arm, Luke?" inquired Sabinus.

"Aha!" Luke chuckled. "Well, it's finally safe to give you these." He handed Sabinus two large brown leather cylinders with scrolls inside. "One is what I call my *Evangelium*, my 'Glad Tidings.' The other is my *Acta*, the record of our faith. I"—he paused and looked at the women with a broad smile—"I've dedicated both treatises to *you*, Prefect, because of how you helped us all."

"*Me?*" Sabinus' eyes widened.

"But in order to spare you any embarrassment or even danger, I've not used your personal name—Titus Flavius Sabinus—but rather a code name—Theophilus—a combination of the beginning sounds of your three names. And since Theophilus means 'friend of God,' I thought it quite appropriate."

Sabinus could not know that someday the entire world would know him, not as Flavius Sabinus, but as Theophilus, because the first scroll would soon be called the Gospel According to St. Luke, and the second, the Acts of the Apostles, both biblical books addressed to a certain "Theophilus." Nor could he know that the scrolls would one day so impress his children and even himself that they would share the Faith also.

EPILOGUE

SABINUS AND PLAUTIA might well have wondered if the future would be dull in comparison with the harrowing past. But the strangest twists lay in store both for Rome and their own family.

The emperor Galba—aged and inept—ruled only seven months before the praetorians killed him in favor of Otho. Otho, in turn, was forced to take his own life after only twelve weeks as Caesar. The Rhine legions replaced him with Aulus Vitellius, the son of Claudius' toady adviser, who proved to be a worthless glutton.

The eastern legions finally lost all patience with the praetorians and the western legions, who had enthroned three worthless successors to an unbearable tyrant. In the summer of A.D. 69, they declared for the commander who was putting down the revolt in Palestine, whose son Titus would conquer Jerusalem while he himself assumed emperorship. Incredibly, it was the former bankrupt mule-trader who got pelted with mud in Rome or turnips in Africa, a man who literally could not stay awake in some circumstances to save his own life—Sabinus' debtor brother, T. Flavius Vespasian. With the proper challenge, he "did something with his life" after all, as one of Rome's ablest emperors. Vespasian gave Rome a decade of peace, prosperity, and freedom, erected the great Colosseum over the ruins of Nero's Golden House, and founded the Flavian dynasty of emperors.

And Sabinus? He gave his life for the Flavian cause, fighting heroically on the Capitoline hill to deliver Rome to his brother. The Senate decreed Sabinus the highest funeral the Empire could bestow and erected his statue in the Forum.

Tigellinus was found—surrounded by mistresses at the sulfur baths down in Sinuessa, where he took a razor and slit his own throat. Locusta, the witch, and Helius, the puppet, were led across Rome in chains and executed. Sporus committed suicide.

Two structures, finally, have a fascinating epilogue of their own. Quintus Lateranus' mansion, confiscated by Nero and retained by succeeding emperors, was given at last by Constantine to the Christian bishop of Rome. Eventually, it became the headquarters of the Western church, the Lateran Palace of the popes and site of the famous Lateran councils—a clear perpetuation of Quintus' name. Today, its base is incorporated in the Basilica of St. John in the Lateran, the mother church of Rome.

And the Egyptian obelisk that witnessed Nero's persecution of the Christians stands today at the center of the great circular colonnade in front of St. Peter's Basilica at the Vatican. St. Peter's itself marks the presumed site of Peter's grave, while the Basilica of St. Paul ("Outside the Walls"), that of the other great apostle.

HISTORICAL NOTE

ALL CHARACTERS and all major and many minor episodes in this book are historical and have been documented in the Notes below. The portrayal of imperial politics under Claudius and Nero is fully authentic. However, the connective material and much of the dialogue was contrived, but done so on the basis of probabilities with no violation of historical fact. Because of missing evidence, some relationships were necessarily presumed. The true name of Sabinus' wife, who bore Flavius and Clemens, is unknown, but she may indeed have been Plautia, an otherwise unrecorded daughter of Aulus Plautius and named for her father, a supposition based on facts explained in the Notes. Plautia's is the only proper name in this book not attested by an original primary source.

Demands of the novel required the trimming away of several minor historical characters to keep the cast from becoming unwieldy, such as Hosidius Geta, who also received honors at Aulus' ovation on the Capitoline, and Antonia, daughter of Claudius by Paetina.

The role of Aquila and Priscilla in this story is partially presumed, but they were leaders of the earliest Christian church in Rome and were closely associated with Paul in both East and West. Since the persons and circumstances involved in Paul's Roman trial(s) and death are almost unknown, they were reconstructed from all shreds of available evidence. Because of the source problem, the role of Peter in Rome was even more difficult to restore, but avoiding, as in the case of Paul, the rich encrustation of legends, the portrayal in these pages has tried to flesh out what faint clues we have.

Finally, Sabinus' efforts in behalf of the Christians are only presumed, but they are, again, in accord with the sources, which show him a noble-minded peacemaker and father of the probably Christian Clemens. His exact role in the overthrow of Nero is unknown. Other items are clarified in the Notes.

NOTES

THE PEOPLE, places, and events portrayed in this book can be documented in the following ancient sources: Tacitus, *Annals*, xi–xvi; *Histories*, i–iii; Suetonius, *Lives of the Caesars*, v–xii; Dio Cassius, *Roman History* (hereafter "Dio Cassius"), lxi–lxiv. Additional evidence for the era A.D. 47 to 69—the time frame in these pages—was derived from the works of Arrian, Aurelius Victor, Eutropius, Josephus, Juvenal, Lucan, Lucian, Martial, Pliny, Plutarch, Seneca, Strabo, and, among Christian authors, Clement of Rome, Luke, Paul, Peter, Tertullian, and others. Archaeology and epigraphy are listed below.

While it would have been possible to document in much greater detail than the references below, only the very significant or disputed items are noted here, particularly where reconstructions have been necessary as a result of missing evidence.

CHAPTER I (Pages 3–19)

T. FLAVIUS SABINUS: Tacitus, *Histories*, i–iv *passim*; Suetonius, *Vitellius*, xv; *Divus Vespasianus*, i; *Domitianus*, i; Dio Cassius, lx, 20; lxv, 17; Plutarch, *Otho*, v; Josephus, *Wars of the Jews*, iv, 11, 4; Sextus Aurelius Victor, *De Caesaribus*, viii; and a mutilated dedicatory inscription in *Corpus Inscriptionum Latinarum* (here-

after *CIL*), VI, 31293. For an inscription recording two letters of
Sabinus to the people of Histria (in Rumania), confirming their
rights at a time when he was governor of Moesia, see *Supplementum Epigraphicum Graecum*, I, 329.

FLAVIUS VESPASIAN: Above references, and Tacitus, *Annals*, iii, 55;
xvi, 5.

THE PLAUTII: For a catalogue of the prominent members of this
Roman gens, see the article "Plautius" in Georg Wissowa, ed.,
Paulys Real-Encyclopädie der classischen Altertumswissenschaft
(Stuttgart: Metzlersche and Druckenmüller Verlag, 1953 ff.),
hereafter Pauly-Wissowa. For the authenticity of Plautia, daughter of Aulus Plautius, see Historical Note above, and the entry
"Plautilla" under Chapter 30 below. Plautius Lateranus' first
name is unrecorded, but since he was doubtless the son of
Quintus Plautius, the consul in A.D. 36, it would most probably
have been Quintus.

CHAPTER 2 (Pages 20–27)

MESSALINA'S STRATAGEM: Incredible as it may seem, Messalina's
method of winning her lovers with apparent imperial approval is
historical. As Dio Cassius states: "Claudius told Mnester to do
whatever he should be ordered to do by Messalina. . . . Messalina also adopted this same method with various other men and
committed adultery, pretending that Claudius knew what was
going on and approved her unchastity" (lx, 22). Since Lateranus
was seduced after Mnester, it is likely that he was subjected to the
same ruse.

CHAPTER 3 (Pages 28–35)

THE GAIUS SILIUS AFFAIR: For the entire extraordinary episode, see
Tacitus, *Annals*, xi, 12, 26–38; Suetonius, *Divus Claudius*, xxvi;
Dio Cassius, lx, 31; and Juvenal, *Satires*, x, 328 ff.

CHAPTER 4 (Pages 36–49)

THE BACCHANAL AT SILIUS': Tacitus, *Annals*, xi, 31–32.

CHAPTER 5 (Pages 50–63)

MESSALINA'S REMARRIAGE A SHAM? Suetonius, *Divus Claudius*,
xxix, suggests, contrary to Tacitus, that Claudius knowingly
signed the contract for the dowry in the supposedly sham mar-

riage to Silius, but I am inclined to agree with Suetonius' own words in introducing this version: "It is beyond all belief. . . ."

THE PUNISHMENTS: Tacitus, *Annals*, xi, 35–38.

CHAPTER 6 (Pages 64–71)

AQUILA AND PRISCILLA: Acts 18:1 ff.; I Corinthians 16:19; Romans 16:3–4. Their contact with the Plautii is only presumed, but tentmaking was their occupation, and they were in Rome at this time.

CHAPTER 7 (Pages 72–83)

THE "CHRESTUS" RIOT: This was undoubtedly the first public notice of Christianity taken by the Roman state, and the earliest chronological reference to Christ by a secular author. In *Divus Claudius*, xxv, Suetonius writes: "Since the Jews constantly made disturbances at the instigation of Chrestus [*impulsore Chresto*], he [Claudius] expelled them from Rome." Some scholars have argued that Chrestus was the name of a Roman Jew who caused the riot, not Christ, and yet Suetonius would probably have used the term *quodam* in that case, "a certain Chrestus." That Chrestus was another form of Christus among Romans of the time is indicated by Tertullian, *Apologeticus*, iii, and Lactantius, *Institutiones Divinae*, iv, 17. The French word for Christian, *chrétien*, reflects this mode of spelling to this day.

EXPULSION OF JEWS FROM ROME: Suetonius, *loc. cit.*, and Acts 18:2, which refers also to the specific expulsion of Aquila and Priscilla and their arrival in Corinth. On the other hand, Dio Cassius, lx, 6, writes: "As for the Jews, who had again increased so greatly that because of their numbers it would have been hard to bar them from the city without raising a tumult, he [Claudius] did not drive them out, but ordered them, while continuing their traditional mode of life, not to hold meetings." Dio cites this in connection with events from A.D. 41, whereas Suetonius seems to suggest a later date, and the reference in Acts coordinates with Paul's visit to Corinth in A.D. 51, where he met Aquila who "recently" came from Rome. Hence A.D. 49, the date cited by Orosius for the expulsion (*Historiarum adversus paganos libri vii*, vii, 6) would seem preferable, since Dio appears to be summarizing some of Claudius' future acts in his lengthy discussion of the first year of the emperor's reign. He is correct, however, in suggesting that

Claudius could not possibly have banished *all* Jews from Rome.

PILATE'S *Acta*: This wording is only presumed, but there is no question that Pilate would have made some reference to Jesus in his official *acta*. For his role in Jesus' trial and the A.D. 33 dating for the Crucifixion, see my book *Pontius Pilate* (Doubleday, 1968) and my article, "Sejanus, Pilate, and the Date of the Crucifixion," *Church History*, XXXVII (March, 1968), 3–13.

THE GRAVE-ROBBERY ORDINANCE: This inscription, discovered at Nazareth in 1878, remained unnoticed until F. Cumont published it in 1930. The Caesar mentioned in the ordinance is not identified, and some scholars claim that it may date back to Augustus, while others have suggested as late as the time of Hadrian. On the one hand, it is unlikely that any emperor would have set up so harsh an edict in any area not under direct imperial control, and Galilee (where the inscription was found) did not return to the Empire until the death of King Herod Agrippa in A.D. 44, ruling out emperors before Claudius. On the other hand, since the epigraphy indicates Greek writing of the first half of the first century A.D., Claudius would, in fact, seem to be the author of the inscription. For further discussion, see F. Cumont, "Un Rescrit Impérial sur la Violation de Sépulture," *Revue historique*, clxiii (1930), 241–66; F. de Zulueta, "Violation of Sepulture in Palestine at the Beginning of the Christian Era," *Journal of Roman Studies*, xxii (1932), 184–97; M. P. Charlesworth, ed., *Documents Illustrating the Reigns of Claudius and Nero* (Cambridge, 1939), p. 17; and Arnaldo Momigliano, *Claudius* (Cambridge, 1961), pp. 35 ff.; 100 f., though the author later changed his mind, see p. ix.

CHAPTER 8 (Pages 84–91)

AGRIPPINA'S AMBITIONS: Tacitus, *Annals*, xii, 8–42. Pallas' successes are reported in xii, 53–54.

CHAPTER 9 (Pages 92–104)

CLAUDIUS ON FLATULENCE AT THE TABLE: Suetonius, *Divus Claudius*, xxxii.

THE DEATH OF CLAUDIUS: Tacitus, *Annals*, xii, 66–69. In addition to the standard account of Claudius' death, Suetonius, *Divus Claudius*, xliv–xlvi, also cites an alternate version that the eunuch Halotus supplied him the poison while he was banqueting with the priests on the Capitoline, but Dio Cassius, lxi, 34, confirms the Tacitean account. See also Pliny, *Natural History*, xxii, 92, who cites Agrippina as serving Claudius a poison mushroom. A few scholars have questioned whether or not Claudius was actually poisoned, but this would seem unduly revisionist. Later, Nero would jest that mushrooms were "the food of the gods," since his father became one by eating them (Dio Cassius, lx, 35), and Seneca's *Apocolocyntosis* is a play on the colocynth or poisonous wild gourd. Cp. also Juvenal, *Satires*, v, 147 ff.; vi, 620 ff.

CHAPTER 10 (Pages 107–23)

SABINUS IN GAUL: His appointment as *curator census Gallici* after his term as governor of Moesia is attested by the inscription in *CIL*, VI, 31293, but Agrippina's interest in him, while possible, is contrived.

CHAPTER 11 (Pages 124–31)

SENECA: Whether or not the philosopher was involved in the death of Claudius has never been proven. Nor have the circumstances causing his exile to Corsica been clarified, other than Messalina's charge of his adultery with Julia. Sources for Seneca are *passim* in Tacitus, Suetonius, and Dio, as well as the philosopher's own writings.

PLATO ON IDEAL GOVERNMENT: Plato, *Republic*, v, 473.

RETURN OF AQUILA AND PRISCILLA: Presumed from Acts 18:18 ff. and Romans 16:3—probably written in A.D. 56/7—in which Paul salutes them in his letter to Rome.

GALLIO: His "hook" remark is attested by Dio Cassius, lx, 35. See also Pliny, *Natural History*, xxxi, 62; Seneca, *Epistulae Morales*, civ, 1; Tacitus, *Annals*, xv, 73. Paul's appearance before Gallio in Corinth is described in Acts 18:12–17. An important inscription found at Delphi records a rescript of Claudius in which "Junius Gallio, my friend and proconsul of Achaea" is mentioned (Dittenberger, ed., *Sylloge Inscriptionum Graecorum*, Ed., 3, 801 D). The inscription is important not only in confirming the account in Acts, but in dating the life of St. Paul, for it styles Claudius as acclaimed emperor "for the 26th time," indicating A.D. 51–52. For further discussion, see F. J. Foakes-Jackson and Kirsopp Lake, *The Beginnings of Christianity* (London: Macmillan, 1920–33), V, pp. 460–64.

CHAPTER 12 (Pages 132-48)

THE DEATH OF BRITANNICUS: Tacitus, *Annals*, xiii, 14-17; Suetonius, *Nero*, xxxiii; Dio Cassius, lxi, 7. Tacitus cites his sources as stating that Nero violated Britannicus some time before he poisoned him, but since this is not confirmed elsewhere, the lurid addendum is relegated to the Notes. Suetonius, *Divus Titus*, ii, has Titus reclining at the side of Britannicus, but Tacitus' version of a separate table for the youth at which they sat upright is preferable.

CHAPTER 13 (Pages 149-57)

SABINUS APPOINTED URBAN PREFECT: Pliny, *Natural History*, vii, 62, suggests that he succeeded Saturninus in A.D. 56. See also *CIL*, VI, 31293.

CHAPTER 14 (Pages 158-68)

PRAEFECTUS URBI: The most complete discussion of the prerogatives of this office is the article so entitled in Pauly-Wissowa.

NERO'S NIGHT GANGS AND JULIUS MONTANUS: Tacitus, *Annals*, xiii, 25; Suetonius, *Nero*, xxvi; Dio Cassius, lxi, 8-9.

CHAPTER 15 (Pages 169-84)

THE TRIAL OF POMPONIA GRAECINA: The text of Tacitus, our sole source, reads as follows: "Pomponia Graecina, a woman of high family, married to Aulus Plautius—whose ovation after the British campaign I recorded earlier—and now arraigned for alien superstition, was left to the jurisdiction of her husband. Following the ancient custom, he held the inquiry, which was to determine the fate and fame of his wife, before a family council, and announced her innocent." (*Annals*, xiii, 32; John Jackson's translation in Loeb Classical Library.)

The identity of the alien superstition (*superstitionis externae rea*) is a matter of some dispute. Lipsius, the great classical scholar of the sixteenth century, first suggested Christianity, and this conclusion has been adopted by the Loeb text and many scholars since that time. However, Judaism, Isis and Osiris, and even Druidism have also been suggested, though without any compelling basis. Some have tried to see in Pomponia's retiring life an early form of Christian asceticism, and there is archaeological evidence that

later Pomponii were indeed Christian, for the Christian catacombs
of Callistus provide inscriptions of a Pomponius Graecinus and of
the Pomponii Bassi, dating from the second century. See G.-B. De
Rossi, *Roma Sotterranea Cristiana*, ii, 364. The objection raised
by some commentators against Pomponia's Christianity, i.e., that
she escaped any penalties in both A.D. 57 and 64, is easily answered: at the former date, Christianity was not yet illegalized,
and at the latter, Nero's persecution by no means eliminated all
the Christians in Rome.

The nature of the prosecution and the defense at Pomponia's
trial is not given by Tacitus, but I have incorporated in the charges
the standard calumnies which Romans raised against Christianity
at this time and subsequently, as cited by Justin, Tertullian, Minu-
cius Felix, and other Christian apologists. Cossutianus Capito as
prosecutor is only assumed in the absence of other evidence, since
he was the most notorious informer of that time (see Tacitus,
Annals, xi, 6; xiii, 33). In the defense—again, Lateranus' role is
only assumed—the verses cited from Paul's letter are Romans 13:1,
7–9, 13.

CHAPTER 16 (Pages 185–204)

OTHO AND POPPAEA: The sources vary widely on how Nero's romance with Poppaea began. The most reasonable version, offered
in the text, follows Tacitus, *Annals*, xiii, 45 f. Tacitus does refer to
an alternate suggestion that Otho *intended* his wife to attract
Nero in order to build his own power over the emperor, but this
seems unlikely and certainly proved to be a foolish plan, if true.

AGRIPPINA INCESTUOUS: There are more scandalous reports regarding Nero and his mother. Tacitus cites his own sources: Cluvius,
for the version which he prefers and I have incorporated; and
Fabius Rusticus, who said that it was Nero who took the initiative
vis-à-vis his mother. Suetonius, *Nero*, xxviii, records that Nero
had incestuous relations with Agrippina as they rode in a litter,
the stains on his clothes betraying it. Cp. also Dio Cassius, lxi, 11.

THE PLOT AT BAIAE: Suetonius, *loc. cit.;* Tacitus, *Annals*, xiv, 3–5;
Dio Cassius, lxi, 12–13. Strabo, *Geographica*, v, 245, provides the
detail that it was an oyster boat which picked up Agrippina.

PAUL'S ARRIVAL AT PUTEOLI: Acts 28:11–13. That St. Paul approached Puteoli on the very night of the collapsible-boat episode
cannot, of course, be documented, but the coincidence has consid-

erable historical basis *if* the apostle reached Italy in A.D. 59, a date favored by many scholars. Paul and his associates wintered "three months" in Malta (Acts 28:11). Since the Mediterranean was technically closed to shipping until March 10, it is at least reasonable to assume that the voyage resumed on or about March 11, since maritime insurance could have been vitiated by an earlier voyage during *mare clausum*. Once resumed, the run from Malta to Puteoli, with stops at the various ports of call mentioned in Acts 28:12–13, took at least nine days, making the estimated date for arrival March 20. Since the Festival of Minerva was celebrated March 19–23, the banquet at Baiae could well have taken place on the second night of the festival, March 20, the same night as Paul's arrival in the above scenario. While hardly provable, then, the coincidence is not as remote as one might assume.

CHAPTER 17 (Pages 205–17)

THE MURDER OF AGRIPPINA: Tacitus, *Annals,* xiv, 6–12; Suetonius, *Nero,* xxxiv; Dio Cassius, lxi, 13–16. Whether or not Seneca and Burrus knew beforehand of the plot against Agrippina is not definite. Dio suggests that Seneca was indeed involved, but his bias against the philosopher is notorious. Tacitus, typically more careful, suggests that he and Burrus only "possibly" were in on the plot. The lurid mention in some sources that Nero carefully examined his mother's corpse, praising its beauty, need not detain us.

PAUL'S ARRIVAL IN ROME: Acts 28:14–16. The Western version of the Greek text at Acts 28:16 has this interesting variation: "When we came to Rome, the centurion handed the prisoners over to the commandant of the camp [*to stratopedarcho*], and Paul was ordered to remain by himself with the soldiers who were guarding him." In commenting on this variant, Theodor Mommsen defined the *stratopedarchos* as the princeps *peregrinorum* ("Zu Apostelgesch. 28, 16," *Sitzungsberichte der Königlich Preussischen Akademie der Wissenschaften zu Berlin* [1895], 491–503). But A. N. Sherwin-White more aptly suggests princeps *castrorum* as the best identification of this officer, for he was the "commandant of the camp" of the praetorians where Paul would most likely have been brought. See A. N. Sherwin-White, *Roman Society and Roman Law in the New Testament* (Oxford: Clarendon, 1963), pp. 108–10.

PAUL AND THE JEWS OF ROME: Acts 28:17-28. Where Paul lived in Rome for two years is unknown, but it must have been in the vicinity of the Castra Praetoria, in a house large enough to accommodate the crowd indicated in Acts 28:23.

CHAPTER 18 (Pages 218-29)

GROWTH OF CHRISTIANITY AT ROME: Paul's reference to praetorian converts is supported by Philippians 1:12-14. He also closed that letter with this salutation: "All the saints greet you, especially those of Caesar's household" (4:22, both RSV). There is some debate over whether the "prison epistles" were written in Ephesus, Caesarea, or Rome, but the scholarly consensus leans strongly to the last, particularly because of the verses here cited. Earlier, Paul had written the Roman church, greeting brethren "who belong to the family of Narcissus" (Romans 16:11), though whether Claudius' secretary is meant here is not known. Paul's claims to Christianity's growth are not inflated, because in just four years, an "immense number" of Christians would die in Nero's persecution, according to Tacitus, *Annals*, xv, 44. Jesus' statement about appearing before kings is Matthew 10:18.

L. PEDANIUS SECUNDUS, not Flavius Sabinus, was *praefectus urbi* in A.D. 61 (Tacitus, *Annals*, xiv, 42). Sabinus certainly succeeded him in office, and because Sabinus served Rome for twelve years as city prefect (Tacitus, *Histories*, iii, 75), most scholars conclude that Sabinus served *two* terms as prefect: A.D. 56-60, and A.D. 61/2-69. See the discussion in Pauly-Wissowa under "166) Flavius Sabinus, der Bruder Vespasians."

SABINUS' BABY: T. Flavius Sabinus was the eldest of Sabinus' children. Though the precise year of his birth is unknown, it is closely estimated to be c. A.D. 60. See Suetonius, *Domitianus*, x; Dio Cassius, lxv, 17. Cp. Tacitus, *Histories*, iii, 69 and CIL, VI, 20, 3828.

CHAPTER 19 (Pages 230-49)

ABSENCE OF PAUL'S PROSECUTION: Another reason may lie in the Temple Wall controversy. Angered that Agrippa II had erected a dining room atop his palace from which he could look into the Temple, the Jerusalem authorities raised the west wall of the Temple so that it obstructed Agrippa's view. Agrippa and Festus ordered them to pull it down, but the priests sent ten of their leaders to Rome to appeal to Nero. Through Poppaea's intervention, Nero permitted the wall to stand. (See Josephus, *Antiquities*, xx, 8, 11.) Accordingly, the Jewish authorities may have decided not to "press their luck" for what must have seemed the comparatively insignificant case of Paul.

PALLAS PROTECTS FELIX: Josephus, *Antiquities*, xx, 8, 9. Why Pallas should still have been in a position to intercede in behalf of his brother after his own fall from power is puzzling. In dismissing him from office, however, Nero did give Pallas extraordinary concessions.

TIGELLINUS: His role in Paul's trial is only assumed. It is known that he came to prominence at this time, and the actual prosecution at Paul's trial, if any, is unknown. But allowing another party to renew an accusation in the absence of the original accusers was permitted under Roman law (*Digestae*, xlviii, 16; x, 2).

PAUL'S ROMAN TRIAL is extremely difficult to reconstruct, since the primary source stops at Acts 28 with only a few hints in the epistles. Some scholars doubt that Paul ever appeared before Nero; others claim he did indeed. The only certainty is that he waited "two whole years" in Rome before any hearing took place (Acts 28:30).

On the basis of all scraps of evidence in the prison epistles (the above passages in which Paul looks forward to a positive resolution of his case), the political situation in both Palestine and Rome, and the known court procedure in appeals to the emperor, I have endeavored to reconstruct the trial as set forth in the text. The general outline would indeed be accurate, in that the basis of accusation would be the same three indictments cited by Tertullus in Paul's first hearing before Felix (Acts 24:1–9). On any appeal, the original character of the case was always preserved.

That Nero heard both accusation and defense on each specific charge before moving to the next was his judicial custom, according to Suetonius, *Nero*, xv. Whether Paul defended himself or had an advocate is not known. Sabinus' role here is only assumed, but Paul would not have disdained such help, for during his second trial he would complain, "At my first defense [in the second trial], no one took my part; all deserted me" (II Timothy 4:16).

Paul's record in Asia Minor, Greece, and Palestine is described in Acts 13–23. The incident regarding Trophimus and the four Jews is Acts 21:17 ff. The Temple notice prohibiting Gentiles (cited by

Josephus, *Antiquities*, xv, 11, 5; *Wars*, vi, 2, 4) has also been discovered by archaeologists. Agrippa's statement absolving Paul (Acts 26:31 f.) would have been powerful evidence for the defense, but whether it was included in any deposition from Festus is unknown.

The most complete discussion on Paul's trial in Rome is Henry J. Cadbury, "Roman Law and the Trial of St. Paul," in Jackson and Lake, *Beginnings, op. cit.*, V, pp. 297–338. Cadbury makes the interesting observation that any Judean prosecution, faced by heavy transportation and legal expenses, might have enlisted the help of Roman Jews for this purpose rather than making the trip themselves, and that the object of Acts 28:21 is to indicate that not even that recourse had been taken. Compare also Sherwin-White, *op. cit.*, pp. 108–119.

NERO DESPISING CULTS: Suetonius, *Nero*, lvi. The goddess in question was Atargatis.

PAUL ACQUITTED? There is strong, though not conclusive, evidence that Paul was indeed acquitted after his first trial at Rome. The pastoral epistles to Timothy and Titus cannot be fitted satisfactorily into the three missionary journeys, and they bespeak Paul's subsequent activities, although the authenticity of the pastorals is much debated.

There is no tradition that Paul was martyred before A.D. 64, and no dating of the apostle's life could reasonably have his two-year imprisonment end in 64. In the meantime, he may well have been released. Clement of Rome, in his epistle to the Corinthians of A.D. 96, states that Paul "reached the limit of the West" [*to terma tes duseos*] before he died (I Clement v, 1–7), which, for a Roman author, would imply Spain or Portugal. (Cp. Strabo, *Geographica*, ii, 1.) Romans 15:24, 28 show that Paul had certainly planned a trip to Spain via Rome, and a second-century document, the Muratorian fragment, states: "Then the 'Acts of the Apostles' were written in one book. Luke says . . . that the various incidents took place in his presence, and indeed he makes this quite clear by omitting the passion of Peter, as well as Paul's journey when he set out from Rome for Spain" (*Canon Muratorii*, xxxviii). This document, however, is somewhat late. Evidence against a trip to Spain is the absence of any local Christian tradition there recalling the apostle's visit. But this would have been brief in any case, and the long Moorish occupation may have expunged it.

While certainty in the matter is impossible, the evidence points to the *probability* of Paul's release after his first trial, and his rearrest, trial, and execution later on (see below). For further discussion of Paul's fate in Rome, see L. P. Pherigo, "Paul's Life after the Close of Acts," *Journal of Biblical Literature*, LXX (1951), 277 ff.; Sherwin-White, *op. cit.*, pp. 108 ff.; and F. F. Bruce, "St. Paul in Rome—Concluding Observations," *Bulletin of the John Rylands Library* (Manchester), L (1967–68), 266–79.

Seneca and Paul: While there is no evidence that the two ever met each other, some contact between Paul and Seneca would easily have been possible at this time. Seneca did, in fact, serve frequently as assessor, and it was his brother Gallio who judged Paul in Corinth. The "golden rule" statement by Seneca is from his *Epistulae Morales*, xlvii, but the famed correspondence between Paul and Seneca is a fourth-century Christian forgery that has no basis in fact.

Luke's Record: The cited passage is Acts 28:30–31, the last verse of Acts and perhaps the most unsatisfactory ending of any book in the Bible. While such an "unresolved fade-out" is very congenial to modern literary taste, it is rather extraordinary for an ancient author, especially one who has pointed his account toward the very matter to be resolved. Why the Acts end so abruptly has been vigorously debated by scholars, see especially Jackson and Lake, *Beginnings, op. cit.*, IV, pp. 349 f. I have suggested an alternative reason in the text.

CHAPTER 20 (Pages 253–66)

The Murder of Pedanius Secundus: Tacitus, *Annals*, xiv, 42–45.

The Death of Burrus: Suetonius states that Nero "sent poison to Burrus . . . in place of a throat medicine which he had promised him" (*Nero*, xxxv), and Dio offers a similar version (lxii, 13). Tacitus, however, leaves open the question as to whether he died from illness or poisoning (*Annals*, xiv, 51). In view of this restraint by a hostile source and the fact that Burrus' symptoms did resemble cancer, Nero may be spared the responsibility for this particular death.

CHAPTER 21 (Pages 267–80)

FLAVIUS CLEMENS: Sabinus' second son probably had "Titus" as his first name, though it is unknown. Suetonius, *Domitianus*, xv; Dio Cassius, lxvii, 14. See discussion on Flavius Clemens in the lengthy note on Chapter 32 below.

NERO'S DEBUT IN NAPLES AND ROME: Tacitus, *Annals*, xv, 33–34; Suetonius, *Nero*, xx–xxi. Petronius' critique of Nero's performance reflects an opinion in the dialogue *Nero*, attributed to Lucian of Samosata, though probably written by the elder Philostratus.

THE ARRIVAL OF PETER: Whether or not Simon Peter ever visited Rome has been debated for centuries. Roman Catholic scholars have been virtually unanimous in insisting that, as first bishop of Rome, Peter must indeed have reached the capital. Protestants have been somewhat divided on the question, although the current consensus agrees that Peter came to Rome.

The evidence *against* Peter's presence in Rome is the silence of the New Testament, particularly Acts, as well as of the second-century Christian apologist who lived in Rome, Justin Martyr.

The evidence *supporting* Peter's presence in Rome is larger. If, as seems probable, "Babylon" were a cryptic name for Rome, then I Peter was addressed from Rome (I Peter 5:13), though there is some debate over its authorship. The crucial, early (A.D. 96) letter of Clement of Rome to the Corinthians strongly links the martyrdoms of Peter and Paul with those of the Roman Christians enduring the Neronian persecution (I Clement, v, vi). A short time later (c. A.D. 107), Ignatius of Antioch's *Epistle to the Romans* contains the revealing phrase: "Not like Peter and Paul do I give you [Roman Christians] commands" (iv, 3). Another early, indirect witness is the first-century apocryphon, the *Ascension of Isaiah*, which implies that one of the disciples—doubtless Peter—was delivered into the hands of the matricidal Nero (iv, 2 f.).

In the second century A.D., there are numerous references in Christian authors to the martyrdoms of Peter and Paul in Rome, and one of these is especially interesting. Eusebius refers to a second-century presbyter, Gaius, who stated: "I can point out the monuments [or trophies] of the apostles: for if you will go to the Vatican hill or to the Ostian Way, you will find the monuments of those who founded this church [Peter and Paul]" (*Ecclesiastical History*, ii, 25). The monuments marked the traditional sites of their martyrdoms and probably their places of burial as well, since Gaius was countering a claim from Asia of apostolic *tombs* in that province. At any rate, the emperor Constantine later erected the basilicas of St. Peter and St. Paul, respectively, at these locations.

Balancing the evidence, the historian is justified in concluding that Peter did, in fact, reach Rome. There is too much in its favor. On the other hand, suggestions that Peter conducted a lengthy, twenty-five-year ministry in the capital and opposed Simon Magus there already at the beginning of Claudius' reign is extremely unlikely, despite Eusebius' discussion of this tradition, *op. cit.*, ii, 13. Such a stay conflicts too grossly with the absence of any reference to Peter's presence or work at Rome in Paul's epistle to the Romans, or in the Acts narrative. The date of Peter's arrival in Rome cannot be determined, although it seems to have been shortly before his martyrdom. For further discussion, see Oscar Cullmann, *Peter—Disciple, Apostle, Martyr* (Westminster, 1962); and Daniel W. O'Connor, *Peter in Rome* (Columbia, 1969).

THE LAKESIDE BACCHANAL: This incredible episode is recounted in Tacitus, *Annals*, xv, 37; and Dio Cassius, lxii, 15. Cp. also Suetonius, *Nero*, xxvii. Dio's version is considerably more sensational —and less believable—than the restrained rendering in the text.

NERO "WEDS" PYTHAGORAS: Tacitus implies that it was a formal marriage (*Annals*, xv, 37), though Dio, lxii, suggests, quite obviously, that it was abnormal in any case. While one is tempted to ignore such reports of degeneracy as concoctions of hostile sources, this pattern is consistent with Nero's later affair with the boy Sporus (see below), and also explains Paul's comments in Romans 1:26 ff.

CHAPTER 22 (Pages 281–93)

THE GREAT FIRE OF ROME: Various versions are provided by Tacitus, *Annals*, xv, 38 ff.; Suetonius, *Nero*, xxxviii; Dio Cassius, lxii, 16–18; Pliny, *Natural History*, xvii, 5; and Seneca, *Octavia*, 831 ff.

The Cause: All ancient sources claim Nero himself as the arsonist, except for the careful scholarship of Tacitus, who begins his famous account with the words: "A disaster followed, whether due to accident or to the treachery of the emperor is uncertain. . . ." Scholars fall into five camps on this issue, concluding 1) that

Nero did indeed send his agents to set fire to Rome; 2) that the first fire arose by accident, but the second was kindled, under Nero's orders, by Tigellinus and his men; 3) that both fires were wholly accidental; 4) that the Christians, or several Christian fanatics, fired the city; and 5) that the Pisonian conspirators (see below) set fire to Rome to incriminate Nero.

Most recent scholarship leans to the third alternative. While some lines in ancient sources can be marshaled in support of all of the above alternatives except 4) and 5), the weight of circumstantial evidence would tend to absolve Nero of any responsibility for the blaze. Accidental fires were all too frequent in Rome, and Nero was miles away at the time—not, of course, a perfect alibi—but a true arsonist would have wished to witness his handiwork soon after its inception. It was the night of the full moon, as C. Hülsen first noted in *American Journal of Archaeology*, xiii (1909), 45. Nor could it have been Nero's violent "slum clearance project," since the worst slums in the Subura were untouched. His noble relief efforts would hardly seem appropriate for an incendiary. And, above all, Nero would hardly have had the fire kindled near the southeastern tip of his Palatine palace to burn down all his own priceless works of art and treasures. Again, this statement must stand: in terms of property destroyed, Nero was far and away the greatest loser in the fire. That it all began from a blaze at an oil merchant's shop is merely assumed, but the general location of its inception is accurate.

The Extent: Most sources exaggerate the devastation of the great fire. According to Dio, "the whole Palatine hill . . . and nearly two-thirds of the remainder of the city were burned" (lxii, 18), while Tacitus says that of the fourteen regions, only four remained intact, "three were leveled to the ground, while in the other seven only a few shattered, half-burned relics of houses were left" (*Annals*, xv, 40). But literary and archaeological evidence shows that the latter is particularly exaggerated, and the fire generally ravaged the areas indicated on the endpaper map. For further discussion, see Gerard Walter, *Nero* (London: Allen & Unwin, 1955); and Jean Beaujeu, "L'incendie de Rome en 64 et les Chrétiens," *Collection Latomus*, XLIX (1960), 5 ff.

DID NERO PLAY WHILE ROME BURNED? Probably the most popular misinterpretation in history is that "Nero fiddled while Rome burned." The violin, of course, was not invented until fourteen centuries after the fire. Tacitus has Nero appearing on a private stage to rhapsodize on the destruction of Troy; Suetonius has him singing, in costume, from the terrace of Maecenas, while Dio has him holding forth on the roof of the palace—an impossibility, since the palace was in flames. An unsensational version of Suetonius' account was used in the text, since Maecenas' terrace was indeed untouched by fire and would have afforded a good vantage point.

THE LOSS STATISTICS are based on a restrained interpretation of Tacitus, *Annals*, xv, 40, while the specific numbers of mansions and houses lost derives from the apocryphal correspondence between Seneca and Paul, Letter xii (Barlow ed.). While no suggestion is made that this correspondence is authentic—it is not—this estimate from a fourth-century author is the *only* surviving statistic we have on the great fire, and it was incorporated because the figures are quite probable in themselves, and the author may well have used an ancient source lost to us.

CHAPTER 23 (Pages 294–305)

THE GOLDEN HOUSE: Tacitus, *Annals*, xv, 42; Suetonius, *Nero*, xxi. Partial remains of the great Domus Aurea are visible today in Rome just northeast of the Colosseum on the sides of the Esquiline. The graffito referring to the expanding Golden House is authentic; see Suetonius, *Nero*, xxix.

CHRISTIANS BLAMED FOR THE GREAT FIRE: Tacitus, *Annals*, xv, 44. This passage, perhaps the most famous in the *Annals*, begins:

Therefore, to scotch the rumor [that he had set fire to Rome], Nero substituted as culprits, and punished with the utmost refinements of cruelty, a class of men, loathed for their vices, whom the crowd styled Christians. Christus, the founder of the name, had undergone the death penalty in the reign of Tiberius, by sentence of the procurator Pontius Pilatus, and the pernicious superstition was checked for a moment, only to break out once more, not merely in Judaea, the home of the disease, but in the capital itself, where all things horrible or shameful in the world collect and find a vogue. (John Jackson's translation in Loeb Classical Library)

That Peter ever made a statement involving the term "fire" which had anything to do with clinching Tigellinus' argument to persecute the Christians is only contrived, but for early Christians to castigate Rome's vices in such language was not untypical. Tigellinus may well have suggested to Nero that he punish the Christians, for this is at least implied in Melito of Sardis, *Apologia*, as excerpted in Eusebius, *op. cit.*, iv, 26: "Of all the emperors, the only ones ever persuaded by malicious advisers to misrepresent our doctrine were Nero and Domitian." At this time, Tigellinus was certainly Nero's principal adviser, and Juvenal, *Satires*, i, 155 ff., seems to link Tigellinus and human torch deaths.

CHAPTER 24 (Pages 306–13)

THE TRIALS OF THE CHRISTIANS: Whether Nero indicted them as a mere police action on the basis of the magisterial *coercitio* (punishing authority) or via a special imperial or senatorial edict against Christianity has long been debated. French and Belgian scholars have tended to follow the latter interpretation, while others, following Mommsen, conclude that the Christians were prosecuted as a police action under existing laws concerning public order. See Theodor Mommsen, "Die Religionsfrevel nach römischen Recht," *Historische Zeitschrift*, LXIV (1890), 389 ff.; and A. N. Sherwin-White, "The Early Persecutions and Roman Law Again," *Journal of Theological Studies*, III (1952), 199–213.

PETER'S LETTER: The phrases are taken directly from I Peter 1–5. There is, of course, some debate over the date and provenance of the epistle.

CHAPTER 25 (Pages 317–31)

NERO'S PERSECUTION OF THE CHRISTIANS: Suetonius, *Nero*, xvi; and the famed source passage in Tacitus, a continuation of *Annals*, xv, 44 (Jackson's translation):

... First, then, the confessed members of the sect were arrested; next, on their disclosures, vast numbers were convicted, not so much on the count of arson as for hatred of the human race. And derision accompanied their end: they were covered with wild beasts' skins and torn to death by dogs; or they were fastened on crosses, and, when daylight failed, were burned to serve as lamps by night. Nero had offered his Gardens for the spectacle, and gave an exhibition in his Circus, mixing with the crowd in the habit of a charioteer, or mounted on his car. . . .

There has been a vast literature on this passage. A few scholars in the last century tried to deny that such a persecution ever existed, on the basis of the following arguments: expressions in the passage unusual for Tacitus, silence of other sources at the time, and silence of the Christian tradition. But the great majority of scholars today accept the authenticity of this passage and of the persecution, since nothing in *Annals*, xv, 44 could not have been written by Tacitus, and recent studies have reaffirmed the validity of this passage, such as H. Fuchs, "Tacitus über die Christen," *Vigiliae Christianae*, IV (1950), 65 ff. Moreover, the secular and Christian sources are *not* silent. Suetonius writes that "Punishments were also inflicted on the Christians, a class of men given to a new and mischievous superstition" (*Nero*, xvi). Cp. also Sulpicius Severus, *Chronica*, ii, 29, and the earlier Christian tradition on this persecution is vocal enough in I Clement vi, and in other documents associated with the apostles cited above and below.

THE SPECIFIC PUNISHMENTS: Besides those indicated in *Annals*, xv, 44, that Christians and condemned criminals suffered in these and other ways may be documented as follows: Ixion (Tertullian, *De pudicitia*, xxii); Daedalus and Icarus (Martial, *op. cit.*, viii; Suetonius, *loc. cit.*). The punishments of Dirce and the Danaides are cited in I Clement vi, 1 ff.: "Besides these men of holy life [Peter and Paul], there was a great multitude of the elect, who through their endurance amid many indignities and tortures . . . presented us a noble example. . . . Women were paraded as Danaides and Dircae and put to death after they had suffered horrible and cruel indignities."

Victims fixed on poles in garments impregnated with inflammables and then set afire is cited not only in *Annals*, xv, 44, but in Juvenal, *Satires*, i, 155–57 and viii, 235; Seneca, *De Ira*, iii, 3; and Martial, *Epigrams*, iv, lxxxvii. The *tunica molesta* and being thrown to the beasts were standard penalties for arson, according to *Digestae*, xlvii, 9, 9, and 12. Several scholars have blunderingly attacked *Annals*, xv, 44 by claiming that the luminous combustion of the human body is physically impossible, but such human torch deaths did in fact take place: the wood of the posts and the *tunica molesta* clothing the bodies would indeed be luminous while the bodies themselves carbonized.

Finally, Hercules in Flames is cited by Tertullian, *Apologeticus*, xv. Other probable tortures, not cited in the text, included Pasiphaë and the Bull (Martial, *De Spectaculis*, v; Suetonius, *Nero*, xii), and Attis (Tertullian, *loc. cit.*)

THE TIME OF THE PERSECUTION: Paul Allard, *Histoire des Persécutions* (Paris, 1903) suggested August, 64 (I, pp. 48 ff.), but since the great fire was not extinguished until July 27, and it would have taken some weeks for planning the Golden House which finally pinned suspicions on Nero, August would seem much too early for the persecution, with October more probable. On the other hand, suggestions that would delay punishments until spring of A.D. 65 founder on Nero's diverting *fresh* public hatreds for suspected arson on the Christians and the fact that in the spring of 65, Nero's full attention was claimed by the Pisonian conspiracy (see below).

CHAPTER 26 (Pages 332–41)

PETER'S MARTYRDOM: Jesus' prediction of his death is given in John 21:18 f. The famous *Quo Vadis* legend first appears in a second-century manuscript, the *Acta Petri* (cp. later, Ambrose, *Epist.*, xxi). A much reduced version of the legend is included in the text because it is both ancient and moving. But it seems certain that if Peter did, indeed, communicate with the spirit of Jesus, he would doubtless have spoken to him in Aramaic, their common tongue, rather than the Latin *"Quo vadis, Domine?"* which would have been foreign to both of them.

The legend that Peter was crucified head downward has been common since Origen, as quoted by Eusebius, *op. cit.*, iii, 1. But this would seem an unnecessary, slightly ostentatious, and—in view of the way crosses were constructed—an unlikely embellishment, even if such crucifixions were not unknown (see Seneca, *Ad Marciam*, xx). But there was no early Roman tradition that Peter was crucified in this way, and the claim has an apocryphal ring.

For the historical sources on Peter's death, see references to Chapter 21 above. Most scholars now agree that Peter was likely martyred in some connection with the Neronian persecution, but the precise date of his death is impossible to determine. Similarly, there is no reliable evidence as to where the apostle was imprisoned, and the tradition pointing to the Mamertine prison is unlikely because it is very late, and the Mamertine was usually used only for high prisoners of state.

As to the location of his burial, Roman Catholic scholars generally concur that his grave lies under the great altar of the current Basilica of St. Peter in the Vatican; see Margherita Guarducci, *La tomba di Pietro* (Rome, 1959). Some Protestant scholars agree, while others conclude that it can only be proven historically that the Christian church of the second century A.D. *thought* that this is where Peter was buried, as Cullmann, *op. cit.*, and O'Connor, *op. cit.*

THE NUMBER OF VICTIMS in this persecution is set at 977 in the *Martyrologium Hieronymianum* (ed. Duchesne-De Rossi in *Acta Sanctorum* [Brussels, 1894], II, p. 84). But this figure need not be considered accurate and might well be reduced in view of the exaggeration of such documents. Tacitus' "an immense multitude" [*multitudo ingens*] in *Annals*, xv, 44 is certainly vague, and the two other places where he uses this expression in the *Annals* (ii, 40; xiv, 8) cannot be reduced to numbers. Clement uses a similar expression in I Clement vi, 1: "a very great number."

CHAPTER 27 (Pages 342–48)

THE PISONIAN CONSPIRACY: Tacitus, *Annals*, xv, 48 ff.; Dio Cassius, lxii, 24 ff. There is some debate as to whether Seneca was part of the conspiracy, but all circumstantial evidence points to his involvement, and most commentators conclude with Momigliano in *CAH*, X, p. 728: "There can be no doubt that Seneca shared in the conspiracy."

CHAPTER 28 (Pages 349–67)

SABINUS' INVOLVEMENT IN THE CONSPIRACY is only presumed, but the fact that so high a magistrate was *not* rewarded for loyalty at a time when his colleagues were would suggest that he was not above suspicion in Nero's eyes. Similarly, Walter, *op. cit.*, p. 196. The fact that Sabinus continued to be popular with both the Senate and the public *after* the fall of Nero, when death for Nero's minions was being demanded, more than demonstrates Sabinus' true loyalties.

CHAPTER 29 (Pages 368–81)

PAUL'S SECOND ARREST: If Philippians offers source material for Paul's first imprisonment, II Timothy provides it for the second. Although some are wary of using II Timothy and the other pastoral epistles as evidence, even critical scholars admit that the letter probably contains authentic Pauline reminiscences in verses such as 1:8 ff., 1:15 ff., 2:9, and 4:6 ff.—which are precisely the references to a second imprisonment in Rome. Evidently Paul did succeed in blunting the charges against him at a *prima actio* or first hearing (II Timothy 4:16–17), though he knew the outcome of the second would result in his death (4:6). Recent attempts to date the pastorals to an earlier, non-Roman imprisonment founder on II Timothy 1:17, as genuine a Pauline fragment as any.

ALEXANDER THE COPPERSMITH: While it is not certain if Alexander came to Rome to prosecute Paul, this may be implied from II Timothy 4:14 ff. Alexander the false teacher (I Timothy 1:19) rather than the Jew of Ephesus (Acts 19:33) seems intended here, and for a former Christian to turn against Paul is very well attested in I Clement v, 2, where the church father says that it was specifically "through jealousy" that Paul was delivered up to death.

THE REIGN OF TERROR: More prominent Romans fell than was possible to mention in the text. A list of other victims is supplied by Tacitus, *Annals,* xvi, 7 ff. and Dio Cassius, lxii, 25 ff. A young Aulus Plautius is a victim cited in Suetonius, *Nero,* xxxi, but he was likely a member of the younger line of the Plautii, and not Aulus' son.

THE DEATH OF PAUL: Nothing is known of the final trial and death of Paul other than that he was most probably executed in Rome under Nero (I Clement v, 5 ff.) Later, Eusebius states that Origen recorded the same fact in his commentary on Genesis (*Ecclesiastical History,* iii, 1). As an early church tradition has it, the execution probably took place outside the Ostian Gate of Rome at or near the present Basilica of St. Paul "Outside the Walls" (see the presbyter Gaius' statement on the "monuments of the apostles" under Chapter 21 above). His grave may be indicated under the high altar of the basilica by the fourth-century inscription, "PAVLO APOSTOLO MART." As F. F. Bruce points out, *op. cit.,* 274, the location may be "accepted provisionally" in default of any rival tradition, and in view of the corporate memory of an ongoing Christian community at Rome ever since the event. The fact that Paul's monument, like Peter's, lay in a pagan necropolis—not the area later Christian piety would have selected—adds a further touch of authenticity.

As to the date of Paul's death, some have suggested that the reference in I Clement v, 7 that Paul gave testimony "before the rulers" [*epi ton hegoumenon*] before he died implies that he was judged by Nero's vicegerents Helius and Nymphidius while Nero himself was away in Greece in A.D. 66–67. While ingenious, this suggestion makes too much of a phrase which is so common in early Christian testimony, that the apostles would have to testify "before governors and kings" (Matt. 10:18; Mark 13:9; cp. Acts 9:15). Paul certainly had already done this before Sergius Paulus, Gallio, Felix, Festus, Publius, Nero, and others. The tradition that Peter and Paul died on the same day, June 29, A.D. 67, on the basis of apocryphal "Acts" of the two apostles, is without historical value.

The names of those attending Paul in his last imprisonment are indicated in II Timothy 4, but whether any of them witnessed the apostle's death is unknown. The presence of Sabinus, Plautia, and Pomponia is only presumed.

CHAPTER 30 (Pages 385–403)

NERO'S "MARRIAGE" TO SPORUS: Suetonius, *Nero*, xxviii, xxxv; Dio Cassius, lxii, 12–13. Even more depravities of Nero are portrayed in the sources, such as his attacking, like an animal, the genitals of nude men and women bound to stakes (Suetonius, *Nero*, xxix; Dio Cassius, lxiii, 13) though regard must be paid the hostility of the sources on Nero. About this time, the emperor also married Statilia, one of his mistresses.

CORBULO: His fate was linked to the Vinician conspiracy against Nero, named for Annius Vinicianus, son-in-law of Corbulo, which broke out at Beneventum in A.D. 66. Details on the nature and extent of this conspiracy are very sketchy, since Tacitus is missing here. See Suetonius, *Nero*, xxxvi; Dio Cassius, lxiii, 26.

PLAUTILLA: While young Flavius and Clemens are the only two children of Sabinus specifically mentioned in the sources because of their later political careers—Clemens as consul in A.D. 95—this does not rule out the possibility that the Plautilla who is mentioned as the "sister of Clement the consul" in the *Acts of Nereus and Achilles* was in fact the third child and daughter of Sabinus. Nereus and Achilles were early Christian martyrs who were originally servants of Plautilla, and ever since De Rossi's discovery of their memorials in the cemetery of Domitilla (*op. cit.*, i, 130 ff.) there is no doubt that they were real persons, an authenticity which should carry over also to their mistress, Plautilla. Since the diminutive "-illa" suffix in a daughter's name usually reflects a mother's "ia" ending, the mother of Plautilla would doubtless be "Plautia," as De Rossi first suggested, and the unnamed wife of Sabinus can provisionally be named after all. For further discussion, see R. Lanciani, *Pagan and Christian Rome* (New York, 1967, reprint), pp. 336 ff.; A. S. Barnes, *Christianity at Rome in the Apostolic Age* (London, 1938), pp. 138 ff.; and G. Edmundson, *The Church in Rome in the First Century* (London: Longmans, 1913), who suggests a slightly different family structure.

CHAPTER 31 (Pages 404–10)

NERO'S LAST DAY, DEATH, AND BURIAL: Suetonius, *Nero*, xlvii f.; Dio Cassius, lxiii, 27–29. Regrettably, the *Annals* of Tacitus break off with the forced suicide of Thrasea Paetus in A.D. 66.

CHAPTER 32 (Pages 411–14)

THEOPHILUS: That Sabinus was so intended by the author of Luke and Acts is only conjecture. But since the man named in Luke 1:3 and Acts 1:1 is cited as "most excellent [*kratiste*] Theophilus," a form of address used elsewhere by the same author only for a Roman official (Acts 23:26; 24:2) and a title accorded Romans of the senatorial class, it may be assumed that the works were dedicated to some Roman of high position. Notes appended to some early manuscripts of the Gospels say that Theophilus was a man of senatorial rank. For the dating of Luke–Acts, see P. Carrington, *The Early Christian Church* (Cambridge, 1957), I, 182 ff., 278 ff.

THE RELIGION OF SABINUS' CHILDREN has long been a subject of scholarly debate. Both Christianity and Judaism have been suggested, on the basis of the epitome of Dio Cassius (lxvii, 14), which states:

. . . And the same year [A.D. 95], Domitian slew, along with

many others, Flavius Clemens the consul, although he was a
cousin and had to wife Flavia Domitilla, who was also a relative
of the emperor [his sister's daughter]. The charge brought
against them both was that of atheism, a charge on which many
others who drifted into Jewish ways were condemned. Some of
these were put to death, and the rest were at least deprived of
their property. Domitilla was merely banished to Pandateria.
(E. Cary's translation in Loeb Classical Library.)

That Sabinus' children, or at least Clemens and his wife, had converted to Judaism is one obvious interpretation of the source, a
view held by some commentators, including E. Mary Smallwood,
"Domitian's Attitude Toward the Jews and Judaism," *Classical
Philology*, LI (January, 1956), 7 ff., who suggests that they were
not full converts to Judaism but only "God-fearers" on the fringe.
    Other scholars, however, think Christianity is intended in the
reference, for Dio otherwise never refers to it by name—an apparently intentional slight—and "atheism" was a term hardly used
for Judaism, a legal religion in Rome, but frequently for Christians (who were also accused of practicing "Jewish ways") in that
they abjured the national religion of Rome. Eusebius, *op. cit.*, iii,
17 f., records Domitian's persecution of the Christians, the second
in history, and claims that the pagan historians recorded Domitilla's banishment for her Christianity, though he considers her
the niece, not wife, of Clemens, a much-debated problem. Since
classical sources do not record such a niece, Eusebius' tradition
would seem to be faulty at this point, and Flavia Domitilla is interpreted as Clemens' wife by most investigators. Synkellos adds
that Flavius Clemens was executed because of his Christian faith
(*Chronographia*, ed. Dindorf, I, 650, 17 f.). Suetonius' description
of Clemens as a man of "most contemptible laziness" seems to
hint at his Christianity (*Domitianus*, xv), since pagan authors regularly faulted Christians for indolence and indifference to public
affairs. M. Goguel, *The Birth of Christianity* (New York, 1954),
p. 532, suggests: "Flavius Clemens may have secretly shared his
wife's convictions but, anxious to preserve his reputation and his
career and not to stand in the way of the future of his sons whom
the emperor [Domitian] had adopted . . . he decided not to enter
the church officially. This explains why he was not remembered
as a martyr."

But his wife Domitilla, not under the same obligations, may well have converted. In 1852, De Rossi uncovered an ancient Christian catacomb which proved to be the "Cemetery of Domitilla," with an inscription, *"ex indulgentia Flaviae Domitill[ae]"* and she is named as "granddaughter of Vespasian" (*CIL*, VI, 948, 8942, 16246). The cemetery had been dug on land that had belonged to Domitilla, which she gave to her dependents as a burial ground.

Finally, that Domitian did indeed persecute the Christians seems strongly supported in a contemporary document of highest authenticity. At the opening of I Clement (i, 1), the author speaks of the "sudden misfortunes and calamities which have fallen upon us one after another," and the date of writing is most probably A.D. 95–96, the tyrannical close of Domitian's reign. See also *CAH*, XI, pp. 254 f.

EPILOGUE (Pages 415–16)

GALBA, OTHO, VITELLIUS, VESPASIAN: Suetonius' *Lives* by those names, and Tacitus, *Histories*, i–v; Dio Cassius, lxiv–lxv.

SABINUS' MONUMENT: *CIL*, VI, 31293.

CHRISTIAN HERALD ASSOCIATION AND ITS MINISTRIES

CHRISTIAN HERALD ASSOCIATION, founded in 1878, publishes The Christian Herald Magazine, one of the leading interdenominational religious monthlies in America. Through its wide circulation, it brings inspiring articles and the latest news of religious developments to many families. From the magazine's pages came the initiative for CHRISTIAN HERALD CHILDREN'S HOME and THE BOWERY MISSION, two individually supported not-for-profit corporations.

CHRISTIAN HERALD CHILDREN'S HOME, established in 1894, is the name for a unique and dynamic ministry to disadvantaged children, offering hope and opportunities which would not otherwise be available for reasons of poverty and neglect. The goal is to develop each child's potential and to demonstrate Christian compassion and understanding to children in need.

Mont Lawn is a permanent camp located in Bushkill, Pennsylvania. It is the focal point of a ministry which provides a healthful "vacation with a purpose" to children who without it would be confined to the streets of the city. Up to 1000 children between the ages of 7 and 11 come to Mont Lawn each year.

Christian Herald Children's Home maintains year-round contact with children by means of an *In-City Youth Ministry*. Central to its philosophy is the belief that only through sustained relationships and demonstrated concern can individual lives be truly enriched. Special emphasis is on individual guidance, spiritual and family counseling and tutoring. This follow-up ministry to inner-city children culminates for many in financial assistance toward higher education and career counseling.

THE BOWERY MISSION, located at 227 Bowery, New York City, has since 1879 been reaching out to the lost men on the Bowery, offering them what could be their last chance to rebuild their lives. Every man is fed, clothed and ministered to. Countless numbers have entered the 90-day residential rehabilitation program at the Bowery Mission. A concentrated ministry of counseling, medical care, nutrition therapy, Bible study and Gospel services awakens a man to spiritual renewal within himself.

These ministries are supported solely by the voluntary contributions of individuals and by legacies and bequests. Contributions are tax deductible. Checks should be made out either to CHRISTIAN HERALD CHILDREN'S HOME or to THE BOWERY MISSION.

Administrative Office: 40 Overlook Drive, Chappaqua, New York 10514
Telephone: (914) 769-9000

The Study of the Bible
Today and Tomorrow

By

MEMBERS AND GUESTS
of the
CHICAGO SOCIETY FOR BIBLICAL RESEARCH

PAUL E. DAVIES
FLOYD V. FILSON
G. ERNEST WRIGHT
Advisory Committee

EDITED BY HAROLD R. WILLOUGHBY

The
Study of the Bible
Today and Tomorrow

THE UNIVERSITY OF CHICAGO PRESS

CHICAGO · ILLINOIS

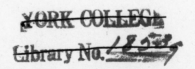

THE UNIVERSITY OF CHICAGO PRESS, CHICAGO 37
Cambridge University Press, London, N.W. 1, England
W. J. Gage & Co., Limited, Toronto 2B, Canada

To the Students of Today
who will become
the Biblical Scholars of Tomorrow

GRATIAS AGIMUS

ON BEHALF of the Chicago Society for Biblical Research we are privileged to express hearty thanks to all who in any way co-operated in the creation and publication of this volume.

President Ernest Cadman Colwell, of the University of Chicago, without knowing that he was doing so, formulated the title. It is a good title. It recalls his own very useful manual, entitled simply *The Study of the Bible*.

Only the editor and the authors know with what diligence the latter prepared the chapters of this book. Every one of them took time from an overcrowded schedule to do a major piece of survey, summarization, or research. Many of them found added time to revise their first copy on the basis of suggestions from the Society's advisory committee or other expert readers. When an author does that, he *is* open minded!

The advisory committee exercised conscientiously and judiciously the normal advisory functions to which they were elected by the Chicago Society for Biblical Research. More importantly and before that, they energetically and stimulatingly contributed to initiating the program for the book.

Numbers of anonymous experts gave freely of time and advice in connection with the great multiplicity of technical problems canvassed in these pages. The proofing of this volume has been mainly the work of Mr. William A. Beardslee, New Testament Fellow in the University of Chicago. He has been assisted in this arduous task by Mr. Wayne E. Barr and Mr. Louis B. Jennings, Fellows in the biblical field in the same institution. To all these and to many others the readers' thanks are due.

H. R. W.

THE HERMITAGE
DISCIPLES DIVINITY HOUSE
Feast of Corpus Christi, 1947

INTRODUCTION

HAROLD R. WILLOUGHBY

University of Chicago

THIS volume is a characteristic record of the interests and activities of an American regional society, the Chicago Society for Biblical Research. For a half-century plus a half-decade this Lakes-region society has been carrying on continuously the sort of investigations and discussions of biblical problems that are here published. During this period the Society itself has developed a group character that is distinctively its own, and it has made peculiar contributions to the advancement of biblical studies on the American side of the Atlantic Ocean.

The Chicago Society got its start in the early nineties as a section of the national Society of Biblical Literature and Exegesis. Mainly on the initiative of George Holly Gilbert, one of the very stimulating New Testament teachers of that period, a "preliminary meeting" was held at McCormick Theological Seminary on the day before Washington's Birthday in 1891. It was attended by ten professors teaching in biblical departments in the Chicago area. They voted unanimously to form "a Chicago Section of the Society of Biblical Literature and Exegesis." They also listened to and discussed a paper on "The Messianic Character of the Twenty-second Psalm," read by Professor Edward L. Curtis of McCormick, who was elected president of the sectional society. For over a year and a half the group experimented with operating as a sectional society of the Society of Biblical Literature and Exegesis. Then, in typically independent mid-western fashion, the group voted to reorganize as a completely autonomous society for biblical research.

The reorganization as the Chicago Society for Biblical Research was accomplished at a meeting held in the fabulous Grand Pacific Hotel on October 29, 1892, under the chairmanship of

President William Rainey Harper. The constitution and by-laws, drafted by George Holly Gilbert for discussion at this meeting, still serve in somewhat amended form to guide and authorize the procedures of the Chicago Society.

For the emphasis on research in the name of the organization and in its very constitution, the Society was indebted to President Harper himself. This was the way the constitution phrased it in Article II:

"The object of this Society shall be to promote the critical investigation of the Bible: and all departments of study which bear upon the interpretation of Scripture shall be considered germane to this object.

"The work of the Society shall be chiefly in the following lines: Biblical Geography and Archaeological Research, Biblical Languages and their cognates, Biblical History, Biblical Exegesis, the Study of Comparative Religions, Rabbinical Theology, Biblical Theology, and those phases of Church History which concern the interpretation of the text of Scripture and the formation of the Canon."

Article III of the constitution continued:

"The Society shall seek to accomplish the above mentioned object by the preparation and discussion of papers on topics in the general sphere of Biblical science, and by such further means as it may from time to time elect."

In view of the present preoccupation of biblical students with theological concerns, it is very interesting to note in the minutes of the reorganization meeting that a proposal to make the society a theological organization was thoroughly discussed—and abandoned.

Eighteen members signed the Gilbert constitution as charter members of the new Chicago Society for Biblical Research. Of that initial group, not one remains alive today. However, at its spring meeting in 1946, the Society conducted a grateful memory service in honor of the Nestor among the noncharter members of the organization, Clyde Weber Votaw. As a young instructor he was the first to join the reorganized group. So near, after more

than a half-century, is the present membership of the Chicago
Society to its very beginnings.

Useful practices, still in vogue in the Society, date back to the
period of reorganization. Now, as then, the Society meets regularly three times a year, in autumn, winter, and spring, for a
three-hour session on Saturday afternoon. At each meeting three
papers, usually, are read and discussed as thoroughly as time
permits. Then the Society adjourns for dinner at six o'clock—
and more discussion. The fellowship feature of CSBR dinners is
greatly appreciated by the members of the Society. Increasingly,
from the start, the Society has functioned as a mid-western regional organization rather than as a merely metropolitan society.

In the course of the decades some very eminent scholars have
served the Society as its president. Names chosen at random from
the presidential list are Harper, Zenos, Mathews, Burton,
Easton, Dickey, Grant, Mann, Eiselen, Case, and Olmstead.
Clayton R. Bowen, of beloved memory, died in office as president. Scholars as eminent have served as secretary or treasurer
of the Society. The manuscript records of Clyde Weber Votaw
are marvels of legibility, and the typed records of Leslie E. Fuller
are models of neatness.

As early as the World's Columbian Exposition in 1893, with
its huge World's Congress of Religions, the Chicago Society developed the habit of hospitality. Since then no famed biblical
scholar, passing through Chicago, could reasonably expect to
avoid an invitation to become a speaking guest of the group. In
the guestbook of the Society may be read the names of Gregory,
Clemen, Abrahams, Von Dobschütz, Gressmann—he left Chicago as ashes—Deissmann, Hempel, and Jaeger—he stayed on in
Chicago for three years. Most memorable was the meeting in
honor of Martin Dibelius at Chicago Lutheran Seminary in
Maywood—February 27, 1937, was the date—when Professor
Dibelius discussed "Present-Day New Testament Scholarship in
Germany," and Dr. D. W. Riddle, a pupil of Dibelius in Heidel-
berg, returned the compliment by reading a paper on "The In-
fluence of German New Testament Scholarship in America."
The practice of hospitality by the Chicago Society is well exem-

plified in the makeup of the present volume. Here are published papers by guests of the Chicago Society as well as studies by its members.

Across a half-century and more of time, members of the Chicago Society have been able to observe and participate in some very signal developments in American biblical research. During the first two decades of our century, Ernest DeWitt Burton discussed with the Society various of his lexicographical studies, which were later incorporated into his *International Critical Commentary on Galatians*. Just after World War I, James Henry Breasted outlined to the Society the unbelievably ambitious program that eventuated in the Oriental Institute at the University of Chicago. S. J. Case submitted various studies in Christian origins to the comradely criticism of the Chicago Society. Even before he located in the "Windy City," A. T. Olmstead began reading to the Society those invaluable inquiries into the life of the Hellenistic period that students are now seeking out from various scholarly publications and are binding together for convenience in study. The amazing Rockefeller McCormick New Testament (Codex 2400) had its first introduction to American scholars at a CSBR meeting. In the early thirties, Ovid R. Sellers regularly reported to the Society his participations in archeological field work in Palestine. Edgar J. Goodspeed was glad to submit his drastic view of *The Meaning of Ephesians* to pre-publication review by the Chicago Society, and John Knox did the same with some of his Philemon studies. President Gruber of Maywood generously shared with the Society his rich collections of manuscripts and Bible printings and his own careful investigations of German and English versions. While he was president of Seabury-Western, F. C. Grant carried through his examination of the Gospels from the point of view of tradition criticism. Altogether, some very important developments in American biblical criticism were matters of firsthand experience and participation to members of the Chicago Society.

Of a piece with all this multifarious experience and activity is the present publication of *The Study of the Bible Today and Tomorrow* by members and guests of the Chicago Society for

Biblical Research. This book, we repeat, is a true and typical expression of the co-operative life and thought of the members of the Society. Specifically, it is a development and enlargement of the program of the Society for the academic year 1945–46.

When it became apparent that the end of World War II was about to break on humanity, it became even more clear that the most valuable thing the Chicago Society could do for biblical research would be to survey comprehensively the present position and the most promising possibilities for biblical studies. The bursting of atomic bombs made this responsibility seem trebly urgent. Certain it was that a new era in human history was upon us. What should biblical researchers do about it? As one of the contributors to this volume phrased it: "Now that World War II has come more or less to an end, it is fitting that every group take account of stock of the past and present in order the better to size up and help plan for the sort of future which is awaiting us all."

Accordingly, the executive committee of CSBR projected the program plans for the society to cover in survey fashion the immediately past accomplishments, the current status, and the immediately future opportunities for biblical research in the main areas of study: Old Testament, intertestamental, and New Testament. A distinctive feature of these plans was the consideration of intertestamental problems on a parity with Old Testament and New Testament matters and in proper sequence between them.

In the 1945–46 sessions of the Chicago Society these plans were actually carried out. At the autumn, winter, and spring meetings various scholars read papers summarizing achievements, status, and possibilities over the main fields indicated. As is customary in the Society, these presentations were rigorously and vigorously criticized by the members of the Society present at the meeting. The final result of all this programming, surveying, discussion, and revision constitutes Part I of this volume, entitled "General Surveys of Main Areas."

Further consideration led to the determination to supplement the main surveys with special investigations of crucial problems

that are engaging scholarly attention at the present time. Outstanding specialists were selected and invited to make such particularized contributions. All these specialists were, of course, exceedingly busy people. It speaks eloquently for the sort of loyalty the Chicago Society commands that only two of the scholars invited to do particular essays found it necessary to decline the invitation. These more concentrated inquiries are grouped together in Part II of this volume entitled "Special Studies of Salient Problems." In this section practiced biblical scholars make specific contributions to the advancement of studies in forefront problem areas, where they have specialized.

Even the casual reader of this symposium is bound to get certain main impressions from the subject matters here published. A revival of interest in both Old Testament and New Testament theology is clearly evident here in certain chapters. Back in the nineties, when the Chicago Society was organized, theological interests were dominant in professional religious circles. Today the Chicago Society is operating in a period when similar theological concerns are gaining domination once again. Basically, this theological revival is doubtless due to the terrifically stressful experiences to which men have been subjected during the last decade and more. Of the religious earnestness back of the current theological drive there can be no doubt. It is to be hoped that theologically interested students of the Bible will succeed in developing a fresh religious vocabulary, truly and accurately expressive of ancient biblical experience and ideology; and that they will further achieve sound discrimination as to the relevance or nonrelevance of the biblical varieties of religious experience to the needs and problems of men in the world today.

Equally evident in various chapters are the reassertions of the validity of historical spirit and methodology in biblical research. There is peculiar appropriateness to this feature in a volume sponsored by the Chicago Society for Biblical Research. In the mid-western area, specifically centered in Chicago, there developed the most coherent social-history group to emerge among the biblical researchers of America. Their applications of social-historical methodology to the investigation of the environ-

ments, the literature, and the history of the early Christians have been quite extensive. Most recently and most significantly, the protagonist of this group has published a truly religious and a truly *Christian Philosophy of History*. It is not surprising, therefore, that historically minded contributors to this volume stand confident in reliance on the usefulness of historical techniques in the investigation of both the Hebrew and the Christian religions. They are greatly concerned at the variety and vastness of the unexplored expanses of social history that must be mastered before the specifically Hebrew and Christian ranges of religious development can be fully known. Each in his own way is working out his own particular religious philosophy of history, as the comprehensiveness of his own knowledge of the historical process enables him to do.

Most conspicuous in this volume of essays is the insistence on the importance of maintaining and carrying forward a comprehensive and balanced program of studies in biblical research. The Gilbert constitution, on the basis of which the Chicago Society for Biblical Research was reorganized as such in 1892, was fairly inclusive in its specification of the different disciplines with which the Society should engage itself. Far more multifarious and exact are the indications of disciplines and techniques to be employed that are specified in the two parts of this volume. Here attention is paid not only to geography and archeology, to languages and history, to interpretation and theology, but also to documentary criticism and tradition criticism, to cultural environment and to social function, to ethics and to world-view, to cult and to organization, to apologetics and to translation, to manuscript study and textual criticism, to religious psychology and to social history, etc. That iconography and iconology were omitted is doubtless a defect in this work! At a time when the gregarious habits of biblical students and scholars are impelling to an unbalanced overconcentration of effort in the single area of biblical theology, this volume sounds a clarion call for a strategic redeployment of scholarly forces more evenly along all important fronts in biblical study and research. Theology is not the only interest in biblical studies; nor is it even the primary concern

for the biblical scholar. At most and best it is only one interest among many others. To quote Professor Edgar J. Goodspeed on a memorable occasion: "New Testament study, to be significant, must be carried forward along a very broad front." Dr. D. W. Riddle's latest phrasing of the ideal reads: "Today all disciplines make their contribution to the attempt to understand and interpret the New Testament correctly." If anything, that is more completely the case for the Bible as a whole than it is for the New Testament by itself.

From what has been written in this Introduction the reader will expect to find in this book an exposition of the working possibilities of *various* methodologies and *different* points of view in biblical study and research. He will not expect to find the elaboration of a single, self-consistent perspective throughout. This volume has not a single author merely, but some two dozen different authors, many of whom very heartily disagree with one another. It is the product of no single group or school but of a fairly large research society that includes in its membership both true conservatives and true liberals, together with numbers of embodiments of conservatism modified by liberalism in between these definite groups. It is scarcely necessary to say that each author has formulated his own findings and his own evaluations, each in his own way. Readers, it is hoped, will not find this juxtaposition of divergent judgments to be a source of confusion, but rather a means for the clarification of their own thought. This book should be read, then, as a record of discussion in progress. If it raises more questions than it answers, that is one of the things it was intended to do.

Comprehensively, the purpose of this volume is to indicate, by general surveys and specific investigations, not only the main current trends in biblical studies but also, and more importantly, what we can be doing and what we ought to be doing in the immediate future. Accordingly, the authors of these essays sincerely hope that the values of this publication will be sought and found, less in its record of past achievements and present problems, and more in its proposals for fresh and important advances in biblical research in the future directly before us.

TABLE OF CONTENTS

PART I. GENERAL SURVEYS OF MAIN AREAS

PART II. SPECIAL STUDIES OF SALIENT PROBLEMS

PART I

General Surveys of Main Areas

CHAPTER ONE

Old Testament Research between the Great Wars

RAYMOND A. BOWMAN
University of Chicago

THROUGH boom-time and depression during the generation between the great world wars (1919–39), Old Testament studies continued to progress. It is impossible to reflect within short compass the breadth of scholarly interest and the nature of the multitude of individual studies wrought during that interval. Since several efforts have already been made to state and evaluate the major contributions of the period, no attempt will be made here to duplicate such work. This study aims, instead, at giving but a brief summary of the prevailing trends of the times.[1]

In this age of specialization we are increasingly aware of the co-operative character of our labors. Trends have a way of becoming attached to the names of persons who first describe them or most capably express them; but this should not blind us to the debt we owe to the unnamed many whose patient efforts, often unrecognized, lie behind the brilliant discoveries of the better-known few. Much of what has been accomplished recently rests solidly upon the research of former generations. Steadily the frontiers of related areas have expanded, broadening the scope of biblical studies and richly supplementing what previously had been largely textual research.

1. G. A. Barton, "The Present State of Old Testament Studies" in *The Haverford Symposium on Archeology and the Bible*, ed. Elihu Grant (New Haven, 1938), pp. 47–78; O. R. Sellers, "The Old Testament Faces 1938 A.D.," *Journal of Bible and Religion*, VI (1938), 67–69; W. A. Irwin, "Fifty Years of Old Testament Scholarship," *Journal of Bible and Religion*, X (1942), 131–35, 183. Much more complete and detailed is the collection of material incorporated in R. H. Pfeiffer, *Introduction to the Old Testament* (New York, 1941).

3

OLD TESTAMENT TEXT

There has been no startling recovery of a Hebrew codex of ancient times to revolutionize our textual study, but some Hebrew fragments of early date have come to light. A pre-Massoretic text of Jer. 48:11, fashioned as a clay stamp for a wine jar, has been found, presumably in Iraq.[2] It is linked in date paleographically with the pre-Massoretic incantation texts from Iraq, which are to be dated possibly from A.D. 200 to 500. The incantation texts themselves are witnesses to early Hebrew texts, for they, too, contain pre-Massoretic biblical quotations in Hebrew characters.[3] These early fragments represent the text as it existed in Babylonia.

An early Western example of Deut. 4:29–31 is now available in an archaic Samaritan script incised into a large marble block, presumably some time before the disruption of Samaria by Justinian in A.D. 529.[4] Its short text contains three variations from the standard Hebrew Bible and appears to be superior to it in all instances.

Owing to a considerable increase in paleographic finds since World War I, it has now become possible to revalue some earlier discoveries. The Nash Papyrus, written in "square" Hebrew characters and formerly usually dated to the second century A.D., has been restudied and is now assigned by Albright, on the basis of its script, to the Maccabean age (150–200 B.C.), thus making it our oldest extant Hebrew manuscript.[5] It contains an introduction to the so-called *Shema*c, which is practically identical with

2. W. A. Irwin, "An Ancient Biblical Text," *American Journal of Semitic Languages*, XLVIII (1931–32), 184–93.

3. J. A. Montgomery, *The Aramaic Incantation Texts from Nippur* (Philadelphia, 1913), pp. 62–64. Among the texts quoted are Num. 6:24–26; 9:23; Deut. 6:4; 29:12, 22; Ps. 91:1, 7, 10; 121:7; 125:2; Isa. 44:25*a;* Zech. 3:2; Cant. 3:7.

4. First mentioned by Pritchett and Pickard in notes to *The Palestine Exploration Fund Quarterly Statement* (1873), pp. 118, 257–58, but apparently unpublished until by W. R. Taylor, "Recent Epigraphic Discoveries in Palestine," *Journal of the Palestine Oriental Society*, X (1930), 18–19.

5. W. F. Albright, "A Biblical Fragment from the Maccabaean Age: The Nash Papyrus," *Journal of Biblical Literature*, LVI (1937), 145–76.

Deut. 4:45, the *Shema*ᶜ itself (Deut. 6:4), and the Ten Commandments in a form closer to the Septuagint than to the Massoretic text.

We have been particularly fortunate in recovering papyrus fragments of the Old Testament in its Greek translation. We now possess Greek fragments from the fourth to the third centuries A.D., and in some instances possibly as early as the second century A.D., of Genesis, Deuteronomy, Isaiah, Ezekiel, Daniel, the minor prophets, Esther, and II Chronicles.[6] Among the more important of these fragments are the John H. Scheide papyri of the late second or early third century A.D., which represent an earlier Greek manuscript of Ezekiel than has been known hitherto.[7] From about the same time we have fragments of Ezekiel, Daniel, and Esther in the Chester Beatty Collection.[8] The Daniel text is particularly significant, for it seems to be located between Ezekiel and Esther and is an early representative of the Septuagint text of the book which has survived elsewhere in Greek only in Codex Chisianus of the eleventh century A.D. Textually the papyrus confirms the accuracy of much of this later codex, which has been generally regarded as being "almost incredibly corrupt."[9] Remarkable, too, is the unusual sequence of chapters in the papyrus, for, by placing chapters 7 and 8 before 5 and 6, thus including a chapter from the Hebrew part of the book, written in the first person, within the Aramaic portion of the book, written in the third person, the papyrus now places the Persian kings in their proper chronological order. Among the papyri in

6. Cf. F. G. Kenyon, *Our Bible and the Ancient Manuscripts* (New York, 1940), pp. 62–66.

7. A. C. Johnson, H. S. Gehman, and E. H. Kase, *The John H. Scheide Papyri* ("Princeton University Studies in Papyrology," No. 3 [Princeton, 1938]); cf. also H. S. Gehman, "Relations between the Hebrew Text of Ezekiel and That of the John H. Scheide Papyri," *Journal of the American Oriental Society*, LVIII (1938), 92–102; and "Relations between the Text of the John H. Scheide Papyri and That of the Other Greek MSS of Ezekiel," *Journal of Biblical Literature*, LVII (1938), 281–87.

8. F. G. Kenyon, *The Chester Beatty Biblical Papyri* (London, 1934–38). The Ezekiel papyrus is believed to belong with the Scheide papyrus of Ezekiel.

9. R. H. Charles, *A Critical and Exegetical Commentary on the Book of Daniel* (Oxford, 1929), p. li; cf. J. A. Montgomery, *A Critical and Exegetical Commentary on the Book of Daniel* (New York, 1927) pp. 13, 35–38.

the University of Michigan is a codex from the early second century A.D. that contains the books Numbers and Deuteronomy.[10]

Most significant of the recently found papyri are those recovered from the cartonnage of an Egyptian mummy case, now called the "John Rylands Library papyri."[11] The text of Deuteronomy in this collection, dated to the second century B.C., is our earliest extant witness to the Septuagint. Considerable portions of Deuteronomy, chapters 23–28, are preserved, in a very fragmentary condition. The text, purer than that of Codex Vaticanus, is believed to lie closer than that codex does to the Massoretic text.

The recovery of early texts of the Greek Old Testament in the papyri has served to push back the problem of the recensions of the Septuagint nearer to the date of its origin.[12] A. Sperber, following the lead of P. Kahle, has insisted that the works of Hesychius and Lucian were independent translations rather than recensions of the Septuagint and that there are traces of two Greek versions, each of which was recognized as the Septuagint, as late as the time of Origen.[13] The majority of scholars, however, are inclined to accept the view that there was but one original text and that all preserved manuscripts of the Greek Old Testament go back, as Jerome has declared, to three recensions made during the third and fourth centuries A.D.: in Egypt (Hesychius; relatively pure in Codex B), Palestine (Eusebius' edition of the LXX in Origen's Hexapla), and Syria (Lucian's text as recovered principally from patristic sources). In addition to these, Margolis

10. Published with Chester Beatty Papyrus VI, with which it belongs, by F. G. Kenyon in *The Chester Beatty Biblical Papyri* (London, 1935), Fasc. V.

11. C. H. Roberts, "Two Biblical Papyri in the John Rylands Library, Manchester: A Ptolemaic Papyrus of Deuteronomy and a Fragment of a Testimony Book," *Bulletin of the John Rylands Library*, XX (1936), 219–44.

12. Cf. H. M. Orlinsky, "On the Present State of proto-Septuagint Studies," *Journal of the American Oriental Society*, LXI (1941), 81–91; cf. also the review of this work by H. S. Gehman in the *Journal of Biblical Literature*, LX (1941), 428–30; F. G. Kenyon, *Recent Developments in the Textual Criticism of the Greek Bible* (London, 1933).

13. P. Kahle, "Untersuchungen zur Geschichte des Pentateuchtextes," *Theologische Studien und Kritiken*, LXXXVIII (1915), 410–26; A. Sperber, "The Problems of the Septuagint Recensions," *Journal of Biblical Literature*, LIV (1935), 73–92, and "New Testament and Septuagint," *ibid.*, LIX (1940), 193–293.

has recognized a Constantinopolitan recension used in Asia Minor and some mixed types.[14]

In general, it may be said that the principles enunciated by P. de Lagarde have been found by later scholars to be sound,[15] even though his actual restoration of the Lucianic recension has been largely repudiated.[16] Margolis and others have still aimed at Lagarde's goal of discovering the purest text of each recension and, finally, through a critical comparison of these, to arrive at a text much closer to the original Septuagint than any that we now possess. Owing to the fragmentary and confused character of the evidence, however, this task is extraordinarily difficult, and no indisputable conclusions have yet been reached.[17]

Study in the Greek Old Testament is considerably hindered by the lack of a critical text of the whole Greek Old Testament. Perhaps still most in use is the text by H. B. Swete, especially in its improved form as expressed in the larger Cambridge Septuagint. This work, of which the Octateuch was completed by 1917, has now grown to include the historical books, through Nehemiah.[18] An excellent critical Greek text of Joshua (to 19:38) has been produced by Margolis.[19] Critical texts also of Genesis, Ruth, and Psalms, edited by Rahlfs, have appeared in the great critical edition that was to have been sponsored by the Göttingen Academy; but the death of Rahlfs and the great war have seriously

14. M. L. Margolis, *The Book of Joshua in Greek*, Parts I–IV (to Josh. 19:38) (Paris, 1931–38).

15. See the inductive work of Margolis (*ibid.*); Montgomery, *A Critical and Exegetical Commentary on Daniel*, pp. 51–55; A. Rahlfs, *Der Text des Septuagintapsalters* (Göttingen, 1907).

16. Cf. G. F. Moore, "The Antiochian Recension of the Septuagint," *American Journal of Semitic Languages*, XXIX (1912–13), 37–62; P. L. Hedley, "The Göttingen Investigation and Edition of the Septuagint," *Harvard Theological Review*, XXVI (1933), 59; J. A. Montgomery, "The Hexaplaric Strata in the Greek Text of Daniel," *Journal of Biblical Literature*, XLIV (1925), 289–302.

17. Cf. Montgomery, "The Hexaplaric Strata in the Greek Text of Daniel."

18. A. E. Brooke, N. McLean, and H. Thackeray, *The Old Testament in Greek* (Cambridge, 1906——). Of the Historical books, I and II Samuel appeared in 1927; I and II Kings in 1930; I and II Chronicles in 1932; and Ezra-Nehemiah in 1935. These books constitute Vol. II. Of Vol. III, Part I (including Esther, Judith, and Tobit) appeared in 1940.

19. *Op. cit.*

endangered that project.[20] A complete text of the Greek Old Testament, with selected variants drawn mainly from the major codices, has been edited by Rahlfs, but it has a relatively small critical apparatus.[21]

Important for biblical study, too, is the recent attempt to establish a better text of the Aramaic version of the Old Testament known as the "Peshitta" by making a critical study of the commentary based on it by Barhebraeus (A.D. 1226–89).[22]

Attempts have been made recently to arrive at a pre-Massoretic Hebrew vocalization by studying Greek transcriptions. Wutz has been able to distinguish several systems of pronunciation earlier than our present type;[23] and Sperber has shown that the Massoretes substituted for the traditional pronunciation, which they regarded as degenerate, a somewhat artificial vocalization which combines various ways of pronouncing Hebrew.[24]

Careful studies have been made, principally by Kahle, of the two schools of Massoretic vocalization—the "Babylonian" and the "Tiberian."[25] More light is available, also, on the two schools of Tiberian Massoretes, Ben Asher and Ben Naftali, since the publication of a list of differences between them compiled by Mishael ben Uzziel soon after their death.[26] The Ben Asher recension is represented in new editions of the

20. A. Rahlfs, *Das Buch Genesis griechisch* (Stuttgart, 1922); *Das Buch Ruth griechisch* (Stuttgart, 1922); *Psalmi cum Odis* (Göttingen, 1931).

21. A. Rahlfs, *Septuaginta* (Stuttgart, 1935).

22. J. H. Breasted, *The Oriental Institute* (Chicago, 1933), p. 419; M. Sprengling and W. C. Graham, *Barhebraeus' Scholia on the Old Testament: Genesis to II Samuel* ("Oriental Institute Publications," Vol. XIII, Part I [Chicago, 1931]).

23. F. X. Wutz, *Die Transkriptionen von der Septuaginta bis Hieronimus* (Stuttgart, 1925); *contra:* Ch. Heller, *Untersuchungen zur Septuaginta: Die Tychsen-Wutzsche Transkriptionstheorie* (Berlin, 1932).

24. A. Sperber, "Hebrew Based upon Greek and Latin Transliterations," *Hebrew Union College Annual*, XII–XIII (1937–38), 103–274.

25. P. Kahle, "Die hebräischen Bibelhandschriften aus Babylonien," *Zeitschrift für die alttestamentliche Wissenschaft*, XLVI (1928), 113–37; *Masoreten des Westens* (Stuttgart, 1930); and "Der alttestamentliche Bibeltext," *Theologische Rundschau*, V (new ser., 1933), 227–38.

26. L. Lipschütz, *Ben Ascher–Ben Naftali: Der Bibeltext der tiberischen Masoreten* ("Bonner orientalistische Studien," Vol. XXV [Stuttgart, 1937]).

Hebrew Bible produced between the wars. It is presented by C. D. Ginsburg, but in a form suffering contamination by Ben Naftali readings.[27] In its purest form it is encountered in the third edition of the Kittel Hebrew Bible as edited by P. Kahle, which no longer uses as its base the Ben Chayyim Bible formerly employed (editions of 1905 and 1912) and now used in the Ginsburg edition (1926), but the Leningrad Codex B19a.[28] In this recent Kittel Bible the collaborators have given the student considerable assistance in the footnotes, by including references to "Babylonian" variants and the readings of the versions as well as some of the recently discovered papyri and, in Genesis, by the use of the newest edition of the Vulgate (1926).[29]

Space will not permit even the listing of other important studies made of the Hebrew text and its versions. Many of these labors are reflected in those other important aids to textual study, the Hebrew grammars, produced since 1919. Hans Bauer and Pontus Leander sought to approach the problem of the Hebrew language historically rather than in the usual descriptive manner in their grammar.[30] Applying the principles and techniques used by grammarians dealing with Indo-European languages, they tried to systematize Hebrew phonetics and to trace each stage in the development of Hebrew words from the "original" forms which existed, hypothetically, in the proto-Semitic speech to those encountered in the Massoretic texts of both the East and the West. Later they produced a similar elaborate and comprehensive grammar of biblical Aramaic.[31] Their thesis that Hebrew is a mixed language, with Aramaean, Akkadian, and Canaanite strata, corresponding to the stages of early Hebrew migrations,

27. C. D. Ginsburg, *The Old Testament Diligently Revised According to the Massorah and the Early Versions, with Various Readings from Manuscripts and Ancient Versions* (London, 1926).

28. R. Kittel, *Biblia Hebraica*, ed. P. Kahle, A. Alt, and O. Eissfeldt (3d ed.; Stuttgart, 1929–37).

29. H. Quentin, *Mémoire sur l'établissement du texte de la Vulgate* ("Collectanea biblica Latina," Vol. VI [Rome, 1922]); and *Biblia Sacra iuxta Latinam Vulgatum versionem . . . . Genesis* (Rome, 1926). The text of Exodus and Leviticus appeared in 1929 and that of Joshua, Judges, and Ruth in 1939; (cf. Pfeiffer, *op. cit.*, p. 126).

30. *Historische Grammatik der hebräischen Sprache des Alten Testamentes* (Halle, 1922).

31. H. Bauer and P. Leander, *Grammatik des Biblisch-Aramäischen* (Halle, 1927).

has won some converts[32] but has been opposed vigorously by Bergsträsser and others.[33] The twenty-ninth edition of the Gesenius' *Hebrew Grammar* was edited by Bergsträsser; but his untimely death in 1933 prevented the publication of the projected section on Hebrew syntax by that capable and promising linguist.[34]

With such improving resources, scholars during the interval between the wars continued to labor at the primary objective of their predecessors—the attempt to recover, wherever possible, the original form of the text. Before World War I, scholarly activity was especially marked by its interest in the text. It was almost the only resource available and, in a real sense, was believed to be fundamental to salvation. Texts and versions were studied intensively; each verse and word was scrutinized. Stylistic and ideological considerations permitted the recognition of accretions to the original text; obvious grammatical errors were corrected; and the text was often "restored" to what appeared to be a more logical order. Conjectural emendations were made where the Hebrew text and the versions were in conflict or where the Hebrew simply made no sense. Excisions were practiced where the rhythmic pattern of poetry was disturbed. By means of an intricate process of source criticism the various strata of complex narratives were disentangled, and attempts were made to date them.

If the results of such enthusiastic and earnest efforts sometimes appeared extreme and, on occasion, even ridiculous, it must not be forgotten that the labor was meant to be constructive, the evidence of a serious concern about the text. Scholars were prone to use all available tools, techniques, and ingenuity in a sometimes desperate attempt to recover the original text.

With the passing years some of the less sound speculations of

32. H. Bauer, *Zur Frage der Sprachmischung im Hebräischen* (Halle, 1924); also in Bauer and Leander, *Historische Grammatik*, pp. 19–22; cf. G. R. Driver, "Hebrew Language," *Encyclopaedia Britannica* (14th ed.; New York, 1929), XI, 353–54, and *Problems of the Hebrew Verbal System* (Edinburgh, 1936), esp. pp. 151–52.

33. G. Bergsträsser, "Mitteilungen zur hebräischen Grammatik," *Orientalistische Literaturzeitung*, XXVI (1923), 253–60, 477–81; B. Landsberger, "Prinzipienfragen der semitischen, speziell der hebräischen, Grammatik," *Orientalistische Literaturzeitung*, XXIX (1926), 967–76; Z. S. Harris, *Development of the Canaanite Dialects* (New Haven, 1939).

34. G. Bergsträsser, *Wilhelm Gesenius' hebräische Grammatik* (29th ed., Leipzig, 1918–29).

earlier scholars have been discarded, but, on the whole, this generation between the wars has considered that much lasting good was accomplished by assiduous application to the text of the Bible. While we regard the former vogue of excessive deletions and emendations on the basis of meter as being out of date, we have come to a renewed appreciation of strophic structure as a critical resource and as an aid to the greater appreciation of Hebrew poetry.[35] We are as much concerned as our predecessors with discovering textual errors and have recently made lists of them.[36] But our own efforts, while applying the same techniques as our predecessors, when necessary, have usually been more moderate. There now prevails a tendency to acknowledge the weaknesses of the Massoretic systems of vocalizations but also a disposition to let the text stand as long as possible and to seek to make it more intelligible, not so much by emendation as by casting light from nonbiblical sources. When correction or emendation is essential, we employ devices that proved helpful in the past, but we try to remember our results for the conjectures that they are and still attempt constantly to understand the received text in the light of new data to be garnered from other sources.

PENTATEUCHAL CRITICISM

Perhaps nowhere in the Bible is concern with the text and its sources better illustrated than in the work done on the Pentateuch, which has always been the citadel of Old Testament

---

35. C. F. Kraft, *The Strophic Structure of Hebrew Poetry* (Chicago, 1938). The older, now usually repudiated, approach to strophic structure is represented by the work of A. Bruno, *Der Rhythmus der alttestamentlichen Dichtung* (Leipzig, 1930). Extremely elaborate patterns of strophic structure, designed according to Greek canons, have been insisted upon in the more radical treatment of the subject by D. Devimeux, *La Genèse, les trois poèmes historiques: Abraham, Isaac, Jacob* (Paris, n.d.). A special aspect of the study is that concerned with the literary form, *chiasmus* (cf. N. W. Lund, "The Presence of Chiasmus in the Old Testament," *American Journal of Semitic Languages*, XLVI [1929–30], 104–26, and "Chiasmus in the Psalms," *ibid.*, XLIX [1932–33], 281–312). A more moderate view of the problem is that held by Kraft, *op. cit.;* by W. A. Irwin, "Critical Notes on Five Psalms," *American Journal of Semitic Languages*, XLIX (1932–33), 9–12; and by K. Fullerton, "The Strophe in Hebrew Poetry and Psalm 29," *Journal of Biblical Literature*, XLVIII (1929), 274–90. Among those least convinced of the strophic structure is T. J. Meek, "The Structure of Hebrew Poetry," *Journal of Religion*, IX (1929), 523–50.

36. F. Delitzsch, *Die Lese- und Schreibfehler im Alten Testament* (Berlin, 1920); F. Perles, *Analekten zur Textkritik des Alten Testaments* (Leipzig, 1922); J. Kennedy, *An Aid to the Textual Amendment of the Old Testament* (Edinburgh, 1928).

criticism. By the end of World War I, the theory of source analysis of the Pentateuch, associated primarily with the names of Graf and Wellhausen, which isolated and named the pentateuchal sources J, E, D, and P, was accepted by all reputable scholars but was still resisted by conservatives, who held to the tradition of Mosaic authorship of the books.

Since 1919 the opponents of the Graf-Wellhausen hypothesis have continued their opposition. The discovery of alphabetic Semitic writing of about 1800 B.C. in the Sinaitic peninsula, as well as other early epigraphic materials in Palestine, made unnecessary the former desperate theories that Moses wrote the Pentateuch in Egyptian hieroglyphs or in cuneiform. Dr. H. Grimme suggested that the proto-Sinaitic texts were written by the Hebrews of the Exodus.[37] He read the names Yahu, Moses, and Sinai in them. But the dating of the material and further study have rendered his hypothesis untenable.[38] J. G. Duncan valiantly, but unsuccessfully, has tried to prove, on archeological grounds, that the sources of the Pentateuch were contemporary with the events recorded.[39] Other conservatives, such as E. Naville,[40] still argue for Mosaic authorship; and A. Šanda, still holding that Moses wrote Genesis, has suggested that from Exodus through Numbers the Pentateuch was based on Moses' diaries.[41] These extreme views have won no following among reputable scholars.

More telling have been the barbs leveled against the Graf-

37. H. Grimme, *Althebräische Inschriften vom Sinai* (Hannover, 1923), and *Die Lösung des Sinaischriftproblems* (Münster, 1926), *Die Altsinaitischen Buchstabeninschriften* (Berlin, 1929), and *Altsinaitische Forschungen* (Paderborn, 1937). He was followed in his interpretation by Sir Charles Marston, *New Bible Evidence* (New York, 1934–35), pp. 178–82, and others.

38. K. Sethe, "Die wissenschaftliche Bedeutung der Petrie'schen Sinaifunde und die angeblichen Moseszeugnisse," *Zeitschrift der Deutschen morgenländischen Gesellschaft*, LXXX (1926), 24–54; cf. H. G. May, "Moses and the Sinai Inscriptions," *Biblical Archaeologist*, VIII (1945), 93–99. Some of the best work done on these inscriptions has been by R. F. Butin, K. Lake, R. P. Blake, *et al.* in *Harvard Theological Review*, XXI (1928), 1–61; XXV (1932), 95–203.

39. *The Accuracy of the Old Testament* (London, 1930), pp. 19–26.

40. *La haute critique dans le Pentateuque* (Neuchâtel, 1921), and *The Higher Criticism in Relation to the Pentateuch*, trans. J. R. Mackay (Edinburgh, 1923).

41. *Moses und der Pentateuch* (Münster, 1924).

Wellhausen hypothesis for its apparent tendency to multiply sources, for the excesses formerly practiced of dogmatically dividing as little as a single verse among several sources, and for the resulting lack of specific agreement among scholars as to the exact limits of the several sources. As might be expected, this reaction was felt first and more intensely in Germany, where the gravest of excesses formerly had been committed. Sellin, who always represents a rather conservative view, wrote in 1924: "If I correctly understand our time, and particularly the trends of Old Testament scholarship, the era of Wellhausen, despite all we have learned from him, may be considered with us in Germany, antiquated and wholly a matter of the past. This is proved by the new crop of scholars whose way of thinking is quite different from that of those who have been brought up on Wellhausen."[42] The new German scholars mentioned, employing an emphasis begun with Gunkel's study of Genesis, would abandon source criticism for a discipline even less objective, concerned with the analysis of traditions and concepts. Such a reaction has delighted the conservatives, who hail the collapse of their opponents with the cries, "There is a strong tendency to abandon textual criticism as far as it is concerned with the dissection of the text" and ". . . . the very foundations of biblical criticism, such as the 'four sources hypothesis' and the theory of the late composition of the Pentateuch are now at stake."[43]

However, even those who believe in the soundness of source analysis as a method deplore the excesses which have rendered it vulnerable. Overzealous scholars are censured and warned to use greater care in the application of the method.[44] The current hue and cry should not blind one to the fact that among the outstanding works of the period, supporting the documentary hypothesis, are the German Eissfeldt's scholarly treatises.[45] Outside of

42. E. Sellin, *Archeology vs. Wellhausenism*, pp. 270 ff., quoted by T. W. Rosmarin, "The New Trend in Biblical Criticism," *Journal of Bible and Religion*, VI (1938), 85–86.

43. Rosmarin, *op. cit.*, p. 83.

44. W. Baumgartner, "Wellhausen und der heutige Stand der alttestamentliche Wissenschaft," *Theologische Rundschau*, II (new ser., 1930), 301 ff.; W. A. Irwin, "The Significance of Julius Wellhausen," *Journal of Bible and Religion*, XII (1944), 166, 168, 170.

45. O. Eissfeldt, *Hexateuch-Synopse* (Leipzig, 1922), and *Einleitung in das Alte Testament* (Tübingen, 1934).

Germany there has been even less defection from the orthodox method of source analysis. Irwin has said: "No such trend [away from Wellhausen] exists. It would be tedious merely to list the names of first-rank scholars of the present day who endorse the familiar documentary theory";[46] and Barton has stated: "In spite of the natural desire of deeply religious scholars to reestablish belief in the tradition that Moses wrote the Pentateuch, the facts on which the documentary hypothesis rests are so incontrovertible that they carry conviction to the mind of all candid persons who really examine them. The investigations of the last twenty years have, accordingly, established more firmly belief in the once separate existence of the great documents J, E, D and P."[47]

Not all who believe in the documentary hypothesis, however, would argue for the existence of *separate* documents, for quite a few consider the editing of the Pentateuch not as a "scissors-and-paste" performance but rather as a supplementing of existing documents. Such a concept of supplementation, which has been recognized as early as the work of A. Klostermann and B. D. Eerdmans, has been supported recently by D. B. McDonald,[48] U. Cassuto,[49] and A. T. Olmstead,[50] among others, all of whom stress the present unity of thought and style in Genesis. But the conception of supplementation is not far removed from the view that separate documents were used in the Pentateuch. Irwin has written:

Since both schools of critics, the documentary and supplementary, consider that the union of JE with Deuteronomy was the work of some member of this later school of thought, there would seem to be little disagreement. We can regard the procedure as a supplementation of D with the JE narratives, or we may take the view that the Deuteronomist merely appended his document to the other. But in regard to the final activity, that of the priestly editors, there is apparently no dis-

46. "The Significance of Julius Wellhausen," p. 170.

47. *Op. cit.*, p. 48.

48. *The Hebrew Literary Genius* (Princeton, 1933), pp. 96 ff.

49. *La Questione della Genesi* (Florence, 1934), pp. 393 ff.

50. "History, Ancient World, and the Bible," *Journal of Near Eastern Studies*, II (1943), 134 and esp. 11–12.

agreement between the two schools of critics unless perhaps in terms and modes of expression, for everyone recognizes that the framework of the Hexateuch is that of P and the incorporation of the JE and D material must have been a sort of supplementation.[51]

The most serious attacks against the Graf-Wellhausen hypothesis during the period between the wars were launched against the D and E documents. Since DeWette in 1805 suggested that Deuteronomy was the basis for Josiah's reform in 622 B.C., Document D, with its fixed date, has been widely regarded as the keystone in the Wellhausen hypothesis. Gramberg in 1829 had suggested that Deuteronomy came from the end of the Exilic period; but during the 1920's some scholars suggested that it came from the post-Exilic period.[52] It was argued that Deuteronomy is later than the Holiness Code (Lev. 17–26) and that it is dependent upon Jeremiah. It was claimed that Josiah's reform was based not on Deuteronomy but upon an early form of the Holiness Code and that Deuteronomy, on the other hand, was a priestly program of reform originating "in the same circles that later showed hostility to Nehemiah."

Countering such arguments for a late date, another group of scholars proposed a rather early one, earlier than the time of Josiah.[53] It was argued that the Deuteronomic Code arose in northern Israel, the result of the work of the earlier prophets, as a warning to the Israelites against the seduction of worship at Canaanite shrines. Josiah's reform was regarded as but a purification of the cultus, and the explicit regulation, centralizing all worship at Jerusalem (Deut. 12:17), was regarded as a later addition to the text. Both positions have been debated furiously but

51. "The Significance of Julius Wellhausen," pp. 166–67.

52. G. R. Berry, "The Code Found in the Temple," *Journal of Biblical Literature* XXXIX (1920), 44–51; R. H. Kennett, *Deuteronomy and the Decalogue* (Cambridge, 1920); G. Hölscher, "Komposition und Ursprung des Deuteronomiums," *Zeitschrift für die alttestamentliche Wissenschaft*, XL (1922), 161–255; F. Horst, "Die Anfänge des Propheten Jeremiah," *Zeitschrift für die alttestamentliche Wissenschaft*, XLI (1923), 94–153, and "Die Kultusreform des Königs Josia," *Zeitschrift der Deutschen morgenländischen Gesellschaft*, LXXVII (1923), 220–38.

53. T. Oestreicher, *Das deuteronomische Grundgesetz* (Gütersloh, 1923); W. Staerk, *Das Problem des Deuteronomiums* (Gütersloh, 1924); A. Welch, *The Code of Deuteronomy* (London, 1924).

have largely counterbalanced one another.[54] They have persuaded but few to abandon the orthodox views regarding the Deuteronomic document and its dating.

In their attack upon the E document, Rudolph and Volz argued sensationally that E was not a variant primary document but represented an incoherent series of résumés or repetitious glosses to the J document.[55] The charge was made that if it were not for the deeply intrenched dogma of the Graf-Wellhausen hypothesis and the inertia and indolence that it fostered, the E document would long since have disappeared as a figment of the critics' imagination. Again, although the issue was debated long and vigorously, there has been no large swing from the commonly accepted view. W. F. Albright says of it: "The recent effort of Volz and Rudolph [1933–38] . . . . has convinced but few scholars and does not do justice to the homogeneity of these additions nor to the principles according to which such compilations were made."[56]

In contrast to the radical views of these men is the work of Mowinckel, who would see the beginning of the E narrative, usually believed to start with Genesis, chapter 12, as far back as the second chapter of Genesis.[57]

Much effort has been expended to discover the possible sources of the earliest document of the Pentateuch, the so-called "J" document. Even before 1919 the unity of J was questioned and the elements of J-1 and J-2 were isolated. Since World War I, J-2 has been shown to be the real J source and to be dated in the time of Elijah-Elisha. The other source (J-1), beginning at Genesis, chapter 2, and continuing to the death of David—popular stories with a primitive theological conception and an inclination to

54. J. A. Bewer, L. B. Paton, and G. Dahl, "The Problem of Deuteronomy," *Journal of Biblical Literature*, XLVII (1928), 358–79.

55. P. Volz and W. Rudolph, "Der Elohist als Erzähler: Ein Irrweg der Pentateuchkritik?" *Zeitschrift für die alttestamentliche Wissenschaft*, Beih. 63 (1933); W. Rudolph, "Der 'Elohist' von Exodus bis Josua," *Zeitschrift für die alttestamentliche Wissenschaft*, Beih. 68 (1938); cf. Irwin, "The Significance of Julius Wellhausen," pp. 169–70.

56. *From the Stone Age to Christianity* (Baltimore, 1940), p. 190.

57. S. Mowinckel, *The Two Sources of the pre-Deuteronomic Primeval History (JE) in Genesis 1–11* (Oslo, 1937).

exalt the life of the nomad—has been called "L" for "Lay" source, in contradistinction to the Priestly source, "P."[58] The criteria for separating J and L operate well in Genesis but tend to function less well elsewhere in the Pentateuch.

The symbol S (for Seir) is used by R. H. Pfeiffer for a source that he believes can be isolated primarily within the J document.[59] Since he holds that the J narrative, like E, begins with the call of Abraham (Gen. 12), the substance of S is largely what has been called "J-1" or "L." Part of S is found in Genesis, chapters 1–11 (what is normally attributed to J), and the rest in the legendary accounts of the origins of peoples of southern Palestine and Transjordania found in Genesis, chapters 14–38. It is to be observed that the hitherto difficult and unstratified block of Genesis, chapter 14, is now assigned to S by Pfeiffer.

As Pfeiffer sees it, the S source is an Edomite document friendly toward Edom and concluding with a list of Edomite kings who ruled before the Hebrew monarchy. It exhibits an interest in the origin of the neighbors of Edom, in the southern part of Palestine and Transjordania, and shows marked antipathy to the Leah tribes of the south, while ignoring the more northerly tribes. The author is envisaged as a person probably living about the time of Solomon; not an original writer but a collector of stories, who carefully selected and arranged about a dozen stories to express his philosophy of history, which was essentially ". . . . the pessimistic observation that cultural progress is accompanied by increased wickedness and unhappiness."

Less well known is the isolation of a pentateuchal source called "K" for "Kenite," found principally within the compass of what is normally recognized as J material.[60] The document is regarded as genuine by Eissfeldt,[61] and its discovery has been called ". . . . the most noteworthy addition to our knowledge

58. Eissfeldt, *Hexateuch-Synopse*, pp. ix and 11 ff.

59. "A Non-Israelite Source of the Book of Genesis," *Zeitschrift für die alttestamentliche Wissenschaft*, XLVIII (1930), 66–73; also his *Introduction*, pp. 159–67.

60. J. Morgenstern, "The Oldest Document of the Hexateuch," *Hebrew Union College Annual*, IV (1927), 1–138.

61. *Einleitung*, p. 147.

of the literary origins of the Pentateuch made during the last twenty years.''[62] Document K, believed to extend from the story of the birth of Moses through the giving of the Ten Commandments, the making of the covenant with Yahweh (Exod. 34), and the establishment of the Tent of Meeting, is thought to have been composed in Judea before 899 B.C. and thus to be the oldest document hitherto isolated in the Pentateuch. It is claimed to have formed the basis for Asa's reforms (I Kings 15:9–15). Both L (J-1) and E are thought to have borrowed material from K, and J (J-2) is believed to have incorporated fragments of it into the J Code (Exod. 34).

Thus, in the face of broad attacks against the documentary hypothesis and the use of source analysis as a method, enterprising scholars have moved from the long-established orthodox view, as from a secure base, to investigate the individual documents themselves, in the hope of arriving at even earlier sources for the Pentateuch. Without first achieving an absolutely uniform agreement as to the exact limits of the different sources J, E, D, and P, individuals examining identical blocks of material have projected these new hypotheses to be tested as the Graf-Wellhausen hypothesis has been, by the efforts of the community of scholars over a considerable period of time. It is still too early to choose dogmatically among the alternatives offered.

The documentary hypothesis seems firmly established. Perhaps our current views, somewhat less loyal to the former scissors-and-paste method, which was so essential in the classical Graf-Wellhausen hypothesis, should not bear the designation ''Wellhausenian,'' but that name has served as well to indicate a belief in multiple sources as over against the former concept of the unity of the Pentateuch. In this sense, at least, the documentary hypothesis still stands. Its critics have nowhere presented a competing explanation that will as adequately account for the literary phenomena of the Pentateuch.

Criticism of the hypothesis has not been in vain, however, for it has resulted in greater caution and a more conservative attitude in textual criticism, as well as in some relaxation of the

62. Barton, *op. cit.*, p. 50.

aggressive dogmatism that characterized the earlier application of the method of source analysis.

ARCHEOLOGY AND THE OLD TESTAMENT

In 1938, G. A. Barton wrote:

As one reviews the trends of Old Testament study during the past two decades, he is impressed with the change of emphasis that has been brought about. We have passed from the stage where documents and literary criticism seem of supreme interest to an intensive effort to recover the inner meaning of the different parts of the Old Testament. This effort has been made possible largely through that increased knowledge of the Near East which exploration and archeological research has made possible. More and more we are coming to see the "situation in life" which called each part of the Old Testament into being.[63]

We realize increasingly that the Hebrews did not live in splendid isolation but were an integral part of the life of the Orient and that the cultures of their Near Eastern neighbors exerted a profound influence upon the expanding life and thought of the Hebrew people. It is customary now to study intently the culture of Israel's neighbors for the light that might be cast on Israel's history, religion, and daily life. The results of such cognate studies have been by no means disappointing.

Knowledge of the Egyptian language has increased at a pace commensurate with that of Old Testament studies, and the production of linguistic aids in Egyptian since 1923 has encouraged the translation of Egyptian materials with historical, and possibly also literary, connections with the Bible.[64] Similarly with Akkadian[65] and Hittite,[66] increased knowledge of the language and improved facilities for translating have opened rich stores of data pertinent to Bible study. The rediscovery of the Horites of

63. *Ibid.*, p. 74.

64. J. A. Wilson, "The Present State of Egyptian Studies" in *The Haverford Symposium*, pp. 205–6, 213–14, 219–22.

65. T. J. Meek, "The Present State of Mesopotamian Studies" in *The Haverford Symposium*, pp. 176–79.

66. A. Goetze, "The Present State of Anatolian and Hittite Studies" in *The Haverford Symposium*, pp. 145–51.

the Bible[67] (Hurrians) in 1918 and the subsequent publication of stores of their tablets have offered explanations for some curious customs found in the patriarchal narratives,[68] while the relatively recent (1929) discovery in Syria of a library of the fourteenth century B.C., principally of religious texts, written in a hitherto unknown alphabet, has presented us with a body of Canaanite literature that, in literary form and sometimes in its very phraseology, strongly resembles the Bible itself.[69] From it we learn much of the religion of Canaan as found by the Hebrews when they entered the land. When the rich finds of tablets recovered at the ancient Amorite city of Mari in Mesopotamia are published, we shall have a better conception also of another of the neighbors of ancient Israel.[70]

Such linguistic advances and the discovery and decipherment of ancient records would have been impossible had it not been for the great strides made in archeological excavation since World War I. It has ceased to be mere treasure-hunting and has become, instead, a scientific pursuit of knowledge with precise techniques for operating and a careful preservation of all records. Riding the crest of the postwar boom, archeology cut deeply into the past and piled up quantities of materials to be examined, digested, and published during the depression years when no funds were available for excavation. Even then, however, sur-

67. R. H. Pfeiffer, "Nuzi and the Hurrians," *Smithsonian Institution Annual Report, 1935* (Washington, 1936), pp. 535–58; E. A. Speiser, "Ethnic Movements in the Near East in the Second Millennium B.C.: The Hurrians and Their Connections with the Ḫabiru and the Hyksos," *Annual of the American Schools for Oriental Research*, XIII (1931–32), 13–54; and *Mesopotamian Origins* (Philadelphia, 1930), pp. 131 ff., 161 ff.

68. C. H. Gordon, "Biblical Customs and the Nuzu Tablets," *Biblical Archaeologist*, III (1940), 1–12.

69. J. P. Hyatt, "The Ras Shamra Discoveries and the Interpretation of the Old Testament," *Journal of Bible and Religion*, X (1942), 67–75; H. L. Ginsberg, "Ugaritic Studies and the Bible," *Biblical Archaeologist*, VIII (1945), 1–58.

70. A. Parrot, *Mari, une ville perdue ... et retrouvée par l'archéologie française* (Paris, 1936); G. Dossin, "Les Archives épistolaires du palais de Mari," *Syria*, XIX (1938), 105–26; "Les Archives économiques du palais de Mari," *ibid.*, XX (1939), 97–113; and "Benjaminites dans les textes de Mari," *Mélanges syriens offerts à M. René Dussaud* (Paris, 1939), II, 981–96; cf. also Albright, *From the Stone Age to Christianity*, pp. 111–13.

face exploration was carried on after 1932 in the previously neglected regions of ancient Ammon, Moab, and Edom.[71]

Biblical study could not help feeling the impact of the new
knowledge of the Near East. Since the discovery of stratified cave
deposits near Mount Carmel in 1934, our horizon of history in
Palestine has been extended to the time of Neanderthal man. We
have an almost unbroken cultural sequence in Palestine from that
period to modern times. Thus we are enabled to witness man's
climb toward civilization and culture and to note the progressive
intermingling of races, Semitic and non-Semitic, in the melting-
pot of Canaan.

Material pertinent to biblical times abounds. The architecture
and countless artifacts recovered bear eloquent witness to the
daily life of the people of the Bible. We know at firsthand the
richness of the late Canaanite cities and the massive structure of
their city walls, which fell before the Hebrews. From nonbiblical
sources—Egyptian, Hurrian, Canaanite, and Amorite—the number of references to the Ḥabiru have been increased and their
character more finely delineated. The objective and datable records of violently destroyed Canaanite cities and of Israelite foundations have aided in clarifying the confused biblical narratives
of the Exodus and the Conquest.

Saul's fortress at Gibeah has been excavated. Solomon's
stables at Megiddo have been recovered, and his mines and
smelteries in Transjordania have been found. In countless ways
our knowledge of Hebrew life through the period of the kingdoms has been illumined. The story of the fall of pre-Exilic Jerusalem is interestingly supplemented by the traces of the destruction of Lachish and by an important series of inscribed potsherds
found there, dating from the time of Jeremiah (587 B.C.), which
mention a prophet and use language reminiscent of that in the
Book of Jeremiah. Seal impressions of Eliakim, the steward of
Jehoiakim, were found at Tell Beit Mirsim, and the seal of "Ge-

71. N. Glueck, "Explorations in Eastern Palestine. I," *Annual of the American Schools of
Oriental Research*, XIV (1934), 1–113; "Explorations in Eastern Palestine. II," *ibid.*, Vol.
XV (1935); "Explorations in Eastern Palestine. III," *ibid.*, Vols. XVIII–XIX (for 1937–
39); *The Other Side of the Jordan* (New Haven, 1940); and numerous articles in the *Bulletin of
the American Schools of Oriental Research* from No. 49 (1933) onward.

daliah who is over the house" was found at Lachish. From Babylonia have come tablets mentioning the deported king Jehoiakin and the dispensing of rations to him and his companions. Also from Babylonia about seven hundred tablets belonging to the banking firm of Murashu and his sons mention the names of a large number of their Babylonian Jewish clients, presumably Jews of the Diaspora, during the days of Artaxerxes I and Darius II (464–405 B.C.). All this and much more have been found. It has served as a stimulus to the restudying of biblical history and the re-examining of perplexing and hitherto unsolved problems in that area.

The influence of archeology has affected both our attitudes and our methodology. The patriarchal narratives in Genesis, which formerly had lost much of their standing as history and were explained frequently as being of mythological or astrological nature, are now regarded more seriously as offering data on the early culture and history of the Hebrews. Some are now prepared to recognize the patriarchs as persons,[72] while others, more cautiously, are inclined to regard the narratives as being ethnographic, preserving in personalized fashion the history of tribes and families. As our knowledge of the Near East increases, the traditions preserved in the patriarchal narratives have a more authentic appearance.

The translation of the law codes of Israel's neighbors (Babylonian, *ca.* 1750 B.C.; Hittite, *ca.* fourteenth century B.C.; and Assyrian, *ca.* twelfth century B.C.) gave an impetus to the re-examination of the pentateuchal laws ascribed to Moses.[73] Jirku has shown that Hebrew laws, although later in date than the other known oriental laws, are culturally more primitive.[74] Morgenstern recognizes two types of laws in Hebrew legislation:

72. Barton, *op. cit.*, p. 59; E. Sellin, *Geschichte des israelitisch-jüdischen Volkes* (Leipzig, 1923–32), I, 22–78; A. Alt, *Der Gott der Väter* (Stuttgart, 1929); C. L. Woolley, *Abraham* (New York, 1936); P. Dhorme, "Abraham dans le cadre de l'histoire," *Revue biblique*, XXXVII (1928), 367 ff., 481 ff.; XL (1931), 364–74, 503–18; Albright, *From the Stone Age to Christianity*, pp. 179 ff.

73. J. M. P. Smith, *The Origin and Development of Hebrew Law* (Chicago, 1931), pp. 181–279.

74. A. Jirku, *Altorientalischer Kommentar zum Alten Testament* (Leipzig-Erlangen, 1923).

a *mishpat* or "casuistic" type ("If a man . . . ."), usually secular in type and perhaps patterned after neighboring codes and probably a compendium of legal decisions; and an "apodictic" type ("thou shalt not . . . ."), which are more ritualistic or religious in nature.[75] A careful study by Alt has led to a similar distinction.[76] He argues that the casuistic type goes back to Sumerian law of the third millennium B.C. and was taken over by the Hebrews from the Canaanites during the period of the judges and the reign of Saul. The "apodictic" category, on the other hand, cannot now be paralleled outside of Israel. Tradition traces such law to Moses, and Alt contends that nothing in such laws conflicts with the conditions in Israel in the time of Moses. However, not all scholars have been convinced by Alt, and there is still considerable debate as to just what, if any, Hebrew law is historically Mosaic.[77]

Archeological results have served sometimes to check a specific trend in criticism. This is true in the case of Exilic and post-Exilic Jewish history, which was long in darkness aside from the Bible narrative. Our best information is found in the contemporary prophecies of Haggai and Zechariah, for the very limited period of 520–518 B.C. Nehemiah's memoirs, too, furnish valuable data. But for the rest of the Bible story we are dependent upon the Chronicler and Ezra. Here is chaos. C. C. Torrey has devoted much energy to demonstrating the insufficiency of the work of the Chronicler and has had a tremendous influence on scholarship in this area.[78] He has shown the Ezra stories to be incomplete, out of chronological order, and concerned with little more than the cultus. Pfeiffer, supporting Torrey, claims: "If we remove from the stories all references to the Law, the Levites, the singers, the ritual practices of the Second Temple,

75. J. Morgenstern, "The Book of the Covenant," *Hebrew Union College Annual*, V (1928), 1–151; VII (1930), 19–258; VIII–IX (1931–32), 1–150.

76. A. Alt, *Die Ursprünge des israelitischen Rechts* ("Berichte der sächsischen Akademie der Wissenschaft, Phil.-hist. Klasse," Vol. LXXXVI, No. 1 [1934]).

77. T. J. Meek, *Hebrew Origins* (New York, 1936), pp. 35 ff., 51 ff.; cf. R. Pfeiffer, *Introduction*, pp. 133 ff., 231 f.

78. "The Composition and Historical Value of Ezra-Nehemiah," *Zeitschrift für die alttestamentliche Wissenschaft*, Beih. 2 (1896); *Ezra Studies* (Chicago, 1910).

and all else in which the Chronicler, writing *after* the Pentateuch was canonized (about 400 B.C.), was interested, hardly anything remains."[79]

Thus, even before 1919, the confusion within Ezra-Nehemiah-Chronicles caused it to be mistrusted as a source. Its story of exile and restoration was widely repudiated, and some even doubted the historicity of Ezra himself.[80] The Ezra-Nehemiah complex was regarded as the Chronicler's fiction. The Chronicler's aim was considered to be ". . . . to establish the fact of the Restoration and to delimit the true and uncontaminated Palestinian 'Israel' . . . . from any other Hebrew religious community."[81] With the repudiation of the Chronicler's story of exile and restoration, historical criticism had to move by dead reckoning, guided solely by Haggai and Zechariah. Torrey popularized the view that, although Judah may have been decimated, it was not depopulated after 586 B.C. and that refugees soon returned to occupy Judean towns. There was no captivity on the scale recorded in the Bible, and Palestine remained, as it always had been, the center of Jewish life and literature. There was little or no restoration from Babylonia to Palestine during the Persian period, and such accounts as we have preserved in Ezra-Nehemiah-Chronicles are but historically worthless propaganda.

The corollary to the proposition was that such biblical literature as Ezekiel and Deutero-Isaiah, which traditionally are believed to have issued from Babylonia and, indeed, to bear internal signs of such origin, would have to be assigned to the Palestinian community where alone Jewish culture was believed to be thriving. Such, in part at least, was the motive for Torrey's sensational treatment of Deutero-Isaiah as a Palestinian work of about 407 B.C.[82] and of Ezekiel as a pseudepigraph from Palestine

---

79. *Introduction*, p. 831.

80. Torrey, *Composition* . . . . , pp. 57, 60; *Ezra Studies*, pp. 238–48; G. Hölscher, *Geschichte der israelitischen und jüdischen Religion* (Giessen, 1922), p. 140.

81. C. C. Torrey, *Pseudo-Ezekiel and the Original Prophecy* (New Haven, 1930), pp. 106–7.

82. C. C. Torrey, *The Second Isaiah: A New Interpretation* (New Haven, 1928).

in *ca.* 230 B.C.,[83] as well as his assignment of Jeremiah, chapters 1–10, and much else to the third century B.C.[84]

But the study of excavated Judean cities has tended to confirm at least the basic outlines of the biblical picture of exile and restoration. An archeologist can now assert:

Excavations in Judah since 1926 have shown with increasing weight of evidence that the Chaldean destruction of Jewish towns was thorough-going and that few of them arose from the ruins. Until the excavations at Bethel (which was in the Assyro-Babylonian province of Samaria) in 1934 no remains of the sixth century which could be dated after cir. 587 B.C. were known; the land was an archeological *tabula rasa* for that period. Work at Beth-Zur and at Bethel has shown that Jewish revival was slow and that the first settlers were few and poor. Innumerable detailed finds, the most important of which have not yet been published, though familiar to the present writer from personal communications, disprove practically every one of Torrey's concrete arguments for his position. The facts are precisely the opposite of what they should be if Torrey's contentions were correct. . . . . In short, we are justified in rejecting his position completely, without any concessions—except that Torrey's searching criticisms of the sources and their interpretation have been of immense heuristic value.[85]

Any future treatment of the Exilic and post-Exilic periods must take archeological data into consideration. Recent work on these periods exhibits, in some respects, a more conservative tendency. Rothstein insists that the editor of the nucleus of Chronicles (Ch-P) lived soon after Ezra (*ca.* 432 B.C.) and made use of the P code and original documents that lay behind the books of Samuel and Kings, while the final redactor (Ch-R) worked *ca.* 400 B.C., using the Hexateuch as a whole and our canonical Samuel and Kings as his basis.[86] Von Rad finds evidence of a Deuteronomic influence in addition to a priestly hand.[87] Welch, greatly

83. Torrey, *Pseudo-Ezekiel*, p. 99.

84. C. C. Torrey, "The Background of Jeremiah 1–10," *Journal of Biblical Literature*, LVI (1937), 208 ff.

85. Albright, *From the Stone Age to Christianity*, pp. 246–47.

86. J. W. Rothstein and J. Hanel, *Das erste Buch der Chronik* ("Kommentar zum Alten Testament," ed. E. Sellin, Vol. XVIII, No. 2 [Leipzig, 1927]).

87. G. von Rad, *Das Geschichtsbild des chronistischen Werkes* ("Beiträge zur Wissenschaft vom Alten und Neuen Testaments," Vol. IV, No. 3 [Stuttgart, 1930]).

influenced by Von Rad, now dates Nehemiah, chapter 10, shortly after 586 b.c., and Chronicles, except for a miscellany in I Chronicles, chapters 1–9, he dates *ca*. 520 b.c. He contends that valuable historical sources were at the disposal of the author of Ezra-Nehemiah, who put them together incorrectly. He argues that there was no return under Cyrus but one under Darius I; that Nehemiah was interested only in building the wall; and that Ezra failed in his attempt to introduce the Law.[88]

Torrey's work on Deutero-Isaiah and Ezekiel created activity in those areas. He was praised for his translation and lauded by some for his defense of the unity of chapters 40–66, which seemed to integrate "a work which criticism had sadly disintegrated";[89] but there was considerable resistance to his excision of references to Cyrus (Isa. 44:28, 45:1) as glosses on metrical grounds and rather more rejection of his late date for the entire work. The great majority of scholars are unconvinced by him and still hold the view advanced by Duhm in 1892 that chapters 56–66 are the work of still another author.[90] In the matter of details, as to the unity or diversity of authorship of each section, the date of the various sections, and such special problems as the identity of the Servant, etc., scholars are still as widely divergent in their views as they have ever been.[91]

Ezekiel has been the storm center of criticism in the period between the wars. Torrey's view that it is a Palestinian pseudepigraphical work of about 230 b.c. falsely set in the days of Manasseh, written to show that the disaster of 586 was deserved by Judah, has not won general acceptance. The earlier, orthodox interpretation is still held by G. A. Cooke (1936)[92] and essentially by Albright,[93] but the current trend is toward a slashing analysis of the work on literary grounds to discover what is original

88. A. C. Welch, *Post-Exilic Judaism* (London, 1935), and *The Work of the Chronicler: Its Purpose and Date* (London, 1939).

89. Barton, *op. cit.*, p. 61.

90. *Ibid.*, pp. 61–62, 76–77, and n. 53; cf. Pfeiffer, *Introduction*, p. 462.

91. For an excellent survey of views cf. Pfeiffer, *Introduction*, pp. 449–81.

92. *A Critical and Exegetical Commentary on the Book of Ezekiel* (Edinburgh, 1936).

93. *From the Stone Age to Christianity*, pp. 248 ff.

and what accretion. Hölscher has found only 143 of the 1,272 verses of the book to be the genuine work of a pro-Babylonian, anti-Egyptian Jerusalemite writing in the period before 621 B.C.[94] The original poems are believed to be set into a prose *ode* pattern that has literary relations in the fifth century B.C. Herntrich holds a Babylonian redactor responsible for the Babylonian setting, the dates, and the perplexing events that have given Ezekiel his reputation as a psychic, ecstatic person.[95] Matthews likewise contends that the author of Ezekiel, chapters 1–39, was a Jerusalemite who worked from 588 to 570 B.C. but is uncertain whether he had gone into exile. He, too, posits a Babylonian editor (520–500 B.C.) who expanded Ezekiel's original work to fit a new situation, stressing theology and cultus as over against the original free prophecy.[96] Irwin, by an inductive approach, has attempted to recover what is original in Ezekiel. Hölscher's poetical criterion was employed with the further stipulation that original material was introduced by the phrase, "And the word of Yahweh came to me, saying 'Son of man. . . . .' " The method severely restricts the original material. Irwin concludes that the author was a native Jerusalemite, neither priest nor ecstatic, but one who spent part of his ministry in Babylonia.[97] Thus the problem remains in controversy. The pattern of attack is observed to have a literary basis, but there is still no solution to which the majority of scholars will assent.

LITERARY CRITICISM

Recent work on Ezekiel, the pentateuchal legislation, the patriarchal narratives, and elsewhere indicates a definite trend toward the use of literary types (*Gattungsgeschichte*) as criteria in current biblical criticism. The application of form criticism to Old Testament material is not new, for it was introduced by

---

94. G. Hölscher, "Hesekiel, der Dichter und das Buch," *Zeitschrift für die alttestamentliche Wissenschaft*, Beih. 39 (1924).

95. V. Herntrich, "Ezechielprobleme," *Zeitschrift für die alttestamentliche Wissenschaft*, Beih. 61 (1932).

96. I. G. Matthews, *Ezekiel* (Philadelphia, 1939).

97. W. A. Irwin, *The Problem of Ezekiel* (Chicago, 1943).

Gunkel long before World War I;[98] but it is increasingly used as a technique to detect earlier strata in existing books and to determine ultimately the initial function of the biblical material and the situation in the life of the people that evoked it. Of the method Albright says: "The student of the Near East finds that the methods of Norden and Gunkel are not only applicable but are the only ones that can be applied . . . . the importance of categories of form is so great that it is a comparatively simple matter to distribute all known compositions among a limited number of categories within which there is surprisingly little variation."[99]

The discovery and translation of the literary works of Israel's neighbors—Egypt, Babylonia, and Assyria and Canaan—have stimulated the interest in form criticism, for we have learned that, however high the theological quality of the content of Israel's religious literature, it is not unique, for there is a strong resemblance in literary form and sometimes even in phraseology to other Near Eastern cultic material. It makes us wonder, then, if it could not be parallel, too, in function and origin.

Nowhere in the Old Testament has the form-history method demonstrated its validity and fruitfulness better than in the Psalter. Its application there has compelled a revision of our conception of the Psalms and has brought us more intimately into an appreciation of the cultus in which they first functioned.

Before 1919 it was the general critical view that the Psalter was the "Hymnbook of the Second Temple," composed of psalms nearly all post-Exilic in date, many from the Maccabean age. There was considerable debate as to whether or not the Psalms voiced individual or group aspirations, and the timeless character of their devotional emphasis afforded little evidence for dating them. What dating was done proceeded principally on subjective bases, and therefore there was but little uniformity in the results.

98. H. Gunkel, *Die Genesis* (Göttingen, 1901), and *The Legends of Genesis*, trans. W. H. Carruth (Chicago, 1901).

99. *From the Stone Age to Christianity*, p. 44.

Since the work of Mowinckel and others, based on form criticism as well as on a study of the liturgy as reconstructed from scattered references within the Bible and by analogy to what is known of the cultus among Israel's neighbors, there is a definite tendency to trace many of the Psalms to pre-Exilic roots.[100] We now have an appreciation of their functional position in the ancient cultus as we recognize a king's prayer (Ps. 18), a prayer for the king (Ps. 20), antiphonal chants (Ps. 24:7–10), ritual for the New Years' Festival (Pss. 24, 96–99 and 132), etc. Sometimes, as in the case of Psalm 104, which strongly resembles an ancient Hymn to Aton composed before 1350 B.C., or Psalm 29, which seems to have Canaanite relations, and others, it is believed that we have in our Psalter an adaptation to Hebrew usage of some of the highest literary and religious literature of other Near Eastern cults.

CURRENT TRENDS

No compendium of all views put forth in Old Testament research between the great wars has been attempted in this study.[101] Many areas have not been mentioned, not because nothing has been accomplished therein but because, with such an abundance of views and contributions as exist, only the most striking, those illustrating the trend, can be considered. The discernible trends appear to be as follows:

1. An acceptance of the sound work of the past and an indorsement of its critical methodology, but a less daring and more conservative application of it in dealing with the text. Scholars are no longer preoccupied with Bible text alone but venture freely into other fields of historical and religious relevance for Bible study, both among the Hebrews and among their neighbors.

2. An increasing interest in archeological study has resulted in a willingness to accept archeological data as a check both on the credibility of the Bible narrative and on critical hypotheses. Although the results of excavation, as at Ai, do not always

100. S. Mowinckel, *Psalmenstudien* (Kristiania, 1921–24); W. O. E. Oesterley, *A Fresh Approach to the Psalms* (New York, 1937); and *The Psalms* (London, 1939).

101. For such a comprehensive purpose Pfeiffer's *Introduction* cannot be matched today.

support the Bible record, the confirmation of biblical narrative at most points has led to a new respect for biblical tradition and a more conservative conception of biblical history.

3. A concern about getting ever earlier documents for Bible study, manifested by a probing behind the existing biblical books for their sources and even, where possible, for the sources of sources already isolated. Thus the Bible books themselves, in their present form, tend to be dated relatively late, as scholarship has ably demonstrated and long insisted, but we are enabled, nevertheless, to push materials back to an earlier and more vital stage in their creation and use. Both source criticism and form criticism serve as fruitful literary techniques in this process, but with full recognition of the dangers of subjectivism entailed. As in the Psalter, the use of these literary techniques tends to produce earlier dates and a more conservative attitude toward biblical materials.

THEOLOGY

A further evidence of the growing conservatism of Old Testament study is to be found in the revived interest in Old Testament theology.[102] At the end of the nineteenth century the term "theology" fell into disuse among students of Old Testament; and, under the influence of the prevailing interest in historical criticism of the Bible, a historical and descriptive, rather than a topical and theological, approach to religion was followed. From the time of Davidson's *Theology of the Old Testament* (1904) to Burney's *Outlines of Old Testament Theology* (1920) this emphasis prevailed, and the term "theology" was avoided in describing work devoted to Old Testament religion.[103] After World War I the designation "theology" was used by Burney and has appeared with increasing frequency in the titles of both English and German works. Scholars are now vitally interested in the

102. J. D. Smart, "The Death and Rebirth of Old Testament Theology," *Journal of Religion*, XXIII (1943), 1–11, 125–36; W. A. Irwin, "The Reviving Theology of the Old Testament," *Journal of Religion*, XXV (1945), 235–46; C. T. Craig, "Biblical Theology and the Rise of Historicism," *Journal of Biblical Literature*, XLII (1943), 281–94.

103. A. B. Davidson, *The Theology of the Old Testament* (New York, 1904); C. F. Burney, *Outlines of Old Testament Theology* (Oxford, 1920).

subject, and learned societies have organized symposiums for the discussion of theological problems. It has already been necessary, lest this pendulum of reaction swing too far, to call attention to the limits of the subject and to the dangers attendant upon its overemphasis. It must not displace the critical approach to Old Testament religion which has come to prevail but must supplement it.[104] Nevertheless, the definite resurgence of the study of Old Testament theology reflects the conviction that the critical, analytical, historical, and descriptive approach to the Bible is not sufficient in itself and that a further approach must be adopted if the entire truth of the Bible is to be known and the full needs of the inner spiritual life of man are to be met. In this task the Old Testament scholar and the theologian must co-operate.

All tendencies are leading to a more conservative attitude in Old Testament study than prevailed among scholars prior to 1919, but there is no sign of an absolute retreat to the earlier uncritical position. There are styles or fads in criticism that have their day and are done. As Sellers has commented: "There is nothing like the Pan-Babylonian theory or the Jerahmeelite hypothesis taking the attention of scholars today."[105] We seem better balanced and more sane in our approach to our task than ever before. There are still widely divergent views wherever inconclusive evidence permits, but there appear to be more charity and less dogmatism and more of a willingness to learn. Much remains to be done, but from this base and in this direction we proceed. Time alone, with its constant critical examination of our results, will prove what is gold and what is dross in the methods and results achieved in Old Testament study during the active and important period between the great wars.

104. Irwin, "The Reviving Theology of the Old Testament."
105. *Op. cit.*, p. 68.

CHAPTER TWO

Intertestamental Studies since Charles's Apocrypha and Pseudepigrapha

J. COERT RYLAARSDAM

University of Chicago

THE publication, in 1913, of *The Apocrypha and Pseudepigrapha of the Old Testament* under the editorship of R. H. Charles was a real landmark in the history of biblical scholarship. For the first time, virtually all the Jewish noncanonical literature, with a critical introduction for each document, appeared in a single publication in English. The work, supervised by Charles, came more than a decade after the German publication of Kautzsch's *Die Apokryphen und Pseudepigraphen des Alten Testaments* (Tübingen, 1900). But it was a more complete work. The introductions provided more detail; and there were editions of IV Maccabees, the Story of Ahikar, the Pirke Aboth, and the so-called "Zadokite Fragment." For the Story of Ahikar the Charles edition utilized the Aramaic papyrus text discovered in 1906–8 at Elephantine. Kautzsch's work was also too early for the Zadokite Fragment, which was recovered by Solomon Schechter.

In his Preface, Charles stated that the value of the noncanonical literature was "practically recognized" on all sides by both Jewish and Christian scholars. The critical-historical method of study was in the ascendancy. Both Jewish and Christian scholars sought to understand their own religious heritage, as well as their relation to each other, in the light of the genetic antecedents of their cultus. There was a great concern to understand Jesus as a historic figure and to see him in relation to the setting in which he arose. The eschatology of the New Testament was being examined in the light of historical movements of thought,

32

especially apocalypticism. The dominant method of study made a rapprochement of Jewish and Christian scholars inevitable and insured their co-operation. The "bridge" of meeting was the area of life and thought recorded in the intertestamental literature. Thus Charles's publication was very timely. It was evoked by current methods and interests. Its appearance facilitated the continued use of the historical method. Its value was cumulative. The work has become a classic.

The co-operation of Jewish and Christian scholars is one of the happy phenomena of our time. Both have recognized that they possess a common heritage and that *all* the materials of *both* traditions must be used in arriving at a true understanding of either one of them. Until rather recently Jewish scholars confined their work to the Old Testament proper and the rabbinic writings. The noncanonical writings and the New Testament were not used because they are outside the main stream of Jewish development. Now, under the compulsion of historical method, it is recognized that these late Jewish and Christian writings sprang from the same roots as the Talmud and can throw light upon its historical growth and show the proportion of its teaching. Similarly, Christians confined themselves to the Old and New Testaments. They were more friendly to the intertestamental literature than were the Jews, but, as long as the confusion of dogmatic and historical methods and concerns persisted, it could receive only passing interest. Rabbinic writings were almost wholly ignored by Christian scholars; they failed to grasp that something of the ground from which Christianity sprang was permanently recorded in them. Today all this has changed. Publications and activities of both Jews and Christians which utilize the entire Judeo-Christian literary heritage have become frequent. The intertestamental literature has become a focus of common interest.

In 1917 the Society for Promoting Christian Knowledge launched a series of publications known as the "Translations of Early Documents." It reflected the new mood. The editors were G. H. Box and W. O. E. Oesterley. Three classes of texts in English translation, provided with brief, popular introductions and notes, were presented: Palestinian-Jewish, Hellenistic-Jew-

ish, and rabbinic. The sponsors were conscious promoters of the Christian cause, and their selections were made because they felt them to be "important for the study of Christian origins." The wider dissemination of the materials used rather than original scholarship was the first concern. In the Preface to his recent book, *The Apocryphal Literature* (New Haven, 1945), Professor Torrey tells us that when he first taught intertestamental literature, in 1894, "few of the students in the Seminary had ever seen an edition of the Apocrypha, to say nothing of the other books." The Society for Promoting Christian Knowledge has done much to overcome that condition. The inclusion of the rabbinic class of texts was especially significant. Indeed, it was tentatively undertaken; only one or two titles were published at first. The demand for these was made the test for proceeding with further publications in this class. In 1920 the editors published *A Short Survey of the Literature of Rabbinical and Medieval Judaism*, the first book of its kind in English since 1852 and entirely unique in its presentation of the rabbinic materials to Christians as a source for the understanding of their own faith.

The new mood and the new method took root and resulted in Great Britain in the organization of the Society of Jews and Christians, in 1924. Ten years later this fellowship sponsored a symposium dedicated to the memory of George Foot Moore and Israel Abrahams. George Yates, the editor, entitled it *In Spirit and in Truth*. The twenty contributors were selected equally from Jewish and Christian scholars. Among them Claude Montefiore discussed the role of the Law in Judaism, and C. F. Burkitt sought to show that the course of rabbinic studies indicates that the influence of orthodox Judaism upon the founding of Christianity is larger than has been commonly assumed.

Hermann L. Strack, a Christian orientalist interested in the conversion of Jews, was so convinced that the understanding of the New Testament demanded a knowledge of rabbinic literature that he founded the Institutum Judaicum in Berlin. In 1921 a fifth edition of his *Einleitung in Talmud und Midrash* was made possible by a subvention from the Central Conference of American Rabbis. The book was translated into English in 1931.

Paul Billerbeck, sponsored and aided by Strack, produced the four-volume *Kommentar zum Neuen Testament aus Talmud und Midrash* (München, 1922–28), which is considered indispensable in New Testament interpretation. Several publications, both by Jews and by Christians, studied the same field. Israel Abrahams' *Studies in Pharisaism and the Gospels* (Cambridge, 1924) compared the teaching of Jesus and the doctrine of the rabbis. Montefiore's commentary on the Synoptic Gospels (1927) was supplemented by his *Rabbinic Literature and Gospel Teaching* (New York, 1930); this supplement Israel Abrahams had hoped to provide.

In America, George Foot Moore's three-volume *Judaism in the First Centuries of the Christian Era* (Cambridge, 1927–30) has deeply influenced all study of the intertestamental period dealing with the nature of Judaism and the beginnings of Christianity. Moore insists that the Talmud and Tannaitic materials demand first place as sources for the study of "normative Judaism." Apocryphal literature, the Gospels, Philo, and Josephus can be considered only as supplementary sources, he feels, since the Talmud ignores or rejects all of them except Ben Sira. Ralph Marcus in *Law in the Apocrypha* (New York, 1928) feels that the doctrines of "normative Judaism" are in preparation in the apocryphal literature and are crystallized in the Tannaitic period.

Hugo Gressmann did much to emphasize the importance of rabbinic studies for the study of the intertestamental literature and the New Testament (*Die Aufgaben der Wissenschaft des nach-biblischen Judentums* [Giessen, 1925]). Under his direction the Berliner Institutum Judaicum, founded by Strack, was transformed into a pure research center. One of its new undertakings was the publication project known as "Judaica: Monumenta et Studia," shared by Gressmann with Torczyner and Lietzmann. When, in 1924, Gressmann succeeded Karl Marti as the editor of the famous *Zeitschrift für die alttestamentliche Wissenschaft*, he gave it the added subtitle "und die Kunde des nachbiblischen Judentums." Among the tasks called "urgent" by Gressmann was the publication of a new critical edition of all the intertestamental literature, a need still unfulfilled.

A desire to recover the immediate historic setting and ante-

cedents of Christianity has greatly stimulated intertestamental studies in our time. The historical method demanded the use of the intertestamental and rabbinic literature to reach this goal. A concern for the historic roots of Christianity evoked the translation series of the Society for Promoting Christian Knowledge. This concern was common. The Englishman, Thomas Walker, writing as a Christian, was so touched by the irenic spirit of Montefiore's work on the Christian sources that he reciprocated by dedicating his work to that scholar and publicly recognizing Christianity's debt to Judaism. But in his first volume, *The Teaching of Jesus and the Jewish Teaching of His Age* (New York, 1923), this fraternal spirit is combined with the labor "directed toward making Jesus better known." He seeks to do this by "giving a connected account of the teaching of the extra-canonical Jewish literature of the period 200 B.C. to 100 A.D." There were two additional volumes in 1937, using the same method and having the same end: *Hebrew Religion between the Testaments* and *Is Not This the Son of Joseph?* This is typical of many similar publications.

The historical method made it clear that Jesus and Paul could never be adequately understood against the background of the canonical Old Testament alone. In the Introduction to his *Story of the Apocrypha* (Chicago, 1939), Edgar J. Goodspeed says: "What makes them [The Apocrypha] of positive importance to the New Testament . . . . is the influence they exerted upon the personalities [of the New Testament] . . . . and the light they throw upon its life and thought." C. C. Torrey includes all the intertestamental literature under the term "apocryphal." In his recent volume of introduction to this literature he speaks of the function of intertestamental studies: "Acquaintance with the Jewish uncanonical writings of the pre-Christian period is now generally recognized as belonging to the equipment of every student of the Bible, in either Testament, for they throw light in both directions." The intertestamental literature stands at the parting of the ways of Christianity and Judaism. It is worked by both for the tribute it will yield for the clearer understanding of the separate traditions. While interest in the historic person

of Jesus may have given way to theological concern, the method of genetic historical inquiry stands. In his *The Historic Mission of Jesus* (London, 1941), C. J. Cadoux says: "The task of our generation is a renewed, untiring investigation of the problem of Gospel origins." For this task intertestamental studies are unavoidable.

Men like Strack, Moore, and Montefiore sought to understand the intertestamental era and Christianity primarily by studying the rabbinic literature. Students emphasizing the apocryphal literature assume, for the most part, a powerful dynamic and an inner integrity for the Hebrew religious tradition. The work of both groups raised anew the question of the relative importance of Palestinian Judaism as compared to the Diaspora and Hellenism in the foundation of Christianity. There is a strong tendency to conclude that Christianity is more directly a product of orthodox, Palestinian Judaism than has been assumed hitherto. Indeed, this tendency is almost powerful enough to constitute a revolt against the direction set by Weber, Schürer, Bousset, Gressmann, Reitzenstein, *et al*. These men were completely under the spell of the Orient as a single cultural area. In their efforts to explain the varied aspects of Judaism and Christianity they were wedded to the comparative-religion method and perhaps overlooked the inner meaning and psychology of Israel's religion. Hugo Gressmann's derivation of the Messiah idea from Egypt graphically illustrates this.

In the third edition of Wilhelm Bousset's *Die Religion des Judentums im späthellenistischen Zeitalter* (Tübingen, 1926) Gressmann, the editor, sought to take note of some of the new emphases which intertestamental and rabbinic studies were producing. Paul Fiebig, who was soon to publish his *Rabbinische Gleichnisse* (Leipzig, 1929), cited several examples of Gressmann's failure to relate properly the contents of the New Testament and rabbinic sources (*Orientalistische Literaturzeitung*, Vol. XXX [1927], cols. 375 f.). Yet Gressmann's effort was indicative of the trend. Gerhard Kittel wrote *Die Probleme des palästinischen Spätjudentums und das Urchristentum* (Stuttgart, 1926) primarily to counteract Bousset's thesis that apocryphal and Hellenistic influences

were paramount in early Christianity. He insisted that the consideration of the Talmudic materials was essential and contended that late Palestinian Judaism was the chief factor in the development and consolidation of Christianity. There is, of course, no final agreement as to which intertestamental documents are Palestinian. In a two-volume work, *Le Judaïsme palestinien* (Paris, 1934), deeply indebted to Kittel, the French Catholic scholar, Joseph Bonsirven, contends that, with the exception of Philo, Diaspora Judaism had no influence upon either Christianity or Judaism. Like Moore, he considers rabbinic literature normative, and with Herford, Klausner, and Elbogen he uses the apocryphal literature as tributaries to it. G. H. Box, in *Early Christianity and Its Rivals* (New York, 1929), also favors the standard Judaism of Palestine as the real source of Christianity. Students of the apocryphal literature seeking for the origins of Christianity have moved almost without exception from it to a study of the Talmud rather than to Hellenistic materials.

R. Travers Herford is that *rara avis*, a Christian scholar with a profound knowledge of rabbinics. In *Judaism in the New Testament Period* (London, 1928) he insists that Pharisaic Judaism was normative and that 90 per cent of Jesus' teachings were Pharisaic. It was only in Palestine that Judaism influenced Christianity. In Galilee, Jesus encountered the Pharisees; in Jerusalem, the Sadducees. These were the cause of his death. In *Talmud and Apocrypha* (London, 1933) he denies the pharisaic origin of any of the apocryphal books. His rejection of apocalyptic as in any sense integral to normative Judaism is vehement. In his first book, *The Pharisees* (London, 1924), Herford showed how deeply he was influenced by Joseph Klausner, whose work on Jesus he had read before its translation from the Hebrew. But Klausner went further by identifying Jesus as a Pharisee. His book reveals a bias against the Herodian and Roman governments that has become quite general for modern Jewish scholarship dealing with the origins of Christianity. Christianity is essentially a Jewish development. "Whatever of primitive Christianity is not derivable from Phariseeism, may be sought for in Essenism" (p. 262, Eng. trans.). Klausner sharply contradicts the position taken in an

earlier day by Moritz Friedländer, who sought to account for the rise of Christianity in terms of the influence of Hellenism upon Diaspora Judaism. The gap parallels that between Bousset and Kittel and illustrates the same trend. Adolf Schlatter's *Geschichte Israels von Alexander dem Grossen bis Hadrian* went through a third edition in 1925. It used the rabbinic materials and assumed the integrity of Judaism. A sharp contrast, sometimes drawn between Diaspora and Palestinian Judaism, was avoided. It has played its role in the contemporary recovery of the Jewish roots of Christianity.

The employment of talmudic and noncanonical Jewish literature as sources has resulted in the tendency to fix the beginnings of Christianity in orthodox, Palestinian Judaism. This "Pharisaic Judaism" is frequently described as a self-contained movement. But there are notable exceptions. Since the rise of rabbinic and apocryphal studies, attempts to discover a transformation of the central Jewish tradition itself by foreign movements of thought have increased. Gustav Hölscher, in his *Geschichte der israelitischen und jüdischen Religion* (Giessen, 1922), draws a sympathetic picture of orthodox Judaism. For the "Roman Period" he uses the Mishnah as well as the patristic and apocryphal literature. At the same time, he makes much of the westward movement of Babylonian-Iranian ideas and relates Israel's religious history to the ethnic psychology and religious development of the Near East as a whole. Similarly, Eduard Meyer, in the second volume of *Ursprung und Anfänge des Christentums* (Stuttgart, 1922), insists upon the gradual transformation of Judaism by foreign rule, paying particular attention to the development of dualism and such related Iranian phenomena as Satan, demons, and resurrection. He considers the Sadducees "orthodox" in contrast to the Pharisees, who yielded to the foreign currents. Indorsing this view, W. F. Albright says: "The Pharisaic movement represents the Hellenization of the normative Jewish tradition" (*From the Stone Age to Christianity*, p. 273). He credits E. Bickerman (*Die Makkabäer* [Berlin, 1935]) with having been the first to see this but finds further illustration of it in the interpretative methods of the Pharisees. These are illustrated by S. Rosenblatt in *The Inter-*

pretation of the Bible in the Mishnah (1935). One wonders whether the entire view does not owe something to Rudolph Leszynski's *Die Sadduzäer* (1912), to which we shall refer again. In a monograph entitled *Hellenistisches in der rabbinischen Anthropologie* (Stuttgart, 1937) Rudolph Meyer presents a great deal of general evidence for the Hellenization of Palestine and also attempts to show that the rabbis taught a Greek, dualistic anthropology. Archeological discoveries, notably those at Dura-Europos, contribute to the complex picture. This group of intertestamental and rabbinic scholars feels that the separate Jewish and Christian traditions root in a Judaism already transformed by Hellenism. But in the nature of the case the transformation is of a very different order from the syncretistic view entertained about the origin of Christianity by such Hellenists as the school of Reitzenstein. The key word is "assimilation."

The use of the historical method in the study of Judaism and the religion of the New Testament has made the intertestamental period and its literature an area of intensive study. Another important aspect of this in our generation has been the interest in the place of apocalypticism in the history of religion, especially its role in the genesis of Christianity. The writings and thought of Albert Schweitzer, continuing the earlier work of Johannes Weiss, did much to stimulate this interest. Translations of some of his books into English, notably *The Quest of the Historical Jesus* and *The Mystery of the Kingdom of God*, turned men from writing biographies of Jesus to a consideration of the eschatological outlook which he inculcated and the general context of thought about final fulfilment in which it appeared.

F. C. Burkitt (*Jewish and Christian Apocalypses* [London, 1914]) and R. H. Charles himself were in the van of this new interest, which struck root early in Britain. In his *Religious Development between the Old and New Testaments* (New York, 1914), still useful, Charles traced historically the development of eschatology in the intertestamental era. He contributed the "International Critical Commentary" volume on *The Revelation of John*, to which he applied the techniques developed in his work on Enoch and Baruch in the pseudepigrapha. In 1922 he published the Schweich Lec-

tures, further elucidating his work on the New Testament Apocalypse. Speaking of the reception given his commentary, he said: "Practically all my reviewers have been brought to admit the necessity of an exhaustive knowledge of Jewish apocalyptic, if we are to understand the Christian Apocalypse. This is something to be thankful for; since, as a rule hitherto, even serious scholars, though possessed of the sorriest equipment in this department of knowledge, readily undertook to expound this great work." Referring more specifically to his methods, he adds: "The contemporary-historical method is indispensable in the exegesis of all Jewish apocalypses. And what is true of such Jewish apocalypses is true also of the New Testament Apocalypse. It refers originally and essentially to the close of the first century of the Christian era." This elementary instruction in method, so recently required is revealing indeed.

The study of the eschatology of the New Testament in the light of its historical antecedents as given in the intertestamental apocalyptic produced great results. New Testament words and themes, such as "Son of Man," "Messiah," and the "Kingdom of God," took on fresh meaning. The new term "realized eschatology" and the intensive studies of the relation between eschatology and ethics in the New Testament were all largely based on a fresh understanding of Jewish expectations of fulfilment and their none-too-successful attempts to state the paradox of Law and grace. Bultmann, Manson, Dodd, and Wilder are only a few of the names of men who came to the New Testament by this new path.

Publications covering the eschatological outlook and problems of the intertestamental period as such have not been wanting. Paul Volz's *Eschatologie der jüdischen Gemeinde im neutestamentlichen Zeitalter* (Tübingen, 1934) pays especial attention to the bearing of the "Zadokite Fragment" (*Damaskusschrift*) and other newly edited materials upon the general eschatological outlook of the period. He also discusses Samaritan eschatology. The Jewish theologian, K. Kohler, and others discussed the sect of the Essenes in the light of apocalyptic literature (*Jewish Quarterly Review*, XI [1925], 145–68). In Βασιλεία τοῦ θεοῦ (Heidelberg, 1926)

A. von Gall, contradicting Gunkel and Gressmann, denied the existence of Hebrew eschatology before the Persian period. For him all expectations of an ultimate fulfilment for Israel recorded in the books of the prophets are later additions, fundamentally opposed to the spirit of the men whose names they now bear. Lengthy articles under the title "apocalyptic" began to appear in Bible dictionaries (e.g., Pirot, *Supplément au dictionnaire de la Bible*, Vol. I [Paris, 1928], cols. 326–54; and, *Encyclopaedia Judaica*, Vol. II [1928], cols. 1142–54). The monographs on special topics would make a long list. Evaluations of the religious spirit represented by apocalyptic have varied tremendously. Many, like Herford, have considered it a sorry excrescence; others discover in it great enduring values. H. H. Rowley, *The Relevance of Apocalyptic* (London, 1943), is a recent contributor to the latter group.

The employment of the religiohistorical method caused Jews and Christians interested in their roots to meet in the intertestamental area; and in their efforts to understand their respective traditions they have remained in this area, attempting to reconstruct the religious, sociological, and political scene in and about Palestine in the two centuries immediately preceding the opening of the Christian era. The center of the quest was normally in Palestine, though its relation to the world outside was never lost sight of. And the study of the noncanonical Jewish literature was often forced upon scholars, whose real concern was an explication of the rabbinic or New Testament traditions. The great progress made in the writing of the social, political, and cultural history of the Near East for the period including the intertestamental era has facilitated the interpretation of the late Jewish writings and demands brief attention.

The twelve-volume series of *The Cambridge Ancient History* (Cambridge, 1923–39) and such works as Michael Rostovtzeff's *Social and Economic History of the Roman Empire* (Oxford, 1926) and *The Social and Economic History of the Hellenistic World* (Oxford, 1941) offer a broad and reliable perspective for the student of the history and culture of the late Jewish era. Similar significance attaches to such cultural histories as William Tarn's *Hellenistic*

Civilization (London, 1927) and Georges Conteneau's *La Civilization phénicienne* (Paris, 1926). The great labor of the late Albert T. Olmstead in this wide field is as yet unpublished.

Against this broad background, general studies on Jewish religious and social-political history of the intertestamental period have appeared. C. Guignebert's study was translated by S. H. Hooke under the title *The Jewish World in the Time of Jesus* (London, 1939). Père Lagrange produced the companion volumes, *Le Judaïsme avant Jésus-Christ* (Paris, 1931) and *Introduction à l'étude du Nouveau Testament* (Paris, 1933). Alfred Loisy's *La Religion d'Israel* and *La Naissance du Christianisme*, both of which appeared in 1933, show a similar attempt to write a connected, genetic account of the story of the Judeo-Christian tradition.

In our period, Old Testament histories acquired the habit of telling the Jewish story through the first century of our era. The popular series known as the "Clarendon Bible" does not go so far as that, but it does contain a volume by G. H. Box on *Judaism in the Greek Period* (Oxford, 1932). Otto Eissfeldt's notable introduction to the Old Testament (Tübingen, 1933) included a treatment of the Apocrypha and Pseudepigrapha as well.

The clarification of the historical situation of the Jews in Egypt has claimed much attention in the recent period. Wilhelm Schubart's *Aegypten von Alexander dem Grossen bis auf Mohammed* (Berlin, 1922) denied that all Jews in Egypt enjoyed Roman citizenship, despite the assertions of Josephus. Harold I. Bell's study, *Jews and Christians in Egypt* (London, 1924), based on the papyrus letter of Claudius to the city of Alexandria, makes this even more definite. Recently a Jewish scholar, V. Tcherikover, has published a book in Hebrew entitled *The Jews in Egypt in the Hellenistic-Roman Age in the Light of the Papyri* (Jerusalem, 1945). Edwyn R. Bevan's work, especially his *History of Egypt under the Ptolemaic Dynasty* (London, 1927), has also done much to provide an intelligible background for the study of intertestamental literature.

General studies on the apocryphal literature during our period have included introductions, translations, and interpretations. Oesterley's *Introduction to the Books of the Apocrypha* (London, 1935) incorporated the results of literaty criticism since his first

book in this field, published in 1914. *The Doctrine of God in the Jewish Apocryphal and Apocalyptic Literature* (London, 1915), by H. J. Wicks, was an interpretative study in which the author declared that it was impossible to assign specific documents to definite religious parties in Judaism. Dr. Goodspeed translated the Apocrypha for the American Bible published by the University of Chicago. While the translation for the American Standard Version was made largely from the Latin, Goodspeed's translation, with the exception of II Esdras, was made from the Greek. C. C. Torrey's *The Apocryphal Literature* (New Haven, 1945) is an introduction covering all the postcanonical Jewish literature. It is the first book of this kind. Professor Torrey speaks of the urgent need for a companion volume giving an English translation, based on critical texts, of all the documents that he treats. But the critical texts are not available. Intertestamental studies have probably progressed least in the area of textual criticism.

Professor Torrey rejects the term "pseudepigrapha" as a title for the postcanonical literature not in the Greek Bible. This is sound, for the term, given currency by Charles, is incorrect and confusing. But Torrey offers no alternative term for separating the "outside" books historically included in our English Bible from those that were not in it. He contends that there never was an Alexandrian Jewish canon that contained our biblical Apocrypha, for canonicity, in Alexandria also, demanded Hebrew or Aramaic originals that antedated the end of the Persian era! Nor, he adds, did the Christians accept the Apocrypha as canonical. They only used them as books "useful for instruction" (II Tim. 3:16). Even if all this were granted, it would still be true that the biblical Apocrypha have had an utterly different history in the Christian tradition than the others, one that it should be possible to indicate by title.

It is no surprise to learn that Torrey assumes Semitic originals for about four-fifths of the apocryphal literature. Only II–IV Maccabees, the Sibyllines, the latter part of Wisdom, and the "letters" in Esther were first written in Greek. This is an extreme position, sharply contradicting that of Goodspeed and others.

But it helps to underline the existence of many unanswered questions in the area of literary criticism. Brief reference can be made to only a few of the conspicuous problems.

Jubilees is a case in point. Charles thought the writer was a Pharisee and therefore dated it before 96 B.C., the time at which Jannaeus broke with the Pharisees. Eduard Meyer dated it a century earlier. Zeitlin said it came from the early post-Exilic period. Box, probably influenced by Leszynski, felt that the author was perhaps a Sadducee. The book, he notes, has little interest in a Messiah and does not teach the resurrection. Tellinek assigned the book to an Essene; Beer, to a Samaritan; Frankel, to a Hellenist; Singer, to a Jewish Christian! But at least it was agreed that it was written in Hebrew. Now Torrey asserts its original was Aramaic. Like Charles, he feels its aim was "to illustrate the normative character of priestly legislation." But it was not just a midrash; it was a targum. Moreover, because it employs the terms *Mastema* and *Beliar*, Torrey feels that it cannot be dated earlier than the last half of the last century before our era. Philological and historical norms do not agree in their findings! Box also questioned the generally accepted view that the Testaments of the Twelve Patriarchs depends upon Jubilees.

The textual history of IV Ezra and its Shealtiel Apocalypse have been problem centers. Bruno Violet continued his textual criticism with *Die Esra Apokalypse, zweiter Teil* (Leipzig, 1923). His thesis is that the Latin version now extant is the daughter of a Greek version resting on a Hebrew original. Box and Kaminka likewise contend for a Hebrew *ur*-text. But L. Gry (*Les Dires prophétiques d'Esdras* [Paris, 1938]) and Professor Torrey posit an Aramaic original. In his commentary for the Westminster series (1933) Oesterley concluded that the Shealtiel Apocalypse is an integral part of the book. What Box and others had considered redactors' interpolations Oesterley described as the incorporation of the general apocalyptic tradition by the author himself.

The identification of the figure "Taxo" has been the *crux interpretum* in the fragment known as the "Assumption of Moses." Charles equated Taxo with the Eleazar of II Macc. 6:18. Hölscher relates him to an Eleazar of the Bar Chochba era (*Zeitschrift für*

die neutestamentliche Wissenschaft, XVII [1926], 108 ff., 149 ff.).
Traditional interpretation, now followed by Lattey (*Catholic Biblical Quarterly*, January, 1942, pp. 17 f.), often equated Taxo with the Shiloh of Gen. 49:10. Rowley is struck by the resemblance between the figure and a man described by Josephus in *Antiquities* xiv. 15. 5. Torrey, assuming an Aramaic original, shows that on the basis of numerical evaluation the figure is a cryptogram for "The Hasmonaean." For him it refers to Mattathias and his sons.

The authenticity of the last three chapters of I Maccabees, very commonly doubted, was given a thorough defense by H. W. Etelaan in *The Integrity of I Maccabees* (New Haven, 1925). The purpose of the book and the circle of its origin have caused much discussion. Oesterley, Torrey, and Goodspeed call the author a Sadducee. Oesterley, speaking in the vein of Leszynski, describes him as a "rigid adherent of orthodox Judaism." In his *Der Gott der Makkabäer* (Berlin, 1937) Elias Bickermann insists that the "Seleucid" persecution was actually produced by a Jewish party that shunned extreme Jewish particularism. He considers I Maccabees a Hasmonaean work that gives this true Jewish orientation of events, while II Maccabees shifts the cause of the outbreak to the Seleucids. Uncertainty about the antecedents of the Sadducees badly complicates this problem also.

Since the publication of the critical edition of *The Odes and Psalms of Solomon* (Manchester, 1916, 1920) by Rendel Harris and A. Mingana, it has been assumed that the Syriac version of this work rested on the Greek translation from the Hebrew. Karl Kuhn's effort in *Die älteste Textgestalt der Psalmen Salomos* (Stuttgart, 1937) to show that the Syriac text came directly from the Hebrew cannot be said to have altered the general opinion. During our period there has been a growing tendency to doubt the Pharisaic authorship of all the Psalms. An interesting attempt to apply the *Gattungskritik* to this late Jewish poetry was made by Ludin Jensen in *Die spätjüdische Psalmendichtung* . . . . (Oslo, 1937).

More than any other part of the apocryphal literature, the Wisdom writings have been studied for their own sake in the interval between the wars, and not primarily for the sake of tracing

the history of ideas. Wisdom literature enjoyed the vogue of being "modern." It appealed to the prevalent mood in liberal religious circles. With or without justification, students under the spell of philosophy of religion have felt that in the Wisdom materials, more than anywhere else in the biblical tradition, they had the record of an outlook and a method that really corresponded to their own approach. D. B. McDonald's *The Hebrew Philosophical Genius* (Princeton, 1936) has probably been the most widely welcomed expression of this mood. One fears that it may have been received somewhat too uncritically. There have, however, also been a large number of more strictly theological interpretations of the Wisdom writings. These are notably represented in the work of such men as Rankin, Duesberg, and Fichtner. Essays in the relation of reason and faith and in the meaning of the concept of revelation have used the Wisdom materials for sources.

It is impossible to speak in detail of work on individual Wisdom documents. The recovery of Hebrew sections of Ben Sira proved less significant than early enthusiasts had hoped. For quite a while there has been virtual agreement that the Hebrew text represents a retranslation of some version, probably Greek. Johannes Fichtner's commentary on the Wisdom of Solomon (Tübingen, 1938) and the study of the eschatological teaching of the same work by Rudolphe Schütz (Paris, 1935) are significant contributions. The question of whether Wisdom is a single document or the work of two authors is perennially discussed. Torrey comes out for a double authorship—one in Hebrew, the other in Greek.

The attempt to write a social history of the Jews for the intertestamental period on the basis of a reconstructed picture of all the religious and political parties and groups that existed and of the role played by each has consumed much time but is far from finished. This is illustrated by the inconclusive results of research on the historic place of the Sadducees and the consequent problems arising in the field of literary criticism.

Leszynski classified the Sadducees as a religious school rather than a social caste or a political party. This view deeply influ-

enced literary criticism; but it has not won the day among historians. While the Sadducees did oppose the introduction of new religious doctrines, the conclusion seems to be that they were not primarily interested in religion. "The religious attitude of the Sadducees, such as it was, favoured conservatism," says Oesterley (*History of Israel*, II, 322). But if the Sadducees were held together by other than religious motives and lacked religious creativity, it becomes dangerous to ascribe apocryphal documents to them simply because they do not affirm belief in resurrection, angels, *et al.*, which seems to be just what Oesterley has occasionally done.

The uncertainty about the Sadducees has contributed to the doubt that still exists about the sect of the "new covenant" that produced the *Damaskusschrift*. Solomon Schechter, its discoverer and first editor, thought it had Sadducean antecedents. Charles, agreeing, called it the "Zadokite Fragment." Gressmann, Ginzberg, Jeremias, and others have argued its Pharisaic origin. Bousset and Büchler dated it in the seventh century and called it a *Tendenzschrift* of the Karaites. Oesterley says flatly: "The sect of the sons of Zadok has nothing to do with the Sadducees" (*History*, II, 322). The attempt to classify documents by parties has not been successful. Judaism was a living organism and must have expressed itself in almost innumerable moods and facets with constantly interweaving patterns of thought. Two or three parties, static and exclusive in our conception of them, cannot reproduce that picture.

It is difficult to relate an account of the study on Philo and Josephus to a survey of intertestamental studies in general. Yet every fresh insight into the life and thought of these two highly individualistic first-century Jews sheds light upon the entire intertestamental era. The critical edition of their writings, with a translation of them, in the "Loeb Classical Library" has greatly furthered their availability. Meanwhile, the recovery of Philonic fragments has continued. Clarification of the status of the Jews in Egypt and in the Empire as a whole has aided in the understanding of both men.

Émile Bréhier and Erwin Goodenough are leaders in a large group who have sought to ascertain the place of Philo in the history of thought. In his very influential *Les Idées philosophiques et religieuses de Philon d'Alexandrie* (Paris, 1925) the former states that the meeting of the Hebrew and Greek spirit in Philo does not produce a fusion. He uses Greek concepts as a philosopher, but his religious experience is Jewish. Thus, he says, Philo knew no philosophical conflict and did not explicitly relate himself to either a Greek or a Jewish view of life. This may explain why it is so difficult to fit him genetically into any larger context. Bréhier thinks the writings of Philo reveal a deep transformation of Greek thought, wrought outside of Judaism. He considers it impossible to recover traces of an Alexandrian school of which Philo's work is representative. The essence of his teaching is a doctrine of salvation worked out by an allegorical transfiguration of Hebrew history.

The Philo that emerges from Goodenough's *By Light, Light* (New Haven, 1935) is rather more Greek than is true in the case of Bréhier. He credits Philo with having worked out a mystery, analogous to the Greek-oriental mysteries, which provided a way of salvation out of matter into the eternal. In his *Introduction to Philo Judaeus* (New Haven, 1940) he denies that he thinks Philo's mystery had a cultic ritual, as some of his critics had concluded. He continues, however, to speak of "Philo's group," a group of which Bréhier found no trace.

Most attempts to understand Philo have used a Hellenistic approach. In *Jewish Studies in Memory of George A. Kohut* (New York, 1925) Ralph Marcus evaluated "The Recent Literature on Philo." Professor Marcus cites two desiderata: a treatment of Philo's relation to rabbinic law by one fully at home in the Talmud as well as in Greek law and philosophy, and a weighing of the influence of Greek-oriental cults upon Philo by one equally familiar with Judaism and Hellenistic religion. Unfortunately, the breadth of specialization implied in these specifications is rare. Professor Marcus is convinced that the weakness of most

interpreters of Philo has been their inability to appreciate his Jewish spirit.

The authenticity of the reference to Jesus in the work of Josephus has been a focus of interest in the period between the wars. This has in large part been due to the discovery of much more extensive references to both John the Baptist and Jesus in a Slavonic version of Josephus than are contained in the Greek. Robert Eisler, in *The Messiah Jesus and John the Baptist* (London, 1931), defended the authenticity of these more extensive passages as well as the historically disputed passage in *Antiquities* xviii. 3.3. He won support from H. St. John Thackeray, possibly the foremost authority in all departments of study on Josephus. But Eisler's position was vehemently disputed by Solomon Zeitlin in *Josephus on Jesus* (Philadelphia, 1931) and other writings. Zeitlin's industry in presenting his rebuttal was illustrated by his trip to Russia. Eisler contended that the Slavonic version rested on an Aramaic edition that had been prepared by Josephus himself, probably for political reasons. Zeitlin rejected this view and propounded the thesis that the Slavonic version was a seventh-century Byzantine paraphrase of Josephus in Greek. He fails to find any Hebraisms in the Slavonic version and shows that the Byzantine writer knew and used the fourth-century Latin text of Hegesippus, also resting on the Greek. Zeitlin traces the Jesus passages in the Slavonic Josephus to "The Acts of Pilate." Those in the original Greek Josephus he held to be interpolations. It is just in this last, crucial step that Zeitlin's arguments do not seem to have settled the problem.

Another prominent emphasis in Josephus studies, very characteristic of the predominent historical method in intertestamental studies generally, has sought to understand the great Jew as a historical figure, the religious and political loyalties that he maintained and the expression of Judaism that he embodied. H. St. John Thackeray's *Josephus, the Man and the Historian* (New York, 1929), excellently represents this interest. A. Schlatter's *Die Theologie des Judentums nach dem Bericht des Josephus* (Gütersloh, 1932) brings to a strong conclusion a study that began twenty

years earlier with his *Wie sprach Josephus von Gott?* Frederick Foakes Jackson comes to many of the same conclusions in *Josephus and the Jews* (New York, 1930). Josephus—the priest's son, Essene, Pharisee, Greek writer, and friend of the Romans— belongs to no single group. He used an exegetical tradition no longer recorded in the same form elsewhere. He is an index to the type of syncretism which, despite the continuing integrity and creativity of the basic Jewish ideas, was never lacking in the intertestamental period.

New Testament Criticism in the World-Wars Period

MERRILL M. PARVIS
University of Chicago

O NE who attempts to make a survey of the New Testament studies that were produced in the two decades that fell between the close of World War I and the opening of World War II must, of necessity, feel that in the ancient Preacher of Israel one can find a kindred soul. When Koheleth observed that of the making of many books there is no end and that much study is a weariness of the flesh, he must have had in mind the consolation of the New Testament student who would undertake such a task.

The volumes of the *International Index to Periodicals* which appeared during the years 1920–40 contain more than sixteen hundred entries under the three general headings "Bible—New Testament," "Jesus Christ," and "Paul, Saint." In the same categories the *Cumulative Book Index*, which catalogues only those books appearing in English, has listed nearly nine hundred entries for the four-year period 1928–32, a period which falls exactly midway between the great wars. It is true that the method of classification used in both these reference works makes it necessary to list many items in more than one category. No attempt was made to tabulate the number of articles and books listed for other New Testament and related subjects or to count those not listed in these two sources. No significance, therefore, can be attached to these figures; but they are at least indicative of the prolific literary activity of this generation of New Testament scholars.

To review, or even to catalogue, every one of the hundreds of

New Testament studies which first saw the light of day during the twenties and thirties of this century is neither possible nor desirable. The great bulk of them perhaps deserve only to be tasted; others may deserve to be swallowed; only a very few deserve to be chewed and digested.

It has been the practice of many generations of New Testament scholars to indicate the fields of their endeavor by such designations as "Linguistic Studies," "Textual Studies," "Synoptic Studies," etc.; these designations will serve us well as a guide for our survey. The limitations of space make it imperative that whole blocks of material be passed over without even so much as a passing reference. We have tried to single out those areas for consideration in which significant trends of thought and method have come to light. There will be those who will insist that some works which we have cited are not worthy of mention in this brief survey; there will be others who will insist that we have omitted significant works that should have been mentioned. Of this shortcoming, we are too well aware.

LINGUISTIC STUDIES

Shortly after World War I, Professor Harold R. Willoughby, in an article which appeared in the *Journal of Religion*,[1] was able to say that, in the linguistic study of the New Testament, critical scholarship had already made its case. The work of Flinders Petrie, Grenfell, Hunt, Deissmann, and others had, once and for all, exploded the theory that biblical Greek was a peculiar language. "Because of the abundance of the new materials," wrote Professor Willoughby, "there remains a seemingly endless amount of work to be done in the field of language study. New Cremers and Thayers and Winers are needed; but the way is cleared for this work."[2]

A survey of articles on the New Testament which appeared during the years 1933–37 in the *Anglican Theological Review*, the *Harvard Theological Review*, the *Journal of Religion*, the *Journal of Biblical Literature*, the *Journal of Theological Studies*, *Religion in*

---

1. "The Next Step in New Testament Study," *Journal of Religion*, II (1922), 159–78.
2. *Ibid.*, p. 160.

Life, and the *Zeitschrift für die neutestamentliche Wissenschaft*, however, revealed only two articles which dealt with grammatical problems.[3] As recently as July, 1945, F. Wilbur Gingrich complained because "the field of lexicography is currently suffering from a neglect which is as dangerous as it is difficult to understand." He wrote:

The poverty of New Testament lexicography is well illustrated by the fact that the English-speaking world has no definitive unabridged lexicon of the Greek New Testament which takes into account the rapid strides which the science has made since 1890. We have introductions and commentaries by the dozen but the great lexicon still goes begging.[4]

Just before this article on lexicography appeared, a group of student and faculty members of the New Testament Club of the University of Chicago set out to find the best available grammar of New Testament Greek. The result of their search may be expressed best in a paraphrase of the words of Dr. Gingrich. Their conclusion was that "the great New Testament grammar still goes begging."

All this does not mean that no advance has been made in linguistic studies since World War I. Much has been done, but much remains to be done. Among the outstanding works which have been published since 1918 are the following:

1. G. ABBOTT-SMITH. *Manual Lexicon of the Greek New Testament*. Edinburgh and London, 1921. 3d ed., 1937.
2. F. M. ABEL. *Grammaire du grec biblique*. Paris, 1927.
3. WALTER BAUER. *Griechisch-deutsches Wörterbuch zu den Schriften des Neuen Testaments und der übrigen urchristlichen Literatur*. 3d ed. Berlin, 1937.
4. A. Debrunner. *Friedrich Blass' Grammatik des neutestamentlichen Griechisch*. 7th ed. Göttingen, 1943.
5. GERHARD KITTEL. *Theologisches Wörterbuch zum Neuen Testament*. Stuttgart, 1932——.
6. H. G. LIDDELL and R. SCOTT. *A Greek-English Lexicon: New Edition, Revised and Augmented by H. S. Jones and R. McKenzie*. Oxford, 1925–40.
7. J. H. MOULTON. *A Grammar of New Testament Greek*, Vol. II: *Acci-*

3. Clarence T. Craig, "Current Trends in New Testament Study," *Journal of Biblical Literature*, LVII (1938), 360.

4. "New Testament Lexicography and the Future," *Journal of Religion*, XXV (1945), 179.

dence and Word Formation. Edited by W. F. Howard. Edinburgh, 1929.

8. J. H. Moulton and G. Milligan. *Vocabulary of the Greek Testament Illustrated from the Papyri and Other non-Literary Sources.* London, 1914–29.

9. F. Preisigke. *Wörterbuch der griechischen Papyrusurkunden.* Berlin, 1925–27.

10. L. Radermacher. *Neutestamentliche Grammatik: Das Griechisch des Neuen Testaments in Zusammenhang mit der Volkssprache.* 2d ed. Tübingen, 1925.

11. A. T. Robertson. *A Grammar of the Greek New Testament in the Light of Historical Research.* 3d ed. New York, 1919.

TEXTUAL STUDIES

The four decades which preceded the close of World War I were witness to many long and bitter battles which concerned themselves with the text of the New Testament. By 1918, however, the theories of Westcott and Hort, at least in broad outline, had won the day. The Alpha text-type (Westcott and Hort's "Syrian"), best known to us through the Textus Receptus, had been abandoned; the Beta text-type (Westcott and Hort's "Neutral") had been generally accepted; and the term "Delta text-type" (Westcott and Hort's "Western") had come to be recognized, not as the designation of a homogeneous text-type but as a general designation for all early non-Beta text-types. H. von Soden's epic work, *Die Schriften des Neuen Testaments,*[5] had been completed. Recently discovered manuscripts, such as the Koridethi and Washington codices, had been made available to students, and the world of textual scholars awaited anxiously the announcement of further discoveries.

These looked-for announcements were not long in coming. By 1933, P. L. Hedley was able to list 157 fragments of New Testament text on parchment, papyrus, and potsherds.[6] Few periods, according to Kirsopp and Silva Lake, have been so rich in the discovery of New Testament documents as the years 1932–36.[7]

5. Berlin and Göttingen, 1902–13.

6. Frederick G. Kenyon, *Recent Developments in the Textual Criticism of the Greek Bible* (London, 1933), p. 32, n. 1; cf. also P. L. Hedley, "The Egyptian Texts of the Gospels and Acts," *Church Quarterly Review,* CXVIII (1934), 23–39, 188–230.

7. "Some Recent Discoveries," *Religion in Life,* V (1936), 89.

It was during these years that the Chester Beatty papyri were found. These documents are so well known that we need do little more here than call attention to the fact that their discovery has been hailed as the greatest discovery of biblical manuscripts since that of the Codex Sinaiticus.[8] The biblical portions of the Chester Beatty papyri have been published in their entirety by Sir Frederick Kenyon.[9] Of particular interest to New Testament students are those documents in this collection which are known as P^{45}, P^{46}, and P^{47}, all dating from the third century. Document P^{45} contains portions of two leaves of Matthew, six of Mark, seven of Luke, two of John, and thirteen of Acts; P^{46} contains eighty-six nearly perfect leaves of Romans, Hebrews, I and II Corinthians, Ephesians, Galatians, Philippians, Colossians, and I and II Thessalonians; and P^{47} contains ten nearly complete leaves of Revelation.

Among the other exciting manuscript finds of this period are three second-century papyri: a fragment of an unknown Gospel, published by Bell and Skeat;[10] a fragment of the Gospel of John, published by Roberts;[11] and a fragment of Tatian's *Diatessaron* in Greek, published by Professor Kraeling.[12] At the present time, there is in the manuscript collection of the University of Chicago a codex of the Gospel of Mark, Codex 2427 (probably from the fourteenth century), which further study may show to contain the oldest form of the text of the earliest Gospel now extant.[13]

It is probably safe to say that during the ten years leading up to World War II more articles were published on textual prob-

8. Frederick G. Kenyon, *The Text of the Greek Bible* (London, 1937), p. 193.

9. *The Chester Beatty Biblical Papyri: Descriptions and Texts of Twelve Manuscripts on Papyrus of the Greek Bible* (London, 1933–41).

10. H. Idris Bell and T. C. Skeat, *Fragments of an Unknown Gospel and Other Early Christian Papyri* (London, 1935).

11. C. H. Roberts, *An Unpublished Fragment of the Fourth Gospel in the John Rylands Library* (Manchester, 1935).

12. Carl H. Kraeling, *A Greek Fragment of Tatian's Diatessaron from Dura* ("Studies and Documents," Vol. III [London, 1935]).

13. Ernest Cadman Colwell, "An Ancient Text of the Gospel of Mark," *Emory University Quarterly*, I (1945), 65; Harold R. Willoughby, "Archaic Crucifixion Iconography," *Munera Studiosa* (Cambridge, Mass., 1946).

lems than upon any other New Testament subject. An important factor in this interest in matters of text was the discovery of new manuscripts.

The recent years also have witnessed a restudy of many of the old manuscripts and, in particular, of the later minuscules, which are known to have preserved old readings. It is now recognized that a so-called "purified" form of the Textus Receptus was the text-type of Antioch, probably as early as the fourth century. Westcott and Hort's neat picture of the "Neutral text" has been overturned. Their Neutral text is now seen to be simply a text-type which was in use in Egypt about the third century. It is now admitted, at least by some scholars, that the work of Westcott and Hort must be done over again.

One of the best-known pieces of work in the textual area that has been done since World War I is that of Canon Streeter on the Caesarean Text and his identification of Family Theta.[14] The extent to which Streeter carried the recognition of codices as Caesarean, however, was unjustified—even though he did classify his witnesses as primary, secondary, and tertiary.

President Ernest Cadman Colwell of the University of Chicago has pointed out that the interrelationships of manuscripts and text-types are so complex that every source contains some element of every other source. In many cases this leads to the identification of some late minuscule as a witness to the Beta, the Delta, or the so-called "Caesarean" text-type when it is actually a witness to some form of the Alpha text-type.

Recent suggestions by the Lakes and others have been made to the effect that it was premature to speak of Family Theta or even of a Caesarean text-type. Our own studies tend to indicate that there are several text-types represented among the witnesses which were classified by Streeter as Caesarean.

In addition to the work done on the Caesarean text-type, there has been a great deal of interest in the reconstruction of other family texts. In this way, much of Von Soden's work in the isola-

14. Burnett Hillman Streeter, *The Four Gospels* (London, 1924), pp. 77–108, 572–89, 598–600.

tion of family groups has been verified; especially has this been true of his K¹, Kᵃ and Kʳ groups.

No great advance has been made in the method of textual study since the days of Westcott and Hort. All the recent critics have, in the final analysis, depended upon the genealogical method—a method which falls short on at least two counts: it cannot get beyond a two-branched family tree, and it does not allow for mixture.

From the great mass of textual studies which have been produced since World War I, we can do no more than mention such valued works as the following:

1. JAMES HARDY ROPES. *The Text of Acts* (London, 1926), which was published as Volume III of Part I of *The Beginnings of Christianity*, ed. F. J. Foakes Jackson and Kirsopp Lake.

2. KIRSOPP LAKE, ROBERT P. BLAKE, and SILVA NEW. "The Caesarean Text of the Gospel of Mark," *Harvard Theological Review*, XXI (1928), 207–404.

3. ALBERT C. CLARK. *The Acts of the Apostles: A Critical Edition with Introduction and Notes on Selected Passages.* Oxford, 1933.

4. JOSEF SCHMID. *Untersuchungen zur Geschichte des griechischen Apokalypsetextes.* Athens, 1936.

5. SILVA LAKE. *Family II and the Codex Alexandrinus* ("Studies and Documents," Vol. V.) London, 1937.

6. WALTER MATZKOW (ed.). *Itala: Das Neue Testament in altlateinischer Überlieferung.* Berlin, 1938, 1940.

7. KIRSOPP AND SILVA LAKE. *Family 13* ("Studies and Documents," Vol. XI.) London, 1941.

No survey of textual studies can be made without a mention of the so-called "new Tischendorf." Using the Westcott and Hort text, Legg published an apparatus to the Gospels of Mark and Matthew.[15] This apparatus, which was received with so much hope, has proved to be a disappointment to the textual critic.

Textual criticism has come to be not only a search for the text of the original autographs but also a historical discipline. It is research in the church history of the periods which produced the manuscripts with which it deals.[16]

---

15. S. C. E. Legg, *Nouum Testamentum Graece* (Oxford, 1935, 1940).

16. Donald W. Riddle, "Textual Criticism as a Historical Discipline," *Anglican Theological Review*, XVIII (1936), 220–34.

SYNOPTIC STUDIES

In the general area of synoptic studies, two developments loom so large in the period between the two wars that, for our purpose, they far overshadow all else. The first of these is the "four-document hypothesis," and the second is "form criticism."

THE FOUR-DOCUMENT HYPOTHESIS

At the close of the first World War one form or another of the two-document hypothesis held the allegiance of most New Testament scholars. It is true that, as early as 1904, Ernest DeWitt Burton had presented a multiple-document theory, but it had failed to win general assent.

In the *Hibbert Journal* for October, 1921, B. H. Streeter first presented in outline a multiple-document theory which was destined to win wide acclaim both in England and in America.[17] His four-document hypothesis was set forth in detail in 1924.[18] Streeter, first of all, warned Gospel critics of three "unconscious assumptions" against which they must be on their guard. They were: (1) the assumption that the authors of Matthew and Luke used no other documents of anything like the same value as Mark and Q; (2) the assumption that that hypothesis is most plausible which postulates the smallest number of sources; and (3) the assumption that it is improbable that the same or similar incidents or sayings should have been recorded in more than one source and that, therefore, if the versions given by Matthew and Luke, respectively, of any item differ considerably, this is to be attributed to editorial modification.

In his investigation Streeter discovered that, if he started with Luke and eliminated Mark, there still remained a Gospel. The Passion narrative in Luke he found to be so different that it is practically independent of Mark. He further observed that, if the discourse document were also eliminated from Luke, there still remained a series of incidents which form the historical framework. This remainder, L, plus Q, gave Streeter his "Proto-

17. Burnett Hillman Streeter, "Fresh Light on the Synoptic Problem," *Hibbert Journal*, XX (1921), 103–12.

18. Burnett Hillman Streeter, *The Four Gospels* (London, 1924), pp. 223–70.

Luke." His theory is that this material was gathered by Luke when he was in Palestine during Paul's Caesarean imprisonment. Later he came upon Mark and combined Proto-Luke with it but gave preference to his own original Gospel. With the addition of the infancy narratives to this composite document, it became our Gospel of Luke. The chief source of Matthew, according to this theory, that is, the material peculiar to Matthew, came from a Jerusalemite document which Streeter designated as "M."

Streeter was not without predecessors in this type of Gospel analysis. Much of what he said had already been advanced by Paul Feine, Bacon, Burton, and Vernon Bartlett. Several outstanding scholars have announced their acceptance of Streeter's hypothesis, at least in so far as the Gospel of Luke is concerned.

FORM CRITICISM

Those who sought the solution of the synoptic problem in some form of the two-document hypothesis were rather generally agreed that in the Gospel of Mark there could be found an accurate historical outline of the life of Jesus. This faith in the general historical accuracy of Mark was shaken by Wrede and Wellhausen.

Wrede came to the conclusion that, although the author of the earliest Gospel had genuine historical material at his disposal, he grouped and interpreted it in accordance with his own dogmatic ideas and the beliefs of the primitive Christian community. Tradition must, therefore, be distinguished from the historical strata.[19]

Wellhausen came to the conclusion that in the Gospels we have a historical picture not of Jesus but of the concept of Jesus which prevailed in the primitive community. Tradition fashioned and transmitted, as the words of Jesus, the ideas which, in reality, arose from the faith of the community.[20]

In 1919, some five years before the announcement of Streeter's four-document hypothesis, K. L. Schmidt undertook the task of

19. Wilhelm Wrede, *Das Messias-Geheimnis in den Evangelien* (Göttingen, 1901).

20. Julius Wellhausen, *Das Evangelium Matthaei* (2d ed.; Berlin, 1914); *Das Evangelium Marci* (2d ed.; Berlin, 1909); *Das Evangelium Lucae* (Berlin, 1904); *Einleitung in die drei ersten Evangelien* (Berlin, 1905).

analyzing the Gospel of Mark in an effort to distinguish the tradition itself from the editorial work of the evangelist.[21] His conclusion was that the Gospel units themselves had existed in a definite, fixed form prior to the composition of the Gospels. The framework of the Gospel is a creation of the evangelist, and it offers neither chronological nor geographical details for a historical life of Jesus.

Within two years, three other German scholars—Martin Albertz, Rudolf Bultmann, and Martin Dibelius—independently produced studies of the various forms of the preliterary traditions concerning Jesus.[22]

Dibelius and Bultmann soon came to be considered the leading exponents of this new critical method. In spite of individual differences in the detailed working-out of the method, they were agreed on their general aims. Their purpose was to study the preliterary transmission of the Gospel materials by the analysis and the classification of forms and to interpret those forms in the light of the life of the primitive community.

The general theory of Dibelius and Bultmann rests on five fundamental principles:[23] (1) The Synoptic Gospels are popular subliterary compositions; they belong essentially to *Kleinliteratur*. (2) They depict the faith of the primitive Christians who created them and not the historical Jesus. (3) They are artificial collections of isolated units of tradition. (4) These units originally had a definite literary form, which can still be detected. (5) This form was created by a specific social situation.

SOCIAL-ENVIRONMENT CRITICISM

If we may be permitted to digress for a few moments from our consideration of form criticism, we may with profit turn once

21. Karl Ludwig Schmidt, *Der Rahmen der Geschichte Jesu* (Berlin, 1919).

22. Martin Albertz, *Die synoptischen Streitgespräche* (Berlin, 1921); Rudolf Bultmann, *Die Geschichte der synoptischen Tradition* (Göttingen, 1921); Martin Dibelius, *Die Formgeschichte des Evangeliums* (Tübingen, 1919).

23. An excellent summary of these principles is to be found in Laurence J. McGinley, *Form-Criticism of the Synoptic Healing Narratives* (Woodstock, Md., 1944). This volume also contains one of the most complete bibliographies of materials dealing with *Formgeschichte* that has thus far been published.

again to the article which was published by Professor Willough-by in 1922.[24] In that article he pointed out that at that time there had just emerged a genuinely historical interest in first-century Christianity as a great social movement. As a result, the Jewish background of primitive Christianity had been carefully studied. The Hellenistic environment, however, was still awaiting ade-quate investigation. Preliminary studies were needed in the field of gentile religions. Early Christianity itself would have to be investigated from a social and genetic point of view. The varied, syncretistic life of the Greco-Roman world provided a host of problems concerning the genesis and function of early Christian-ity for the New Testament student who was willing to do pioneer work. Typical of the whole problem-complex were questions concerning the hope, the present experience, the agent, and the guaranties of salvation. The developments marked in first-cen-tury Christianity demonstrated how the new movement strove to meet the needs of Gentiles in the Greco-Roman world.

How well this work of "criticism by social environment," as it is called by McCown,[25] has been developed, is amply demon-strated by the great amount of work that has since been done in studying the mass of rabbinic materials in order to gain a better understanding of first-century Pharisaism; by the work that has been done on Philo in order to show him to be the representative of a religious movement that had gone far in the first century to-ward absorbing the Hellenistic mystery into Judaism; by the work done in archeology in order to demonstrate how deeply Hellenistic culture had penetrated even into Palestine itself; and by the work done by the men of the so-called "Chicago School," such men as, for example, Shirley Jackson Case, Harold R. Wil-loughby, and Donald W. Riddle.

Before the development of the form-critical method and before the rise of the "Chicago School," however, the method of "criti-cism by social environment" was used by Burkitt, Bacon, Loisy,

---

24. "The Next Step in New Testament Study," pp. 159–78. See, further, by the same author, "The Study of Early Christianity," in *Religious Thought in the Last Quarter-Century*, ed. G. B. Smith (Chicago, 1927), pp. 42–69.

25. Chester Charlton McCown, *The Search for the Real Jesus* (New York, 1940), p. 196.

and others. The basic principle of the method was stated by Professor Riddle when he wrote: "Agreement with known environment is the criterion by which a datum is identified as authentic, that is, having actually come from Jesus or as having been produced by a Christian community."[26] The basic element in both form criticism and the more general "criticism by social environment" is, thus, the "life-situation."

In our opinion, as we come to a consideration of the results of this method of "criticism by social environment," we come to the crisis of New Testament criticism in the world-wars period. The method, as it was used by some, led eventually to a thoroughgoing historical skepticism.[27] In 1926, Rudolf Bultmann was led to write: "I do indeed think that we can now know almost nothing concerning the life and personality of Jesus, since the early Christian sources show no interest in either, are moreover fragmentary and often legendary; and other sources about Jesus do not exist."[28] Shirley Jackson Case, in spite of the fact that he was writing what purported to be a biography of Jesus, asserted that in a very real sense a biography of Jesus was impossible.[29]

One of the classic expressions of the skeptical mood which resulted from this form of criticism was that given voice by Frederick Clifton Grant in his presidential address before the Society of Biblical Literature and Exegesis in 1934. He said:

One of the main results of the modern critical view of the New Testament, one that was probably entirely unforeseen in the earlier days of criticism but is now becoming perfectly clear, is this: The New Testa-

---

26. Donald W. Riddle, *The Martyrs: A Study in Social Control* (Chicago, 1931), p. 210.

27. In all fairness, we should hasten to state, as does Taylor in his very excellent critique of form criticism, that this is "not the necessary trend of the method; on the contrary, when its limitations are recognized, Form-Criticism seems . . . . to furnish constructive suggestions which in many ways confirm the historical trustworthiness of the Gospel tradition" (Vincent Taylor, *The Formation of the Gospel Tradition* [London, 1933], p. vi).

28. Quoted from the English translation of Rudolf Bultmann's *Jesus*, which was made by Louise Pettibone Smith and Erminie Huntress and published under the title *Jesus and the Word* (New York, 1934), p. 8.

29. *Jesus: A New Biography* (Chicago, 1927).

ment alone, and taken by itself, provides neither an adequate historical explanation of the rise of Christianity nor even a thoroughly satisfactory narrative of its origins. . . . . It used to be thought, by some, that when all the "later accretions" to the Gospel had been stripped off, and we really got "back to Jesus" himself and his genuine teaching, we should have discovered the central dynamic of Christianity. . . . . I will simply point out that from the critical point of view it is now next to impossible to "strip off all accretions" and have anything left. . . . . "Christianity According to Christ" cannot be distinguished, at least by these methods, from that "According to Mark" or "According to Q," or according to the Church's earliest teachers in Jerusalem or Antioch or Caesarea or Joppa or Samaria or Damascus or Rome.[30]

It is here, perhaps, that we reach the high-water mark in the New Testament criticism of the interwar period. Just when the clouds of skepticism looked their blackest, a light broke through from the east—not a light from the ancient east, to be sure, but a light from the east, nevertheless.

In 1934, Rudolf Otto's *Reich Gottes und Menschensohn* (Munich) appeared.[31] Although we may find fault with Otto's knowledge of technical New Testament studies and with his handling of his sources, we cannot deny his influence on theology since his day. C. H. Dodd, in particular, has been greatly influenced by Otto and his theory of realized eschatology.

In 1936, Frederick C. Grant, a very different Grant from the one who so recently had delivered his presidential address before the Society of Biblical Literature and Exegesis, reviewed Martin Dibelius' newest publication.[32] In his review Grant said:

Students who are concerned to get at the very basis of our knowledge of Jesus and to strip off as far as possible the accretions which have gathered about the earliest tradition might well make a beginning with this attractive little book. Form-Criticism has not done away with our knowledge of the historical Jesus; on the contrary, it has brought him and the earliest body of his followers far closer to us than ever before.[33]

---

30. "The Spiritual Christ," *Journal of Biblical Literature*, LIV (1935), 1–15.

31. This was translated into English by Floyd V. Filson and Bertram Lee Woolf and was published under the title, *The Kingdom of God and the Son of Man* (Grand Rapids, Mich., 1938).

32. *Die Botschaft von Jesus Christus* (Tübingen, 1935).

33. *Anglican Theological Review*, XVIII (1936), 103.

When he translated this work of Dibelius into English, Grant said of it:

In his little book . . . . the author has endeavoured to set forth the results to date of Form-Criticism, as applied to the oldest materials in the Gospels. He has removed the later accretions, whether oral or literary, which have gathered about the traditions of Jesus' words and deeds, his teachings and healings, his sayings and parables and the reports of his "mighty works." As a result the pristine evangelic tradition stands out with great freshness and unity of appeal.[34]

Otto and Dibelius, each in his own way, are outstanding among those scholars who succeeded in turning the New Testament critic away from a thoroughgoing skepticism, which threatened his effectiveness in the world in which he lived. At the risk of being accused of leaving the field of New Testament criticism and entering that of theological speculation and with a willingness to allow the interpreter to call his method what he will, we must turn our attention to the so-called "modern school"—a school of thought that has had profound influence on the New Testament critic of the last decade.

THE MODERN SCHOOL

Dodd has, perhaps, best expressed the principles of this "modern school," and his words are worth quoting at some length. He says:

The study of the Gospels has recently entered upon a fresh phase. The aim of nineteenth-century criticism was defined as "the quest of the historical Jesus." Its method was the minute analysis and assessment of the Gospels as historical documents. Its assumption, avowed or implicit, was that this method would succeed in eliminating from the records a mass of intrusive material due to the faith and thought of the early Church (*Gemeindetheologie*). When this was done, the residue would lie before us as a solid nucleus of bare fact upon which we might put our own interpretation, without regard to the interpretation given by the early Church in the documents themselves. Christianity might thus be reconstructed upon a basis of historical fact, scientifically assured.

The modern school speaks with a different voice. It emphasizes the character of the Gospels as religious and not historical documents. It

34. Martin Dibelius, *The Message of Jesus Christ*, trans. Frederick C. Grant (New York, 1939), pp. vii f.

tends to decry the significance of mere facts of history, supposing they could be ascertained, and to doubt the possibility of ascertaining them. . . . . The older method of criticism, in its search for bare facts, set out to eliminate whatever in the Gospels might be attributed to the faith or experience of the church. In doing so, it deliberately neglected in them just those elements which in the eyes of their authors made them worth writing. They did not write to gratify our curiosity about what happened, but to bear witness to the revelation of God.[35]

Here, then, we have the turning-point in the New Testament criticism of the decades which lie between the great wars. What we have to say concerning New Testament criticism from this point on may seem to be in the nature of an anticlimax—not that it is unimportant within itself but that its importance suffers in the light of what has gone before.

No survey of Synoptic studies during this period can be made without at least a mention of a problem which has called forth much discussion—discussion which, perhaps, is out of all proportion to the importance of the problem and to the results achieved. The generally accepted view that the Gospels originally were written in Greek has been challenged by a group of Semitists, who feel that they originally were written in Aramaic. The most active exponents of this view are C. F. Burney and C. C. Torrey.[36] They have been opposed by E. J. Goodspeed, F. C. Grant, E. C. Colwell, and others.[37] Four facts thus far have weighed heavily against the Semitists: (1) There is no written Aramaic literature from the time when the Gospels were written; (2) the Gospels were written at a comparatively late date; (3) up to now, no two Semitic scholars agree on lists of so-called "Aramaisms"; (4) the overwhelming majority of the so-called "Aramaisms" appear in the nonbiblical Greek of the papyri and Epictetus.

35. C. H. Dodd, *History and the Gospel* (New York, 1938), pp. 11–14.

36. C. F. Burney, *The Aramaic Origin of the Fourth Gospel* (Oxford, 1922); C. C. Torrey, *The Four Gospels* (New York, 1933), and *Documents of the Primitive Church* (New York, 1941).

37. Edgar Johnson Goodspeed, *An Introduction to the New Testament* (Chicago, 1937); Frederick Clifton Grant, *The Earliest Gospel* (Nashville, 1943); Ernest Cadman Colwell, *The Greek of the Fourth Gospel: A Study of Its Aramaisms in the Light of Hellenistic Greek* (Chicago, 1931).

LIFE OF JESUS STUDIES

Professor McCown has already given us a very admirable survey of the studies in the life of Jesus which had been made up to the opening of World War II.[38] "The nineteenth century," he says, "ended with the destruction of its characteristic 'liberal' portrait of Jesus. It would appear that after nearly forty years, the twentieth-century has discovered none at all of its own."[39] Jesus has, in a very real sense, become all things to all men. He has become, in turn, socialistic agitator, small-town man, and Rotary Club member. Even when one turns to the so-called "scientific" treatments of the life of Jesus, one finds no consensus among scholars.[40] The first eschatological life of Jesus published between the world wars was that of Rollin Lynde Hartt (*The Man Himself* [1923]), a book that has been characterized as being a strange mixture of scholarship and wisecracks. This was followed by Joseph Warschauer's *The Historical Life of Jesus* (1927) and by Francis Crawford Burkitt's *Jesus Christ: An Historical Outline* (1932).

Shirley Jackson Case's *Jesus: A New Biography* (1927), we have mentioned already as being an example of "criticism by social environment." It presents Jesus as believing himself to be, not the Messiah but the forerunner, and as preaching a thoroughgoing, apocalyptic, transcendent eschatology.

Maurice Goguel, in his *Vie de Jésus* (1932), and James Mackinnon, in his *Historic Jesus* (1931), find much in the Fourth Gospel that can be used in reconstructing a life of Jesus. Guignebert and Loisy are skeptical about the value of the material preserved in the Gospel of John.

Guignebert, Loisy, and the German form critics find but little in the Synoptic Gospels that can outline the life of Jesus. On the other hand, Goguel, Easton, Scott, Taylor, and Dodd find in the Synoptics a solid substratum of fact with regard both to the deeds and to the teaching of Jesus.

One of the greatest of the lives of Jesus which this century has

38. *Op. cit.*

39. *Ibid.*, p. 278.   40. *Ibid.*, pp. 284 ff.

produced is that of the Jewish scholar, Joseph Klausner.[41] In this work, which first appeared in Hebrew in 1922, Klausner presents what McCown has described as "actually a 'liberal,' Unitarian Jesus."[42]

McCown concludes that the failure to find a consensus among scholars regarding Jesus is not because the historical methods of criticizing and evaluating documents are at fault or that the Gospels as source materials have not been critically treated. The fundamental difficulty is philosophical. The real problem is that of Jesus' relation to history and revelation. This involves not only historical method but also the philosophy of history.

FOURTH GOSPEL STUDIES

The studies of the Fourth Gospel have been tied in with the whole problem of the relationships of early Christianity with the Hellenistic world. In speaking of this Gospel, Craig says: ". . . . the crucial problem of today concerns the Fourth Gospel. It is certainly not to be interpreted in a vacuum, but is the point of contact Greek Dionysiac religion, an international myth of the 'redeemed redeemer,' Philo's Hellenistic Judaism, rabbinic Judaism, or an ambitious group of social climbers?"[43] In similar vein, when discussing the Fourth Gospel, Dodd said: "The understanding of this gospel . . . . is the crucial test of our success or failure in solving the problem of the New Testament as a whole."[44]

W. F. Howard has given a valuable survey of the work done in this area before 1931 in his book *The Fourth Gospel in Recent Criticism and Interpretation* (London, 1931). In a posthumous publication, which was edited by Carl H. Kraeling, B. W. Bacon in his *The Gospel of the Hellenists* (New York, 1933) interprets historically "the message of the Ephesian Elder." He finds that much can be learned of his character and purpose from our increasing knowledge of contemporary thought in Asia Minor and in Syria.

41. *Jesus of Nazareth: His Life, Times, and Teaching*, trans. Herbert Danby (New York, 1925).

42. *Op. cit.*, p. 282.   43. *Op. cit.*, p. 364.

44. C. H. Dodd, *The Present Task in New Testament Studies* (New York, 1936), p. 29.

In 1936, Ernest Cadman Colwell in his *John Defends the Gospel* (Chicago) approached the problem from the viewpoint of "criticism by social environment." Among the more recent important studies which our period has produced is that of R. Bultmann, *Das Johannesevangelium* (Göttingen, 1937–41).

The question of Greek or Aramaic origin has been argued for the Fourth Gospel just as it was for the Synoptic Gospels. This problem already has been referred to in our discussion of Synoptic studies.

ACTS AND PAULINE STUDIES

We may well consider the recent studies in Acts and in the life and letters of Paul together. Perhaps the outstanding tendency of this period in regard to Acts has been the emphasis that it is Volume II of Luke's two-volume work. This work of Luke is seen by most scholars to be history; it is history as the Greeks conceived it—an art and not a science. Luke-Acts is seen to have as its purpose the telling of the story of Christianity's rise and expansion. For the early chapters of Christianity's origin it is our sole authority.

Without doubt the most outstanding study of Acts which the world-wars period has produced is the five-volume work, *The Acts of the Apostles*, which appeared as Part I of *The Beginnings of Christianity*, edited by F. J. Foakes Jackson and Kirsopp Lake (New York, 1920–33). Among the other works which have contributed to our understanding of Acts and of the earliest period of the church's history are the following: H. J. Cadbury's *The Making of Luke-Acts* (New York, 1927); C. H. Dodd's *The Apostolic Preaching and Its Developments* (Chicago, 1937); and Johannes Weiss's *The History of Primitive Christianity*, trans. F. C. Grant (New York, 1937).

In the area of Pauline studies, perhaps the great bulk of the work done should be classed not as New Testament criticism but as theology, or, if we so desire, as biblical theology.[45] For our purpose only three studies need be mentioned: (1) the theory set forth by E. J. Goodspeed as to the place of Ephesians in the Pauline corpus and the importance of Acts in the collecting of the

---

45. Cf. the chapters in this volume by D. W. Riddle and A. N. Wilder.

letters;[46] (2) the suggestions of John Knox concerning the place of Philemon among the letters of Paul, which formed the basis for a new view of the chronological sequence of the letters;[47] and (3) D. W. Riddle's emphasis on the Pauline letters as primary source materials for the life of Paul.[48]

PASTORAL AND CATHOLIC STUDIES

So far as we have been able to determine, there have been very few studies in these areas which have made unusual contributions to New Testament criticism since World War I. Among the exceptional few should be cited Bishop Carrington's *Primitive Christian Catechism* (Cambridge, 1940). In the area of the Pastorals, attention should be given to P. N. Harrison, *The Problem of the Pastoral Epistles* (Oxford, 1921). In this book it is argued that these epistles, as they now stand, are the work of a Paulinist who lived in the early years of the second century. By a series of linguistic studies, the genuine Pauline sections are isolated.

APOCALYPTIC STUDIES

World War I brought about a renewed interest in apocalyptic. In general, the apocalyptic studies of the period that are the work of critical scholarship approach the book from the point of view of "criticism by social environment." The Revelation of John is seen as a work that was written to steady the churches of the late first century in time of persecution. It was written to meet the needs of its time. Most scholars are agreed that it is the work of one author who leaned heavily upon earlier sources, particularly upon earlier Jewish apocalypses. There are those, as, for example, R. H. Charles, who hold that in its present form the Apocalypse is the work of a later editor. Major contributions to

46. *New Solutions of New Testament Problems* (Chicago, 1927); "The Place of Ephesians in the First Pauline Collection," *Anglican Theological Review*, XII (1930), 189–212; *The Meaning of Ephesians* (Chicago, 1933); *New Chapters in New Testament Study* (New York, 1937); *An Introduction to the New Testament* (Chicago, 1937).

47. *Philemon among the Letters of Paul* (Chicago, 1935); " 'Fourteen Years Later': A Note on the Pauline Chronology," *Journal of Religion*, XVI (1936), 341–49; "The Pauline Chronology," *Journal of Biblical Literature*, LVIII (1939), 15–30.

48. *Paul, Man of Conflict* (Nashville, Tenn., 1940).

our understanding of Revelation have been made by S. J. Case, R. H. Charles, A. S. Peake, and E. F. Scott.

Of particular interest to us was the fact that in this area, almost alone, critical study was motivated by the contemporary scene. Professor A. S. Peake wrote: "It had never been my intention to write a book on the Revelation of John, but I chose this subject as the one . . . . timely in the present conditions. . . . ."[49] R. H. Charles, in his exhaustive two-volume commentary, wrote: "The publication of this commentary has been delayed in manifold ways by the War. But these delays have only served to adjourn its publication to the fittest year in which it could see light, that is, the year that has witnessed the overthrow of the greatest conspiracy against right that has occurred in the history of the world, and at the same time the greatest fulfilment of the prophecy of the apocalypse."[50] In 1917, Shirley Jackson Case wrote: "In the name of religion, it is maintained that human efforts to make the present world a safer and better place in which to live are wholly misguided. On the contrary, God is said to will that conditions shall grow constantly worse as the impending doom approaches."[51] In order to counteract this mistaken conception, he wrote his book.

It is interesting to observe that there was but little parallel to this interest in apocalyptic in World War II. What interest has been shown in the Apocalypse of John is often found in those religious groups which some are wont to call "the lunatic fringe."

Other important studies on the Apocalypse of John are:

1. SHIRLEY JACKSON CASE. *The Revelation of John*. Chicago, 1919.
2. ERNEST FINDLEY SCOTT. *The Book of Revelation*. New York, 1940.

CONCLUSION

Throughout the two decades which fell between the great wars, there ran one unifying thread. It was an ever recurring plea

49. *The Revelation of John* (London, 1920), p. vi.

50. *The Revelation of St. John* ("International Critical Commentary," Vol. LXVI [Edinburgh, 1920]), p. xv.

51. *The Millennial Hope* (Chicago, 1917), p. v.

for an interpretation of the New Testament that would make that book—if we may be permitted to call the New Testament that—of practical use to this generation.

Professor Montgomery, in his presidential address before the Society of Biblical Literature and Exegesis in 1918, said:

> The world has been unified, it is calling upon all to pool their interests and capitals, and those causes which can show no worth-value, spiritual or material, will no longer be quoted in the world's market. This is particularly true of Bible knowledge. Despite all skepticism and varieties of religious belief, the world has fostered and propagated Bible study because of its assumed value to humanity. For the science of the Bible . . . . it has little care . . . . unless the technical study keeps the interpretation of the Bible up to modern needs as well as standards and vivifies it for the ever-changing life of society.[52]

In the following year (1919) Edgar Johnson Goodspeed, also in a presidential address before the Society of Biblical Literature and Exegesis, said:

> . . . . The greatest tasks before American biblical scholarship are not archaeological but interpretative. We are the custodians of the greatest of spiritual values. Fascinating as is the technique of the subject, it would be fatal to be absorbed by it. The Bible's final worth to the world we live in is religious and moral.[53]

In 1936, again in a presidential address before the Society of Biblical Literature and Exegesis, Professor Henry J. Cadbury gave voice to the thoughts of his predecessors in that office as he said:

> . . . . There is a sense in which fidelity to the strictest standards of scholarship about the Bible demands . . . . from us a responsibility for constructive forces that would counterweigh any destructive, unspiritual results of our labors. No more than the inventor of poison gases in his laboratory can the Biblical scholar remain in his study indifferent to the spiritual welfare which his researches often seem to threaten or destroy. He may be in his processes faithful to the cold standards of history and literary criticism, he must not be indifferent to moral and spiritual values and needs in contemporary life.[54]

---

52. James A. Montgomery, "Present Tasks in American Biblical Scholarship," *Journal of Biblical Literature*, XXXVIII (1919), 2 f.

53. "The Origin of Acts," *Journal of Biblical Literature*, XXXIX (1920), 84.

54. "Motives of Biblical Scholarship," *Journal of Biblical Literature*, LVI (1937), 2 f.

We have seen that, except in almost isolated instances, the New Testament critic of the last quarter-century has not been motivated by the conditions which have existed in his own world. He has worked with seeming disregard for world wars, world-wide depressions, and human misery of every sort. He has said, in effect, "leave such concerns to the minister and to the theologian," until the results of his labors have become, in the eyes of some at least, trivial and unprofitable. But the New Testament critic, by and large, is the teacher of the minister and the theologian, to whom he would pass the burden of making practical the teachings of the Christian faith.

If the past years have taught us anything at all, they have taught us that the work of the New Testament critic, as has already been pointed out by Dodd and McCown, involves not only historical method but also the philosophy of history. History must be viewed as consisting not merely of occurrences but of events, which are occurrence plus meaning. The past years have shown us also that the critic of the New Testament must, after he has worked out his philosophy of history along with his historical method, find a way to disseminate the results of his findings. But they must be results worth disseminating. They must be vital to the world in which he lives. No longer can the critic of the New Testament be content to sit in his study, engaged in academic research that his contemporaries will call trivial and unprofitable, while those same contemporaries manufacture atomic bombs potent enough to blow both him and themselves from the face of the earth.

CHAPTER FOUR

The Present State of Biblical Archeology

G. ERNEST WRIGHT
McCormick Theological Seminary, Chicago

ARCHEOLOGY is the study of the life and culture of the human race as it is revealed through excavation. What is biblical archeology? The term is often used in almost synonymous parallelism with Palestinian archeology; but a moment's reflection makes it obvious that much with which the latter deals has little to do with the Bible, and it is equally obvious that the range of biblical study extends far beyond the borders of Palestine. In the past the term has been used by some to include virtually the whole of pre-Mohammedan archeology in biblical lands. Yet here again it is obvious that biblical archeology is something more definite and confined, since Near Eastern archeology has long since thrown off any real or primary interest in the Bible; while classical archeology has rarely had such an interest.

To me at least, biblical archeology is a special "armchair" variety of general archeology, which studies the discoveries of the excavators and gleans from them every fact that throws a direct, indirect, or even diffused light upon the Bible. It must be intelligently concerned with stratigraphy and typology, upon which the methodology of modern archeology rests; but its chief concern is not with strata or pots or methodology. Its central and absorbing interest is the understanding and exposition of the Scriptures.

To evaluate the "present state" of this subject is in a sense an attempt to assess a nonexistent abstraction, because this "state"

74

is the rather nebulous line of demarcation between the product of past research and the possibilities for the future. The aim of this paper is not to present a list of the epigraphic and nonepigraphic discoveries from the various sites which throw light upon the Bible but rather to attempt a perspective treatment of the subject as it is impinging on the present and future course of biblical studies.

I

At the outset it is necessary to say that biblical archeology is laboring under several handicaps. The first and obvious handicap is the paucity of workers. In Britain today, except for papyrologists, there are no outstanding scholars in this field. Before the war, the school of Albrecht Alt in Germany had done exceedingly important work, particularly in topography and territorial history;[1] but the future of scholarship on the Continent, particularly in Germany, is most uncertain. In Palestine the research of a few men connected with the American School of Oriental Research, the Dominican École Biblique, and Hebrew University has been significant. In America the scholars who control the sources and labor intensively in this area can be numbered on the fingers of one hand. The Oriental Institute, which can be said to be the outstanding center of Near Eastern archeology in this country, has, to my knowledge, never had a biblical archeologist on its staff. The one figure who looms head and shoulders above all others, not only on this side of the Atlantic but on the other as well, is W. F. Albright. The revolutionary implications of archeology for biblical studies have been seen by him as by no other, with the result that the real range and importance of the subject are often regarded as nothing more than the individual views of one scholar. Yet one does not need to agree with all of Albright's conclusions to see that such an opinion is not the fault of the facts; it is due to the scarcity of trained workers. As a consequence of this handicap, we may say that the true significance and meaning of archeology have been slow in affecting biblical studies, though there is no doubt that the books produced by the

1. I omit here mention of the important work in linguistics and philology (e.g., that on the Ugaritic tablets).

next generation, at least in the Old Testament field, will be considerably different in content and approach from those which have been most widely used by the last two generations.

A second handicap under which biblical archeology labors is occasioned by the confusion which exists between many of the reports of the excavations, by the inadequacy of many of the publications, and by the lack of competence on the part of a surprising number of excavators. The situation has gradually improved since the establishment of the various departments of antiquities, particularly in Palestine; and we are entitled to hope for still higher standards in the postwar era. The type site for ancient Palestine today is Tell Beit Mirsim because the quality of excavation and publication has made it so, though it is a comparatively small and unimportant mound.[2] Judging from the amount of money expended, Megiddo should be the focal center of Palestinian work; but thus far, at least, it has not become so.

A third handicap to the biblical archeologist is the fact that professional archeologists and the scholars who interpret their findings often fail to exhibit a broad cultural interest and training. Specialists in architecture, pottery, and linguistics are necessary and extremely important. Yet archeology is a branch of the humanities; its aim is the interpretation of the life and culture of ancient civilization in the perspective of the whole history of man. This requires a broader, *as well as* a more intensive, training than our graduate schools have in the past been providing. Heretofore, the primary question which we have asked of ourselves and our students is not so much what ought to be studied and what is most important as it is what details we can study so as to enable us to write a book or an article in the not too distant

2. See W. F. Albright, "The Excavation of Tell Beit Mirsim I" and "IA" in *Annual of the American Schools of Oriental Research*, Vols. XII and XIII (1932 and 1933); these works actually form the introductory manual to the study of Palestinian pottery. See, further, Albright, "The Excavation of Tell Beit Mirsim II" and "III," *ibid.*, Vols. XVII and XXI-XXII (1938 and 1943). These discuss the stratification and remains of the ancient town in the light of our present knowledge of Palestinian archeology; they draw on information from all other countries which in any way illuminates the history and artifacts of the site.

future![3] This pragmatic and rather self-centered aim has succeeded in making too many of our journals and books little more than repositories of odds and ends of pedantic research, some of which is good and stands the test of time, but most of which is of little significance and is "like the chaff which the wind driveth away." Because the Bible is the type of literature that it is and because its intensive study today is largely carried on by those interested in prospering the life of church and synagogue, biblical archeology cannot remain content with the mere pedantics of scholarship. It must insist on knowing to what end the matters of technique and detail lead; and it is even more interested in the conceptual life of Israel's neighbors than it is in their pottery and grammar, when the latter are conceived as ends in themselves. Thus far, however, it has received far too little help from the specialists in contiguous fields, because too many of the scholars have failed to keep in focus the primary end for which they and their disciplines exist.

II

Turning from these negative considerations to a more positive evaluation of the present state of our subject, we shall pass all too quickly the areas of topographical, textual, and linguistic research in order to concentrate on certain historical and religious issues, the significance of which is not yet widely appreciated.

One of the most satisfying areas to survey today is biblical topography and geography. There are still many knotty problems which defy solution; yet, within the last twenty years, progress has been so striking that the preparation of biblical maps can be carried on with much more assurance than before the first World War, when the basic work for the Smith and Guthe atlases was done.[4] Since the labors of Edward Robinson and the survey of western Palestine in the last century,[5] the most

3. This, of course, is an exaggerated caricature, and the writer is himself included in the criticism.

4. G. A. Smith, *Atlas of the Historical Geography of the Holy Land* (1st ed., 1915); Guthe, *Bibelatlas* (1st ed., 1911).

5. Edward Robinson, *Biblical Researches* (2d ed., 1856); Conder and Kitchener, *The Survey of Western Palestine* (1881–83).

important events in the history of Palestinian topography have been the establishment of the German Evangelical Institute for the Archeology of the Holy Land (1902), headed, first, by Gustav Dalman and, since 1922, by Albrecht Alt;[6] the work of the American School of Oriental Research since 1922 under the successive direction of W. F. Albright and Nelson Glueck;[7] and the monumental publication of Père F.-M. Abel's *Géographie de la Palestine*, Vols. I (1933) and II (1938). The German school introduced far greater precision than had been used heretofore, particularly in the study of the documentary sources and in the attempt to reproduce Arabic place names correctly. The American school was the first to make systematic use of the pottery criterion. This is of obvious importance, since there is no use in discussing a particular site as a candidate for a biblical place if the former was unoccupied at the time the latter was supposed to have been inhabited. Abel's work suffers its greatest limitation at this point, though it is now the basic source for the study of biblical geography and topography. In sum, we may say that in no other country has this type of research been carried on with the same precision and intensity as it has in Palestine; as a result, few of the important biblical towns and cities remain unidentified.[8]

Progress in the field of linguistic research has been so rapid, particularly since the first war, that biblical lexicons are woefully out of date. A new dictionary of New Testament Greek which utilizes the papyri and the LXX, together with a controlled and inductively established theological treatment, is sorely needed. A complete lexicon of the Greek of the LXX in a modern language has never been compiled[9] and is now desperately needed.

6. See esp. the successive issues of *Palästinajahrbuch*.

7. See esp. the successive issues of the *Bulletin of the American Schools of Oriental Research; Annual of the American Schools of Oriental Research*, Vols. II–VI, XIV–XV, XVIII–XIX; Glueck, *The Other Side of the Jordan* (1940), and *The River Jordan* (1946).

8. Cf. Wright and Filson, *The Westminster Historical Atlas to the Bible* (1945). Future work should be greatly aided by the cadastral survey of western Palestine, which has been completed but not yet released by the British War Department. Southern Transjordania has never been properly mapped.

9. Cf. Schleusner, *Novus thesaurus philologico-criticus: sive, lexicon in LXX et reliquos interpretes Graecos, ac scriptores apocryphos Veteris Testamenti* (1829).

Old Testament lexicography is in a much worse state than that of the New Testament. Numerous Hebrew, Aramaic, and Canaanite inscriptions and documents have been coming to light.[10] Continuing study of the cognate languages, particularly of Akkadian, and the revolutionary results of Ugaritic research have combined to make the need for a new Hebrew and Aramaic lexicon imperative.[11] In the light of the present state of Near Eastern lexicography and particularly that of northwestern Semitic, what is needed is not merely a new revision of Gesenius but a fresh restudy of the whole vocabulary of the Old Testament. The meanings of innumerable words will be clarified, and further progress will be made in the reduction of the large number of hapaxlegomena for the meaning of which we have been able to do little more than make astute guesses.

What has been said for lexicography is equally true for grammar.[12] Here, again, the progress of research, especially in northwestern Semitic, has been so rapid that our understanding of the whole setting and background of the Old Testament languages has been revolutionized. Indeed, the contributions made to Hebrew morphology, phonology, and syntax accumulate with almost every inscription discovered in Palestine and Syria. Arabic, which once was the primary language for comparative grammar, while still important, now must take second place to the languages, contemporary with Israel, which archeology has recovered.

Likewise, the majority of our basic commentaries, particularly in the Old Testament field, were either produced before the first

10. Cf., e.g., Diringer, *Le Iscrizioni antico-ebraiche palestinesi* (1934).

11. Cf., particularly, Gordon, *Ugaritic Grammar* (1940); Harris, *A Grammar of the Phoenician Language* (1936), and *Development of the Canaanite Dialects* (1939). It is instructive to note that the Brown-Driver-Briggs revision of Edward Robinson's translation of the Gesenius *Handwörterbuch* began to appear in 1891 (completed in 1906). The Buhl revisions in German of Gesenius began with the 12th ed. in 1895 and concluded with the 17th ed. in 1921. The König *Wörterbuch*, first published in 1910, can scarcely be said to have been brought up to date by the fifteen pages of *Nachträge* in the 5th ed. of 1931.

12. The English translation and revision by Cowley of the Gesenius *Hebräische Grammatik* in accordance with the 28th ed. of Kautzsch was published in 1910. In German the latest edition of Gesenius, edited by Bergsträsser (29th ed.), and Bauer and Leander, *Historische Grammatik*, both began to appear in 1918.

World War or reflect the state of research and the point of view of that period. In other words, the period between the two wars was not productive of the basic tools which the biblical scholar must use. Yet it was the time when archeology grew into maturity. The greatest single task of the postwar era must be the preparation of new lexicons, grammars, and commentaries which not only endeavor to deal adequately with the wealth of new factual data now at hand but also reflect the new points of view and perspective which archeology necessitates.

III

As we turn to matters of historical interpretation, we are on much more debatable ground. In general, however, the discoveries have demonstrated that far more trust in the substantial reliability of the narratives is now in order and that lateness of a written record does not necessarily mean complete unreliability. When the basic attitudes of higher criticism were being formed in the last century, there was an insufficient amount of extra-biblical data to serve as a check to hyperskepticism. Consequently, passage after passage was challenged as being a literary forgery, and the possibility of "pious fraud" in the compilation of written documents was exaggerated beyond the limits even of common sense. When such a critical attitude is established, constructive work becomes increasingly difficult, since emotional as well as rational factors are involved in the general negativism. The shift in attitude which is now taking place is difficult to assess, but it is perhaps the most important change which archeologists have forced upon biblical scholars. Attitude is a subtle factor, not easily described; but it certainly plays a major role in the determination of the use to which the tools of scholarship are put.

There are numerous illustrations of the service which archeology has rendered along this line. Perhaps the most noteworthy is the partial "recovery" of the patriarchal period of biblical history. Our written sources for this period, dating as they do between the tenth and fifth centuries B.C., necessitate the supposition of a long period of oral transmission of the patriarchal tra-

ditions before they were partially, and then wholly, committed to writing. Evidence of the later hands and the "modernization" which took place is easy to assemble. It is small wonder, then, that the dominant point of view before the first World War was that, while the stories probably contain some kernel of tradition, they actually reflect the environment of ninth–eighth-century Israel.

Archeological discoveries have changed this attitude to no small degree. While no evidence has been, or probably ever will be, found of the actual characters, many of their names are now seen to fit squarely within the onomasticon (compiled from several sources in northern Syria, Mesopotamia, and even in Egypt) which dates from the first half of the second millennium B.C., but not in the corpus of names of any later period.[13] Several of the names of partiarchal ancestors have been recognized as names of towns in the Haran (Ḥarran) area.[14] The Nuzi tablets elucidate many a custom typical of the patriarchal age in the second millennium, but not of Israelite life in the first.[15] Analogy suggests that the traditions regarding the God of the Fathers are not completely secondary in origin. Alt and Lewy have illustrated the practice of each patriarch's choosing his God for himself by numerous examples from Aramaic and Arabic paganism, from the contract tablets of fifteenth-century Nuzi, and from Old Assyrian documents of the nineteenth century.[16] In fact, the more we have learned about the western Semitic or Amorite civilization of the first part of the second millennium, the more striking have the parallels with the patriarchal traditions become, and the more

13. Albright, *From the Stone Age to Christianity* (1940), pp. 184 ff.; *Journal of Biblical Literature*, LIV (1935), 173 ff.; *Bulletin of the American Schools of Oriental Research*, LXXXI (February, 1941) 16 ff.; LXXXIII (October, 1941), 30 ff.; Bauer, *Die Ostkanaanäer* (1926).

14. Albright, *From the Stone Age to Christianity*, pp. 179 f.; cf. also *Journal of Biblical Literature*, XLIII (1924), 385 ff.

15. See Gordon, *Biblical Archaeologist*, Vol. III, No. 1 (February, 1940), and *The Living Past* (1941), chap. viii; Pfeiffer and Speiser, "One Hundred Selected Nuzi Texts," *Annual of the American Schools of Oriental Research*, Vol. XVI (1936).

16. Alt, *Der Gott der Väter* (1929); Lewy, *Revue de l'histoire des religions*, CX (1934), 50 ff.; Albright, *Journal of Biblical Literature*, LIV (1935), 188 ff. The date given here for the Cappadocian tablets is that of Albright in *Bulletin of the American Schools of Oriental Research*, LXXXVIII (December, 1942), 32.

probable it is that the Fathers of Israel were one small branch of the Amorite movement.[17] As such, and with a center at Haran in the heart of western Semitic territory in the pre-Hurrian period, they undoubtedly came into contact with the Sumero-Akkadian culture, which was the dominant influence in the civilization of early western Asia. If so, we should be in a position to explain a most peculiar fact about Israel in Palestine: the possession of creation stories which show an undeniable influence from Sumero-Akkadian epics, but none whatever from Canaanite.[18] A far more conservative view toward the antiquity of such traditions is probably called for.

Evidence from Egypt and from Palestinian excavations and exploration has also pointed in the same direction. The simplicity of life in Palestine of the Amorite period, as contrasted with the rapid growth of feudalism in the Hyksos age; the distribution of towns during the early second millennium, as known from exploration and also from the Egyptian execration texts; the revival of nomadism in Transjordania and the rapid growth of settled agrarian society in western Palestine; the history of the Jordan rift in connection with the Sodom and Gomorrah incident;[19] the Egyptian parallels to the Joseph story; the possible connection between Hebrew tradition and the four-hundred-year era of Tanis; the absence of any evidence for the familiar fertility-cult cycle in Genesis[20]—all these items and many more illustrate

17. The theory, especially popularized by Dussaud on the basis of a questionable interpretation of certain Ras Shamra texts, that the patriarchal traditions are merely the reflection of Canaanite prehistory in the Negeb and in Palestine has little to commend it either philologically or historically (cf. Dussaud, *Les Découvertes de Ras Shamra [Ugarit] et l'Ancien Testament* [2d ed., 1941]). Contrast, e.g., Albright's reconstruction in "The Role of the Canaanites in the History of Civilization," *Studies in the History of Culture*, Waldo G. Leland Volume (1942), pp. 11 ff.

18. This statement can now be made with considerable confidence as a result of our present knowledge of Canaanite mythology (cf. Albright, *Archaeology and the Religion of Israel* [1942], chap. iii; Eissfeldt, *Ras Schamra und Sanchunjaton* [1939]; Gordon, *The Living Past* [1941], chap. vii, and *The Loves and Wars of Baal and Anat* [1943]).

19. Cf. Harland, *Biblical Archaeologist*, Vol. V, No. 2 (May, 1942), and Vol. VI, No. 3 (September, 1943).

20. Cf. Graham and May, *Culture and Conscience* (1936), chap. iii, esp. p. 94.

the wealth of data from the patriarchal age with which we now have to deal.[21]

A second major illustration of the conservative trend which archeology is bringing about has to do with the Conquest and the settlement of Israel in Palestine. Heretofore, the Conquest has been regarded as a gradual one by osmosis, wherein Israelites and Canaanites were progressively amalgamated. That there is much truth in this belief can be easily shown. However, the violent destruction which occurred at such sites as Bethel, Lachish, and Debir during the thirteenth century indicates that we must take seriously the biblical claims for a storming of at least central and southern Palestine with such violence and such contempt for the inhabitants that there was small opportunity or desire for amalgamation on a large scale. The supposed conflict between chapters 10–11 of the Book of Joshua and chapter 1 of the Book of Judges has been exaggerated, and a new point of view regarding the historicity of the Conquest is necessitated.[22] This means that we must reckon with an Israel which in the earliest days of her life in Palestine was a dynamic cultural and national entity. Syncretism, while there was much of it, particularly during the period of the judges and the age of the monarchy, must not be exaggerated to the extent that we lose sight of this fact.

A great deal has been written on the date of the Exodus and the Conquest. In the past, three main theories have been held: (1) that the Exodus was the Hebrew echo of the expulsion of the

21. With the appearance of the new inscription of Amenophis II, which lists and numbers the ͨApiru along with other peoples of Canaan, the whole question of ͨApiru-Ḫapiru (Ḫabiru)–Hebrews may be reopened. It is becoming increasingly difficult to deny the relation of the Hebrews to these other groups, and it is also increasingly difficult to interpret the ͨApiru-Ḫapiru as nothing more than nomadic people in an inferior social status. The inscription in question is published by Ahmad M. Badawi, *Annales du service des antiquités de l'Égypte*, XLII (1943), 1 ff. While this volume has not yet reached this country, a copy of the inscription is in the possession of Dr. John Wilson of the Oriental Institute, to whom this reference is due.

22. Cf. Wright, "The Literary and Historical Problem of Joshua 10 and Judges 1," *Journal of Near Eastern Studies*, Vol. V, No. 2 (April, 1946).

Hyksos from Egypt, *ca.* 1550 B.C.;[23] (2) that it occurred during the Eighteenth Egyptian Dynasty, *ca.* 1440 B.C.;[24] and (3) that it took place during the reign of Merneptah in the Nineteenth Dynasty, *ca.* 1230 B.C.[25] None of these theories now appears entirely adequate. Albright's study of the Amarna tablets indicates that there were four main city-states in southern Palestine during the first part of the fourteenth century.[26] Letters from the kings in northern Gilead and Bashan indicate that this area was likewise organized within a city-state system, while the silence of the Amarna correspondence concerning southern Transjordania, together with the results of Glueck's survey, indicates that this area was still inhabited by a nomadic people. In the Book of Joshua, however, we encounter nine city-states in southern Palestine, in addition to those of Jericho, Bethel, and the Hivite tetrapolis, while from the Book of Numbers we learn that an entirely new system of affairs existed in Transjordania, for the area is divided into four kingdoms (those of Og, Sihon, Moab, and Edom); and a fifth, the Ammonite, had come into being by the time of the judges.[27] Obviously, a later date than the Amarna period of the fourteenth century is presupposed by this state of affairs. In addition, the lack of evidence for royal building in the Egyptian delta during the Eighteenth Dynasty points to the Nineteenth Dynasty for the Hebrew construction of Pithom and Raamses (Exod. 1:11). This fact, together with the destruction of Bethel, Lachish, and Debir about the middle and third quarter of the thirteenth century, leads us to Albright's view that the Exodus must have occurred sometime in the early part of the

23. Cf. Josephus *Against Apion* i. 73–105; Hall, *Ancient History of the Near East* (1913), pp. 403 ff.; *Quarterly Statement of the Palestine Exploration Fund* (1923), pp. 125 f. There may be some truth in this view in the sense that certain of the tribal groups, if they were ever in Egypt, left there at that time (so Meek and Albright).

24. Cf. especially Garstang, *The Foundations of Bible History: Joshua-Judges* (1931), pp. 51 ff.; *The Story of Jericho* (1940), pp. 129 ff.

25. This has been the dominant view of critical scholarship, though held with numerous variations: see most recently, Meek, *Hebrew Origins* (1936), pp. 42 f.; Rowley, *Bulletin of the John Rylands Library*, XXII (1938), 243 ff.; *Bulletin of the American Schools of Oriental Research*, LXXXV (February, 1942), 27 ff.

26. *Bulletin of the American Schools of Oriental Research*, LXXXVII (October, 1942), 32 ff.

27. Cf. Wright and Filson, *op. cit.*, pp. 35 f. and Pls. IV–VI.

reign of Rameses II (1301–1234 B.C.).[28] The problems of Jericho and Ai, however, remain and prevent us from oversimplifying the picture. The final history of Jericho is still obscure. That it was abandoned by the second or third quarter of the fourteenth century, however, seems certain. Consequently, we must assume that behind the present narratives of the Conquest there was a more complex situation than first meets the eye.[29] Yet this fact cannot obscure the substantial historicity and violence of the main wave of the Conquest in the thirteenth century.

There is an equally large amount of evidence bearing on the settlement of Israel in Palestine. For the first time, the hill country became dotted with newly established towns, the ruins of which can be distinguished from those of the great Canaanite centers left standing and from the towns under the political and economic control of the Philistines.[30] The disturbed conditions described in the Book of Judges are also reflected in the strata of all excavated towns of the period, indicating that the struggle for power and control among the various groups in the country was intense.[31] The excavations also indicate the change which began with the united monarchy of David and Solomon. A far greater degree of stability was achieved; the general prosperity and rise in population and standard of living are witnessed; the last centers of Philistine and Canaanite culture (except, of course, those along the coast to the north of Mount Carmel) were either destroyed, as was Beth-shan, or brought under the political and economic control of the hill country for the first time in the country's history.[32]

28. Cf. Albright, *Bulletin of the American Schools of Oriental Research*, LVIII (April, 1935), 10 ff.; LXVIII (December, 1937), 22 ff.

29. See, further, Burrows, *What Mean These Stones?* (1941), pp. 72 ff.; Wright, *Biblical Archaeologist*, Vol. III, No. 3 (September, 1940); McCown, *Ladder of Progress in Palestine* (1943), pp. 79 ff.; Finegan, *Light from the Ancient Past* (1946), pp. 129 ff.

30. Cf. Wright, *Journal of Biblical Literature*, LX (1941), 27 ff.; *American Journal of Archaeology*, XLIII (1939), 458 ff.

31. See reference in n. 22.

32. The wealth of information for the ages of David and Solomon cannot be surveyed here: for the reign of David the best recent survey is that of Bright, "The Age of King David," *Union Seminary Review*, LIII (1942), 87 ff. For Solomon, see Hyatt, "Solomon in All His Glory," *Journal of Bible and Religion*, VIII (1940), 27 ff., with references cited there;

The combined linguistic, historical, and archeological treatment of the list of levitical cities in Joshua, chapter 21, by Albright indicates that this list is almost certainly from a tenth-century compilation of still older material and that the establishment of these cities is not an idealization of the post-Exilic priestly school, a view which has been commonly held.[33] In my opinion the same can be held for the lists of tribal cities and perhaps even for the boundaries in Joshua, chapters 15–19; at least it is difficult to explain on other grounds the presence among them of such cities as Sharuhen (Tell el-Fârᶜah) and Gezer, which by the ninth century had been virtually abandoned. If this is the case, then there is no reason whatever to ascribe these lists in Joshua to the priestly writers of the post-Exilic period; in fact, powerful support is given to Martin Noth's recent study, which indicates a high probability that the P stratum in Genesis, Exodus, Leviticus, and Numbers is not to be found in the Book of Joshua at all but that the book is to be considered as a Deuteronomic work in the same sense as are Judges, Samuel, and Kings.[34] The system of land tenure in Israel; the special group (the tribe of Levi) set apart for the priesthood which had certain cities but no land allotted to it; the Tabernacle and Temple cultus, supported, not by grants of land, but by tithes and other contributions, are characteristic Israelite institutions, which are thrown into bold relief when contrasted with the variant institutions of surrounding countries. They cannot be adequately explained as being late priestly idealizations; they are too basic to the whole Israelite economy. If so and if the lists in Joshua, chapters 15–21, are early in origin as they are here claimed to be, then we have reached certain conclusions, the implications of which are widely at variance with the views which have been

---

Glueck, *The Other Side of the Jordan*, chaps. iii–iv; Albright, *Archaeology and the Religion of Israel* (1942), pp. 119–55; Wright, *Biblical Archaeologist*, Vol. IV, No. 2 (May, 1941); Burrows, *op. cit.* (use index).

33. Albright, "The List of Levitic Cities," *Louis Ginzberg Jubilee Volume, English Section* (1945), pp. 49 ff.

34. Martin Noth, *Überlieferungsgeschichtliche Studien*, Vol. I: *Die sammelnden und bearbeitenden Geschichtswerke im Alten Testament* (1943).

commonly held in the past. A complete restudy of the institutions of early Israel is necessitated, and a new evaluation must be placed upon the priestly stratum of the Pentateuch.

When it is sometimes said that recent study has done little to disturb the basic tenets of the Graf-Wellhausen hypothesis, we should not fail to observe that the statement is confined to the continued recognition of the basic documents and the acceptance of certain dates for their completion. There is more, however, to Wellhausenism than this. It is primarily a reconstruction of the whole institutional history of Israel in line with Hegelian developmental patterns and based upon the assumption that the material within a given document is more of a reflection of the age in which the document was compiled than of the age which it purports to describe. Archeological discoveries and the new perspective which they are bringing about are attacking this aspect of Wellhausenism, with the result that many of its basic tenets are being revised.

To continue the list of archeological discoveries which illustrate Israel's history and which lead us to a more conservative treatment of the sources would consume far more space than is here available. Reference can be made only to the basic surveys now at hand.[35] The excavations certainly bear clear witness to the gradual decline in the material prosperity of Palestine during the second half of the eighth century and throughout the seventh century, when the country was controlled and repeatedly ravaged by the great powers. Even more vivid witness is borne to the devastating havoc wrought by the Babylonian conquest of Judah, in which town after town was destroyed, many never to be reoccupied. It was three centuries before the country again attained something of its former prosperity. Any attempt to minimize in any way the importance of this traumatic event in biblical history is thus doomed to failure.[36]

35. See references to Albright, Burrows, McCown, and Finegan in nn. 13, 29, and 32. Cf. also Galling, *Biblisches Reallexikon* (1937); Watzinger, *Denkmäler Palästinas*, Vols. I (1933), II (1935); Barrois, *Manuel d'archéologie biblique*, Vol. I (1939).

36. Such as that of Torrey. At least it would seem that Albright has the better of the argument in the discussion with him of what the latter actually said and meant (*Journal of Biblical Literature*, LI [1932], 104, 179 ff., 381 f.). For a brief review of the period of the

No discoveries for the period of the New Testament compare in importance with those for the Old. This is inevitable, since the New Testament covers little more than a century in time, while the Old carries us through more than fifteen hundred years. The most spectacular event in recent New Testament archeology has been the publication of newly found manuscripts dating from the second and third centuries A.D.[37] These, together with those manuscripts long known, provide more evidence for the text of the New Testament than for any other book from antiquity. The recent discoveries, by and large, have supported the text of our best Greek manuscripts, and few new readings of much significance have been discovered. Aramaic inscriptions, especially on Jewish ossuaries, keep coming to light; but, until more of them have been discovered and until all the evidence has been assembled, the vexing question of the Aramaic origin of the Gospels will not be settled to the satisfaction of many scholars. Except for the work of Glueck and others in the exploration of Nabataea, archeological work in Palestine has dealt primarily either with pre-Christian or with post–first-century monuments.[38] Accordingly, archeology has not had the same historical implications for New Testament scholarship as it has had for Old Testament studies. The new conservatism regarding oral tradition in the Old Testament, however, ought to have a challenging effect on those whose skepticism has viewed the Christian Gospels as largely the creation of the early church, especially since the period of oral transmission in this case was so short.

Exile and Restoration, see Albright, *Biblical Archaeologist*, Vol. IX, No. 1 (February, 1946); cf. also *From the Stone Age to Christianity*, chap. vi.

37. Cf. Kenyon, *The Chester Beatty Biblical Papyri* (1933–37); Roberts, *An Unpublished Fragment of the Fourth Gospel in the John Rylands Library* (1935); Bell and Skeat, *Fragments of an Unknown Gospel* . . . . (1935); Finegan, *op. cit.*, chap. vii.

38. See, further, Finegan, *op. cit.*, chaps. viii–ix; McCown, *op. cit.*, chaps. xvi–xxi; *Westminister Historical Atlas* . . . . , pp. 75–96; various articles with bibliography by Filson, May, McCown, McDonald, Parvis, and Willoughby in *Biblical Archaeologist*, Vol. II, Nos. 2, 3; Vol. III, No. 2; Vol. IV, No. 1; Vol. V, No. 3; Vol. VI, No. 2; Vol. VII, Nos. 1, 4; Vol. VIII, No. 3. The majority of the discoveries in the Greek and Roman cities which bear directly on the Bible have long been known. In Palestine the work at such sites as Scythopolis (Beisân), Samaria, and Gerasa bears unmistakable and astonishing witness to the progress of Hellenization in that country.

IV

As we turn to a brief consideration of the effect which archeology has had upon the study of biblical religion, we are immediately plunged into an area in which heated disputes have been taking place. The conservative trends to be observed in German scholarship between the two wars have been drawn together, greatly amplified, and focused with erudition and a large compilation of the relevant archeological data in the writings of Albright.[39] A majority of the scholars in England and America have not been convinced by such an assertion as that of Mosaic monotheism;[40] yet, even so, the discussion is having a healthy effect. Issues are being clarified, and a new perspective is being achieved, so that future writing by up-to-date scholars, on the question of Old Testament religion at least, will be very different from that in the past. What are the issues in this discussion?

The Graf-Wellhausen reconstruction of the history of Israel's religion was, in effect, an assertion that within the pages of the Old Testament we have a perfect example of the evolution of a religion from animism in patriarchal times through henotheism to monotheism. The last was first achieved in pure form during the sixth and fifth centuries. The patriarchs worshiped the spirits in trees, stones, springs, mountains, etc. The God of pre-prophetic Israel was a tribal deity, limited in his power to the land of Palestine. Under the influence of Baalism he even became a fertility god and sufficiently tolerant to allow the early religion of Israel to be distinguished little from that of Canaan. It was the prophets who were the true innovators and who produced most, if not all, of that which was truly distinctive in Israel,[41] the grand culmination coming with the universalism of II Isaiah.

39. See especially *From the Stone Age to Christianity* (1940); *Archaeology and the Religion of Israel* (1942); *Journal of Biblical Literature,* LIX (1940), 85 ff.

40. For the chief reviews of the point of view of the works cited in n. 39, see Meek, *Review of Religion,* 1940, pp. 286 ff.; *Journal of Biblical Literature,* LXI (1942), 21 ff.; *Journal of Near Eastern Studies,* II (1943), 122 f.; Burrows, *Journal of the American Oriental Society,* LXII (1942), 343 ff.; McClellan, *Theological Studies,* III (1942), 109 ff.

41. For the most recent assertion of this view see Snaith, *The Distinctive Ideas of the Old Testament* (1944), p. 51; cf. also Longacre, *The Old Testament: Its Form and Purpose* (1945), pp. 116 ff.

Thus we have animism, or polydemonism, a limited tribal deity, implicit ethical monotheism, and, finally, explicit and universal monotheism. The second and third stages have been variously grouped by scholars under polytheism, henotheism, and monotheism, depending upon the particular emphasis of the individual scholar.[42]

Now it should be noted that this view was first established between 1850 and 1880, when the archeological recovery of the ancient world was barely in its swaddling clothes. No synthesis of Near Eastern cultural history was possible, and inability to understand Israel's environment would inevitably make it difficult to place Israel's religion in its proper evolutionary background.

Only in the last ten years has a real archeological synthesis become possible; small wonder, therefore, that its revolutionary effects on biblical study are only beginning to be felt. In any event, we can assert with confidence that by the time of the patriarchs the religion of all parts of the Near East was a long distance removed from the animistic stage, if the latter in any approved textbook form ever existed at all. As early as the Neolithic period, before the appearance of pottery, we find a building at Jericho, which is almost certainly a temple, with remarkable statues of deities in the triad of man, woman, and child.[43] The Ghassulian paintings of the Chalcolithic period in the Jordan Valley bear witness to an exceedingly complex religious imagination, with indications of a belief in high gods.[44] At least three temples of the third millennium are known from Palestine,[45] while both the fourth and the third millenniums bear witness to a highly developed cultus in Egypt, Mesopotamia, and prob-

42. The pattern of Hegelian dialectic is evident behind this reconstruction: thesis (pre-prophetic), antithesis (prophetic reaction), and synthesis (nomistic stage).

43. Garstang, *The Story of Jericho*, pp. 47 ff.; Albright, *From the Stone Age to Christianity*, pp. 95, 127.

44. Mallon, Koeppel, and Neuville, *Teleilāt Ghassūl*, Vol. I (1934), Frontispiece and Pls. 55–56, 66–67.

45. At Jericho, *ca.* 3000 B.C. (Garstang, *The Story of Jericho*, p. 71); at Megiddo, *ca.* 3000 B.C. (Loud, *Illustrated London News*, November 19, 1938, p. 926); and at Ai, *ca.* 2500 B.C. (*Syria*, XVI [1935], 325 ff. and Pls. L–LI).

ably in Syria.[46] Thus it can confidently be said that, when Oesterley and Robinson in their *Hebrew Religion: Its Origin and Development*[47] take one-fourth of their book to describe the animistic and magical background of Israel's religion, they are dealing neither with pagan nor with patriarchal religion but chiefly with Stone Age survivals or relics, the true importance of which either in Israel or in contemporary polytheism is inadequately understood and overemphasized. It cannot be objected that patriarchal nomads would naturally be more "primitive" than the inhabitants of contemporary Palestine. While this may have been true relatively, a study of the evidences for Amorite religion, particularly in the Amorite onomasticon, and the indications of such sources as the Egyptian Tale of Sinuhe, lead us a long, long way from the picture which Oesterley and Robinson have painted. The details of patriarchal religion we shall never know. That it was a branch of Semitic "El" religion seems probable, but we have no clear evidence as to its exact nature.[48]

It seems to me quite probable that these remarks would find general agreement today among a majority of informed scholars. A far greater degree of disagreement exists regarding the nature of early Israelite religion. With what assured facts does archeology confront us? Perhaps the first fairly obvious one which should be mentioned is that each of the great polytheisms, we now know, was a cosmic system, of which the gods were the personified natural forces, phenomena, and the like. The gods had no geographical limitation other than the limitation of that portion of nature which they personified.[49] Accordingly, when the earliest poetry and documents of Israel speak of Yahweh's complete charge of nature and all its substance, we are warned against assuming a geographical limitation on his power which not even the polytheists imposed on their deities. In fact, it

46. E.g., the temple complexes at Tepe Gawra, stretching back to the beginning of the Obeid period, *ca.* 4000 B.C. (see, provisionally, *Bulletin of the American Schools of Oriental Research*, LXXI [October, 1938], 23; and *Asia*, September, 1938, pp. 536 ff.).

47. 2d ed., 1937.

48. Cf. Albright, *From the Stone Age to Christianity*, pp. 184 ff.; May, *Journal of Biblical Literature*, LX (1941), 113 ff.

49. See Frankfort, Jacobsen, Irwin, and Wilson, *The Intellectual Adventure of Ancient Man: Speculative Thought in the Ancient Near East* (Chicago, 1946).

seems quite obvious that, since divinity in the Old Testament was one and not many,[50] the designation of Yahweh as a fertility-god or as a mountain-god or by any other such term derived from polytheism is misleading. In our earliest, preprophetic sources he is all these and more, because he is no personification of nature. He transcends nature and is nature's god.

In view of the archeological evidence, therefore, it seems to me that Albright is quite justified in raising his questions about henotheism.[51] It is extremely difficult to put one's finger on any parallel phenomenon in the conceptual life of Israel's neighbors; and, while there are several verses in the Old Testament which appear to indicate certain tendencies toward it, the weight of the evidence seems to point away from a dominating henotheism known thus far from the textbook definitions, at least within the official Yahwism of early Israel. An illuminating source of study is the attitude taken toward the holy sites, Tabernacle, and Temple in the preprophetic literature. Yahweh used them all, even former Canaanite sacred sites, as places where he revealed himself, without in any way being bound or geographically limited by them.[52] Consequently, those who still wish to retain the term "henotheism" will have to define it very differently from the way in which it has been customarily used in biblical circles in the past.

It has been frequently asserted that the early religion of Israel had little to distinguish it from the religion of Canaan. Today such a view seems almost preposterous. Certainly, that portion of the long-lost Canaanite literature which has been found at Ugarit sounds very different from anything we have in the Old Testament. According to the Deuteronomic editor of Judges and Kings, great numbers of people did "play the harlot" after other gods. Even here, however, we may perhaps be in danger of as-

50. There was, of course, a belief in angels, but it would seem that their divinity was dependent or derived. The main point is that there was no pantheon of deities (e.g., biblical Hebrew has no word for "goddess").

51. Albright, *From the Stone Age to Christianity*, pp. 219 f.; *Journal of Biblical Literature*, LIX (1940), 102 ff.

52. Cf. Eichrodt, *Theologie des Alten Testaments*, I, 44 ff.; and Wright, *Biblical Archaeologist*, VII, No. 4 (December, 1944), 71 ff.

suming too much, for, though statues of male deities are frequently found in Canaanite sites, not a single clear example has thus far been found within the tons and tons of debris removed from Israelite sites. The evidence in this case is so striking that it cannot be dismissed as a questionable argument from silence. The basic character and antiquity of the Second Commandment thus receives as strong a support as archeology will probably ever be able to provide for it. At the same time, however, large numbers of figurines, representing probably the Canaanite mother-goddess and fertility-goddess, have been found in Israelite sites, furnishing unquestionable evidence of syncretism among the common people. These two pieces of evidence suggest that the syncretism, while it certainly existed, did not go so far as to displace Yahweh as Israel's national and all-controlling God. It seems to me quite possible that the real source of danger in early Israelite theology lay not so much in an equating of Yahweh with a pagan deity as in the comparative freedom which angelology might allow for the importation of many pagan notions.[53]

The absence of typical mythology of polytheistic type and the concentration, instead, upon the will of God as expressed in election and covenant is another fundamental element in preprophetic, as well as in prophetic, religion.[54] The virtual absence of therio-

53. E.g. Gen. 6:1–4 and later Jewish angelology. The evidence of personal names for the equating of Baal with Yahweh is exceedingly tenuous. Beginning in the period of the judges, the appellative "baal" was borrowed, of course, for Yahweh, though, even so, it remained rare and not nearly so common as such borrowed appellatives as El, Elohim, Elyon, and Adon. In any event, a great confusion exists in the writing on this subject because little account has been taken of the vast subject of divine appellatives in the ancient Near East.

54. Professor W. A. Irwin has informed me that in the work cited in note 49 he maintains that the covenant first appears in Israel's literature about the time of Hosea, though the idea of election was much older. This view, to my mind, would necessitate the dating of both the J and the E strata of the Pentateuch after the time of Hosea (cf., e.g., Exod. 19:5, 24:7–8, 34:10–27). More important, it denies what, in my view, Eichrodt and Pedersen have clearly demonstrated, namely, that even early Israel's *Weltanschauung* was based on the covenant conception. The more one studies the conceptual life of Babylon, Canaan, and Egypt with the aid of the materials which archeology is providing, the more these doctrines of election and covenant are set in bold relief as peculiar to Israel and decisive in determining the course of her conceptual history. To my mind they cannot be separated, since, in the Old Testament sense, election has little meaning apart from covenant.

morphism in official Yahwism[55] and the apodictic, as distinguished from the casuistic, type of law[56] are further evidence that even in early Israel there was a distinct cultural and religious point of view, which was never lost but was held to tenaciously, and which was not invented but was clarified by the prophets. Thus the more information which archeology has provided for an understanding of the contemporary polytheisms, the more we are forced to emphasize the distinctive, the revolutionary, mutation, which was Israel's true significance among the ancient religions. In fact, the break in continuity with these religions is becoming increasingly easy to describe, while the evolutionary process between the one and the other is increasingly obscured. Relation, dependence, and influence in many conceptual items and practices are clear; but the organic wholeness of the Israelite point of view (as expressed in the conceptions of God, man, covenant, law) cannot be delineated solely by evolutionary criteria.[57]

The purpose of this brief discussion is not to list all the evidence which archeology presents for the study of biblical religion but to point out its most significant contributions: namely, the presentation of evidence which proves that the Graf-Kuenen-Wellhausen reconstruction of the history of Israel's religion is a

55. It seems to me that the archeological evidence is overwhelmingly on the side of Albright for the interpretation of Jeroboam's bulls as podia for the invisible Deity (a parallel to the "enthronement" of Yahweh on the cherubim in the Solomonic Temple [cf. *From the Stone Age to Christianity*, pp. 228 ff.]). While the cherubim in Jerusalem were not open to public view, the bulls of Dan and Bethel undoubtedly were. In any event, there is no doubt that in the course of time many people came to worship the bulls themselves.

56. Cf. Alt, *Die Ursprünge des israelitischen Rechts* (1934). The apodictic, or command, type of law was, of course, typical of the covenantal conception of society, which was a distinguishing mark of Israel.

57. Cf. Eichrodt in his review of Fosdick, *Guide to the Understanding of the Bible* in *Journal of Biblical Literature*, Vol. LXV, No. II (June, 1946). Up to this point I have purposely avoided the term "monotheism," because a final decision about its use does not lie in the province of archeology. So much depends on the definition of the term and on the interpretation of such accommodating exclamations of praise as: "Who is like unto thee among the gods, O Yahweh!" (cf. the writer, *Biblical Archaeologist*, VI, No. 1 [February, 1943], 14 f.).

vast oversimplification. In its circular reasoning,[58] in its exclusive attention to the extreme simplification of the historical process along unilateral evolutionary lines, in its abnormal preoccupation with what is "primitive" and "advanced" according to an a priori scale of ethical judgments (under the guise of "objectivity"), and in its inevitable naïveté regarding the conceptual life of the ancient world, it has been shown, and will be increasingly proved, to be utterly inadequate as a final interpretation of the religious data which the Old Testament presents. For this reason the Old Testament is a wide-open field today for research and study as it has not been for fifty years.

V

The limitations of space have made it necessary to leave many subjects untouched; the attempt has been to deal more with matters of perspective than to catalogue discoveries irrespective of their relative importance. The New Testament field particularly has been slighted; yet, when the Bible is taken as a whole, it is obvious that archeology, while extremely important for all phases of study, has played the most significant role in the exposition of the Old Testament.

What are the urgent tasks of the future?

1. The first and foremost task is the recruiting and training of able men and women, particularly those who have a broad background, a great fund of the indispensable common sense, and a good personality, so that they can be placed in teaching positions throughout the country and at the same time be encouraged to continue their study.

2. Next in importance is the preparation of new biblical lexicons, grammars, and commentaries which will repair the tremendous lag that now exists between such handbooks and the present state of our knowledge. This is perhaps the major task of the postwar era, though its successful completion is dependent upon the rearing and training of young scholars adequately prepared for the task. To my mind there is little use at the moment

58. That is, a theory is established on the basis of biblical passages, and then by means of the theory the same passages are dated ("on internal evidence").

of launching a large commentary project, for example, since people who are adequately trained in archeology, linguistics, and biblical theology are few in number. An eclectic hodge-podge of data and rival points of view would scarcely fill the need.

3. Money must be found in this country both for publications and for excavations. As a result of the devastating effect of the war upon England and the Continent, America must take the lead in furnishing the resources which our discipline requires and this places a rather heavy burden of responsibility upon us. The undisputed leadership of Germany in our fields of study is a thing of the past. The question, however, is whether we here possess the qualifications necessary to carry on that leadership without a serious drop in quality of output.

4. Perhaps more than anything else today, the biblical student needs an understanding of the conceptual life of the ancient world, particularly along the lines staked out by *The Intellectual Adventure of Ancient Man: Speculative Thought in the Ancient Near East*, by Frankfort, Jacobsen, Irwin, and Wilson. The time has come when such interpretative syntheses are possible, and specialists in the cognate fields must labor far more along such philosophical and theological lines if they expect their research to bear fruit for modern culture. This means that more works are needed of the type represented by Werner Jaeger, *Paideia: The Ideals of Greek Culture* (Vols. I–III [1943–45]); C. N. Cochrane, *Christianity and Classical Culture* (1940); and W. F. Albright, *From the Stone Age to Christianity* (1940).

5. New compilations of the archeological data which bear on the Bible are badly needed. Burrows' *What Mean These Stones?* (1941) and Galling's *Biblisches Reallexikon* (1937) are excellent as far as they go; but what is especially imperative are up-to-date works along the line of Barton's *Archeology and the Bible* (7th ed., 1937) and Gressmann's *Altorientalische Texte und Bilder zum Alten Testament* (2d ed., 1927).

6. The continued study of the Ugaritic, Sumerian, and Akkadian literature will undoubtedly throw much more light on literary forms and allusions in the Old Testament. The structure

and nature of Israelite poetry should become much clearer,[59] and the background of many allusions, quotations, and forms of expression, many of which cannot now be recognized, should be established.

7. Many new excavations are desirable, since archeological techniques and control have vastly improved within the last twenty years. Specifically, New Testament sites have rarely been dug in Palestine, and more attention should be paid to them. Further excavations in Syria and Lebanon, particularly in Iron Age sites, are sorely needed. In Palestine the areas of Galilee, Transjordania, and Samaria have scarcely been more than touched. Such an important site as Hazor should certainly be dug, and renewed studies of such old sites as Gezer, Eglon (Tell el-Ḥesī), and Gerar with new excavations should make the older reports more usable.

This list of things to be done could be indefinitely expanded: e.g., the renewed study of personal names in the light of the whole corpus of ancient names; the collection and study of all Aramaic documents; the study of Israelite cultic objects and practices; the attempt to identify the tools and weapons mentioned in the Bible with those found in the excavations, in order that more accurate translations of the terms in question may be made; continued research on Israelite institutions in the light of their background; etc. The discovery of the Ugaritic, Mari, Lachish, and ʿAuja el-Ḥafîr documents certainly whets our appetites for more, and leads us to hope that even the impossible may be possible! Perhaps enough has been said, however, to indicate that biblical archeology, far from being a stale subject that has reached the state of diminishing returns, has barely outgrown its adolescence. Its revolutionary contributions and implications are only now being clarified, and no one can predict just how disturbing it may become in the future!

59. Cf. Patton, *Canaanite Parallels in the Book of Psalms* (1944), pp. 1–11.

CHAPTER FIVE

Contemporary Trends in Jewish Bible Study

FELIX A. LEVY[1]

Emanuel Congregation, Chicago

THE Jew has always looked upon his Bible (the Old Testament to the Christian) as the word of God, which he revealed to his people, Israel. Rabbinic dictum might declare, "Scripture speaks the language of man," thus permitting interpretation and even critical study; but the divine origin and nature of Holy Writ were scarcely ever doubted. While Jews were the original expositors and even critical students of the Bible, they rarely reached the extreme positions of the earlier modern Protestant schools.

Bible criticism had become a department of Protestant dogmatics, and, regardless of what mode of approach was utilized—literary, historical, or cultural—the Christian student was anxious to prove the superiority of Christianity to Judaism and the appearance of Jesus as the greatest event in history. The new covenant, according to Christians, was a natural and inevitable outgrowth of the old and superseded the latter. This attitude has not yet disappeared and is expressed by Professor Peake: "The chief aim of the study of the Old Testament is not to analyze the Hexateuch into its component parts, but to understand the

1. The author herewith expresses his thanks to Rabbi Solomon Goldman and to Professors Samuel I. Feigin and Ovid R. Sellers for reading this paper and for their valuable suggestions. Some of the topics in this paper are treated in Meyer Waxman's *History of Jewish Literature* (New York, 1938–41), which has frequently been consulted.

course which was taken in the education of Israel to prepare for the coming of Christ.''[2]

The first reaction, therefore, of Jewish scholars to biblical criticism that sought to prove the inferiority of Judaism was natural resentment. They felt that they were best fitted to understand their own literature; and they rejected almost entirely the findings of the dominant school of biblical criticism of a half-century ago.[3] The Old Testament was not, to them, the forerunner of Christianity but of a Judaism and a Jewish life which had a development of their own. These students did not accept generally the division of the Hexateuch into J, E, D, P, and R, or the theory of a ''straight-line development''[4] of Israel's culture and religion. They did not put prophecy before Torah and make the latter a deterioration of the former, nor did they agree to the statement that all Israel's prehistory is fiction[5] and that its recording was late because ancient Israel was analphabetic. A Jewish scholar, Siegmund Jampel,[6] has given the best summary of what might be called the ''Jewish'' point of view by his analysis of the theories of Wellhausen and Eduard Meyer and his proof of their untenability. He supports his own arguments by draw-

2. A. S. Peake, *A Guide to Biblical Study* (New York, 1897), p. 16; cf. also Norman W. Porteous, ''Prophecy,'' in *Record and Revelation*, ed. H. W. Robinson (Oxford, 1938), pp. 247 ff. See two recent studies by Wilhelm Vischer, *Das Christuszeugnis des Alten Testaments* (Leipzig, 1935), and *Die Bedeutung des Alten Testaments für das christliche Leben* (Zürich, 1938).

3. Not all Jewish scholars, particularly at the beginning of our period, entered the lists against the higher criticism. Simon Bernfeld, an excellent popularizer in Hebrew, wrote the first, and practically the only, Jewish introduction to the Bible in a radically critical spirit. Simon Dubnow pens the story of Israel's early career in his *Weltgeschichte des jüdischen Volkes* (Berlin, 1925–29) and in his Hebrew writings in accord with the findings of the dominant German Protestant school. Lurie and Menes portray the cultural growth of ancient Israel in agreement with the tenor of investigation and the forced conclusions of Eduard Meyer from unestablished premises of a rather late cultural development in Israel. Similarly, M. J. Gorion's posthumous *Sinai und Garizim* (Berlin, 1926) analyzes the legal development of the Hexateuch with reference to Talmudic and other rabbinic works and espouses the case for the priority of the Joshua-Gerizim over the Moses-Sinai tradition.

4. Championed by Wellhausen.   5. Propounded by Eduard Meyer.

6. *Vorgeschichte des israelitischen Volkes und seiner Religion*, I (1928), 11.

ing upon the work of Gressmann[7] and Gunkel,[8] who have gone a long way from their teachers. In general, Jewish study has attacked the theory of development, particularly the claim that anything of a high ethical or religious character must be late, post-Exilic; the documentary hypothesis, or the possibility of recovering the original sources; and the late dating of the books.[9]

Jews have been extraordinarily interested in the Hebrew language, particularly since it has become the vernacular for many of them, and they have made special contributions to the study of the meanings of words, to the understanding of the literary art of the Bible, and to comparative philology. We shall now proceed to a more detailed account of what actually has been done by Jewish scholars in the last semi-centennial period.

The first Jewish scholar of consequence to break a lance with the "critics" was Joseph Halévy (1827–1917) in his *Recherches bibliques*. The author was a competent philologist, who used his knowledge of language to good stead by proving on linguistic grounds the impossibility of certain theses that cut up the Pentateuch into bits.

Harold M. Wiener, in his voluminous writings[10] early in this century, maintained the Mosaic authorship of the Pentateuch. He admits that the Massoretic text is often inaccurate, and he repudiates completely the documentation based on the usage of the

7. Who asks: "Whether knowledge gains [by such methodology] and whether this discipline can claim to be a science." "What one cannot define, is regarded as post-exilic" ("The Task of Old Testament Investigation," *Zeitschrift für die alttestamentliche Wissenschaft*, XLII [1924], 5 ff.).

8. Ideas expressed in the prophets and in Genesis, chap. 1, can be very old, even though they may have been written down in the Babylonian Exile (*Schöpfung und Chaos* [Göttingen, 1895], pp. 135 ff.).

9. Jews, of course, have not been alone in their refusal to accept currently popular theories. One has but to recall the various "fashions" in biblical criticism and the reactions to the sweeping explanations of the various "pan" schools. The present tendency among Christian scholars is in almost entire accord with the Jewish claims of the profound trustworthiness of biblical tradition. For example, Lohr ascribes to Moses the greater part of Deuteronomy, and Regel holds for its great age.

10. *Studies in Biblical Law* (London, 1904); *Essays in Pentateuchal Criticism* (Oberlin, 1909); *The Origin of the Pentateuch* (Oberlin, 1910); *The Prophets of Israel in History and Criticism* (London, 1923).

divine names. His study of text and style is meticulous, and, as a result of his analysis, he opposes differing dates for the legal sections of the Pentateuch. While he made little impression upon his opponents, he did demonstrate that the Graf-Wellhausen thesis was vulnerable. David Z. Hoffmann (1843–1921), a magnificent scholar, supplied what Wiener lacked in preparation for the assault on his opponents. There is astute and encyclopedic learning, sound logic, and critical acumen in much of his *Die Wichtigsten Instanzen gegen die Graf-Wellhausensche Hypothese* (1904), *Leviticus* (1905–6), and *Deuteronomium* (1913). He argues against a separate Holiness Code in Leviticus, inserted by P, and asserts, as do other Jewish scholars after him, that Ezekiel shows dependence on the Pentateuch and not vice versa. Hoffman was followed by a host of others who maintain the traditional stand that the Hexateuch in its present order is chronologically correct and natural and that there is more or less a unity of narrative and content, that does not permit of the usual carving up into fragments, so colorfully blocked by the Polychrome Bible. It is strange that Christian scholars have almost unanimously neglected this meritorious work and that none has deigned to answer the author.

Isaac Halévy in his Hebrew history of Jewish literature, begun about 1900 and called *Dorot Ha-Rishonim*, continues what Hoffmann began. The most recent volume of his work, the sixth (1939), takes the literary-critical theory apart and shows its weakness and futility. Approaching the problem from another angle, Chaim Tchernowitz in his Hebrew *History of the Halakhah* (not yet completed), by tracing the growth of the law from within, shows the documentary hypothesis, with its ideas of a "straight-line evolution" that assumes differing literary sources, to be wrong. Like most Jewish scholars, he gives much more credit to the priests than to the prophets, to whom usually most merit is extended for the growth of Israel's religion, especially its moral purification. He does not think that D is the book found by Josiah, and he avers that the Levites had a military function. A. Kaminka, strongly conservative in religious outlook, in various scattered essays has espoused the cause of the

unity of the Pentateuch and even of Isaiah.[11] He refers the Psalms to a time before the Exile.

In Palestine, particularly at the Hebrew University, there may be said to be an original and specifically Jewish school of biblical investigators.[12] Ephraim Yerushalmi[13] (P), in a series of studies in Hebrew, takes issue with the commonly accepted hypothesis of religious evolution. He studies the cult in its manifold phases —Sabbath, holy days, cleanness and uncleanness, etc.—in a masterly fashion and arrives at the conclusion that the present order of Scripture reveals the actual development of Israel's religion; that D is not the work of Josiah; that "Yahweh" refers to the Lord, the God of the people; and that Elohim is a household or chthonic deity.

Ezekiel Kaufman (P) is the contemporary leader, if such there be, of the attack on the older critical school. In his *History of the Religion of Israel*,[14] a monumental work in Hebrew, he scrutinizes and analyzes every contention of the critical school in detail and, in this writer's opinion, has dealt the old theory its death blow. He maintains that D is later than P and that the Aaronide priesthood goes back to a period before Samuel. The Torah does not follow the prophets but the reverse is the case; and Jewish monotheism is not the result of the prophets' labors but was there before these men appeared. Torah and prophecy are two strands of Jewish life and thought, each cultivated by its respective proponents, the former being the older. Israel was free of all those mythological features that characterized other folk religions and from the beginning had a pure monotheism, at least doctrinally, if not in practice. Kaufman rejects completely the J-E-D-P-R division, not because the Bible may not be composite but because the original documents can no longer be determined. The quest for these is useless. Certainly, the composite character of Scripture does not follow the generally accepted pattern as outlined by the critical school.

11. *Le Prophète Isaïe* (1925); Hebrew essays entitled *Mekharim*.

12. "(P)" after names refers to Palestinian scholars.

13. *Historical and Religious Investigations* (1929–31) and *The Acts of Josiah and His Generation* (2d ed., 1935–36).

14. Five vols. (1937–42).

Kaufman's theory is reinforced by the work of a married couple of Palestinian scholars, Deborah and Matthew Gershman (P) (Hebrew name, "Abidob"), whose *Paths in the Examination of Scripture* (1940) is a fine bit of pleading for the old age and priority of P to D. On internal evidence these writers seek to prove that the book that Josiah promulgated was not D; at most, it could have been only chapter 28, containing the Blessings and the Curses. No reform was instituted by this king (reminiscent of Kaufman at this point) because the so-called "Book of Josiah" (Deut., chaps. 12–26) betrays not the least trace of such origin, nor for the same reason can it have emanated from a period near to the date of the king's reign. It has resemblances to the age of Saul.

Umberto Cassuto[15] (P) analyzes the divine names and decides that "Elohim" is the general word for "god," used as a common noun, while "Yahweh" is the specific proper name for Israel's deity. The few apparent deviations from this rule, he justifies. Cassuto has a remarkable gift of understanding the Hebrew literary idioms as well as the art of ancient narrative. He draws on the Ras Shamra texts and the Lachish seals as well as on other ancient sources in and out of the Bible, particularly for his creation of the ancient pre-Israelitish mythology, which, with much ingenuity, he succeeds in restoring. As an example of his fine perception of language, he points out that the use of *Hōṣiᵓ* and *Haᶜaleh* in reference to the Exodus is not due to the idiosyncrasies of different scribes, but to the fact that when the stress is on the leaving of Egypt, the former word is employed and when on Palestine, the latter; the one referring to the place of origin of the journey, the other to the destination. Similarly, *Yālad* and *Hōlīd*, which have been the cues for the differentiation of documents, he shows to be false criteria. Each has its specific meaning, necessary in the context and to the thought to be expressed. *Kārōth Bᵊrith* means the laying-down of conditions of a covenant, while *Hāqīm*

---

15. Numerous articles in journals, some of which are mentioned in Robert H. Pfeiffer, *Introduction to the Old Testament* (New York, 1941), and in the *Encyclopaedia Judaica;* more specifically *La Questione della Genesi*, and his Hebrew works, *The Documentary Hypothesis* (1941) and a new commentary on Genesis, chaps. 1–15, *From Adam to Noah* (1945).

signifies its fulfilment. A proper understanding of these and other Hebrew idioms does not indicate a variety of authors; on the contrary, a single narrator would have to write in this wise. It is only fair to say that Cassuto was anticipated by Christian scholars. Cassuto, too, maintains that the repetitions and other duplicating features which are so often taken as evidence of a double narrative are simply elements of oriental style; so do Franz Rosenzweig[16] and others who have studied the art of the Hebrew bard. We cannot judge the tales of the Bible by the literary standards of a modern story-teller or historian. Cassuto does not say that there are no documents but that these are not those that the Graf-Wellhausen school has disentangled. He thinks that there are discernible a popular and a learned tradition or accounts of the early legendary material, in prose and in poetry, which a later compiler has utilized to arrive at the present form. The theory is different from O. Eissfeldt's, which posits an L, or Lay, source. The Torah precedes the prophets. Unlike Kaufman, however, Cassuto does not make these divisions represent two separate movements but explains the difference in character of the recensions on the score of the mythology underlying the ancient sagas of Genesis. For Cassuto, as for practically all the Jewish scholars, as well as for many non-Jewish, monotheism goes back to Israel's very beginning. At first, idolatry was not considered the serious deviation from monotheism that it was later; hence the two could flourish side by side. The Ten Commandments, therefore, with their injunctions against serving other gods, are not necessarily late, but easily could be as early as Moses.

M. H. Segal (P) has retraced the steps taken by the original investigators of the names of deity, thus furnishing the first clue for the supposition that differing accounts explained the use of "Yahweh" or "Elohim." He studies carefully every occurrence of these nouns and does a similar task for the words "David" and "king," as well as for "Jacob" and "Israel," frequently tabulating his results. He finds that in certain parts of the Hexateuch, particularly in stories in Genesis and in legal sections else-

16. In scattered articles.

where, "Elohim" is used. Otherwise "Yahweh" is preferred, and occasionally the two are combined. He concludes from his highly detailed analysis that the choice of the divine name is not due to an external factor such as a source, or even change of meaning (as Cassuto holds) and content, but that it depends upon psychological causes. The two appellations of God are synonymous. Therefore, there is no basis whatever for the division into documents on the score of the usage of divine names.

Torczyner (P), in a series of articles published in Hebrew, maintains the apparently satisfactory theory that the writers of the books of the Bible, like the Arabs, had the habit of inserting speeches and laws, words of wisdom, and songs which only at a later date were removed and arranged as separate units into tales. Feigin, following this theory, proves that in Exod. 21:1—22:15 (with the exception of a few older regulations) we have a bit of pre-Mosaic legislation given to Moses by Jethro.

Martin Buber began his critical studies of Scripture in *Das Königtum Gottes* (1936), of which only the first part has appeared. This work gives a most provocative and stimulating account of the beginnings and growth of the concept of God's kingship and its reference to the human monarch and the relations between God and people and king and people. His method, which he describes in his Hebrew *Doctrine of the Prophets* (1942) and which he uses in these books and in other articles, printed and unprinted, is what he terms the "scientific intuitive approach." Even if there be literary sources, such as the common theory holds and which he claims cannot be satisfactorily demonstrated, literary analysis proves nothing about religious growth. Early religious ideas may be found in late documents and vice versa. The prophets (or the prophetic strain) always existed in Israel, and their function was the preaching of the relationship between Israel and its God. The seers interpreted events in accordance with the teachings of their religion; they expounded God's will and exhorted the nation to repentance; they interpreted deity. Judaism owes its concept of God not so much to their innovations in ideas as to their activity.

In the study of the language, Jews have made outstanding con-

tributions. Since the recovery of Hebrew as a spoken tongue, no phase of linguistics has been neglected. In grammar and lexicography, neglected by us for almost half a century after Gesenius, we have recovered primacy. Beginning with Bacher, Barth, Levias, and Margolis in the nineteenth century, the twentieth[17] has seen a tremendous growth in knowledge, which often sheds new light on the biblical text. Eliezer ben Yehuda's *Thesaurus*, though often unreliable, is a great aid, as are David Yellin's many studies, which include the discovery of a new stem *hippael*. A number of grammars in various languages have appeared. Alexander Sperber's challenging work[18] bids us to re-write completely our Hebrew grammars. H. Torczyner's discovery of the *Semitische Sprachtypus*, a landmark in its realm, is well known to all students.

Some good Hebrew commentaries are: Joshua Steinberg's commentary to his Russian translation of the Pentateuch, Joshua, Judges, and Isaiah (Wilna, 1899–1906); S. L. Gordon's popular work, which draws on all the previous literature, Jewish and Christian, comparable to the *Cambridge Bible Commentaries;* Arnold B. Ehrlich's *Hebrew Scripture According to Text* (in Hebrew, 1890–1901, in three volumes), with "scholia," as he calls them, on certain passages. He is neutral, Jewishly speaking, and accepts the documentary theory, though it plays no role in his exegesis. The Pentateuch, he maintains, is a book of religious instruction. Occasionally he tampers with the Massoretic text and here and there achieves a brilliant result. The book is marred by attempts at overcleverness. His *Randglossen* in six volumes (1909–13) is more radical in its treatment of text, preferring often the LXX and sometimes other readings to that of the Hebrew. His *Psalmen* (1905) gives a new translation and is no departure from his usual method. In spite of an occasional unreliability, Ehrlich's research has been a solid and monumental piece of work. Abraham

---

17. Mordecai Hillel Schneider, *The Study of the Hebrew Language in Its Development*, in Hebrew, a splendid analysis of syntax and morphology; Israel Burztyn, *Grammatik der alt- und neu-hebräischen Sprache* (1929), with much that is new in morphology and in analysis and comparisons of conjugations.

18. *Hebrew Grammar* (New York, 1943) and *Biblical Exegesis* (New York, 1945).

Kahana (P), at the head of a group of selected experts, published, in Hebrew, *The Bible, with Scientific Commentary*. A few books are missing.

All these writers are competent critics and are freer in their critical treatment of the books following the Pentateuch than they are with the Torah itself. The exegetic material has been culled from old Jewish and non-Jewish sources and for the most part is learned, scientifically satisfactory, and Jewish in tone. The critical approach to the Pentateuch is relegated to footnotes for the scholar, while the running commentary takes no regard of the documentary character of the Five Books; Isaiah is credited with about a third of the present book bearing his name, chapters 24–27 are attributed to the time of Alexander; II Isaiah and other portions are given a post-Isaianic date. The Psalms are of non-Davidic origin and as late as the Maccabean period. The Scrolls, except Esther, which is unhistoric, and the Song of Songs, which belongs to the Solomonic period, are Exilic or post-Exilic at the latest.

The work of a few other men might be mentioned: H. Torczyner has written, among other articles and books, *Das Buch Hiob* (recently completely revised in a Hebrew edition) and *Die Bundeslade*. The author is a profound scholar with an exceedingly wide range and variety of learning. His explanations are often brilliant and sometimes startling; yet, because of his proneness to depart from the "safe, sane and conservative," one must be careful in accepting them. He turns the whole book of Job in his recent Hebrew work topsy-turvy, actually manhandling the text. His tremendous learning occasionally degenerates into pendantry and, despite his brilliant flashes of insight, he cannot always be followed confidently.

B. Jacob's *Das erste Buch der Tora* (1934) is a translation and explanation, as his subtitle states, of Genesis. He maintains the unity and integrity of the book against the documentary hypothesis. Step by step he supports his view with many fine arguments, replete with an incomparable knowledge of his subject. Every student ought to read his Preface. He insists that the text is almost free from error; that, while there may be literary sources,

these are not P, E, or J; and that the editor is the author. He likewise rejects the "development theory" of Israel's religion. He strives to give a Jewish commentary, scientific in character, yet pious in tone. A similar work on Exodus is about to appear. Jacob has Cassuto's penetration into the mysteries of language and his keen appreciation of the art of biblical narrative.

We owe to Julian Morgenstern, the best-known of American Jewish biblical scholars, the important *Amos Studies*, of which the first volume has appeared (1941). His work is a mine of information and has by some been put on a par with that of Wellhausen. Morgenstern, like the great German professor, is fond of Arabian parallels, and like him, is a vigorous academician, careful and painstaking, though often building up his scientific structures on insufficient evidence. He comes nearest, at least among present-day Jews, to the ideal of complete neutrality in his studies and has, as a result, the defects of such virtues. His work shows little Jewish influence and has had little influence on Jewish scholarship. His theories and conclusions are accepted by some Christian scholars; while others reject them as violently as do his own Hebrew-writing co-religionists. He has done valuable work in the comparison of religious practices, e.g., marriage, the Ark of the Covenant, and so forth.

Moses Buttenwieser writes lovingly of the prophets.[19] He adheres to the old theory, which very few Jewish scholars have accepted, that monotheism was the result of prophetic endeavors, particularly of Jeremiah, and that the seers raised the moral and religious standards of their people. Kaufman denies them this supreme influence. The universal element alone in Israel's faith is important for Buttenwieser; and, because of his infatuation with it and his failure to understand its dependence on the national features of Israel's life, he could not properly evaluate, as does the average Jew, its particularistic features, especially Torah. Buttenwieser did not always understand Judaism, so much so that he believes there is nothing valuable in the particularistic elements of Israel's religion. Despite his excellent training in grammar, the spirit of the language all too frequently escapes

19. *The Prophets of Israel* (New York, 1914).

him, and he falls into misconceptions and even mistranslations. He is all too ready to change the text to bolster up his own theories. His *Job* contains much of value, for all his shuffling of passages. Any statement in it that contradicts his thesis that the burden of the book is that virtue is its own reward is excised—the simplest way of meeting a difficulty but not of solving it. His voluminous *Psalms* follows the same pattern and leads very frequently to conclusions as untenable as those of Briggs, whose treatment is equally cavalier.[20]

The Jewish Publication Society has projected a series of commentary helps to its translation on each book of the Bible. These are called *The Holy Scripture with Commentary: Micah* (1908) by Max L. Margolis, *Deuteronomy* (1937) by Joseph Reider, and *Numbers* (1939) by Julius H. Greenstone. These are serviceable, critical, popular, and, in general, defend the traditional point of view of pentateuchal unity and priority of date. They reject the literary documentation.

Jewish exegesis differs from the Christian, in that it does not ascribe to the prophet the superlative place assigned by the Christian scholar, and it emphasizes the role and supreme value of "the Law" and its guardians, the priests. Jacob Hoschander, who began his career by maintaining the historicity of Esther,[21] has made a study of the relationship between the two groups in his *Priests and Prophets* (1938) and of their contribution to Israel's religion. His book shows clearly that the priests are as responsible for the greatness of Israel's religion as are the prophets.[22] Many passages of the Bible are illumined by this author's insight and knowledge. C. Z. Reines, in a work with the same title in

20. A few single works may be noted here: Morris Jastrow, *Book of Job* (Philadelphia and London, 1919); *The Gentle Cynic* (1921) and *The Song of Songs* (1921). Each book is accompanied by a commentary, and each is adjudged late and composite by the author; Reuben Levy, *Deutero-Isaiah* (1915). To my mind, Robert Gordis has given the best English translation of, commentary on, and introduction to Ecclesiastes in his *Book of Ecclesiastes* (New York, 1945).

21. His *Book of Esther* (1923), puts the time and place of this tale in Persia during the reign of Artaxerxes II and attributes authorship to one of the Scribes.

22. Cf., however, Elias Auerbach, *Die Prophetie* (1921), with its insistence on Jeremiah's superlative role in the development of Israel's religion.

Hebrew, follows a similar thesis. I. S. Zuckerbram who draws largely on Tchernowitz's work on the development of Halakhah, maintains in his Hebrew *The Age of Jeremiah* (1944) that the priests were responsible for the reformation of Josiah and that the prophets were simply moral reformers. Jeremiah's work in this regard was outstanding. The author discusses the Passover festival, particularly its development from the original feast of unleavened bread to the form given by Hezekiah and Josiah, which set the pattern for its final celebration. Hayyim Schauss, influenced largely by the critical school, has written, mostly in Yiddish, on festivals and other religious institutions.

Many important studies of the Massoreh—always a Jewish preoccupation—have been made during our period. These investigations began with the splendid contributions of Christian David Ginsburg, who, in addition to four volumes on the Massoreh, has to his credit an *Introduction to the Hebrew Bible*, dealing largely with textual matters, and an edition based on his studies of the Hebrew Bible itself. Recently, a great deal of stimulus has been given to this discipline. Robert Gordis[23] has made a study of the various aspects of the Kethib-Qerē problem, collating all the material and correcting the earlier work of Z. Frankel, *Vorstudien zu der Septuaginta*. The writer rejects the views either that the variants K and Q are due to different readings or that Q is the correction of K. In its early stages the use of Q was a safeguard to the synagogue reader against blasphemy by utterance of the ineffable tetragrammaton and a guide to correct reading before the invention of vowel points. At a later period K is the archtype of a code that was adopted as correct and of which Q is the variant. This dates from the year 70 c.e.

David Kahana in *Massoret Seyog Mikrah* finds an explanation for the twenty-eight pauses placed in the Bible by the Massoretes, the correctness of whose text he defends; and on the basis of this fact he tries to refute the documentary hypothesis. The stops, he contends, were not a device to mark a faulty text or deletions, as has been suggested, which the Massoretes left out because they could not understand them. Rather they were used to mark state-

23. *The Biblical Text in the Making* (Philadelphia, 1937).

ments that deal harshly with biblical heroes, aspersions upon whom a later adoring generation could not tolerate. Victor Aptowitzer in *Das Schriftwort in der rabbinische Literatur* investigates biblical quotations in Jewish postbiblical literature up to the fifteenth century, when printed Bibles became available. Aptowitzer is scrupulously critical and notes few classes of deviations: (1) those due to a context in which the quotation is found; (2) those of a high probability, because they are supported by readings in the ancient versions; (3) those that are probable because they are supported by manuscript readings; and (4) those with the highest degree of possibility because they are found in all sources. Ernst Ehrentreu in his *Untersuchungen über die Massora* (1925) has given us a history of its development and shows its reliability. He has scoured the Jewish sources and analyzed the classic *Oklah W'oklah* for his material. He maintains that study of this branch is an important ancillary science and of great aid to the understanding of the language of Scripture. Perhaps here ought to be mentioned the work of Felix Perles, in the earlier portion of our period, on the text. He deals with changes of letters, abbreviations, textual errors, false vocalization, and exegesis and makes many valuable contributions.

Translations have always occupied Jews. I mention a few of the most recent and popular attempts. There is the splendid English rendition, the best in all respects in this or any other tongue in my opinion, despite some exasperating stylistic perpetrations, issued by the Jewish Publication Society of America in 1917 under the editorship of Max L. Margolis in collaboration with other Jewish scholars and based on the earlier English versions; and the German translation *Die Schrift* by Martin Buber and Franz Rosenzweig, begun in 1926. Their rendering, characterized by great literary beauty and religious fervor, succeeds often in capturing the rhythm and picturesqueness of the original, though it is not free from frequent turgidity of style, due in part to somewhat bizarre artifices employed for the rendition of an ancient Semitic tongue into modern German, e.g., their translation of the names of God and their use of the pronouns for deity. Torczyner has edited *Die Heilige Schrift*, a new and excellent

translation. Jehoash has translated the Bible into Yiddish, producing an excellent version, reflecting the archaic flavor of the stately Hebrew in this Jewish German dialect. Space does not permit the recording of single volumes.

Jews devote themselves in large numbers to the auxiliary sciences of Bible study. Semitic linguistics, decipherment and interpretation of inscriptions, and their bearing on the Bible owe much to the labors of Julius Lewy, student of Assyrian and Hurrian, whose many articles, scattered throughout the journals, not only prove an early date for Israel's monotheistic ideas and cult practices but, in so doing, dispose of the contention that the prehistory of Israel, as given in the Bible, has no scientific validity. I might state that the old view that no nation knows the truth of its origins does not apply to Israel. Its birth and childhood were in the Near East; and from whatever people or peoples the nation sprang, when it appeared as Israel, it was already full grown, so to speak, in nationality and in cult, and its accounts of its national origins cannot therefore be cavalierly dismissed as a later historical fiction.

In the early period the well-known American Assyriologist, Morris Jastrow, was outstanding in his field and was especially prolific of books and articles, all well known, on the Babylonian religious and cultural life and Israel's relationship to these. More recently, Torczyner has done valuable work in the general field of Semitics and was first to edit the Lachish letters. Skoss has turned to Arabic for his speciality; Samuel I. Feigin, who writes in English, Hebrew, and Yiddish, to Assyrian. In his many articles in the various journals and in his recent Hebrew volume, *From the Secrets of the Past* (1943), he deals largely with Hebrew origins. He maintains, for example, that in the creation story "the image of God" refers to bicorporality and that Adam and Eve were created Siamese twins and that later the woman was separated from Adam; that Jephtha is the adopted son of Yᵓair ha-Gilᵓadi; that Solomon and Adonijah's contest was not only a dynastic struggle but one between two cult and political centers, Jerusalem and Hebron. He is in the Jewish trend of thought when he insists on the antiquity and originality of the

Hebrews as a people who were in Palestine before Joshua, and that their language was that of Canaan.

H. L. Ginsberg has gone to the Ras Shamra inscriptions for light. Some of these studies are written in Hebrew and hence are inaccessible to the student unacquainted with its modern idiom. Archeology is indebted to Nelson Glueck for the pioneering and magnificent work he has done in Transjordania, thus opening another door to our science; Benjamin Maisler's excavations at Bet Shearim have shed new light upon an ancient period. He has also written an excellent *History of the Land of Israel* (1938), to which his own researches have contributed, of which only the first part that deals with the beginnings to the kingdom has been published; and he has given us an excellent *Biblical Atlas*. All these works are in Hebrew.[24]

Cyrus Gordon has shed additional light on the life of the Bible by his description of life in Nuzu. He has also written the only Ugaritic grammar. A. Speiser has done solid work in Hurrian, and Z. Harris in Phoenician; both men have published grammars in their respective language fields. The former has given us the report of *Excavations at Tepe Gawra* (1935) in addition to many papers on archeology. Ralph Marcus has worked in the domain of Hellenistic literature, including the Septuagint.

On the whole, the efforts of these men have resulted in establishing the fact that the Bible account is reliable, that Israel's unique religion goes far back into its antiquity, that there was far more originality in Israel's culture than was commonly supposed, and that Israel was as highly civilized in many respects as were its brilliant neighbors.

I could not end this review without mentioning some of the work being done on the versions. Hayyim Heller, writing in Hebrew and German, defends the superiority of the Massoretic text. He tries to show that all deviations from it found in the Samaritan Pentateuch or in other ancient translations—particularly the Peshitta—as well as the Hebrew manuscripts collected by Kennicott, did not arise from differences in the original Hebrew text but were either deliberate alterations by translators for pur-

24. Cf. also Elias Auerbach, *Wüste und Gelobtes Land*, Vols. I (1932) and II (1936).

poses of explanation or were due to negligence of copyists. The Samaritans, he claims in his work on the Samaritan Pentateuch, deliberately altered the text (this has been challenged) to suit their own purposes, frequently following Jewish explanations. Changes are sometimes the result of differing grammatical usages of Hebrew which were adopted by the Samaritans or of their way of writing words. In his *Peshitta* he continues along these lines and makes many pertinent observations and discoveries. His *Untersuchungen zur Septuaguinta* rejects Wutz's theory of a Hebrew text written in Greek characters and finds other explanations for variants from the original. He has also shown in *The Septuagint References in Mandelkern's Concordance* (1943) the unreliability of the latter in a great many of its references to the LXX. Joseph Reider, in his *Prologomena to a Greek-Hebrew and a Hebrew-Greek Index to Aquila*, gives a list of the words involved and discusses Aquila's translations and transliterations. The greatest work in the area of Greek versions is Margolis' authoritative collation of *The Book of Joshua in Greek*, a masterpiece of its kind.

Moses Ginsburger began our period with his edition of *Das Fragmententhargum: T. Jerushalmi zum Pentateuch* (1899). Hayyim Heller's earliest work was in this very field. Sperber, cited above, has given us some Septuagint studies and has, ready to publish, a critical edition of the Targum in manuscript, of which very small samples have been printed. Pinhas Churgin, in the *Targum to the Prophets*, analyzes the "Jonathan" to the prophets and holds its authorship to be composite, as is that of Onkelos, and as having developed out of official synagogue translations used in public worship. Some of the "Jonathan" dates from a time prior to the destruction of the temple. The author has continued his studies in a Hebrew book on the *Targum of the Writings*.

A. E. Silverstone[25] defends a very interesting thesis anticipated by Meyer Friedman of the last century—that these two names, Aquila and Onkelos, represent the same person. He studies the literature and on the basis of internal and external evidence, in Targum, Septuagint, and Peshitta, arrives at his conclusion.

This paper cannot take into consideration the numerous arti-

25. *Aquila and Onkelos* (Manchester, Eng., 1931).

cles that have appeared in Jewish scientific journals in many languages or those in other periodicals or such as exist in yearbooks. I must, however, call attention to a new edition of the Hebrew Bible under the editorship of Cassuto, which is soon to be published by the Hebrew University—the first time in the history of printing that Jews are issuing their own classic.

Much could be added, and the author is aware of omissions. Jews are engaged in the fields of biblical research and the allied disciplines and, as always, are doing their part to make the Book understandable. Whether there are any trends here that are not observable in the Gentile world of scholarship is questionable. The Jew of tradition will seek to reconcile it with his scientific outlook. The Christian makes a similar reconciliation. If the Graf-Wellhausen hypothesis has been demolished by Jews, Gentiles also have been engaged in a similar enterprise. The canons of criticism as such should not be formulated to suit the religious proclivities of the investigator. Scientific method will always remain, and the results of this or that professor's or school's scrutiny will always be challenged; old theories go, new ones appear. There is no Jewish mode in archeology, philology, or history; nor yet a Christian one, despite Max Weber. There is, however, a Jewish understanding and sympathy both in regard to language and in regard to thought; for, even as Shakespeare is England's, so the Bible is ours. It has grandeur, originality, beauty, and worth, for it expresses the Jewish spirit; in it the soul of the Jew is made vocal. Therefore, for us at least, it never has been, nor can it ever be, superseded. By our nature, by its character, we understand it best, in the manner that the lover knows his beloved.

CHAPTER SIX

Current Trends in Catholic Biblical Research

JAMES HARREL COBB

Kansas Wesleyan University, Salina, Kansas

IN ORDER to define the current trends in Catholic biblical research, this paper will survey briefly the significant works of Catholic scholars since 1918, to discover the major areas of interest represented and to name those books which should prove the most serviceable both in introducing the student to the field and in providing a foundation for continued study.[1] Since the readers of this essay will be, in a large measure, liberal Protestant scholars, it seems advisable to put before the discussion of areas of interest a clear-cut statement of the factors which condition and, in fact, control the thought of the Catholic scholar when he interprets Scripture.

Catholic and liberal scholars hold widely divergent world views, which necessarily result in radical differences in both the method and the results of interpretation. Liberal scholarship, as a whole, has adhered to a philosophical position which emphasizes cultural, social, and religious evolution in terms of various types of environment and in terms of natural causation and human motivation. Thus the liberal scholar regards the Bible as differing in no essential way from other literature. It was created, he maintains, by men; and it has been transmitted through men, subject at every stage to the limitations, prejudices, and even errors of its creators and custodians. Just like other litera-

---

1. The author acknowledges numerous courtesies, during the preparation of this paper, from the Rev. William A. Dowd, S.J., who called his attention to several books of merit but who is in no sense responsible for the development and interpretation of the subject as here presented.

116

ture, the Bible reflects the ideas, ideals, aspirations, customs, interests, and literary conventions of the periods in which its various parts were produced. Its real meaning can be ascertained only through a critical analysis of its form and content and by the proper placement of its several parts in the pattern of cultural development. Scholars who maintain that interest in the official organization of the church was a post-Pauline development must, of course, deny the traditional authorship of the Pastoral Epistles on the basis of the type of interests reflected in these writings. Moreover, the liberal scholar examines and evaluates biblical literature with more or less independence of creeds, dogmas, and traditions, either Jewish or Christian. It is this freedom, in fact, which constitutes the basis for objectivity. In most instances the liberal scholar has defined revelation, inspiration, and prophecy in such a way as to exclude supernatural contexts. Moreover, he has endeavored to minimize the miraculous by explaining the miracles in naturalistic and psychological terms or as the deposit of periods in which there was widespread, uncritical popular belief in the nature and character of supernatural activity in history.

The Catholic scholar, on the other hand, begins with Scripture and tradition, the total deposit of the faith as, and only as, this is officially interpreted by the living *magisterium* of the church. Thus he adheres to its dogmatic theology and to the special rulings of its constituted authorities. He participates as priest or layman in the devotional life of the church, which culminates in the Mass. He shares in the habits, attitudes, ideals, associations, and disciplines which, as an integrated pattern, constitute the Catholic way of life. The things which the church teaches, he holds to have been committed to it by the Lord Jesus Christ. The deposit of faith thus committed to the Apostles has been preserved in a pure, accurate, and complete form in the church. The constant and effective guidance of the Holy Spirit keeps the church from error in its interpretation in matters of faith and morals.

From the standpoint of method, the Catholic never begins his study of the Christian movement with an analysis of contem-

porary religious life or with a survey of culture patterns and their interaction. He does not start with philosophical theories of the nature and significance of values, moral and spiritual. He begins with the teachings of the church. He cannot doubt the reliability of the channels by which the biblical literature has been transmitted, nor can he consider portions of it as mere myth, legend, fiction, symbol, etiological explanation, or apologetic. He cannot employ one portion of it to disprove the factual character of another portion. To illustrate, when accounts of a given event, such as the resurrection narratives, differ widely in detail, he must harmonize the records in such a way as to affirm both the truth of the detail and the truthfulness of the total story of which it is a part.

Of course, what is distinctively Catholic does not appear with equal prominence in every type of writing. Lexicographical and linguistic studies, works on archeology and biblical geography, frequently contain little or nothing that would seem strange to the liberal scholar. In contrast, when the Catholic writes about Jesus, messianic prophecy, and the doctrines expressed in the various New Testament books, he is controlled at every point by loyalty to the teaching church. Of course, Scripture is not for the Catholic the sole rule of faith. It is, in fact, a partial, insufficient, remote rule; what it teaches must be viewed in the context of the total defined doctrine, that is, the dogma of the church.

The Catholic scholar looks upon the Gospels as inspired in a supernatural, and not in just a literary, sense. They therefore constitute an accurate, dependable, objective report of events as these occurred, either as they were viewed personally by those who saw them or as they were learned from the eyewitnesses or other sources of unquestioned reliability. For example, the birth narratives must be interpreted to affirm the Virginity of Mary, both before and after the birth of Jesus, as well as the reality of the Incarnation. The resurrection narratives must be analyzed in such a way as to support belief in the physical resurrection. The Jesus of history and the Christ of faith are one to the Catholic, and the real Jesus is the Lord, God and Man, who is enshrined in the worship of the church. The Catholic places complete trust in

the historical reliability of the Fourth Gospel both as a record of facts and as a correct interpretation of them. Its theology, no less than its narrative, is held to be a true picture of the historic life of Jesus.

The classical summary of the teaching of the church against modernism is the Decree of the Holy Office *Lamentabili* (July 3, 1907). These principles should be supplemented, so far as biblical interpretation is concerned, by the replies of the Pontifical Biblical Commission. Among other things, Catholics reject the Graf-Wellhausen theory of the composition of the Pentateuch and all its variants. They reject the theory of a Second and Third Isaiah. The book, they hold, was the work of the pre-Exilic Judean prophet. Psalms cited in the Old and New Testaments as Davidic are considered to be written by King David himself. Catholics reject the theory that Mark is the first Gospel in point of time and a primary source for the parallel narratives in Matthew and Luke. The Book of Acts is held to be by Luke, the companion of Paul and the author of the Third Gospel. The Fourth Gospel and the three letters bearing the name of John are to be attributed to John the Apostle. The Pastoral Epistles must be attributed to Paul. These representative examples illustrate the trend: Catholic biblical scholarship supports views radically at variance with those which have become axiomatic with liberals.

Tradition, dogma, and general agreement among Catholic scholars define the path along which the Catholic travels. Equally important is the fact that the Catholic biblical scholar, as priest or layman, is a devout participant in the worship of the church. Consequently, Jesus is always the object of divine worship—the Redeemer, Savior, and Lord. In his presence anything less than adoration and reverential commitment is insufficient. For the Catholic scholar the teaching of the church in its totality faithfully adhered to is a prerequisite for an accurate, well-proportioned view of biblical literature and its cultural significance.

The studies in biblical literature produced by Catholic scholars may be classified conveniently into eight areas: biblical introduction and journals, biblical backgrounds (archeology, geography, history, and culture), collective commentaries, Old Testament

commentaries, New Testament commentaries, Jesus, Paul, and translations and language studies.

The place to begin any study of Catholic biblical scholarship is John E. Steinmueller's *A Companion to Scripture Studies* (3 vols.; New York, 1941–43). These volumes are organized like the long-standard two-volume work of Rudolf Cornely, revised by August Merk, *Introductionis in Sacrae Scripturae libros compendium* (2 vols.; Paris, 1934). The first volume of the English work is devoted to a general introduction to the problems of biblical study. The major topics are canon, texts, versions, and principles of interpretation. The second and third volumes deal, respectively, with the Old and the New Testaments. In their proper places the texts of the decisions of the Pontifical Biblical Commission are given. There are lengthy bibliographies which list books by both Catholic and Protestant scholars. The discussions of the individual books indicate the divergent views held by Catholic scholars in areas open to debate. The views of liberal scholars are stated succinctly and criticized in terms of the interpretative norms of the Catholic church. A very compact introduction and concise commentary, replete with details, is the revision of R. P. Hadriano Simón's *Praelectiones biblicae ad usum scholarum* by Johannes Prado; three volumes appeared in 1942 and 1943.

There are several journals of exceptional value for keeping abreast of the current activities of Catholic scholars. For English readers the best single periodical is the *Catholic Biblical Quarterly* (1939———), published by the Catholic Biblical Association of America. An especially valuable feature of this publication is its survey of articles in other learned journals, both Catholic and Protestant. Because of the organic relationship which exists between the theological disciplines and biblical study, it is important to follow *Theological Studies* (1940———), published by the Theological Faculties of the Society of Jesus in the United States. Scarcely an issue appears without a review of some book on biblical interpretation. The *Revue biblique* (1915———) reflects the best Catholic scholarship of France; the superlative materials in this journal must never be neglected by any serious investigator. Of equal significance are the articles produced by members

of the Pontifical Biblical Institute and other scholars appearing in *Biblica* (1920——). The annual bibliographies in this journal are especially worthy of attention. The same institute publishes the *Verbum Domini* (1921——), which seeks to interpret the Bible for priests. (*Verbum Domini* has suspended publication temporarily.) It is scholarly in content but nontechnical in presentation. The standard text on the doctrine of inspiration is Christian Pesch's *De inspiratione Sacrae Scripturae* (Freiburg, 1925–26).

The liberal and the Catholic scholar are closest together in viewpoint when the Catholic writes on geography, the secular historical background of the Bible and the biblical languages. Félix Marie Abel's *Géographie de la Palestine* (2 vols.; Paris, 1933–38) is the most comprehensive scholarly work on its subject in any language. The first volume treats physical and historical geography. The second deals with political geography; the material on specific sites appears in dictionary form in the rear of the second volume. Much material of interest is presented in Barnabas Meistermann's *Guide to the Holy Land* (New York, 1923). The plans of ancient buildings are particularly valuable. Significant, too, are the writings of Hugues Vincent, in the later of which Father Abel collaborated. From Vincent's pen there are studies on Jerusalem (1912, 1926), Hebron (1923), and Emmaus (1932).

Giuseppe Ricciotti in his *Storia d'Israele* (1932–34) ably summarizes the history of Israel from the earliest times down to the last revolt (A.D. 132–35). An English translation is soon to appear.

Dr. Joseph Felten's *Neutestamentliche Zeitgeschichte* (2 vols.; Regensburg, 1925) is a remarkably comprehensive and well-documented study. The first volume deals with the political and social relationships of the Jewish people in New Testament times, while the second volume treats the theological views of the Jews and the total picture of pagan life in this period. The latter occupies two-thirds of the second volume. Compact but well-documented is André Marie Jean Festugière and Pierre Fabre's *Le Monde greco-romain au temps de Notre Seigneur* (2 vols.; Paris, 1935). These volumes are the best introduction to the cultural

backgrounds of early Christianity in any language. Festugière has dealt with the Greek world particularly in *L'Idéal religieux des grecs et l'évangile* (Paris, 1932). Two books are especially complete on the Jewish background: Joseph Bonsirven's *Le Judaïsme palestinien au temps de Jésus-Christ* (2 vols.; Paris, 1935) and Marie-Joseph Lagrange's *Le Judaïsme avant Jésus-Christ* (Paris, 1931). Practically the complete corpus of intertestamental literature with compact notes appears in P. Riessler's *Altjüdisches Schrifttum ausserhalb der Bibel übersetzt und erläutert*, which was published in 1928. While still a Dominican, Augustin Georges Barrois wrote his compact *Précis d'archéologie biblique* (Paris, 1935) and the relatively full *Manuel d'archéologie biblique* (Paris, 1939).

The major collective commentaries present some of the best work of Catholic scholarship. In Latin the most significant of these is the *Cursus Scripturae Sacrae* (Paris, 1908–38). The German *Die Heilige Schrift des Alten Testamentes* (Bonn, 1932——), edited by F. Feldmann and H. Herkenne, and *Die Heilige Schrift des Neuen Testamentes* (Bonn, 1932——) edited by F. Tillmann, are wholly interwar projects. The French "Études bibliques" (Paris, 1903——) include critical commentaries on both Testaments. In this series appear the excellent commentaries on the Gospels by Père Lagrange. As Dr. Robert Pierce Casey has remarked: "His commentaries combine philological competence in both the Greek and Semitic fields which is almost unparalleled among his contemporaries. His intimate acquaintance with Palestinian ways and places, owing to his long residence there, is also a striking advantage in his work." A very compact collective commentary by a single scholar is Hugh Pope's *The Catholic Students' Aids to the Study of the Bible* (5 vols.; London, 1926).

Catholic and liberal scholarship represent as widely divergent types in the field of the Old Testament as in that of the New. The differences are most comprehensively treated in Joseph Coppens' *The Old Testament and the Critics* (Paterson, N.J., 1942). Augustinus Bea's *De Pentateucho* (Rome, 1928) covers exceptionally well its limited field. The best sources for materials on Old Testament interpretation are the collective commentaries just mentioned. Two areas have had special attention: Psalms and the prophets.

There are three recent commentaries on the Psalms—Patrick Boylan's *The Psalms* (2 vols.; Dublin, 1926–31), Thomas E. Bird's *A Commentary on the Psalms* (2 vols.; London, 1926–27), and Cuthbert Lattey's *The First Book of Psalms* (*I–XLI*) (London, 1939). The prophetic literature has been treated as a whole in E. Tobac's *Les Prophètes d'Israel*, which should be consulted in the edition by Joseph Coppens (Malines, 1932). Because of its importance as a major source of messianic prophecy, as well as for its general religious merits, the writing of Isaiah has received much attention. One of the ablest of the critical Catholic commentaries on the prophet is that by Edward J. Kissane, *The Book of Isaiah* (2 vols.; Dublin, 1943). He has also issued an excellent commentary on the Book of Job (New York, 1946).

There are three compact summaries of Catholic thought on the New Testament. Cuthbert Lattey's *The New Testament* (London, 1939) and Hugh Pope's *Layman's New Testament* (New York, 1934) represent the work of single scholars. The special feature of Father Pope's work is the fact that the text appears on the left-hand page and the comments on the right. More recent is the publication by the scholars belonging to the Catholic Biblical Association, *A Commentary on the New Testament* (New York, 1942). The collective commentaries previously mentioned ought not to be neglected. On the Synoptic Gospels there is an excellent study by John Chapman, *Matthew, Mark, and Luke* (London, 1937), while on all the Gospels there is the study by Charles J. Callan, *The Four Gospels* (New York, 1942). Robert Ormston Eaton has been a prolific writer on biblical interpretation. He wrote on *Mark* (1920), *Colossians and Philemon* (1934), *Thessalonians* (1939), *The Catholic Epistles* (1937), and the *Apocalypse* (1930). Patrick Boylan produced a commentary on *Romans* (1934) and Cuthbert Lattey one on *First Corinthians* (1928). Joseph MacRory covered the whole Corinthian correspondence in his *Epistles of St. Paul to the Corinthians* (Dublin, 1935).

Because of the importance of patristic thought in the interpretation of the Bible, it is well for the student to have at hand a good history of the field. For completeness the best is Otto Bardenhewer's *Geschichte der altkirchlichen Literatur* (5 vols.; Freiburg,

1913–32). Good single-volume treatments are Joseph Tixeront's *A Handbook of Patrology* (St. Louis, 1920) and Fulbert Cayré's *Manual of Patrology* (Tournai, 1936). The latter is the best single-volume treatment of the subject in existence. The history of the period is concisely presented in the first volume of Philip Hughes's *A History of the Church* (New York, 1934).

Continental and English Catholic scholarship has been especially active in producing lives of Jesus. Some of these have as their specific aim the criticism of liberal scholarship. Typical of this class are Hilarin Felder's *Christ and the Critics* (2 vols.; London, 1924) and Léonce de Grandmaison's *Jesus Christ: His Person, His Message, His Credentials* (3 vols.; New York, 1930–34). An ideal introduction to Catholic thought on Jesus is Marie-Joseph Lagrange's *The Gospel of Jesus Christ* (2 vols.; New York, 1938–39). This author had also previously produced massive, critical commentaries on each of the Gospels, as well as a synopsis. The merit in this study lies in the fact that the entire procedure of Catholic scholarship is carried out with singular lucidity and with a minimum of polemic. Of course, Jesus is presented as the person defined in the creeds, and all the Four Gospels are drawn upon as historically reliable. Perhaps the greatest life composed between the wars was that by Louis Claude Fillion, *The Life of Christ* (3 vols.; St. Louis, 1928–29). This work covers background, the life itself, and, in a series of appendixes, the Catholic case against the conclusions of liberal scholars. Because of its size and the extensive scholarship of the author, this life is the most complete statement of all aspects of Catholic thought on the mission and message of Jesus. There is particular emphasis on the teaching of Jesus by a scholar well-versed in early Christian thought in Jules Lebreton's *The Life and Teaching of Jesus Christ Our Lord* (2 vols.; London, 1934). Two lives emphasize the human life of Jesus as lived in a specific historical context—Alban Goodier's *The Public Life of Our Lord* (2 vols.; London, 1930) and Franz Michel Willam's *The Life of Jesus Christ* (St. Louis, 1936). Ferdinand Prat has produced a very incisive study of Jesus in his *Jésus-Christ, sa vie, sa doctrine, son œuvre* (Paris, 1933).

The Catholic and liberal views on the person of Jesus and the

historicity of the primary sources diverge at so many points and so completely that it is difficult to find common ground. On the other hand, in the area of Pauline study there is much in the Catholic field with which the liberal scholar will agree. The principal divergences are two. The Catholic accepts the historicity of Acts and a Pauline corpus which includes Ephesians, the Pastorals, and Hebrews. Second, the Catholic will vigorously object to attributing distinctive Pauline ideas to pagan sources. There are two monumental studies of Pauline thought by Jesuits. First, there is F. Prat's *Theology of St. Paul* (2 vols.; New York, 1926–27; 2 vols.; London, 1933; also reprinted with special emendations: 2 vols.; Westminster, Md., 1946); the work had gone through nineteen French editions up to 1939. The text presents both a life and an analysis of Pauline thought. The author has read widely and with discrimination in patristic and medieval sources; and, so far as Continental scholarship is concerned, he appears to have read, digested, and evaluated everything of worth in the modern literature. He writes with lucidity and candor. Less well known but equally solid as a work of scholarship is Lino Murillo's *Paulus et Pauli scripta* (Rome, 1926). Only the first volume of this study has appeared; but this volume contains the biography and a systematic topical analysis of Pauline theology. Especially valuable are the sections which deal with Paul's conceptions of Judaism and his relationship to Judaism both before and after his experience on the road to Damascus. William J. McGarry's *Paul and the Crucified* (New York, 1940) might well bear his own subtitle "St. Paul's Theology of the Cross." The work makes no pretense to completeness, and it presupposes acquaintance with Catholic thought, but the matters which it discusses are handled brilliantly. Rudolph G. Bandas, who spent six years of research in preparing his doctoral dissertation, *The Master Idea of St. Paul's Epistles* (Bruges, 1925), interpreted his task as the presentation of the whole of Pauline thought. Charles J. Callan has produced a commentary on the traditional Pauline corpus in *The Epistles of St. Paul* (2 vols.; New York, 1922, 1931). For the general reader, Joseph Holzner's *Paul of Tarsus* (New York, 1944) is a vividly written introduction.

The period between the wars has been characterized by great activity on the part of Catholic scholars engaged in preparing modern-speech translations on the basis of a conservative text. These translations fall into two groups: those based upon the Greek and Hebrew originals and those based upon the Latin. The fact that the Latin text is the text of Catholic scholarship means that it is always an influence to be reckoned with. Two translations seek to present the New Testament in modern, lucid, dignified English without undue experimentation in new and radical patterns. The first of these is the *Westminister Version of the Sacred Scriptures* (4 vols.; 2d ed.; London, 1927–38), edited by Cuthbert Lattey and Joseph Keating. It is paralleled by the work of an American, Francis Aloysius Spencer (d. 1913). Though the text of his New Testament was prepared prior to the first World War, it did not appear, with notes and headings from other hands, until 1937. In contrast to the relative conservatism of these translations is the freedom to follow new patterns, to use vivid and popular diction, and to interpret freely the meaning of Greek particles, as found in James A. Kleist's *Memoirs of St. Peter* (Milwaukee, 1932), a translation of Mark. The text is printed in sense-lines; and the notes, both factual and interpretative, are placed in the rear of the volume. Father Kleist is at work on other translations, notably one of Luke.

Two distinguished renderings from the Vulgate have appeared recently. The American translation was produced by a committee of scholars under the patronage of the Episcopal Committee of the Confraternity of Christian Doctrine. This version appeared in 1941. The Old Testament version will be translated from the Hebrew, Aramaic, and Greek and will be accompanied, like the New, by a compact commentary. In England, Ronald Knox prepared a translation of the New Testament, which appeared in 1944. He has paid special attention to the qualities of English style. He handles the problems of Latin translation with the deftness of a man who has enjoyed from youth the disciplines of classical education.

The Latin version of the Psalms, which has been in use since 1570, has occasioned difficulties because of obscurities in the

translation. The groundwork for a change was laid by Francisco Zorell in his *Psalterium ex Hebraeo Latinum* (Rome, 1928). In 1945 there appeared, with authorization for use in the Office by Pope Pius XII, the *Liber Psalmorum cum canticis breviarii Romani*, produced by a committee of scholars. One of these, Augustinus Bea, wrote about the methods employed in its production and the principles followed in the *Catholic Biblical Quarterly* for January, 1946. The Latin edition contains both critical and historical notes, which enable the student to see in detail the exact procedure followed.

Francisco Zorell has prepared two massive lexicons: a *Lexicon Graecum Novi Testamenti* (Paris, 1931) and a *Lexicon Hebraicum et Aramaicum Veteris Testamenti* (Rome, 1940———). These treat the biblical languages both linguistically and theologically. The treatment is such that the student can see where the theological interpretation begins. Incidentally, the volumes are a mine of information for the theological usage of terms and are of extremely high quality as language tools. There are two important Greek-Latin critical editions of the New Testament. The most complete of these manual editions is the second, by August Merk, *Novum Testamentum, Graece et Latine* (Rome, 1942). More compact is Joseph Maria Bover's *Novi Testamenti biblia, Graeca et Latina* (Madrid, 1943). Félix Marie Abel has composed an excellent advanced grammar, *Grammaire du grec biblique* (Paris, 1933). This volume surveys comprehensively the language of the New Testament in relation to the Koiné of the papyri. One of the most exhaustive language studies is that of Paul F. Regard, a student of Antoine Meillet, entitled *Contribution à l'étude des prépositions dans la langue du Nouveau Testament* (Paris, 1919).

Beginners in the area of textual criticism will find no better introduction than Léon Vaganay's *An Introduction to the Textual Criticism of the New Testament* (London, 1937).

During the period between the wars, Catholic scholarship was active in every area of biblical study; the present scanty survey gives no idea of the voluminous production of advanced and highly technical studies. Books designed for the general reader have made much of this material available for the layman. Apart

from the Psalms, more attention has been paid to the New Testament than to the Old. The Catholic interpretation of Jesus has been elaborately worked out in studies not likely to be superseded in this generation. The same may be said of studies on Paul and his place in Christian thought. Catholic interest in, and facilities for producing, studies in Palestinian geography, archeology, and culture will no doubt contribute to much valuable work in this field. Linguistic studies will be pursued with thoroughness. It is to be hoped that Catholic scholars will prepare a critical edition of the Peshitta, for example. There will be in all fields erudite technical works, and these will be mediated to the general public in appropriate, dignified, and scholarly popularizations. Catholic scholar and layman alike are traditionalists and conservatives. There is a unity of thought and viewpoint in the church. From the child's catechism to the most erudite theological tractate, that unity is produced by dogma in the field of thought, by the sacraments in the field of worship, by the ideal of sanctity in the field of ethics, and by countless habits of piety, shared by rich and poor, by learned and unschooled alike, in everyday life. Everything in the Catholic church is designed to emphasize and impress upon the minds of men one single, dominant idea: Jesus Christ is Lord and Savior, Son of the Living God, God made manifest in human flesh, God granting, with infinite compassion, faith and grace to those who trust him and obey him. This religious response to a person, possessing both divine and human natures, is the dynamic center of Catholic faith, its organizing principle, the heart and lifeblood of Catholicity. Scripture study, learned and scholarly, becomes an act of worship the moment the Gospel is discussed. The Jesus of history and the Christ of faith are one in the mind of Catholicism.

CHAPTER SEVEN

The Status and Prospects of Research concerning the Psalms

OVID R. SELLERS

McCormick Theological Seminary, Chicago

IN SOME ways the Book of Psalms may well be considered the most important portion of the Old Testament. While the critical study of it has not stirred up much controversy, as has the analysis of the Pentateuch or the division of Isaiah into sections, it has been read more frequently than any of the other books. This is partly because of the beauty of the Psalms and partly because they are the most available. In many pocket editions of the New Testament the Psalms are included. The member of the armed forces who carries with him the Testament which he has received as a gift from his church or from the American Bible Society can easily turn to a Psalm. Moreover, excerpts from the Psalms are printed in many hymnals, and the custom of reading responsively from the Psalter has increased in churches during recent years. So the person who participates in any Christian or Jewish activities is almost certain to gain at least a little familiarity with some of the Psalms.

Scholarly research has had little to do with the general attitude of reverent church attendants or of casual readers toward the Psalter. The great majority of people who receive comfort, consolation, encouragement, and aesthetic pleasure from reading the Psalms have no concern at all with research. In most of our churches the questions which have engaged scholars are ignored. Even in some sophisticated congregations the Davidic authorship of at least those Psalms which bear his name in the titles is taken for granted, and the people piously repeat their parts of

the responsive reading with little or no thought of what the words meant to the one who composed them or what significance they might have for life today. The readers sense in Psalm 23 a message of assurance; in Psalms 8 and 24 they feel an awe for the mighty works of God as revealed in nature; Psalm 51 they repeat as a confession of sin; but, if they wonder about its significance, they see from the title that David wrote it after being rebuked by Nathan for his sin with Bath-sheba. They may have repeated Psalm 91 when their sons and brothers were going to war and wondered if the psalmist was not exaggerating a bit when he said, "A thousand shall fall at thy side and ten thousand at thy right hand; but it shall not come nigh thee." They like to repeat the refrain in Psalm 136, "for his mercy endureth forever"; but probably they know only about the portions which are printed in the hymnal, leaving out such harsh verses as, "To him that smote Egypt in their firstborn: for his mercy endureth forever," and "To him which smote great kings: for his mercy endureth forever." They may have repeated or sung the part of Psalm 137 which deals with sitting by the rivers of Babylon and hanging harps on the willows; but the anthem or the Psalter passage based on this Psalm will omit the last verse about taking and dashing the little ones against the stones.

We can say confidently that research has had little effect on the use of the Psalms by the general Christian and Jewish public. In fact, some mistranslations that were pointed out generations ago still persist as they have become set in the English language. For instance, "the beauty of holiness"[1] is a phrase often repeated in sermon and in prayer. For a long time scholars have known that the expression does not represent the Hebrew *haḏraṯ-qōḏĕš*, which is better translated "holy array" in the American Standard Version and the Chicago Bible, "festal attire" by Moffatt, and *"heiligem Schmuck"* by Martin Luther; but "beauty of holiness" is such an attractive phrase that it bids fair to remain in the English language.

Likewise, there remains the question, "If the foundations be destroyed, what can the righteous do?"[2] The verb *pāʿal* is in the

1. Ps. 29:2; 96:9; I Chron. 16:29; II Chron. 20:21.   2. Ps. 11:3.

perfect, however, and so is better translated by a past. Thus it is in the Chicago Bible, "what has the righteous done?" and in *Die Schriften des Alten Testaments*,[3] "*was hat der Fromme geschafft?*" For a long time, however, we may expect to hear sermons from the text, "What can the righteous do?"

I

Though the extensive amount of research done on the Psalms has had little effect in the popular conception of the poems, it has caused a great deal of academic discussion. There is scarcely an Old Testament scholar who has not published at least an article about some aspect of the Psalms.

One of the first fields to arouse speculation concerned the historical settings of the separate compositions. Certain Psalms were assigned to historical situations in the life of David (e.g., Nos. 51, 52, 54, 56, 57, 59, 60). This urge to define the historical settings was early; for we find the titles reproduced in the Septuagint, though with considerable variation. By the fourth century A.D. there had been developed a more critical attitude on the part of advanced scholars. Theodore of Mopsuestia questioned the authenticity of the titles and, though he would not repudiate the Davidic authorship, said that various Psalms referred to historical events long after the time of David, even down to the Maccabean period.

With the rise of the critical school in Germany and its emphasis on history, there came naturally the desire to fix every Psalm in its historical environment. This desire spread over the Continent, to England, and to America. Commentaries which appeared in the nineteenth century and through the first three decades of the twentieth devoted a great deal of attention to questions of date and authorship, and scholars with amazing confidence and even more amazing diversity of opinion would assign the separate Psalms to exact periods of history. Besides the commentaries, there have been innumerable attacks on individual Psalms, as a casual glance through any of the European or Ameri-

3. Abteilung 1, Band 2, verbesserte und vermehrte Aufl., von D. Dr. W. Staerk (Göttingen, 1920).

can journals in the biblical field will show. Doctors' dissertations were written on separate Psalms, and many of them, through the influence of sponsoring professors, were published in periodicals.

Of the various criteria for dating individual Psalms there were four most cogent: theological conceptions, references to known events or conditions, language, and poetic form. Working on the Hegelian hypothesis of development, the school of Wellhausen and his followers could place a Psalm at the period when its idea of God corresponded with the idea supposed to be prevalent in Israel at that time. For instance, Psalm 50, with its idea of the immanence of God and of his concern for ethical conduct above sacrifice, reminds us of the eighth-century prophets. Hence it is easy to place its date in the late eighth or early seventh century.[4] Likewise, any Psalm which seemed to express a high ethical monotheism was to be dated after Second Isaiah, who was supposed to be the first prophet in Israel to attain such a lofty concept. Psalm 23 was considered impossible at the time of David because of its advanced theological content.

References to known events or conditions were much more reliable. A Psalm like 137, dealing with the Jews in the Exile, must have been written after the deportation, though there have been differences of opinion as to whether it was written by a poet in the Exile or by a later singer who was meditating on the Exile. From references to the Exile and to the fallen temple it is reasonably safe to assign some passages to the period when the temple was in ruins.

It is much more difficult to identify historical incidents to which there is allusion. Psalm 2 seems to be on the occasion of some coronation, and various commentators have referred it to different kings, from David to Aristobulus. Psalm 45 is called "a nuptial ode," and it clearly refers to some royal marriage, but scholars have varied widely in their attempts to identify the couple.

Language in some ways is of considerable help, though dependence on it can be overdone. In the course of time a great

4. So Davison, *The Psalms* ("The New Century Bible" [New York and Edinburgh, n.d.]), and Moses Buttenwieser, *The Psalms* (Chicago, 1938).

many old expressions doubtless were modernized in transmission, and, on the other hand, as in much poetry, there was a conscious archaizing. But, taken in connection with poetic form, language can be of some help in making plausible conjectures as to date. Poems which are almost certain to be early, such as the Song of Deborah[5] and David's lament over Saul and Jonathan,[6] are in what seems to be early language and are irregular according to all our metrical studies; while Psalms with definitely late vocabulary are likely to be regular, some of them using the artificial device of the acrostic.[7] One criterion accepted by many scholars today concerns the personality of the speaker. If the Psalm speaks for the nation, it is presumably early; if it is individualistic, it is considered late. At the turn of the century there was a strong tendency to consider all the Psalms communal. That is, when the Psalmist said "I," he was supposed to mean "we"; when he said "my," he was supposed to mean "our"; when he said "me," he was supposed to mean "us." We were told that the Israelite seldom considered himself as an individual, that his only conception of immortality was the survival of the nation. So, presumably, the Psalms expressed the feelings not of the individual but of the people. A few Psalms, such as 38, were too definite in their personal implications to be assigned to the whole nation; but most of the hymns could be applied to the community. Since World War I, however, there has been growing the conviction that many of the Psalms were written to be used by individuals. John P. Peters[8] in an original study held that many of the Psalms were used for liturgical purposes, some by groups and others by individuals in the offering of gifts and prayers at the temple. S. Mowinckel[9] also presented the theory that many of the Psalms were used in pre-Exilic celebrations in the temple. While no other scholar has followed Peters or Mowinckel completely, they were influential in curbing the tendency to date all the Psalms in late post-Exilic days. Moreover, they both gave good evidence that some of the Psalms were for individual application. H. Gun-

---

5. Judges, chap. 5.

6. II Kings 1:19-27.

7. E.g., Pss. 111, 112, 119, 145.

8. *The Psalms as Liturgies* (New York, 1922).

9. *Psalmenstudien* (Christiania, 1921–24).

kel[10] also proposed to take many of the Psalms as pre-Exilic, some of them going back to the period of the judges and others showing a high degree of development typical of the eighth century.

Even after all the efforts of erudite scholars to establish general principles for dating the Psalms, we cannot claim very much in the way of positive results. There is scarcely a Psalm which can claim anything like general agreement as to its date. Buttenwieser's commentary marks a high point of assurance in this field. He arranges the entire Psalter in a chronological scheme, ranging from the premonarchical period to the Hellenistic. A large section he assigns to the crisis when the Persian army overran Palestine in 344 B.C. Even the Psalms which are "of uncertain date" he divides into pre-Exilic and post-Exilic. The latest commentary,[11] excellent in most respects, still makes valiant attempts to assign dates; but, though the author is less dogmatic than Buttenwieser, he is not more convincing than his predecessors. As an example of what may be done when the only evidence is internal, we may take Psalm 18. Davison says: "If there is any Davidic Psalm in the Psalter, this is one." Buttenwieser with equal certainty dates it in the time of Artaxerxes II Mnemon. Oesterley, while admitting the possibility of Davidic elements, dates the Psalm in its present form as late pre-Exilic. With such disagreement on the part of experts, we must admit that little progress has been made in the dating of individual Psalms since the Greek Fathers began to question the Davidic authorship.

II

More tangible results have come from the study of metric forms in the Psalms. We have no rules of versification from the Israelites, but we may be certain that there were principles which the poets of the Old Testament observed. Through the centuries of the Christian era there have been writers, such as Philo and Jerome, who felt that the Psalms were poetic; but the first known attempt to formulate rules for Hebrew verse was by Robert Lowth in 1753. He pointed out three kinds of parallel-

10. H. Gunkel and J. Begrich, *Einleitung in die Psalmen* (2 vols.; Göttingen, 1928, 1933).

11. W. O. E. Oesterley, *The Psalms* (2 vols.; London, 1939).

ism: synonymous, antithetic, and synthetic. Thus he covered the field; for any kind of sentence could be arranged in synthetic parallelism. His observations were sound and still are used as the starting-point for any study of Hebrew meter.[12] Edouard Sievers, a competent classical scholar, spent a good deal of energy in applying the canons of Greek and Latin poetry to the Hebrew.[13] Generally he was followed in the early days of this century; largely under the influence of his studies, though disagreeing in detail, Briggs wrote his commentary.[14] Later study, however, has shown that Hebrew meter is quite different from the classical. The basic difference is in the verse. In classical poetry, as in English hymns, the number of syllables in a foot, or in a verse, is important. In Hebrew it is only the number of beats in a line which counts.

While there are some differences of opinion as to detail, there has come fairly general agreement among scholars as to the first principles of Hebrew versification:

1. The verse (line) is the unit, and it is divided into two parts (occasionally three). The whole line is called a "stich" and the two parts "hemistichs"; or each of the parts may be called a "stich" and the whole line a "distich" (or, where there are three parts, a "tristich"). Scholars vary in their use of these terms.

2. The lines which exist in sufficient quantities to be easily recognized are the 3 + 3 (the most common), the 3 + 2 (so-called "Qina" because it prevails in the Book of Lamentations), and the 2 + 2 (not so common, but frequently used to denote excitement or tense emotion). There seem to be a few passages of 4 + 3, which correspond to the common meter in English

12. There have been published several good treatments of Hebrew versification in recent years. Among them are Oesterley, *op. cit.*, pp. 20–23; C. C. Torrey, *The Second Isaiah* (New York, 1928), pp. 151–82; Cyrus H. Gordon, *Ugaritic Grammar* (Rome, 1940); John H. Patton, *Canaanite Parallels to the Psalms* (Baltimore, 1943); Charles Franklin Kraft, *The Strophic Structure of Hebrew Poetry* (Chicago, 1938).

13. *Studien zur hebräischen Metrik* (Leipzig, 1901).

14. Charles Augustus Briggs and Emelie Grace Briggs, *A Critical and Exegetical Commentary on the Book of Psalms* ("The International Critical Commentary" [2 vols.; New York, 1906, 1907]).

hymnology; but there still is some question as to whether the number of lines in this pattern is sufficient to establish it as an accepted form.

3. The lines may be joined in couplets (as in Ps. 121) or in triplets (as in Ps. 23). There are clearly some longer strophes. For example, in Psalm 119, the great acrostic, under each letter of the alphabet there are eight verses, or four couplets. As yet, however, there has been no successful attempt to show any rules about long stanzas or anything like the sonnet.

These principles have been remarkably confirmed by the Ugaritic, or Ras Shamra, alphabetic cuneiform tablets.[15] And the Ugaritic poetry has also proved that chiasmus and definite schemes for building up the sentence were well known in pre-Israelite Canaan.[16] An example of chiasmus is in Ps. 2:1:

> *Lammâ rāḡĕšû gôyîm   u-l'ummîm yehgû rîq?*
> Why rage nations   and peoples meditate emptiness?

There is in the first hemistich the order of verb and subject, and in the second hemistich, subject and verb. Many such lines may be found in the Psalms; often in the English translation the chiasmus is lost.

Another pattern found repeatedly in the Psalms and also in Ugaritic is the so-called "abc," "abd," an example of which is Ps. 67:4 repeated in verse 6:

> *Yôdûḵā ꜥammîm Ĕlôhîm   yôdûḵā ꜥammîm kullâm.*
> Praise thee peoples, O God;   praise thee peoples, all of them.[17]

Studies in the poetic principles of the Psalms have, then, yielded some definite results. One principle has to do with rhythm and the other with the order of words or ideas. We know that the poet composed certain kinds of lines and that he could arrange his words for rhetorical effect.

15. James A. Montgomery, "Recent Developments in the Study of the Psalter," *Anglican Theological Review*, XVI (1934), 185–98; Gordon, *op. cit.*; Patton, *op. cit.*; H. L. Ginsberg, "Ugaritic Studies and the Bible," *Biblical Archaeologist*, Vol. VIII (May, 1945).

16. Nils W. Lund (*Chiasmus in the New Testament* [Chapel Hill, 1942]) points out a number of cases of chiasmus in the Psalms, some of them rather elaborate. While few scholars go all the way with Lund, most agree that he has demonstrated cases of undoubted chiasmus.

17. For other examples see Patton, *op. cit.*, pp. 8, 9.

Metrical reconstructions on the basis of these recognized principles have been greatly overdone, as is generally recognized today. Duhm, Budde, and Haupt would determine the pattern of a poem and make of it a Procrustean bed. If a line seemed too long, it was easy to discover which part was a gloss; if a line were too short, a word could be added. There is a good deal of such reconstruction of the text in nearly all modern commentaries, and, as in dating, there is great diversity of opinion as to which words should be deleted and what additions are necessary. There is no doubt that the Massoretic text is corrupt in many places; but attempts to restore the original text are often palpably subjective. On the other hand, many emendations proposed on the basis of meter are plausible and attractive.

III

Naturally, many students of the Psalms have discussed the religious or theological aspects. Montgomery[18] makes a distinction between religion and theology. Theology, he says, "is the property of a few elevated souls, like Aken-aten with his monotheism, or the Hebrew Prophets who seem to be separated from the people by a great gulf." The Psalms, like the hymns of the modern church, are the expressions of the poets, who can voice the yearnings and aspirations of the people, rather than the logical formulations of abstract thinkers. In the first three decades of this century, accordingly, there was more discussion of the religion of the Psalms than of their theology. A popular study along this line was that of the late J. M. Powis Smith.[19] Recent revival of interest in theology, however, has had its impact on the study of the Psalms. Oesterley has given the problem considerable attention.[20] So far, as would be expected, the study has been based largely on the theory of historical development. Thus a Psalm which was frankly anthropomorphic was considered as representing an early stage of theological development and was there-

18. *Op. cit.*, p. 193.

19. *Religion of the Psalms* (Chicago, 1922).

20. *A Fresh Approach to the Psalms* (New York, 1937), in which chaps. xii–xiv are devoted to theology. Chapter x of his commentary deals with the general subject, and in the study of individual Psalms the theological aspects receive attention.

fore given an early date, while a definitely monotheistic Psalm was considered post-Exilic.

There is, however, a growing recognition of the difficulty of dating the Psalms,[21] so that any study of development of religious ideas is precarious. In the first place, there always arises the question of whether the poet expects his words to be taken literally. For instance, in many Psalms God is pictured as having hands; but it would be absurd to date all these Psalms early because of the anthropomorphism.[22] It may be that the many anthropomorphisms of the Psalms reflect a primitive conception of the deity, who walked about on earth, held face-to-face conversations with men, and gave exhibitions of human emotion. It would be hazardous to say, however, which of the anthropomorphic expressions show the actual beliefs of the writers and which merely carry over the old verbiage. Many modern prayers, even in the most cultured churches, contain anthropomorphic and even theriomorphic expressions. We repeat the plea, "Hide me under the shadow of thy wings,"[23] and confidently we have said to our boys going to battle, "He shall cover thee with his feathers and under his wings shalt thou trust."[24] It is hardly likely that there ever was a general belief that Yahweh had wings and feathers; there is no evidence at all that this was an early conception which was outgrown in the religious development of Israel. One frequently quoted and often misunderstood theriomorphism is "the Sun of righteousness with healing in his wings."[25] This phrase refers to the Egyptian sun-god, pictured on countless monuments as the winged sun-disk.[26] It is hardly likely, however, that Malachi actually believed in the Egyptian sun-god.

Probably a great many Israelites, like many people today, thought of God in human form, with eyes, ears, and face.[27] But

21. As pointed out by Oesterley, *ibid.*, p. 206.

22. Ps. 119:73 has "Thy hands have made me and fashioned me." But clearly this Psalm, the great acrostic glorifying the legal aspect of the Yahweh religion, is late post-Exilic.

23. Ps. 17:8.   24. Ps. 91:4.   25. Mal. 4:2.

26. James H. Breasted, *The Dawn of Conscience* (New York, 1935).

27. Ps. 34:15, 16.

that the Psalmists who spoke of the parts of Yahweh's body actually believed that he had a human physical form does not follow. In fact, it is the poet's business, and always was, to stir the imagination, to produce an emotional response, and not to teach physiology. Many have pointed out the difficulty of saying anything about God without getting into anthromorphic phraseology; when we use the pronoun "he" in referring to deity, we are out of the purely spiritual. So none of the attempts to trace the development of the idea of God from the theriomorphic and anthropomorphic to the incorporeal has carried much conviction.

There is similar frustration in trying to trace through the Psalms any development from polytheism to monotheism. There are some Psalms, it is true, which seem to picture Yahweh as one among other gods. He is said to be the greatest among the gods and the judge of the others; there are few passages proclaiming him as the sole God.[28] Oesterley has taken this scarcity of monotheistic dogma as another indication that more Psalms are pre-Exilic than were considered so by scholars of the preceding generation.[29] Even the post-Exilic poets, he believes, were slow to accept the monotheistic teaching of Deutero-Isaiah. On the other hand, it is not certain that the Psalmists who mention other gods believed in the reality of those gods any more than Milton and Dante believed in the actuality of all the pagan gods paraded through their poems. For instance, Psalm 82, which pictures God as standing in the congregation of the mighty and judging among the gods, may mean simply that God is judging human rulers, who considered themselves divine. In fact, we read in verse 7, "But ye shall die like men, and fall like one of the princes," which would indicate that those addressed were not gods but mortals. Likewise Ps. 86:8, "Among the gods there is none like unto thee," does not necessarily mean that the gods are real and that Yahweh is merely chief of the pantheon. It may mean that Yahweh is the only genuine God.

28. Psalm 115 contrasts the God of the Psalmist with the heathen gods, which are only idols, the work of men's hands. Ps. 86:10 is definitely monotheistic: "For thou art great, and doest wondrous things; thou art God alone."

29. *A Fresh Approach to the Psalms*, pp. 211–12.

As the Psalms fail to show any steady development in belief about God, they also have yielded scant results when scholars have tried to show in them a gradual development in the idea of immortality. There are some passages which seem to deny immortality and some which either take it for granted or declare it,[30] but no convincing attempt has been made to set these passages in a chronological order.

IV

In one aspect of the study of the Psalms, H. Gunkel has had a large influence in Europe and America. His work corresponded to what in New Testament circles is known as *Formgeschichte*. There had been previous classifications of Psalms, such as Baethgen's "sad, joyful, and restful"; but Gunkel's designation of types seems to have had greater influence and has been adopted by a good many other scholars. His types, as translated by Fleming James,[31] are: Hymns, Songs of Yahweh's Enthronement, Laments of the People, Royal Psalms, Laments of the Individual, Thanksgivings, and Wisdom Poetry. These designations show what were presumably the intentions of the authors as to the use to which the Psalms were to be put. The identification of the so-called "Enthronement Psalms" has called forth a large amount of discussion. The theory of the Enthronement Psalms rests on the supposition that at an annual feast, the New Year, the Israelites celebrated Yahweh's mounting the throne after the manner of early Egyptian kings. For the ceremony certain Psalms proclaiming "Yahweh is king" were used. Mowinckel went further than Gunkel in identifying these hymns; Oesterley, though more cautious than Mowinckel, accepts the principle, as does Fleming James. But, as James points out, the theory rests on "indirect evidence," and it has met with considerable opposition. For instance, Psalm 97, one of Gunkel's and Mowinckel's Enthronement Psalms, is taken by Oesterley and Adam C. Welch[32] as eschatological.

30. *Biblical Archaeologist*, VIII (February, 1945), 12–14.
31. *Thirty Psalmists* (New York, 1938), p. 9.
32. *The Psalter in Life, Worship, and History* (Oxford, 1926), p. 26.

V

From the standpoint of objective research the most tangible recent contributions have come from discoveries in comparative literature. Decipherment of the Babylonian cuneiform and the Egyptian hieroglyphic in the last century made available a large store of ancient oriental literature with many affinities to the Hebrew. Further research in these fields during the first third of the present century has shown a great many similarities between the Babylonian and Egyptian poems and the Hebrew Psalms, both in poetic form and in subject matter. Like the Hebrew, both Babylonian and Egyptian have the line consisting of two hemistichs. Particularly striking are the Babylonian penitential psalms and the Egyptian hymns to the sun-god.[33] Psalm 38 is very much like a poetic petition to Ishtar by one who is suffering bodily ill because of his sin. Psalm 104 has so much in common with Ikhnaton's hymn to Aten that some have thought there was direct influence.[34]

More pertinent than the Babylonian and Egyptian parallels, however, are those from the Ugaritic alphabetic cuneiform. The first decipherment of this material was scarcely more than fifteen years ago, and the most important studies have appeared only in the last decade. A great many of the texts still are obscure, and a large amount of work must be done before all the texts which have been discovered are understood. Among the scholars who have made significant contributions in this new field are Hans Bauer, E. Dhorme, W. F. Albright, U. Cassuto, René Dussaud, J. Obermann, A. Goetze, H. L. Ginsberg, Cyrus H. Gordon, T. H. Gaster, C. F. A. Schaeffer, C. Virolleaud, J. A. Montgomery, and Z. S. Harris.[35]

These scholars have shown that, for all practical purposes, the Ugaritic and the Hebrew may almost be considered one language. A great many of the thought-patterns of the Psalms, such as Yahweh's riding on the clouds, giving forth his voice as thunder from heaven, enduring from generation to generation, acting as father to the fatherless and judge of the widow, and crushing

33. Oesterley, *The Psalms*, pp. 34–43, 226.   34. Breasted, *op. cit.*, pp. 281–86.
35. There is a good bibliography in Patton's thesis (*op. cit.*).

sea monsters, are found in the Ugaritic. In view of the fact that the Ugaritic texts, coming from the fifteenth to the thirteenth centuries B.C., are considerably older than any of the biblical passages, it is evident that the Canaanite writers influenced the Hebrew Psalmists. Psalm 29 is clearly taken over from a Ugaritic poem to Baal, with Yahweh substituted for the Canaanite deity. Other Psalms which show particularly strong Canaanite influence are Nos. 18, 45, 68, 88, and 89. Patton has pointed out similarities to the Canaanite in one hundred and twenty of the Psalms. This does not mean that all the expressions cited were borrowed directly from the Ugaritic, but it shows that the older Canaanite thought-patterns persisted in Israelite times.

In none of the commentaries has this wealth of material now available from Ugaritic studies been utilized. Buttenwieser wrote his commentary before the material was well disseminated, and Oesterley has only a few brief allusions to Ras Shamra. Any future writer on the Psalms will have to familiarize himself with the Ugaritic hymns if he expects to make any impression on the scholars. The Ugaritic is of high importance in the study of the religion of the Psalms and in the corresponding lexicography. This is a rich field for a young scholar.

VI

Prospects for research concerning the Psalms are encouraging. There will be more work in the Ugaritic field, which has not yet reached the point of diminishing returns. There is still research to be done in the interpretation of texts already discovered, and there is the possibility of the discovery of new texts when excavation is resumed. Already the Ugaritic has shown that some of the Psalms must be dated much earlier than the times to which previously they had been assigned. New light will be thrown on many words and phrases, and it will be increasingly evident that the Psalms as we have them are not merely the hymnbook of the second temple.

Another aspect of the Psalms which probably will receive some attention is their merit as poetry. There have been many appreciations of the poetic excellence of the Psalms according

to the older conceptions. Poetry, as distinguished from mere verse, has been considered "the embodiment in appropriate language of beautiful or high thought, imagination, or emotion, the language being rhythmical, usually metrical, and characterized by harmonic and emotional qualities which appeal to and arouse the feelings and imagination."[36] According to this definition, most, if not all, of the Psalms are good poetry and as such have received wide acclamation. There have been, however, marked changes in the evaluation of poetry since the days of R. G. Moulton. In our day W. B. Yeats, Robert Frost, Carl Sandburg, and Archibald MacLeish have not written according to the old patterns, and yet they are accepted as poets of merit. The teachers of literature are formulating new standards in the evaluation of poetry.[37] It will be interesting if one of the rising schools of literary critics undertakes to investigate the poetic merit of the Psalms.

Undoubtedly, there will be in the next few years further studies of the theology of the Psalms. Old treatments purporting to show the steady development of theological ideas are outmoded. The new interest in theology stemming from Barth, Brunner, Niebuhr, and other representatives of the neo-orthodox movement has caught the attention of some of the leading young scholars in the Old Testament field. Frequently voiced in the past few years is the need of a biblical theology in English along the lines of Eichrodt's work in German.[38] There is so much about God, man, and salvation in the Psalms that we may feel certain that someone with the current urge will undertake a formulation of the theology contained in them.

Certainly, the Psalms will continue to be read and quoted by millions who will receive from them courage, cheer, comfort, and inspiration. They will also be the subject for research, and from this research we may expect increasing knowledge and understanding of an important portion of the Word of God.

36. *Webster's New International Dictionary*.

37. Cleanth Brooks, *Modern Poetry and the Tradition* (Chapel Hill, 1934).

38. To some extent this need has been met by Millar Burrows, *An Outline of Biblical Theology* (Philadelphia, 1946).

CHAPTER EIGHT

Current Progress and Problems in Septuagint Research

HARRY M. ORLINSKY
Jewish Institute of Religion, New York City

THE main purpose of this essay is to describe and analyze what has been done in Septuagint research in the past few decades and to outline the more important aspects of this discipline which demand attention in our own time.

THE RECOVERY OF THE ORIGINAL SEPTUAGINT TEXT

1. Far and away the greatest value of the Septuagint (LXX) is to be found in the data offered by this version for the Hebrew text with which the "Seventy-two" translators operated. However, before this Hebrew *Vorlage* can be recovered, it is first necessary to determine the original text of the LXX, the text which the translators brought into being (Proto-LXX). No one saw better than did Paul de Lagarde (1827–91) in the latter half of the nineteenth century the special problems and correct methodology pertaining to the recovery of the text of the Proto-LXX.[1] The work of Alfred Rahlfs (1866–1935), Lagarde's successor at Göttingen and for over a quarter of a century director of studies in the Septuagint at the Gesellschaft der Wissenschaften at Göttingen,[2] and that of James Alan Montgomery (1866–——), of the

---

1. Cf. A. Rahlfs's appraisal of *Paul de Lagardes wissenschaftliches Lebenswerk im Rahmen einer Geschichte seines Lebens dargestellt* ("Mitteilungen des Septuaginta Unternehmens," Vol. IV, No. 1 [Berlin, 1928]); G. Bertram, "Theologische Kritik und Textkritik bei Paul Anton de Lagarde," *Kirche im Angriff*, XIII (1937), 370–81. The new interest in Lagarde's religious *Anschauung* (the principles of German fascism were largely anticipated by Lagarde, and loved by him!) is indicated also by such an article as "Paul de Lagardes religiöse Entwicklung," by W. Hartmann, in *Theologische Blätter*, XX (1941), 334–41.

2. Someone should appraise the important studies of Rahlfs in some detail. In the meantime see "Alfred Rahlfs," by Walter Bauer, in *Nachrichten von der Gesellschaft der Wissen-*

University of Pennsylvania, advanced the problem nearer to solution.[3] The solution itself, in the most concrete manner, was offered by Max Leopold Margolis (1866–1932) of the Dropsie College.[4]

It may be worth while to describe here briefly the nature both of the problem and of the solution.

2. The textual critic finds himself in possession not of any one manuscript containing the original LXX translation of the Hebrew Bible, but of many Greek manuscripts, uncials and cursives, each one containing a text differing from the others to a greater or lesser extent. Furthermore, there are available to him scores of manuscripts of translations from the LXX into Latin (second century), Sahidic-Bohairic (second–third centuries), Armenian (fourth century), Gothic (ca. A.D. 350), Ethiopic (fourth–fifth centuries), Georgian (fourth?–fifth centuries), Arabic (seventh?–eighth centuries), and Slavonic (ninth–tenth centuries).[5] The critic thus finds himself confronted at once by the task of determining which manuscript or group of manuscripts, whether in Greek or in any of the languages enumerated just above, has preserved the original, or the nearest to the original, text of the LXX.

3. Margolis compared these secondary versions of the LXX with the many Greek manuscripts representing the LXX, and

---

schaften zu Göttingen, 1935, pp. 60–65; J. L. Seeligmann, "Problemen en Perspectieven in het moderne Septuaginta-Onderzoek," Jaarbericht No. 7 van het Voorariatisch-Egyptisch Gezelschap, Ex Oriente Lux, 1940, pp. 359–90e passim.

3. See especially Sec. III ("Ancient Versions," pp. 24–57) of the Introduction in Montgomery's International Critical Commentary on Daniel (New York, 1927), and the corresponding section in his forthcoming Kings in the same series.

4. The Book of Joshua in Greek (Paris, 1931——) (Parts I–IV cover 1:1—19:38), with which should be studied his "Specimen of a New Edition of the Greek Joshua," in Jewish Studies in Memory of Israel Abrahams (New York, 1927), pp. 307–23. For an analysis of the problem as a whole, cf. Orlinsky, On the Present State of Proto-LXX Studies ("American Oriental Society Offprint Series," No. 13 [New Haven, 1941]). An interesting sketch of Margolis' life and works was written by Alexander Marx for the Proceedings of the Rabbinical Assembly of America, IV (1933), 368–80 (reprinted in Alexander Marx, Studies in Jewish History and Booklore [New York, 1944], pp. 418–30).

5. For a graphic representation of these data see the chart in the Biblical Archaeologist, Vol. IX, No. 2 (May, 1946).

these same Greek manuscripts one with another and with the citations from these manuscripts and other pertinent material in the various editions of the *Onomasticon* of Eusebius and in the writings of such early authorities in the church as Justin, Origen, Eusebius, and Theodoret. Margolis chose the Book of Joshua of all the books in the Bible because it lent itself admirably to textual and exegetical analysis and—what is of supreme importance—because it contained hundreds of proper names whose *Überlieferungsgeschichte*, in context, could readily be traced. Margolis found:

The sum of the witnesses yields four principal recensions, PCSE, and in addition a number of MSS. variously mixed which I name M. At the outset it must be remarked that all of our witnesses are more or less mixed; the classification has in mind the basic character of a text, which alone is the determinant. P is the Palestinian recension spoken of by Jerome, that is the Eusebian edition of the Septuagint column in Origen's Hexapla-Tetrapla [then, as in the case of CSEM below, follows a sketch of the more important manuscripts which belong to this recension]. . . . . C is a recension which was at home in Constantinople and Asia Minor. We are helped in localizing the recension by the aid of the Armenian version. . . . . Whether the recension had any relationship to the fifty copies ordered by Constantine from Eusebius, as CONYBEARE suspects, must remain a matter of conjecture. Jerome says nothing of a fourth recension; but then he is by no means exact, or the recension was at his time just in the process of formation. . . . . S is the Syrian (Antiochan) recension. . . . . An outstanding characteristic of the S recension is the correction of the Greek style, as shown by the substitution of Attic grammatical forms for Hellenistic. . . . . The Egyptian recension, E, is preserved with relative purity in B [Codex Vaticanus]. . . . . The Coptic and Ethiopic versions unmistakably point to the Egyptian provenance of their text. Hence the designation of the recension [as Egyptian]. There remain a number of MSS. which may be classed together as M, i.e. mixed texts. Mixture is the general characteristic, the elements coming from the four principal recensions in diverse processes of contamination. . . . . The road to the original text of G [the LXX] leads across the common, unrevised text. In order to get at the latter, we must abstract from the recensional manipulations. . . . . A study of the translator's mannerism of rendition becomes imperative. . . . . The scope of my edition is to restore critically the original form of the version. I print the critically restored text at the top of the page. Below follow the forms assumed in the four classes, E, S, P, CM. Omis-

sions and contractions of the text, by which certain witnesses or groups of witnesses step out as silent on the textual form, receive a rubric of their own. Then follow individual variations of class members, such as leave the characteristic class reading undisturbed in its main features. Lastly marginal readings in so far as they have not been embodied above. . . . .[6]

4. What Margolis has done for Joshua needs to be done also for the other books of the Old Testament. Yet it is very doubtful that there will arise in the future other scholars of the quality of Margolis to perform this task. Consequently, our hopes and plans for the coming several decades must be modest.

a) There is a considerable amount of preliminary work to be done in the recovery of the Proto-LXX. This work revolves about the determination of the family relationship of the manuscripts containing the text of the LXX and of the secondary versions. It seems to the writer that a very acceptable sort of subject for a doctoral dissertation would be the analysis of, say, the Ethiopic or Arabic or Old Latin, etc., in relation to the manuscripts containing the LXX text, with a view to determining the recensional affinity of these data, viz., whether the recension be Syrian (Lucianic) or Palestinian (Origenian) or Egyptian (Hesychian) or Constantinopolitan. Thus a number of students of Montgomery's wrote such theses (Benjamin, Gehman, Haupert, Wyngaarden, Yerkes); and Gehman, in turn, has some of his students working on such topics.

b) In this connection it is important to make readily available

6. "Specimen of a New Edition of the Greek Joshua," pp. 308–16. It is of the greatest significance that Montgomery, working independently and on another book altogether, found the facts and interpretation in Joshua to hold true essentially also for Daniel (for the references, not only to Montgomery's work but also to the important work done by Henry S. Gehman, see n. 9 of the writer's work cited in n. 4 above). It should not go unnoted that, working on Joshua independently of Margolis, Otto Pretzl (1893–1941) came to the same conclusions with regard to the LXX manuscripts as Margolis did ("Die griechischen Handschriftengruppen im Buche Josue untersucht nach ihrer Eigenart und ihrem Verhältnis zueinander," *Biblica*, IX [1928], 377–427); for a sketch of Otto Pretzl, see A. Spitaler, *Zeitschrift der Deutschen morgenländischen Gesellschaft*, XCVI (1942), 161–70. "The List of Levitic Cities," by W. F. Albright (*Louis Ginzberg Jubilee Volume* [New York, 1945], English section, pp. 49–73; see esp. pp. 50–51 and n. 4), goes a very long way in demonstrating the correctness of Margolis' method. Cf. R. Marcus, "Jewish and Greek Elements in the Septuagint," *Louis Ginzberg Jubilee Volume*, English section, p. 227, n. 2; and Giovanni Cardinal Mercati, *Nuove note di letteratura biblica e cristiana antica* (Vatican City, 1946), chap. v.

both for the student who is working on such a project and for the general biblical scholar two kinds of data: (i) critical editions of the secondary versions, utilizing all the manuscripts still available even after the destruction wrought during World War II (this is an urgent desideratum for all the secondary versions of nearly every book in the Old Testament);[7] (ii) a critical apparatus containing the variants of all the LXX manuscripts of the Old Testament. From 1798 to 1827 the Oxford Press published, for the scholarly world, Holmes and Parsons' *Vetus Testamentum Graecum cum variis lectionibus*, still the greatest and, generally speaking, a reliable enough collection of variant readings of no less than three hundred and eleven LXX manuscripts and, in Latin dress, of some secondary versions: Old Latin, Coptic (Memphitic and Sahidic), Arabic, Slavonic, Armenian, and Georgian; and since 1906 the Cambridge Press has been making available Brooke and McLean's (and Thackeray's) *The Old Testament in Greek* with its more select and reliable collection of variants.[8] In view of the fact that quite a bit of Holmes and Parsons' material has not been duplicated in the work of Brooke and McLean and is not readily accessible anywhere else, it becomes obvious at once how much indebted biblical scholarship would be to the Oxford Press if this great institution were to reproduce Holmes and Parsons' critical apparatus.[9]

7. Oscar Löfgren has published *Die äthiopische Übersetzung des Propheten Daniel nach Handschriften* . . . . (Paris, 1927) and *Jona, Nahum, Habakuk, Zephanja, Haggai, Sacharja and Maleachi äthiopisch* . . . . (Uppsala, 1930). Heinrich Dörrie published in 1938 a very fine critical edition of the Old Latin of IV Maccabees (*Passio SS. Machabaeorum, die antike lateinische Übersetzung des IV. Makkabäerbuches* [Göttingen]); there has now come to hand the same scholar's useful article "Zur Geschichte der LXX im Jahrhundert Konstantins," *Zeitschrift für die neutestamentliche Wissenschaft*, XXXIX (1940), 57–110 (on which see G. Mercati, "Di alcune testimonianze antiche sulle cure bibliche di San Luciano," *Biblica*, XXIV [1943], 1–17). In 1923, A. Dold made available *Konstanzer altlateinische Propheten- und Evangelienbruchstücke* . . . . (Leipzig); cf. its enthusiastic reception in Montgomery, *Daniel*, p. 30).

8. Yet note even here the extent to which Margolis was able to make "Corrections in the Apparatus of the Book of Joshua in the Larger Cambridge Septuagint," *Journal of Biblical Literature*, XLIX (1930), 234–64.

9. The writer is aware of the criticism leveled at the *apparatus criticus* of Holmes and Parsons who "entrusted no small part of the task of collation to careless or incompetent hands"; cf. Edwin Hatch, *Essays in Biblical Greek* (Oxford, 1889), pp. v–vi and 131–33; and now J. Ziegler, *Zeitschrift für die alttestamentliche Wissenschaft*, LX (1944), 121–23.

THE USE OF THE LXX AND ITS DAUGHTER-VERSIONS IN
THE TEXTUAL CRITICISM OF THE HEBREW BIBLE

Whether or not the (nearest to the) original Septuagint text of any book in the Old Testament has been recovered, there still remains the task of using the primary and secondary versions properly in order to determine their Hebrew *Vorlagen* for comparison with the Textus Receptus of the Hebrew Bible, the Massoretic text.

5. There can be little doubt that the field of Old Testament textual criticism has not been worked since the end of World War I by as many and as skilful workers as in the epoch preceding. First, it was the disciplines of Egyptology, cuneiform studies, and comparative Semitic linguistics and, later on, archeology and northwestern Semitic which drew away many thoroughly competent scholars who would have advanced materially the discipline in which we are here interested. But another, no less important, factor in the general decline of the textual criticism of the Hebrew Bible has been, strange as it may strike the reader, the publication of Swete's edition of the LXX (also Rahlfs's edition in 1935) and Kittel's *Biblia Hebraica*.

a) Ever since the appearance of Swete's Smaller Cambridge Septuagint (1894; 2d ed., 1899), it has become increasingly customary for the average biblical critic, when turning to the Septuagint translation of whatever word or passage in the Hebrew Bible he wishes elucidated, to consult this convenient handbook. But whether the critic is aware of it or not, the "Septuagint" in the edition of Swete (as of Rahlfs) was never meant to be more than "a portable text . . . . taken from the Vatican MS., where this MS. is not defective, with the variations of two or three other early uncial MSS." (Swete, *Introduction to the Old Testament in Greek*, p. 189).[10] The average critic has come to look upon the

10. Margolis had this to say about Swete's edition: "For the uncials [of Joshua] I have used the phototypic editions. . . . . I say this because I have discovered numerous inaccuracies in Swete's edition" (*American Journal of Semitic Languages*, XXVIII [1911–12], 3). And Ziegler ("Bei der Ausarbeitung des Dodekapropheton für die grosse Göttinger Septuaginta-Ausgabe," *Zeitschrift für die alttestamentliche Wissenschaft*, LX [1944]) has this to say after a study of Swete: "Diese Nachkollation von Amos zeigt zur Genüge, dass die Handausgabe von SWETE für die wissenschaftliche Erforschung der Textkritik, die sauberste Arbeit ver-

impressive fourth-century uncial, Codex Vaticanus, as *the* "Septuagint" and has almost completely lost the habit of consulting the variants in the critical apparatuses of Holmes and Parsons and Brooke and McLean. Professor Montgomery has put it this way:

.... Scholars have perpetrated the mistake of baldly citing B as though it were ultimate, with no attempt to criticise it apart from its group and to recover the original text .... [*Daniel*, p. 40]. In many cases they (Sahidic-Coptic) help to correct B where it can otherwise be proved to be untrue to its group .... [p. 42]. [The Old Latin] is of great value in showing the antiquity of errors, glosses, etc., in B .... [p. 43]. Codex A must be extremely discounted as a witness; an early listing has disclosed more than 175 errors, some of them most glaring. .... Its colleague [the Arabic translation] .... is infinitely superior in the text it represents to A .... it must have been made of an early authoritative codex of which A is a base offspring ... . [p. 52].

Nine years later (*Journal of Biblical Literature*, LV [1936], 309–11), Professor Montgomery criticized Sir Frederic Kenyon (who edited the Chester Beatty papyri) and C. H. Roberts (who edited the Rylands papyri) and, three years after that (*Journal of the American Oriental Society*, LIX [1939], 262–65), some of the editors of the Scheide papyri, because they compared their newly discovered material with only two or three uncial manuscripts. At best such an "analysis" can be but inconclusive; at worst, it can be, and too often has been, utterly misleading.

b) In 1900 the Dutch scholar, Henricus Oort (1835–1927), conceived the excellent idea of putting within the confines of one book some of the results of the textual criticism of the Hebrew Bible (*Textus Hebraici emendationes quibus in Vetere Testamento Neerlandice vertendo*, usi sunt A. Kuenen, I. Hooykaas, W. H. Kosters, H. Oort). In 1905–6 there appeared the much more elaborate project of Rudolf Kittel (1853–1929), *Biblia Hebraica*[2] (3d ed., 1929), which was composed of the Hebrew text of the second edition of the Bomberg Bible, edited by Jacob ben Chayyim (Venice, 1524–25), and a critical apparatus, consisting essen-

---

langt, ungenügend ist .... " (p. 128). Rahlfs's edition, on the other hand, he says: ".... in dieser Hinsicht Lob verdient. Gewiss finden sich auch verschiedene Mängel und Versehen; aber im Vergleich zu den oben besprochenen Werken sind sie verschwindend gering .... " (pp. 128–29).

tially of various readings from Hebrew manuscripts, the versions, and conjecture. It is a pity that one usually remembers this statement by S. R. Driver, the master-critic: "The best collection both of variants from the versions and of conjectural emendations is that contained in Kittel's *Biblia Hebraica*" (*Notes on . . . . Samuel*², p. xxxv, n. 6), whereas it has become all but forgotten that Driver followed up with the following strong *caveat:* "But in the acceptance of both variants and emendations, considerable discrimination must be exercised."[11]

(1) It is no exaggeration to assert that the critical apparatus in this edition of the Hebrew Bible has become to many scholars more sacred and authoritative than the Hebrew text itself. The average critical student of the Bible only too infrequently goes beyond the convenient collection of footnotes in *Biblia Hebraica*²,³, unless it is to look at Swete's or Rahlfs's edition of Codex Vaticanus and their all too meager apparatus.

(2) Were the critical notes in *Biblia Hebraica*²,³ generally reliable, there might be some justification for the nonspecialist in not going beyond them. It so happens, however, that the overwhelming majority of the twenty-four books in the Hebrew Bible were done by scholars whose *forte* was not textual criticism (notable exceptions were Driver in *Biblia Hebraica*² and Bewer in *Biblia Hebraica*³). The writer does not consider it an exaggeration to assert that nearly every line of their footnotes swarms with errors of commission and omission, as regards both the primary and the secondary versions.[12]

11. A posteriori, no one should really be surprised that the textual criticism of the Hebrew Bible, involving the correct use of the LXX and other primary, as well as secondary, versions, is so poorly done in Kittel's *Biblia Hebraica*. A perusal of Kittel's useful study, *Über die Notwendigkeit und Möglichkeit einer neuen Ausgabe der hebräischen Bibel* (Leipzig, 1901) ("Zur Feier des Reformationsfestes und des Übergangs des Rektorats [of the University of Leipzig] auf Dr. Eduard Sievers . . . .") will show that in the chapter (iii) devoted to "Das erreichbare Ziel" (pp. 32–47) the author failed to grasp the character and problems of the textual criticism of the Hebrew Bible.

12. For some years the writer has been waging virtually a one-man battle against the footnotes in Kittel's *Biblia Hebraica* (cf. the remarks in the *Journal of Biblical Literature*, LXIII [1944], 33, and in n. 18, the references to the specific instances which are discussed in detail elsewhere). He is now happy to welcome into the fold a ranking textual critic, Joseph Ziegler, whose extremely valuable "Studien zur Verwertung der Septuaginta im Zwölfprophetenbuch" have just come to hand (*Zeitschrift für die alttestamentliche Wissen-*

(*a*) It is too often forgotten that the Septuagint translation of the Hebrew Bible is not only a thoroughly Jewish work but also that it was popular among the Jews until after they lost their sovereign state in A.D. 70–135 and (Judeo-)Christianity, with the LXX rather than the Hebrew original as its Bible, had become a distinct and increasingly powerful group. The unique Greek translation by Aquila, in keeping with the Jewish exegesis current in the first and second centuries, replaced the LXX, until its use in the Synagogue was forbidden by the Code of Justinian (A.D. 555).[13] The failure to bear the LXX in mind as a Jewish work and to treat it as such in the textual criticism of the Hebrew Bible, far from being purely an academic problem, has resulted in an enormous waste of talent, time, and paper in the unscientific use of the LXX for the "elucidation" and "restoration" of the text of the Hebrew Bible.

(*b*) The Hebrew Bible was read, studied, and interpreted by the Jews during the Maccabean, Mishnaic, and Talmudic periods, no less than it was before the second century B.C. and after the sixth century A.D. It is only reasonable to assume that where the LXX points, or appears to point, to a Hebrew reading which differs from the reading preserved in the Hebrew text currently in use, there may be involved not two variants, of which only one can be original, but only one reading, of which the LXX is simply an interpretation. This interpretation, of identical or similar character, should be sought in the vast literature which the Jews produced from the Maccabean through the Talmudic periods, a literature which is a mine of information for the discerning biblical scholar. It was the great contribution of Rabbi Zecharias

---

schaft, LX [1944], 107–31). At the end of his "Kritische Bemerkungen zur Verwendung der Septuaginta im Zwölfprophetenbuch der Biblia Hebraica von Kittel [3d ed., 1937]," pp. 107–20, we read: "Bei einer Neuausgabe der Biblia Hebraica des Dodekapropheton muss das gesamte G-Material, wie es die eben erschienene Göttinger Septuaginta-Ausgabe vorlegt, neu bearbeitet werden."

13. The earlier attitude of the Jews toward the LXX is found in the Letter of Aristeas and in the works of Philo and Josephus; the later attitude is expressed, e.g., in the tractates, Megillat Taᶜanit and Masseket Soferim. English translations of these and other materials are conveniently available in Thackeray, *The Letter of Aristeas* (London and New York, 1918), Appendix.

Frankel, of Dresden (1801–75), to one phase of correct LXX and Bible study that he collected and classified material of this kind in such works as *Vorstudien zu der Septuaginta* (1841), *Über den Einfluss der palästinischen Exegese auf die alexandrinische Hermeneutik* (1851), and *Zu dem Targum der Propheten* (1872), demonstrating the manner in which the LXX exhibits the kind of exegesis (and sometimes the *eis*egesis, too) found in the Targumim, Mishnah, Tosefta, Midrashim, and Gemara. Had they kept this important approach in mind, would such better-known critics as Briggs, Duhm, Ehrlich, Gunkel, and Marti—not to list dozens of others equally or less known—have so recklessly and indiscriminately emended the preserved Hebrew text in accordance with what they supposed must have been the reading in the Hebrew manuscripts used by the LXX translators?[14]

(*c*) The Hebrew Bible was to the Jews a collection of sacred books. They turned the Bible from Hebrew into Greek precisely because their Sacred Scriptures had to be made accessible to those Jews who no longer knew enough Hebrew to read the original (cf., e.g., the *raison d'être* of the Aramaic Targumim, Saadia's Arabic translation, and the English version published by the Jewish Publication Society of America). Is it reasonable to sup-

14. To cite but one, hitherto unnoted, case in point: nearly all critics have emended drastically either the LXX or the Massoretic text (or both) in Job 3:10, where the latter's "(And the servant) is free (from his master)" is reproduced in the former by "does not fear." Yet all that we have here, as so often in the LXX of this book, is a nice interpretation of the Hebrew; and it is interesting that a medieval Jewish commentator, Zeraḥiah ben Isaac ben Shealtiel, of Barcelona (quite independently of the LXX!), has precisely the same exegesis, viz., What does *ḥofshî* "free" mean here? *lōʾ yifḥád* "he does not fear." The reader will find it to his advantage to pore over and apply the sober statements to be found, e.g., in Driver's *Notes on . . . . Samuel*[2] (pp. lv–lxix) and Montgomery's *Daniel* (pp. 35–38).

It should be observed here that only infrequently will the critic meet an anomalous LXX rendering of the Hebrew also in rabbinic literature. It is primarily the critic's knowledge and "feel" of early Jewish exegesis which will help him comprehend the true character of the Jewish exegesis, which constitutes the LXX. Among the recent attempts in this direction may be cited: A. Kaminka, "Septuaginta und Targum zu Proverbia," *Hebrew Union College Annual*, VIII–IX (1931–32), 169–91; Ch. Heller, *Die Tychen-Wutzsche Transskriptionstheorie* (Berlin, 1932) and *The Septuagint References in Mandelkern's Concordance* ([in Hebrew] New York, 1943); S. Lieberman, *Greek in Jewish Palestine* (New York, 1942), chaps. i and ii, and "Two Lexicographical Notes," *Journal of Biblical Literature*, LXV (1946), 67–72; D. Daube, "κερδαίνω as a Missionary Term," *Harvard Theological Review*, XL (1947), 109–20.

pose that these same Jews wilfully and/or negligently altered and corrupted their Hebrew Bible between the time the LXX was made (third–first centuries B.C.) and the *floruit* of Theodotion and Aquila (second century A.D.) to the extent that the footnotes in *Biblia Hebraica*[2, 3], would indicate? Is it not so much more reasonable for scholars first to have made an independent and thorough study not only of the preserved Hebrew text of whatever book in the Bible they were commenting on, but also of the LXX? Had they done so—and not one of the better-known critics mentioned above, or most of their fellow textual critics, ever did so—they would not have abused the LXX so frequently and unjustifiably as to create from it a Hebrew *Vorlage* which never existed outside their own imagination. They should have realized that there must be something fundamentally wrong with an approach to the LXX such as theirs which resulted in such a far-reaching divergence between the preserved Hebrew text, on the one hand, and, on the other, the Hebrew text which they derived from the LXX.

6. From the foregoing it will have become clear why the writer believes that a real and urgent need for the textual criticism of the Hebrew Bible is the proper analysis of the LXX and of its daughter-versions in relation to it. Very much has already been accomplished in such works as Wellhausen's *Der Text der Bücher Samuelis* (1871); S. R. Driver's unexcelled *Notes on . . . . Samuel*[2] (1913) and footnotes to Deuteronomy, Joshua, and Ecclesiastes in *Biblia Hebraica*[2]; Rahlfs's *Septuaginta-Studien* (1904–11)—studies in the books of Kings and Psalms—and *Studie über den griechischen Text des Buches Ruth* (1922); Dhorme's *Le Livre de Job* (1926); Montgomery's *International Critical Commentary on Daniel* (1927) and forthcoming commentary on *Kings* in the same series; Margolis' *The Book of Joshua in Greek* (1931——); Ziegler's excellent *Untersuchungen zur Septuaginta des Buches Isaias* (1934); and Bewer's footnotes to Ezekiel in *Biblia Hebraica*[3].[14a]

14a. The work of Peter Katz should not go unnoted here. Cf. such articles of his as in the *Theologische Literaturzeitung*, LXI (1936), 265–87; *ibid.*, LXIII (1938), 32–34; *Journal of Theological Studies*, XLVII (1946), 30–33, 166–69; "Eyes to the Blind, Feet to the Lame," in the German Refugee Pastors' Volume in honor of the Bishop of Chichester (Cambridge, 1942); *Journal of Biblical Literature*, LXV (1946), 319–24; and an unpublished book on the text of the Septuagint.

When biblical scholarship comes to realize the many and serious shortcomings in Kittel's *Biblia Hebraica*, a grand opportunity will arise for biblical societies in the United States and Canada to organize and sponsor the sort of major project which should replace it. Time alone will tell whether or not we shall successfully meet the challenge.

THE RISE AND FALL OF THE (TYCHSEN-)WUTZ TRANSCRIPTION THEORY

7. The two decades between the end of World War I and the beginning of World War II saw both the resurrection of an interesting theory and its demise. It was in 1772 that the learned and eccentric Olaus Gerhard Tychsen (1734–1815) first advanced the rather novel theory that the LXX translation of the Hebrew Bible (as also the versions of Aquila, Theodotion, and Symmachus) was made from a text written not in Hebrew but in Greek characters (see his *Tentamen de variis codicum Hebraicorum Vet. Test. MSS. generibus* [Rostochii], Sec. I, pp. 59–134). Tychsen based his theory on a fair amount of inductive material and theoretical reasoning, but no one else followed it up in any detail. Passing reference to Tychsen's *Tentamen* is about all one finds in the nineteenth century, and that in few works (cf., e.g., Eichhorn, *Einleitung in das Alte Testament*[3] [Leipzig, 1803], I, 249–50; König, *Einleitung in das Alte Testament* [Bonn, 1893] p. 92, n. 1; Frankel, *Vorstudien*, pp. 31–32, n. *r*, 183, n. *j*, 204–5, n. *c;* Blau, *Zur Einleitung in die heilige Schrift* [Budapest, 1894], pp. 80 ff.).

8. In 1925 (Part II was published in 1933) there appeared the entirely independent work by Franz Xavier Wutz (1883–1938) of the Catholic Philosophico-theological Institute in Eichstätt, *Die Transkriptionen von der Septuaginta bis zu Hieronymus*, advancing essentially the same theory but basing it on a mass of evidence and drawing many far-reaching conclusions. Rudolf Kittel, editor of *Biblia Hebraica*[2], greeted the work in the following words (*Deutsche Literaturzeitung*, Vol. XLVI [1925], cols. 657–64): ".... *amicus Plato, amica 'Biblia Hebraica,' magis amica veritas* [col. 659]. .... Meine Absicht ist nicht, zu zensieren, sondern die Leser auf eine grosse weittragende Entdeckung hinzuweisen,

die vielleicht bestimmt ist, eine gewaltige Revolution in unserer
ganzen Bibelforschung, der griechischen wie der hebräischen,
hervorzurufen [col. 664]."[15] More skeptical were the comments,
e.g., of Margolis (*Jewish Quarterly Review*, XVI [1925–26], 117–25)
and Montgomery (*Daniel*, p. 27, n. 2). Since most of the important literature on the subject has been cited on pages 378–79 of
J. L. Seeligmann's excellent review article cited in note 2, the
writer will limit himself here to but a few observations.

a) In his very stimulating work, *Zur Einleitung in die heilige
Schrift* (pp. 89–90), Ludwig Blau demonstrated the use of transliterations into Greek of the Hebrew text of the Pentateuch and
of those portions of the Prophets and the Hagiographa that were
read in the Synagogue as Haftarot and Megillot. And both Epi-
phanius (in the so-called "essay" *De mensuris et ponderibus*, sec. 7)
and a Latin scholium found in an Arabic manuscript of the Pentateuch (Hody, *De Bibliorum textibus originalibus* [1705], p. 597)
attest to the use of the second column of the many-columned
Bible of Origen (viz., the vocalization in Greek characters of the
consonantal Hebrew text of the first column) by Christians who
could not read the first column.[16] A priori, therefore, Wutz's
theory is reasonable enough.   .

b) Certainly, in this case "the proof of the pudding is in the
eating." In the decade and a half following the appearance of
Wutz's work, so many scholars published detailed, critical studies of various words and passages discussed by Wutz that his transcription theory has already become nothing more than a curiosity. P. A. H. de Boer (*Research into the Text of I Samuel I–XVI*
[Amsterdam, 1938], p. 86) has put it into classical form: ". . . .
he [viz., Wutz] is caught in a vicious circle, when he . . . . speaks
in his final conclusion, which gives a remarkable agreement of G
[= the LXX] and M [= the Massoretic Hebrew text], of: 'Be-

15. It will be seen even from this brief excerpt that the *Philadelphia Ledger* of April 25,
1925, was not justified in paraphrasing Kittel's review of Wutz to the effect that "his own
life's work of research [in biblical research] had been rendered worthless."

16. On the proposition that the columnar order of Origen's many-columned Bible was
determined by pedagogic considerations, see the *Jewish Quarterly Review*, XXVII (1936–37),
137–49, to which the writer can now add considerably more data. This view has been accepted most recently by Giovanni Cardinal Mercati, *Biblica*, XXVIII (1947), notes on pp.
6 f.; cf. also his *Nuove note di letteratura biblica e cristiana antica*, p. 145, n. 3.

stätigung der Richtigkeit der Methode.' This agreement is no more than an agreement of G, revised by Wutz, with M, revised by Wutz!''[17]

c) It has not generally been noted, however, that Wutz himself gave up his transcription theory. It is true that Wutz did not admit this openly, but on pages 15–16 of his commentary on *Das Buch Job* (1939), where "Septuaginta und Urtext" are discussed, the reader will learn that the LXX of Job, along with Psalms—the key book in the Bible for Wutz's theory—was made directly from a Hebrew text, no mention being made at all of any transcription text (cf. *Journal of Biblical Literature*, LIX [1940], 529–31).

THE LXX AS A SOURCE FOR THE SEMANTICS AND LINGUISTICS OF BIBLICAL HEBREW

9. It has long been known that any ancient primary translation of the Hebrew Bible constitutes an important source for the determination of the meaning and grammatical form and function of words and combinations of words in biblical Hebrew; those rabbis of the Talmudic period who were interested in determining the form and meaning of some biblical word must have turned to the Greek and Aramaic translations for aid. The Jewish biblical philologians of the Golden Era in Spain and other countries under Moslem influence, who knew little or no Greek, made extensive and systematic use of the Targumim (as of Arabic) with that end in view. In recent times much work has been done by commentators in the use of the LXX and Targumim for the grammar of biblical Hebrew, usually in complete ignorance of the work already accomplished almost a millennium earlier by such lexicographers, grammarians, and exegetes as Saadia, David ben Abraham, Yefet ben ʿAlī, Judah ben David Ḥayyūj, Abulwalīd Merwān ibn Janāḥ, and many others, not to mention the "Big Three"—Rashi, Abraham ibn Ezra, and David Qimḥi.[18]

17. W. F. Albright's study of "The List of Levitic Cities" in Joshua, chap. 21 and I Chronicles, chap 6 (see end of n. 6 above) has convinced him that it is impossible to operate with Wutz's transcription theory (cf. pp. 50–51 and nn. 4 and 6).

18. It is a pity that one is justified in adding the words "and their modern successors" to this statement by A. Eustace Haydon: "Unfortunately, the immense library of linguistic knowledge, the brilliant achievements of the Jews in biblical scholarship, were ignored by the medieval Schoolmen" (pp. 240–41 of his chapter on "The Influence of Medieval Ju-

As in medieval, so also in modern, times the biblical scholar is not infrequently a commentator, lexicographer, and grammarian rolled into one (cf., e.g., the scholars mentioned just above and, in modern times, Gesenius, Böttcher, Stade, König, S. R. Driver, Briggs). Withal, there is very much more work which remains to be done.

10. Of course, the cognate languages are a primary source for the etymology and semantic history of biblical Hebrew. Yet by themselves they are not sufficient; the usage of the word(s) involved, within the Bible itself, is paramount (cf., e.g., the pertinent remarks of Professor Meek, *Journal of Religion*, XXI [1941], 408–9). For this usage such early Jewish primary versions of the Hebrew Bible as the LXX and Targumim constitute a source no less primary than the cognate languages and should be used together with them. As cases in point, cf. Otto Eissfeldt, "Der Maschal im Alten Testament" Beihefte zur *Zeitschrift für die alttestamentliche Wissenschaft*, XXIV (1913), 21–25; Robert Stieb, "Die Versdubletten des Psalters," *Zeitschrift für die alttestamentliche Wissenschaft*, LVII (1939), 102–10 (biblical *sĕlāh* according to the LXX); Orlinsky on *tpś*, "lay hold of," in *Jewish Quarterly Review*, XXXIV (1943–44), 281 ff., and XXXV (1944–45), 351–54; Israel Lévi, "La Racine ʿyp-yʿp et sa traduction dans la Septante," *Revue des études juives*, LXIV (1912), 142–45; S. H. Blank, "The Septuagint Renderings of Old Testament Terms for Law," *Hebrew Union College Annual*, VII (1930), 259–83; C. H. Dodd, *The Bible and the Greeks* (London, 1935), Part I, pp. 3–95, "The Religious Vocabulary of Hellenistic Judaism," *passim;* Georg Bertram, "Der Sprachschatz der Septuaginta und der des hebräischen Alten Testaments," *Zeitschrift für die alttestamentliche Wissenschaft*, LVII (1939), 85–101; N. H. Snaith, *The Distinctive Ideas of the Old Testament* (Philadelphia, 1946), chap. viii.

11. Everyone knows that the phonology and morphology of biblical Hebrew are much better analyzed than is the syntax.[19]

---

daism on Christianity," in *Environmental Factors in Christian History*, ed. McNeill, Spinka, and Willoughby [Chicago, 1939]).

19. See most recently Professor Meek's presidential address, *Journal of Biblical Literature*, LXIV (1945), 1–13.

Our knowledge of this phase of biblical Hebrew would be considerably increased if the LXX and Targumim were studied more carefully from the point of view of grammar. In a forthcoming article in the *Journal of the American Oriental Society* (Vol. LXVII, No. 2 [April–June, 1947]) the writer has made extensive use of these primary versions to help determine the presence and widespread use in biblical Hebrew of the verbal noun.

12. This continent could have been foremost in the study of the Greek and Latin transcriptions of the Hebrew Bible in the intertestamental period; the writer has in mind the studies of Margolis, Speiser, Sperber, and Staples. The Old World, between the two world wars, contributed to this aspect of Greek and Hebrew through the writings of Pretzl and Wutz, and now there has come to hand the most detailed *Studien über hebräische Morphologie und Vokalismus auf Grundlage . . . . der zweiten Kolumne der Hexapla . . . .* (Leipzig, 1943), by Einar Brønno, with full discussion both of the hexaplaric material and of the treatment of this material at the hands of the aforementioned scholars.[19a]

THE LXX AS A LANGUAGE IN ITS OWN RIGHT

13. It is only since the turn of the century that the LXX has come to be regarded as a language which really lived in the mouths of people. It is no longer considered to be an artificially contrived vehicle for expressing the Hebrew Bible in Greek form. As is well known, it is essentially the discovery of so many Greek papyri deriving from the Mediterranean world of the intertestamental period which has given us the correct perspective, as the generation preceding ours was thrilled to discover in Adolf Deissmann's *Licht vom Osten* (as also in his [*Neue*] *Bibelstudien*).[20]

19a. See also Giovanni Cardinal Mercati, *Nuove note di letteratura biblica e cristiana antica*, chap. i; *Il problema della colonna II dell' Esaplo* (Vatican City, 1947; reprinted from *Biblica*, XXVIII [1947], 1–30, 173–215), with reference in the Post Scriptum on p. 75 to a work I have not yet seen, G. Lisowsky, *Die Transskriptionen der hebräischen Eigennamen des Pentateuchs in der Septuaginta* (Basel, 1940).

20. One should be careful to distinguish between the form and the substance of the LXX. This is brought out clearly by placing side by side these two statements from "Jewish and Greek Elements" by Ralph Marcus (*Louis Ginzberg Jubilee Volume*, English section [New York, 1945]), pp. 233 and 244: ". . . . the language of the LXX is part of the Egyptian Koiné and differs from contemporary pagan Greek only because it is translation-Greek

14. The Greek of the New Testament has been rather well studied in the light of the Greek of the classical, Hellenistic, Roman, and Byzantine periods; this is, however, not true at all of the Greek of the Old Testament. An excellent beginning in this direction was made by that careful scholar, Edwin Hatch, in his *Essays in Biblical Greek;*[21] of especial interest are his Essays II ("Short Studies of the Meanings of Words in Biblical Greek" [pp. 36–93]) and III ("On Psychological Terms in Biblical Greek" [pp. 94–130]). In 1916 there appeared Karl Huber's very useful *Untersuchungen über den Sprachcharakter des griechischen Leviticus* (Giessen), following upon Martin Flashar's very fine "Exegetische Studien zum Septuagintapsalter" in 1912 (*Zeitschrift für die alttestamentliche Wissenschaft*, Vol. XXXII). In 1926 Martin Johannessohn published (in *Zeitschrift für vergleichende Sprachforschung*, LIII, 161–212) a detailed study of "Das biblische καὶ ἐγένετο und seine Geschichte"; and in 1942–43 (*Zeitschrift für die alttestamentliche Wissenschaft*, LIX, 129–84) he supplied the corollary, "Die biblische Einführungsformel καὶ ἔσται"; these studies must be consulted by anyone who wants to study the syntax of biblical Hebrew. Worthy of note is προφήτης, *Eine sprach- und religionsgeschichtliche Untersuchung* (Giessen, 1927) by Erich Fascher, especially chapter iii (pp. 102–65). Easily the finest study of the LXX per se of any book in the Bible is Joseph Ziegler's *Untersuchungen zur Septuaginta des Buches Isaias* (1934).[22]

---

and not because the Jewish translators spoke a peculiar Jewish Greek jargon" and ". . . . the Greek elements of the LXX are merely superficial and decorative while the Jewish elements are deep-lying, central and dominant." There has just come to hand F. Büchsel's "Die griechische Sprache der Juden in der Zeit der Septuaginta und des Neuen Testaments," *Zeitschrift für die alttestamentliche Wissenschaft*, LX (1944), 132–49. Cf. also S. E. Johnson, *Journal of Biblical Literature*, LVI (1937), 331–45

21. Not to be overlooked even now are the labors of Schleusner, *Novus thesaurus philologico-criticus sive lexicon in LXX et reliquos interpretes Graecos . . . . Veteris Testamenti* (5 vols.; Leipzig, 1820–21).

22. Also to be consulted are the works of Dodd and Bertram, cited at the end of sec. 10 above. It will readily be seen that no attempt has been made here to catalogue everything that has been done in recent decades on this aspect of the LXX, e.g., E. Schwyzer, "Altes und Neues zu (hebr.-)griech. σάββατα (griech.-)lat. sabbata usw.," *Zeitschrift für vergleichende Sprachforschung*, LXII (1934), 1–16; A. Fridrichsen, "ἰσόψυχος [Ps. 55(54):14]," *Symbolae Osloenses*, XVIII (1938), 42–49; W. S. van Leeuwen, *Eirene in het Nieuwe Testament:*

15. What H. G. Meecham has done for the Greek of *The Letter of Aristeas* (Manchester, 1935) and what Ziegler has done for the LXX of Isaiah, it is important that scholars do for the LXX throughout. And it should be noted that it must be primarily the Old Testament scholar who must perform this task; unfortunately, the scholar who comes to this task from the classical side lacks the specialized training which is so necessary for the proper treatment of the Greek-Hebrew of the Bible.

Limitation of space prevents the writer from touching on other aspects of the LXX, e.g., the *alleged* tendency on the part of the LXX translators to avoid the anthropomorphisms and anthropopathisms in their Hebrew original (cf. the *Crozer Quarterly*, XXI [1944], 156–60); the width of the columns in the earliest manuscripts of the LXX; the kind of alphabet used in the Hebrew *Vorlage* of the LXX (cf. the *Biblical Archaeologist*, IX [1946], 31–33). However, the interested reader will find abundant food for thoughtful digestion in the splendid review article by J. L. Seeligmann (cited at the end of n. 2 above).[23]

Een semasiologische, exegetische Bijdrage op grond van de Septuaginta en de joodsche Literatuur (Wageningen, 1940); cited from *Zeitschrift für die alttestamentliche Wissenschaft*, LVIII (1940–41), 153.

23. The writer has refrained from citing anywhere Otto Stählin's detailed contribution to Wilhelm von Christ's *Geschichte der griechischen Litteratur*, ed. Wilhelm Schmid [6th ed.; München, 1920]), II, 1 [= Vol. VII of Iwan von Müller's *Handbuch der klassischen Altertums-Wissenschaft*), for the simple reason that in no one section of this reference monograph (pp. 535-656, "Die hellenistisch-jüdische Litteratur") is there any indication that the vast range of the fundamentally important literature produced by the Jews in Hebrew and Aramaic in the postbiblical period has been worked. The primary source, which is the rabbinic literature, has remained a closed book to Stählin. Such a procedure is tantamount to utilizing only the rabbinic sources for a study of the New Testament period in the Greco-Roman world! Nor is it only this procedure of "omission" which vitiates so much in the monograph under discussion; there is also the no less grave error of "commission," viz., the prejudice against the idea that the Jews in the intertestamental period could and did write reliable history. It is the direct continuation of the work and spirit of Schürer (himself an able scholar who, however, was devoid of any direct knowledge and use of the all-important rabbinic literature), who branded so much of the literature which he did not know directly as "Jewish Propaganda under a Heathen Mask" when, in reality, Schürer, himself was guilty of "anti-Jewish propaganda under a scholarly mask." American scholarship has before itself the important and urgent task of re-writing and understanding correctly the history and literature of the intertestamental period, of which the LXX is a part.

CHAPTER NINE

The War in Europe and the Future of Biblical Studies

W. F. ALBRIGHT

Johns Hopkins University, Baltimore, Maryland

I. THE PRESENT SITUATION

AS THE effects of the second World War wear off, we are becoming aware of the tremendous cultural and spiritual problems which confront us. It is already evident that the future historian will attribute to the war many consequences which extend far beyond the sphere of politics. Obvious among these non-political consequences is the rapid decline of European cultural influence. Great Britain, France, and the Netherlands are fast losing their imperial status as they become transformed into loose federations of autonomous national units, if not into relatively small countries with clusters of minor colonies and groups of independent commonwealths attached to them only by vague historical ties. Russia is shifting the focus of its huge empire eastward into Asia, while America is becoming a great Pacific power, with correspondingly less interest in Europe. In the light of such transformations it is clear that no humanistic discipline relying on Europe for inspiration can possibly escape drastic modifications.

The most immediate result of the devastation brought about by the war is the virtual suppression of Germany as a normative intellectual center for the generation now growing up. Because German scholarship ruled the world of learning with undisputed authority for a good century, from the 1830's to the 1930's, it will be hard for us of the older generation to become accustomed to a new world of the spirit in which there is no organized Ger-

man intellectual élite to set the pace and to impose standards of accomplishment. Yet this unexpected situation is now a hard fact, to which we must adapt ourselves as rapidly as possible under the circumstances.

It would, however, be a mistake to focus our attention too narrowly on the results of the war without taking the larger historical pattern into account. The process of intellectual decentralization had begun during the first World War, and after 1933 it proceeded with accelerated momentum. The wholesale flight of intellectuals from Germany after 1933 strengthened the scholarship of other countries even more than it weakened that of Germany, whereas increasing *Gleichschaltung* within the German universities reduced the relative amount of worth-while research to a point well below that of surrounding countries. The destructive effects of the war were thus only the culmination of a long-continuing process.

Within Germany itself there was, moreover, an increasing tendency to break away from academic domination of the spirit, a tendency noted a generation ago. During the Weimar Republic it developed apace, and the universities became more and more dissociated from the intellectual life of the nation as a whole. That it did not become evident to all the world at the time we may attribute largely to the fact that the primary place assigned to technology in the German system of education could scarcely be challenged successfully as long as technology provided most of the means for economic and commercial expansion. The more remote from utilitarian goals any discipline was, the more apparent the popular revolt from academic domination. And so, to the horror of university faculties, anthroposophy and all kinds of quack philosophies grew apace; spiritism won multitudes of adherents; the Deutsche Astrologische Gesellschaft had more members and a longer list of publications than did half-a-dozen comparable scientific societies. Even in practical "science" the *Rutengang* (dowsing with a willow twig) replaced serious geomorphology, and geophysics was tainted with more than a little quackery. Academic psychology was almost displaced for the ordinary person by graphology, "characterology," and especially by all

kinds of psychoanalysis. In the historical field pseudo-scientific research like that of Spengler obtained immense popularity, however much academicians might inveigh against his alleged quality as a typical *Gymnasiallehrer*. Even the wild vagaries of Hermann Wirth's *Ura Linda* enjoyed wide diffusion. Among extramural specialists in the Near East, pan-Babylonianism was rampant. It was a time when anti-Semitism and other pathological forms of romantic nationalism gained followers in great numbers from the *petite bourgeoisie* and among intellectual misfits and failures. Literature and art fell increasingly under the influence of impressionistic and postimpressionistic theories of form and content. In short, Germany was perhaps the land most affected by the spiritual malaise which swept around the world in that period. Yet so great was the *esprit de corps* existing in the universities and so solidly intrenched were the *Fachgenossen* in their positions that it required the triumph of the Nazis to prove to the world that the power of the university élite in Germany was just as illusory as the power of the French aristocracy of birth on the eve of the French Revolution.

At present, the German universities have been reconstituted as faculties, though they are mostly without libraries or laboratories. The four-zone division of the country, with the *Eisenvorhang* separating East and West, bids fair to block academic reconstruction almost as completely as it threatens to bar the way to a peaceful future for the German people. Such famous old universities as Breslau and Königsberg have ceased to exist, with the mass expulsion of the Germans from Silesia and East Prussia. On the other hand, Leipzig, Halle, and Jena have been reorganized under Russian auspices and are functioning after a fashion. The distinguished Old Testament scholar, Otto Eissfeldt, was appointed rector of the University of Halle. Alt and Leipoldt are teaching single-handed in their old chairs in Leipzig. In the American zone such universities as Munich, Heidelberg, Marburg, and Erlangen have been reopened, though Giessen has been almost completely obliterated and Würzburg is little better. Bonn, Göttingen, Hamburg, and other universities in the British zone have been reorganized, and the same is true of Tübingen in

the French zone, where a new university has been opened at Mainz. A surprising number of well-known biblical scholars escaped from the holocaust and are lecturing again; among them are Hölscher and Bultmann, Barth, Dibelius, Noth, Von Rad, Rudolph, Galling, Jeremias, Rost, Albertz, Lohmeyer, Fascher, Klostermann, Bertram, Balla, Baumgärtel, Horst, Schaeder, Weiser, and others. Two of the most violent and dangerous Nazi scholars came, unhappily, from the ranks of outstanding New Testament scholars: Gerhard Kittel, editor of the *Theologisches Wörterbuch zum Neuen Testament*, and Emanuel Hirsch, neo-Marcionite and existentialist theologian of the German Christian movement. In view of the incredible viciousness of his attacks on Judaism and the Jews, which continued at least until 1943, Gerhard Kittel must bear the guilt of having contributed more, perhaps, than any other Christian theologian to the mass murder of millions of Jews by the Nazis; an *apologia pro vita sua* written by him about the beginning of 1946 (for which the writer wishes to thank Miss Carlotta Knoch) paints an utterly amazing picture of a diseased conscience. Through the equal viciousness of his long-continued campaign against the Old Testament and the Jewish elements of the New and through his systematic teaching that the German state could do no wrong, Emanuel Hirsch prepared the way for the collective breakdown of Protestant conscience, without which the excesses of the Nazi movement would scarcely have been conceivable. Among Old Testament scholars only two appear to have been dismissed from their posts because of their Nazi record so far: Johannes Hempel and Anton Jirku.

Without journals or other facilities it is hard to see what German scholars can publish in the near future, but we may be sure that their colleagues in Great Britain and this country will do their utmost to provide channels for publication, as well as to help restore their libraries. But nearly all the great German publishing houses have been destroyed, among them Hinrichs, Brockhaus, and Harrassowitz in Leipzig. However, such firms as Kohlhammer and Vandenhoeck and Ruprecht have escaped harm, and they will probably undertake modest publishing pro-

grams in the biblical field as soon as they can get paper—which may prove a very difficult problem to solve. Lack of paper may also prevent the reprinting of many important works and essential handbooks for which we formerly went to Germany, such as Kittel's *Biblia Hebraica* and Rahlfs's *Septuaginta*, the plates of both of which fortunately escaped destruction when the Bibelanstalt in Stuttgart was destroyed.

One of the most heartening aspects of the present situation, as far as biblical scholars are concerned, is the energy shown by Protestant scholars in the neutral countries of Switzerland and Sweden. In Switzerland the Old Testament scholars of Basel, W. Eichrodt and W. Baumgartner, ably assisted by their pupils and colleagues, have continued to work vigorously and effectively. A new theological journal has been founded, and plans for publication are active. The long-delayed new edition of Gesenius' *Handwörterbuch* (which last appeared in a new edition in 1915) by Köhler and Baumgartner is finished and will be published by Brill in Leyden. In Sweden, Nyberg (Uppsala) and Nygren (Lund), ably seconded by their colleagues and pupils, have published many biblical studies, particularly in the fields of comparative and historical religion. Now that the war is over, the occupied countries of Denmark and Norway, whose universities escaped material harm, may be expected to re-enter the arena of biblical studies actively and effectively. S. Mowinckel and Johannes Pedersen are already hard at work making up the arrears of the war years.

In Holland and Belgium the hand of the German oppressor weighed heavily on all strata of the population. Universities and scholars were particularly hard hit, with a sad record of destruction and martyrdom. It is astounding to see what the devoted scholars of these two little countries accomplished in spite of all difficulties and how many important publications were issued. In Holland two new journals were launched: *Bibliotheca orientalis* (1943——) and *Oudtestamentische Studiën* (1942——). Old Testament scholars formed a small society in which Catholics and Protestants collaborated on an equal footing. In spite of the de-

struction of the Louvain library in 1940, Belgian scholars there continued to work and to publish.

In France the situation was more difficult than anywhere else, since Germans and men of Vichy vied with one another in restricting biblical study. Père Vincent was compelled to change the title of the *Revue biblique* to *Vivre et Penser*, which continued to appear during the first part of the war in the same format as the journal which it superseded—and, needless to say, with exactly the same type of content. The liquidation of the French University of Strasbourg brought an almost complete end to the activity of French Protestant biblical scholarship in France for the duration of the war.

In contrast to the general picture of decline of Protestant interest in biblical studies throughout the world during the past generation must be set the extraordinary revival of interest in the Bible and in biblical scholarship throughout the Catholic world. This interest grew slowly through the nineteenth century, reaching its culmination in the foundation of the *Revue biblique* (1892), followed by the famous encyclical of Leo XIII, *Providentissimus Deus*, in which the Pontiff laid down the basic principles governing Catholic biblical research and strongly advocated systematic biblical scholarship. Interest developed slowly but steadily until after the first World War, and in 1920 the Pontifical Biblical Institute in Rome, first established in 1909, launched the journal *Biblica*. During the following two decades before the outbreak of the second World War, interest in the Bible grew rapidly in Catholic countries. In 1937 the newly founded Catholic Biblical Association of America created the *Catholic Biblical Quarterly*, followed in 1939 by Mgr. Straubinger's *Revista biblica* in the Argentine. At the same time there was a remarkable revival of biblical interest in Spain, with new journals and publications of various kinds, culminating in 1944 in a complete translation of the Bible from the original languages— the first of its kind to appear in Spanish. In 1945 a new Latin translation of the Psalter was published by the Pontifical Biblical Institute in Rome; it is designed to supplant the Vulgate for

many devotional and liturgical purposes. Meanwhile, the Vatican celebrated the fiftieth anniversary of *Providentissimus Deus* by issuing a new encyclical, *Divino afflante spiritu* (1943), in which both serious research in biblical philology and archeology and increased religious use of the Bible were authoritatively recommended. The effect of this great encyclical has been particularly marked in English-speaking countries; in this country work on the new translation of the Old Testament under Fr. Arbez's editorship has been accelerated, encouraged by the extraordinarily wide diffusion of the recent translation of the New Testament. Further examples of the trend are too numerous to mention and amply justify our expectation that Catholic biblical scholarship will soon take the lead in such fields as biblical languages, textual criticism, historical background, and Palestinian archeology. It is true that contemporary Catholic scholars do not have license —or, perhaps, liberty—to indulge in the literary and historical criticism characteristic of many Protestant circles; but, when one seriously examines the enormous mass of subjective speculation and labored ingenuity which fills most critical libraries in our field, one cannot altogether regret a limitation which prevents Catholic scholars from adding appreciably to the Protestant chaos.

In Protestant and Jewish circles throughout the English-speaking world biblical studies may be said to be holding their own, on the whole. In Great Britain there has been a reaction against the stagnation into which they had fallen about the time of the first World War. In 1917 the Society for Old Testament Study was founded, and by the middle twenties it had begun to exert marked influence on the field as a whole. By the outbreak of the second World War, both Old and New Testament studies had become more active than they had been in a generation, and new blood was beginning to make itself felt in the universities. Productive biblical research in Great Britain is now largely restricted to Protestant circles in and around the universities.

Non-Catholic biblical research in America is at the moment in a position of unstable equilibrium. With biblical studies continuing to lose ground slowly in liberal Protestant circles, at the

same time that serious research is being undertaken in conservative circles, it is already evident that the balance of emphasis is shifting steadily to a more conservative orientation. The proportion of really competent scholars in the field as a whole was perhaps never lower than it is now; but this unfortunate situation is counterbalanced somewhat by a burst of organizing and publishing activity, illustrated especially by the programs of the Westminster Press in Philadelphia and the "Interpreter's Bible" in New York. Moreover, there is intense and still growing interest in biblical archeology, kept alive by the group of scholars affiliated with the American Schools of Oriental Research.

II. TENDENCIES AND PROSPECTS

We have painted the present situation in broad strokes; it remains to evaluate the situation in terms of its potentialities. It is, however, idle to attempt to predict specific developments of concrete character, since there are too many variables in our equations. In any country concrete movements are too likely to depend on the dynamic quality of single leaders, whose emergence is quite unpredictable. Moreover, political happenings may upset the best prediction. Who would have ventured to predict the present fate of Germany fifteen years ago? I vividly recall a lecture given about that time by an eminently sober and well-balanced historian, E. P. Cheyney, of the University of Pennsylvania, in which he discussed the range of reasonable prediction in history, venturing a few very cautious predictions—every one of which was falsified in a few years! If the Bolshevist regime in Russia should be unexpectedly overthrown, as appears increasingly possible to many observers, the immediate future of Western civilization will appear in a decidedly different light. The advent of nuclear energy as an effective force for destruction and as a potential force for construction makes concrete prediction doubly dangerous.

On the other hand, it is quite possible to evaluate the theoretical prospects for biblical studies in the two epistemological domains of judgments of typical occurrence and value-judgments, which are relatively little affected by unexpected constellations

of facts. I shall propose two positive judgments in the domain of typical occurrence, and I shall venture two complementary value-judgments, where the available facts seem to support our extrapolations.

The decentralization of biblical scholarship is a phenomenon supported by so many obvious facts that little explanation is needed. The collapse of German scholarship has left the rest of the world with no measuring rod by which to assess the *consensus eruditorum* in the field of biblical research. No longer can opinions be swayed throughout the Western world (with suitable lags in peripheral regions) by the dicta of the school of Wellhausen or by the latest work of Dibelius. There may be a Lund school or a Louvain school, but each of our extant schools is essentially local or national, without any claim to dominating the international scene in its specialty, as was once true of Tübingen or Leipzig. America, where a disproportionate number of *soi-disant* biblical scholars is now located, is itself thoroughly decentralized, both religiously and academically. What comes out of Methodist circles in Boston does not interest Presbyterian circles in Chicago. What Catholic scholars may write is not read by most Protestant scholars, who snobbishly perpetuate the Lutheran dictum: *Catholica sunt, non leguntur.* The *Journal of Biblical Literature* is an olla-podrida, containing samples of every conceivable variety and school of biblical research existing in Protestant and Jewish circles; no unprejudiced reader can fail to be impressed by the democratic anarchy which reigns in its pages. Nor have the efforts of the Pontifical Biblical Commission since the turn of the century to unify Catholic biblical scholarship had much success in detail, as may be testified by any neutral scholar who compares recent publications by Catholic scholars in the Low Countries, by French Dominicans, and by German Jesuits. The views of Wutz were accepted for a time by nearly all German Catholic scholars, but the response abroad was almost wholly negative from the start.

Another typical trend of our day, which is supported by a plethora of facts, is the steady increase everywhere of attention to the study of the Bible in the light of its *Umwelt*. Thanks to the

astonishing progress of archeological discovery in the Near East and to the no less remarkable refinement of our interpretation of both written and unwritten remains of antiquity, it is no longer possible to understand the Bible as a human document without the aid of archeology—archeology in its broadest sense, of course. This is not the place to list the triumphs of collective human intellect over enormous masses of *disjecta membra* from the remote past; it will be sufficient to recall the tablets of Mari and Ugarit, the Zenon Papyri and the Dura excavations, the Lachish letters and the Chester Beatty papyri. Just to illustrate, I may mention a volume published toward the end of 1945 and received from the author just as I write these pages: Maurice Dunand's *Byblia grammata*, where we find full publication of all known documents in two scripts whose very existence was unknown twenty years ago. But so rapid has been the progress of discovery and interpretation of the primary Near Eastern sources that the average biblical scholar is relatively ignorant of their bearing on his specialty. In one great university, where ancient Near Eastern studies are cultivated with extraordinary success, there is almost no cross-fertilization, and the biblical field remains sterile. One may safely predict that this situation will not continue long.

In the full tide of discovery and of application one may easily overlook pertinent facts and forget that it was not always so. As is well known, Wellhausen drew his basic scheme of religious and institutional development from Wilhelm Vatke, whose major work, *Die Religion des Alten Testamentes*, appeared in 1835, when he was a young Hegelian enthusiast of only twenty-nine. In those years not a single ancient Near Eastern script except Egyptian had been deciphered, and Champollion's solution of the hieroglyphic puzzle, still incomplete and widely rejected, had yielded virtually no new historical results. For all one's admiration of the young *Privat-Docent*'s acumen, his judgments on ancient civilization and his antiquarian footnotes strike a qualified modern reader as grotesque.

I shall now proceed to make two judgments with regard to the trends of tomorrow which can scarcely be divested of some valua-

tional coloring. Yet they are not simple value-judgments but are complementary inferences from present trends, where each is the natural result of the other and where both can be documented and explained in the light of historical conditions. My two judgments are that the current trend away from evolutionary historicism will continue and that the complementary trend toward increased attention to biblical theology will become accelerated for some time to come. In other words, I expect that the emphasis on diachronic approach which has prevailed for over a century will yield to emphasis on synchronic treatment of the material. It is, of course, no secret that there is just now an increasingly strong reaction against the normative Hegelianism of the founders of German historical criticism—Vatke, Wellhausen, and F. C. Baur, whose basic approach has continued to dominate the field ever since. It is also a matter of common knowledge that the output of books and papers dealing with biblical theology has been steadily increasing of late and that more and more of these publications have taken a strong stand with W. Eichrodt against evolutionary historicism.

To say that such a trend exists at the moment does not explain its background or yield any insight into its historical meaning. In order to catch some glimpse of the underlying historical meaning of the tendency, we must remember that Wellhausenism is a Hegelian structure, which flourished naturally under the conditions of the German Reich but was already alien to the spirit of the Weimar Republic and could be introduced into England and America only by the creation of *ad hoc* ideological patterns which could not last long. To the nationalistic Wellhausen there was something inspiring in the progress of biblical institutions from early Israelite anarchy to national unity and from alleged primitive fetishism to abstract monotheism, which foreshadowed the reign of the Hegelian *Geist*. In the Weimar Republic this concept ceased to exert much basic ideological appeal, and in the reorientation which followed the debacle of 1918 it became easy for a Rudolf Kittel to say (in 1921): "Es fehlte dem Gebäude [*sc.*, of the Wellhausen school] das Fundament, und es fehlten den Baumeistern die Massstäbe." When transplanted to the positivistic liberal

atmosphere of Victorian England and to the sociologism and instrumental pragmatism of America, Wellhausenism proved an essentially refractory foreign body. To be sure, both British and Americans welcomed the evolutionary idea, which was thoroughly congenial to the intellectual atmosphere of the late nineteenth century. But the notion of an evolution by Hegelian dialectic from concrete disunity to abstract unity remained totally foreign to English-speaking thought, which has never been hospitable to any form of Hegelianism. So the general acceptance of Wellhausenism in English-speaking lands has provided the best means by which to insure the extinction of Old Testament studies in liberal Protestant institutions.

The reaction toward renewed interest in biblical theology has come about in two principal ways: through philosophical dissatisfaction with a Wellhausenism which could not be squared with the facts of archeology and which was out of step with the phenomenological and organismic trends of the day; through religious dissatisfaction with a system of interpretation which has lost all meaning for an age of crisis, an age in many respects singularly like the age of the great prophets of Israel. European scholars were the first to see the utter lack of accord between Wellhausenism and ancient Near Eastern fact; it is no accident that the first Americans to take a similar stand were precisely those who were in closest touch with European thought. European scholars were quick to recognize the fundamental tragedy of modern existence and to break away from the evolutionary meliorism in biblical interpretation, which had kept their immediate predecessors from understanding the underlying identity of biblical and modern experience. Since 1914, life has been little more than an uninterrupted series of catastrophes and disillusionments for the European, just as it was for the Israelite from 735 to 538 B.C., when most of the great prophetic utterances were delivered. The prophetic message has thus acquired a new meaning, greater in poignancy than ever before in the history of the Christian church. In America we have been saved from most of the tragedy and destruction which have visited Europe during the past third of a century; we have suffered inconvenience and even

serious discomfort, but that is all. To us technology is still essentially a means for the provision of greater material well-being, not an engine of dehumanizing etatism and pervasive devastation. Hence we can still believe in evolutionary meliorism and treat the Old Testament as a long-outmoded document of an exotic ancient faith and the New Testament as a spiritual drug by which to evade the bitter realities of a world ruled by inexorable cosmic justice as well as by love. But such fatuous childishness will no longer satisfy a European who has been matured by suffering, to whom mercy is inconceivable without justice, and to whom faith is useless unless it has been tempered on the anvil of pain.

The imperious demands of life are thus bringing renewed interest in biblical theology. This interest need not become divorced from history in order for us to recognize the eternal values of the Bible; these eternal values become still more real when they are followed through the vicissitudes of history. And, since true history has far greater effectiveness than unreal reconstructions which offend our reason at every turn, we may be sure that archeology, philology, and other ancillary branches of history will play a fundamental role in the revival of biblical theology in the world of tomorrow.

CHAPTER TEN

Problems Ahead in Old Testament Research

FREDERICK C. PRUSSNER
University of Chicago

WHATEVER shortcomings our modern science of the Old Testament may have exhibited in the past, it certainly cannot be accused of a lack of vigor or thoroughness. Ever since it first began to take form, more than a century and a half ago, it has applied itself with unwavering zeal for, and penetrating insight into, the task of interpreting Israel's account of its life and faith. Every conceivable aspect of this record has undergone closest scrutiny. Even areas only remotely related have been examined with the greatest care in the hope that they, too, might in some way help to further our understanding of the Scriptures. It is not surprising, therefore, that Old Testament scholarship should have achieved results rarely duplicated in any other field of ancient literature.

At the same time, however, the very excellence and comprehensiveness of the work already done also leave us with a feeling of concern for the future of our science. Is there anything which has hitherto escaped attention? Will it be possible to move beyond, or to improve upon, the accomplishments of the past? In fact, can we hope to play any other role than that of transmitting to the next generation the large body of knowledge which our elders have amassed? The apprehensions implied in such uneasy questions are, unfortunately, not entirely groundless. The truth of the matter is that, in many respects, we actually seem to have reached the point of diminishing returns. For the Old Testament, despite its importance, is, after all, a relatively small book, especially when compared with the literary remains of other peoples. This restriction and previous research together explain why

175

progress in every direction is no longer to be expected. Textual criticism and literary introduction, both areas of study which, in the years gone by, have yielded some of the richest returns, are cases in point. Opportunities for significant advance in these two fields appear to be nearly exhausted, not because all questions have by now been answered adequately but, rather, because we lack the facts or the source materials with which to solve the remaining ones.

And yet this is only one side of the picture. However often we might feel tempted to repeat the doleful words of that Jewish skeptic, "whatsoever has been done is that which will be done,"[1] the future is not so hopeless as that. There are, to anticipate some of the findings of this survey, even in the more technical fields not a few problems which thus far have been either neglected or treated inadequately. Furthermore—and this almost goes without saying—archeology should continue to be the scene of real pioneer labor and the source par excellence of new data enabling us to push beyond the present limits of our knowledge of Israelite civilization, history, and religion. Finally, important gaps still exist in that area which, in theory if sometimes not in practice, has always been the ultimate concern of critical investigation, namely, the religion of the Old Testament. It is particularly at the last-named point that the days ahead seem to hold out their greatest challenge; for it is here that the future fate of Old Testament research as a whole will, in all likelihood, be decided. If we can show to a world which is becoming increasingly dubious about matters of religious faith that the convictions of the Old Testament about the ultimate nature of things have validity and timeliness, men will go on to be vitally interested in what this book has to say to them. If we cannot, the world will presently pass it by and place its loyalties elsewhere. No, the time has not yet come when we can relax our efforts and suppose that Old Testament criticism has for the most part completed its mission.

What, accordingly, seem to be the various tasks which today face students of the Old Testament? There are several which, because they are more general in nature, ought to be mentioned at

1. Eccl. 1:9.

the outset. In the first place, it is quite certain that the future will lay upon us, who belong to the English-speaking nations, a responsibility greater than any we have had before. Thus far the position of leadership in our field has fallen, by and large, to Continental-European scholars, notably to Germans. Events of the years just passed may, however, change this situation completely; for, even though at present it is not yet apparent what effect the recent world conflict and all its ramifications will have on biblical learning on the other side of the Atlantic, there is every possibility that it may never again attain the pre-eminence that it enjoyed before the war. Should this happen, the focal point of Old Testament research may very likely move westward; and we shall, consequently, be called upon to shoulder a much heavier part of the burden of high scholarly achievement than heretofore.

The second task is no less important, though arising from a different need. It is becoming increasingly difficult, as every teacher of Old Testament subjects no doubt agrees, to give even graduate students an adequate grasp of their field of specialization because of their inability, all too frequently, to make thorough use of the materials available only in other languages. The failure of our secondary schools and colleges to provide a really effective knowledge of foreign languages is now beginning to make itself felt in our area of scholarship. Dependent as we still are for the best in Old Testament studies upon works usually written in German, we cannot safely ignore this development, especially since it interferes so seriously with our efforts to raise up new generations of well-trained and qualified experts. One possible way of meeting this emergency would be to establish a definite program for the creation of the necessary textbooks in English, particularly of the advanced kind, either by translating existing books or, better yet, by writing new ones. The responsibility is a grave one. It can scarcely be shirked without the greatest detriment to the future of our science.

Such a program, once started, need not stop at the requirements of the relatively restricted field of graduate training. It could be extended easily enough to any of the groups interested

in the Bible. As things stand now, these language barriers make it nearly impossible for seminary students, ministers, and lay readers to familiarize themselves at firsthand with the current status of Old Testament research. Because of this, participation in the discussion of Old Testament problems is not much wider than the circles of the critics themselves, whereas, on the other side, ignorance about the activity of these scholars is all but universal. To a large extent this may be laid to the deplorable apathy toward the Bible which is progressively gripping many Protestants. But a part of the blame must also be placed on us, for we have certainly not done all we could to keep the English-speaking world abreast of every new and significant advance made elsewhere. In instance after instance, as the following pages will show, we have failed to match in English what can now be had, for the most part, only in German. Time was when Old Testament scholarship, under the spell of the ideal of science for its own sake, might have acted as though it were largely obligated only to itself. In the present age of declining moral and religious values it cannot afford to ignore its responsibilities toward others.

The tasks discussed thus far apply to the whole area of Old Testament research. Each individual field, however, also presents its own problems. To these we now turn. They are of all kinds— some are technical and detailed; others are far-reaching and complex. Together they demand every type of talent. The linguist, the literary critic, the historian, the sociologist, the theologian —all will have ample opportunities to make worth-while contributions.

Let us look, first, at the study of *Old Testament languages*. As far as this field is concerned, the most immediate needs seem to be grammatical. Especially called for is an advanced Hebrew grammar. We still have nothing in English which could in any way compare with Bauer and Leander's historical grammar,[2] although that work is now almost a quarter of a century old. This is all the more painful, since, with the exception of a few hints

2. H. Bauer and P. Leander, *Historische Grammatik der hebräischen Sprache* (Halle, 1922), Vol. I.

here and there, our smaller Hebrew textbooks like Harper's *Elements of Hebrew*[3] and Davidson's *Introductory Hebrew Grammar*[4] ignore the historical approach altogether. What is true of the morphology of Hebrew is even more so with respect to its syntax. Adequate treatments of it are almost completely lacking. About the only systematic discussion of syntax available is that found in the second half of the *Hebrew Grammar* by Gesenius and Kautzsch.[5] None of the introductory grammars shows more than a passing concern for it. As a result, students usually find themselves forced to learn Hebrew syntax in a wholly haphazard fashion.

The other Semitic languages bearing more immediately on the Old Testament—Aramaic and Syriac—exhibit the same shortcomings. In both instances there are no satisfactory textbooks in English from which the rudiments of these languages could be learned. The only exception is Stevenson's *Grammar of Palestinian Jewish Aramaic*,[6] a compact manual of Targumic Aramaic, which is, however, not too well suited for the learning of biblical Aramaic. Indispensable here, too, is a historical grammar patterned, in this case, after Bauer and Leander's excellent *Grammatik des Biblisch-Aramäischen*.[7]

It is unbelievable that such basic tools should be practically nonexistent in English. This is particularly so, since truly creative research is thereby made almost totally impossible, dependent as it is upon the closest acquaintance with the original text of the biblical records. That these tasks require prompt attention can hardly be emphasized enough.

In the realm of *textual criticism* it seems that our work is all but over. The reason for this is not, of course, that the textual critic has succeeded in solving all the many problems of the text

3. W. R. Harper, *Elements of Hebrew by an Inductive Method* (12th ed.; New York, 1890).

4. A. B. Davidson, *An Introductory Hebrew Grammar*, revised by J. E. McFadyen (21st ed.; Edinburgh, 1921).

5. F. H. W. Gesenius, *Hebrew Grammar*, ed. E. F. Kautzsch, trans. G. W. Collins, revised by A. E. Cowley (Oxford, 1898).

6. N. B. Stevenson, *Grammar of Palestinian Jewish Aramaic* (Oxford, 1924).

7. H. Bauer and P. Leander, *Grammatik des Biblisch-Aramäischen* (Halle, 1927).

of the Old Testament. At times it would appear that some of the the most crucial and tantalizing of the corrupt passages are also those on which textual criticism can shed the least light. The truth is that we have simply exhausted the materials with which we can carry on our attempts to recover the original text of the Old Testament writings. There is, of course, always the remote hope that the discovery of new manuscripts will help to clarify a few more difficulties. Furthermore, it may well be that when we possess critical editions of all the more important versions of the Old Testament, a number of textual riddles will be solved. On the whole, however, it does not look as though we shall be able to pierce appreciably the thick wall still separating us from the original text.

It is also not easy to assess the future contributions of *literary criticism*. In the past, some of the most penetrating, and at the same time most controversial, results of Old Testament research were achieved by the literary critics. When we recall that for the first century of our modern study of the Scriptures, or from Eichhorn to Wellhausen, this method of investigation prevailed—chiefly because the biblical records were, by and large, the only sources available—we may understand why literary criticism became the exhaustive and detailed investigation it is. However, partly as a reaction to the incongruities which this concern for minutiae frequently produced, partly because archeology and the study of the civilization and religion of the ancient Orient provided us with new facts with which to assess the place and meaning of the Old Testament records, and partly also because literary criticism did not always yield the desired results, the last decades have witnessed a noticeable lessening of interest in this area. The Pentateuch is a case in point. The great battles of the past over its sources have all but stopped. Even the attempt made by Volz and Rudolph[8] to disprove the separate and independent existence of the E document has not been able to bring about a gen-

---

8. P. Volz and W. Rudolph, "Der Elohist als Erzähler: Ein Irrweg der Pentateuchkritik?" *Zeitschrift für die alttestamentliche Wissenschaft*, Beih. 63 (Giessen, 1933); W. Rudolph, "Der 'Elohist' von Exodus bis Josua," *Zeitschrift für die alttestamentliche Wissenschaft*, Beih. 68 (Berlin, 1938).

eral abandonment of the now almost traditional theories attached to Wellhausen's name. Perhaps this is caused in some measure by a kind of spiritual lethargy, which resists the reopening of these old issues; but in part it is also due to a generally felt confidence in the main results of the literary work done in the past.

This is not to say that literary studies have come to a standstill or that they will do so in the future. Within the last few decades the Book of Ezekiel has, for example, been freshly examined, with the troublesome result that our earlier faith in its essential unity and trustworthiness as a record of Ezekiel's life and thought is now no longer shared by all.[9] Equally of recent date the interrelationship of the various strands within the Book of Jeremiah has received further treatment.[10] These are good indications that the interest in literary analysis is not dead and that it will not die.

One area of literary criticism which hitherto has been almost completely neglected in our country is that for which the Germans use the term *Literaturgeschichte*, namely, the "study of the history of literature." The nearest thing to this is Bewer's *Literature of the Old Testament*,[11] especially the first part, with its discussion of the primitive forms of Hebrew literature. But otherwise it is really an introduction to the books of the Old Testament, except that it is arranged historically and not canonically. There is nothing that can compare, for example, with Hempel's *Althebräische Literatur*,[12] with its broad sweep of Hebrew literature from its beginning in popular legend and song to its decline in the Jewish writings of the Hellenistic period. Here is surely an area for significant research, which should, among other things, do full justice to the modern desire for synthesis.

Another subject which deserves a much more thorough treat-

9. Most recently, W. A. Irwin, *The Problem of Ezekiel* (Chicago, 1943).

10. H. G. May, "Towards an Objective Approach to the Book of Jeremiah: The Biographer," *Journal of Biblical Literature*, LXI (1942), 139–55.

11. J. A. Bewer, *The Literature of the Old Testament in Its Development* (2d ed.; New York, 1933).

12. J. Hempel, *Die althebräische Literatur und ihr hellenistisch-jüdisches Nachleben* (Potsdam, 1934).

ment than it has received among us is *Hebrew civilization*, that matrix which produced the literature now collected in our Old Testament. While books describing the social customs of the Bible lands are to be had in considerable variety, very little effort has been expended to give a connected view of Hebrew life in its more secular aspects and to describe such phases of the life of the Jews as the development and functioning of their government, the place of the state, their civil laws, their art, industry, and commerce. Perhaps more significant than these questions about the external manifestations of Hebrew culture is the problem of discovering the unifying elements of that culture, of learning how it compared with the surrounding civilizations, and of determining in what ways it was peculiarly fitted to produce the religious ideas of the Old Testament. A magnificent prototype for such a study exists in Johannes Pedersen's *Israel: Its Life and Culture*.[13] The disadvantage of this book today is that it is now twenty years old and, therefore, did not have the full benefit of the tremendous advance in our knowledge of Canaan and Syria brought about since the end of the first World War. To some extent this failing is remedied by a book like Graham and May's *Culture and Conscience*,[14] with its wealth of more recently uncovered material. However, because its main emphasis is placed largely on the development of moral and religious thought in Canaan and surrounding areas and only secondarily on the civilization of these countries, it is not too adequate a supplement. To put it briefly, the history of Palestinian civilization still remains to be written.

Linked to this problem of the nature of Hebrew culture, but well worth further independent treatment, is a sociological and economic analysis of the life of the Hebrews and Jews. Wallis is just about the only person to have attacked this problem with any seriousness.[15] The findings of archeology should in this respect, too, give a firmer basis for such an examination than has

13. London, 1926.

14. W. C. Graham and H. G. May, *Culture and Conscience* (Chicago, 1936).

15. L. Wallis, *Sociological Study of the Bible* (Chicago, 1912); *God and the Social Process: A Study in Hebrew History* (Chicago, 1935); *The Bible Is Human: A Study in Secular History* (New York, 1942).

been hitherto possible, besides helping immeasurably to round out our picture of Hebrew social life.

The problems of the *history of the Hebrews and Jews* are, as we might expect, largely tied to those two periods about which we know very little: first, their origins or the time from their earliest appearance to the establishment of their monarchy, and, second, the centuries between the end of the Exile and the Maccabean revolt. The first of the two is without doubt also the most troublesome. Nobody who has tried to discuss in class or elsewhere the premonarchical development of the Hebrews can have failed to be almost completely baffled as he sought to bring them on the scene of history with the help of a few bits of archeological evidence and of literary records upon which he could not place too much reliance. The relationship of the patriarchal narratives to the facts of history, the date and course of the Exodus and of the Conquest, the earliest relationships between the southern and the northern tribes, the validity of the so-called "two-invasion theory"—all these are but a few of the puzzles we should like to have solved. We have every reason to hope, of course, that the work of the spade in Palestine and elsewhere will turn up new facts, as it has in the past with the Tell el-Amarna tablets and the excavations at Jericho and Bethel.

The other dark age in Israelite history—the Persian period and the first century of the Greek era—is in certain respects not quite so depressing. We have a rough picture of the course of Jewish history after the Exile and can also follow without too much difficulty the general religious development of the Jews. What we wish for is a greater amount of detail with which to fill out our sketchy knowledge. One of the still unanswered problems of this period is whether the Chronicler's order, with Nehemiah following Ezra, should not actually be inverted. Indeed, at this point a yet more disturbing question has been raised, namely, whether Ezra himself is not wholly the product of the Chronicler's imagination,[16] thereby placing in doubt the commonly held belief that Ezra was instrumental in bringing about the establishment of normative Judaism in Palestine.

16. R. H. Pfeiffer, *Introduction to the Old Testament* (New York, 1941), pp. 824 ff.

Historical problems have, of course, not all been solved for the other periods. One of the most important of these, the chronology of the kings between Saul and the fall of Jerusalem in 586 B.C., still remains to be worked out more definitively. Since, however, real progress can be registered within the last years,[17] a final solution is perhaps not too far off.

One last area of study now remains to be discussed. It is also by far the most important and the most promising field for future research. We have in mind the *religion of the Old Testament*. Some of the issues here are of a factual kind, but others touch the very core of our Old Testament science, challenging, among other things, its purpose and its right to exist or demanding that it direct its efforts away from so-called "antiquarian" interests toward a more serious concern for the religious problems of the present. As a matter of fact, one of the trends of which we are all aware, because it has steadily gained strength within the last decade, shows the Old Testament scholar adding to his functions as a scientist the interests of the theologian, seeking to present the religious thought of the Old Testament as a unified system of belief and to demonstrate the vitality of this belief for our own day.

It will not be easy to serve as scientists as well as theologians; but, whether we desire it or not, the obligation to do just that is being thrust upon us with ever increasing force. In a very real sense this development in our circles is due to the challenge with which Christian religion is faced on practically all sides. Old Testament scholarship cannot ignore these larger issues in favor of its own little world of research. To do so would be clear proof of its own spiritual poverty and of its betrayal of the great heritage of which it claims to be the interpreter.

However, before we pursue this discussion of the place of theology in Old Testament research during the years ahead, let us

---

17. E.g., E. R. Thiele, "Chronology of the Kings of Israel and Judah," *Journal of Near Eastern Studies*, III (1944), 137–86. More briefly, W. F. Albright, "The Chronology of the Divided Kingdom of Israel," *Bulletin of the American Schools of Oriental Research*, December, 1945, pp. 16–22.

pause for a moment to consider a different aspect of the study of Hebrew religion. It seems hard to suppose that this new interest in theology will completely put an end to the kind of investigations which until recently were the only ones thought to be appropriate, that is to say, the type of scientific inquiry associated with the term "history of religion." We still need to gather facts, and for this no better method has been devised than the historical one, with its techniques. That a rich harvest still awaits the historian of religion is shown by the epoch-making discoveries in the ruins of Ugarit in northern Syria. Though these findings have yet to receive their final interpretation, they have already yielded extremely important results for our knowledge of Canaanite religion and the environment in which Hebrew faith was molded. The conflict of the prophets with the popular worship of their times, the mythology, the moral values, and the practices of the fertility cults—all have gained new meaning and greater clarity for us. We can confidently expect similar gains in the future. They, too, will have to be analyzed and assessed and their bearing on the Old Testament determined. This explains why historical studies of religion will continue to be a part of the program of Old Testament research, even if they are relegated to a position of secondary significance.

Belonging to this field of historical studies and definitely needing further treatment is the question of the psychology of the prophets. Since Hölscher[18] no one has attempted a thorough investigation of the prophets from this point of view, but his work is clearly outmoded, based as it is on psychological theories no longer accepted. Especially pertinent would be an examination of the prophetic religious experience for the purpose of determining the extent to which we can speak of the prophet as either a mystic or an ecstatic. Hölscher's efforts to find epistemological value in the prophetic experience itself, notably to regard the ecstatic trance as the real source of the prophet's religious knowledge, can no longer be considered seriously; but there can be no

18. G. Hölscher, *Die Profeten* (Leipzig, 1914). See also J. Lindblom, "Die literarische Gattung der prophetischen Literatur," *Uppsala Universitets Arsskrift*, 1924, pp. 1–122.

doubt that we shall require something to take its place as an authoritative discussion of this matter.

After this digression we are ready to return to the much more problematical area of Old Testament theology. As was said before, all trends seem to indicate that the real emphasis of future research will be here. In the past, major stress has largely been laid on determining the content and the historical development of Hebrew and Jewish religion or of the more significant of its concepts, while only little effort has been given to a presentation of the faith of the Old Testament as a unified whole. There can be no uncertainty about the desirability of such a synthesis, but it is equally true that some very important questions will have to be answered first.

What, therefore, seem to be some of the fundamental problems of Old Testament theology? The first one suggests itself immediately: *What is Old Testament theology?* Is it "the historical presentation of revealed religion during the period of its growth," as Schultz[19] defined it in the last century? Is it the study of the Old Testament basis of New Testament doctrines, as Wilhelm Vischer[20] seems to think? Is it concerned with throwing light on the inner nature of the religion of the Old Testament and with understanding its inner structure in comparison with the religions of the world around it or with the various types of religion which the history of religion has established, as Eichrodt[21] has maintained? Or is it, as it is to Eissfeldt,[22] the systematic discussion of the divine revelation, that is, God's Word, which is believed in by some particular confessional group? These are some of the answers given. The lack of any unanimity illustrates conclusively the need for a clear definition of what one holds Old Testament theology to be.

The next basic question concerns the *possibility of a systematic*

19. H. Schultz, *Alttestamentliche Theologie* (Göttingen, 1896).

20. W. Vischer, *Das Christuszeugnis des Alten Testaments* (Leipzig, 1935).

21. W. Eichrodt, "Hat die alttestamentliche Theologie noch selbständige Bedeutung innerhalb der alttestamentlichen Wissenschaft?" *Zeitschrift für die alttestamentliche Wissenschaft*, XLVII (1929), 83 ff.

22. O. Eissfeldt, "Israelitisch-jüdische Religionsgeschichte und alttestamentliche Theologie," *Zeitschrift für die alttestamentliche Wissenschaft*, XLIV (1926), 1 ff.

presentation of Old Testament religion. Considering the many varieties of religion which historical analysis has taught us to recognize and taking into account, also, the fact of development, is synthesis conceivable? Are there unifying elements—or, perhaps, one single element—around which we may group in an integrated form the multitude of religious ideas found in this book? Prophetic and priestly writings, with all their differences, are basically on common ground in their insistence on the absolute centrality of God, in their demand for man's complete loyalty to God, and in their emphasis on man's sinfulness. This convergence of the prophetic and priestly patterns of thought[23] was furthered by the Deuteronomic redactors, who thereby gave to the Old Testament a unity which it might otherwise not have had. However, can we also include in such a systematization the thought of the Wisdom movement? Do we have in this strand of the Old Testament something which stands too far outside the dominant prophetic-priestly tradition because of its pragmatic temper, its search for truth through observation and experiment, and its corresponding neglect of divine revelation? It is noteworthy, for example, that Eichrodt in his *Theologie*[24] can make only minor use of the Wisdom literature and that he finds none of his major principles of Old Testament thought therein. Does this mean that, actually, a theology of the whole Old Testament is out of the question because one of its major components resists integration?

The possibility of synthesis is contingent, furthermore, upon the solution of another and, perhaps, more serious problem, that of the *method to be employed.* The chief point in dispute here is, in effect, the relationship of the historical method to the doctrinal method of systematic theology. Must the former be ignored in favor of the latter because it cannot help us in our quest for the permanent values and the ultimate meaning of Old Testament faith, as Eissfeldt[25] has suggested? Or should our method be basically doctrinal, without, however, losing sight of the growth in Israel's thinking, a point of view recommended par-

23. See Aubrey R. Johnson, *The Cultic Prophet in Ancient Israel* (Cardiff, 1944).

24. W. Eichrodt, *Theologie des Alten Testaments* (3 vols.; Leipzig, 1933–39).

25. *Op. cit.*

ticularly by Eichrodt,[26] Sellin,[27] and Köhler?[28] Or, finally, ought we to retain the historical approach, in which case Old Testament theology would still be essentially a history of Hebrew religion, but a rearranged one, treating not so much the various epochs and their peculiarities as the development of individual concepts? These three possibilities, conflicting and in part contradictory, make it clear that the nature of the method to be used is a prime issue, concerning which we shall need to come to some kind of agreement.

Such are the not always easily answered questions of principle arising from our interest in Old Testament theology. They will undoubtedly loom large in any future discussions of the religious ideas of this book. By no means, however, do they represent the only matters calling for our attention. We shall need, for example, to give more thought to the unifying elements in the Old Testament in contrast to our usual concern for analysis, the discovery of differences, and the tracing of development. As Eichrodt has so suggestively demonstrated with the idea of the covenant, genuine integration and systematization are best achieved when they are based on such elements. Furthermore, extensive study will have to be devoted to the task of determining the content of the various concepts which are characteristic of Old Testament thought. Excellent illustrations of this type of work are provided by Glueck's treatment of the word *hesed*[29] and Kittel's theological dictionary of the New Testament.[30] These word studies, seeking as they do to ascertain the religious as well as the linguistic meaning of the vocabulary of the Old Testament, should be particularly helpful in laying a solid groundwork for the theological structure we shall be attempting to erect. Lastly, a distinctive part of this theological enterprise will be the formula-

26. *Theologie des Alten Testaments.*

27. E. Sellin, *Alttestamentliche Theologie auf religionsgeschichtlicher Grundlage* (2 vols.; Leipzig, 1933).

28. L. H. Köhler, *Theologie des Alten Testaments* (Tübingen, 1936).

29. N. Glueck, "Das Wort Ḥesed im alttestamentlichen Sprachgebrauche," *Zeitschrift für die alttestamentliche Wissenschaft*, Beih. 47 (Giessen, 1927).

30. *Theologisches Wörterbuch zum Neuen Testament*, ed. G. Kittel (Stuttgart, 1932——).

tion of a doctrine of Sacred Scripture. We are especially obligated to do so because most of contemporary Protestantism urgently requires something that will take the place of the Reformation teachings concerning the place and meaning of the Bible—teachings which, to a large extent, were robbed of their strength by the work of the biblical critics. Having torn down, we also have the responsibility of building up again.

The awakening interest in theology represents one of the most heartening signs of life in the field of Old Testament research and augurs well for the future. It gives us real reason to believe that biblical studies are actually far from coming to a standstill. It is particularly reassuring in an age when our Hebrew-Christian ideals and beliefs are being attacked with ever growing bitterness, for only by such vitality can we hope to maintain ourselves in the ideological struggles into which man now appears to be descending.

CHAPTER ELEVEN

The Future of Intertestamental Studies

RALPH MARCUS

University of Chicago

IT WOULD take a person of stronger character than the present writer to resist two temptations in discussing the future of intertestamental studies. One is that of taking the title to include the history and religion of the Jews in the Hellenistic-Roman period. The other is that of indicating what studies ought to be made rather than (or in addition to) what studies are likely to be made. Furthermore, in drawing up this prospectus, the present writer has particularly in mind the needs and interests of American readers, not for narrow nationalistic reasons but simply because our country seems likely to be a center of scholarship for a long time to come. With this confession of wilfulness, the writer will proceed to discuss the subject under a number of convenient headings.

I. JUDAISM AS A WHOLE IN THE HELLENISTIC-ROMAN PERIOD

There are two schools of thought concerning the possibility and desirability of undertaking ambitiously synthetic works in fields in which knowledge is far from complete or is rapidly increasing. There are those who advise postponement of synthetic studies until gaps have been filled and many detailed inquiries have been completed. The other school, to which the present writer belongs, holds that it is always desirable to attempt to give a synthesis of any field of knowledge, no matter how many important special problems remain unsolved, on the theory that every generation is entitled to make its own synthesis and that there will always be important new problems in history for the future to solve.

It is now almost forty years since the publication of the last

190

edition of Emil Schürer's *Geschichte des jüdischen Volkes im Zeitalter Jesu Christi*,[1] of which only the first edition, all too sketchy, was translated into English. It is a rather impressive fact that through four decades Schürer's work has remained the most useful one on the period as a whole, in spite of the fact that its detailed narrative begins only with the reign of Antiochus Epiphanes. No fair-minded person will deny the great merits of this three-volume work, its thoroughness in analyzing the sources, its wealth of detailed information, its conveniently classified bibliographies. But at the same time we must all recognize that the time has come to revise and amplify this work and to produce a new synthesis that will incorporate the many important discoveries that have been made since 1907. What we need at the present time is a "new Schürer," that is, a work of about the same scope written by a person who equals Schürer in classical knowledge and surpasses him in knowledge of rabbinics as well as in objectivity and who will, of course, make use of recent literature as thoroughly as did Schürer in his time.

In addition to such a monumental work, most teachers of biblical history in English-speaking lands would be glad to have a compendious book of the same scope as Schlatter's *Geschichte Israels von Alexander dem Grossen bis Hadrian* or Lagrange's *Le Judaïsme avant Jésus-Christ* or the second volume of Eduard Meyer's *Ursprung und Anfänge des Christentums* or the relevant volumes of the histories of the Jews written by Dubnow in Russian (better known in German translation), by Ricciotti in Italian, and by Klausner in Hebrew. What is here suggested is a one-volume work to cover the Hellenistic-Roman period in a general way. There are, to be sure, a few books in English which, at first sight, seem to serve this need, for example, the second volume of Oesterley and Robinson's *History of Israel*, which covers the post-Exilic period to about A.D. 100. But experienced teachers of this period will agree that Oesterley's book is far from being adequate to present-day needs.

In the field of the religion of the Jews in Palestine and the Dias-

---

1. For a comprehensive bibliography of the Jews in the Hellenistic-Roman period, covering the years between 1920 and 1945, see the present writer's article in the *Proceedings of the American Academy for Jewish Research*, Vol. XVI (1947).

pora (Palestinian religion will be discussed separately below) there has been no well-documented general treatise since Hugo Gressmann in 1926 brought out a third and revised edition of Bousset's *Die Religion des Judentums im späthellenistischen Zeitalter*. Except for the fact that Gressmann was not entirely successful in removing traces of Bousset's antirabbinic bias, the volume deserves praise for its representative selection of passages and its attention to external influences on the development of early Judaism. But here again we may be justified in thinking particularly of the needs of the English-speaking student and express the hope that an English adaptation or counterpart of the useful German treatise will soon appear. The contents of such a future work need not differ greatly from those of the Bousset-Gressmann volume, but there should, of course, be a change in emphasis where needed, and the perspective must be corrected to allow for our somewhat different estimate of the weight and variety of pagan influences on Palestinian and Diaspora Judaism, as well as our greater insight into the problem of the relation between Diaspora and Palestinian religion. To some aspects of these general problems we shall return.

At this point we should also speak of the need of a general orientation on the synagogue as an institution common to Palestine and the Diaspora. The latest detailed book on the subject is Samuel Krauss's *Synagogale Altertümer*, which was published as long ago as 1922. Since that time a great deal of important archeological material has been uncovered, which throws new light on many details of synagogue architecture and decoration and on the religious and secular aspects of the synagogue as a community center. Some of these new discoveries were summarized in E. L. Sukenik's Schweich Lectures of 1930, published in 1934 under the title *Ancient Synagogues in Palestine and Greece*. But many more discoveries have been made even more recently, notably at Dura-Europos on the Euphrates, where the synagogue wall-paintings illustrating biblical scenes have revealed a whole new field of Jewish religious art. And so it seems clear that we are ready for a new work along the lines of Krauss's book. It may be that such a book will be written in Hebrew by some of the

Palestinian scholars who have been particularly productive in this field. If they should bring out such a work, they should make it accessible to the larger audience of non-Hebraists by providing an English translation.

We now come to the subject of intertestamental literature as a whole. We have all been heavily indebted to Canon R. H. Charles for his editorship of the imposing two-volume corpus called *The Apocrypha and Pseudepigrapha of the Old Testament*, with its excellent translations by various British scholars, and the useful introductions, critical and explanatory notes, and Index. But it came out more than thirty years ago; and as in the case of the works by Schürer and Bousset-Gressmann, so in the case of the Charles *Apocrypha*, we are ready for a new collection of annotated translations. Such a new collection should not only represent scholarly progress but should also be an improvement in respect to pedagogical and practical convenience. The two volumes of Charles are now prohibitively expensive for the average student and young instructor. They are also rather heavy and clumsy to handle. In the third place, the critical apparatus to each book seems disproportionately large in the absence of the original text. Finally, in respect to the amount of pseudepigraphic material included, the work falls short of the one-volume German translation of intertestamental literature published by Paul Riessler in 1928 under the title *Altjüdisches Schrifttum ausserhalb der Bibel*. One might think of the "Translations of Early Documents" put out by the Society for Promoting Christian Knowledge as meeting the need, but the expense of so many volumes, if the series were completed, and the amount of shelf-space required would be a serious drawback. To the present writer it seems most desirable to have the Oxford Press plan a new, revised, and enlarged edition of Charles. Such an edition might include more pseudepigraphic works and, at the same time, be less bulky and expensive if the present critical apparatus and introduction to each book were reduced and thinner paper were used. The loss of detail in the critical apparatus would be compensated by the publication of such separate works as will be suggested in the following paragraph.

Probably all biblical students today would agree that intertestamental books are as deserving of a place in a series of biblical commentaries as are books of the Old and New Testament. But not even in German is there a complete set of critical and exegetical commentaries on the Apocrypha and pseudepigrapha, though such an undertaking seems to have been planned by Otto Eissfeldt as editor of a *Handbuch zum Alten Testament* and by F. Feldmann and H. Herkenne as editors of *Die Heilige Schrift des Alten Testaments*. For the sake of piety one should parenthetically mention the wonderfully learned series of commentaries edited by Otto Fritzsche some seventy years ago, but these did not include the pseudepigrapha. At the present time the scholar who wishes to do exegetical work in this field is obliged to consult scattered volumes written over a long period of time. The writer would therefore suggest that some enterprising body like the Society of Biblical Literature plan a series of commentaries on the intertestamental literature that will be less detailed than the volumes of the "International Critical Commentary" and more detailed than those of the Eissfeldt series or of the Hebrew series edited by A. Kahana.

As for introductions to the literature of this period, we seem to be in a better situation. C. C. Torrey, the venerable and distinguished Semitist of Yale University, who began working in this field over fifty years ago, has just given us a brief survey called *The Apocryphal Literature*. This book does not pretend to be an exhaustive study, but, like most of Professor Torrey's works, it is original and challenging enough to stimulate further research along several lines (some of which will be discussed below). There is also reason to believe that Robert Pfeiffer, whose wide reading, freshness of approach, and skill in exposition make his *Introduction to the Old Testament* the best book of its kind, will soon complete a similar work on the Apocrypha and pseudepigrapha.

II. HISTORY OF THE JEWS IN PALESTINE

Thanks largely to archeological discovery, our knowledge of the economic, social, and political history of the Jews in Palestine has increased considerably in the last twenty-five years.

Thanks also to the application of the methods of religious sociology worked out by Max Weber and his followers, a conscious attempt has been made by biblical historians to maintain a truer balance between political history, on the one hand, and economic and social history, on the other.

But some of the new discoveries and recent sociological theories have not yet been adequately fitted into the general literature on this particular period of Palestinian history. So far as the present writer knows, there is not in any language an up-to-date economic and social history of the Jews in Palestine in the intertestamental period or even a political history that gives a satisfactory account of the increase of our knowledge since the end of the first World War.

This negative statement does not mean that the writer fails to appreciate the value of recent work done in the fields of Palestinian economic, social, and political history and in the auxiliary fields of topography, numismatics, epigraphy, monumental archeology, and the like by such men as Abel, Avi-Yonah, Bickermann, Dalman, Heichelheim, Jeremias, Klein, Momigliano, Narkiss, Reifenberg, Schalit, Schwabe, Tcherikover, and many others. What is meant here is simply that the time has come for a new summing-up of the advances in our knowledge of Palestinian history in the Hellenistic-Roman period. We need a work that will fully take account of the new finds and the reinterpretations based on those finds, as well as of the philological innovations arising from more critical and more comparative methods of interpretation. An example of how a hitherto vaguely known area has been illuminated is the admirable way in which Tcherikover has used the Zenon Papyri to give us a reconstruction of the economic and social structure of Ptolemaic Palestine.

Turning to more specialized desiderata, we find that many archeological finds from this period have not yet found their proper historical evaluation, even though they have been brought to the attention of the nonspecialist in such competently and attractively written books as those put out by Carl Watzinger, Millar Burrows, and Jack Finegan between 1933 and 1945. One would like to see the late Père Jean-Baptiste Frey's *Corpus*

inscriptionum Judaicarum continued and provided with a volume on the Greek and Semitic inscriptions of Palestine as ably treated as were those of Europe by the lamented French scholar. Another desirable work would be a revision of that minor classic, the *Essai sur l'histoire et la géographie de la Palestine* by Josèphe Derenbourg, which after eighty years is still the best thing of its kind; but such a revision should include the rabbinic passages on the early Hellenistic period, barely treated by Derenbourg.

III. PALESTINIAN JEWISH RELIGION

There is no lack of convenient and fairly recent handbooks of the religion of the Palestinian Jews in the intertestamental period. In addition to the relevant sections in such general works on early Judaism as those by Bousset-Gressmann, Causse, and others, we have at least two monumental works on Palestinian Judaism which provide a wealth of information based on source material, though the two books are very different in outlook and emphasis. These two works are George Foot Moore's *Judaism in the First Centuries of the Christian Era* and J. Bonsirven's *Le Judaïsme palestinien au temps de Jésus-Christ*. This is not the place to attempt to give an estimate of either book, but it will be necessary to speak briefly of Moore's *Judaism* in order to make a point concerning the need of further works in the same field.

No one who has used Moore's volumes can fail to be impressed by the architectonic qualities of the work, even if he does not happen to know that it represents the mature judgment of a keen and objective mind, learnedly engaged for over forty years in sifting intertestamental and Tannaite sources. But Moore's *Judaism*, for all its learning, breadth, and accuracy, does not exhaust the possibilities of synthesis in this field. In the first place, it is concerned almost exclusively with Pharisaic Judaism and has almost nothing to say of other early Jewish movements and groups. In the second place, it is restricted to the Haggadah and thus gives us only the theological views of the more articulate and influential circles.

But in order to understand the social-psychological pattern of an ethnic or cultural community it is essential to know not only

their myths and theology but also their folkways, religious ceremonies, and legal institutions. And it is important to know the philosophical or religious or ethical principles underlying those ceremonies and institutions. For example, the Jewish law of debt provides that a man accused of not repaying the entire amount of a loan may establish his innocence by swearing that he has repaid the full amount, whereas a man accused of not paying back any part of a loan and denying that he has received the loan at all is acquitted by his mere denial. This seems to us a bizarre and illogical ruling. But it is based on sound moral and psychological principles. Since loans to fellow-Jews were made without charging interest, it was assumed by the rabbinic authorities that no Jewish debtor would be so lacking in simple decency as to deny receiving any loan at all, whereas a weak-willed or hard-pressed debtor might yield to the temptation of trying to get out of repaying the whole debt; hence they required an oath of innocence in the latter case but none in the former.

This is merely one instance of the importance of the Halakah or the civil and ceremonial law contained in the Mishnah and other Tannaite writings in establishing the ethos and the ethics of Palestinian Judaism. What the writer would therefore like to see undertaken is a substantial volume on the religious and moral philosophy of early Judaism as they are represented in the halakic portions of intertestamental literature. Such a volume would be a most welcome parallel and supplement to Moore's *Judaism* if it were written with the same objectivity and insight that Moore showed in interpreting the Haggadic portions of early rabbinic literature.

Another welcome *novum* would be a volume on the daily life of the average Jew in the Tannaite period, which would give an account of the various religious and social ceremonies that were observed by men of various schools at different seasons. A course on this subject has for several years been given at the Jewish Theological Seminary by that distinguished Talmudist, Louis Ginzberg. Since Professor Ginzberg, who is now in his seventies, is immersed in his Hebrew commentary on the Palestinian

Talmud, of which three volumes have been published to date, it seems unlikely that he can be persuaded to undertake the writing of such a work in English. But perhaps one of the younger scholars whom he has trained will some day give us such a book, which will treat the social and religious aspects of the daily life of individual Jews and communities in a quite different way from that followed in an archeological handbook like Samuel Krauss's *Archäologie der Talmud*, however useful the latter may be in its own way.

It was in the intertestamental period that the Jewish liturgy was essentially formed and canonized. The normative prayers and the system of Scripture readings in the synagogue, which, incidentally, were of great importance for the early Christian church, were during this period given the form and function that they have retained for almost two milleniums. The development of the liturgy as a whole is admirably presented in the late Ismar Elbogen's *Der jüdische Gottesdienst*, of which a third revised edition appeared in 1931. However, only half the book is devoted to the liturgy of our period; also, a number of important studies in the history of the early liturgy by V. Aptowitzer, Jacob Mann, A. Marmorstein, Louis Finkelstein, and others have been published within the last decade or so. Moreover, the contents and nature of the prayers contained in nonrabbinic intertestamental literature have not yet been adequately studied and related to the prayers known from Tannaite sources. Another neglected subject is the theology of the prayers in the intertestamental literature as a whole; it would be most instructive to have popular piety compared with that of the rabbinic authorities. All these aspects of the liturgy might well be combined in a study that would also incorporate the material published since Elbogen's work appeared.

The Jewish parties or "sects" (to use the term traditionally representing the Greek word *haireseis* applied to them by Josephus) deserve special mention in this section. The two most important groups, Pharisees and Sadducees, have been almost exhaustively discussed ever since Abraham Geiger in 1857 opened the modern period of evaluation with the publication of his

Urschrift und Übersetzungen der Bibel. From that time on there has been a tug of war between two groups of scholars, each of them including Christians and Jews, over the question of whether the differences between the Pharisees and the Sadducees were primarily economic, social, and political, on the one hand, or theological and philosophical, on the other. Most contemporary scholars seem to be coming around to the reasonable opinion that both sociological and theological differences are involved, for what now seems the obvious reason that the Jews of that period did not make any such distinction between sociology and religion as we are accustomed to make.

But beyond this general position (which, incidentally, is not yet too firmly established), it remains to determine just what differences in social or religious philosophy were involved. In this field the most original and, at the same time, the soundest theories, in the writer's opinion, have been put forth by the late Professor Jacob Lauterbach and especially by Louis Ginzberg, who has been mentioned above. Although Professor Ginzberg's theories have not been published in extensive and detailed form in a special work on the Pharisees and Sadducees, they are implied or alluded to in a number of his studies on early rabbinic literature. The nearest thing to a formal and systematic presentation of his views on the subject is perhaps the reprint of a Hebrew lecture which he delivered in Jerusalem in 1931 under the title, *Meqomah shel ha-Halakah be-Hokmat Yisrael* ("The Place of the Halakah in the Study of Judaism"). This lecture we can only summarize with the bare statement that it most ingeniously explains the puzzling controversies over some ritual regulations by using the sociological method. Although this little essay was published in 1931, it is merely the partial distillation of his oral instruction, which goes back several decades. Ginzberg's theories have been adopted and applied to similar aspects of the Halakah by several of his talented pupils, notably, Louis Finkelstein, now president of the same institution in which he sat at the feet of Professor Ginzberg. In two important works Professor Finkelstein has attempted to find a formula that will harmonize the varying, and in part incongruous, accounts of the sects given by the ancient

sources and modern interpretations. The first of these was a long article published in the *Harvard Theological Review* in 1929; the second was an enlarged and revised presentation of his original thesis, with the addition of a sketch of Jewish religious history from the prophetic to the Tannaite periods, which appeared in 1938 in two volumes with the title, *The Pharisees: The Sociological Background of Their Faith.*

Even a miniature critique of Finkelstein's theory would be out of place and take too much time in this survey. But the present writer must say just enough about it to justify his opinion that it does not end the search for a fully satisfactory explanation of the essential nature of the various Pharisee-Sadducee controversies. It is Finkelstein's merit to have conveniently assembled the sources in Josephus, the Gospels, and rabbinic literature and to have called attention to the importance of the sociological method so successfully applied by his teacher to specific controversies. But in his laudable ambition to discover a master-theory and perhaps subconsciously influenced by the desire to see in the Pharisees prototypes of American Puritans, he has stretched his rural-urban theory so far and so thin that it does not hold together the various differences mentioned in the ancient sources. Even if we were to grant (which the present writer would only tentatively do) that the Pharisees were predominantly an urban group and the Sadducees predominantly a rural group (a supposition that was rigidly formulated in the monograph and modified so as to be more fluid in the two-volume work), this theory would not fit all the controversies discussed by Finkelstein, though he has made a desperate attempt to see elements of "rural tenderness" in Galilean peasants and to discover "lower lay patricians" in Jerusalem, contempt for book-learning among the "assimilationist" Sadducees, and other strange combinations. A less ingenious, but probably sounder, explanation of the basic difference between the two groups would seem to lie waiting for us on a different level; it might be formulated briefly as follows: The Sadducees were the aristocratic and wealthy priests whose special rights and privileges, including ecclesiastical benefits, were guaranteed by the constitution (*politeia*) of the theocratic Judean

state, namely, the Mosaic law in written form. Whatever ameliorative legislation the Pharisaic scholars wished to promote in the interests of the middle and lower classes had to be obtained through construction of the written law or by novel enactments.

As for their religious or philosophical differences, it is unsafe to read as much into Josephus as does Finkelstein, for the simple (or perhaps not so simple) reason that his account of the sects, which is probably drawn from Nicolas of Damascus (though that is not a primary consideration), is not the factual testimony of an insider but the retouched rhetorical exposition made for the benefit of cultured pagans by a would-be philosopher (for the moment), who in part explicitly, in part implicitly, compares the Pharisees with the Stoics and the Sadducees with the Epicureans —Eduard Meyer (*Ursprung*, II, 297, n. 1) to the contrary notwithstanding.

This divagation from the proper subject of our paper may be excused on the ground that it was needed to make clear why there is need for a new study of the two leading Jewish "sects." Such a study should make full use of the extremely useful materials furnished by recent workers of both the sociological and the theological schools of thought; but it should strive for greater objectivity than has yet been shown by those who have written ambitious treatises on this subject. It is hardly necessary to add that the future historian should also strive to maintain that disinterested and sympathetic attitude toward the Pharisees with which liberal Christian scholars like Strack, Moore, and Herford have sought to replace the narrowly prejudiced attitude of earlier scholars like Wellhausen and Charles. At this late date it should not be too much to expect biblical scholarship to have emancipated itself from the polemical spirit of ancient Christian and Jewish writers.

That enigmatic group, the Essenes, has been a subject of learned speculation since the early Christian centuries, but we do not know much more about it now than did scholars of preceding generations. The fundamental problem of whether or not the Essenes are to be identified with groups with like-sounding names mentioned in rabbinic literature has not been solved. Nor

has any scholar convincingly shown whether Jewish or Greek or oriental influence is paramount in their beliefs and practices. The first seems most likely but has not yet been demonstrated to the satisfaction of all who have wrestled with the problem. But that is no reason why new attempts should not be made.

Even more complicated and less extensively studied is the problem of Jewish gnosticism. Here, too, one must deal with the gnarled problem of the relations of Jewish gnostics to the *Minim*, though this particular aspect of the problem does seem to be as near a definitive solution as can reasonably be expected. When Heinrich Graetz published his *Gnosticismus und Judentum* just a hundred years ago, his analytical talents were restricted by the paucity of material to be found in Tannaite literature, in the *Sepher Yeṣirah*, and a few other sources. Since that time our knowledge of Hellenistic gnosis has been enormously increased by the discovery of Coptic, Manichaean, and Mandaic documents and by comparative studies relating Hellenistic gnosticism to ancient oriental beliefs as well as to movements in early Judaism and Christianity. This wealth of material is beginning to be more fully utilized by biblical scholars, though not always cautiously. It must be admitted, however, that there is much more gnosticism in both Apocalyptic Judaism and Pauline Christianity than was formerly believed, in spite of the fact that both the rabbis and Paul were professed opponents of gnosticism. We understand more clearly today than did our predecessors how ambivalent the attitudes of religious thinkers, especially mystics, may be. It would be a great contribution to our knowledge of Hellenistic religions if some scholar would give us a comprehensive study of early Jewish gnosticism comparable in insight and learning with the masterly work on later Jewish mysticism, which Gershom Scholem has given us in his *Major Trends of Jewish Mysticism*.

IV. PALESTINIAN LITERATURE

A part of the work that might be laid out (not too didactically, the writer trusts) for students of Palestinian apocryphal literature has already been mentioned in the first section. Here we may suggest a few tasks of immediate interest. One of these is

the restudying of the problem of the original language of some of the late biblical and apocryphal works. There has recently been a tendency, exemplified by C. C. Torrey, Frank Zimmermann, and L. Gry among others, to regard Aramaic rather than Hebrew as the original language of Daniel, Ecclesiastes, Enoch, IV Esdras, the Additions to Esther, and so on. In the case of books like Daniel and Esther there is no a priori reason why they should not have been written in Aramaic, since they purport to describe events that happened in Babylonia and Persia in post-Exilic times. But that books like Enoch and the Assumption of Moses, which passed as the writings of Palestinian patriarchs, should have been published (not merely drafted) in Aramaic rather than Hebrew is a theory that would compel assent only if it were supported by more compelling philological arguments than have so far been made.

It would also be useful to have a careful collection of Old Testament quotations in the apocryphal literature with analyses of their textual and theological nature. There is also room for fresh studies of some of the quasi-sectarian books like Jubilees and the Damascus Covenant, which abound in all sorts of historical and halakic problems. Perhaps some student of Louis Ginzberg will give us a continuation of his teacher's valuable commentary on the Damascus Covenant, as well as a comprehensive treatment of the Book of Jubilees; the varying views concerning its character and authorship, which have been expressed in recent times by experts like Louis Finkelstein, Solomon Zeitlin, Hanoch Albeck, and others, call for a new critical and exegetical commentary. There are also various problems of a literary nature connected with the apocalyptic books that remain to be solved.

Considerable progress has been made within the past few decades in the critical editing and translating of Tannaite literature. With the publication of Louis Finkelstein's edition of Siphre to Deuteronomy in the *Corpus Tannaiticum*, which was almost complete in page proof before the Nazi plague struck down the Jews of Germany, we shall have excellent texts of all the halakic Midrashim. Whether a critical edition of the Mishnah is possible some eminent Talmudists seriously doubt. But we may

cherish the more modest hope that there will some day be a *Handausgabe* of the Mishnah giving a Textus Receptus based on early printed editions and including variant readings from the Cambridge, Parma, and Kaufmann manuscripts and the citations in the commentary of Maimonides (in those portions where the text has been reliably ascertained).[2] English readers have been fortunate in being provided with the useful translation of the Mishnah by Canon Danby and the authoritative translation of the Mekilta by Jacob Lauterbach. The series of translations of Hebrew literature, recently established at Yale University under the editorship of Julian Obermann, will probably soon give us competent English translations of other Tannaite books. Another boon to students of early rabbinic literature will be the completion of the series of concordances to the Tannaite writings which was begun by J. Kassowsky of Jerusalem. Finally, it is to be hoped that some society or foundation will soon make possible the publication of Alexander Sperber's critical edition of the Targum to the prophets. This work is mentioned here because of the present writer's conviction that Targums to the Pentateuch and to the prophets existed in written form before the first century A.D.

With these indispensable tasks well in hand, we should begin to plan for the further utilization of early rabbinic literature in the interpretation of early Judaism. A number of specific projects may be suggested, such as a translation of Tannaite texts arranged under theological headings, a work on the theology of the Targums, and a dictionary of Tannaite Hebrew and Aramaic. Also desirable would be a companion work to Louis Ginzberg's *magnum opus*—the *Legends of the Jews*—which would give the original texts of the apocryphal and Tannaite Midrashim there paraphrased and identified in the notes.

But, since Palestinian Jewish studies have already taken up a disproportionate amount of space, we must hastily turn to the subject of Hellenistic Judaism.

---

2. As this paper goes to press, the writer is glad to receive the first volume of a new critical edition of the Mishnah with English translation and commentary, published by the Fellows of the Harry Fischel Institute in Jerusalem.

V. HELLENISTIC JUDAISM

Anyone who wishes to present a well-rounded economic, social, and political history of the Jews in the Hellenistic Diaspora would do well to keep before himself as a model Michael Rostovtzeff's *Social and Economic History of the Hellenistic World*, a remarkable synthesis of widely scattered materials. At the same time, our prospective historian would find his task simplified by making use of the great amount of bibliographical material assembled by Jean Juster some thirty years ago in his *Les Juifs dans l'empire romain*, but he should bring it up to date. Another important task is the completion of the admirable *Corpus inscriptionum Judaicarum* begun by the late Père J.-B. Frey, of which the first volume contains the inscriptions found in Europe. For the compilation of a second volume containing the inscriptions found in Asia and Africa we might look to one of the able epigraphists trained by Moses Schwabe of Jerusalem. A clear desideratum is a revised and enlarged edition of Theodore Reinach's *Textes d'auteurs grecs et romains relatifs au Judaïsme*, which appeared back in 1895. Such a new edition was planned by Hans Lewy of the Hebrew University, but the work so brilliantly begun in his studies of Hecataeus, Tacitus, and other classical writers on the Jews was ended by his untimely death in the summer of 1945.

Coming, now, to the histories of separate Jewish communities, we are glad to note that V. Tcherikover of Jerusalem expects to bring out a corpus of papyri and ostraca relating to the Jews of Egypt. How much valuable information these sources yield has just been demonstrated by Tcherikover in his excellent work, *The Jews in Egypt in the Hellenistic-Roman Age in the Light of the Papyri*. Though the book is written in Hebrew, Western readers will find its chief conclusions stated in a thirty-page English summary. No doubt the same author will some day give us a definitive history of the Jews in Egypt on the basis of the literary sources as well as the papyri and ostraca. We have had recent sketches of the history of the Jewish communities in Rome and Antioch by Père Frey, H. Vogelstein, Carl Kraeling, and others, but more comprehensive and detailed studies of these important

Jewish centers remain to be written. For Alexandria much historical and archeological information can be gleaned from the works of Philo. Then, too, there is the neglected field of the history of the Jews in Asia Minor and Mesopotamia. Perhaps future discoveries as revealing as that of the synagogue at Dura-Europos will enrich our knowledge of these little-known areas of Jewish settlement.

The cultural and religious problems of Hellenistic Judaism have received increasingly careful consideration in recent years. We are gradually coming to understand more clearly the relation of Hellenistic Judaism to gentile culture, on the one hand, and to Palestinian Judaism, on the other. The degree of assimilation to Greek culture undergone by the Greek-speaking Jews of the Diaspora and the extent to which they differed from their Palestinian coreligionists are involved problems which require all the resources of philology and cultural anthropology to approach with confidence. In the writer's opinion the recent studies of such scholars as Georg Bertram, Isaac Heinemann, and (*sit venia verbo*) his own point to the conclusion that most educated Hellenistic Jews underwent a high degree of assimilation to the external forms of pagan culture (Philo being a conspicuous example and not merely an exception) but continued to be inwardly at one with the spirit of Pharisaic Judaism.

Nevertheless, many special problems remain to be clarified. What, for example, was the relation of the synagogal observances of the Therapeuts to those of more typical Alexandrian Jews? How seriously are we to take the thesis championed some twenty years ago by L. Cerfaux that certain Jews in Alexandria were organized into a Jewish mystery cult and practiced a non-normative *Kyrios* mysticism? Perhaps the researches now being pursued by Erwin Goodenough in the archeology of Hellenistic Judaism will throw more light on this question.

An especially promising field of study from the point of view of the Hellenization of the Hebrew religion is to be found in the study of the vocabulary of the Septuagint, as Adolf Deissmann showed many years ago. There is a good deal of material relevant to this study in the still unfinished *Theologisches Wörterbuch zum*

Neuen Testament, edited by Gerhard Kittel (who has perhaps disqualified himself from continuing as editor by his un-Christian conversion to Nazi ideology), but the Septuagint deserves a theological lexicon of its own. Incidentally, it is high time that biblical lexicologists begin to plan a new and revised edition of Schleusner's *Novus Thesaurus*, which after a hundred and twenty-five years of faithful service deserves the recognition of honorable retirement.

As for the field of extra-biblical Hellenistic Jewish literature, we must content ourselves with briefly mentioning the works that are in progress. The critical editions and annotated translations of Philo and Josephus in the "Loeb Classical Library" are gradually nearing completion. That remarkable octogenarian, F. H. Colson, fortunately lived long enough to complete the tenth volume of his admirable series of Philo translations in the "Loeb Library" during the past year. An eleventh volume, containing a translation of Philo's *Quaestiones* from the Armenian with partial retranslation into Greek, is being prepared by the writer, who hopes to complete the "Loeb" Josephus reasonably soon after the Philo volume appears. The *Greek Lexicon to Josephus*, begun by the late St. John Thackeray and continued by the writer, is slowly progressing, and new fascicles may be expected to appear in a year or so if the European publisher and printer succeed this year in putting their war-harassed businesses in order. Beside these helps the scholar in the field of Hellenistic Judaism would be greatly assisted by the publication of a new collection and critical edition of fragmentarily preserved writers like Eupolemos, Artapanos, and Aristobulus and the Jewish apologists using pagan literary names, since Wallace Stearns's *Fragments from Graeco-Jewish Writers* is out of date and hard to obtain.

The subject of Philonic studies is too large to be touched on in casual fashion. A glance at Goodhart and Goodenough's *Bibliography of Philo* will reveal the enormous increase of literature on Philo during the past few decades. By the time this paper is published, there will have appeared a study of Philo's religious philosophy and its influence on later thought, by that distinguished historian of philosophy, Harry A. Wolfson, of Harvard, whose

avowed purpose is to rehabilitate Philo as a major philosopher. It may be safely predicted that Professor Wolfson's ambitious work will evoke a large number of supplementary studies.

VI. CONCLUSION

This survey, addressed to professional students of the Bible, has necessarily taken the form of a bibliographical commentary. But the writer would consider it unfortunate if a casual reader were to glance at this paper and dismiss it as a piece of trivial scholarship on the ground that this age of crisis demands the discussion of ideas rather than books. The writer ardently believes that the Judeo-Christian religion has an even more fateful part to play in the drama of modern civilization than it had in ancient times. Now, the prophetic teachings of social justice, world brotherhood, and the kingdom of God in all the richness of its meaning were crystallized in the Jewish writings of the intertestamental period and in those of their Christian successors. In this period the Judeo-Christian religion was given its classical form. And to interpret this religion and to reveal its insights to the desperately groping minds of modern men is the task of the scholars who have laboriously, skilfully, and reverently sought to feel their way into this older time.

For such reasons we have sought to present a plan of study to younger scholars and to indicate, however inadequately, how they can contribute to the understanding of early Judaism and nascent Christianity. In the days of Nehemiah "everyone with one of his hands wrought in the work, and with the other held a weapon." In our own day let every scholar do his work with one hand, so to speak, and with his other let him hold the weapon of prophetic zeal to defend Judeo-Christian civilization.

CHAPTER TWELVE

Urgent Tasks for New Testament Research

PAUL SCHUBERT

University of Chicago

I

IT WOULD be comparatively easy to discuss a small or large number of possible and desirable research projects for scholars and Ph.D. candidates in New Testament research. If the list were longish, some of the suggestions might possibly qualify as urgent tasks. It would not be too difficult to produce a rather good list of such research items, since the compiler could rely on a respectable number of competent discussions recently published.[1] Singly and taken together, they nearly exhaust the possibilities of urgent tasks and exhibit a large number of specific problems with which New Testament research faces the future.

1. Diagnoses and prognoses are frequently made in all fields of research. For New Testament study the following representative items may be mentioned: *American:* B. W. Bacon, "Ultimate Problems of Biblical Science," *Journal of Biblical Literature,* XXII (1903), 1–14; J. A. Montgomery, "Present Tasks of American Biblical Scholarship," *Journal of Biblical Literature,* XXXVII (1918), 1–14; C. T. Craig, "Current Trends in New Testament Study," *Journal of Biblical Literature,* LVII (1938), 359–75; C. Jackson, "The Seminary Professor and New Testament Research," *Journal of Religion,* XVII (1937), 183–94; H. J. Cadbury, "The Present State of New Testament Studies," in *The Haverford Symposium on Archaeology and the Bible,* ed. Elihu Grant (New Haven, 1938), pp. 79–110, a full and well-balanced discussion; by the same author, "The New Testament in the Next Generation," *Journal of Religion,* XXI (1941), 412–20; M. Dibelius, "The Text of Acts: An Urgent Critical Task," *Journal of Religion,* XXI (1941), 421–31; M. Enslin, "The Future of Biblical Studies," *Journal of Biblical Literature,* LXV (1946), 1–12; C. C. McCown, "In History or beyond History," *Harvard Theological Review,* XXXVIII (1945), 151–75. *British:* C. H. Turner, *The Study of the New Testament: 1883–1920* (Oxford, 1920); W. Sanday, *The Study of the New Testament: Its Present Position and Some of Its Problems* (Oxford, 1883); J. Moffatt, *The Approach to the New Testament* (London, 1931), esp. chaps. iv–viii; C. H. Dodd, *The Present Task in New Testament Studies* (Cambridge, 1936). *German:* J. Weiss, *Die Aufgaben der neutestamentlichen Wissenschaft in der Gegenwart* (Göttingen, 1908); J. Leipoldt, *Gegenwartsfragen in der neutestamentlichen Wissenschaft* (Leipzig, 1935).

Some of these surveys, especially those by C. H. Dodd and C. T. Craig, first discuss in the conventional and approved fashion the present state of New Testament research, grouping the problems according to the traditional fields of specialization within which New Testament research is usually carried on. Their real burden, however, is to suggest a new, urgent task for New Testament scholarship. Craig arrives at the following conclusion:

Research in the New Testament cannot escape this question: is there any religious reason why its discoveries should still be disseminated? Has the disinterested love for truth destroyed every compelling reason why these documents should be studied outside of a small group of scholarly specialists? Such questions will not be answered in the same way by every individual, but they must be faced by every sincere student of the New Testament. Speaking for myself, I would say that everything depends upon the significance which we still find in the essential apostolic faith. If that no longer has any meaning for us, then the New Testament has only antiquarian interest. It records what the men believed in whose spiritual lineage we stand. But it is no longer central if our faith has become a different one. It should be clear, however, that such a conclusion is forced upon one not by history but by individual faith. It is inevitable that the New Testament speaks the language of the first century rather than the fourth, or the sixteenth, or the twentieth. But for those who find abiding significance in the apostolic message, the New Testament must still stand at the center of religious faith.[2]

There is in Craig's questions and in his own answer an apparent suggestion that the disinterested love for truth may become dangerous and that in the study of history it can, at best, have only antiquarian interest. Craig seems to say that "every sincere New Testament student" is forced into an inescapable dilemma. One task of his is to study the New Testament with disinterested love of truth; the other is to interpret it in the light of individual faith. In the article here quoted both tasks seem to be necessary; but they are separate, if not irreconcilable, since it is suggested that they may lead to opposite results. However, it seems that in his larger work, *The Beginning of Christianity*,[3] he brings the two tasks together.

2. *Op. cit.*, p. 375.

3. New York, 1943.

Dodd's problems are the same. His analysis of the situation is as follows:

The influence of analytical criticism upon the interpretation of the New Testament was far-reaching, and not in all respects beneficial. . . . . [It] was in its time of quite incalculable value for clear thinking, and opened a fruitful period of investigation. But its exclusive dominance led to a piecemeal treatment of early Christian thought, which in the end made it more difficult to understand the New Testament as a whole, and left the mind bewildered by its diversity.[4]

From this analysis follows Dodd's view of the urgent task ahead for New Testament scholarship. This task is

. . . . to approximate by degrees to a clear and conclusive understanding of the essential purport of the New Testament in its various parts and as a whole, which is the goal of all interpretation. Interpretation in this sense culminates in biblical theology, which is the ἀκρογωνιαῖον of the whole building.[5] . . . . The emphasis laid in some recent work upon this principle of inner unity, as controlling all specialized research in the New Testament field, is a sign that we have entered upon a new stage of interpretation.[6] . . . . Our study is in the first place historical, for it aims at the interpretation of that significant phenomenon in history which is early Christianity. Such study is peculiarly relevant to a religion which so emphatically announces itself as an historical revelation. But the interpreter I have in mind will be one who, having penetrated to the historical actuality of first-century Christianity, has received an impression of the truth in it which lies beyond the flux of time, and demands to be restated in terms intelligible to the mind of our own age.[7]

Thus Dodd insists that the basic task of New Testament research is historical; but not many historians who have "penetrated to the historical actuality of first-century Christianity" receive the Platonic impression "of the truth in it which lies beyond the flux of time." In fact, they receive such widely different impressions, expressed in such a variety of notions and value-judgments that New Testament interpretation, if its aim were generally accepted in Dodd's terms, would result in the same confusion as before.

Nevertheless, Craig's and Dodd's suggestions as to *the* urgent task of New Testament research should be taken as well-consid-

4. *Op. cit.*, pp. 32 f.   5. *Ibid.*, p. 8.   6. *Ibid.*, p. 35.   7. *Ibid.*, pp. 37 f.

ered answers to vital questions which, in one way or another, occupy the minds of all New Testament scholars, at least of all those who consider themselves as historians of early Christianity. Even though Dodd and Craig cannot be labeled as extremists, it is clear that their views of the aims and tasks of New Testament research differ considerably from those recently expressed by M. S. Enslin and C. C. McCown.[8] In timely, if overalarmed, words the latter express the fear that growing theologism may overwhelm intrenched historism.

In view of this somewhat unsettled situation, which could be documented much more profusely, it would seem helpful, if not imperative, to ask what the urgent task of New Testament *research* is and to illustrate this task by a consideration of representative, concrete projects.

II

To envisage the urgent tasks ahead in New Testament research is a legitimate undertaking only if such research is, at least to a degree, objective and if it achieves a substantial measure of permanent and solid results. The history of New Testament research during the last one hundred and fifty years fully confirms these assumptions. In so far as it has produced scientifically valid results, it has been a historical science. It has a future only if this fact will at long last be fully recognized and consistently acted upon.

On the one hand, mere so-called "historical criticism" which has made up its mind that the work of the historian is simply to push the question mark behind certain *uncertain* results indefinitely back and back, or back and forth, must not be confused with his real task. A historian who works that way does not do so as a historian but because he is philosophically a skeptic. The deep-seated bias against history and historical science, so widely current and so fashionable since Nietzsche, the rise of twentieth-century positivism and of the crisis theologies, also have their origin in philosophic pessimism or skepticism.

While these attacks from within and from without against the relativism of historical science call valid attention to the

8. See above, n. 1.

limitations inherent in it, they cannot be said to shake or to tear down its old and lasting foundations. The facts of history, i.e., the sum total of human experiences in the setting of time and space, are the facts out of which every actual and every conceivable world view arises. Historical, as well as ahistorical and antihistorical, world views are not merely historically conditioned. What is more important, they are part and parcel of historical processes. Therefore, the adequacy of a world view may be most adequately judged by the way in which it accounts for the empirically knowable facts of empirical history.

Moreover, Western man has no choice in the matter. Historical consciousness has been a central part of his heritage since pre-Christian times. Chiefly through Herodotus, Thucydides, and Plato,[9] Greece bequeathed to Western culture not only a full-blown concept of universal history but also the elements of historical science—ἰστορία. Through the Hebrew prophets[10] another, no less decisive, type of historical consciousness, whose influence has been continuous, entered into Western culture. Since the confluence of those two older cultures during the early centuries of the Christian era, all Western world views in general, and all views of history in particular, have been mere variations, combinations, elaborations, compromises, criticisms, denials, or reaffirmations of the ancient themes.[11]

Over against this inescapable and age-long historical consciousness of Western man, the relatively modern phase of historical consciousness, defined by Christopher Dawson as "a dis-

9. Various views on Greek historiography may be studied in J. B. Bury, *The Ancient Greek Historians* (London, 1909); W. W. Jäger, *Paideia: The Ideals of Greek Culture*, trans. G. Highet, Vols. I–III (1939–44); C. N. Cochrane, *Christianity and Classical Culture* . . . . (New York, 1940), pp. 456–74. Both Greek and Hebrew-Christian historiography are briefly characterized in a noteworthy article by Karl Loewith, "The Theological Background of the Philosophy of History," *Social Research*, XIII (1946), 51–80.

10. See W. Eichrodt, *Theologie des Alten Testaments* (Leipzig, 1933–39); L. H. Köhler, *Theologie des Alten Testaments* (Tübingen, 1936); R. B. Y. Scott, *The Relevance of the Prophets* (New York, 1944); J. Muilenburg, "The Faith of Ancient Israel," in *The Vitality of the Christian Tradition*, ed. G. F. Thomas (New York, 1944); N. N. Glatzer, *Untersuchungen zur Geschichtslehre der Tannaiten* (Berlin, 1933).

11. In other cultures, too, historical consciousness of a high order has developed. For ancient and modern China see H. H. Dubs, "Chinese Histories and the First Dynastic History," *South Atlantic Quarterly*, XXXIX (1940), 185–94.

tinct consciousness of the essential characteristics of different ages and civilizations," is a development of minor significance and no decisive advance. According to Dawson, it is the particular result of the Renaissance and of the Romantic movement. It is also the rationalistic reaction, led and exemplified by Voltaire, against Bossuet's neo-Augustinian, Christian view of history. It is a highly sophisticated, skeptical, and tired reaction. It may be true, as Dawson says and Nietzsche agrees, that modern man's sense of history "is not all gain, since it involves the loss of that noble self-sufficiency and maturity in which the great ages of civilization culminate"[12]—but such maturity, historically speaking, has always been beyond the grasp of Western man. What intellectual maturity he does possess forces him to recognize that ultimate questions can find a valid solution only when he has defined his own place in history. Empirical historical science, however limited its scope may be, is the only safe and sane starting-point for thought, because thought itself is a historical phenomenon and man is characteristically a historical being. The historical scene must also be the end-point of all thought, because it is on the stage of history, at the very edge and under the stage lights of the future, that each human generation plays its role.

III

It was noted that, as a historical science, New Testament research has achieved permanent and objective results. It is equally true that, more than any other special field of historical study, New Testament research has always suffered from a curious inability to be thoroughly historical in method and in aim. That this inability has been increasingly obvious in recent years is only an additional reason to inquire more specifically into its essential causes. The future of New Testament research is bleak indeed, if these causes are not clearly understood and taken into account.

Fifty years ago, the eminent church historian, Gustav Krüger, took to task the New Testament scholars of his day, especially

---

12. Christopher Dawson, *The Kingdom of God and History* ("The Official Oxford Conference Books," III [Chicago, 1938]), 197.

Harnack and Holtzmann, for their failure to conceive of their work as strictly historical. In a lecture entitled *Das Dogma vom Neuen Testament*[13] he charged that New Testament scholarship claims an exclusiveness for the New Testament, dictated by unjustifiable theological and historical interests and by the equally serious inability of scholars to do away with unscientific specialization into such disciplines as history of New Testament times, introduction to the literature of the New Testament, history of the canon and text, biblical theology, life of Jesus, history of the apostolic age, and history of the postapostolic age.[14]

The real danger inherent in this division is that each discipline starts from its own presuppositions and becomes an aim in itself. Each single discipline can be pursued properly only when its specific problems are seen as part and parcel of the same historical processes. The one abiding and ever urgent task of New Testament scholarship is the history of earliest Christianity. Within this over-all task the various disciplines find their true function and their scientific justification.

Krüger's criticisms and constructive suggestions are even more valid in 1946 than they were in 1896. During this half-century, atomistic specialization has increased by leaps and bounds. Textual criticism, archeology, epigraphy, and papyrology have grown into vast and intricate disciplines of research. Philological studies, involving the lexicography and grammar of half-a-dozen languages and dialects, are making increasing demands on the New Testament student. The "history of New Testament times" has grown from a study of Palestinian-Jewish religious and political institutions into the study of numerous Mediterranean histories, cultures, and religions. Lately it has become particularly fashionable to study and sharply distinguish between "normative" Judaism, Hellenistic Judaism, and pagan, oriental-occidental Hellenism as three types of "background" of early Christianity. As a result, specialists have too often become absorbed in preliminaries, or they have too easily generalized from the narrow viewpoint of a specialty. Klausner's, D. W. Riddle's, and Reitzenstein's reconstructions of the "preconversion career" of

13. Giessen, 1896.   14. *Ibid.*, pp. 36 ff.

Paul[15] are the inevitable results, respectively, of these three over-sharp distinctions.

Equally dangerous and perhaps more obvious is the resurging insistence on a religious and theological interpretation of the New Testament. The validity of this interest cannot and need not be denied.[16] From the point of view of the historian, the New Testament itself is a collection of writings, basically religious and theological in orientation and content, produced in the course of the first century of Christian history. No modern theological viewpoint is needed to recognize the religious and theological character of the New Testament documents.

For instance, the modern theological question—In what sense is the New Testament "the Word of God"?—may be a legitimate and necessary question, although even the question, to say nothing of the answer, is less simple than it looks. The answer certainly must depend upon, and square itself without evasion with, the demonstrable historical facts. They show that the New Testament itself is a product of a long and well-known historical process, a process which began with the very beginnings of Christianity and was not yet finished by A.D. 200. The answer must square itself with the equally well-known variety of views about "the Word of God" held by the successive representatives and generations of the early Christians. Of course, we may call this, with equal right, a short process, if we wish, but we *must* call it a measurable and knowable historical process. To describe it with fulness, within the framework of early Christian history, is an urgent task of New Testament scholarship. Apart from the elementary and basic spadework of scholars like Westcott, Zahn, Leipoldt, and Gregory,[17] supported more recently by valuable,

15. J. Klausner, *From Jesus to Paul* (New York, 1943); D. W. Riddle, *Paul: Man of Conflict* (Nashville, 1940); R. Reitzenstein, *Die hellenistischen Mysterienreligionen* (3d ed.; Leipzig, 1927), and *Studien zum antiken Synkretismus aus Iran und Griechenland* (Leipzig, 1926).

16. The theological study of the New Testament is dealt with in this volume by A. N. Wilder.

17. B. F. Westcott, *A General Survey of the History of the Canon of the New Testament* (6th ed.; Cambridge, 1889); Th. Zahn, *Geschichte des neutestamentlichen Kanons* (Erlangen, 1888–92); J. Leipoldt, *Geschichte des neutestamentlichen Kanons* (Leipzig, 1907–8); C. R. Gregory, *Canon and Text of the New Testament* (New York, 1907).

programmatic suggestions,[18] little has been done to fill this large gap.

Let us take another historically important question, since it also arises from the New Testament itself—the question of Christology. Whatever else the various New Testament writers have to say about Jesus in their various ways, in the earliest and most important of them Jesus bears the characteristics of what we moderns rightly call a "historical person." Therefore, the critical examination of the sources and the historical presentation of its results remain an ever urgent task. That historians at this task do, in fact, quite radically disagree in specific methods and therefore also in results is perhaps regrettable, but not fatal. Their disagreements are not so radical as are the disagreements between philosophers, between psychologists, or between sociologists. The disagreements within these types of study are structurally similar. In the last analysis they are epistemological. Historians enjoy the great advantage, however, that they interpret the facts of human experience by describing them; the other sciences attempt to deduce laws from them.

Great as the difficulties may be, they do not excuse the historians of early Christianity from their most urgent task—the best possible reconstruction of the history of early Christianity. Whatever the critical conclusions of a given scholar may be about the historical Jesus or about the history of his sources or about the formation of the canon or a hundred other "critical problems" with which he has to deal, he cannot shirk that responsibility. It rests on a simple, demonstrable fact: Any single historical problem can find its adequate solution only in the given context of antecedent and subsequent historical facts. Thus a student's view of the historical figure of Jesus will depend on his understanding of first-century Judaism, the habitat of Jesus. It will also depend on the student's view of the history of the Christian movement almost to the end of the first century, if it is granted that the Synoptic Gospels, which are his primary sources, were

18. A. Harnack, *Die Entstehung des Neuen Testaments und die wichtigsten Folgen der neuen Schöpfung* (Leipzig, 1914); E. J. Goodspeed, *The Formation of the New Testament* (Chicago, 1926).

produced in, by, and for the church during the last third of that century. Also, the letters of Paul have much more to contribute to the historical criticism of the Synoptic Gospels than is usually realized; they even yield a few obvious, but very basic, data for the life of Jesus.[19]

The best works on Jesus are those in which this combined method of criticism and reconstruction is best practiced. Contrary to widespread misunderstanding, the *formgeschichtliche* study of the Synoptic Gospels cannot be criticized as a rival of the historical method. It was meant to be, and is to a large extent, a more rigorous practice of the historical method. Of late, *Formgeschichte* has been extolled[20] as the harbinger of a new theological "approach" to the Gospels. It is no such thing. *Formgeschichte* is *Geschichte*, i.e., historical reconstruction of the Gospel-making period. That "form" is one specific criterion in this task of reconstruction is simply due to the fact that written and oral words constitute the sources and that the observation of the formal structure of these words is a marvelously objective criterion of the historical processes which shaped these forms. Moreover, the so-called "form historians" have not invented this technique of historical study; they have only exploited its possibilities more fully than their predecessors did. It is also clear that with Dibelius the practice of the technique is more historical, while with Bultmann it is more form-critical. But "form criticism" in either case is a misleading translation of *Formgeschichte*.[21]

The best practitioners of the form-historical and of the social-historical methods have begun the task of writing the history of

19. Profitable use is made of these materials by M. Goguel, *The Life of Jesus* (New York, 1944), in a brief chapter on "The Pauline Evidence" (pp. 105–33), which precedes the analysis of the evidence furnished by the Synoptic Gospels.

20. See, e.g., Paul Minear, "Form Criticism and Faith," *Religion in Life*, XV (1945–46), 46–56.

21. The best brief evaluation of *Formgeschichte* as a technique of historical research is by an impartial authority, H. Lietzmann, *The Beginnings of the Christian Church*, trans. B. L. Woolf (New York, 1937), pp. 56–59.

Jesus and of the Gospel-making age as one historical process. The complete fulfilment of this task is perhaps the most urgent single task ahead. Such a history must attempt to place every Gospel pericope, every part and every phrase of it, at their proper points in the total historical process.

The difficulties of this task are obvious and, at first glance, staggering. It is perfectly true to say that the sources are scanty, fragmentary, and biased and that they therefore do not answer every possible question. Consequently, it may be said, the reconstruction of early Christian history requires too large a measure of subjective speculation. But this reasoning is really circular. The judgment that the sources are scanty is possible only on the basis of a knowledge of what is lacking. If this judgment is truly historical and scientific, the areas of the historian's ignorance can and must be clearly defined. They can be so defined only by placing the fragments of extant sources in their proper places.

When this is done, the history of Jesus and of the Gospel-making age will have been written as well as it can be written. It will then become clear that the extant sources are not too scanty, because every word in the Synoptic Gospels, in Acts, and in the letters of Paul are authentic source materials for this history; and there is much material in the canonical and extra-canonical sources of the subsequent periods to fill in many a gap. Moreover, the necessary work of subjective and speculative historical reconstruction is the only reliable critic *of itself*. Subjectivism and speculation can thus, and thus only, be recognized for what they are. The total result is bound to re-establish confidence in the work of the constructive historian. Finally, an irreducible element of subjective speculation remains in all historical work. For the historian of a modern period it merely takes different forms. His trouble may not be the scantiness, but rather the profusion, of available source materials; but in the last analysis the elicitation of historical facts and their interpretation require the same kind of subjective imagination. Historians of antiquity would do well to pursue—at least as a serious hobby—the study of a modern historical period.

IV

Before exploring more fully the scope and nature of the historical task with which New Testament scholarship is faced, it may prove profitable to consider a few additional specific tasks as parts of the whole.

One of the encouraging signs of recent times is that textual criticism, one of the oldest and noblest concerns of New Testament scholarship, is no longer considered an opportunity for the indulgence in mechanical skills, in soothing routines, in statistical ingenuity, interrupted by adventurous journeys through dusty bookshops, dark attics, somnolent libraries, solemn monasteries, and spooky tombs. It should no longer be called "lower criticism," a hoary term borrowed from hoary, classical philology. For classical text critics, who have at their disposal relatively few medieval manuscripts for their work, e.g., on the dialogues of Plato, the term may be good enough. In the case of the New Testament the transmission of the text is a vital and exciting part of the history of early Christianity, especially so from the second to the fourth century. Text criticism is well on its way toward becoming a historical study of the highest order.[22]

As regards the Synoptic Gospels, one further suggestion may be made. It is vital, but not enough, to deal with them as sources for the history of the first century; they must also be appreciated and explained, without parsimony and without extravagance, as eminent, creative fruits of the life of the early church. It is not enough when the critic, magician-like, resolves them into the process which brought them forth.

There is a larger and more significant area of general agreement, i.e., of permanent and solid results, on what is known and what is knowable about Jesus than is sometimes realized. Even the extreme and opposite solutions of the problem, which is

22. See, e.g., B. H. Streeter, *The Four Gospels* . . . . (New York, 1925); D. W. Riddle, "Textual Criticism as a Historical Discipline," *Anglican Theological Review*, XVIII (1936), 220–34; B. M. Metzger, "The Caesarean Text of the Gospels," *Journal of Biblical Literature*, LXIV (1945), 457–89; W. G. Kümmel, "Textkritik und Textgeschichte des Neuen Testaments 1914–37," *Theologische Rundschau*, X (1938), 206–21, 292–327, and XI (1939), 84–107.

often described as the messianic consciousness of Jesus, overlap in no small measure. As regards Paul and his letters there is no notable agreement on any major issue. Cadbury's discerning diagnosis of this paradoxical situation and his prognosis deserve to be carefully weighed:

> That modern scholars can hold such variant views in the case of a man so well recorded is a testimony not so much to their perverse ingenuity and quarrelsomeness as to the actual manysidedness of Paul himself. . . . . In contrast with the obscure figure of Jesus and with the unidentified mind and personality behind the gospel of John, Paul of Tarsus provides the relief of a vivid, recoverable and placeable historical personage. . . . . Paul's letters give us an intimate and unquestioned insight into his mind. Here if anywhere New Testament study has a field for clear-cut appreciation of unquestioned historical facts and a well-known actor. The opportunity for vivid history and biography is scarcely used to the full by modern theologians. The known and knowable do not attract the speculative mind, and therefore even in the case of Paul the unanswered and perhaps unanswerable questions receive the most attention. . . . . Paul is the natural starting point for the study of Christianity.[23]

From F. C. Baur to Schweitzer, Bultmann, and Lohmeyer,[24] Paul has been explained as the great creative, systematic theologian of early Christianity. From Renan and Nietzsche to Wrede, Deissmann, D. W. Riddle, and Klausner, he has been pictured, vividly and sometimes extravagantly, as the dynamic, if not frantic, man of action, emotionally high strung and unstable, physically strong, yet ridden by a morbidly fascinating disease; his mind was immensely receptive rather than systematic, a meeting place of any and all ideas which might be helpful to the missionary enthusiast or to the scheming mob leader. Matthew Arnold,[25] followed by many middle-of-the-road professional students, makes out Paul to have been the prototype of the early Victorian *bourgeoisie*, of "sweet reasonableness." To what refined

23. *Op. cit.*, pp. 100–104.

24. F. C. Baur, *Paulus der Apostel Jesu Christi* (Stuttgart, 1845); A. Schweitzer, *The Mysticism of Paul the Apostle*, trans. W. Montgomery (New York, 1931); R. Bultmann, in *Die Religion in Geschichte und Gegenwart* (2d ed.; Tübingen, 1930), IV, 1019–45; E. Lohmeyer, *Grundlagen Paulinischer Theologie* (Tübingen, 1929).

25. *St. Paul and Protestantism* (London, 1870).

conclusions on fine points academic guesswork may lead is well illustrated by the fact that, for Deissmann, Paul belonged to the lower stratum of the middle class, for Schwartz to the middle stratum of the middle class, for Nock and Dodd to the upper stratum of the middle class.[26]

The areas of the unknowable in Pauline research are quite large. A real biography of Paul is quite out of the question, in spite of D. W. Riddle's most valuable book of this type. It is possible only in the most general terms and on an oversharp interpretation of real and so-called "autobiographical" passages in the letters. Paul never reminisces for the sake of reminiscence. The personality of Paul is knowable indeed, but only in so far as each letter portrays the author's state of mind and heart in the situation in which he wrote each letter. This is the only proper and promising starting-point for the study of Paul the man. It is an urgent task, since in each letter Paul is freely, wittingly and unwittingly, self-communicative.

His letters as such continue to raise a number of problems. Even the question of their precise dating is still a matter of heated debate on the part of scholars who know more than can be known. The precise date, place, destination, and occasion of the composition of Galatians may indeed be unanswerable problems.

As regards the authorship of Paul, seven letters are at present generally conceded it. Occasional doubts, beyond the seven, attach only to II Thessalonians and to Colossians. Since Holtzmann no thorough examination of the problem of the authorship of Colossians has been made.[27] Its re-examination is an urgent task, since, among other things, the solution has a bearing on the interpretation of Paul's christological ideas.

26. A. Deissmann, *St. Paul* . . . . , trans. L. R. M. Strachan (London, 1912), pp. 49–54; Ed. Schwartz, *Charakterköpfe aus der antiken Literatur*, Zweite Reihe (Leipzig, 1919), pp. 105 f.; A. D. Nock, *St. Paul* (New York, 1938), p. 21; C. H. Dodd, "The Mind of Paul: A Psychological Approach ,"*Bulletin of the John Rylands Library*, XVII (1933), 94 ff.

27. H. J. Holtzmann, *Kritik der Epheser- und Kolosserbriefe* (Leipzig, 1872); see also K. Lake and S. Lake, *An Introduction to the New Testament* (New York, 1937), pp. 140 ff. According to Lake, the view that Colossians is Pauline and that Ephesians is not "fails to explain the close similarity between Colossians and Ephesians. Both or neither of these epistles may be genuine, but a 'straddle' which accepts one and not the other combines all the difficulties and solves none" (p. 141). This judgment is sound and unanswerable.

The old question of interpolations within the extant text of Paul's letters was recently raised once more by Hawkins.[28] His work is a timely reminder that this problem needs to be restudied. Methodologically, this task is especially attractive, because it demands and permits the use of highly objective criteria, namely, a detailed and full analysis of the style, i.e., of the vocabulary and the syntax of the letters. Such a study, moreover, would yield objective conclusions of great value for the questions of interpolations, authenticity, and the psychological understanding of Paul's personality. All other types of psychological interpretation are too intuitive and impressionistic.

The study of thousands of papyrus letters has much advanced our understanding of Paul's letters, but the bulk of those letters —"private letters" as Deissmann called them—are neither the only nor the chief clue to the understanding of Paul's letters as letters. The whole range of Hellenistic letter-writing, from private billets to literary and official letters, must be studied for the exegesis and the appreciation of the specific species and literary quality of the letters of Paul.[29]

The ultimate task of the historical student of Paul is to determine his place and influence in the Christian movement during its first three decades. Renan's answer that Paul, even though no thinker, was yet the originator of Christian theology, is still widely popular but no longer seriously defended. Wrede's judgment that Paul was the *second* founder of Christianity is in no better case. Hellenistic Christianity existed before Paul and has a long and important history alongside Paul without receiving vital impulses from him. To see in Paul the creator or even the one great figure in the history of the first century is a case of misplaced hero-worship.

Another major problem in Pauline studies is the question of his Jewishness and of his Hellenism. For a hundred years the answer

28. R. M. Hawkins, *The Recovery of the Historical Paul* (Nashville, 1943).

29. A most promising program for the stylistic study of Paul's letters was initiated by E. von Dobschütz, "Zum Wortschatz und Stil des Römerbriefes," *Zeitschrift für die neutestamentliche Wissenschaft*, Vol. XXIII (1924); see also Paul Schubert, *Form and Function of the Pauline Thanksgivings* (Berlin, 1939).

has swayed back and forth between these alternatives. The more recent compromise view that Paul was a Jewish Hellenist could be regarded as a decisive advance if we knew more about Jewish Hellenism. Even then the answer would not be final, because the question of Paul's Jewishness and Hellenism is not only a quantitative but also a qualitative one. In a valid sense Paul is thoroughly and wholly Jewish, in his own way. In an equally valid sense Paul is thoroughly and wholly Hellenistic, in his own way. The quality of Paul's Jewishness and Hellenism could be more precisely appreciated by a thorough and detailed comparison of Paul with Philo and Josephus, the two other familiar Jewish Hellenists of the first century.

V

The question of Paul's Jewishness and Hellenism brings once more to a focus the larger task of the historians of early Christianity. What is the scope of their work, geographically, chronologically, and in terms of interpretation?

That Christianity had its rise in Palestinian Judaism is a fact which New Testament scholarship did not need to discover. The New Testament itself makes that plain. The church knew and proclaimed it throughout its history. That there never was a Christian church without the Hebrew Scriptures at the base of its own canons of sacred writings is but an external, though significant, sign of that primeval consciousness.[30] Thus the study of Judaism became automatically and early an important concern of technical New Testament scholarship. All the more significant, therefore, is the phenomenal progress made in the study of Judaism during the last fifty years, due in the main to the intensive and combined labors of Christian and Jewish scholars. Of course, first-century Judaism is, in any view, a highly complex and mature culture. It is the result of centuries of experiences suffered and made by one of the most gifted peoples of the ancient world.

---

30. Marcion's canon is no exception to this rule. In fact, it is a particularly impressive example of it. His deliberate *rejection* of the Hebrew Scriptures is indeed the basis of his canon. That he "chose" the Gospel of Luke and ten letters of Paul was not so much a matter of positive preference as it was a matter of choosing what was best for his purposes. It proved to be not good enough.

Its understanding means the understanding of the Near East, in so far as it conditioned the history of the Hebrew-Jewish nation. Since the analysis and forecast of research in this field are set forth in other chapters of this volume,[31] no more is necessary here than to mention some principles of importance to the historian of early Christianity.

It is well known, but not always remembered, that Christianity had its rise in a mature and high culture. The student must, when necessary, speak of the quantitatively small beginnings of Christianity; but there is no scientific justification for calling Christianity in the period of its emergence "primitive." When the historian inadvertently ignores this fact, his conception of the genesis of early Christianity is bound to result in a perverted account of the facts.

Historical research in all periods is subject to fads and fashions. Any new discovery of materials and any new critical technique of study are liable to result in rash generalizations. Thus we have, of recent years, heard much of apocalyptical versus normative or of Palestinian versus Hellenistic Judaism. A more sober judgment, based on the study of all facts and factors involved, seems to be in the making.[32]

The point that Judaism had for centuries been part and parcel of a wider oriental culture need no longer be labored. That Judaism also was part and parcel of the Hellenistic civilization for three centuries before Jesus and for several centuries after him is not yet quite so certain. It is known, however, that Judaism was "unaffected" by Hellenism only where it was genuinely isolated, i.e., in hinterland, rural regions. Wherever Judaism is consciously and militantly anti-Hellenistic, it is, in being so, profoundly influenced by Hellenism. Without the historical necessity for such opposition, the course of Jewish history would have been quite different. The old, widespread, and strong Jewish "Diaspora" is thoroughly Hellenistic in various modes and in various degrees, from thorough, enthusiastic assimilation to thorough, enthusiastic particularism. The full application of these facts and

31. See the chapters in this volume by Wright, Prussner, Marcus, and Rylaarsdam.

32. On this point see Professor Marcus' chapter in this volume.

principles to the writing of early Christian history is an urgent task ahead; it also poses a great many specific items of research.

More intensive work in the study of pagan Hellenism is no less needed. Paul Wendland's monumental work,[33] definitive as it still remains in many respects, needs not only to be revised but to be re-written. It should be re-written as a history of Hellenism, including Christianity, from the first to the fourth century A.D. It is difficult to reconstruct some aspects of Hellenistic history, and none is more difficult than the history of Hellenistic religions —the forerunners, fellows, and rivals of Christianity from its very beginnings.

The needs for research in this area are large. Archeology, papyrology, and epigraphy will retain all their present importance; but once more it becomes necessary to re-examine, in the light of these studies, the whole range of Hellenistic literature—religious, philosophic, historical, scientific, journalistic, epistolographic, fictional, and poetic.

With little hesitation scholars have made prolific use of sources from the second, third, and fourth centuries A.D., in order to shed light on the history of first-century Christianity. In principle this procedure is entirely sound, but it can be made sounder. The same critical and meticulous attention which is paid to the genetic development of early Christianity must be paid to that of all Hellenistic religions. They must first be studied for their own sake. Hellenism is not just a body of miscellaneous sources for the writing of Christian history, it is *the* over-all historical reality of which Christianity, for the first six centuries of its history, is only a part.[34]

As early as the second century A.D.—indeed, much earlier—we can see with the naked eye that Hellenistic religions, philosophic

33. *Die hellenistisch-römische Kultur in ihren Beziehungen zu Judentum und Christentum* (3d ed.; Tübingen, 1912); one of the best among more recent studies in this field is A. D. Nock, "Early Gentile Christianity and Its Hellenistic Background," in *Essays on the Trinity and the Incarnation*, ed. A. E. J. Rawlinson (London, 1928), pp. 51–156.

34. This principle does not prejudge the question of whether early Christianity was or was not "just another Hellenistic religion." It does not even suggest the question. The principle is invoked because it alone makes it possible to study and understand Hellenism and early Christianity in all the varieties of their historical manifestations.

thought, and imperial statesmanship combine with increasing energy to establish a unified culture. The efforts to include Christianity into this superintegrated, planned syncretism constitute a considerable part of the history of the Roman Empire and of Christianity throughout the third century; they vitally affect its course in the two subsequent centuries.

Thus New Testament scholarship must carry its task well into the fourth century. Gustav Krüger, in the program referred to at the beginning of this chapter, gives good reasons for extending the task at least into the third century.[35] One important reason for this seemingly extravagant extension is the principle of genetic interpretation. It is just as vital, and certainly more fruitful for the understanding of first-century Christianity to know its second- and third-century stages of development as it is to know Judaism from Maccabean times to Herod the Great. The best New Testament scholars, at their best, have always understood this necessity.

One further concrete problem which equally affects the first and the fourth century may be briefly stated to illustrate the point—the historical interpretation of the issues at stake in the so-called "Trinitarian" controversies. What actual role did the New Testament play in this process, which found a dramatic, though temporary, solution in the fourth century? What part was played by Greek academic metaphysics, by pagan and Christian gnosticism, by the mystery religions, and by imperial and ecclesiastical policies? By which routes and in what manner did each of these contributory, historical forces make their way from the first century to the First Council of Constantinople? What more objective method is there for determining the relative degree and mode of Hellenization of first-century Christianity than a full exploration of Hellenistic history from the first century to the meeting of the Christian bishops under Theodosius I in 381?

Harnack, Loofs, and R. Seeberg, the great historians of Christian "dogma," as they called it, from the first to the sixth century, have too long held the field and cast their shadows on New

35. *Op. cit.*, pp. 35 f.

Testament research.[36] Sharply as they differ from one another, all three conceive of this history too much in terms of *internal* development within the Christian church. They wrote without adequate appreciation of the fact that Hellenistic influence on Christianity increased with each successive century.

It is neither the yearning for greener pastures nor the naïve urge to establish a professional monopoly that should drive New Testament scholars to become historians of Mediterranean history from Alexander the Great to Augustine of Hippo. It is the urge for self-preservation and self-assertion which thrusts this responsibility upon them. No single scholar can ever master every section of this immense field. But he can master no single important phase within it without an intelligent and real vision of the whole. When the W. Durants and the H. G. Wellses of this world can communicate to the world their amateurish visions of the centuries and milleniums, it is not only possible but also urgent that the professionals stay not too far behind.

It may be the legitimate task of the sociologist to discover general laws which govern the behavior of men in any possible or actual social group. It always has been and always will be the task of the historian to show what happened to the people of a given age and what they did about it; to show what seeds they sowed and what fruits they produced by which succeeding generations lived; for man does not live by law alone, but by every word and deed that proceedeth out of the course of history, of history in general, and of early Christian history in particular.

36. More recently two histories of dogma have appeared, Walther Köhler, *Dogmengeschichte als Geschichte des christlichen Selbstbewusstseins* (Zurich, 1938); Martin Werner, *Die Entstehung des christlichen Dogmas problemgeschichtlich dargestellt* (Berne, 1941). The latter is an attempt to confirm Schweitzer's reading of the history of dogma. The former is more suggestive and less biased; it is discussed in a notable review article by Gustav Krüger, "Eine neuartige Dogmengeschichte," *Theologische Blätter*, XVIII (1939), 91–94.

PART II

Special Studies of Salient Problems

The Geographical Conditioning of Religious Experience in Palestine

CHESTER C. McCOWN
Pacific School of Religion, Berkeley, California

IN THE present state of geographic studies, final conclusions as to the effects of environment upon the development of Hebrew and Christian religious ideas are impossible. In spite of the mass of geographic literature dealing with the relations of culture to environment, on many points even tentative agreement has not been reached. The question of the relation of religion to environment is so delicate, difficult, and controversial that geographers are chary of attacking it. Often they are not competent to do so because of inability or failure to control the archeological and documentary sources; archeologists and philologians lack the necessary familiarity with geographic science. Realization of the demands of full competence in these fields makes for diffidence in approaching the subject.

The progress which has been made, within the last twenty-five years, in enlarging the content and improving the methods of archeology, history, and cultural studies, although it warrants neither dogmatism nor pride of achievement, is nevertheless sufficient to justify attention to this difficult theme. Scientific excavation and exploration, which were but in their infancy before the first World War, have made remarkable progress in both the quantity and the quality of their results. Ancient documents, both written and unwritten, have been unearthed, published, and interpreted with increasing competence and intelligence. New alphabets and languages have been deciphered and interpreted. Much remains to be done. But a vast amount of material is already at hand. A fuller appreciation of the nature of the prob-

lems to be solved will render archeological and historical research more fruitful as time goes on.

The superabundance of, and also the many lacunae in, the material now available for such a study are alike depressing. A bibliography of the fundamental geographical studies already made would exceed the limits of this essay. Yet little has been written on this immediate subject, and much remains to be done in preparatory research. Sir George Adam Smith's great work abounds in genial suggestions, but it emphasizes the relation of terrain to the "wars of Yahweh" and of others.[1] Père F. M. Abel's thoroughgoing study covers practically all the details of geomorphology and historical geography, with much that bears upon the use of the land and the development of culture; but it attempts no interpretation of social, and especially religious, history in relation to environment.[2] W. F. Albright's *From the Stone Age to Christianity*[3] well illustrates the complexities and difficulties of the theme and makes numerous contributions to its discussion. Yet not only is there need of many careful geographical studies and much scientifically reported excavation, but the analysis and interpretation of the mass of available data wait upon the development of more rigorous method and the collaboration of many conscientious students.

The dangers involved in such a study must be fully realized—dangers to cherished theories of theology and geography and history. What is actually implied by the subject must be stated at the outset, both negatively and positively. Ill-considered guesses may plausibly deceive as to the part played by geographical influences on the development of religious ideas. Generalizations based upon single instances, however common in popular speech,

1. *The Historical Geography of the Holy Land* (London, 1894). The only real revision (1931) consists largely of accounts of Allenby's conquest.

2. *Géographie de la Palestine* (2 vols.; Paris, 1933, 1938).

3. Baltimore, 1940. See the series of cultural studies in John T. McNeill, Matthew Spinka, and Harold R. Willoughby (eds.), *Environmental Factors in Christian History* (Chicago, 1939), for a further illustration of the complications of the subject; likewise, W. C. Graham and H. G. May, *Culture and Conscience: An Archaeological Study of the New Religious Past in Ancient Palestine* (Chicago, 1936).

can have no scientific standing.[4] Two major errors in attempts to relate geographic environment to history have been mechanistic explanations and oversimplification. Both arise from want of a well-considered methodology. The chief difficulty is the combination of material and cultural, or human, factors.

It has long been recognized that geography is a subject which cannot be pursued in abstraction from man and his culture. Its chief, almost its only, interest lies in human ecology—land as man's home, as the scene of his activities and his development. Topography is the identification of his places of habitation on the land. The study of geology, soils, and relief determines its usefulness. Climatology and meteorology seek to discover the conditions under which man lives and uses the land. The landscape is constantly changed by man's activities, even as he is affected by the landscape. In modern geography the center of gravity has shifted from nature to man. A geographer has recently remarked that knowledge of the peoples of the world is the core of his science.[5] Knowledge of the peoples who produced the Hebrew religion is an essential to the understanding of our religion. "Human geography" is the accepted term to describe the modern geographer's ultimate interest. It has a far from passing concern for the student of the Bible.

The *Geisteswissenschaften*, the "sciences of the spirit," and the *Naturwissenschaften*, the "natural sciences," are both sciences, in that the members of each group can develop an ordered and systematic body of knowledge derived from observation, generalization, and classification of data leading to the construction and testing of hypotheses. But the nature of the data in the "sciences of the spirit" is such that valuations cannot be based upon foot-rules or balances; they cannot be adequately expressed in arithmetical figures or diagrams or formulas. Mathematics and things of the spirit are incommensurable. Mechanistic and, consequently, deterministic interpretations of history are excluded because history is human experience. That does not mean abandonment

4. See C. C. McCown, *The Genesis of the Social Gospel* (New York, 1929), pp. 37 ff., for mention of some of them.

5. H. J. Fleure in the *Geographical Review*, XXXIV (1944), 515.

of the concept of causation in social and cultural processes.[6] But it does seriously complicate the problem. On the other hand, the presence of the often apparently irrational human factor cannot be pleaded as an excuse for neglecting method.

The methodology of cultural studies is only in process of becoming. But order is beginning to appear out of an earlier chaos. The student of religion cannot afford to overlook the discussions of method in cultural studies. Philology and literary criticism are only the beginning. Historical criticism involves anthropology, sociology, and psychology, as well as what is more narrowly defined as historical method and the philosophy of history.[7]

The dangers of oversimplification need to be stressed most emphatically, since the complexity of the problems involved gives them a most forbidding aspect and has resulted in the proposal of many inadequate solutions. Heredity and environment are too often treated as if they were mutually exclusive. Racialism has recently been overemphasized, with infinite loss to culture in all the world. Yet the eminent contributions of certain societies to cultural history cannot be denied; and it must be acknowledged that natural and social selection has worked to produce the superior types which have made these contributions. What, then, are the agents of selection? That geographic factors are basic no one will deny. But which among the many elements in the geographic environment are the more important? What do the geographic and corresponding economic and political relationships contribute to the development of national character? How are psychological factors and the activities of man to be assessed? Above all, the danger of singling out some "key cause" must be avoided.[8]

Unfortunately, the theological pendulum has recently swung too far away from the scientific attitude. Oversimplification often

6. Cf. R. M. MacIver, *Social Causation* (Boston, 1942), esp. pp. 35–69.

7. To illustrate, I may refer to certain typical works: R. H. Lowie, *The History of Ethnological Theory* (New York, 1937); Bronislaw Malinowski, *A Scientific Theory of Culture and Other Essays* (Chapel Hill, 1944); A. L. Kroeber, *Configurations of Culture Growth* (Berkeley, 1944), as well as that of MacIver, *op. cit.*

8. Cf. R. M. MacIver, *Society* (New York, 1929), pp. 61–139; *Social Causation*, pp. 73–120; Wilson D. Wallis, *An Introduction to Sociology* (New York, 1927), pp. 92–234.

takes the form of an inadequate conception or a denial of social causation. With many persons recent unhappy social experience in the world has weighed more heavily than has scientific thought. Theories which carry the burden of ancient eschatology or prescientific dogma can only prove thoroughly confused and confusing.[9] The revival of a healthy interest in the philosophy of history is a favorable sign. In the last thirty or forty years and especially in the last decade or two, attempts too numerous to mention have been made to work out a philosophy of history that can satisfy the scientific thought and the social experience of the twentieth century. Evolution in both the biological and the social areas is a fact which will eventually wreck any theory that neglects it. The attempt to carry over into the modern world ideas of miracle and magic which prevailed in biblical times is certain to mislead. Satisfactory and permanently useful conceptions of history cannot start from theological, economic, or social dogmas or presuppositions but must be based upon the data of experience, scientifically interpreted.

To illustrate the nature of the problems involved, three studies by Louis Wallis may be mentioned as serious attempts to approach the subject from a scientific point of view and to work out definite relations between the historical process and the ethical and religious thought of the Hebrews.[10] Wallis is right in his fundamental contention that there can be no division of history into sacred and secular and that Hebrew history is subject to the same social and economic laws as that of other nations. Reviews of *The Bible Is Human* have rightly agreed that Wallis' reconstruction of the history of the Hebrews is based upon a peculiar social theory and cannot be substantiated by what is known of their documents and their archeology.[11] A satisfactory interpre-

9. Cf., e.g., N. P. Jacobson, "Niebuhr's Philosophy of History," *Harvard Theological Review*, XXXVII (1944), 237–68; C. C. McCown, "In History or beyond History," *Harvard Theological Review*, XXXVIII (1945), 151–75.

10. *Sociological Study of the Bible* (Chicago, 1912); *God and the Social Process* (Chicago, 1935); *The Bible Is Human* (New York, 1942).

11. C. T. Craig, *Christendom*, VIII (1943), 124 f.; H. G. May, *Journal of Bible and Religion*, XII (1944), 98–106, with a useful summary of pertinent literature; J. C. Rylaarsdam, *Journal of Religion*, XXV (1945), 284 ff.

tation of geographical influences can hardly be based upon an undemonstrated and highly hypothetical construction of history. But a debatable theory of history should not obscure the fact that history is "human."

H. G. May goes on to a positive statement of principles with which one can only agree. An "ecological or holistic approach" to such problems is demanded. As May insists, such an approach includes both science and religion. It includes religion as it does music and art. It involves cosmic relations, since the ecology of the human spirit must take religious beliefs into account. Religion cannot be studied apart from culture, just as culture is a mere torso, without religion. But religious ideologies are as dangerous as are social ideologies. Fundamentalism and Marxism are equally dogmatic and equally alien to scientific thinking.

Man transcends the physical world to which his body belongs; he also transcends the society to which he owes his techniques, his language, his concepts, and all that makes him something more than one of a herd of cattle or of a swarm of bees. As a whole he is infinitely more than the sum of his parts. Environmental influences can no more explain the whole of culture than chemistry can explain life. But culture is unintelligible apart from environment.

To say that the Hebrews discovered God in their historical experience and developed their conceptions of him out of it is surely not to be guilty of atheism or naturalism. James Henry Breasted's *Dawn of Conscience*[12] suggests how complicated the process was. It cannot be discussed within the limits of this essay; but it must be said that environmental factors play an impressive role in the development of any people's religious ideas and that their belief in God is a response, direct or indirect, to the challenge of environment. If the student of religion wishes to avoid obscurantist theorizing, he should recognize two facts: (1) What man knows he acquires from his contacts with his material and social environment; all that is valuable in practical techniques, in social customs, and in the theoretical principles which are supposed to guide his conduct comes ultimately from these two

12. New York and London, 1933.

sources. God speaks to man through his environment. (2) Techniques, customs, and theories undergo a constant process of change. Although geographic, economic, and historical determinism of every kind has proved quite unequal to interpreting the data of experience, yet every individual and every generation are caught in the rushing stream of change. Man's physical evolution is so slow that development in body and brain has not been discoverable since the beginning of history. But his cultural evolution is comparatively rapid. The Hebrews lived in a world which, as they saw it, was vastly different from ours. The world of Paul of Tarsus was little like that of Saul of Gibeah. To understand their world and their religion, with its slow but certain development, and to understand our world, our religion, and our development we must know what made the Hebrews what they were and what caused them to change as they did. That involves three problems: what they were, what their environment was, and what they made out of their environment. Their religious experience enters as a decisive factor into the answers to all three problems, for the interaction of all these factors appears in their religion.[13]

In this essay the foregoing survey of materials available and discussion of method, both all too brief, call for illustration. Certain outstanding features of the geographic environment and certain peculiarities of Hebrew culture may be compared in order to discover whether there seems to be a positive correlation between them. Those chosen are well marked and should be well known and generally recognized. They cannot here be described at length. The environmental features are (1) the physical limitations of Palestine in size, resources, and productivity; (2) the climate with its favorable and unfavorable effects; (3) the variety of landscape—stimulating, divisive, and isolating; (4) the steppe, nomadism, and the cultural conflicts involved in the intermediate situation of the land; and (5) the geographical and resulting cultural relations of Palestine and its inhabitants.

13. See the writer's previous discussions of some aspects of the subject in *The Genesis of the Social Gospel*, esp. pp. 37–101; *Journal of Geography*, XXIII (1924), 333–49; *Journal of Religion*, VII (1927), 520–39.

The infinitesimal area of Palestine, as compared with the world which its religion has influenced, seems rarely to be understood. It measures 6,000 square miles west of the Jordan and possibly 4,000 on the eastern side. But size is not its only limitation. It consists so largely of mountains, sharply and deeply cut gorges, uncultivable wastes of rock, waterless steppe, and desert that hardly more than 2,300,000 acres are claimed for agriculture, even by optimistic Zionists. Its mineral resources are small and were not located in the areas ordinarily under Hebrew control. Humus is lacking in the soil. Many of the best fields have but a thin layer of earth over the limestone rocks which form the backbone of the land. They are usually full of stones. The one saving feature is the fertilizing effect of the disintegrating limestone. In the absence of level areas, aside from the plains of Esdraelon and Jezreel and the maritime plain, fields are very small and are often made and maintained only by arduous and continued labor at terracing. In ancient times wine and oil were abundant, wheat and barley less so. There were many other food products available, but the population of Palestine could never count on a life of luxury and ease.

The climate of Palestine had both favorable and unfavorable features. A Mediterranean climate, with summer drought and winter rains, and otherwise much like that of southern California, provided a favorable environment for primitive man. Its very moderate extremes of heat and cold put no great strain upon his resistance. Its abundant sunshine made for health; its aridity and its variations were stimulating. It was such as to produce a healthy, vigorous, and prolific population.

On the other hand, its limited and capricious rainfall, the lack of stores of water underground or in the snows of lofty mountains, and the high rate of evaporation made agriculture extremely hazardous. Because of its scarcity of rivers and springs, as well as of level areas accessible to its limited waters, irrigation could never have been practiced on a large scale. Palestine was also subject to the common pests of a Mediterranean climate. In short, its climate sharply limited the production of its limited area.

The variety of the landscape surely contributed to the wide acceptance of the Bible in all lands. Its language is full of refer-

ences to nature and of similes and metaphors which are intelligible to people everywhere in the world. The land's variety of terrain contributed to the health and stimulation of its population, for, nearly everywhere, within a few miles there are varieties of climate running from subarctic to subtropical. But a land so varied and so irregular in relief was a paradise for regionalism and parochialism. The political divisions—Judea, Samaria, Galilee, Edom, Moab, Gilead, and Bashan—correspond to different landscapes.[14] The Jordan gorge never connected, but always divided, eastern and western Palestine. The Shephelah and the maritime plain, like upper and lower Galilee, were likewise distinct regions, each demanding differences of custom and providing differences of contact with the outside world. The isolating effect of the terrain, especially of Judea, is particularly to be noted. Its rugged mountains, the dangerous gorges through which it had to be approached, and the poverty to which its barren and rocky hills condemned it set it off by itself. It was a poor prize for a military expedition; it offered little to the merchant; its people could not but be different from their own fellow-countrymen and from the rest of the world.

What has already been said culminates in another feature of the utmost importance—the nomadic influence in Hebrew culture. Low rainfall and the absence of water for irrigation condemn great areas of fertile fields in southern and eastern Palestine to a sparse growth of winter grasses. Partly for the same reason, partly because of its broken terrain, the deeply eroded eastern flank of the watershed of the central range is likewise *midhbār, erēmos*, waste, uninhabited, uncultivable land. The "wilderness" along its eastern border gives to Judea a most unusual character. Similar, but smaller, areas are to be found here and there in all parts of the country. Consequently, along its borders and in its mountain areas Palestine was as largely pastoral as it was agricultural.

14. G. E. Wright and F. V. Filson (*The Westminster Historical Atlas to the Bible* [Philadelphia, 1945], p. 57) are quite wrong, as I see it, in denying George Adam Smith's distinction (*op. cit.*, pp. 323–37) between Judea and Samaria in terrain and correspondingly in culture. Here is precisely the kind of area in which geography plays a decisive role. It is true that there is no clearly marked boundary between the two regions, but the difference between the landscape about Jerusalem and that about Samaria is as great as between Denver and Omaha.

There were always on its borders nomads ready to raid or invade. All through its history, slow and silent infiltration or mass invasion has been going on. The land lies on the border between the desert and the sown, with no natural boundary between.

Likewise, Palestine lay among the great civilizations of antiquity at the center of the world. The stone vase and globe in the Greek Katholikon in the Church of the Holy Sepulcher, which marked the center of a Ptolemaic earth, aptly symbolize the former geographical and cultural relations of the Promised Land. It promised much more than its Israelite conquerors guessed. From the beginnings of Western civilization in the valleys of the Nile and the Euphrates until the rise of the Parthian Empire and the Roman conquest of Palestine, this centrality was a dominant fact. The land lay between the desert and the sea, between the temperate zone and the subtropical; it looked north and south, east and west. It was a natural focus on which to concentrate the influences of all the nations from which Western civilization was derived. All nations had long been flowing into the little city set upon the forbidding mountains of Judea.

What the Hebrews were when they entered the strange environment that eventually made them a peculiar people is a mystery hidden in the fogs of legend. We do not know even what language they spoke. Doubtless, there was a large Semitic strain in them. But, as the tribes which eventually came to call themselves "Israelite" entered that corridor of conquest and commerce, they inevitably absorbed many alien elements beside the Gibeonites. It is one of the "ironies of history" that the facial characteristic which is supposed to mark the Jew is not found in a large majority of them and is not even a Semitic feature but must have been borrowed from the Hittites, the Hurrites, the Mitannians, or some Armenoid source. Not a few names and references to aliens domiciled among the Hebrews indicate what the recovery of more and more information from recent discoveries proves—that the Hebrew race in the time of the monarchy already was far from "pure" and that, as time went on, more and more non-Semitic, or at least non-Hebrew, elements were absorbed. The people which by 100 B.C. was priding itself on its ex-

clusiveness and racial purity had received its racial character, like Nazi Germany, through the most extensive mixture.

Hebrew culture went through the same historical process. The notable characteristics of Hebrew religion are many. But they are not to be credited to some strange originality of the Hebrew race or to the geographical conditioning of that race. On the contrary, a considerable proportion of their allegedly unique contributions to religion was not of their own discovery. They were not the only, or the first, people to approach the idea of monotheism. Their laws, including some of their most highly ethical elements, were to be found, even with improvements, in the Code of Hammurabi. Their ideals of the universal justice of God, of his disregard, even hatred, of wealth and power, and of his care for the poor, the orphan, and the widow had already been proclaimed in Egypt or Babylonia or both, long before the birth of Abraham.

In the beginning, their ideas of prophecy reflected those of the surrounding peoples. Their conception of the new age and of the perfect prince who should rule in righteousness they held in common with others of their neighbors. The mythology which formed the basis of their cosmology and their eschatology they shared with the Semitic world. They probably borrowed their conception of the resurrection, the coming reign of God, and other features of their eschatology from the Persians. They did not escape the influence of Greece, although Hellenism reached them when they were already beginning to react toward isolation.[15] How much they owed to still other races, lost or imperfectly known, we may never learn.

The unique characteristic of the Hebrews is that, while they borrowed from many sources, yet in nearly every item they eventually altered and improved upon the ideas which they had received. Likewise, these seminal ideas were preserved by the Hebrews for the use of future generations, whereas they disappeared from other cultures in the course of time and are now recovered by the scholar only as fossils, preserved in buried and forgotten documents. It is difficult enough to understand how the beautiful

15. Cf. *The Genesis of the Social Gospel*, pp. 102–18, 160–75, 187–291.

hymn of the heretic king, Akhenaton, to his sole god, Aton, is preserved in Psalm 104. It is much more difficult to explain why the Hebrews, alone of all the nations of antiquity, preserved the prayers and hopes for peace and happiness, for security and justice, which for more than twenty-five hundred years had been upon the lips of men throughout the Near East.

The problem of Hebrew monotheism is too complicated and too highly controversial to attack here. Like every other such problem, its solution must be sought in the total social history of the nation. Other answers lie nearer the surface. The conditions under which the Hebrews lived quite obviously drove them to certain conclusions. Among these conditions, the limited area and physical resources, the aridity, and the poverty of the land, with resulting austerity of life, are unmistakably to be included. The result in limiting the population must be noted, for size of population is reflected in nearly every phase of culture.

Ancient "censuses" are, of course, completely unreliable. The only safe basis of argument is the amount of arable land and the size of the present population. Without going into details it may be said that the present population of 1,600,000 represents over-crowding, according to modern standards, in both Arab and Jewish areas. Ancient agricultural methods can hardly have surpassed those now in use. Ancient commerce can hardly have been more rewarding than the tourist trade and commerce of today. Remembering that during most of their history the Hebrews and the Jews were confined to their mountains and that the coastal plain was always inhabited chiefly by non-Jews, one can but conclude that the real Hebrews in Palestine could never have numbered more than a few hundred thousand. The Hebrew kingdom of Isaiah and Jeremiah consisted of hardy mountaineers, partly agricultural and partly pastoral, inhabiting the smaller, and the roughest and least productive, part of the small land that bulks so large in the patriotic stories of its grandeur. Poverty and hardship, drought and famine, taxes and tribute, wars and invasions —these were their constant lot. For the greater part of them neither ease nor security was ever possible.

Intimate connection with the steppe and familiarity with

nomad life are outstanding factors in Hebrew culture. According to their traditions—and traditions are in themselves weighty determinants of culture—their ancestors, the patriarchs, were nomads or semi-nomads. Their tribes had wandered in the wilderness, most of them doubtless far longer than forty years. Some of their clans—the Kenites and the Rechabites—clung always to the black tent. Many of the villagers reverted to nomadic life at times for various reasons. Their literature is still marked by love of nomadic life and dislike of settled agricultural life. Cain, the peasant, found Yahweh unfavorable; while Abel, the shepherd, was blessed. The cry, "To your tents, O Israel," meant "Return to your homes." The "wilderness" with its simple, austere life came eventually to symbolize true righteousness and pure religion. The riches of Canaan had corrupted the nation. Only a return to their original way of life could save them.[16]

To the Hebrews nomadic life was more than a symbol. From their first entry into the "Promised Land" there had been a constant conflict between the ideals and customs of nomadism and those of agriculture. It was not merely the fertility cult which was alien and corrupting. Nomadism called for at least a measure of individual independence and initiative. It demanded toughness and self-reliance but also mutual helpfulness within the circle of the family and the clan. The life of the peasant called for less showy qualities; and it often involved yielding to control. As the few became rich and added house to house and field to field until they dwelt alone in the midst of the land, the peasant could not but envy the freedom of the nomads who wandered throughout the country. The character of the land helped keep alive the old ideal; and even the agricultural conception of true happiness, when every man should sit under his own vine and fig tree with none to make him afraid, preserved the essence of the nomadic notion of individual and family independence.

Since Yahweh was a God of the steppe and of the nomad, the cultural conflict was also a religious conflict. The return to nomadism was a party cry based upon economic conditions, a false historical perspective, and religious conservatism. In this it is

16. *Ibid.*, pp. 133–48, with references given there.

clear that the geographic conditioning of economic experience influenced the expression of religious experience. The conservative trend was reinforced by the obvious antimoral characteristics of the fertility cults connected with agriculture and Baal worship and by the sufferings of the poor consequent upon the transition to a new economic order. Control of the means of livelihood by the few in their selfish interest progresses from the ownership of flocks and herds to that of land. Commercial practices hasten the process.

The introduction of commerce, inevitable as it was in a land situated like Palestine, aroused all the same prejudices and caused all the same difficulties which a transition to agriculture had occasioned, and others in addition. It involved contacts with strange peoples, the use of foreign wares, and the introduction of alien mores and religious practices. Since it brought with it economic dislocation, the rapid increase of wealth of the few who adapted themselves to the new order, and the impoverishment, both relative and actual, of the many, it was immoral and antireligious. Yahweh must be against it.

It must be noted that geographic conditioning does not, in these matters, affect basic religious experience. Only the expression of it reflects the environment. The same experience of economic and social disturbance comes continually to all cultures, and the sense of injustice aroused by economic difficulties which the mass of the population suffers arouses religious opposition, which is expressed in various ways but is based upon essentially the same arguments as those which the ancient Hebrew exponents of nomadism used. The biblical prohibition of the loaning of money at interest, which represents the agriculturalist's reaction against a common and necessary commercial practice, has created difficulties all down through the centuries.

The idea of a return to nomadism is thus a particular expression of an almost universal human experience. In another respect Hebrew social experience and its religious expression were less usual. The Hebrew and Christian religions, therefore, acquired a peculiar trend and limitation. It is generally agreed that the prophetic movement—that unique element in Hebrew religion

which eventuated in Christianity—represents a protest against official religion and upper-class mores. The prophets were, in a sense, a minority party, although actually they spoke on behalf of the submerged majority for whom the upper classes had little regard. The prophets were the party of the opposition and, except possibly in the time of Josiah's abortive and inconsequential reform, never controlled, although they occasionally modified, national policy.

They were, therefore, a minority within a nation which was itself a pitiful minority in the great world of oriental culture. The same situation continued into Christian times and marks the character of both first-century Judaism and the first three centuries of Christianity. How the Hebrews came to regard themselves as the "chosen people" of the one God who ruled the universe and directed history is too complicated a problem to discuss here. It is a matter of great importance that the early Christians arrogated to themselves the same pre-eminence. In the present connection the point is that, for the Hebrews, the geographic conditions completely and emphatically invalidated any such belief. Yet they held tenaciously to it. Almost all their actual political history denied the legitimacy of their faith. The highly exaggerated traditions of the military might of David's armies and of the glories of Solomon's reign formed a basis for this unshakable faith, and the adventitious successes of the Maccabees, which were due chiefly to Syria's weakness, gave it vitality.

The weakness and poverty of the little Judean nation during the post-Exilic period led to the adoption of the prophetic message of hope for the poor as applying to the nation as such, and thus to the preservation of a literature and a point of view, representing the oppressed and submerged "people-of-the-land," which elsewhere have disappeared. The hopelessness of this conception led to its etherealization into an expectation of an overthrow of their enemies and of all evil by a miraculous act of God, and thus it made the whole apocalyptic eschatology possible. The Book of Daniel and its contemporary apocalypses were the natural product of a hope doomed to be turned into despair by geographical conditions.

The legal literature of the Bible is thus the expression partly of nomadic, partly of agricultural, experience, both of the simplest and most meager kind. Its entire attitude is colored by the deficiencies of its geographic environment. The prophetic literature is the expression of an attitude of the "opposition," not of the dominating party which is responsible for the nation. It is a literature of protest. It is largely negative, and deficient, although not wanting, in positive elements which can guide a majority party in its control of the state. It looks to God, not man, to overcome the evil in human nature and in social relations. The ethics of the Bible, both the Old Testament and the New, presupposes an economy of scarcity, not one of abundance.

There are many more possible approaches to the theme of this paper. In a fuller treatment various categories which A. J. Toynbee has developed should be discussed. His idea of the "challenge" of conditions and the "response" of a people, for example, applies most suggestively to the Hebrews.[17] It would be most enlightening to work out the idea of evolutionary selection in the development of the Hebrews and to discuss their isolation, in contrast to their interrelations with their neighbors, in its effects upon their religion. Likewise, in their social evolution there is a clear illustration of the interplay, which Sir Arthur Keith has pointed out, between two codes which work side by side in human evolution—the cosmical and the ethical—the cosmical, which he considers to be the way of evolution, and the ethical, which, he says, seems to contradict evolution; the cosmical, which is indifferent to moral values and works by isolation, and the ethical, which calls for the extension of moral attitudes to an ever enlarging neighborhood.[18] It is a problem of the first magnitude which can be profitably studied as it appears in Hebrew history. However, perhaps enough has been written here to make clear something of the significance, as well as the limitations, of the geographical conditioning of religious experience in Palestine.

17. *A Study of History*, II (London, 1934), 49–55.
18. *Essays on Human Evolution* (London, 1946), esp. pp. 3–7, 93–109, 129 ff.

CHAPTER FOURTEEN

Revelation in the Old Testament

WILLIAM A. IRWIN
University of Chicago

THE problem of divine revelation is of an importance such as to call for no demonstration; with entire appropriateness it has in recent years been the object of keen interest. Yet an examination of the results of this revived activity provokes disquiet. The authors commonly pour out much learned theological terminology upon the theme, they talk at length of the distinction of "natural" and "special" revelation, they offer much platitudinous comment on the uniqueness of Christ as divine revelation; but few of them disclose any adequate realization of the historical aspects of the matter which they undertake to discuss. The problem, it would appear, has become an occasion of theological speculation, when it should have been treated as a sequence of historic events; for the essential fact is that the reality which we call "divine revelation"—and rightly so—is a process in history and is susceptible of study, just like any other historic process and largely by the same methods of verification, analysis, and generalization.

Set in this proper perspective, it becomes immediately clear—it should never have been obscured—that the Bible is the great classic of divine revelation. That is and has been its prime function; and in this realm it is unrivaled. Conceding, if one will, that there may have been other genuine mediums of revelation, nowhere has this attained the elevation or the clarity evident in the Scriptures. Valid and indispensable also as are the methods of the philosopher and theologian, it must, nonetheless, be realized that these may speak of man's knowledge of God only after the biblical scholar has spoken. Lacking the facts and insights

contributed by the latter, speculation on the mode or nature of revelation is in grave danger of reducing to empty theorizing, as, indeed, is painfully evident from some recent writing on the subject.[1]

Now, when the question is returned to that biblical centrality from which it should never have shifted, the striking fact emerges that it is the Old Testament which offers highest promise for fruitful results of study. This is due both to the greater wealth of incidents there related, which exhibit wide variations in the process of revelation, and also to the greater freedom of inquiry felt, by Christian investigators at least, in studying the Old Testament. What progress might be expected by beginning, for example, with the consciousness of Jesus, inextricably obscured as it is with theological presuppositions? Instead, one can approach this question effectively only with the background of dependable results attained elsewhere in the Bible. The problem of the reality, the nature, and the means of divine revelation is thus, in the first instance, a problem of Old Testament history and interpretation.

But still the great bulk and diversity of relevant material may well baffle investigation. However, this will be found to fall loosely into three classes: in general, Old Testament revelation came through the priest, the prophet, and the wise man. There is, it is true, much of the literature which will not obviously organize into such classes; further, the distinction is only one of con-

---

1. An excellent illustration is provided by *Revelation*, a volume of essays by foremost theologians, edited by John Baillie (1937). But, of the eight contributors, not a single one, apart from the editor and the then Archbishop of York, manifests the slightest realization of the factual character of revelation; it is for them nothing but an area of theological speculation. Of very different character is Baillie's own volume, *Our Knowledge of God* (1939); H. Richard Niebuhr's *The Meaning of Revelation* also deserves serious attention. Both of these emphasize the historic aspect of revelation; but it is primarily, if not exclusively, Christian revelation with which they deal. If one may judge from the course of their thought, they would doubtless both admit the reality of a pre-Christian revelation; yet their failure to give it attention deprives the treatments of that illumination which can come to this topic only through the scope of its complete setting. An excellent discussion which does not labor the historic approach, yet nonetheless employs historic results, is J. E. Turner's *The Revelation of Deity* (1931). On the other hand, B. B. Warfield's *Revelation and Inspiration* (1927) demonstrates conclusively that a copious use of the Bible carries no assurance of sound thinking on this matter.

venience, for in actual life the types mix and overlap, so that few individuals can be regarded as belonging exclusively to any type. Nonetheless, it will be found that these three lines of approach will take account of all that was of significance in the religious discovery of ancient Israel. We turn first to the priest.

I

As it is known in the pages of the Old Testament, the priesthood is an august institution, the heir of a long tradition, a more or less developed cultus, and a wide popular authority. Its prestige is well symbolized in such a man as Simon, the son of Onias, of whom Ben Sira wrote that, when he came out of the sanctuary,

> He was as the morning star in the midst of a cloud,
>   and as the moon at its full,
> as the sun shining upon the temple of the Most High,
>   and as the rainbow that illumines the clouds.[2]

The lips of the priest kept knowledge, and the people sought the law at his mouth, for he was to them the messenger of the Lord of Hosts, as the prophet Malachi relates. But the source of such mystic knowledge at this late time, it is clear, was in an ancient tradition. A very long process of accumulating knowledge of procedures, cultic and ethical alike, had made the priesthood the dignified and elevated institution that it was. If we would understand it, we must delve back into its beginnings.

In essence the priest was, just as later literature describes him, the minister of the god, that is, his personal attendant. His beginnings were in utmost anthropomorphism. The god was a great nobleman, with his house and property and his retinue of slaves, just like the rest of the aristocracy.[3] Various of these slaves did menial work about his estate, but he reserved certain ones to wait upon his personal needs. Thus it was the nascent priest who was responsible for entering the god's chamber in the morning, opening his windows, perfuming the air with incense, scattering

2. Ecclus. 50:6–7.

3. See J. H. Breasted, *A History of the Ancient Egyptians* (1908), pp. 62–65; *Encyclopedia of Religion and Ethics*, VI, 251b; X, 278–80.

fresh sand on the floor, giving the god his bath, and, at the right moment, serving him his food. By and by, visitors would arrive; it was the priest's duty to instruct them in the etiquette proper for their admission to the divine presence. As the day wore on, a variety of responsibilities devolved upon the god, until the tedium of the hours dulled his spirit. He needed entertainment with music and dance; it was the priest who knew what best would soothe and revive the flagging divine energies. Just as the attendants of other landed gentlemen of the environment came to know the idiosyncrasies of their masters, so, too, the priest, out of his long association, understood the will and the tastes of the god.

Yet the god was but a block of stone or a gaudily adorned piece of wood. Admitting that even primitive religions were, in general, spiritual and that they conceived of the symbol as only the abode of that vital reality which was the power and person of the deity, yet for all practical purposes the image was the god. And, obviously, that inanimate mass of matter was just as uncommunicative as any other stone or stick. But it should be recalled that "actions speak louder than words." The priest learned of the god's thought and will by what he did, or was alleged to have done—which is the same thing for this level of religious speculation. Let us suppose that some inexperienced priest on a casual day offered his divine master a meal of boiled beef and horse-radish; then soon after, there fell a disastrous and terrifying storm with thunder and lightning—as soon as the timid servant could command courage again to enter the divine presence, he was ready to make confession of sin and to seek means of propitiation! Never again would he offend the godly tastes with boiled beef and horse-radish; instead, next day he brings in a sizzling platter of roast beef garnished with leeks, and abundant flagons of wine. And all goes happily; the sun shines benignly, wealthy visitors come with rich presents, the prayers of suppliants are fulfilled, good news comes from afar, and happiness and prosperity smile upon all. Clearly, the god is pleased. Now the priest has discovered a fundamental truth: the god doesn't like his beef boiled!

This may appear a deliberate effort to burlesque a serious matter. It is nothing of the sort. Here we deal with simplest beginnings of a system that in the course of many centuries came to express itself in dignity and exaltation, such as are manifest in many high-minded individuals of Israel's history and in the insights of the priestly element in the Old Testament. And while the illustrations employed are imaginative, yet several incidents of Old Testament story seem to provide documentation of some such process as here sketched. What was it that actually happened when Nadab and Abihu, sons of Aaron, were mysteriously struck down in the very performance of their duties in the presence of Yahweh (Lev. 10:1–7)? We are told that "fire went out from the presence of the Lord and consumed them." Was it a sudden shaft of lightning? Through the half-score of centuries when Hebrew ritual expressed itself on hosts of hilltops throughout the land, there may well have been numerous occasions when lightning fell right into the sacred inclosure and destroyed priests actually officiating in the ritual. Ancient psychology could not have avoided interpreting this as a direct act of the god, incensed by the procedure of that precise moment. And so we have it in this very passage; Moses undertook to explain what was wrong and why Yahweh took his drastic course. Similar is the incident of Uzzah's instantaneous death on touching the sacred ark (II Sam. 6:7). The natural cause may have been any one of several; for the witnesses, it was a clear case of intervention by an angry God.

Thus the priest in his function as medium of the will of God was an interpreter of events. By his keen intelligence he was set off, apart from, and above the common crowd—lacking that, he would not have been a priest. He played on their credulities with various deceptions, now transparent to critical eyes. An example is provided by a stone figure of a falcon, representing the god Horus, now in the museum of the Oriental Institute; from its beak through to the back of the stone a hole has been drilled. Evidently this was connected to a tube, so that at a convenient distance the priest might make responses in the god's name to the inquiries of the credulous worshipers. But of more significance was

the application of this superior intelligence to reading the deeper meaning of events and circumstances of the time. The priest who had learned the mind of the god through the small affairs of personal attendance found himself drawn into the role of interpreter of all events—natural, social, and political—that impinged on the life of his community. And, with the enlarging limits of the community as city-states grew into empires, the priesthood came to be the spokesmen of the god and the mediator of his will as expressed in matters of high politics. The great conquering monarchs consulted their religious advisers on projected ventures; they turned to them for explanation of portents and signs. Solemnly the auguries were taken, and the will of the gods was declared from what the priests had learned through age-long study of the viscera of sacrificed victims or from the movement of oil on water or the flight of birds or whatever else might be considered to reveal the divine mind. An illuminating little text comes to us from ancient Assyria. It says:

To the king, my lord, thy servant Babua: May Nabu and Marduk bless the king, my lord. On the seventh day of the month Kislev a fox came into the midst of the city. In the garden of Assur it fell into a well. It was drawn out and killed.[4]

Now foxes are timid creatures, living in solitary places; for one to venture into an inhabited city was a remarkable event; it was a portent. The priests had centers for collecting such data. Apparently, they had more or less organized the entire empire for this purpose, with local reporters responsible for transmitting records of unusual occurrences. It would seem that these reports were then filed away; and the priests waited to see what would happen. Presently, let us say, an invading force was overwhelmed and destroyed by the royal troops. There it was: Whenever a fox came into a city and was killed, one might know that the king was to win a victory over invaders!

If we may but concede the presuppositions of the ancient prognosticators that coming events do cast their shadows before, it will be apparent that the priest was a logical, indeed an induc-

4. Friedrich Delitzsch, *Assyrische Lesestücke* (1912), p. 88.

tive, thinker in his methods not unlike a modern scientist. He accumulated data, observed relevant phenomena, then drew conclusions.

Yet one must be careful to avoid confining the entire priestly activity of the long centuries of the ancient world within the compass of these practices. As evidenced in Israel and, doubtless, in varying measure in other lands, there were among the priests high-minded individuals, who in deep sincerity sought to serve the religious needs of their generation. There is no doubt that from the priests there flowed influences of ethical insight and social righteousness. In part we are, perhaps, to postulate that men of this character found their moral principles along the empirical lines already suggested. But much more important must have been their response to feelings of justice and decency that stir in the hearts of all. However, in this direction borders grow vague, and priestcraft merges into prophecy.

Unlike his great colleague, the prophet was one who heard the voice of God deep within his own consciousness. Doubtless largely for this reason, the problem of his knowledge of God is of central importance in Christian thought, for, in varying degrees but with striking unity, Christianity has placed emphasis upon the individual's immediate experience of God. Yet intimately related to this in the church's high appraisal of the prophetic books is the fact that, from its earliest days, it has seen in them some sort of anticipation of the coming of Christ.

In earlier times in Israel the prophetic experience had been the occasion of certain emotional and psychic excesses. The contagious frenzy of their communal ecstatic practices, the artificial stimuli employed to induce religious hysteria, the abnormal phenomena that accompanied or were integral to these states, are all familiar to every student of Old Testament prophecy. In fact, an approach through such psychological phenomena has been a marked feature of studies of the Hebrew prophets through the last thirty years.[5] But a notable development in the character of

5. One of the earliest expressions of the view was by Gustav Hölscher in his *Die Profeten* (1914). An important study was that of H. W. Hines, "The Prophet as Mystic," *American*

prophecy is apparent from about the middle of the eighth century B.C. In the experiences of the writing prophets the crudities of the older practices fell into disrepute, artificial stimuli for inducing the ecstatic state ceased to be employed; but the persistence of a firm belief in actual contact with ultimate spiritual reality through a vivid personal experience was typical of the stream of Hebrew prophecy to the end. The great prophets, while different, yet stood in the succession of the older *nebi'im*.

The experience of these newer prophets can be well studied in the account of the vision of Isaiah in chapter 6 of his book, one of the great and well-known stories of the Old Testament. The narrative gives no interpretation of its incidents; we are obliged to supply what elucidation we can from other sources. It was in the year of King Uzziah's death that Isaiah saw the Lord seated on his exalted throne with the seraphim, in rapt awe, serving before him. That was, according to a recent treatment of the chronology of Hebrew history, the year 740 B.C. Two years before, the vigorous Assyrian monarch, Tiglath-Pileser III, had captured and sacked the northern Syrian city of Arpad. The ruthless conquerors, well known from their incursions of a century before, were once again on the warpath. They were in northern Syria. From there a natural and easy road led south to Israel. And, in Judah, King Uzziah was dead. The long period of peace and stability associated with his reign had come to an end. Uncertain days lay ahead. Thus in thoughtful mood a young Judean went up to the Temple to ponder on the menace of the days and its religious meaning for him and for his people. As he stood there, lost in thought, the scene was transformed, and for him the priests in their cultus no longer ministered in the earthly house; instead, he saw heavenly ministrants soaring in the presence of the Lord and crying, "Holy, holy, holy is the Lord God of Hosts; the whole earth is filled with his glory." He heard the voice of the Lord saying, "Whom shall I send, and who will go

Journal of Semitic Languages, XL (1923–24), 37–71. Since that time the point of view has permeated in various ways most works on prophecy. As a reaction against excesses of the trend, Abraham Heschel's *Die Prophetie* (1936) is of importance. Relevant is J. Lindblom's *Die literarische Gattung der prophetischen Literatur* (1924).

for us?" And, responding with personal dedication, Isaiah received from the Lord himself a message of rebuke and doom for his people.

The incident is of basic importance for an understanding of Isaiah's career. Obviously, it was his "call" as a prophet. In it, too, are evident attitudes and points of view that were to dominate him throughout the entire forty difficult years of his religious leadership. Here we observe that conviction of the holiness of God which was a notable feature of Isaiah's continuing teaching; here, too, his unquestioning faith in the supremacy of God and the finality of His purposes in history; and here likewise we detect the ethical and religious idealism that was to manifest itself in self-forgetting activity through the following years. Still more important, however, is it that we recognize the reality of the whole incident. Isaiah was wrestling with a crucial problem, the poignancy of which we in the modern world have unusual advantages for understanding, through recollection of the steady and insidious aggression of the Nazis in the later 1930's. His experience was a part of the quest, pursued by thoughtful men in all ages, for a reality deeper than the transient things of the common days, however overwhelming these may chance to be. Further, the essential truth of the revelation that came to him on this occasion has been attested in the course of religious history through the succeeding centuries.

But precisely at this point we come to grips with our present problem; for, however highly we may appraise the incident and whatever may be our respect for the worth of Isaiah's convictions, how did he come to these convictions?[6] The tendency—indeed, the traditional attitude—has been to accept the validity of the ancient claim that, in the trance-experience, Isaiah and the other prophets likewise actually did come into contact with unseen reality. In that abnormal state he and they bridged the gulf

6. Significant discussion will be found in the following: Johannes Hänel, *Das Erkennen Gottes bei den Schriftpropheten* (1923); Friedrich Haeussermann, *Wortempfang und Symbol in der alttestamentlichen Prophetie* (1932); H. W. Hertzberg, *Prophet und Gott* (1923); W. F. Lofthouse, "Thus Hath Jahweh Said," *American Journal of Semitic Languages*, XL (1923–24), 231–51; H. W. Robinson, "Hebrew Psychology," in *The People and the Book* (1925), esp. pp. 371–75, and "The Psychology and Metaphysic of Thus Saith the Lord," *Zeitschrift für die alttestamentliche Wissenschaft*, Vol. XLI (1923).

between this world of sense and the unseen world that religious folk have been prone to speak of as the "supernatural"; and thus their accounts of seeing the Lord or of hearing him, as well as their accepted formula of declaration, "Thus saith the Lord," are all to be taken at face value.

Yet this facile interpretation ignores a wealth of relevant facts. The prophets were not the only persons of whom such abnormal experiences are related. Down the centuries one recalls the phenomena of the beginnings of the Christian church, notably the incident of Paul on the Damascus road. Then there follow in train the great Christian mystics and many leaders, such as George Fox and John Wesley. We would gladly dismiss practices such as those of the primitive shaman and medicine man or in later times the hypnotic neuroses of those who claim the "gift of tongues." But we may not. They are all of one class. As phenomena, the visions of the prophets and saints belong together with the strange behavior of the crude medium and of modern ecstatic cults, in so far as these latter are genuine and do not merely assume a psychic experience not actually present.

The issue is of more than passing importance; for it will be apparent that, when we assume the right so to assess the worth of religious visions, by the same act we confess that they in themselves are not the source of religious authority and that for religious knowledge they are of dubious worth. Yet there is no escape from this course. Otherwise, we surrender ourselves as victims of every mad notion concocted by any empty-headed fellow who can establish that he has seen a "vision." Further, if we need authority for it, the New Testament strictly enjoins that we "try the spirits, for many false spirits have gone forth." And by what criteria are we to "try" them? The answer is obvious. The test of their religious validity lies in their conformity with the highest standards and ideals that we know. These may have come out of the long heritage of the past, or they may have been shaped in the crisis of contemporary issues, though again by influences and concepts derived perhaps unconsciously from the total of the best thinking of the age. It was not less so in Isaiah's day or in Moses' or Abraham's, long before him. And if we postu-

late that Moses was influenced by Akhenaton, we have but pushed the ultimate origin a step further back along the same path of our common human wrestle with the issues of life.

Isaiah's great vision, then, was not a source of religious knowledge. It is of interest to see that along this line we have reached the conclusion which psychologists also attain by their analysis of the phenomena of ecstasy. The ecstatic vision is no source of knowledge, they tell us, but all the factual content which the "mystic" brings out of the vision he has first taken into it. Yet this is not to say that the experience is of no worth. Such a view is at once belied by a study of the prophets; it is clear that for some of them, at least, the remarkable certitude they manifest is the direct result of the clarity and convincing reality of the religious experience that came to them in the form of a vision. This, it is apparent, is the function of the vision. It focuses thought; it clarifies issues with which the individual has been struggling, even if somewhat unconsciously; it throws moral and religious matters into a relief as bold as that of black on white. Briefly, the vision constituted the prophet's *inspiration*. But his *revelation* had its source elsewhere.

This conclusion receives considerable corroboration from a study of the formula "Thus saith the Lord." It is simply out of the question that this oft repeated phrase relates at each occurrence the outcome of yet another ecstatic "vision." That would be to turn the prophets into hysterical neurotics whose chief occupation almost every day was throwing themselves into a mad fit. Such frequency of the divine frenzy, it is clear to anyone who understands its physical results, would inevitably have brought on early and complete nervous breakdown, such as, indeed, overtook King Saul under comparable circumstances. For this and for other reasons it is recognized that prophetic utterances usually took their origin in more common experiences and derived their authority from "visions," if at all, only through some basic experience which then, the prophet believed, authenticated all his teaching. His precise psychological relation to these several utterances it is obviously impossible to trace; probably the use of the formula had a tendency to run off into professional formal-

ism. But, on the other hand, we may well believe that, in general, it evidences some deep conviction of unusual insight which the prophet could and did interpret as the stirring of the divine spirit within him. The content of the unusual phenomena in the ecstatic "vision" and the common teaching of the prophet day by day thus alike derive from mental and spiritual activity such as are characteristic of normal human thinking. However much their endowment may have set them apart from the rest of us, it is apparent that the source and origin of the prophets' knowledge of God lay in their own human endowment of thought and feeling. They pondered deeply, devoutly, and long on the issues of their days, and they were profoundly concerned about them; out of such activity there came to them the convictions which they have set down for us as revelations of the will of God.

The wise man is soon dealt with. Certain of his utterances we must presently invoke as revealing a profound insight into the nature of the problem that now occupies us, but in himself he claimed no heavenly raptures or supernatural revelations. He would have been the most surprised man imaginable if one had accosted him with an ascription of divine inspiration. The wise men were the scholars of the ancient world. They were versed in the learning and speculation of their times. In particular, they were students of human life. The neat aphorism of Alexander Pope well describes much of their engrossment: "The proper study of mankind is man." Finding its earliest expressions in a thoroughly practical undertaking to train young men for positions at court, the Wisdom movement had continued through the ages, studying the nature of the good life and the courses of conduct that were conducive to it. In other words, the sages were students of the theory and practice of ethics. But circumstances forced them to broaden their interests to metaphysical problems as well. They became scholars and philosophers. Their convictions came to them through normal intellectual processes. However high their moral teaching, however true their religious insights, all was derived from what we may for the moment describe as purely "human" thinking.

Along these three lines, then, which comprise all that is significant in Old Testament revelation—priesthood, prophecy, and Wisdom—we are forced step by step to the admission that Israel's knowledge of God, in all its height and all its incomparable significance for religious thought, came about through very human processes which we may call, in the better sense of a much-abused term, "commonplace."

Where, then, have we arrived? Man's knowledge of God was attained by human and natural channels, if we may use without discrimination terms that lie open to misinterpretation. Yet such a conclusion seems to be nothing other than a denial of the reality of divine revelation—a view to which, indeed, the critical movement came close at one point in its development but from which it has happily turned away. Yet, before one may jump lightly to this conclusion, it will be well to consider that a remarkable development of almost unique importance was taking place in the centuries of Israel's history. One may well wonder at the strange, almost incredible, fact that this little nation, intimately related as it was by blood and intercourse to the peoples inhabiting a very similar region just a few miles away across the Jordan, stirred with an uneasy aspiration which led it ever upward to nobler concepts of God and man, while they, so far as we can discern, remained largely stagnant in a common paganism much like that from which Israel originally emerged. The consideration will scarcely suffice to point the direction of a final answer to our inquiry, but at least it may serve to deter hasty abandonment of the conviction, traditional among religious persons, that God revealed himself in some unique way in Israel's history; for the problem has now assumed the following form: How are we to understand divine revelation, since its notable expressions in the three great modes of Israel's religious leadership were, in their ultimate analysis, fully natural and human?

II

Whatever position one may assume on the much debated issue of human progress, it seems to be generally admitted that, when set in the full measure of man's career, the question is susceptible

of only one answer. No one disputes that the race has progressed since the Java man. Indeed, the contrast here is such as to arouse feelings of wonder. How can it have come about that such a simian half-man begot a race which has striven and aspired, ever lured on by things unseen, to yet more intangible goals? In this strange stirring that would not let us alone, which refused to let us remain beasts but carried us onward and upward, however hard and dangerous the way, we sense one of the most profound mysteries of the universe. It will not do to dismiss the matter lightly as still another illustration of adaptation to survival needs. What has the writing of poetry or the building of Gothic cathedrals to do with biological survival? The course of biological safety and allurement is precisely that from which we have resolutely turned. As a vestigial remain of our brute ancestry, there are still those—even outside Hollywood—who dream with nostalgic longing of southern seas, where life is easy and biological urges allegedly are uninhibited. But the fact is that at one time we had enough of that and to spare and turned away at a sterner call, which summoned us to endure toil and surmount peril and pain. And why? Why could we not have been content with mere physical things? How attractive to lie all a summer's day like well-fed cows in rich pasture! Why did we not loll under a banana tree and wait for the ripe fruit to fall into our hands— probably we would not have grudged then the effort to carry it to our mouths! But no; we have gone the course that has brought us to sit,

> with blinded eyesight poring over miserable books.

Was it that some remote ancestor, as he lay on a chance day staring up through treetops, scratched his hairy hide and remarked sententiously: "This is no life for a man. We ought to have poets, musicians, architects, dreamers: I'll send my boys to college"? How absurd! If that had happened, it would in itself have been a miracle scarcely less than what we are pondering. Besides such impulse would have spent itself ages ago; and we would now be still in the treetops, with never a faintest realization of the great dream of this lone prophet of the race. The proc-

ess has been far too deep for such a solution. It is in us and of us. It is of our deepest selves. "A spark disturbs our clod." Some reality far beyond our choosing, greater than ourselves, individually or even racially, has caught us up in the sweep and purpose of endless eons and carried us whither we would not and where we did not know. Intimately of ourselves, it is yet far greater than we. It is human nature, but human nature as a product and expression of the process that is the universe. From out of the remote past it has operated to create man, a being with unmeasured powers to aspire and achieve; and it is still carrying him forward to ends that he cannot discern. Man, not alone in his biological being but in his best and highest, is a child of the universe; he is an expression of some mysterious cosmic reality that is infinitely beyond him and yet most intimately of him.

A striking result emerges when we now adduce the thinking of the Hebrew sages as preserved in the eighth chapter of the Book of Proverbs. In poetic imagery the author presents the figure of Wisdom standing in the busiest spots of the city or beside the thoroughfares, calling to all and sundry who pass by:

> You simple ones, learn life's planning,
>   and you foolish, learn to think.
> Listen, for I speak of noble things,
>   with equitable things I open my lips.
> My mouth murmurs truth
>   but wrong my lips detest. . . . .
> Accept my instruction in preference to money,
>   and knowledge rather than finest gold.
> For wisdom is better than pearls,
>   and of things sought after none compare with her.

Wisdom was earlier described in terms which show that the word covers all the finest values of life, its spiritual quality, the total of that higher element which distinguishes man from the brute. And here in chapter 8 that intangible reality is represented as accosting men wherever they may be: in life's busiest spots, in the concourse of traffic, by the wayside, there comes to them the never ceasing challenge, "Accept my instruction; learn, listen, for I speak of noble things."

But in a moment the writer goes on in astonishing sequence. Wisdom has become a cosmic quality:

> The Lord possessed me in the beginning of his ways,
>   before his works of old;
> In eternity I was poured out,[7]
>   ages before the world was.
> When there were no deeps I was born,
>   when there were no fountains filled with water. . . . .

And so the passage runs on in description of primeval ages when Wisdom already was at work:

> When he set for the sea its bound
>   where the waters should not transgress his command,
> When he marked out the foundations of the earth:
>   then I was beside him, a master workman,
> I was daily his delight,
>   and I found pleasure before him at all times.
> I took pleasure in his fruitful earth,
>   and my delight was in the sons of men.

No one may doubt the meaning of this poetic passage. To debate whether this Jewish writer conceived of another person alongside of God in creation and the immeasurable ages before is to confess a prosaic mind incapable of understanding symbolic description. Wisdom here is clearly an attribute of God himself; it is the quality through which he performed his acts of creation, by which also that creation is most highly characterized. Observe the care with which the writer has chosen his words to support this thought. Contrary to certain recent translations, God did not "create"[8] wisdom; the famous word in the cosmogony of Genesis was available if the writer had wished to express without equivocation the idea of creation. But he said God "possessed" wisdom: it was an attribute of him. Also wisdom was "poured out"—not "established" as many would render the word—"in far eternity," an expression remarkably similar to

7. The verb is usually believed to be, rather, of the root "to establish." But the thought of the passage favors the alternate meaning here followed.

8. Gen. 14:19, 22; Deut. 32:6; and Ps. 139:13 are commonly cited as corroborative; but a brief examination shows that, in these passages likewise, "create" is an inaccurate equivalent of the Hebrew word.

later Gnostic notions of divine emanations. But Wisdom most of all was characteristic of human life; there she found her chief delight. And there her high function was to lead men into higher ways of thought and living.

The passage is of profound thought, with far-reaching implications. For our present concern, however, it will be apparent that in the universal and inescapable appeal of the divine wisdom, which, like Francis Thompson's "Hound of Heaven," pursues one down the following years, there is expressed much of what Christian doctrine ascribes to the work of the Holy Spirit. Here, it is apparent, we have the sages' understanding of divine revelation: God works in the hearts of all men everywhere, calling, persuading, insistently urging and imploring them to higher things. And here, too, the sages give their answer to the problem which engaged much of the thought of the ancient Orient: Why is man different from the beasts? What has made him take the course that we call "civilization"? All the finest achievements that history has known, the sages explain, are an expression of the divine wisdom operative in the hearts of men.

And so the thinking which we followed a little ago, pointing the mystery of man's upward climb from his brute ancestry, dependent as such thought appeared to be upon the scientific discoveries of the past hundred years, is really very old. We have been merely rediscovering realities which the thinkers of Israel discussed ages ago. And we can do no other than agree with them that in the mighty process, the direction of which is evident across the immense ages of the human career, we are to discern the self-revelation of God.

The "wisdom of God," by whatever name one may choose to call it, is the supreme fact of history. It has given us all art and literature; it has stirred in the aspirations of poet and saint; the passion of reformers and the indignation of prophets have attested its moving within the human spirit. This strange reality that is intimately of us and yet beyond us has not been fickle in its favors or partisan in its working. All races and all men have experienced it. The fact is all too inadequately realized, even by prominent thinkers in our own day, that God has no favorites!

The divine leading operates upon the heart of every man. Some religious thinkers are fond of stressing the lost estate of man "apart from God," and the consequent need of accepting the particular style in theology which they advocate. Doubtless, there is something to this; man apart from God would probably be a pitiful creature "lost and broken by the fall." But what is the use of talking about him? Such a being has never existed and, as far as we can see, never will. Theology of this kind is nothing but intellectual shadow-boxing, which may have some value for the theologian as a mental exercise but is divorced from reality. The wisdom of God is universal. The difference between a good man and a bad one is not that one is "apart from God"— it would be a strange perversion of Christian thought which would deny even to the most depraved the pleading of the divine Spirit—the difference is only in the measure of conscious devotion which individuals may yield to the mysterious impulses to better things that stir without discrimination in the hearts of all. The concept of "man apart from God" is both an intellectual absurdity and a religious apostasy; but "man with God" is a reality which the course of human history demonstrates. The mystery of man's being is that he is shot through with that reality which we call "the divine." God is in man, not less truly than man is in God. Such is the teaching of the sages; it is the thought attributed to Paul by the author of Acts, whose famous quotation gathers into neat expression the fundamental reality of divine revelation, "In Him we live and move and have our being."

A study of the actual process of growing religious knowledge enforces this understanding of it. The prophet is an individualist. He is liable to eccentricity; many within the total of the movement have been freaks. The problem, which became acute in Israel about the seventh century B.C., of the authentication of prophecy was an expression of the functioning of social tests and checks upon the individualism of the prophet. The common members of society learned to look skeptically upon the claims of self-appointed leaders and accepted or rejected according as they were convinced. And while it would be absurd to argue that the

views of some ignorant peasant were better based than those of, say, Jeremiah, still it is apparent that the Judean community as a whole was assessing prophetic oracles in accord with the best that they knew and felt. The "wisdom of God" spoke through the great prophets; it operated also in the "natural law" felt by their commonplace contemporaries. In the restraint and skepticism of these, provoking and nullifying though they often were, the total truth was being clarified. Revelation ultimately is a social process. It does not suffice that the seer should mount the heights and gain a glimpse of the celestial city; he must show it to his fellows; for, whether in minute measure or in soul-consuming devotion, all the Lord's people are prophets!

Divine revelation, the Old Testament discloses with clarity, is far greater than, traditionally, we have supposed. To recognize our common human nature speaking in inspired prophets and thinkers does not rob us of the voice of God, but makes it real and near. Divine revelation is no pale abstraction of theologians mulling over the alleged supernaturalism of ages long gone by; it is a living presence. It is a process as wide as the race and as long as time. It transcends the limits of human life. Just as the great thinker in the Book of Proverbs asserts, the stirring that manifests itself in human aspiration is the same as that which operated through the long ages before man came upon the earth. It made a habitable world; it created living beings; it evolved man; it led him ever upward through the dreary stagnation of the stone ages, through the growing light of early cultures, and with increasing clarity ever onward to higher realization of his own true destiny. The voice that spoke through prophet and sage in ancient Israel has been heard by men everywhere since first the race emerged from its brute ancestry. It is heard in our own days, in the might and terror of the testing through which we have just passed, in uneasy stirrings toward a real human brotherhood, and in quiet aspirations in our deepest souls; but, because of the heaviness of our ears, we hear less clearly than did some men of old.

The Bible is not the single and sole "inspired" literature. Other great religious books, we are compelled to affirm, in so

far as they have recorded and stimulated man's quest for a better life, take their place also as valid revelations of God. But then the pre-eminence of the Bible is not a matter of partisan loyalty. Its true place can be understood only through an objectivity that will approach each sacred literature in complete fairness, ready to ascribe to all their proper merit. Yet those who love the Bible need fear nothing from such a test. While the greatness of other scriptures must not be disparaged, still the Bible stands supreme in the exaltation of its knowledge of God, in the nobility of its vision of human duty, and in its power to seize and quicken the imagination with a vision of possibilities that lie open to the human spirit. In this sense one may make concession to those who seek for a "special revelation" in Israel. The Bible is the great classic of divine revelation.

Comment is frequently made on the strangeness of the fact that in this modern world of scientific wonders we continue to read solemnly in services of worship passages from the literature of a little people of a remote time who knew nothing of "our glorious gains" but lived in a simplicity and baldness of material conditions such as would now seem little less than barbaric. But the reason is apparent. That brief segment of history which we call the "life of ancient Israel" was of unique significance in the whole long human story. The fact of distinctive national traits cannot be disputed. The Greeks excelled in literature and thought, the Romans in law and organization; in later times there arose the art of Italy, the painting of Holland, the poetry of England. Israel's genius was in religion. Great as have been the spiritual attainments of others, in this realm Israel was supreme. But religion is, in essence, a sensitivity to finer things; it is of a piece with aesthetics. Ethics is but aesthetics within the area of conduct. The prophet was an artist in religion. How clear this becomes in certain of the confessions of Jeremiah:

> If I say I will not mention him
>   nor speak any more in his name,
> then there is in my heart as a burning fire
>   shut up in my bones,
> and I am weary with forbearing
>   and cannot withhold [Jer. 20:9].

In those words there speaks the inner urge of the artist who expresses himself in his chosen medium, not because it is his living or because he wants to do so, but because of an inner compulsion by which he cannot refrain. Who would dare set limits to the mystical power of the human personality to apprehend truth? Along that path Israel's seers went far beyond our lowly course; they transcended the great of other times and places. They heard the voice of God.[9]

9. The discussion has been restrained within chosen limits. Three further questions are so intimately related as well to be considered a part of the problem. To the view held by Old Testament prophets and thinkers of their inspiration only meager attention has been given. The highly important issue of the validity of the experience of these men as a revelation of God has likewise been dismissed with no more than allusion or inference. Also the inspiration of the Old Testament, in the sense of its religious value for the modern reader, has received even less attention. These deficiencies have not been due to oversight, much less to indifference, but, rather, because a proper discussion would in each case occupy space comparable with that claimed for the present study. Consequently, attention has been narrowed to the question of how that reality called "divine revelation" has come about, with the scope of discussion enlarged, at the most, only to set the Hebrew experience in its full context. The study is objective, concerned with facts, in so far as these are recoverable. As hinted above, the evaluation of these facts and their integration into organized religious statement is the valid task of the theologian.

CHAPTER FIFTEEN

Propaganda Analysis Applied to Alexandrian-Jewish Apologetic

A. HAIRE FORSTER

Seabury-Western Theological Seminary, Evanston, Illinois

O F ALL the movements of history, none are more fitted to attract our curiosity than those by which Jew and Greek first came into contact: when the minds were confronted and the spiritual heritages began to be exchanged, whose concurrence and interaction were destined to exercise so enormous an influence upon civilization."[1]

If the consequences of this culture contact are considered, these words of a distinguished Old Testament scholar are fully justified. This mingling of Jew and Greek resulted in a Greek Old Testament with additions and in a Greek, not an Aramaic, New Testament. It produced Paul. It created, with the help of imperial Rome, that "fulness of time" in which a world religion became possible; for, even if the Jews held their main positions, they had to adopt the weapons of the Greeks in order to do so.

In Palestine the issue was decided, for a time at least, by force of arms: the Maccabees and dissensions in the Seleucid Syro-Greek empire checked the tide of Hellenism, so that the "Holy Land" was not completely submerged and Judaism remained in its integrity.[2] In Alexandria the Jews were in no position to meet the Greeks with the sword, and so they used another weapon— the pen. They launched a propaganda campaign, both defensive

---

1. G. A. Smith, *Jerusalem* (New York, 1908), II, 367.

2. The "isolationist" policy of the Palestinian Jews resulted rather curiously in the inclusion of non-Jews in the covenant of Israel; the conquests of Hyrcanus (135–105 B.C.) forced Idumaeans and Itureans to accept circumcision and the Jewish Law (Josephus, *Ant.* xiii. 9. 1 and 11. 3).

and offensive, and such a campaign should have a special interest in this, "the propaganda age." If their methods were not always fair, Christians should be the last people to cast a stone at them, for early Christian writers not only imitated their methods but adopted, with additions, some of their most daring inventions.

It would be both tedious and unnecessary to survey the propaganda literature which came from Alexandria; such a survey is easily accessible in Schürer's *History of the Jewish People in the Time of Jesus Christ.*[3] It can also be found in I. G. Matthews, *The Jewish Apologetic to the Grecian World in the Apocryphal and Pseudepigraphical Literature.*[4] The most recent survey is that of Otto Stählin, *Die hellenistisch-jüdische Litteratur.*[5]

Before examining the methods used by the Jewish apologists, the writer will describe the situation, to survey, as it were, the field of this battle of the books.

Alexander the Great showed himself more than a military strategist when he chose the site of Alexandria. It became a great and flourishing city almost at once and remained so for nearly four hundred years. Racial and religious riots led to its decline; and the Mohammedans replaced it as capital by the city now known as Cairo. Since A.D. 1800, when the population was only five thousand, the city has regained its earlier place as a great Mediterranean port. For the subject of this study it is the first three centuries of Alexandria's history that are important.

"Alexandria," Zeller wrote, "was the place where first and most completely the connection of Greece with the East was realised. In that centre of commerce, for three centuries, East and West entered into a connection more intimate and more lasting than in any other centre."[6]

Strabo, who visited Alexandria in 25 B.C. and stayed there for five years, described it as "the greatest commercial centre of the world." It was the meeting place of the merchandise of the Medi-

3. (New York, n.d.), Div. II, Vol. III, § 33.
4. Chicago, 1914.
5. Munich, 1921.
6. *The Stoics, Epicureans and Sceptics* (London, 1870), p. 29.

terranean and the Nile; and, before the time of Strabo, the literary interests of the first Ptolemies had made it an intellectual capital as well. The city was built on a neck of land, two miles broad, between Lake Mareotis and the sea. It was situated west of the Nile mouth, so that the harbors were not choked by the Nile mud, which is carried east by the current. Strabo was impressed by its climate. "At the beginning of summer," he tells us, "the Nile, being full, fills the lake also and leaves no marshy matter which is likely to occasion malignant exhalations. At the same period, the Etesian winds blow from the North over a large expanse of sea and the Alexandrians in consequence pass their summers very pleasantly."[7]

Two of the intersecting streets of Alexandria were a hundred feet in breadth and lined with colonnades. Of the public buildings, the Museum was founded by the first Ptolemy (305–285 B.C.); and this was essentially a home of research, not a teaching institution. It has been called "the first example of a permanent institution for the cultivation of pure science founded by a government."[8]

The Museum of Alexandria had no "students" in the usual sense of the term, but it was a "University" in the truest meaning of that word. Some of its members were Aristarchus, who anticipated the Copernican theory by eighteen centuries; the geometer Euclid, whose book on geometry was a textbook for more than twenty centuries; and Eratosthenes, who was the first to measure a degree of latitude on the earth's surface and who calculated the circumference of the earth to within a few hundred miles of the correct figure.

Developments in medicine were as remarkable as those in astronomy and geometry; and Alexandrian physicians became world famous. The glory of the Museum was in science. In literature it was erudite and pedantic, a school of commentators and philologists, who, in the study of the great poets of Greece, missed nothing except their poetry.

7. *Geography* xvii. 1.

8. A. Holm, *The History of Greece* (London and New York, 1894–98), IV, 317.

Although the Museum itself was primarily a research center, it was possible to attend lectures in Alexandria; and Philo gives a sarcastic account of those who listened to them.[9]

The population of Alexandria was made up of four more or less distinct groups.[10] First were the native Egyptians in Rhacotis on the west side; this element became more important in each century, especially after the battle of Raphia (217 B.C.), when the Egyptian contingent in his army gave Ptolemy IV (Philopator, 222–205) the victory over Antiochus the Great (223–187). Then there was the Greek element, settled for the most part in the New City toward the east; among these the Macedonians were naturally pre-eminent. These, with the mercenary soldiers, were the upholders of Greek rule. There was also a hybrid element, a "mixed multitude" from the intermarriage of Greeks and Egyptians. These Eurafricans, along with the native Egyptians, probably made the largest part of that Alexandrian mob which was so infamous in the city's history. Philo refers to polytheists as "men who do not blush to transfer that worst of evil constitutions, mob rule—from earth to heaven."[11] The fourth element was Jewish. They had come to Egypt at various times, as mercenaries, merchants, captives, and refugees; but in the time of Ptolemy I they were introduced in large numbers, so that Philo says: "Jews that inhabited Alexandria and the rest of the country were not less than a million men."[12] In Alexandria, their location was in the northeast corner of the city, on the coast, east of the promontory of Lochias. According to Philo, they occupied two out of the five quarters of the city.[13] Their political position was known as *isopolity*,[14] or "potential citizenship," that is, a Jew could become a full citizen if he agreed to worship the city gods. Obviously, such a status would increase the temptation to apostasy.

---

9. *De congressu eruditionis gratia* 13.

10. Cf. Strabo xvii. 12.

11. *On the Creation* 61.

12. *In Flaccum* 6.

13. *Ibid.* 8.

14. W. W. Tarn, *Hellenistic Civilisation* (London, 1927), p. 176.

On the Alexandrian Jews generally, the evidence supports the statement of Theodor Mommsen: "In acknowledged independence, in repute, culture and wealth, the body of Alexandrian Jews was, even before the destruction of Jerusalem, the first in the world."[15]

The situation at Alexandria was therefore something like this: the "university people" were probably rather contemptuous of the Jews. Aristeas in his *Letter* is careful to note the applause of the *philosophers* at the answer of one of the Seventy (§ 235). The native Egyptians disliked and were disliked by the Jews. They could scarcely have failed to notice that the great annual Jewish festival, the Passover, was anything but flattering to Egyptians; and the result must have been something like that of the annual celebration of the Battle of the Boyne in Ireland. The court was favorable to the Jews, because they made loyal and industrious citizens. The Jews themselves were numerous and prosperous but were exposed to constant attacks by non-Jewish writers on charges connected with their history and their peculiar way of life and also to a greater, because more subtle, danger—the apostasy of their members. For instance, Philo's nephew, Tiberius Alexander, deserted his religion and became procurator of Palestine and afterward prefect of Egypt, and then crowned his apostasy by aiding Titus in the war that was distinguished by the destruction of the Temple of Jerusalem.

So the champions of Judaism in Alexandria had these problems: How were the Jews who had read Plato and those who were attracted by Greek culture and way of life to be kept in the Faith? How were Gentiles to be persuaded that the Pentateuch was on a level with Greek philosophy and that Jewish history was as ancient and contained as great names as that of any other nation? The more honorable answered these questions by allegorizing the Law, the less honorable by falsifying the (gentile) prophets and by redecorating their own writings. Philo is an example of the first type, the redactor of the Sibylline Oracles of the second, Artapanos of the third. It must never be forgotten that

15. *The Provinces of the Roman Empire* (New York, 1887), II, 291.

the Alexandrian age was an age of literary license. "The whole age was now full of literary dishonesty" is Sir John Pentland Mahaffy's characterization of the period. Allegory, forgery, falsification, plagiarism, were rampant; and when so many were using these dubious means for their own glorification or to promote unworthy ends, it is not surprising that a few Jews were tempted to use them, as they thought, to promote the glory of the one true God. Freudenthal makes a vigorous defense of the Jewish apologists and shows by numerous instances that, though they were not blameless, the other side was just as guilty. He writes of some of these Jewish productions: "Sie bleiben eine verwerfliche Erscheinung innerhalb der hellenistischen Litteratur; doch sie sind durch die allgemeine Sitte oder Unsitte der Zeit erklärt und in gewissem Sinne entschuldigt."[16] Even Solon, long before the Alexandrian age, is said to have added lines to Homer to support his side in a dispute with the Megarians, and Solon was the great lawgiver of the Greeks.

As an example of Jewish manipulation of Greek masterpieces, the following specimens are taken from Aristobulus, who is supposed to have lived in the time of Ptolemy Philometor (182–146 B.C.): "Homer and Hesiod declare what they have borrowed from our books that it [the seventh] is a holy day." To prove this he quotes Hesiod, *Works and Days*, line 770: πρῶτον ἔνη τετράς τε καὶ ἑβδόμη ἱερὸν ἦμαρ; but Hesiod means that the first and fourth are holy days as well as the seventh, and these are days in the first period of the month when the moon is waxing. Later on (l. 819) he says that the *fourth* of the midmonth is a day holy above all. Again he quotes the *Odyssey* v. 262: ἕβδομον ἦμαρ ἔην, καὶ τῷ τετέλεστο ἄπαντα ("it was the seventh day and all was done"); but the correct reading is τέτρατον ("fourth"). He also quotes, as from Homer, another line which may be translated, "Then, the seventh day returned, a holy day." The line in Greek is a hexameter; but it is not in Homer. It is not certain that Aristobulus himself altered the text of Homer, but the alterations are, at any rate, the work of an Alexandrian Jew and an example of one of

16. *Hellenistische Studien* (Breslau, 1875), p. 194.

their propaganda devices. Pseudo-Hecataeus is suspected of being the originator of these textual falsifications.[17]

One of the most curious products of the Jewish Alexandrian apologists is a dramatic poem in Greek iambic trimeters by Ezekiel, whose date is assigned to the second century B.C. The poem is named the "Exodus" ('Εξαγωγή); and the existing fragments bring the story of Moses up to Exod. 15:27.

After the fashion of the Greek dramatists, an Egyptian messenger, escaped from the Red Sea, relates ιthe story of that disaster. It was clearly intended to be read by Greeks and even to be acted; but a Greek accustomed to the plays of Euripides must have smiled as he read or listened to an iambic line such as this: Ἀβραάμ τε κ' Ἰσαὰκ κ' Ἰακώβου τρίτου. Perhaps, however, he was impressed by the story and overlooked the style, for the story showed that the Jews had a hero, Moses, who might be compared, and not unfavorably, with the lawgivers and leaders of Greece. The Sibylline Oracles had already been fabricated by, or in the time of, Berosus, a priest of Bel, in the interests of Babylonian prestige. Berosus lived in the time of Antiochus Soter (280–262 B.C.), one of the early Seleucid kings, who wished to stage a "Babylonian" revival.

Alexandrian Jews took the hint from "Berosus," and the origin of Book III of the Sibyllines is described by Bate in these words:

Conceive, then, an Alexandrian Jew—in whose hands is a work already accepted as Sibylline, but containing—in a pagan form, of course —the stories of the Deluge and the Tower of Babel——. What "Berosus" had begun, the Jew could not fail to continue. A few touches only were needed to expunge the polytheism of the Berosian stories: the rest could be incorporated en bloc.[18]

The resultant work might be described as a missionary appeal to the Greeks. "Judgment is near, therefore renounce idols and turn to the One Most High God" is its theme. The style is turgid, and the composition chaotic; it contains an odd mixture of Babylonian traditions and Greek myths, but the ultimate author has

17. On the critical questions concerning Aristobulus and his writings cf. Stählin, *op. cit.*, pp. 604–6.

18. *The Sibylline Oracles: Books III–V* (New York, 1918), p. 20.

no uncertainty that "the people of the Great God" are to be the guides of life to all mankind, οἳ πάντεσσι βροτοῖσι βίου καθοδηγοὶ ἔσονται (1. 195). It is a Doomsday Book, but the tone softens for Greece (11. 545–67), and who could resist such an appeal, for it comes from a Sibyl who is a true prophetess and, furthermore, is the daughter-in-law of Noah!

Falsifications of history are to be found among the writings of Alexandrian Jews, but in this they were equaled, if not surpassed, by their opponents. The great event of Jewish history was the Exodus; yet Egyptian historians turned this into an ugly story about the expulsion of a horde of lepers and cripples. The great glory of the Jewish people was their Temple at Jerusalem, but an Egyptian writer spread the story that in it was worshiped an ass's head. In the face of such insults, it is not surprising that they went to extremes in magnifying their history and their Temple. The grandeur of the Temple is certainly made the most of in the Letter of Aristeas, and the writer who most exaggerated Jewish history was Artapanos. Freudenthal is of the opinion that these two writers are one, but his arguments do not amount to proof. In his enthusiasm for his people, Artapanos becomes a syncretist: Moses is identical with the Greek Musaeus, the teacher of Orpheus; he did more than teach Orpheus, he taught the Egyptians their religion. He also interpreted the hieroglyphics and, in consequence, was honored like a god and given the name "Hermes." He was, in fact, the originator of all culture, both religious and otherwise. Such embellishments as these, found in Artapanos and others, indicate the sources of the marvels about Moses which Josephus adds to the Bible story.

The Alexandrian version of the Old Testament, known, unfortunately, as the "Septuagint," is sometimes classed as Jewish apologetic, and it did so function; its original purpose, however, was plainly for synagogue use. It is remarkable how completely Greek replaced Hebrew in the Dispersion. Philo can write: "The name is, as the Hebrews say Phanuel, which translated into *our* language means. . . . . " Mahaffy came to the conclusion that there is a basis of truth in the Aristeas legend and that Ptolemy II may have requested a translation of the Jewish Law for his li-

brary; but there are sections of Isaiah which suggest a translator who was forgetting his Hebrew and had not got very far in his Greek. Thus the Pentateuch, to which alone the name "Septuagint" belongs, may have been made for the royal library. Some parts of the rest of the translation could be just the distillation of Jewish targuming. This famous product of Alexandrian Judaism is dealt with at length in chapter viii.

The use of allegory as an apologetic method will always be associated with the great name of Philo; yet, again, it was a *Greek* method long before his time, he only adopted a foreign weapon. He was following the Cynics and Stoics, who exercised their ingenuity in allegorizing the Greek myths; they called the process θεραπεία ("doctoring"). Democritus used it about 420 B.C., and even Aristotle at times. By this method, men of culture were enabled to accept beliefs hallowed by long tradition but repulsive to their ethical discernment. The method was not strictly valid; it carried truths into myths and then out, but it was ἀντιφάρμακον τῆς ἀσεβείας ("an antiseptic against impiety"), and what strange methods are used even today in the interests of piety!

It is unnecessary to multiply examples of allegory; however, when Philo finds the four cardinal virtues in the four rivers of Paradise, not only is he, after his fashion, allegorizing the Bible, but he is bringing it into line with Greek philosophy; he is expressing his fundamental idea: the identity of the truths of philosophy with those of revelation.

So the works of the Jewish Alexandrian writers are, at best, an attempt to combine the faith of the Synagogue with the thinking of Greece by means of allegory; at worst, an attempt to approach the Greek world by forgeries and falsifications of history and of poetry. Such forgeries and falsifications were not confined to any one race or group; they were a feature of the Hellenistic age. These Alexandrian Jews were propagandists, and propagandists are not always overscrupulous; read, for example, *The Fine Art of Propaganda*[19] in order to see what modern propagandists can produce. Indeed, some of the devices of our present-day propagandists had not been discovered by these ancient writers. *Name-*

19. Alfred M. and Elizabeth B. Lee (eds.) (New York, 1939).

Calling, giving a group a bad label, was sometimes used: for example, Jews called Greeks "atheists," and Greeks returned the compliment. Today we call those with whom we disagree "Communists." *Glittering Generalities*, associating something with a "virtue" expression like "science," might be illustrated by the Book of Wisdom, at least in its later chapters. *Transfer*, carrying the prestige of something revered over to something else in order to make the latter acceptable, is the device of those who "padded" the Sibylline Oracles with Jewish, and later with Christian, doctrines. *Card Stacking*, selecting the facts or falsehoods that suit one's own case, seems to be inevitable in all propaganda, both ancient and modern; but the other three common devices of today, know as *Testimonial*, *Plain Folks*, and *Band Wagon*, are not prominent in the ancient world. In order to flourish, these need Hollywood stars and a democratic age.

Whether the apologetic or propaganda of the Alexandrian Jews proved successful cannot be decided with any exactness. There is not and could not be any evidence of the number of those who were kept in the Jewish Faith by the arguments and appeals of the apologists.

There is, however, considerable evidence that many proselytes were brought in. Izates, king of Adiabene, with his whole household, and the women of Damascus in large numbers are recorded by Josephus.[20] Roman writers attest similar results;[21] and, in addition, a notable statement of Seneca is quoted by Augustine: "Cum interim usque eo sceleratissimae gentis consuetudo convaluit, ut per omnes jam terras recepta sit; victi victoribus leges dederunt."[22]

Such successes may have been due in some cases to the writings of the Jews, yet it is probable that the majority of proselytes had never read any of these and that the most effective propaganda agencies of the Jews were not their literature, but their simple, dignified, and *congregational* Synagogue service, beginning with

20. *Ant.* xx. 2. 4. and *BJ* ii. 20. 2.

21. Horace *Sat.* i. 4. 142 f.; i. 9. 68; Juvenal *Sat.* xiv. 96 f.

22. *De civ. Dei* vi. 11.

its impressive proclamation of the Unity of God, and also their family life, so far superior to anything that the majority of Greeks, Egyptians, or Syrians were able to produce.

SOME IMPORTANT BOOKS AND ARTICLES NOT QUOTED DIRECTLY

CAUSSE, A. "La Propagande juive et l'hellénisme," *Revue d'histoire et de philosophie religieuses*, III (1923), 397–414. Deals only with Sibyllines and the Book of Wisdom.

MAHAFFY, J. P. *Greek Life and Thought*. 2d ed. New York, 1896.

———. *The Empire of the Ptolemies*. New York, 1895.

EUSEBIUS. *Preparation for the Gospel*, trans. E. H. GIFFORD. 2 vols. Oxford, 1903. The main source for the extant remains of most of the Jewish Alexandrian apologists.

SUSEMIHL, F. *Geschichte der griechischen Litteratur in der Alexandrinerzeit*. 2 vols. Leipzig, 1891–92.

BURY, J. B., and OTHERS. *The Hellenistic Age*. Cambridge, England, 1923.

FAIRWEATHER, W. *The Background of the Gospels*. 4th ed. Edinburgh, 1926.

BRAUDE, W. G. *Jewish Proselyting in the First Five Centuries of the Common Era*. Providence, R.I., 1940.

CHAPTER SIXTEEN

The Relevance of Apocalyptic for Ancient and Modern Situations

PAUL E. DAVIES

McCormick Theological Seminary, Chicago, Illinois

APOCALYPTIC has suffered so severely at the hands of its self-styled champions that its proper friends have very often failed to appreciate its true character and relevance. If only to offset false interpretation in these days after the war, the students of the Bible have a duty to demonstrate the clear relevance of this type of literature. The question of relevance is, of course, part of the larger question of the place of all ancient writing in the modern scene and is in part connected with the question of the value and authority of Scripture for the man of today. But, by comparison with other literature from that time, apocalyptic labors under special handicaps. Its claim to be "revelation" warns off at the outset. The speculations of the apocalyptist concerning things heavenly and eschatological seem to put it out of touch with the real life that was the concern of the prophet, and its extravagant language tends to discredit any claim it might have to represent serious revelation. The reader tries, often in vain, to present to the imagination the figures and symbols with all their wings and heads and fiery splendors. Then again, while the prophet spoke his message in his own name with all the vigor of his own personality behind it, most apocalyptic authors hid behind the mask of an assumed name; and this circumstance cut the direct appeal. The remoteness of these apocalypses is further increased by their marginal standing in relation to the canon of Scripture, only Daniel and Revelation having a place in the regular canon. Even Revelation had difficulty in certain areas.

And the question may be asked, "What relevance can these marginal writings have when their predictions of world-shaking events have not been fulfilled?" Then, to make the case worse, the millenarians in the face of nonfulfilment have reinterpreted these predictions with reference to modern history and with little or no regard to the original meanings. It is small wonder that these writings are closed books to the average reader and that they seem to convey no meaning for our times. But such neglect does scant justice to a very considerable body of literature and to a point of view which played an important part in early Judaism and Christian beginnings.

APOCALYPTIC IN RELATION TO PROPHECY

Apocalyptic in its main line of development between 200 B.C. and A.D. 200 may be defined as that literature which deals with matters which, by their nature, must be revealed. Cosmic explanations, heavenly scenes, eschatological details, are beyond the usual range of knowledge and must be made known to man through visions, angelic visitors, or ecstatic experiences. But apocalyptic in its proper sense cannot be adequately defined apart from its genesis in prophecy. The Hebrew prophet uttered short oracles bearing upon particular situations and indicating what God intended to do with his people. The prophet was directly concerned with the moral outcomes for God's people, and so he transcended the present in predicting the future, often in relation to the Day of the Lord. God was a factor in the future as in the present, and through it all he was working out his purposes. In the later stages of prophecy we find a more elaborate imagination playing upon the future hopes of the nation as in Deutero-Isaiah and Ezekiel. Prophecy actually supplied much of the material which was worked over and interpreted by apocalyptic.

The time came when the voice of the prophet gave way to the authority of the Law. Then the nation fell under the dominance of pagan empires, Greco-Syrian and Roman, and the cause of God's people and their religion was endangered. How could this impossible situation stand in the light of their faith in the power

of a righteous God?[1] The prophet had interpreted the suffering of the people in terms of God's judgment on the nation in the light of the Day of the Lord. But such a solution in terms of God's working in and through this perverted world appeared hopeless. The pressure of this conflict between the hopeless situation and the will of a sovereign God resulted in a break with the prophet's linear view of God's working in this world. Actually, the prophets in their visions and their projections of an ideal restoration had already pointed the way. Now, to cope with the moral and religious urgency of the situation, this revival of the prophetic function took the form of revelations that penetrated beyond the limits of ordinary knowledge. They recognized the evil in this world, but, at the same time, they asserted their strong faith in God's sovereignty with respect to the ultimate issues. In the end God would intervene catastrophically to assert his will and vindicate his people. This resolution of the seer's sense of frustration resulted eventually in the two-age succession in time—the present evil age and the age to come. The limit to human knowledge, once surmounted in terms of historical issues, was also exceeded in the direction of all time from the beginning and of the ordering of the heavens. Where the occidental mind, faced with a similar demand for more knowledge and an ordered world, would have resorted to philosophical abstractions, the apocalyptic mind overleaped the barrier through vision, angel visitor, or heavenly tour and objectified the spiritual world in terms of symbolic and concrete imagery. The result was a practical dualism, consisting of this frustrated evil world and God's order in historical determinism and in heavenly economy.

Yet there remain fundamental similarities between prophecy and its "problem child," apocalyptic. Both proceed from a strong faith in God, both take seriously the evil in the world, and both believe in a future under God when evil will be conquered. Both transcend the visible factors in the present situation, prophecy in the direction of God's power working in the present scene and

---

1. II Esd. 3:30, 31a: "For I have seen how thou sufferest them sinning, and hast spared the ungodly doers, and hast destroyed thy people, and hast preserved thine enemies; and thou has not signified unto any how thy way may be comprehended."

apocalyptic in God's ultimate interference. Actually, apocalyptic is the direct outcome of later prophecy, and typical apocalyptic elements can be traced in the prophetic literature of Ezekiel and after. The apocalyptists spoke of themselves as "prophets"[2] and of their writing as "prophecy."[3] Within the range of the similarities the relevance of the prophets may be extended to the apocalyptists.

It must be recognized, however, that the differences are in certain areas crucially important for the relevance or lack of relevance of these writings. The prophets in their own personalities are relevant,[4] but the mask of pseudonymity generally hides the identity of apocalyptic writers. The prophet's call to the nation for repentance in the light of God's judgment was vital with his own faith and sense of urgency. But the apocalyptist allowed his faith to carry him away on the wings of imagination, unchecked by temporal realities, and he frequently lost his reader on the way. The prophet in the earlier stage uttered his message with the authority of direct experience and the spoken word. The apocalyptist wrote down the record of his visions and heavenly conversations for his own or later(?) generations to read.

Recognizing the similarity and difference in relation to prophecy, can we, then, estimate the relevance of apocalyptic? At the outset we face the very real difficulty of giving any over-all conclusions for a literature of so vast a range. Its range in time of production covers four hundred years, and the literary classification covers many writings of the greatest variety. The author of II Esdras numbered seventy (or sixty) books in this category,[5] and II Enoch refers to three hundred and sixty-six books.[6] The modern editor, R. H. Charles, lists eight apocalypses in the pseudepigrapha. There are Jewish apocalypses, such as Jubilees, and Christian apocalypses, such as Revelation and the Shepherd of Hermas and the Apocalypse of Peter. The problem becomes more complicated when we find apocalyptic passages and elements scattered through other writings. Isaiah, chapters 24–27,

2. II Esd. 1:1.   3. Rev. 1:3.

4. Cf. R. B. Y. Scott, *The Relevance of the Prophets* (New York, 1944), chap. x.

5. II Esd. 14:44.   6. II En. 23:6.

has been usually classified as apocalyptic, although H. H. Rowley has recently questioned it. Joel and Zechariah are definitely tinged with it. As for the New Testament, it has been said recently: "There is not a single book of any size in the New Testament except John which is not written against the background of this apocalyptic framework."[7] The "little apocalypse" in Mark is commonly recognized. Even such a prosaic book as James refers to *apocalypsis*.

Furthermore, the material itself is not at all uniform. Its major bearing is upon eschatology, predicting the woes and glories of the end and the judgment. But its speculation ranges out to the ordering of the system of nature or the successive heavens, as in II Enoch, a sort of prescientific explanation of earth and high heaven. We also find extensive reviews of world history in the guise of predictions by ancient seers, for example, the Book of Jubilees or the Testaments of the Twelve Patriarchs.

The ideas presented vary within wide limits. The messianic era may be four hundred years or a thousand years, or it may be spiritually conceived. The resurrection is literally conceived in II Baruch; spiritually conceived in the Ascension of Isaiah; or not conceived at all, as in Jubilees. Within a single book concepts will vary. In I Enoch, chapters 12–36, it is taught that the spirit and the body will rise, but in the Similitudes of I Enoch (chaps. 37–71) it is a spiritual body that will rise. The Messiah appears in some of this literature but plays no part in other portions. These varied materials and concepts scattered through many writings complicate the problem: How can the general relevance of this amorphous material be demonstrated? The consideration of a single writing could be the subject of this chapter.

RELEVANCE—GENERAL AND SPECIFIC

Relevance has to do with bearing, applicability, or pertinence and may be construed in the most general sense or with a narrower meaning in a particular area. There is a sense in which all this material is relevant for the historian as a varied exhibit of a stream of literary and religious tradition in the centuries 200

7. W. A. Smart, *The Spiritual Gospel* (New York, 1946), p. 51.

B.C.–A.D. 200. The apocalypses were written out of the pressure of a real situation; and they are of aid to the historian in the reconstruction of that situation, particularly on the inner side of the feelings and emotions involved.[8] In fact, it has been recently maintained that apocalyptic in its genesis owed more to the historical circumstance of its rise in the Maccabean age than to prophecy or to foreign influences.[9] It was generally a reaction to a specific situation of conflict, and therefore it becomes evidence of one side of the particular struggle. Daniel and Revelation betray the reaction to Syrian and Roman oppression, respectively. Daniel gives history as prophecy, and so he can describe the four successive empires and the symbol of the fourth empire (Macedonian-Syrian) as a terrible beast with a little horn. Rome is symbolized as a beast in Revelation, but in II Esdras, chapters 11 and 12, it is a mighty eagle with many wings.

But there is the narrower or deeper relevance which has to do with the intended message and religious purpose of the authors. If they had a vital message for their own times, they probably have a message for our day. Forty years ago F. C. Porter wrote:

> If we could grasp the underlying faiths that have clothed themselves in these strange forms, faith in the kingship of God, and the sure triumph of good over evil, and the heavenly blessedness of those who hold to God's side amid whatever shame and abuse and in the face of death; if through the peculiar imagery and obscure symbolism of the books we could feel the power of the unseen world and gain a fresh sense of its reality; then this use, call it literary, or call it devotional, would be the best use to which the books could be put, and even most in accordance with the highest mood and real purpose of their writers.[10]

This kind of relevance ties in with the intended purpose on the part of the apocalyptic writers and with their success in realizing that purpose. Here at the outset we may note an important difference from prophecy: whereas prophecy comes to us with the authority of a great experience mediated through personality, apocalyptic is more conscious of the author as writer and of its purpose as literary and, to a degree, intellectual. There is, of

8. F. C. Porter, *The Messages of the Apocalyptical Writers* (New York, 1905).

9. H. H. Rowley, *The Relevance of Apocalyptic* (London, 1944).

10. *Op. cit.*, p. xiii.

course, the possibility of a real experience of trance in some instances, such as might follow the fasting of Esdras. But the vision usually appears as a literary device or vehicle of the "revelation." The center of meaning therefore shifts from experience either to the content of the revelation, more or less intellectual and imaginative, or to the author's conscious purpose in presenting this material.

How cogent are the ideas and details of these visions and heavenly descriptions? Modern interpreters make much of them. The apocalyptic cosmology represents an ideal knowledge of the universe as ordered in the determined counsel of God. The angel showed Enoch "what is first and last in the heavens in the height, and beneath the earth in the depth, and at the ends of the heaven, and on the foundation of the heaven." The explanation of the natural forces of snow and wind and sun and moon did not transcend the ordinary knowledge of these things, the important element being an attempt to give a spiritual interpretation of the forces of natural providence.

In a similar ideal way the seer arrived at a complete theological understanding of the world and all life. The hierarchies of angels, beneficent and malign, were described in detail. God and Beliar and the Messiah all found their places in the theological picture, for the seer believed that the ultimate solution of human problems was to be found in the invisible world.

Looking forward to the end, the apocalyptist gave glowing descriptions of the supra-historical vindication of the suffering individual and nation and of God himself. The present scene was all frustration. The individual would be vindicated in the great resurrection. The nation would at last witness the judgment of God upon the enemy. And God himself would be avenged in that judgment.

Thus apocalyptic in its own way covered science, history, theology, and philosophy. In terms of ideas and details corresponding to any known reality, what do we have? At times the pictures are elevated and beautiful, but generally the ideas are vague and chaotic and often inconsistent. How could it be otherwise, since they were describing the indescribable and limiting the illimit-

able with human language? Apocalyptic moves in an otherworldly scene, and who has terms to describe it? Enoch's language verges on poetry in the description of the day of resurrection and its joy:

> In those days shall the mountains leap like rams,
> And the hills also shall skip like lambs satisfied
>   with milk,
> And the faces of the angels in heaven shall be
>   lighted up with joy.
> And the earth shall rejoice,
> And the righteous shall dwell upon it,
> And the elect shall walk thereon.[11]

But, for all his poetry, he gives very little in the way of clear ideas. Frequently, the description turns to simple negation of all that the natural earth means, as, for example, when the Slavonic Enoch describes the final state of the righteous as characterized by "neither labor nor humiliation nor anxiety nor violence nor night nor darkness but great light." Or, again, the description of the spiritual heaven is mixed with the forces and constellations of nature.

The poverty of ideas in this field becomes most acute when the seer tries to describe the presence of God. "Fire" and "light" are the most frequent terms used by apocalyptists. So I En. 71:2:

> And I saw two streams of fire,
> And the light of that fire shone like hyacinth,
> And I fell on my face before the Lord of Spirits.

Slavonic Enoch (chap. 22) adds little to the description: "Thus I saw the appearance of the Lord's face, like iron made to glow in fire and brought out, emitting sparks and it burns. . . . . The Lord's face is ineffable, marvellous and very awful, and very, very terrible." Levi, in the Testaments of the Twelve Patriarchs, describes heaven and declares that "the Holy One of the Holy Ones is above all holiness." This means little or nothing! It has been well said that the apocalypses fell into the danger of attempting to surmount human terms in describing God, and as a result they fell below them. The very fact that apocalyptic bor-

11. I. Enoch, chap. 51.

rowed language and figures so readily is an indication of its poverty in any exact terms to describe the ineffable. The inconsistency of details shows that they did not take these details very seriously.

Thus the apocalyptists, for all their externalizing and objectifying of the invisible, made little progress in making real the spiritual world. By their thoroughgoing externalization of religion in pictorial fashion, they presented in most acute form the problem of religious knowledge: How far can material terms ever express spiritual realities?

One set of details bearing on the time factor in prediction is worthy of special treatment, because later students of apocalyptic have built their whole interpretation upon them. The predictions of the end are accompanied by a recital of woes and a warning of its speedy arrival. It requires no close reading of apocalyptic to observe that these writers generally had their own generation in mind when they wrote. The second person of direct address is used repeatedly.[12] The message was for the writer's own time, and that time was short.

It was only by the illusion of history as prophecy that apocalyptic was able to give years and periods. The author writing in the name of Enoch, Daniel, or Moses could predate his prediction and arrive at wonderful accuracy as to kingdoms and periods. When, however, he came to his own time and looked ahead, he became immediately vague. When there was real and not assumed prediction, the authors of these apocalypses resorted to simple sequence of events, one following the other without precise dating. Even simple sequence broke down if we understand with many interpreters of Revelation that the seals, bowls, and trumpets repeat themselves.

There are some definite time periods in these projections of the future. "Time, times, and half a time" is a phrase repeated from Daniel. In Revelation the devil is bound a thousand years while the saints reign with Christ. But for the apocalyptic mind in general, events were determined—predetermined in the will of God

12. Cf. Jesus' Beatitudes in Luke, or Paul in I Cor. 15:51: "We all shall not sleep but we shall all be changed."

and not by a controlling time schedule. God might cut short the time of woe before the end, and the whole time scheme itself would come to an end in God's great consummation. It cannot be said that the relevance of apocalyptic rests on such details of any time schedule. For these apocalyptists the time factor was simply the necessary exponent of any future, however brief, in a continuing world, and it was usually limited to the speedy realization in the writer's own time.

All these observations raise the question of whether it was the apocalyptic writer's first purpose to convey esoteric information of a time schedule of the end. The imagery gives the impression of objective reality, and these writings must have been stimulating to the imagination of the first readers. But the modern reader discovers that now and again the seer breaks through the vision form to show that he was writing a message for *people* and to satisfy the needs of *people*. The appeal to men is seen in such passages as II Esd. 8:51, 52: "But understand thou for thyself, and of such as be like thee seek out the glory. For unto you is paradise opened, the tree of life is planted, the time to come is prepared. . . . ." The seer wrote for men, sometimes to satisfy their curiosity about the unseen but in the more intense moments to give men comfort and assurance and faith in the face of great obstacles and terrible frustration.

The working of the apocalyptic mind is suggested in II Esd. 10:5–7: "Then left I the meditations wherein I was, and answered her [Sion in disguise] in anger, and said, Thou foolish woman above all other, seest thou not our mourning, and what hath happened unto us? how that Sion the mother of us all is full of sorrow, and much humbled."[13] The period of concentrated meditation on the sad condition of the nation issued in deep emotion, which grappled with the fact of suffering and defeat in the guise of symbols and figures. Then the apocalyptic mind overleaped these hampering limitations to lay hold on the larger realities of heaven and earth, the past and the future. This purpose, no matter how deviously conceived, to affirm the realities in the larger spiritual context of life marks the direction of the primary

13. W. O. E. Oesterley, *II Esdras* ("Westminster Commentaries" [London, 1933]).

relevance of apocalyptic. The apocalyptist could not deny either the fact of evil in his world or the apparent victory of evil for the time. But, with true religious feeling, he affirmed God's justice in the ultimate issues of the historical scene. Men were to bear their suffering for the time and to live in hope of God's vindication and restoration. The prime importance of the imagery and symbols rests in their contribution to this end. Through these successions of vivid scenes and horrendous actions the reader will realize afresh the transcendent power of God and the final ruin of evil.

RELEVANCE FOR RELIGION

Within this true religious context many of the ideas of these writers must have come home with the vitality of real insight. God is transcendent and holy, yet his purpose of providence and justice and righteousness is mediated by angelic representatives. His ultimate design remains for the end and rests for men in the hope of restoration through his Messiah, earthly or heavenly. These writers were deeply concerned with the problem of suffering: they saw evil rampant in the world, and they could not adjust its present power to the immediate working of a just God. Refusing to acquiesce in this moral confusion,[14] they restricted the sway of evil to this present age and to the very last phase of the present age. The suffering before the end was already upon them. God's power was so vividly present to their believing minds that they felt it must be displayed immediately in the defeat of evil and the victory of the righteous.

The idea of resurrection receives extensive development in these writings, and the New Testament emphasis upon it cannot be explained apart from this literature. Side by side with much narrow nationalism, the individual becomes a center of real interest. They felt that the relation between God and the individual had a future—a future that would continue beyond judgment into the coming age. The fortunes of the individual in that future fluctuated between rather grossly material prosperity and a refined spirituality, but in any case the hope was part of God's concern for the righteous.

14. II Bar. 70:3-6.

The ethical temper of apocalyptic has been challenged, because these writers did not echo the prophet's call for moral reform but simply counseled patience and forbearance until the end. Did the apocalyptists cut the nerve of effort? In actual fact they took evil in the world seriously; they declared that evil was more than individual wickedness, that it was in the very spirit of the times; and they affirmed that only God's power could deal with it. At the same time they sounded again and again the call to repentance. In the Shepherd of Hermas the moralizing occupies most of the book. While apocalyptic generally did look to a catastrophic change, there were some apocalypses, such as Jubilees, which expected a gradual reformation on the basis of the supremacy of the Law. In general, we may say that the woes of the wicked and the rewards of the righteous are, within their limits, the expression of a conviction that the roots of the moral order go deep and extend beyond the bounds of this life. Many of the grotesque pictures of natural elements changed (sun, moon, and stars darkened; rivers motionless; etc.) are simply forms of poetic sympathy in harmony with the radical moral change. The ideal pictures of the messianic age, while often in materialistic terms, are painted in terms of the ethical fitness of things in the larger framework of divine justice.

APOCALYPTIC AND EARLY JUDAISM

The relevance of these apocalypses for early Judaism follows most naturally, for they correspond to the crises in the life of the nation and they reflect certain phases of its inner spirit. "They are," wrote F. C. Burkitt in the Schweich Lectures of 1913, "the most characteristic survival of what I will venture to call, with all its narrowness and its incoherence, the heroic age of Jewish history, the age when the nation attempted to realize in action the part of the peculiar people of God."[15] Thus in the early Maccabean struggle Daniel played its part in sustaining the spirit of the nation. In the struggle with Rome the apocalyptic hope of God's intervention must have spurred them on in the Zealot movement and even in the hopeless effort of A.D. 132–35.

It is impossible to estimate the popularity and representative

15. *Jewish and Christian Apocalypses* (London, 1914), p. 15.

character of these writings for the Jewish people. The large number of these apocalypses witnesses to their acceptance and popularity. When the apocalyptic viewpoint appeared in the Christian movement, it was treated, not as something strange and marginal, but as a pattern of familiar language and ideas. Jesus came preaching the Kingdom without troubling to define the idea. Some of the Pharisees shared in these apocalyptic views, for the Assumption of Moses and the Testaments of the Twelve Patriarchs appear to have been written by Pharisees, and II Baruch is strongly pharisaic in character. For a time, at least, there was no sharp cleavage between loyalty to the Law and the espousal of apocalyptic ideas, for Jubilees asserts the supremacy of the Law in the Kingdom of the Messiah. But when the Jewish canon was closed, only Daniel was included, and Judaism turned its back upon the rest of these apocalypses and centered upon the study of the Law. Johanan ben Zakkai said that God revealed to Abraham this world, but he did not reveal the world to come. F. C. Burkitt is convinced that this saying implies the Jewish rejection of an apocalyptic kingdom.[16] According to Louis Ginzberg, the Jewish schools of Jabneh and Tiberias did not directly oppose and reject these writings but deliberately ignored them; and he is able to state that "in the entire Rabbinic literature of the first six centuries of the Common Era there is not one quotation from the now extant apocalyptic literature."[17] The apocalyptic character of early Christianity undoubtedly played its part in this reaction on the part of Judaism,[18] and it is perfectly apparent that many of the ideas in apocalyptic would not be at home in the atmosphere of rabbinic Judaism. However, the apocalyptic temper appears again and again in later Judaism,[19] and there is a "little apocalypse" in the Mishnah.[20]

16. *Ibid.*, p. 12.

17. "Some Observations on the Attitude of the Synagogue towards the Apocalyptic-Eschatological Writings," *Journal of Biblical Literature* XLI (1922), 115–36.

18. Cf. George Foot Moore, "The Definition of the Jewish Canon and the Repudiation of Christian Scriptures," in *Essays in Modern Theology and Related Subjects* (New York, 1911).

19. C. C. McCown and Simon Cohen, "Apocalyptic Literature," *Universal Jewish Encyclopedia* (New York, 1939).

20. Sotah 9:15.

Still, for the period under discussion, the apocalypses are relevant for the inner life of Judaism in a critical time,[21] and this is particularly important because it was with this side of Judaism that Christianity was most closely connected. Here we find not only the hopes and fears of the people but also their theology of a more speculative character. We may not take this extravagant eschatology as typical of all first-century Judaism, but these apocalypses are representative of that "higher theology of Judaism, which culminated in Christianity."[22]

APOCALYPTIC IN RELATION TO CHRISTIAN ORIGINS

The real interest in this literature is connected with Christian origins, for, while rabbinic Judaism turned away from it, Christianity was in a real sense an apocalyptic-eschatological movement. No book of the New Testament is unaffected by this outlook. We have in apocalyptic what has proved to be a critical factor for interpreting the Christian movement in the light of its background and for understanding the idea of the Kingdom, Jesus' consciousness of his own mission, and the primitive Christian community. In many ways it is basic for all New Testament thinking. The history of the interpretation of Jesus can be gauged by the recognition of this factor in the Gospel record.[23]

Schweitzer pointed to Reimarus (d. 1768) as the first, after eighteen centuries of misconception, to grasp the eschatological (apocalyptic) character of Jesus' message in its true Jewish setting. Other scholars after Reimarus rejected this element; and it was only after the recognition of the Jewish pseudepigrapha that this factor was given its true weight in appraising the thought of Jesus. It was Johannes Weiss in his book, *The Preaching of Jesus concerning the Kingdom of God*, who recognized that Jesus preached a kingdom as wholly future, present only in the paralysis of the kingdom of Satan. Jesus simply proclaimed its coming. Schweitzer put the alternatives bluntly:

On which of the two presuppositions, the assumption that His life was completely dominated by eschatology, or the assumption that He

---

21. Porter, *op. cit.*, p. x.
22. R. H. Charles, *Apocrypha and Pseudepigrapha* (Oxford, 1913), II, 163.
23. Albert Schweitzer, *The Quest of the Historical Jesus*, English trans. (London, 1911).

repudiated it, do we find it easiest to understand the connexion of events in the life of Jesus, His fate, and the emergence of the expectation of the Parousia in the community of His disciples?[24]

Schweitzer would answer this question by his "thoroughgoing eschatology," by which he would apply the apocalyptic-eschatological explanation to the whole ministry and preaching of Jesus, interpreting it in the light of Jewish apocalyptic literature.

While all do not agree with this extreme view, it is commonly recognized that there are apocalyptic sayings and ideas in every strand of Jesus' teaching in the Synoptic Gospels. (The supposition that the early church imposed these views on the record of Jesus' ministry has scant basis, although it is possible that the apocalyptic element has been heightened by the church or the evangelist; cf. Matthew, chaps. 24–26.) The Baptist sounded the call to judgment, and Jesus picked it up as a call to prepare for the Kingdom. His teaching was in the language of apocalyptic, but with a difference. He spoke of the heavenly realities with constant restraint, and his pictorial representation of last things was meager by comparison with the extravagant revelations before him. Jesus on occasion refused to calculate times and seasons in true apocalyptic fashion. His eschatology is mixed with much teaching that has little bearing on an apocalyptic consummation, and it is only by radical reshaping that his ethics can be called "interim ethics."

A strict eschatological theory must be balanced by those elements in Jesus' teaching which point to the present character of the Kingdom. Rudolph Otto[25] and others have pointed to Jesus' exorcism (Matt. 12:28; Luke 11:20) as evidence of the Kingdom's presence: "He does not bring the kingdom, but he himself, according to the most certain of his utterances, is in his actions the personal manifestation of the inbreaking divine power."[26] The parables of the Kingdom touching on growth, while they cannot be cited for a program of gradual development, nevertheless are evidence that the final Kingdom stands in some relation to a

24. *Op. cit.*, p. 256.
25. *The Kingdom of God and the Son of Man*, English trans. (London, 1938).
26. *Ibid.*, p. 104.

present reality.[27] Any interpretation of the Kingdom "among you" or "in your midst" must point in the same direction.

C. H. Dodd[28] has developed a variant hypothesis, denominated "realized eschatology." He sees the early church living in the age of fulfilment. The Kingdom, "the age to come," had been inaugurated in the coming of Christ and would be consummated in the return of Christ.[29]

Not a few scholars would find in apocalyptic only the framework and external form of Jesus' thought, which he took from his background but which he filled with his own content. So Maurice Goguel distinguished between eschatology and apocalyptic, and he found in Jesus' ignorance of the time of the sudden Parousia a weakening of strict apocalyptic.[30] The ethics of the Kingdom, according to Amos N. Wilder, are not "interim ethics" (Schweitzer), neither do they bear the simple sanction of rewards and punishment. Their sanction is derived from the nature and character of God as presented by Jesus.[31]

The apocalyptic factor figures also in our interpretation of the messianic career of Jesus. The Gospels assume that Jesus was acknowledged during his lifetime as the Messiah by the demons, by disciples, and by his own declaration before the high priest. Jesus also looked forward to the coming of the Son of Man in the near future. During his lifetime there were few indications of glorious messiahship; it was only after the Resurrection that the full dignity of the heavenly Messiah could be applied to him. Was it then that the church and the Gospel writers read back the messiahship into the earthly career and the Synoptic account? Did tradition put this messianic secret back into the life of Jesus, as Wrede suggested?

Jesus applied to himself the apocalyptic term "Son of Man." Daniel was probably referring to Israel when he described "one

27. The term "kingdom" is used in the general sense of "reign" and not in the sense of "realm."

28. *The Apostolic Preaching and Its Developments* (Chicago, 1937).

29. *The Parables of the Kingdom* (London, 1936).

30. *The Life of Jesus*, English trans. (New York, 1933), pp. 569–72.

31. *Eschatology and Ethics in the Teaching of Jesus* (New York, 1939).

like unto a son of man" coming on the clouds of heaven,[32] while I Enoch individualized the conception as a heavenly judge. In some instances the Gospel writers used the term, "Son of Man," simply as "man" or "I";[33] but in most characteristic uses they referred either to a glorious coming or to a career of suffering. Opinion varies between a strict apocalyptic future sense by which Jesus applied the term proleptically to himself and a transformed sense by which Jesus filled the little-used term by his own understanding of the messianic career.

The primitive church took over the eschatological outlook from Jesus and lived in expectation of his speedy return. The Resurrection of Jesus, the gift of the Spirit, and the miraculous powers and gifts were to the early Christians an earnest of the glorious age which would break upon them shortly. The coming of the messianic age was a part of the apostolic preaching,[34] and the glow of that expectation suffused the life of the early church. Paul's letters are witness to the apocalyptic hope from the Thessalonian correspondence to Philippians. Hebrews and the Fourth Gospel were written from a different viewpoint, but still the earlier apocalyptic expectations of the Coming and the Judgment shine through. The delay in the Coming had to be explained in the later writings;[35] but the persistence of this type of thinking in Christian circles is seen in such writings as the Book of Revelation, Shepherd of Hermas, and the Christian portions of II Esdras. Eventually, the Greek patterns of thought prevailed, and to that end apocalyptic served as a halfway house from the Hebrew thought of God's direct action in history to the Greek dualism, in which emphasis rests on the spiritual over the material. But for the period of Christian origins, apocalyptic was an important factor in their thinking and their living, and the knowledge of the larger range of this literature throws a flood of light for the understanding of the new movement.

32. Dan. 7:13.

33. Examples of these meanings are found in Mark 2:28, Luke 6:22, Matt. 16:13.

34. Dodd, The Apostolic Preaching, p. 28.

35. II Tim. 2:18; II Pet. 3:4.

RELEVANCE FOR TODAY

Thus far we have sketched the relevance of apocalyptic for Jewish and Christian origins. It remains to inquire as to its relevance for us today. Is it to be for us a curious exhibit of the extravagant speculation and unfulfilled hope of the ancient past? Or does it have a message for our time?

In certain respects it has no relevance. So far as it was the response to a specific historical situation, its meaning is lost on us, for our historical situation has changed and history does not repeat itself. Lost on us are the details of world creation and heavenly management; their pictures have value for us only as symbols of their faith. Their deterministic view of history and predictions of the end have no permanent standing for the guidance of life. The details of their speculations of time, space, and destiny do not correspond to any reality that we know.

Here it should be noted that the history of the interpretation of apocalyptic has followed a peculiar pattern. The first writers appear to have used imagery and symbolism, details of time, and portents to bring home their message of comfort and encouragement. Later generations have mistaken the framework for the fact and have taken literally what was intended figuratively and symbolically. The imaginative projections of strong faith become the certainties of theology and eschatological planning.

The ideals and hopes of any people are always significant, and these apocalyptic writings are the vivid projections of the human spirit, often out of the torture and agony of a crisis. Surely, these books, which have been the inspiration of martyrs, cannot be without meaning for us today.

It is in the religious context, however, that their truest relevance will be found. These writers gave what might be called a "religious philosophy" of history, for they believed that the ultimate issues of life and destiny are in the hands of God and that, as God's rule could be seen in a predetermined plan of history, so God would triumph in the end. The historian today is not impressed by that determinism, and he finds this view of history lacking in a sense of the inner relations. But today there are

not lacking voices to tell us that the meaning of history must come from beyond history; and this in the largest sense was the message of the apocalyptist.

For the religious mind today the eschatological outlook on time and history makes an important contribution. The meaningless continuity of ordinary historical time gives way to the tension of the claim of God's will on life; faith is quickened, conscience is stirred, and the ideal is put in its true spiritual setting.

The moral tone of apocalyptic at times falls below the level of the prophets. But within its scope apocalyptic still has a message, for it affirms the faith that righteousness cannot forever remain as an ideal, that it must come to realization—and that right soon! The immediacy of the ideal in the national hope or in the Kingdom of God comes of the sure conviction that the ideal is real in the power of God. The Kingdom is God's kingdom, and He will bring it to pass.

The over-all relevance of apocalyptic lies in its message of faith in God through suffering and in crisis. The present suffering is a prelude and sign for the demonstration of God's power, and the crisis may be only the signal of a great new advance. Even the crisis of death must issue in resurrection! To this transcendent reality the church and the Christian through faith must bear witness.

CHAPTER SEVENTEEN

The Teachings of Jesus and First-Century Jewish Ethics

FREDERICK C. GRANT
Union Theological Seminary, New York City

THE late F. C. Burkitt once observed that "the Gospel ethics need criticism more, not less, than the Gospel miracles."[1] That was in 1906. During the forty years since then the interests of New Testament scholars have been more fully concentrated upon another field—not the miracles but eschatology, as a consequence of the tremendous impact of the "eschatological school" upon modern theology and exegesis. We are still at about the same place, relatively to the ethics of the gospel, where we were in 1906, though considerable accumulation of material has been made during the interval—materials which are indispensable for an accurate interpretation. Such materials are, chiefly, the vast stores of information upon Tannaite Judaism in the commentaries of Strack and Billerbeck[2] and of Montefiore[3] and in other modern works, such as the magnum opus of the late

1. *The Gospel History and Its Transmission* (1906), p. 282: "We do not get rid of the real difficulties of the Gospel, though we make jettison of all the miracles, if we leave the Sermon on the Mount. The Gospel ethics need criticism more, not less, than the Gospel miracles; and for this reason, that it is more for the ethics than the miracles that the Gospels are permanently valuable. We need to put the Gospel morality into its due relation to time and place. If Christ said, 'Give to every one that asketh thee,' and, 'Unto him that smiteth thee on the one cheek, offer also the other,' we need to understand the social conditions of Christ's day, and those of our own also, before we can turn these maxims into a rational command for fellow-believers."

2. Hermann L. Strack and Paul Billerbeck, *Kommentar zum Neuen Testament aus Talmud und Midrasch*, Vols. I–IV, Part II (1922–28).

3. C. G. Montefiore, *Rabbinic Literature and Gospel Teachings* (1930), suppl. to his *Commentary on the Synoptic Gospels* (2d ed., 1927); see also Israel Abrahams, *Studies in Pharisaism and the Gospels* (2 ser., 1917, 1924), originally designed to supplement the *Commentary*.

George Foot Moore, *Judaism in the First Centuries of the Christian Era: The Age of the Tannaim*,[4] or the more recent work of J. Bonsirven, *Le Judaïsme palestinien*.[5]

The question is now more sharply put than ever before (it was scarcely raised, in many quarters, in the nineteenth century): Can the teaching of Jesus fairly be described as "ethics"? Was it ever intended to be put into general practice? Was it not essentially an "interim ethic," valid only during the brief interval to precede the Day of Judgment? Was his teaching addressed to mankind in general or to Jewish society in general or only to his own immediate followers as they faced the approaching crisis of the last things? Was the teaching set forth, or even systematically thought out, upon the basis of certain axiomatic principles of a philosophic or religious character? That is, coming back to the original question, was the teaching of Jesus "ethics," after all?

On the other hand, we are coming to see more clearly than ever before that Judaism in the first century was not a systematic creed but a religion of revelation and that its ethics were purely inferential, i.e., derived by exegesis (usually homiletical) from the sacred Scriptures.[6]

Judaism, during the Tannaite period, was in process of transition. The far-reaching reform movement of Ezra—or of the "Men of the Great Synagogue"—had laid the foundations of a community exclusively devoted to the observance of the entire revealed will of God. Nothing secular, nothing pagan, nothing indifferent, was to find a place in it. The very harness bells on the horses were to be inscribed with the legend, "Holiness unto Yahweh"; and every pot in Jerusalem and in Judah was to be consecrated—like the sacred vessels in the Temple—to the Lord; not a single "Canaanite" (or perhaps "trader") was to enter the house of God in the holy city (Zech. 14:20 f.). The whole nation was to be dedicated once more, as once long ago it had been dedicated at Sinai, to the full observance of the entire Law; that is, the nation's response to the divine self-revelation in the Torah was to

4. Vols. I–II (1927); Vol. III: *Notes* (1930).
5. Two vols. (1934–35); see also B. H. Branscomb, *Jesus and the Law of Moses* (1930).
6. See my book, *The Earliest Gospel* (1943), p. 246.

be perfect and complete. They were to be "a kingdom of priests, a holy nation" (Exod. 19:6); "Ye shall be holy, as I am holy," saith the Lord (Lev. 11:44 f.). During the later years of the Persian domination, we gather, this puritanical movement of reform, of consecration, and of renewed zeal was carried through successfully. Foreigners—including Samaritans and "Canaanites"—were excluded from the cult and from intermarriage with Jewish families, amid much bitterness and lasting grief. The small restored "nation of the Jews" lived about their Temple in southern Palestine, under the rule of their high priest, and with slight interference from the officials of the Persian regime. The ideal of this restored community, the "Second Commonwealth," was entirely theocratic. They had no concern with the rest of the world and recognized no responsibility for or to the nations outside. It was an isolated, self-contained religious community, like other temple communities in the Near East at that time. In spite of a few scattered protests, the dominant spirit and outlook of this era left a deep and permanent impress upon the Scriptures, which were then being collected and edited, upon many of the Psalms, and upon the whole fundamental formulation of Jewish belief, practice, and teaching. There was no such thing as "ethics" in this earliest Judaism. The duties of men were entirely and exclusively religious. The observance of the Sabbath and the tradesman's use of honest weights were on a par—both were demanded by God's Law, and both were equally religious duties. The ethics of the Wisdom literature was also religious, though its antecedents included not only the Law (as in Sirach and the Wisdom of Solomon) but also the vast tradition of popular lore, widespread in the Near East and centuries old.

If Judaism had been permitted to continue as a closed community in Palestine, though enjoying considerable contact with the Jewish communities in Babylonia and elsewhere, the history of that religion—and of the world—would have been very different. But this was not to be. Reluctantly and against their will, this people that occupied one end of the land bridge between Asia and Africa was forced into contact with other peoples. First came the Macedonian conquest, followed by the long and

relatively peaceful dominion of the Ptolemies, though during this period the whole of Judaism was affected by the leaven of "Greek" ideas—not all of them of the best or the most fruitful kind, as the Book of Ecclesiastes amply shows. The Wisdom literature as a whole reflects this leavening. The slow but steady process of secularization, the religious dry-rot and crumbling of conviction, which were symbolized by the athletic contests at Jerusalem and even by the wearing of the "Greek hat"[7]—all this led to the internal disunion which made possible the events of the early days of the Seleucid era. But again a wave of retrenchment, exclusion, and renewed zeal arose—the Maccabean revolt and the movement of the Chasidim, at first in alliance with the Maccabees, before that heroic family compromised with secularism and entered the arena of world politics. The whole of later Jewish history, down to the war under Hadrian and even later, is the story of an intense conflict, far more significant internally than externally, in the course of which Judaism was being slowly and painfully transformed. The nucleus of uncompromising devotees of the Law continued heroically to resist the encroachments of the ever more worldly minded Maccabees, then of the Herods, and, finally, of the Romans. Their resistance was like that of the oyster or the turtle, withdrawing into its shell or closing it securely, when the rest of the world demanded that Israel open up and become as one of them; become a mere ethnic group in the midst of the vast melting-pot of Hellenistic culture; dissolve its religion in the fluid syncretism of the times; and abandon all its peculiar ways and customs—circumcision, Sabbath, the food laws, its empty and statueless Temple, its strange Scriptures written in a barbarian tongue, its marriage regulations, and whatever else characterized Judaism and distinguished it from the cults and customs of the surrounding world. It was this Jewish resistance to an external, enforced, secular cosmopolitanism which accounts for the tremendous internal strains of the period from the end of the Greek domination to the establishment of "normative" Judaism in the second Christian century. Groups within

7. See A. T. Olmstead, "Wearing the Hat," *American Journal of Theology*, XXIV (1920), 94-111.

the nation that were willing to compromise, and thus to yield, were as bitterly opposed as any external group. Fanatics at the opposite extreme—the Zealots or Sicarii or, earlier, the family of Judas in eastern Galilee—were sometimes favored, sometimes opposed; but their achievements were mainly detrimental both to the Jews as a nation and to Judaism as a religion (as Josephus points out), and their influence was evanescent. At last, out of the chaos and catastrophe of the wars with Rome, ending in the fall of Jerusalem in A.D. 70 and its total destruction in 135, there emerged a consolidated, unified, "normative" Judaism (as Moore called it), which has survived to this day. It entered the conflict a nation; it emerged a church, a religion. This formula may be too simple—but it recognizes and stresses the main facts.

It was this period of tension and transition that formed the background of the life and teaching of our Lord. He lived at about the middle of the period—his public career, of perhaps two or three years' duration, ended in the year 29 or 30, when he was put to death under Pontius Pilate, the Roman governor (procurator) appointed to manage affairs in Judea and Samaria. That tragic event itself, singled out in the creed, is extremely significant; for he lived among a people who were no longer free but were under a foreign domination; a people who never became reconciled to this state of affairs but were determined to recover their freedom—or at least prayed unceasingly for its restoration by God—and to restore (or to let God restore) the ancient theocratic government which was the fundamental presupposition not only of their religion but of their ordinary everyday life as Jews. Jesus, we might say, was caught in the cross-fire of this intense conflict and yielded his life, the devoutest of Jews, upon a Roman cross, the most ignominious of the conquerors' instruments of torture and annihilation.

Now these are all factors that must be borne constantly in mind if we are to interpret Jesus' "ethics" with any degree of historical reality or sound sense. It will not do to lift his teaching out of its context, as used to be done, and to make the Parable of the Workers in the Vineyard a solution of the wage prob-

lem in twentieth-century America or to equate his teaching on nonresistance of enemies with the theory of pacifism as a principle of national policy.

In the first place, as we have seen, Judaism itself had nothing—in the first century—that might be described as philosophical ethics. There was the traditional "wisdom" of the scribes or, rather, of the earlier Ḥakamim as summed up in such books as Proverbs, Ecclesiasticus, or the "wisdom" elements in I and II Enoch and the Testaments of the Twelve Patriarchs. But this was purely prudential sagacity or shrewdness in the conduct of practical affairs, in dealings with other men, or in the management of one's own life—a proverbial, sententious kind of lore which rarely rose to the level of general principles. On the other hand, the casuistry of the scribes was purely exegetical in form, and, though it was often noble in expression, it likewise dealt almost exclusively with particular cases as they emerged in practice. As Père Bonsirven observes, at the beginning of his volume on Jewish moral theology:

The doctrines contained in Jewish theology are not expounded or even considered by themselves, as an end in themselves; they are all connected with living and orientated toward practice. Life itself, a rule of life, this is what above all interested every Jewish soul. That is why, in their theodicy, they scarcely thought of God in any other way than in His relations to His creatures; and in their studies and preoccupations they gave chief place to what is concerned with living: wisdom was the science of life, of physical life quite as much as spiritual. And it was also inevitable that, in their teaching, practical directions took precedence, in numbers and almost in importance, over pure theory. . . . . It is in the domain of morals and religion that one sees most clearly the excellence of Judaism. On this point it surpasses the [other] ancient religions and philosophies, as was to be expected of the nation which was the depository of revelation and the zealous guardian of ethical monotheism.[8]

Dr. Moore likewise emphasized this feature in Judaism:

Right and wrong were for them not defined by the reason and conscience of men, naïve or reflective, nor by national custom or the *consensus gentium*, but by the revealed will of God; and constituted a dis-

8. *Op. cit.*, Vol. II: *Théologie morale: vie morale et religieuse* (1935).

tinctive Jewish morality which as a whole was different from that of other peoples, as the observances of Judaism, whatever their resemblance to the rites and ceremonies of other religions, constituted a distinctive Jewish cultus and observance.[9]

At the same time, it is possible both to classify the rulings of this casuistry (as Moore, Bonsirven, and others have done) and also to write the ethical history of early Judaism and to show (as Finkelstein, Montefiore, and others have shown) how the main tendency of Tannaite teaching was in the direction of moderation, mildness, restraint, and, in general, a "humanitarian" interpretation or modification of the rigorous older codes. But even here the governing principle was *religious;* for it is the goodness of God, who gave the Law, which must be the highest principle in its interpretation, as it is the welfare of men which constitutes the end which the divine Lawgiver intended. In this respect the general tendency of Jewish casuistry was in the direction followed by Jesus in his interpretations of the ancient Law. It was simply a tragedy for Judaism that Jesus was ostracized by the religious leaders of his time and that his influence was neutralized and rejected; it was equally a tragedy for Christianity that the teaching of Jesus was torn up by the roots and transplanted into the alien soil of Greek popular philosophy and Roman law and treated as a complete code in itself, with slight reference to the Old Testament and with none at all to the contemporary Jewish religious world in which he had lived and taught.

Jesus' teaching on the subject of human duty—since we can scarcely use the term "ethics"—*presupposes* the teachings of Judaism, based as they were on the Hebrew Scriptures. He deepened and reinforced that teaching, in some directions; in others he criticized and corrected it; in still others he flatly rejected the current interpretations and went back to the Scripture, or even back of the Scripture to the will of God, the Creator and Lawgiver. He did so as a prophet, or prophetic teacher, speaking with direct, unmediated authority. He did not, apparently, require submission to his own person or acceptance of the authority of his own *ipse dixit*—though some theologians (following

9. *Op. cit.*, II, 79.

the lead of the Fourth Gospel) have assumed the contrary—the authority with which he spoke was authority *for him*, as for others. This authority was the pure will and purpose of God, the divine intention in the giving of the Law, in the revelation which God had made of himself to Israel and to the world. This, of course, raises the question, "How could Jesus be so sure?" And before that question is fully answered, we shall, no doubt, be led back once more to the doctrine of the Incarnation. But in its first expression—say, in Galilee or in controversy with the Jerusalem scribes—Jesus simply does not demand, first, the acceptance of his own personal authority as the new lawgiver and then the acceptance of his teaching as based on this authority. The authority with which he speaks is still that of the Law—or, rather, of the divine Lawgiver, whose will he interprets. His "I say unto you" is authoritative; but it does not take the place of the divine utterance. And it is misconceiving his purpose to assume that he is setting forth a complete system of duties in place of the old; he came, "not to destroy but to fulfil." In brief, the medieval (and essentially Roman) concept of the *nova lex* as a substitute for the old Law is quite wrong; it simply will not tally with the New Testament records.

What Jesus was concerned with was the same thing that concerned other Jewish teachers; viz., the interpretation and application of the divine revelation to the whole practice of religion. Only, he went further in this direction than any other teacher went, with the consequence that the principles embodied in his teaching were revolutionary and would have changed the whole outlook and orientation of Judaism, had they been adopted and put into practice.[10] The Christianity of the gospel of Jesus was not gentile Christianity but Christian Judaism. It is no use saying that this means "reducing" Jesus to the stature of a Jewish reformer; for, as we Christians hold, had his teaching been accepted by the religious leaders of his own people, Judaism would then have become the final religion, the divinely revealed faith and practice for all mankind—that is what we believe Christianity to be.

10. See John A. Hutton, *The Proposal of Jesus* (1921).

The headings under which the Jewish "ethics" of the period may be classified—if, for once, we may use the term "ethics"—are more or less as follows (as in Moore, *op. cit.*, Vol. II, Part V):

1. The *source* and *authority* for the definition of human duty, as found in the Scriptures;
2. The *motivation* of moral conduct, viz., obedience to the will of God, and the desire to gain his approval or the resulting benefits ("rewards") or final salvation; sometimes the motive is the lower one of escaping punishment;
3. Duties to *rulers*, viz., obedience, so far as this did not contravene religious loyalty;
4. *Family* duties, marriage, divorce, the rearing of children, the status of women, respect for parents, slavery, employers, and hired workers;
5. *Property*, gain, fair dealing in business, fair prices, interest;
6. *Slander*, calumny, *forgiveness*, reparation;
7. Relations of social *classes*, neighborliness, rich and poor;
8. Private and public *charity*, care of the poor and of orphans, loans, charitable giving, loving kindness, community funds for the poor, self-support;
9. The concept of *justice*, judicial procedure, evidence, sentences;
10. The concept of *truth*, truthtelling, hypocrisy, personal integrity;
11. The ideal of *peace*.

At the end, the whole subject merges into that of piety, for the "ethics" of Judaism are (as we have seen) part and parcel of the religious observance which characterized it.

It should be clear at once, from even as brief a survey of the headings as this—and it is clearer still from a full reading of Moore or Bonsirven—that the subject matter of Jesus' teaching is much the same: as a *chasid*, or lay teacher of religion, he dealt with the traditional round of subjects. At the same time, it is clear that on some points he laid no emphasis at all, or else that the Gospel tradition failed to include such subjects. Moreover, he "taught as one having authority, and not as the scribes," for he went directly to the source in the divine revelation, and interpreted it, not in accordance with the views of this or that earlier teacher or school, but directly, guided by his own unerring insight or by the immediate, fresh revelation which he

himself had received. The scribes also went back to Scripture and the will of God; but there was a difference: they belonged to a school of interpreters, and they recognized earlier expounders as their guides and authorities—Jesus did not.

1. For him, as for other Jewish teachers, the source and authority for the definition of human duty was to be found in the Scriptures.

2. The motivation of moral conduct was the same—obedience to the will of God, desire for his approval, even for "reward," and for final salvation—in some cases, the fear of punishment. Every one of these points could be illustrated from the Gospels, but the passages are too obvious to require citation.

3. The third section, duty to rulers, seems not to have been greatly emphasized by our Lord. His eschatological conviction, viz., the nearness of the coming reign of God, made such a concern wholly secondary, if not irrelevant. For him, as for his followers, even a generation or two later, "the fashion of this world [was] passing away," and so the subjection of Israel to Rome was no longer a serious problem. At the same time, his dictum, "Render to Caesar the things that are Caesar's, and to God the things that are God's," sums up perfectly the thought of many of the best Jewish teachers of his age—those who counseled co-operation and submission, with prayers for the government and sacrifices for the emperor.[11] I think it is as much a mistake to look for something abstruse and esoteric in this saying as it is to find in it the sufficient authorization for the medieval conception of the two empires. Jesus did not go the full length of hearty co-operation—let alone promote an armed revolt (as Eisler and others have supposed)—nor did he, on the other hand, counsel anything like "passive resistance"—he was neither a Caiaphas nor a Theudas nor a Gandhi. Why should he be? The reign of God was at hand!

4. On family duties Jesus simply took for granted the teaching of the Law and severely criticized those who ruled that a dedica-

11. See Moore, *op. cit.*, II, 117 f. This view is more probable than the recherché one of Herbert Loewe, *Render unto Caesar* (1940).

tion as "Corban" released a son's property from use in support of his parents. Here Jesus was not criticizing Judaism but was uttering the conscience of genuine Judaism as against its contemporary perversion.[12] As to divorce, he took a much higher stand than any other teacher of his time, unless it was the obscure author or authors of the "Zadokite" fragments (Frag. 7:1–3 may refer only to polygamy). On the "adultery of the eyes," his teaching is like that of other Jewish teachers.[13] Slavery he simply took for granted, as did everyone else, though the mitigation of its worst features was a necessary consequence of his central teaching of love. Paul's classic little note to Philemon shows how it worked out in practice. He had no counsels to give on employment or the duties of employers or employees, though he quoted—or perhaps even originated—the proverb, "The laborer deserves his keep." The Parable of the Workers in the Vineyard is not designed to show how laborers should be paid but how God's goodness exceeds all human deserving—as Adolf Jülicher rightly said.[14]

5. On property questions he refuses to be made an arbiter (Luke 12:14, quoting, or at least alluding to, the words of Exod. 2:14), and, in general, the Gospel tradition does not represent him as really concerned with questions of business, trade, interest, or profit. In part this may be due to his eschatological outlook; but in part it must also be due to the fact that his background and surroundings are rural, not urban.[15]

6. On human relations in general, including the duty of forgiveness and reconciliation, his teaching belongs in the setting of the noblest Jewish ethics. If his words are more memorable than those of other teachers, it is because they were more pointedly expressed and leave behind them every concession, limitation, and compromise—our forgiveness is to be like God's, as we are to be "perfect, as He is perfect" (Matt. 5:48; Luke 6:36).[16]

12. See Branscomb, *op. cit.*, pp. 165–75.

13. See Bonsirven, *op. cit.*, II, 271.

14. *Die Gleichnisreden Jesu*, II (2d ed., 1910), § 41, 459–71.

15. See W. Bauer, "Jesus der Galiläer," in *Festgabe für Adolf Jülicher* (1927), pp. 16–34.

16. See *The Earliest Gospel*, chap. x, esp. pp. 218–23.

7. He had nothing to say about the continuous duty of the rich toward the poor;[17] but he blessed the poor, as those who were to possess the Kingdom of Heaven, and he bade the rich sell their goods and give to the poor—a counsel of perfection set forth in word and deed by more than one saintly rabbi.[18] At the same time, his point of view is that of the common people; what goes on in "kings' houses" and among the rich is known to him only by hearsay (e.g., Luke 7:25), not from experience. He is a "commoner," though he never makes capital of it. There is no ground in the gospel for any theory of "class war," though certain Marxian writers have done their best to make out a case for their views. The "tension of the times" in first-century Palestine was political and religious—and in some degree economic—not sociological or industrial.[18a]

8. Private charity was strongly emphasized by our Lord; whether or not he also stressed public charity we do not know. Presumably, the "box" that Judas carried was for the offerings in support of Jesus and his disciples on their journeys, not for a settled community; though the "community chest" among the Christians in Jerusalem, as described in Acts (4:34–37), was a natural outcome of the disciples' practice and thoroughly in consonance with Jewish practice in religious communities or groups. What Jesus said about "giving to everyone that asketh thee," which sounds so extreme to Anglo-Saxons, was not only a recognized virtue in Judaism but was even laid down as a *duty* by the rabbis.[19] That it would have been balanced by the duty of self-support, wherever this is possible, seems clear from one of the earliest New Testament writings, where Paul insists: "If anyone will not work, neither let him eat" (II Thess. 3:10).

17. See Mark 14:7; the statement, "You always have the poor with you," echoes Deut. 15:11 and may be secondary—as is perhaps the whole pericope in its present form.

18. See Strack and Billerbeck, *op. cit.*, I, 346 ff., 391 f.

18a. See my *Economic Background of the Gospels* (1926).

19. See Moore, *op. cit.*, II, 168: "When Jesus said, 'Give to him who begs of thee, and do not turn away him who wants to borrow from thee,' (Matt. 5:42), it is not, like the preceding injunctions of nonresistance, what the Jews called conduct that keeps 'inside the line,' but an exact summary of what they laid down as prescribed by divine law. To lend to a would-be borrower is not optional but obligatory, and no less obligatory to give to the poor according to the measure of his need and to the ability of the giver."

9. As Joseph Klausner maintains, Jesus had no advice to give the judge on the bench or the lawyer or administrator concerned with the ordinary affairs of court and market.[20] He could use a story of an unfair judge—or of a dishonest steward or of a band of murderers who had seized a vineyard—in order to illustrate some point in his teaching, without saying a word in reproof of their morals—though why should he? The story itself either condemned them or took for granted his hearers' condemnation of their behavior.[21] But, it is true, he was not interested in courts of law; he was no lawyer (*nomikós*) or administrator (*oikonómos*)—their affairs were on another plane than that of his interests.

10. As for truthtelling, no one has ever stated more bluntly the duty of saying "Yes" to mean "Yes," and "No" to mean "No," for whatever goes beyond this, as in the taking of oaths, is a concession to evil. Hypocrisy he excoriated with burning words.

11. As for peacemaking, he made it a duty, with a blessing, as fully as any rabbi of his time or later (Matt. 5:9).

Thus the "ethics" of Jesus, if we may again use the term, are Jewish, through and through; they spring from no philosophical consideration of the ends of human life, or of the motives or "characters" of men, or of human nature, or of the best possible harmonization of conflicting interests, or of the ideal state; instead, they are derived directly from the revealed character of God and from his purposes for men. Contrast, e.g., the classical ethics of Aristotle, or of Cicero or Epictetus, or of the Stoics generally—as in the full survey which Diogenes Laertius gives in his (fragmentary) Book vii. That is, his ethics are purely and simply and completely religious, inseparable from his religious faith. Further, they presuppose the divine revelation which was the foundation of Jewish religion. They are in line with the highest development of Jewish ethics in his time, though he went further on some points than other teachers went. They are not "ethics of the Kingdom" or "ethics of discipleship" or "interim ethics,"

20. *Jesus of Nazareth*, trans. H. Danby (1925), pp. 361–414.
21. See Martin Dibelius, *The Message of Jesus Christ* (1939), pp. 148–55.

save for those few admonitions which were addressed specifically to his personal followers and to those who had responded to his message and were concerned with preparation for the immediate coming of the reign of God. On the other hand, they are not addressed to men generally, but to Israel. And yet their eschatological orientation is scarcely greater than that of the religion of Israel as a whole. Judaism was itself an "eschatological" religion. Its concept of history was no series of cycles continuing in endless repetition, or any permanent continuance of the "status quo," let alone a steady decline to extinction, bogged down in a world of intractable matter; but it was a straight line of divine purpose, thwarted now and then for a time, but triumphant in the end. This teleology in the Jewish concept of history springs directly out of its eschatological religious view, nurtured on the teaching of the prophets. The will of God is the clue to history—and that will, now thwarted, now obeyed, is certain to triumph in the end, in "the latter days," when God's Anointed is to reign and the whole plan which God inaugurated in the creation of the world and in the election of Israel is to be manifested, justified, established forever as universal and all-controlling. Nor are Jesus' ethics those of a sect or school, though their formulation came in time (even before the New Testament was complete) to bear that kind of impress. As first delivered, his teaching was addressed to ordinary Jewish men and women and took for granted the same religious presuppositions that other Jewish teachers assumed, except that Jesus belonged to no school and had received no formal education as a scribe or as a "disciple of the wise." It is a grave mistake to sever his teaching from its context, to center it exclusively in his assumed "Messianic consciousness," and relate it solely to the approaching end of the age. A study of contemporary Jewish ethics shows this to be unnecessary and even impossible.

Finally, as against those theological interpreters in our day who maintain that Jesus' teaching was never meant to be put in practice but was, instead, the statement of the "pure will of God" by which men were to be confronted with the divine judgment and thus forced to repentance, we can only say that this is

not the way other Jewish teachers viewed their task, nor was it the way the earliest Christians viewed Jesus' teaching, nor was it the way he himself viewed it.[22] "Why call ye me Lord, Lord, and *do* not the things that I say?" "Everyone who hears these words of mine *and does them*, I will show you what he is like. . . . ."

Does it distress us that Jesus was "after all only a first-century Jewish teacher"? But why must we use the word "only"? For one thing, his uniqueness does not disappear when his teaching is studied in its proper historical setting. For another, the world —Jewish, Christian, and pagan—has not yet risen to the height of those "mere Jewish moralists" of the first century; hence that word "only" does not sound well on our lips. Moreover, Paul and other New Testament teachers did not hesitate to view Jesus as a Jewish teacher, "a minister to the circumcision" (Rom. 15:8), and to describe his teaching as the fulfilment and completion of the noblest course of religious and ethical development, based upon divine revelation, that mankind had ever known—the religion of Israel. In the vast new world now opening before our eyes, a world which we hope and pray is to be in truth "one world," with one divine Sovereign, one dominant purpose, one interrelated human family under God, it will help to break down the barriers and dividing walls which have for so long separated us if we can realize that Judaism and Christianity are not, fundamentally, two different religions, but one. By the

22. See Hans Windisch, *Der Sinn der Bergpredigt* (2d ed., 1937); see also M. Dibelius, *The Sermon on the Mount* (1940).

On the question of "interim ethic," compare what Moore says (*op. cit.*, II, 152): "This theory ignores a striking feature of the biblical legislation itself. By the side of laws which represent ancient custom and the amendments made necessary by experience or changing conditions, there are laws that leave the ground of reality altogether and set forth in statutory form ideals which in the world of reality are manifestly impossible—take for a single example the law of war in Deuteronomy 20. It is more serious that those who entertain this theory take no account whatever of what I have called the utopian element, not alone in the ethical maxims of the rabbis and in commendations of ideal standards of conduct such as we expect from moralists, but in the prosaic pages of the laws about bargain and sale, usury, and the like. . . . . It would be easy to multiply indefinitely illustrations from other fields of this tendency to interpret and apply the biblical law in the spirit of equity and charity. That this often carries them beyond the strict letter of the law they were well aware."

accident—or rather by the misfortune—of history, the church and the synagogue drew apart and went their separate ways, from a very early date; but in Christ we should be one, in the teaching of Jesus we ought to be one, in the things that he stressed above all else we can be one. For the chief emphasis in all his teaching was the duty of obedience to God, likeness to God, and the privilege that is ours of entering his Kingdom as sons and servants of the one Father in heaven. Perhaps our Jewish brethren will see this sometime and cease to "cast out his name as evil." Perhaps Christians will see it, too, and begin by giving to Judaism the place of confidence and affection, of trust and of honor, to which that ancient faith is entitled, as "keeper of the oracles of God" (Rom. 3:2), the rich olive root into which the wild branches ("contrary to nature"!) have been grafted (Rom. 11:17–24).

Reassessing the Religious Importance of Paul

DONALD W. RIDDLE

University of Illinois at Chicago

AT THE close of World War I, international scholarship in the Pauline field had reached a high point in the *religions-geschichtliche* approach. Paul's gentile environment received major attention, on the basis of excellent studies of Hellenistic cults. Concerning his Jewish background the greater volume of work had been accomplished in studies of the apocalyptic literature.

But in the study of New Testament and early Christian literature in connection with Paul, little had been done that was not traditional. Indeed, there was only one feature in which the traditional viewpoint had been disturbed: in Germany and in England the "Ephesian imprisonment" was being urged by a small minority as a means by which the Pauline letters might be differently and better understood. Deissmann adopted this revision in his enthusiastic application of his study of nonliterary Greek to the illumination of Paul's letters.

In the decades following the war, however, new approaches, new viewpoints, new applications of current methods, and genuinely new methods of the study of Paul, his letters, and his religion were developed. It is interesting and a matter of gratification that some of the most distinctive of these were made by members of the Chicago Society for Biblical Research. Professor Goodspeed in his studies of the New Testament and early Christian literature conceived a distinctive view of the so-called "Let-

ter to the Ephesians"[1] and from this advanced his stimulating and fruitful hypothesis of the publication of Paul's letters.[2] Professor Willoughby and the present writer made applications of the religious-historical method to the area of religious experience—the former studying the gentile salvation cults with reference to their central function as religions of regeneration,[3] the latter surveying the entire field of the writings of the New Testament and apostolic writings as products of early Christian life.[4] Professor John Knox offered his radically new and different view of the chronology of Paul's life and letters.[5]

Concurrently, important fresh contributions were being made, generally in the field of the religious background of early Christianity and specifically in Pauline studies. Further studies of gentile cults were produced, and, of very high importance, Professor Goodenough offered several studies of Hellenistic Judaism.[6] In this difficult field the advances in the knowledge of rabbinical Judaism, although they but slightly applied to the study of Paul, were of great value. The difficulty of this aspect of the study of Paul was illustrated in the volumes on Paul's ethical teaching by Professors Enslin[7] and Andrews;[8] the former leaned too heavily upon the sources which reflect "normative" Judaism, while Miss Andrews was much more successful in demonstrating the influence of Dispersion Judaism upon Paul.

Thus in the years between the two world wars work upon Paul presented two trends. On the one hand, there was the attempt to

1. *New Solutions of New Testament Problems* (Chicago, 1928).

2. *The Meaning of Ephesians* (Chicago, 1933); *Christianity Goes to Press* (New York, 1940). A thorough test of the fundamental hypothesis was made by Barnett and published in his *Paul Becomes a Literary Influence* (Chicago, 1941).

3. H. R. Willoughby, *Pagan Regeneration* (Chicago, 1923).

4. D. W. Riddle, *Early Christian Life* (Chicago, 1936).

5. " 'Fourteen Years Later': A Note on the Pauline Chronology," *Journal of Religion*, XVI (1936), 341–49; "The Pauline Chronology," *Journal of Biblical Literature*, LVIII (1939), 15–30; "A Conjecture as to the Original Status of 2 Corinthians and 2 Thessalonians in the Pauline Corpus," *Journal of Biblical Literature*, LV (1936), 145–63.

6. Especially *By Light, Light* (New York, 1935), and, for bibliography, *The Politics of Philo Judaeus* (New Haven, 1938).

7. *The Ethics of Paul* (New York, 1930).

8. *The Ethical Teaching of Paul* (Chapel Hill, 1934).

bring to bear new data upon the traditional portrait of the apostle—to improve the picture which had been generally accepted on the basis of the harmonization of the story of Acts and the usually followed sequence of Paul's letters. On the other hand, the opportunity was presented to make an entirely new and fresh approach and thus to produce a genuinely new view of Paul's life, letters, and religion.

To be sure, there were minor modifications of the traditional picture in certain studies of Paul. Few scholars accepted the Pastoral Epistles as authentic documents of Paul. Curiously, Michaelis as an advocate of the Ephesian imprisonment utilized this so as to regard Ephesians, Philippians, Colossians, and Philemon as written in the earlier Ephesian imprisonment and the Pastorals as written by Paul during his later Roman imprisonment.[9] Too, Harrison's minute study of the vocabulary of the Pastorals[10] enabled some writers to find fragments of genuine letters imbedded in them. But more usually such departures from the tradition as occurred were made on the basis of the judgment, for example, that Galatians was Paul's earliest letter.[11]

In the main, the character of studies of Paul's life was determined by the all but universally accepted procedure of harmonizing Acts and Paul's letters. While such elements of the tradition as Paul's rabbinical study under Gamaliel had been questioned,[12] and although some doubt had been thrown upon the correctness of the schematized "missionary journeys,"[13] it was usual to construct the story of Paul's life on the basis of the narrative in Acts. That such basis was patently inadequate did not counter the general trend.

This is the more curious, inasmuch as the techniques of scien-

9. See Deissmann, *Paul* (London, 1926), pp. 17 ff., n. A member of the CSBR, the late Professor Clayton R. Bowen, contributed to this theme: "Are Paul's Prison Letters from Ephesus?" *American Journal of Theology*, XXIV (1920), 112–35, 277–87.

10. *The Problem of the Pastoral Epistles* (Oxford, 1921).

11. Emmet, *St. Paul's Epistle to the Galatians* (London, 1912); Duncan, *The Epistle of Paul to the Galatians* (London, 1934).

12. Enslin, "Paul and Gamaliel," *Journal of Religion*, VII (1927), 360–75.

13. E. Schwartz, "Zur Chronologie des Paulus," *Göttinger Nachrichten*, III (1907), 263–99.

tific biography were fully developed and admirably illustrated in numerous examples. Further, the study of the life of Jesus was at this time exhibiting notable advance, and this research had been thoroughly and brilliantly applied to the Gospel section of Luke-Acts. Professor Lake and associates were at this time publishing thorough studies of Acts.[14]

The possibilities of improvement upon this almost uniform picture of Paul are what still present themselves as demands for reassessment in the entire field of Pauline study. The present writer offered a new biographical sketch of Paul, in which the viewpoints of Knox and Goodspeed were followed as the basis.[15] It is to be hoped that, together with new studies reassessing Paul's religion, examples of full-scale biography and complete treatments of Paul's letters will be made, since the exhaustive analysis of any single phase of Pauline research involves all others.

For example, work on Paul's letters is by no means complete. It is a striking fact that, while highly important new work has been done on the Greek text of the Gospels and of Acts,[16] with conclusions which radically revise the older generalizations, almost nothing has been done on the various types and local texts of Paul's letters. Further, Professor Schubert's work on the Pauline thanksgivings[17]—a highly important application of *Formgeschichte* to the Pauline field—is a brilliant example of what is yet to be accomplished in almost purely literary study of Paul's letters.

As a still further illustration of needed work on the letters of Paul, the growing acceptance of the Ephesian imprisonment hypothesis offers some prospect. This is particularly promising in view of Goodspeed's work on Ephesians; for it is no longer sim-

14. Foakes Jackson and Lake, Cadbury and Lake, *The Beginnings of Christianity* (5 vols.; London, 1922——).

15. D. W. Riddle, *Paul, Man of Conflict: A Modern Biographical Sketch* (Nashville, 1940).

16. The reference is particularly to work on the so-called "Western Text" (see A.C. Clark, *The Primitive Text of the Gospels and Acts* [Oxford, 1914]).

17. *The Form and Function of the Pauline Thanksgivings* (Diss., University of Chicago Libraries, 1935). This valuable investigation has been published as Beiheft 20 to *Zeitschrift für die neutestamentliche Wissenschaft*. Another example of the literary study of the form of the Pauline letters is Bultmann, *Der Stil der Paulinischen Predigt und die kynisch-stoische Diatribe* (Göttingen, 1910).

ply the question of whether Ephesians is a genuine or a pseudon-
ymous letter of Paul's. Previous to Goodspeed's work, the old
study of Holtzmann was the only genuinely scholarly work on
that difficult problem;[18] unless the modern scholar accepts Goodspeed's view, he has no alternative but to follow Holtzmann;
and few indeed are the readers—whether they be teachers or students—who have mastered that formidable book. The vital
problem of Ephesians is not the elementary question of whether
or not Paul wrote it but the discovery of the place of Ephesians
as a product of early Christian life. What does it reveal of the
current development of the Christian movement? How did it
come out of the religious situation in Asia? Its Paulinism is obvious and unquestionable; but is it an immediate reflection of
Paul's preaching or an application of Paul's leadership by a successor?

Similarly, the literary problems involved in the making of a
single "Letter to the Philippians" of several fragments require
attention. Lightfoot long ago showed ample reason for regarding
Philippians as an "earlier" letter;[19] the hypothesis of the Ephesian imprisonment not only makes possible the demonstration of
this but further enables the relegation as late and editorial of the
otherwise incomprehensible reference to bishops in the editorial
introduction. In the same manner the numerous valuable contributions to our knowledge of gentile cults make it possible
to view Colossians as early and as a product of the Ephesian imprisonment; for one can bring together what is known of gnosticism and other such quasi-philosophical cults and the now familiar facts of the influence of Paul's gentile environment upon
him. When this is done, there is no sufficient reason to shy away
from the acceptance of Colossians as a genuine letter and a letter
which might have been written as early as the time of the Ephesian imprisonment. And Professor Knox's work fully illustrates
what can be accomplished when a new point of view is brought
to bear upon the little note, miscalled the "letter to Philemon."

The promise lies in the willingness to entertain a genuinely

18. H. J. Holtzmann, *Kritik der Epheser- und Kolosserbriefe* . . . . (Heidelberg, 1878).

19. *St. Paul's Epistle to the Philippians* (London, 1868).

new and different viewpoint. So long as the harmonization of Acts and Paul's letters controls one's study of the primary sources, there is not much hope for the reassessment of Paul's religion. The traditional viewpoint altogether inhibits the application of available knowledge of Dispersion Judaism; for, by following Acts, the alleged rabbinical study under Gamaliel must answer all the questions. By the same token, the old sequence and dates of the letters must necessarily preclude all but a little of the use of current information of Paul's gentile religious environment.

But if one is willing to entertain the possibilities offered by the work of Knox and Goodspeed, there is fair prospect of a valuable reassessment of Paul's religion; for thus one begins from the point that several years elapsed between the death of Jesus— the beginning of what emerged as the Christian movement—and the experience which brought Paul into emerging Christianity. One thus can see that in those several years the transition to gentile environments not only occurred but had considerable development. One can bring to bear at this point what is known of Dispersion Judaism.

These three aspects: pre-Pauline Christianity, the gentile environment of Paul, and the nature of Dispersion Judaism are the central problems of background. In none has the full work been accomplished, and in all three important work already done gives the promise of future advance.

Much has been developed in the study of the gentile environment of Paul and of Christianity, to be sure; but only the beginning has been made of the application of an immense amount of research and production to the specific factor of the influence of this gentile background upon Paul. The crux of the problem is exactly that so ably presented by Professor Willoughby in his *Pagan Regeneration*, plus the element so well begun by Professor Goodenough in his *By Light, Light*, namely, the focusing of knowledge of gentile religions and Dispersion Judaism to the point of actual religious experience, behavior, and living.

The situation is readily perceived by inspecting the literature which deals with the influence of gentile religions upon Paul.

The viewpoints, differ widely, ranging from the practical denial of any such influence to the opposite conviction that Paul had joined the Orphic cult. The negative (or, if it is not wholly negative, the conservative) conclusion is untenable in the light of recent contributions to our knowledge of Judaism: nothing is more obvious than that the religious life reflected in Paul's letters cannot be understood as the religion of a representative of normative Judaism. Nor can one accept the judgment that Paul became a member of the Orphic or any other gentile cult if, as obviously he must do, he sees that Paul not only had been but regarded himself all through his life as a Jew.

The apparent *impasse* disappears as soon as the student applies the criterion of religious experience. Once this is done, there is slight need of collecting "parallels" between Christianity and its contemporary religions, whether Jewish or gentile. Recognizing, as Goodenough pointed out, that, by their very nature, parallels never meet, one sees that the development of Christianity, Judaism (Palestinian and Dispersion), and the gentile religions had mutually effective relationships. The history of religions means the study of function. It is only then, and upon that basis, that use can be made of theology and of the purely literary study of religion.

The application of this method is not difficult, although much further study of primitive Christianity and especially of Dispersion Judaism must be accomplished before the story can be fully written. More than the scanty information of non-Jews and of gentile culture and religion in Palestine must be known before the whole story of the rise of Christianity in the Land of Israel can be told. We know *that* what became Christianity had its beginning when, in Palestine, certain of the followers of Jesus had experiences which convinced them that he was alive after they had supposed him to have been put to death and began to tell stories of their experiences to others. We know *that* it was much easier for non-Jews than for Jews to accept these stories; and we know *that* some Jews and some non-Jews believed them and thus became the beginning of the Christian movement. But it is possible to know *why* and *how* these developments occurred only as

we learn of the presence and the function of salvation cults in Palestine and elsewhere.

Then, as the facts of one's study take him to extra-Palestinian localities, it is necessary to accept what is known of Dispersion Judaism; it is further necessary for this information to be greatly extended—especially in areas of the northern Mediterranean seaboard; and it is necessary to apply the criterion of religious experience. One cannot stop, for one cannot find his answers, with either the further descriptive and statistical information of Jewish life in the Mediterranean world or with the observation of similarities and differences between what is known of Dispersion Judaism and what is seen in Paul's letters. At this point Goodenough's work is of immense helpfulness.

It is curious that students of the history of religion have been reluctant to perceive that Judaism, both Palestinian and Dispersion, was the actual living religion of human beings. It would appear that, to Christian scholars, Judaism was a closed system of theology and that it existed solely for the purpose of becoming the parent of Christianity and, further, since it was the parent of Christianity, that it could not possibly have been affected by any foreign cultural influence. Moreover, it seems that, for many Christian scholars, all that is necessary to understand a given feature of Christianity is to be able to cite a literary parallel in biblical Judaism for the corresponding element in Christianity.

However much the foregoing characterization is exaggerated, it is only thus that one can understand the reluctance of scholars to accept the work of Böhlig[20] and Goodenough, not to mention the work of Jewish scholars, on Dispersion Judaism. It is not easy to see why there should be hesitation in recognizing that Judaism, in Palestine and elsewhere, was the living religion of living persons and in realizing that its significance for Christianity lies not in its theological generalization or in its literary relations but in its constant change, as its people lived it in successive periods and in various localities. Once this is done, it is possible to understand Jesus, Paul, and primitive Christianity.

It is regrettable that the paucity of source materials makes it

20. *Die Geisteskultur von Tarsos* (Göttingen, 1923).

impossible to know in full detail the transition of Christianity from Palestine to gentile localities, and, by the same token, to learn in desirable degree of pre-Pauline gentile Christianity; for, as is well known, Paul's letters are themselves a major source of information of early gentile Christianity. But, in so far as data are available, they enable a well-based generalization. Clearly, Paul was neither the only nor the first exponent of gentile "Christianity"; he, too, was one of its products. But when that point in the study of Paul has been reached, if in reaching it the lead of Willoughby and Goodenough has been followed, the understanding of Paul is wholly possible on the basis of the knowledge of Dispersion Judaism, gentile redemption cults, and the little that is known of genuinely primitive emerging Christianity.[21]

From this point the new view offered by Professor Knox affords the great potentiality for the reassessment of the religious importance of Paul. The full possibility requires, of course, the adoption of judgments and findings of less fundamental importance, such as the hypothesis of the Ephesian imprisonment. What is basic in the entire matter is the abandonment of the principle of harmonizing the story of Acts and the data of Paul's letters and the complete commitment to the use of the letters as primary sources. This requires, by necessary implication, a complete willingness to restudy the letters with no prepossession concerning their sequence and relative dates. It may be that some portions of the Pastoral Letters may prove to be indicative of elements of Paul's religion, although the fragments identified by Harrison as genuine are negligible in this respect. Certainly, scholars will be required to face the probable necessity of the further partitioning of Pauline letters; in addition to Philippians, as already remarked, the Corinthian correspondence presents questions of historical and biographical reconstruction which must be worked out.

21. The "apocryphal" sources must be gleaned in this connection, and, properly utilized, they throw much light on the religious life of minority groups. Such a work as Schmidt's edition of *Prakseis Paulou: Acta Pauli, nach dem Papyrus der Hamburger Staats- und Universitäts-Bibliotek* (Hamburg, 1936) is a mine of information. Reference may also be made to such a study of nonconformist groups in the Pauline communities as that of Lütgert, *Freiheitspredigt und Schwärmgeister in Korinth* (Gütersloh, 1908).

But it is in genuinely historical aspects that the application of Knox's view promises to be of enormous fruitfulness. When Paul's life is understood upon the basis of Knox's criteria, the central importance of the province of Asia in his work emerges unmistakably; and it is precisely here that our information of Hellenistic religions is especially abundant. It is indeed striking how Knox's view enables the application of viewpoints and judgments long ago developed by the ablest scholars of preceding generations. For example, the basic elements of the religious situation which constitute the background of the letter to the Galatians thus become illuminating. When brought to bear in the light of Knox's work, Paul's activities in the communities addressed in that letter appear to be of the nature of midway and of way-station developments in rural surroundings, even though the communities were, by their situation on Roman highways, well within the Empire's life-stream of commerce and communication. Paul's statements to the Galatians are thus seen to be not some early articulation of his evangelistic methods but mature formulations forged in the heat and travail of his protracted work in the province of Asia. So, too, it is readily perceived that there was ample reason why Paul wrote nothing more to the Ephesian community than the little letter introducing Phoebe to the people of the Ephesian church (now imbedded in Romans, chap. 16). No "Letter to the Ephesians" was required, in view of Paul's relatively long and continued relationship with these people.

One must recognize that Paul's residence and work in Asia thus brought him into relationship with all sorts and conditions of men and with all types of contemporary religion. One must see the effect upon him of being thus confronted by various types of religious life. When these facts are observed, it is no longer difficult to consider that Paul might as characteristically have written the Letter to the Colossians as his letters to the Thessalonians or to the Romans. When it is seen that Paul, the zealous and precocious Jew, had a revolutionary experience in which he adopted a form of individual redemption, it is no longer difficult to comprehend that, why, and how he—remaining within Juda-

ism as he understood it—accepted so much of the fundamental processes of various gentile religions. It has long been recognized that Paul was an ecstatic, a charismatic, a pneumatic person; so far from being overemphasized, this aspect is usually given a place of lesser importance in understanding him than the facts require. Presumably, this is because such a type of religious living is uncongenial to moderns; one finds no difficulty in admitting that Paul was ecstatic, for it is not difficult to concede that the ancients were different from us—but it is not so easy to make full utilization of the fact that Paul's ecstatic behavior is the basis for understanding him.

The implications of this fact, as well as the fact itself, must be fully accepted in order to appreciate Paul's religious significance and importance. It must be recognized, too, that Paul was but one of many persons involved in the transition of emerging Christianity to gentile environments and to gentile character. It must be borne in mind that much of Paul's importance in subsequent Christianity and thus to modern Christianity is the accident that he wrote and that some of his writings have been preserved. No small part of the value of the *formgeschichtliche* study of the Gospels lies in what this method shows of the many "heralds," who in face-to-face contact with hearers told their stories and made their exhortations. In the written Gospels we find some, but by no means all, of the results and effects of their work. In Paul's letters there is another precipitation, in a different medium, of what was part of the same effort. Paul's letters, when interrogated historically with the further application of the criterion of religious experience, at the same time throw light upon the expansion of Christianity and enable the understanding of how the transition and expansion were accomplished.

Illustrations are abundant. Consider, for example, what may be called the "paraenetic" teaching of Paul's letters—generalized teachings which were intended to apply to any community, such as Rom. 12:9-21. It is immediately apparent that these teachings closely parallel sayings of Jesus in the Gospels. But it is gratuitous to conclude that Paul was quoting; certainly, he was not quoting gospels as yet unwritten, nor is it necessary to suppose

that he was quoting the teaching of Jesus as known in oral tradition. Paul was here formulating a teaching which was becoming, or had become, "Christian," and he was doing this as one of the early Christian leaders who brought Christianity to that articulation of standards and teachings which it thus achieved in the interrelationship of leaders and publics. The story of the rise of Christianity will never be told by those who look to writings as the ultimate or immediate sources of the preaching of the early heralds, sources of the Gospels, or sources of either Paul's "ideas" or of his letters. Paul is understood when it is seen that he and many others developed these teachings by their own religious experiences in relationship with people.

It is thus that one can understand Paul, the zealous Jewish youth, as a pursuer and coercer of Jews who, before him, had identified Jesus as apocalyptic Lord; as himself in ecstasy making the same identification and then throwing his zeal and ardor into the formerly persecuted cause. It is thus that one sees how he, still the Jew, adopted some of the modifications of Judaism indicated by Goodenough's fascinating study. So, too, one sees why and how he adopted many of the values and processes of pagan cults of individual salvation. Thus one sees the manner in which Paul discharged what he solemnly believed to be a divine commission to take this religion to the nations. Students today have the open opportunity to reassess Paul's religion.

It is regrettable that those contributions to the understanding of Paul which were made previous to World War II were not more widely utilized. The war inevitably interrupted publication, if not research, in the Pauline field. Only a few volumes and articles appeared, and these include some of slight value. Professor Stinespring deserves the gratitude of all New Testament scholars and students for his translation of Klausner's *From Jesus to Paul*;[22] such negative evaluation of this otherwise admirable volume as is here made is that it follows the outmoded method of harmonizing Paul's letters and Acts; but apart from this the volume is one of the all too few scientific studies of Paul by

22. Klausner, *From Jesus to Paul*, translated from the Hebrew by William F. Stinespring, of Duke University (New York, 1943).

Jewish scholars. Hawkins in his *Rediscovery of the Historical Paul*[23] works a field of some promise: the discrimination of accretions from the genuine writings of Paul in his letters. But, unfortunately, Hawkins exhibits no evidence of any objective scientific method in his attempt; he merely begins with a conclusion of what is genuinely Pauline and rejects all else, without applying linguistic, syntactical, or textual criteria. In documents with so long a manuscript transmission as the Pauline letters, it is inevitable that accretions occurred, and it is a part of the obligation of scholarship to discriminate them—but not to reject them, as Hawkins does; the accretions also reflect religious living and are source materials for the study of Christianity's history. Professor Paul Minear's article, "The Jerusalem Fund and Pauline Chronology,"[24] is welcome as a further consideration of Knox's viewpoint. Harris Hirschberg's "Allusions to the Apostle Paul in the Talmud"[25] is also to be welcomed as a contribution in a field so highly specialized that only the few experts are competent in it.

Little, in the nature of the case, is yet known of work done by German scholars during the war. Dibelius in 1944 published in a Swedish journal an article, "Vier Worte des Römerbriefs, 5:5, 5:12, 8:10, und 11:30 ff."[26] It is to be hoped that Dibelius, now dean of the Theological Faculty of Heidelberg, will find it possible to resume publication.

An article by a Swedish scholar, Bo Reicke, may also be mentioned, although the present writer has not had the opportunity to have it translated for him: "Lagen och denna världen bos Paulus, Nagra tanken infor Gal. 4:1–11."[27]

23. Nashville, 1943.

24. *Anglican Theological Review*, XXV (1943), 389 ff.

25. *Journal of Biblical Literature*, LXII (1943), 73 ff.

26. In "Symbolae biblicae Upsaliensis," Vol. III (Supplementhäften till *Svensk Exegetisk Årsbok*, Vol. IX [1944]). The present writer owes this and most of the following references to his friend, Professor Sherman E. Johnson, of the Episcopal Theological School, Cambridge, Massachusetts, to whom his thanks are gratefully expressed.

27. Bo Reicke, in *Svensk exegetisk Årsbok* (Uppsala), VIII (1943), 49 ff. Other work on Paul published during the war may be cited: F. W. Beare, "Note on Paul's First Two Visits to Jerusalem," *Journal of Biblical Literature*, LXIII (1944), 407 ff.; H. F. Rall, *According to*

Reassessing the religious importance of Paul is thus a task for the present generation of scholars. It is indicative of much hope that Jewish scholars, as well as Christian scholars competent in Jewish studies, are engaged in the Pauline field; for no problem of Pauline research is more basic, more central, than the Jewishness of Paul; and, obviously, the co-operative work of Jewish and Christian scholars is required to solve it. But the task is one of complete co-operation; it involves all aspects of the study of the history of religion.

Members of the Chicago Society for Biblical Research have already made important contributions to Pauline study. It is to be hoped that the continuing fellowship of that Society will utilize, correct, and advance their work and that, with them, others will share the labor of producing studies of Paul which will be a part of the future achievements of biblical scholarship. Work in the Pauline field possesses many advantages. For instance, while doctrinal positions will doubtless influence scholars and their findings, the study of Paul, as is not the case in the study of Jesus, does not involve a religious leader who is at the same time a religious object. Further, neo-orthodoxy need have but slight, if any, effect in the study of Paul; Barth's commentary is sufficient illustration of the barrenness of that position, and this example is not likely to be followed. Indeed, the current perception of the nature of early Christianity as inclusive and as containing numerous trends, which subsequently with the arrival of Catholic Christianity were, and only then were, denominated as sects, points to the central emphasis in the task.

This central emphasis is properly subsumed in the title of the present chapter: the task is that of reassessing the religious importance of Paul. The sheer interest in religion will insure continued effort in Pauline research—it is not merely interest in

Paul (New York, 1944); F. R. Crownfield, "The Singular Problem of the Dual Galatians," *Journal of Biblical Literature*, LXIV (1945), 491 ff.; M. H. Shepherd, "Paul and the Double Resurrection Tradition," *Journal of Biblical Literature*, LXIV (1945), 227 ff.; Pierson Parker, "Paul Kept the Faith," *Anglican Theological Review*, XXV (1943), 399 ff.; C. W. Quimby, *Paul for Everyone* (New York, 1944); W. L. Knox, *St. Paul and the Church of the Gentiles* (Cambridge, 1939); R. Martin Pope, *On Roman Roads with St. Paul* (London, 1939); A. M. Hunter, *Paul and His Predecessors* (London, 1940).

Christianity but interest in religion which offers the prospect of further advance in what, on the face of it, might appear to be New Testament study. The goal is much more than the poring over New Testament documents or the generalization of Christian theology. It is the understanding of religion as a force which moved and moves people that sufficiently impels further work upon Paul. He as a leader of great force and result in world history is the subject of part of the total effort applied by the university of scholars in the broad field of the history of religion, and the reassessment of his religion promises rich reward.

The Central Problem concerning Christian Origins

FLOYD V. FILSON

McCormick Theological Seminary, Chicago, Illinois

HOW is the rise of Christianity to be explained? A comprehensive answer to this question must follow the course of the Christian movement until the solidly organized ancient Catholic church appears.[1] For the present purpose, however, we focus attention on the first century, because that is where the issues concerning Christian origins center. "The origin of anything is its beginning considered esp. with reference to that from which it springs."[2] Our study must take account of the background and setting of Christianity; it must seek to understand the emergence and initial stages of the new movement.

Christian leaders and critical scholars should agree on the necessity and value of this study. The second-century Marcion asserted that Christianity was a *de novo* revelation; like Melchizedek, it was "without father, without mother, without genealogy."[3] The church rejected this view, and rightly, for the Christian faith has deep roots in a rich background which forms a proper field of study. The biblical view is that God made himself known and acted for the salvation of men in a series of events which started far back in the life of Israel, came to a climax in Jesus Christ, and received confirmation, interpretation, and trustworthy attestation in the apostolic church.

1. Concerning the emergence of the church in this full sense see the discussion by Sherman E. Johnson, below, in chap. xx.

2. *Webster's New International Dictionary of the English Language* (2d ed.; Springfield, Mass., 1934), *s.v.*

3. Heb. 7:3.

Nothing could be more alien to the biblical outlook than the attempts which some philosophically minded people have made to extricate Christianity from its involvement in history and identify it with ideas which can then be treated without reference to specific events. The biblical message is so presented and involved in a specific history that those who take it seriously can never consider the story a dispensable and now outmoded scaffolding.

Thus historical study is as necessary for the healthy life of the church as it is accepted to be in the field of the humanities. Literary criticism, historical study, and attention to background and setting are not alien and hostile methods foisted upon a transparent and immediately intelligible Christian message; they rather follow inevitably from the basic nature of that message. The Christian and the independent critic share a common task. In the end, as we shall see, they come to a radical divergence. But each tries to explain the rise of the Christian faith and church. Let us look at five ways in which scholars have done this.

I

The first and least important explanation is that Christianity is a garbled form of some conjectured cult and world view which antedated the Christian period. Such a theory may deny the historicity of Jesus, or it may consider him an innocent historical bystander who, without personal creative contribution of any kind, has become merely the name-peg on which an already existing faith was hung. With older forms of this type of explanation we need not concern ourselves.[4] Among the most significant of recent attempts to find the origin of essentials of the Christian faith in a pre-Christian cult is that of the Frenchman Paul-Louis Couchoud, whose view is clear from the title of his 1937 book, "Jesus, the God Made Man."[5]

Such a view is both serious and negligible. It is serious, for, if

4. See M. Goguel, *Jésus de Nazareth, mythe ou histoire?* (Paris, 1925) (Eng. trans., *Jesus of Nazareth—Myth or History?* [London, 1926]); S. J. Case, *The Historicity of Jesus* (2d ed.; Chicago, 1928); C. C. McCown, *The Search for the Real Jesus* (New York, 1940), chap. v.

5. *Jésus le Dieu fait homme* (Paris, 1937). See also Couchoud's earlier book, *Le Mystère de Jésus* (Paris, 1924).

accepted, it undermines the validity of Christianity, which roots in certain permanently significant events. A view such as that of Couchoud asserts that the gospel message is a story of things which did *not* happen. This is to deprive the gospel of all effective truth and worth. Yet this view is negligible, for, as the adequate replies of such scholars as Goguel and Loisy have once more proved,[6] such attempts to find the creative center of Christianity without taking seriously the reported events of ancient Palestinian history lack any convincing evidence. They show a fatal deafness to the substantial testimony of all available witnesses that the origin of the substance and basic tradition of Christianity must be sought in first-century history.

II

The second explanation of the origin of Christianity identifies in the background and setting of the nascent faith determinative forces which are regarded as the real key to the problem. This type of explanation may take many forms; and it, like certain other explanations, may be offered only as a partial or contributory explanation of Christian origins. One form stresses economic factors and holds that Christianity was essentially shaped by reaction to unfavorable economic circumstances under which certain classes labored. Extreme older views, of which an example was Kalthoff's theory that Christianity was the "product of a social proletarian element,"[7] have proved untenable. But economic facts play a role in other interpretations of the first-century developments. Taxes in Palestine in the day of Jesus were about 30–40 per cent of income.[8] This suggests that economic factors may have aroused political resentment against Roman rule, created interest in apocalyptic promises of the triumph of God's oppressed, and stimulated popular response to Jesus as the prophet of a better day. Many may have hoped that Jesus was about to

6. See Goguel, *op. cit.*, for a reply to Couchoud's 1924 book. A. Loisy, "Was Jesus an Historical Person?" *Hibbert Journal*, XXXVI (1937–38), 380–94, 509–29, states and answers the theory of Couchoud.

7. L. Salvatorelli, "From Locke to Reitzenstein: The Historical Investigation of the Origins of Christianity," *Harvard Theological Review*, XXII (1929), 345.

8. On this subject see F. C. Grant, *The Economic Background of the Gospels* (Oxford, 1926).

introduce—not "the century" but the millennium of "the common (overtaxed) man."

L. Finkelstein has sketched a picture of Old Testament times which makes much use of economic and social factors to explain party differences within Judaism, and he has expressed the view that the conflict between Jesus and the Pharisees was largely due to the fact that he did not come from the same economic and social situation as the Pharisees and so misunderstood them.[9] Class conditions are thus supposed to give a partial explanation of the rise of Christianity, which, then appears too much like an unfortunate mistake.

Political and geographical factors throw some light on the emergence of the Christian movement.[10] Political factors, of course, are never divorced from racial and cultural conditions and trends, but political setting determines to a considerable degree what influences operate in an area and with what strength. The position of Palestine was highly significant. It was on the land bridge between Mesopotamia and Egypt, Egypt and Syria, Arabia and the West. Moreover, in the first century it was on the eastern frontier of the Roman Empire. Both the political unrest of the subject Jews and the tension between Rome and the Parthian enemy to the east constituted a ferment which could not fail to produce results in the life and thought of the people. The concentrated intrusion of Greek ways of life into Palestine aggravated this situation. Such intrusion began as early as the seventh century B.C.[11] and was accelerated by the conquests of Alexander the Great and the political influence of the Ptolemies and the Seleucids. Its promotion was a definite political policy under the Romans and the Herods. At the same time, oriental groups and background continued. Racially, politically, culturally, and religiously, Palestine was a key friction-point in the first half of the first century, and the study of Christian origins cannot ignore this fact. Moreover, the later development of Christianity was

9. *The Pharisees* (2 vols.; 2d ed.; Philadelphia, 1940); see esp. I, 32.

10. On questions of historical geography see C. C. McCown's discussion, above, in chap. xiii; also G. E. Wright and F. V. Filson, *The Westminster Historical Atlas to the Bible* (Philadelphia, 1945).

11. W. F. Albright, *From the Stone Age to Christianity* (Baltimore, 1940), p. 259.

notably conditioned by the large Dispersion in leading cities of the Roman Empire,[12] by the use of Greek by Jews in both Palestine and the Dispersion,[13] and by the political orientation of Palestine toward the West rather than toward the East.

The main environmental influence behind Christian origins was, of course, religious. The obvious thing is to look for this influence chiefly in Judaism. This has long been done. It has been observed that from the time of the Exile two lines of development can be traced in Judaism. One chose the way of isolation to protect the heritage of Israel; it led to Pharisaism, rabbinism, and modern orthodox Judaism. The other stressed the mission of Israel; it found expression in Deutero-Isaiah and the Book of Jonah, in the proselyting movement of Judaism, and in the epochal adaptation of this sense of universality and mission in the Christian church. This viewpoint need not deny to Christianity an original element.

Other views, however, tend to move the creative center which produced Christianity out of the period of the New Testament events and to locate it in certain developments in Judaism. To be sure, attempts to find the explanation in the Essene movement do not deserve serious consideration.[14] But three other lines of approach are more important.

1. An insistent effort is being made to show that what Jesus and perhaps his earliest followers presented was essentially Pharisaism.[15] This view may stress the points that the Sermon

12. F. M. Derwacter, *Preparing the Way for Paul* (New York, 1930).

13. For the Dispersion we need only refer to the making of the Septuagint for use by Greek-speaking Jews and to the writings of Hellenistic Jews. As for Palestine, S. Lieberman (*Greek in Jewish Palestine* [New York, 1942]), is concerned with the second to the fourth centuries A.D. but throws some light on the first century. Papyri found in Egypt and inscriptions found in Jerusalem show that Greek was constantly used in Palestine by traders and travelers and hence must have been used by resident Jews.

14. K. Kohler (*The Origins of the Synagogue and the Church* [New York, 1929], Book II, chaps. ii, iii, iv, v) argues for heavy Essene influence.

15. Finkelstein (*op. cit.*) tends in this direction; so does D. W. Riddle, in *Jesus and the Pharisees* (Chicago, 1928). R. T. Herford (*The Pharisees* [New York, 1924]) sees both kinship and conflict between Jesus and the Pharisees, but says (p. 212) that the "only" difference between early followers of Jesus and unconverted Jews was that the former believed Jesus was the Messiah.

on the Mount is thoroughly Jewish teaching, that practically
all the teaching of Jesus is repetition of previously current Jewish
instruction, and that Jesus shared the essentials and general
practices of Pharisaism. Discordant elements are explained as the
product of later ecclesiastical rivalry of church with synagogue.
The theory involves two disputable features; first, Christianity is
virtually equated with the teaching of Jesus, to the exclusion of
Christology, atonement, and resurrection faith; and second, no
basic issues of principle and conviction adequately motivate the
separation of Christianity from Judaism.

2. Another view sees in primitive Christianity simply a form
of apocalypticism, which, whatever its original sources may
have been, came into Christian circles from the Jewish background.[16] Then, whatever qualifies this extreme and consistent
apocalyptic view is the later adaptation of the church to a world
which was lasting too long and was unresponsive to Jewish
apocalyptic. This point of view contains much truth. However,
it can be carried too far. Every Gospel and practically every
writing of the New Testament includes a nonapocalyptic accent
on the present working of God and the present offer of redemptive power.

3. A third view seeks light on Christian origins in Hellenistic
Judaism.[17] This latter term, be it noted, includes more than the
Dispersion; Hellenistic Judaism was present in Palestine also.
Concerning the life and thought of the Dispersion we are not too
well informed, and the temptation is almost irresistible to take
Philo as the sufficient voice of what must have been a vastly more
varied segment of Judaism than his writings reflect. However,
Philo has recently suggested new possibilities of Jewish influ-
ence on Christian origins. It has often been thought that Judaism
was inherently hostile to mysticism, although the appearance of

16. A. Schweitzer has done most to focus attention on this question (see his *The Quest
of the Historical Jesus* [London, 1910]). R. H. Charles did much to further study of apocalyptic writings; he published important studies of individual works and edited *The Apocrypha
and Pseudepigrapha of the Old Testament* (2 vols.; Oxford, 1913).

17. E.g., C. Guignebert, *The Jewish World in the Time of Jesus* (New York, 1939); note
his conclusion on p. 261.

mystical strains of thought in the later rabbinical line could have given ground to challenge such a view. E. R. Goodenough now argues that Philo himself reveals the presence of a mystical phase of Judaism, which can rank as a true mystery religion.[18] This disputed view at least suggests that the discovery of a mystical strain in the New Testament is not an automatic proof of gentile influence.

The gentile environment may also be studied for the real clue to the rise of Christianity. The search may move in more than one direction. Greek philosophy will not prove very productive, except in providing instructive material to help in understanding the setting of the apostolic and ancient church; attention to Plato and the Stoics is most productive here. The theory of direct influence of Eastern religions also fails to produce decisive results. The study of apocalyptic, of angelology, and of the Logos-concept may receive light from research into oriental faiths and thought, but such light will show influence on Christianity almost entirely through Judaism rather than directly.[19]

This question of oriental influence comes to a head in the problem of the extent to which gnostic tendencies and the mystery cults produced or shaped Christian attitudes and views.[20] The mystery-religion type was not peculiar to any one part of the

18. See his By Light, Light (New Haven, 1935), and An Introduction to Philo Judaeus (New Haven, 1940), pp. 183 ff. Goodenough does not claim that the "Jewish mystery" required mystic rites as fixed and prominent as those characteristic of pagan mystery cults.

19. W. Bousset, Die Religion des Judentums im späthellenistischen Zeitalter (3d ed., rev. by Hugo Gressmann; Tübingen, 1926), deals extensively with Eastern influences. R. Otto (Reich Gottes und Menschensohn [2d ed.; Munich, 1940]) (Eng. trans., The Kingdom of God and the Son of Man [London, 1938]) finds in Jewish apocalyptic and the ideas of Jesus strong influence from Persian and Indian sources or from their roots. On an Eastern source for the Logos-concept see Albright, op. cit., pp. 145 f., 285 f.

20. On gnosticism, which cannot be regarded as the creator of Pauline or pre-Pauline Christianity, see S. Angus, The Religious Quests of the Graeco-Roman World (New York, 1929), chaps. xx, xxi; F. C. Burkitt, Church and Gnosis (Cambridge, 1932). Among noteworthy books on the mystery religions are H. A. A. Kennedy, St. Paul and the Mystery Religions (London, 1913); S. Angus, The Mystery Religions and Christianity (New York, 1925); R. Reitzenstein, Die hellenistischen Mysterienreligionen (3d ed.; Leipzig, 1927); H. R. Willoughby, Pagan Regeneration: A Study of Mystery Initiations in the Graeco-Roman World (Chicago, 1929).

gentile world. It was a long-standing type of pagan religious life. It had one early expression in the Canaanite fertility cults of Old Testament days and, by the opening of the Christian era, was undergoing a purification, elevation, and expansion which was to reach its maximum expression in postbiblical days. A few scholars have claimed that Christianity in its later orthodox form was essentially the creation of mystery-religion influence, which took the simple religion of Jesus and his first followers, introduced a dying-and-rising-god network of thought and experience into a faith which had previously lacked it, and thus created what we know as "historic" Christianity.

The strongly Jewish character of New Testament Christianity throws suspicion upon such a theory. The late date of the actual evidence for the mystery cults is a fact far too lightly passed over by those who claim mystery influence on Christian developments in New Testament days. The focus of Christianity on a historical Jew, whose death and resurrection were central facts of Christian preaching in Jewish circles from the very beginning of the Christian church, makes suspect any attempt to explain redemption ideas as intrusions from gentile environment. Furthermore, competent scholarship must note differences as well as similarities and advance past details to seek the creative center and drive of each religious movement. In the discharge of its task it cannot explain Christianity by appeal to religions which in spiritual power, moral vigor, social concern, and intellectual vigor fail to offer a real parallel. The involvement of the usual mystery cult in primitive sex features also renders suspect the idea of a mystery-religion source of Christian origins. The one effective mystery-cult rival of ancient Christianity was Mithraism, and it attained influence too late to explain the origin of Christianity. These mystery cults illumine the setting of early Christianity, show the background and significance of details of Christian terminology and usage, and help us to understand trends which Christianity followed in the next few generations; but they do not explain how the Christian gospel came into being. We must look for that explanation not in mythology but in history.

III

· The third way to explain the rise of Christianity is to find the real center of vitality in the apostolic church rather than in the teaching, action, and person of Jesus. This view takes many forms. One curious variant seeks to explain Christianity as a spiritual reinterpretation of what was originally a political movement. Robert Eisler, for example, asserts that Jesus was a revolutionary who succeeded in seizing the Temple in Jerusalem and holding it for a time, only to be seized in the end and executed as an insurrectionist.[21] Solomon Zeitlin says that the Christian movement was, at first, a political movement, which only with the passage of time became a religious fellowship.[22] He considers that the messianic claim of the first disciples marks them as a political group. Common to the otherwise greatly different theories of Eisler and Zeitlin is the idea that the politically quietistic and spiritually centered message of the New Testament was a later development of a movement which originally had a political orientation. This tendency to blur the essentially spiritual and moral character of the initial form of Christianity has no future. We are dealing with a religious movement and must seek its explanation in faith-centered, worship-grounded circles.

The former idea that Paul was the real originator of Christianity is less popular today, although it is still heard; Joseph Klausner, for example, urges it, although with some important qualifications.[23] Moreover, E. W. Parsons denies that Jesus spoke any words about his death and its meaning for his followers, and he is inclined to ascribe to Paul the whole atonement doctrine, which Parsons identifies too narrowly with the penal substitution idea.[24] This makes Paul largely responsible for the classic form of Christianity, for a Christianity with no word about the Cross is not New Testament Christianity. But Paul explicitly states that he *received* the doctrine that "Christ died for our sins

21. *The Messiah Jesus and John the Baptist* (London, 1931). Eisler was effectively answered by J. W. Jack, *The Historic Christ* (London, 1933).

22. *Who Crucified Jesus?* (New York, 1942), chap. xi.

23. *From Jesus to Paul* (New York, 1943), chap. xii, esp. pp. 581 f.

24. *The Religion of the New Testament* (New York, 1939), pp. 27 ff.

according to the Scriptures."[25] The church from the first had to deal with the meaning of Jesus' death, and the fact that a third of the Gospel material deals with the last week of his life indicates that the significance of Jesus' death was a subject of Christian teaching from the first.

On essential matters of Christology, the Cross, and the Resurrection, Paul shows no consciousness of being a lone voice; he rather says that the church in both its gentile and its Jewish constituency shared the main features of his own faith.[26] His career and contribution to the life, expansion, and thought of Christianity were unsurpassed; but the origin of the essentials of historic Christianity cannot be dated so late as the time of Paul's known leadership. The significance of this fact is tremendous when it is remembered that Paul's conversion came but a very few years after the death of Jesus and that nowhere in his writings does he betray the consciousness of any radical difference between the faith he found in the church at the time of his conversion and his faith at the time he wrote the letters preserved for us.

Certain leaders of critical scholarship in recent years have looked for the creative center of Christian origins not in Paul but in the short period between Jesus and the letter-writing period of Paul's ministry. Three such attempts should be noticed. One is the attempt of such scholars as W. Bousset[27] to find in Hellenistic Christianity—later than the most primitive stages in Palestine but early enough to be prior to the decisive leadership of Paul—a development which notably altered the Christian message so as to give it a Lord acceptable to the religious habits and desires of the Hellenistic world. Indeed, the alterations which Christianity underwent in being transplanted into the gentile world were considerable and call for constant attention. But this change can be overstated. In the first place, all evidence shows that, from the outset, Jesus was regarded as the unique

25. I Cor. 15:3.

26. Gal. 2:1–10; I Cor. 15:1–11.

27. *Kyrios Christos* (3d ed.; Göttingen, 1926). Among the answers to Bousset note A. E. J. Rawlinson, *The New Testament Doctrine of the Christ* (London, 1926), esp. pp. 231–37.

and final expression of God's mind and will to men, and that the church at every stage gave him the highest titles at its command. In the second place, Hellenistic Judaism was present in Palestine; and followers of Jesus included, from the first, Christians of that type, as the presence of Barnabas and Stephen attests. The developments of which Bousset writes began in the presence of personal friends of Jesus, a fact which argues against radical distortion of his role and significance.

A second attempt to find the center of Christian origins in the period between Jesus and Paul is that of C. C. Torrey.[28] He argues that Judaism possessed a completely developed messianic expectation, that Jesus let this expectation strictly alone, but that the first thing the apostolic church did was to adopt it and attach it to Jesus *in toto*. The adoption of this set of ideas appears then to be the decisive point of Christian origins. But the curious isolation of Jesus from a set of ideas which everyone else had on the tip of the tongue is suspicious; the rigid ready-to-wear form in which they are said to have existed does not ring true; the connection of this theory with the view that Greek-speaking Christianity was a late and, from a literary point of view, parasitical development weakens it; and the view fails to explain how the personal followers of the completely nonmessianic Jesus adopted so unhesitatingly a group of ideas which had no roots in what he had taught them.

Far more influential is the third way in which the search for Christian origins centers in the period between Jesus and Paul. It finds the origin in the disciples' social experience and adaptation to environment. I refer, of course, to form criticism.[29] It

28. *Our Translated Gospels* (New York, 1936), pp. xv–xlix.

29. Outstanding works of this type include K. L. Schmidt, *Der Rahmen der Geschichte Jesu* (Berlin, 1919); M. Dibelius, *Die Formgeschichte des Evangeliums* (2d ed.; Tübingen, 1933) (Eng. trans., *From Tradition to Gospel* [New York, 1935]); R. Bultmann, *Die Geschichte der synoptischen Tradition* (2d ed.; Göttingen, 1931); F. C. Grant, *Form Criticism* (Chicago, 1934) (Grant here translates and discusses very briefly works by R. Bultmann and K. Kundsin). The first thorough evaluation of the method was by E. Fascher, *Die formgeschichtliche Methode* (Giessen, 1924). For discussion in English see B. S. Easton, *The Gospel before the Gospels* (New York, 1928); V. Taylor, *The Formation of the Gospel Tradition* (London, 1933); E. B. Redlich, *Form Criticism* (London, 1939); D. W. Riddle, *The Gospels: Their Origin and Growth* (Chicago, 1939); and my *Origins of the Gospels* (New York, 1938), chap. iv.

puts much of the development of New Testament Christianity later than the first generation of the church, but it places the beginning of the social process which produced historic Christianity in the common life of the earliest Christians. It tends to find the source of the Gospel material not in Jesus or any leader or writer but rather in the group and the process; in its extreme form it denies individual creativity and magnifies the contribution of the group. It may qualify the group contribution by ascribing much of the Gospel material to outside sources, from which the disciples are said to have borrowed.

The method itself is not determinative of the results; the presuppositions which guide its use have more effect than is sometimes realized. Some form critics end in a practical denial that we know anything about the historical Jesus; in such a case the origin of the church and the Gospel is due to undisciplined appropriation from environment or to creative capacities in the community itself. Yet, in spite of such devastating results, some emphases of form criticism point in another direction. This method of study indicates that the Gospel tradition, including especially the story of the Cross and the Resurrection, was known and constantly used in the church from the earliest days, even though not in its fully developed later form. The earliest documentary sources of our Gospels cannot be dated much later than A.D. 50, and the prior use of Gospel tradition in the life of the church is not a situation in which radical distortion and unrestrained addition seems reasonable. This constant use of the tradition in the church, coupled with the fact that the message of Paul and of the first-generation church contained teaching about Christology, Cross, and Resurrection, constitutes a bridge which nearly spans the period between Paul's letters and Jesus, and the idea of complete transformation of the tradition in so short a period becomes exceedingly difficult, or—as I would say—impossible, to maintain. Either the Christian message underwent a thoroughgoing transformation almost immediately after the death of Jesus, so that the failure to reflect what he stood for was due to, or at least approved by, his personal companions; or the historic

Christianity we know runs back through the early years of the apostolic age to the mind and career of Jesus himself.

One fact is not open to question. If the early disciples made essential and far-reaching alterations in the Christian message and way of faith, they never suspected what they were doing. Their unanimous and unwavering conviction was that the creative center of their movement was not in their group but in Jesus, and not merely in his teaching and example but also in his death and resurrection. Although apostolic leaders show differences of temperament, background, cultural contact, and individual purpose, the reverent centering of faith and life in Jesus is the only faith we find in the apostolic church.

IV

The preceding statements support the fourth view of Christian origins—that the creative center was in Jesus himself. This view focuses attention not only on the public career of Jesus but also on his death and resurrection; it likewise includes the apostolic interpretation in the essential Christian message. But it holds that this interpretation was in line with the purpose and work of Jesus and considers the later development the result, rather than the eclipse, of his total action.

On such a view Jesus' extensive dependence on Judaism does not exclude vital creative originality. In one way or another this originality has been recognized by recent scholars. C. G. Montefiore[30] and J. Klausner[31] have pointed to aspects of Jesus' teaching which, if taken seriously, result in a religion with a universal appeal. Karl Holl,[32] Maurice Goguel,[33] and Rudolph Otto[34] have united in the view that the message of Jesus contained original elements which gave ground for a new development.

In two respects, however, this long-standing view of Christian

30. See *The Synoptic Gospels* (2 vols.; 2d ed.; London, 1927), esp. comments on Mark 7:1–23 and Luke, chap. 15.

31. *Jesus of Nazareth* (New York, 1925), pp. 369–80.

32. *The Distinctive Elements in Christianity* (Edinburgh, 1937).

33. *Au seuil de l'Évangile: Jean-Baptiste* (Paris, 1928), pp. 264 ff.

34. *Op. cit.*, pp. 393–95.

origins is strongly challenged today. Many question whether Jesus ever thought of himself as the Messiah.[35] The tradition explicitly states that Jesus so regarded himself, and the New Testament puts it beyond dispute that the apostolic church did so from the first. This does not prove the claim true but only insists that the issue is important. The argument for the claim will appeal to the fluid character of messianic expectations; it will state that, while Jesus avoided public use of messianic terminology because of aspects of it which he could not accept, yet he held to it because it asserted a fulfilment of Jewish spiritual hope which he found in his role; it will point to first-century apocalyptic usage to show that Son-of-Man terminology and messianic concepts were at least occasionally combined;[36] it will note that the execution of Jesus was on the charge of claiming to be the Jewish king, i.e., Messiah; and it will give great weight to the fact that Jesus' own companions evidently asserted from the earliest days of the apostolic church that he was and knew himself to be the Messiah.

The other point of Synoptic tradition which is strongly challenged today is its representation that Jesus foresaw his death and attached religious significance to it. These repeated forewarnings and the story of the Last Supper are ascribed by some scholars to the creative imagination of the apostolic church, which then becomes the real source of some outstanding features of the theology and worship of later Christian life.[37] The variations in the tradition of Jesus' words on this subject certainly show that we cannot determine with literal accuracy what he said; the question is whether he is responsible for the substantial content which all versions of these sayings contain. To regard the

35. Epoch-making in this field of study was the work of W. Wrede, *Das Messiasgeheimnis in den Evangelien* (Göttingen, 1901). A summary of and answer to Wrede's argument is given by A. E. J. Rawlinson, *St. Mark* (London, 1925), pp. 258–62. Among those who deny that Jesus referred to himself as the Messiah are S. J. Case, *Jesus: A New Biography* (Chicago, 1927), pp. 360–78; Parsons, *op. cit.*, pp. 42–56.

36. See W. Manson, *Jesus the Messiah* (London, 1943), Note C, "Interconnection of the Concepts Davidic Messiah, Servant of the Lord, and Heavenly Son of Man."

37. See n. 24, and, for a fuller reply to this position, see my *One Lord, One Faith* (Philadelphia, 1943), chap. viii.

tradition as the creation of the apostolic church reflects needless-
ly on the mentality and memory, if not on the integrity, of the
church. But it also neglects to explain the situation of Jesus. It
implies that he faced the fact of opposition, the threat of death,
and the resultant threat to his work, and yet never found for himself or gave his followers a way to relate this crisis to his ministry
and cause. Such a picture of a baffled and defeated leader cannot
make so strong a claim to historical credibility as the explicit
statements of the sources that he faced and interpreted the situation and, by teaching and symbolic action, gave a positive meaning to it.

V

The fifth explanation of the origin of Christianity is that
which the New Testament gives, that the gospel and the Christian movement have their explanation only in God's purposeful
working through Jesus Christ for the salvation of men. How are
scholars to deal with this clear claim? The prevalent solution is
to regard it as a matter of personal faith and to limit the discussion to the area which seems open to objective study. Does
not this rather subtly imply that the New Testament explanation of Christian origins is not true, or at least that it is so unimportant or so disconnected from the actual operation of life that
the movement can be studied, understood, and explained as a
humanistic phenomenon? To raise this point is not to belittle historical study, which is indispensable in dealing with a faith
which has roots in history. The purpose is rather to point out
that to exclude the New Testament view from the study of origins not only results in a decidedly incomplete view but must dis-
tort the significance of the factors which are taken into account.

Many will condemn the foregoing statement as a surrender of
objectivity. What is objectivity? Is it not that honest and careful
facing of evidence which will prevent personal prejudice and im-
perfections from warping the conclusions? We certainly have to
face the facts and find the truth. But the key question is whether
God is a fact. In a world in which there is no purposeful, competent God, the explanation of a noteworthy religious development as the working of God is absurd. But in a world where God

is the Creator and Lord and acts through Jesus Christ, the explanation of the spiritual history of man without reference to divine action may bring out many facts but can never give more than a relatively unimportant fragment, and I do not see how it can treat the subject without giving a misleading impression.

The task of scholarship in tracing the rise of Christianity can be conceived in two ways. We may exclude the question of divine working from the field under study and seek to grasp the issues concerning Christian origins within the realm of the tangible data and the human outlook which remains. Or we may consider that the fact of God and the New Testament explanation of his working are so essential to any true grasp of the subject that they demand the fruitful co-operation of personal attitude and honest study. Because I believe that this is one of those life-issues on which there is no valid neutrality, I hold that we cannot complete the task of scholarship without working into our picture a personal response for or against the New Testament explanation.

CHAPTER TWENTY

The Emergence of the Christian Church in the Pre-Catholic Period

SHERMAN E. JOHNSON

Episcopal Theological School, Cambridge, Massachusetts

I

HOW did the Christian church emerge into the light of history? When was the ancient Catholic church "founded"? These questions became insistent when scientific historians distinguished several levels in the New Testament, formulated sharp pictures of the religion of Jesus and that of Paul, and asked what genetic relationship existed between the apostolic age and the Catholicism of Irenaeus and Tertullian. Though Neander touched on these questions,[1] the lines of future study were marked out by Rothe's theory that the fall of Jerusalem led to the coalescence of Jewish and gentile Christianity and the formal institution of a monarchical episcopate.[2] The work of F. C. Baur followed immediately. To the Tübingen school belongs the credit for opening up the field.

Baur found the key to the first two Christian centuries in the conflict between the Jewish Christian and Pauline parties, which persisted for some time and can be observed in the Book of Revelation and the Clementine writings. As a movement toward peace and unity developed, such books as Hebrews, I Peter, and Barnabas represented "Jewish Christian" attempts at theological *rap-*

---

1. P. Batiffol, *Primitive Catholicism* (London, 1911), pp. 143–44; A. Neander, *Allgemeine Geschichte der christlichen Religion und Kirche* (Hamburg, 1825–52), I, 292–313, 325–46; *General History of the Christian Religion and Church* (10th American ed.; Boston, 1866), I, 190–201, 207–17.

2. R. Rothe, *Die Anfänge der christlichen Kirche und ihre Verfassung* (Wittenberg, 1837), Part I, pp. 340–551.

prochement, while Ephesians, Colossians, and the Pastorals marked a similar effort on the gentile side. The Book of Acts is a second-century *irenicum*, designed to show that Paul and the Jerusalem apostles had lived in harmony; while in the Fourth Gospel we find Jewish and Pauline doctrine blended into a higher unity.[3]

Thus the Catholic church was founded in the second century. It received its permanent form in the course of the conflict with gnosticism and Montanism. On the dogmatic side, it appealed against them to Scripture and tradition; on the practical governmental side, its bulwark was the hierarchy.[4]

Baur has often been stigmatized as a mere *Tendenz* critic, with a dogmatic philosophy of history derived from the Hegelian school. Of course, his theory of synoptic relationships has not stood the test of time; his dates for most books are too late; he rejected some genuine Pauline letters; he assigned to Jewish Christianity too long a span in space and time; and, in short, his view of the grand plan of early Christian development controlled his approach to the details. But no one has done more to perceive and state the important issues. He looked at his documents as wholes, not as collections of texts, and saw them as productions of a living and developing community which achieved unity out of diversity. His works are a permanent source of inspiration, and his severest critics have appropriated something of his point of view.[5]

While A. Schwegler agreed that the Jewish and Pauline movements reacted on each other, he assigned most of the decisive de-

3. *Über den Ursprung des Episcopats in der christlichen Kirche* (Tübingen, 1838); *Church History of the First Three Centuries* (3d ed.; London, 1878–79), esp. I, 25–31, 79–80, 84–85, 115–54; II, 1–61.

4. Baur, *Church History*, II, 15: "Tradition is the substantial element of the Catholic Church, the principle which, however widely the Church expands, preserves its apostolicity and unity: but it is from the episcopate alone that tradition derives its concrete reality."

5. For appreciative statements see H. S. Nash, *The History of the Higher Criticism of the New Testament* (2d ed.; New York, 1906), pp. 128–32, 142–45; S. J. Case, *The Evolution of Early Christianity* (Chicago, 1914), p. 13; W. Dilthey, *Gesammelte Schriften*, IV (Leipzig and Berlin, 1921), 403–32.

velopments to the Pauline side.[6] According to A. Ritschl, Jewish Christianity ceased to be influential after the Bar Kokhba revolt, and later Catholicism developed out of Paulinism. Its fundamental characteristic is its insistence that Christianity is a new law.[7] While Ritschl was right to discount the influence of Jewish Christianity and to deny that books like Hermas were its products, he was mistaken in minimizing the struggle between Paul and the Judaizers, in reckoning most of the later books as "Pauline," and in failing to perceive the interaction of different types of Christianity. Like most of his contemporaries, he failed to realize that there might be several kinds of non-Pauline gentile Christianity.[8]

Because of their theological bent, Baur, Ritschl, and their followers assumed that an "essence" of primitive Christianity and an "essence" of Catholicism could be isolated. Like most other Protestants, they regarded Catholicism as a deviation from primitive Christianity and held that the earliest Christians formed autonomous communities which only later were confederated. The earliest church's doctrine of its own being was thus congregational and atomistic. But, unlike the conservatives, they assumed that primitive church order was modeled on secular types of organization, and they sought to discern an unbroken development toward later Catholicism.[9]

Ernest Renan, who was no follower of the Tübingen school, placed the gnostic crisis and the most important developments of early Catholicism in the reign of Hadrian. By 130 the Catholic church was in every important respect complete. Even ritualism

6. *Das nachapostolische Zeitalter in den Hauptmomenten seiner Entwicklung* (Tübingen, 1846).

7. *Die Entstehung der altkatholischen Kirche* (2d ed.; Bonn, 1857), esp. pp. 21–23, 249–50, 259, 274–97, 312; cf. G. V. Lechler, *Das apostolische und das nachapostolische Zeitalter* (3d ed.; Karlsruhe and Leipzig, 1885–88), and also Neander, *Allgemeine Geschichte* (2d ed.), I, 331–33, who anticipates Ritschl's idea that Catholicism developed out of Paulinism. For Baur's criticism of Ritschl see his *Church History*, I, 100–104.

8. On this point cf. B. H. Streeter, *The Primitive Church* (New York, 1929), p. 48. The same limitations are to be observed in F. J. A. Hort's *Judaistic Christianity* (London, 1894).

9. O. Linton, *Das Problem der Urkirche in der neueren Forschung* (Uppsala, 1932), pp. 24–25, 29. The "consensus" of nineteenth-century critics assumed "that the individual devotee and his experience and conviction were the primary datum and that the church was a congregation" (p. 26). A few German High Churchmen protested against this, but they were not critical scholars (pp. 28–29).

and sacramentalism were part of the church's heritage from the gnostics. His massive knowledge of the sources, his literary skill, and his delightful humor and irony combined to make his work uncommonly persuasive. Not the least of his merits was his attempt to see the rise of Christianity in its setting as a part of world history and to assess the outside movements which operated upon it.[10]

In England, two names stand out. Bishop Lightfoot's famous *Dissertation* is mainly concerned with the origin of the ministry, but it is clear that he regarded Catholicism as a product of the late first and early second centuries.[11] Edwin Hatch, whose assumptions were largely those of the German "consensus,"[12] turned his powers to the task of investigating external influences on Christianity. Not only was the episcopate modeled on secular forms, but the Christian confederation itself was formed partly in response to political forces and was not achieved until the Council of Arles.[13]

The latter years of the nineteenth century saw the publication of many critical editions of sources and special studies, which were of great importance for future research.[14] The great conservative, Theodor Zahn, investigated the history of the New Testament canon,[15] and Kattenbusch and others dealt with the origin

10. *L'Église chrétienne* (3d ed.) ("Histoire des origines du christianisme," Vol. VI [Paris, 1879]) (English trans.: *The History of the Origins of Christianity* [London, n.d.], Vol. VI). Cf. his *Lectures on the Influence of the Institutions, Thought and Culture of Rome on Christianity and the Development of the Catholic Church* (3d ed.; London, 1885).

11. J. B. Lightfoot, "The Christian Ministry," in his *Saint Paul's Epistle to the Philippians* (4th ed.; London, 1878). What is decisive is the elevation of a single president over the presbytery. "In this way, during the historical blank which extends over half a century after the fall of Jerusalem, episcopacy was matured and the Catholic Church consolidated" (p. 207). Cf. his answers to the Tübingen school in *Saint Paul's Epistle to the Galatians* (10th ed.; London, 1892), pp. 292–374.

12. Linton, *op. cit.*, p. 35.

13. E. Hatch, *The Organization of the Early Christian Churches* (3d ed.; London, 1888), pp. 172–73; see also pp. 170–71, 173, 187–89.

14. On this and other matters covered in this article see H. R. Willoughby, "The Study of Early Christianity during the Last Quarter-Century," *Journal of Religion*, VI (1926), 259–83; H. Windisch, *Harvard Theological Review*, XIX (1926), 95–103, 105–8.

15. *Forschungen zur Geschichte des neutestamentlichen Kanons und der altkirchlichen Literatur* (Erlangen, 1881–1929), and *Geschichte des neutestamentlichen Kanons* (Erlangen, 1888, 1890).

of the Apostles' Creed.[16] There were numerous publications on the history of doctrine. Bryennios' discovery of the Didache evoked a flood of publications, some of the most important of them from the pen of Harnack—for example, his translation of Hatch's book and his contribution to the second volume of the new "Texte und Untersuchungen" series.[17] One might say that the century closes with Weizsacker, a Tübinger who had abandoned many of Baur's positions.[18] While he interprets Paul from his letters and is conscious of the seriousness of the apostolic conflict, he uses Acts, with judicious care, as a trustworthy source. His attitude to the book is similar to that of Jülicher: Paul was not Judaized, nor was Peter Paulinized, but both were Lucanized or Catholicized.[19] What is most striking about Weizsacker is that he operates simply as a historian, without any dominating theological or philosophical point of view.

II

Of all historians of the postapostolic period, Harnack has been the most influential, because of his immense learning, breadth of vision, theological competence, and literary power. Though he was a Ritschlian, he was able to investigate historical problems with unusual detachment. His most famous conclusion may be stated thus: While Christianity as a syncretistic religion was not complete until the time of Origen, the Catholic church was in a real sense founded in the last quarter of the second century, in

16. For literature see A. C. McGiffert, *The Apostles' Creed* (New York, 1902).

17. *Die Gesellschaftsverfassung der christlichen Kirchen im Alterthum.* Übersetzung . . . . besorgt und mit Excursen versehen von Adolf Harnack (Giessen, 1883); *Die Lehre der zwölf Apostel nebst Untersuchungen zur ältesten Geschichte der Kirchenverfassung und des Kirchenrechts* ("Texte und Untersuchungen," Vol. II, Nos. 1–2 [Leipzig, 1884]).

18. C. von Weizsäcker, *The Apostolic Age of the Christian Church* (London, 1899); see esp, I, 201–2; II, 149, 206–7. Acts is the focal book for Christian origins. The historian's judgment on developments in the apostolic and postapostolic periods depends to a large extent on his evaluation of Acts. The issue affects the origin of worship, the sacraments, the ministry, the content of early Christian preaching, and the isolation of non-Pauline influences (see the articles in *The Beginnings of Christianity*, ed. F. J. Foakes Jackson and K. Lake, Part I, Vol. II [London, 1922], pp. 363–433).

19. A. Jülicher and E. Fascher, *Einleitung in das Neue Testament* (7th ed.; Tübingen, 1931), p. 431; cf. A. Meyer, *Die moderne Forschung über die Geschichte des Urchristentums* (Freiburg i. Br., 1898), p. 13.

competition with gnosticism and Montanism, through the development of three defenses: the rule of faith, the canon of Scripture, and the apostolic succession of bishops.[20]

Such a judgment involves work in a number of fields, to all of which he made contributions. For example, in his studies of the canon, he laid down the principle that evidence for a book's use is not proof of its formal acceptance; the New Testament canon begins only with Marcion. His studies of the ministry and the doctrine of the church are built on foundations laid by Hatch, Sohm, and others. But he rejected Sohm's extreme position that the earliest idea of the church was entirely charismatic and non-legal, and he drew a distinction (perhaps too sharply) between the universal charismatic ministry and the local noncharismatic type.[21]

Sohm's work has received less attention in America, but it is of comparable importance.[22] Like Weizsäcker and Harnack, he realized that, long before the founding of a Catholic organization, there existed (in Paul's teaching) the idea of one spiritual, universal church. With rigorous consistency he pictured the primitive community from the Pauline letters and the Didache as a charismatic body without any church law except the guidance of the Spirit. Bishops, like apostles, were originally charismatics, marked out to preside at the Lord's Supper. Sohm emphasized the cultic and prophetic aspect of early Christianity; financial and governmental functions were, so to speak, incidental duties of those who handled the Word of God. Since law, in the usual sense, was foreign to apostolic Christianity, a doctrine of the in-

20. A. von Harnack, *Lehrbuch der Dogmengeschichte* (4th ed.; Tübingen, 1909), I, 353–54 (English trans., *History of Dogma* [London, 1894–1900], II, 18–93); see also I, 337 (English trans., II, 1). This was not an entirely new idea, for others had recognized the significance of Tertullian's statements (*De praescr. haer.* 36), but Harnack gave it a new turn and was able to establish it as the prevailing opinion of non-Catholic scholars.

21. Harnack's great thesis, of course, rests on more than these three points. He shows himself also as a social historian in *Die Mission und Ausbreitung des Christentums in den ersten drei Jahrhunderten* (4th ed.; Leipzig, 1923) (English trans.; *The Mission and Expansion of Christianity in the First Three Centuries* [2d ed.; New York, 1908]).

22. R. Sohm, *Kirchenrecht*, Vol. I (Leipzig, 1892). Part of Sohm's conclusions were presented by Walter Lowrie in an important and sadly neglected volume, *The Church and Its Organization in Primitive and Catholic Times: The Primitive Age* (New York, 1904).

visible church, like that of Luther, should have developed. But it did not, and the door was open for the entrance of Catholicism, whose essential characteristic is a fixed church law claiming divine right, not "Hellenization" and moralism, as Harnack thought.[23] As soon as there existed a congregation in the legal sense and a fixed college of bishops and as soon as a bishop had a right to his office, Catholicism was present. I Clement was immensely influential in bringing this about. The weakest part in Sohm's reconstruction is his subtle idea of church law.[24]

Von Dobschütz essentially agrees with Harnack, though he places less emphasis on the Hellenization of Christianity and more on its increasing worldliness and loss of the primitive enthusiasm.[25] A. Sabatier,[26] A. C. McGiffert,[27] and Williston Walker[28] largely adopted Harnack's point of view and did much to introduce it to theological students. Goodspeed, in his studies of the canon and of early Christian literature, draws a distinction between the "Catholic" and "pre-Catholic" periods. H. Lietzmann builds on Harnack's foundations.[29] B. J. Kidd's book, written from an Anglican point of view, gives a mild and qualified acceptance of Harnack's position.[30] The same is true of Jackson, though he holds that in the first century of its existence the church had already done much to consolidate its institutions.[31]

Harnack's influence can be seen in his opponents also, and

23. Sohm, *Wesen und Ursprung des Katholizismus* (2d ed.; Leipzig, 1912), pp. v ff.

24. *Kirchenrecht*, I, 156, 167; cf. Linton, *op. cit.*, p. 57. Harnack's criticism of Sohm is given in *The Constitution and Law of the Church in the First Two Centuries* (London, 1910), pp. 176–258.

25. E. von Dobschütz, *Probleme des apostolischen Zeitalters* (Leipzig, 1904), pp. 110–32; cf. also his more recent article, "Die Kirche im Urchristentum," *Zeitschrift für die neutestamentliche Wissenschaft*, XXVIII (1929), 107–18.

26. *Religions of Authority and the Religion of the Spirit* (New York, 1904).

27. *A History of Christian Thought* (New York, 1932), Vol. I, chap. viii.

28. *A History of the Christian Church* (New York, 1918), esp. pp. 59–60.

29. *Geschichte der alten Kirche* (3 vols.; Berlin and Leipzig, 1932–38). The first two volumes are translated as *The Beginnings of the Christian Church* (New York, 1937) and *The Founding of the Church Universal* (New York, 1938).

30. *A History of the Church to A.D. 461* (Oxford, 1922), Vol. I, chap. x.

31. F. J. Foakes Jackson, *The History of the Christian Church from the Earliest Times to A.D. 461* (New York, 1933), esp. pp. 144–46.

Batiffol's *Primitive Catholicism* was written partly to answer him. While Harnack emphasized the vast changes that took place in a century and a half, Batiffol called attention to the continuity of development and brought into high relief all the "Catholic" elements which can be seen in first-century Christianity, insisting that gnosis was a protest against an already existing Catholicism.[32]

The principal weakness of Harnack's thesis is not difficult to discover. Behind it is the theological idea, eloquently expressed in *Das Wesen des Christentums*, that there is an essential kernel which can be isolated as primitive Christianity and contrasted with Catholicism, which has a *Wesen* all its own.[33] It was this point which Loisy attacked with such skill.[34] On the other hand, Roman Catholic writers pointed to a *Wesen* of Catholicism and insisted that it was present from the beginning.[35] And both Harnack and the Catholics wished to make direct use of their results for theological purposes.

The historian must therefore ask himself what he means by "the emergence of the church." At least it cannot mean anything as concrete and formal as the founding of a new denomination like the United Church of Canada. Actually, history cannot operate with the concept of "the founding of the Catholic church" except as a convenient generalization which must be defined carefully and not pressed too hard. We may picture the several communities of the apostolic age; the social and doctrinal movements of the next century or two, both centripetal and centrifugal; the formation of a canon; and the rise of synods and coun-

32. L. Duchesne's temperate and noncontroversial manual (*Early History of the Christian Church from Its Foundation to the End of the Third Century* [New York, 1909]) takes it for granted that Catholicism was a gradual and continuous development. An excellent example of more recent Catholic historiography is G. Bardy, *The Church at the End of the First Century* (London, 1938).

33. A. von Harnack, *What Is Christianity?* (London, 1901). Just so, Von Dobschütz insisted that the apostolic age was unique; its religion is not a slightly modified Judaism, nor is it shot through with gnosticism and later Catholicism (*Probleme des apostolischen Zeitalters*, pp. 121–32).

34. A. Loisy, *The Gospel and the Church* (New York, 1904).

35. E.g., Batiffol, *op. cit.*, pp. vi–vii.

cils. Which of these shall we call *the* foundation? The answer is that there is no one "essence," and at no point is a hard-and-fast line to be drawn. Every new period is different from the last, and the whole development is a continuous stream.[36] This is not to say that the development has no theological significance but that history must speak for itself and not be controlled by an interpretation imposed upon it.

III

As the twentieth century opened, research began to be more independent of theology. Wernle and others found the beginnings of Catholic theory and institutions already present in the first century.[37] It was the eschatological and *religionsgeschichtliche* schools which principally turned history-writing into new channels. No longer could one suppose that Jesus intended to found a church; the church idea thus receives its great impetus when eschatology wanes. At the same time, outside influences came in early, and "Catholic" elements entered the picture almost as soon as there was a church idea. Pfleiderer regarded Luke-Acts, and Matthew even more, as products of nascent Catholicism.[38] Johannes Weiss traced the concept of apostolic authority, which was to be so significant, to Paul's charismatic apostleship. No sharp line can therefore be drawn between spirit and office. The Didache and the mission discourses in the Gospels exhibit some of the first developments, and Harnack's three "apostolic norms"

36. As C. C. McCown says, in *Munera studiosa* (Cambridge, Mass., 1946), p. 54: "History is a seamless garment. It represents both a time and a space continuum." Cf. also G. P. Wetter, "La Catholisation du christianisme primitif," *Revue d'histoire et de philosophie religieuses*, VII (1927), 17-33.

37. P. Wernle, *The Beginnings of Christianity* (New York and London, 1903-4), II, 1-10; A. Meyer, *op. cit.*, p. 7. One must, of course, realize that Wernle passed an unfavorable judgment on these developments. We have already alluded to Weizsäcker.

38. O. Pfleiderer, *Primitive Christianity* (London, 1906-11), II, 379 f.: "In its combination of the most heterogeneous elements, the Gospel of Matthew shows itself to be an ecclesiastical Gospel-harmony . . . . The tendencies which were to culminate in the dogma, ethics, and organisation of the Church Catholic are all visible in this Gospel." See also B. W. Bacon, *Studies in Matthew* (New York, 1930), especially Part I, chap. x, and Parts II and IV; F. C. Grant, *The Growth of the Gospels* (New York, 1933), chap. vii; D. W. Riddle, *The Gospels, Their Origin and Growth* (Chicago, 1939), pp. 156-60.

have their beginning in the early period. Weiss believed that Catholicizing additions (e.g., in I Cor. 1:2; Col. 2:1–2) were made to the Pauline letters, perhaps when they were collected, and that Ephesians is an important early Catholic document.[39] The newer approach thus removed the sharp line between the apostolic and the postapostolic periods, between primitive Christianity and Catholicism.[40]

The historians of religion have provided us with an immense amount of material, only part of which has been used up to now in reconstructing the origins of the church.[41] One immediately thinks of their researches into the origins of the sacraments and christological doctrine, and especially Bousset's *Kyrios Christos;* the various studies of popular Hellenistic philosophy, the origins of gnosticism, and particularly the Hermetic religion, Mandaeism, and Manichaeism. Investigators like Walter Bauer turned their attention to the "apocryphal New Testament" and

39. J. Weiss, *The History of Primitive Christianity* (New York, 1937), II, 752, 673–87; cf. Linton, *op. cit.*, pp. 127–31. The later chapters of Weiss contain much information about the period; some of them are by Rudolf Knopf. Knopf's *Das nachapostolische Zeitalter* (Tübingen, 1905) is a most useful book, but it is largely descriptive and not a genetic history. By comparison with Weiss, the sections on church origins in Eduard Meyer's *Ursprung und Anfänge des Christentums* (Stuttgart, 1921–23), III, 214–29, 249–57, are disappointing. Though Meyer was a great ancient historian, he disregarded many of the results of New Testament study. Yet it is worth pondering that he regarded Acts as a trustworthy source and held that the church's organization existed practically from the beginning.

40. H. Weinel, *Die Wirkungen des Geistes und der Geister im nachapostolischen Zeitalter bis auf Irenäus* (Freiburg i. Br., 1899), showed that pneumatic phenomena lived on for some time, and not only in Montanism.

41. See, e.g., H. Gunkel, *Zum religionsgeschichtlichen Verständnis des Neuen Testaments* (Göttingen, 1903), which develops the thesis that Christianity is a syncretistic religion; the literature listed by Willoughby in his article cited above; and by H. Windisch, *Harvard Theological Review*, XV (1922), 206–16, and XIX (1926), 108–14; also G. P. Wetter, *Der Sohn Gottes* (Göttingen, 1916); H. Schlier, *Religionsgeschichtliche Untersuchungen zu den Ignatiusbriefen* (Giessen, 1929); E. Schweizer, *Ego Eimi* (Göttingen, 1939); E. Peterson, ΕΙΣ ΘΕΟΣ (Göttingen, 1926); E. Fascher, ΠΡΟΦΗΤΗΣ (Giessen, 1927); Nils Johansson, *Parakletoi* (Lund, 1940); K. Holl, *Urchristentum und Religionsgeschichte* (Gütersloh, 1925); G. Kittel, *Die Religionsgeschichte und das Urchristentum* (Gütersloh, 1932), which contains many bibliographical suggestions and some striking plates; A. D. Nock, "Early Gentile Christianity and Its Hellenistic Background," in *Essays on the Trinity and the Incarnation*, ed. A. E. J. Rawlinson (London, 1928), pp. 51–156; cf. also his *Conversion* (Oxford, 1933), esp. chap. xii, which describes early Christianity in terms of its social and religious environment. See also W. Bauer, *Rechtgläubigkeit und Ketzerei im ältesten Christentum* (Tübingen, 1934), and *Das Leben Jesu im Zeitalter der neutestamentliche Apokryphen* (Tübingen, 1909).

THE EMERGENCE OF THE CHURCH

other popular Christian writings and studied the relation of "orthodoxy" to "heresy." Both Catholics and Protestants investigated liturgical origins and archeological remains. What once had been called "Jewish Christianity" was now analyzed into several non-Pauline gentile movements, some of them strongly influenced by the Diaspora synagogue.[42]

In the later work of Alfred Loisy one sees the confluence of Catholic modernism, Harnack's researches, the history of religions, and the eschatological school.[43] Because Loisy continues to date Hermas in the times of Pius, even though his doctrinal looseness fits badly with the rejection of Marcion, he finds it necessary to postpone the development of monarchical episcopacy and to connect it with the gnostic struggle. This, together with his late dates for Ephesians, Matthew, Luke-Acts, and John, explains why he does not put the rise of Catholicism earlier. On the other hand, if he regards Tertullian's thought as the kernel of Latin Catholicism, complete Catholicism does not exist until after the Montanist movement has failed.[44]

Lietzmann's three volumes are even richer and more suggestive. Though the author stands in the Harnack tradition and emphasizes the three "apostolic bulwarks," he sees the church as the product of a manifold development. Lietzmann sets the idea of the church in the perspective of the early Christian world view. He utilizes a great variety of source material—literary and nonliterary, Christian and non-Christian, religious and profane—including his own researches into liturgical origins and the apostolic symbol, the latest investigations of episcopacy in Egypt, and the insights of Bauer's *Rechtgläubigkeit und Ketzerei*. Further study must follow some such lines as these.

42. Note especially W. Bousset, *Kyrios Christos* (3d ed.; Göttingen, 1926), esp. chaps. viii–x; B. W. Bacon, *The Gospel of the Hellenists* (New York, 1933), chap. viii; D. W. Riddle, "The So-called Jewish Christians, " *Anglican Theological Review*, XII (1929), 15–33.

43. *La Naissance du christianisme* (Paris, 1933), chap. x. This mature volume summarizes conclusions reached over a period of years and stated in Loisy's commentaries and elsewhere.

44. Loisy's compatriot, C. Guignebert, *Le Christianisme antique* (Paris, 1922), dates the rise of Catholicism earlier. His idea of the origin of the monarchical episcopate is similar to that of Sohm. Cf. also his book *Le Christ* (Paris, 1943).

IV

Another development has been the study of the church from the sociological point of view. H. Achelis' work appeared in 1912[45] and Case's pioneering book in 1914.[46] Not only was Christianity now studied in relation to the surrounding society, but its own social thought and inner social structure were investigated.[47] Interest centered, at first, in the earliest period, but Troeltsch gave full attention to the postapostolic age and rightly emphasized the sociological importance of the sacraments. George LaPiana's remarkable article on "The Roman Church at the End of the Second Century,"[48] without direct dependence on the "social-approach" school, interpreted the consolidation of the church in Rome as due to social factors and placed it in the setting of that new juridical development which fell in the period from Marcus Aurelius to the end of the Severan dynasty. LaPiana showed that this consolidation was due to practical, rather than doctrinal, interests; that it was undertaken consciously and deliberately; that tradition was brought under hierarchical control; and that the Roman settlement was of decisive importance for church life everywhere.[49]

Form criticism, with its doctrine that community interests controlled the formulation of Gospel material, made added information available for the study of church origins. K. Kundsin attempted to reconstruct the thought and life of an early Christian group.[50] Case and Riddle, without emphasizing the *forms* of

45. *Das Christentum in den ersten drei Jahrhunderten* (Leipzig, 1912). Von Dobschütz had already published his *Christian Life in the Primitive Church* (London, 1904).

46. *The Evolution of Early Christianity* contains little on the postapostolic age, though some important suggestions are to be found in the final chapter.

47. Among the important works are E. Troeltsch, *The Social Teaching of the Christian Churches* (New York, 1931); L. P. Edwards, *The Transformation of Early Christianity from an Eschatological to a Socialized Movement* (Menasha, Wis., 1919); K. Kautsky, *Foundations of Christianity* (New York, 1925), a Marxian treatment; C. E. Hudson and M. B. Reckitt, *The Church and the World* (London, 1938), Vol. I; F. H. Stead, *The Story of Social Christianity* (London, 1924), Vol. I.

48. *Harvard Theological Review*, XVIII (1925), 201–77.   49. *Ibid.*, p. 235.

50. "Primitive Christianity in the Light of Gospel Research," in F. C. Grant (ed.), *Form Criticism* (Chicago, 1934); cf. also his *Topologische Überlieferungsstoffe im Johannes-Evangelium* (Göttingen, 1925).

the oral tradition, used a similar method. Case pictures the development of Catholicism as beginning in the last quarter of the first century, when need was felt to control the human agencies "through whom the Holy Spirit was assumed to work."[51] Heresy is "fundamentally a social phenomenon rather than an intellectual problem." He lays no unique weight on the gnostic and Montanist dangers but stresses nonintellectual factors: the separation from Judaism, the interest of the Roman church in moral teaching and social control, the desire of Christians to find a place in world society, the need for propaganda among pagans. The Romans consciously and deliberately institutionalized Christianity.

D. W. Riddle develops these and other ideas with much skill.[52] By the late first century "the cults of Jesus were now a general Church." The most characteristic part of the Fourth Gospel (chaps. 14–17) is not merely a manual for personal devotion; its principal object is the guidance of the New Community. From this point to the time when Jude and II Peter were written, the institutional development is entirely unbroken.[53]

V

Many valuable special studies have appeared in recent years. The early church's doctrine regarding itself has been dealt with by George Johnston, but his conclusions are not completely clear, and the weakest part of the book is the chapter on the subapostolic age.[54] Investigation of the origins of the baptismal

51. S. J. Case, *The Social Origins of Christianity* (Chicago, 1923), esp. chap. v.

52. *Early Christian Life as Reflected in Its Literature* (Chicago, 1936).

53. Among other American publications the following may be mentioned: E. F. Scott, *The Gospel and Its Tributaries* (New York, 1930), and *The Varieties of New Testament Religion* (New York, 1943); MacKinley Helm, *After Pentecost* (New York, 1936); W. W. Hyde, *Paganism to Christianity in the Roman Empire* (Philadelphia, 1946).

54. *The Doctrine of the Church in the New Testament* (Cambridge, 1943). Most of the important items are to be found in Johnston's bibliography or in Linton, *op. cit.;* see also B. S. Easton, "The Church in the New Testament," *Anglican Theological Review*, XXII (1940), 157–68; R. Dunkerley (ed.), *The Ministry and the Sacraments* (London, 1937), pp. 287–367; C. T. Craig, *The Nature of the Church* (Chicago, 1945), pp. 9–18; and S. Hanson, *The Unity of the Church in the New Testament: Colossians and Ephesians* (Uppsala, 1946). There is certainly some significance in the fact, now increasingly realized, that, even before the Crucifixion, Jesus' preaching had attracted large numbers of people and had created a movement. One

symbol has gone on steadily. A creed was probably in existence
by the middle of the second century, and perhaps even as early as
Pliny's governorship in Bithynia, while anticipations of it are
to be found in the New Testament books.[55] Harnack's researches
on Marcion, and other studies of eccentric movements, remind us
of the variety of early Christian thought; and investigators are
now beginning to use this vast material from popular and heretical sources.[56] Martin Werner's recent book is the most important
study of early Christian doctrine to appear since Harnack's *Dog-*

---

of the necessary conditions for emergence of the church was thus already present (see, e.g.,
F. C. Grant, *The Gospel of the Kingdom* [New York, 1940], pp. 1–6; A. D. Nock in *Journal of
Biblical Literature*, LXIII [1944], 61–62).

55. For literature from 1914 to 1920 see G. Krüger, *Harvard Theological Review*, XIV
(1921), 341–43. For later literature see K. Lake, "The Apostles' Creed," *Harvard Theological
Review*, XVII (1924), 173–83; G. Krüger, *Harvard Theological Review*, XXVI (1933), 188–
90. Note especially H. Lietzmann, "Symbolstudien. XIV," *Zeitschrift für die neutestamentliche Wissenschaft*, XXVI (1927), 75–95, and "Die liturgischen Angaben des Plinius," in
Geschichtliche Studien Albert Hauck. . . . dargebracht (Leipzig, 1916), pp. 34–38, and "Carmen =
Taufsymbol," *Rheinisches Museum für Philologie*, LXXI (new ser., 1916), 281–82.

56. A. von Harnack, *Marcion: Das Evangelium vom fremden Gott* (2d ed.; Leipzig, 1924);
J. Knox, *Marcion and the New Testament* (Chicago, 1942), and the literature cited there; P. N.
Harrison, *Polycarp's Two Epistles to the Philippians* (Cambridge, 1936). For gnosticism see
G. Krüger, *Harvard Theological Review*, XXVI (1933), 201–5; W. Bousset, *Die Hauptprobleme
der Gnosis* (Göttingen, 1907); E. de Faye, *Gnostiques et gnosticisme* (2d ed.; Paris, 1925); P.
Hendrix, *De Alexandrijnsche Haeresiarch Basilides* (Amsterdam, 1926); F. C. Burkitt, *Church
and Gnosis* (Cambridge, 1932); J. N. Sanders, *The Fourth Gospel in the Early Church* (Cam-
bridge, 1943); J. T. Carlyon, "The Impact of Gnosticism on Early Christianity," in J. T.
McNeill, M. Spinka, and H. R. Willoughby (eds.), *Environmental Factors in Christian History* (Chicago, 1939), pp. 114–30. For the persistence of Jewish thought-forms and teaching
methods see P. Carrington, *The Primitive Christian Catechism* (Cambridge, 1940); A. Meyer,
Das Rätsel des Jacobusbriefes (Giessen, 1930); E. G. Selwyn, *The First Epistle of St. Peter*
(London, 1946), pp. 365–466. We may hope that Professor B. S. Easton will shortly publish his commentary on the Pastoral Epistles. Much remains to be done in investigating
the currents of thought which produced the Revelation of John and other Christian apocalypses. Important suggestions on other points may be found in such volumes as K. Lake,
Landmarks in the History of Early Christianity (London, 1920); A. C. McGiffert, *The God of
the Early Christians* (New York, 1924); in the volumes of the "Handbuch zum Neuen Testament"; R. Bultmann, *Das Evangelium des Johannes* (Göttingen, 1937–39) and other recent
commentaries in the Meyer series; Sir E. C. Hoskyns, *The Fourth Gospel* (London, 1940);
C. H. Dodd, *The Johannine Epistles* (London, 1946); W. L. Knox, *Some Hellenistic Elements in
Primitive Christianity* (London, 1944); and in G. Kittel (ed.), *Theologisches Wörterbuch zum
Neuen Testament* (Stuttgart, 1933———); also C. C. Richardson, *The Christianity of Ignatius of
Antioch* (New York, 1935), and the literature cited there.

mengeschichte; and, in the light of it, Case's judgment is seen to be one-sided, for heresy is something more than a social problem.[57]

In the last generation the study of liturgical origins has made great strides, and early Christian worship is increasingly being recognized as an important factor in ecclesiastical development.[58] The church was not merely an ethical and didactic society but, first of all, a community of worship; and it is significant that a distinctive Christian cultus, including the Lord's Supper, developed quite early.[59]

The introductory problems of postapostolic literature and the history of the canon are intimately related. Recently, there has been increased interest in the literary relationships of the New Testament writings and other books.[60] Harnack, Goodspeed, and others have extensively studied the collection of the Pauline corpus of letters,[61] and the debate over the formation of a four-Gospel canon continues.[62] At the present time we possess excel-

57. M. Werner, *Die Entstehung des christlichen Dogmas problemgeschichtlich dargestellt* (Bern and Leipzig, 1941). Werner takes full cognizance of the problems raised by "consistent eschatology" and form criticism and utilizes the popular "apocryphal literature." Cf. also W. Köhler, *Dogmengeschichte als Geschichte des christlichen Selbstbewusstseins* (Zürich and Leipzig, 1938).

58. M. H. Shepherd, Jr., "The Function of Church History Studies in the Liturgical Movement," *Anglican Theological Review*, XXIII (1941), 118–33.

59. The later books of the New Testament give ample evidence of the existence of Christian liturgical materials (see, e.g., E. J. Goodspeed, *The Meaning of Ephesians* [Chicago, 1933], pp. 20–22, 60). For recent studies of eucharistic origins see the bibliography in A. Arnold, *Der Ursprung des christlichen Abendmahls* (Freiburg i. Br., 1937); also G. Dix, *The Shape of the Liturgy* (Westminster, 1945); W. Lowrie, *The Lord's Supper and the Liturgy* (London, 1943); F. L. Cirlot, *The Early Eucharist* (London, 1939).

60. A. E. Barnett, *Paul Becomes a Literary Influence* (Chicago, 1941), is a valuable supplement to earlier works. Unfortunately, the monograph of Lloyd V. Moore, "The Use of Gospel Material in Pre-Catholic Christian Literature" (University of Chicago Libraries, 1929), remains unpublished. See also Harrison, *op. cit.*, E. J. Goodspeed, *An Introduction to the New Testament* (Chicago, 1937), and *A History of Early Christian Literature* (Chicago, 1942).

61. A. von Harnack, *The Origin of the New Testament* (London, 1925), and *Die Briefsammlung des Apostels Paulus und die anderen vorkonstantinischen christlichen Briefsammlungen* (Leipzig, 1926); E. J. Goodspeed, *The Formation of the New Testament* (Chicago, 1926); Knox, *op. cit.*

62. Besides Goodspeed's *Formation*, see Sanders, *op. cit.*; R. M. Grant, "The Fourth Gospel and the Church," *Harvard Theological Review*, XXXV (1942), 95–116, and "The Oldest Gospel Prologues," *Anglican Theological Review*, XXIII (1941), 231–45; D. de Bruyne,

lent editions of the Apostolic Fathers and apologists and reasonably good collections of the "apocryphal New Testament," but one great need is a new Greek-English critical text of short works and fragments which can be assigned to the period before 200.[63]

Though the episcopate is only one among several institutions involved in the emergence of organized Christianity, the problem of its origin has received much attention, particularly in England, because it is of great practical importance for the reunion of the modern churches. Indeed, in some quarters "emergence of the church" means "emergence of the episcopate"! Up to 1929 in Protestant circles, five principal theories had prevailed: (1) according to Lightfoot, the monarchical episcopate arose out of the presbytery by the elevation of a single presbyter to be president;[64] (2) Hatch distinguished presbyters and bishops from the beginning but traced their origin to secular models; (3) Sohm held that all church functionaries were originally charismatics and that the church, as a spirit-filled body, had a unique structure and law of its inner life independent of any secular organization and that presbyters were originally the unordained, but tried and tested, older men of the church from whom a bishop was chosen as leader of the Eucharist; (4) Harnack posited two types of ministry: the charismatic apostles, prophets, and teachers and the local ministry of presbyter-bishops and deacons, which grew up according to models of secular law and ultimately replaced the former; (5) Bishop Gore and others held various forms of the traditional Catholic view that bishops were

---

"Les plus anciens prologues latins des Évangiles," *Revue bénédictine*, XL (1928), 193–214; A. von Harnack, "Die ältesten Evangelien-Prologe und die Bildung des Neuen Testaments," *Sitzungsberichte der Preuss. Akad. der Wissenschaften, Phil.-hist. Klasse* (1928), pp. 322–41; Bauer, *Rechtgläubigkeit*, chap. ix.

63. The older work of E. Preuschen, *Antilegomena* (2d ed.; Giessen, 1905), was very useful, as were his *Analecta* (Freiburg i. Br. and Leipzig, 1893). The need is partly met by R. M. Grant's *Second-Century Christianity* (London, 1946). I have listed some of the other materials in my article, "Stray Pieces of Early Christian Writing," *Journal of Near Eastern Studies*, V (1946), 40–55.

64. Cf. T. M. Lindsay, *The Church and the Ministry in the Early Centuries* (New York, n.d.).

successors of the apostles. Whatever the original "presbyters" had been, the later ones were given only subordinate authority.[65]

What Streeter added was not so much a new theory as a reconciliation of old ones.[66] After determining, so far as possible, the date and provenance of the sources, he used them to reconstruct the church order of the several localities, concluding that a great variety of ministers and types of polity had existed and that they had no unitary origin. In his view that "bishop" and "presbyter" were originally the same, Streeter followed the lines laid down by Lightfoot.

Though Streeter's book has been immensely influential, interest in Sohm's hypothesis has recently revived.[67] Future research must build on this double foundation. Nothing is more antecedently likely than variety in early Christianity, and one would expect some localities not only to follow synagogue organization but to look on Christianity as a new law,[68] while in other places, where the charismatic was predominant, Sohm's theory furnishes the best explanation.

VI

The origins of the Christian church are to be traced along the lines laid down by Baur. Early Christianity was a network of diverse movements, which interacted to achieve unity. Though the Jewish Christians soon came to be in the minority, we can trace in the New Testament and other early writings several types of gentile Christianity. The merit of Goguel's most recent

---

65. C. Gore, *The Church and the Ministry*, new ed. revised by C. H. Turner (London, 1919); C. Jenkins and K. D. Mackenzie (eds.), *Episcopacy Ancient and Modern* (London, 1930).

66. B. H. Streeter, *The Primitive Church* (New York, 1929).

67. Linton (*op. cit.*) obviously inclines to follow Sohm. For recent modifications of Sohm's theory see F. Gerke, "The Origin of the Christian Ministry," in *The Ministry and the Sacraments*, ed. R. Dunkerley, pp. 343–67; and M. H. Shepherd, Jr., "The Development of the Early Ministry," *Anglican Theological Review*, XXVI (1944), 135–50. These two articles cite some of the most important literature to appear since the publication of Linton's book.

68. See, e.g., Carrington, *op. cit.*, esp. pp. 67–73; B. S. Easton, *The Apostolic Tradition of Hippolytus* (New York, 1934).

book is that it is written in the light of this important insight.[69] Goguel, indeed, goes back to the Tübingen school in his view that, while the Jewish war was decisive for the victory of gentile Christianity, a small Jewish wing continued to be influential for some time. The Elkesaite heresy was a gnosis which developed in the *milieu* of Ebionitism. Other survivals of Jewish Christianity are indicated by the controversy over the Nicolaitans in the Book of Revelation, by Ignatius' trouble with "Judaism," and by the Quartodeciman dispute. But the principal emphasis is properly placed on the various forms of gentile Christianity. One of these is "Deutero-Paulinism," which Goguel sees in the Synoptic Gospels, Acts, I Peter, and the Pastorals.[70] Other types include the Johannine theology, the "moralism" of James and the Didache, and the "pre-Catholicism" of I Clement. The last-named document shows

certain traits which mark the physiognomy of ancient Catholicism, notably the narrow solidarity of a theological conception of which moralism is an important element, and of a theory which, associating a stable organization of the church with true doctrine, makes of it a framework within which the life of the Christian develops in the way of salvation, guided by a ministry which is exercised in virtue of divine institution.[71]

Ancient Catholicism could not come into being until doctrine and organization were fixed. Before this could happen, eschatology had to retire into the background, and pneumatism or free prophecy had to be brought under control. The gift of the Spirit, which once had been the means of innovation, became an organ of conservation. The process was completed only toward the end of the second century. Originally, Clement and the Fourth Gospel merely represented local forms of Christianity. No one at the beginning of the second century had the power to impose his doctrine as the only one or to put heretics outside the church.

69. M. Goguel, *La Naissance du christianisme* (Paris, 1946). See also Streeter, *op. cit.*, p. 50; F. C. Grant, "The Significance of Divergence and Growth in the New Testament," *Christendom*, IV (1939), 575–87.

70. But see B. S. Easton's important article, "Post-Pauline Paulinism," in *Munera studiosa*, particularly pp. 80–84.

71. Goguel, *op. cit.*, p. 417.

The best that Ignatius was able to do was to create centers of resistance against heresy around bishops who held the traditional doctrine and to insist that the church really existed only in these groups. But this strategy was finally successful, for to it was joined a more reasoned and precise statement of the unity and homogeneity of sound doctrine in opposition to the diversity of the heresies. Finally, this unification was greatly favored by the fact that the church of Rome attracted to itself Christians from all regions.[72]

My own view of church origins does not differ greatly from that of Goguel. However, I should identify the several strands of gentile Christianity somewhat differently. One group of believers probably collected and preserved the traditions underlying the Synoptic Gospels. Another group depended largely on the Greek Old Testament and the ethical traditions of the Diaspora synagogue. Christians of this type largely made up the church in Rome, which, as we know, was independent of Paul. While Paul was able to give orders to his own communities, he could do no more than offer the Romans a "spiritual gift."[73] A third group (which may overlap the others) comprises the Hellenistic Christians of Syria. A fourth is made up of the followers of Paul in various parts of the Empire. These groupings are not altogether homogeneous. For example, several types of Christology and piety can be detected in the Q and L material, the pericopes underlying Mark, and the source material of Acts. Some Antiochene Christians, no doubt, used the Old Testament, while others did not. The Pauline churches showed marked variety even in the lifetime of the apostle; and one can imagine that after his death some of his successors turned in a Marcionite direction, while others relied on free prophecy or tried to develop a new law. It was, however, the work of Paul, which, more than any other factor, established the church as a movement independent of Judaism.[74]

72. *Ibid.*, pp. 282–85, 469, 472.

73. Cf. Ed. Schwartz, *Charakterköpfe aus der antiken Literatur*, II. Reihe (2d ed.; Leipzig, 1911), p. 139.

74. See, e.g., A. D. Nock, *St. Paul* (London, 1938), pp. 245–47.

When one recalls that the gentile Christians did not live in a vacuum but were in daily contact with Jews, Jewish Christians, and religious pagans, it does not surprise one that serious dangers faced the communities after the year 70. But almost immediately a drive toward unity can be detected in Luke-Acts and Matthew, whose writers took the decisive step of establishing the concept of "apostolicity." The "apostles" of the mission field were assimilated to the Twelve, and the basic teachings and practices of central Christianity were traced (not without some justice) to the "apostles." Thenceforth, all Christians who constantly used the Old Testament and the deeds and teachings of Jesus had a basis for unity.

The earliest Catholicism of Rome rested intellectually on a synthesis of the Synoptic and Pauline strands and the "Septuagintal" religion of Clement, though it was able to embrace so eccentric a prophet as Hermas. This basis was strengthened when, in the conflict with Marcion and his canon, the Gospels, the Acts, and the Pauline letters were coupled with the Old Testament as Scripture. In the East there were far more variants of Christianity, some of them dangerous, and the Gospel of John represents a *via media* between the older Gospel tradition and the radical religion of prophets and teachers who were far more ready than others to accept religious influence from the surrounding world. When the Roman and Johannine influences were at last brought into a higher unity, ancient Catholicism was complete.

Such are the broad lines of doctrinal development. Many points remain to be investigated, such as the possible relation of Judaism and Jewish Christianity to gnosticism, the later developments in churches founded by Paul, and the place of the Book of Revelation, the Odes of Solomon, and various lesser-known writings, in the total picture. In the New Testament period there were other types of Judaism besides that rabbinic variety which became "normative," and one must not discount the interaction of Judaism, Hellenistic religion, and Christianity.[75] We must

75. See, e.g., W. L. Knox, *St. Paul and the Church of the Gentiles* (Cambridge, 1939), and the extensive literature on Philo which has recently appeared.

always realize, too, that while the theological development was taking place the institutional framework was being perfected. Theological and social factors are of equal importance, and they are not separate but interrelated. The origins of the church are to be seen not alone in the formation of scriptural canon, creedal basis of union, and episcopate but also in the shaping of a distinctive worship, piety, sacramental life, and congregational discipline; in the growing self-consciousness of a unique community within the Empire, which possessed an independent inner social life; and, finally, in the increasing contact of the several congregations with one another. The church was a doctrinal, cultural, social, and liturgical achievement.

The Role of the Bible in the Reformation

ARTHUR A. HAYS

McCormick Theological Seminary, Chicago, Illinois

WHATEVER else the Reformation manifested, it was certainly characterized by a great outpouring of religious energy. The source of this power that changed the course of history was universally attributed by the reformers themselves to the Bible. A careful study of this fundamental phase of the Reformation is most timely, since from several points of view the situations at the beginning of the sixteenth century and in our own age present striking similarities. Four hundred years ago the mind of man was on the march, and a hitherto unknown continent had just been discovered. Today science is bringing into view a vast new world full of marvelous materials and of limitless atomic energy, for whose organization there is no known pattern and before whose problems and potentialities all men of insight stand aghast.

Then all ethically minded men were keenly aware that organized Christianity, in spite of many attempts, seemed powerless to correct known abuses. Today the impotence of the church is cried to heaven by two world wars within one generation, which it was too feeble to prevent.

If scholarly researchers can point the way to the recovery of the golden secret of those valiant men who in their time laid the foundations for a truer Christianity, they will have served well their day and generation. With the hope of aiding not only scholars but all men of good will everywhere, who are striving to bring to a proper birth the brave new world that is struggling to be born, we in this paper will aim to discover the distinctively Protestant use of Scripture.

A careful study of the early Reformation will show plainly that, essentially, Protestantism was not, as many still assert, a bare negation; on the contrary, it protested because it was tied to a compelling affirmation. It did not begin in a denial, it began when Luther found peace with God through the truth of justification by faith.

It is true that he achieved this position only after he had failed to win a gracious God through his monastic practices. However, it was only slowly that Luther realized that his positive truth involved the denial of many beliefs which he had cherished hitherto. Protestantism was born in a positive experience. There would have been no protest, unless there had first been something to affirm. And this something Luther found in the Bible.

If we are to understand adequately why the Bible played the central role in the Reformation, it will be necessary to note carefully the forces that thrust it into its pre-eminent position. The first of these was an unquestioned belief in a fiery hell, into whose scorching flames an angry Deity cast all sinning souls at death. Of this not one of the reformers had the slightest doubt. It was because Luther believed in hell that he sought the way to heaven so earnestly. He strove to appease the wrath of God because he believed in the devil. Medieval art is crowded with pictures of the Day of Judgment, in which the scenes of the joys of the forgiven move one little, but the lurid agonies of the damned make one's blood run cold. Even so Christian a soul as Michelangelo, in his famous painting in the Sistine Chapel, presents Christ more as a judge who is intent on condemning guilty souls to everlasting torment than as the Redeemer of mankind. His right arm is raised, not in blessing but in wrath, to hurl sinners to hell. The Bible, then, held the foremost place in the minds of all the reformers because they believed that it alone provided the true way of escape from the fiends and fires of hell.

This leads us directly to the second reason for the supreme role of Scripture. The Roman church, for a thousand years and more, had claimed and men had undoubtingly believed that to her had been committed the keys of heaven and hell; hence submission to her was altogether necessary for salvation. A formula of priest-

ly absolution of 1516 reads: "I remit for you all the penalties due in purgatory. I close for you the gates of hell and open the portals of paradise."[1] It was in conflict with these claims of Rome that the reformers more and more exalted the Bible. With such a certain belief in the power of the church over a Dantean hell, little wonder that a Henry IV went to Canossa, a Henry III bared his back to the lash at the tomb of Thomas à Becket, and an Innocent III strode the world with the powers of Deity, the vicar of Christ on earth.

Plainly, the views of the reformers were irreconcilable with these exclusive claims of Rome, and a conflict was inevitable. It was in this struggle that the Bible was more and more exalted.

Since the medieval church based its claims on Scripture and had as high a doctrine of inspiration as ever was current in Protestantism, it will be well to look a little more closely at its teaching. Over against all the fallible knowledge obtained by man's natural powers, the doctors of the church placed the infallible Scriptures. True, the apostolic traditions were also considered of divine origin; but these, so it was held, never contradicted the canonical writings; hence they were, in practice, the court of last appeal.

The role of the Bible in the Reformation era was not due to a new doctrine of revelation but, rather, to a new attitude and use of it. Traditionally, men believed that in Peter alone was the prayer of Christ fulfilled, "That thy faith fail not." This meant that the divinely guided Roman church was to be forever "the pillar and ground of the truth"— and should never err. Hence she alone could determine what books were of divine inspiration, and her interpretations must be accepted implicitly; for, even though the Bible was a revelation from God, its meaning was so obscure — so enigmatic, in fact—that all private interpretations were sure to contain some heretical and damnable errors. Accordingly, the private reading of the Bible was not encouraged or held a means of grace; indeed, even candidates for the priesthood, like Luther, gave more attention to Peter Lombard than to it. As the

---

1. B. J. Kidd, *Documents Illustrative of the Continental Reformation* (Oxford, 1911), p. 10.

Vulgate was believed to be an inspired translation, the study of the Hebrew and Greek Testaments had been neglected for centuries; and, to make matters even worse, the plain, literal sense was commonly disregarded in favor of the traditional allegorical, tropological, and anagogical interpretations. The infallibility of Scripture we may well call "transferable," since the Schoolmen believed they could derive such perfect major premises from it that their logically deduced dogmas were as trustworthy and binding as the biblical truths themselves. Thus there had been developed a system of doctrines concerning God, creation, man's duty, and destiny that were held necessary for salvation, for no unbeliever could ever hope to escape eternal destruction.

This divine institution, the church, founded by Christ on Peter and led by his successors, possessed ortho-polity—outside her there was no salvation; her faith alone failed not, she was the sole teacher of orthodoxy; in her alone was found ortholatry— that worship which was acceptable to God; and he who would perform those deeds that merited salvation must learn orthopraxy from her. *Securus judicat orbis terrarum.* In her the unshakable decrees of God would be realized—the triumphant City of God would vanquish all her foes. When one considers that the Roman church, thus grounded in divine revelation, was backed by a thousand victorious years, he begins to comprehend the magnitude of the role played by the Bible in the hands of the reformers when they broke with Rome.

As we now begin our examination of the role of the Bible, it may be well to state that, owing to the limitations set for our paper, we shall quote mainly from Luther and Calvin, as it was they who determined the part it was to play and from their widely circulated words we can best discover how it affected the men of the sixteenth century.

What did the Bible do for Luther? It gave him an experience of God. While he was still trying to find a gracious God by monastic practices, he had "very often endured such torments . . . . so great and infernal as to be beyond the power of tongue to tell or pen to write."[2] From this agony he was delivered by the Word

2. J. Koestlin, *Theology of Luther*, trans. C. E. Hay (Philadelphia, 1897), I, 58.

and wrote: "I was filled with joy surpassing all others."[3] The revolutionary change that took place in Luther after his experience of hearing God's voice is very apparent. Before he understood fully what had occurred in his soul, he wrote of the Pope: "I shall recognize his voice as the voice of Christ speaking in him."[4] But when he began to suspect that Rome would not uphold him, he was held in the grip of his experience and wrote: "I won't make myself a heretic by contradicting that which made me a Christian. I will die first by fire, or be exiled and cursed."[5] Calvin, too, had perceived in the Scriptures "the undoubted energies of the divine power."[6] No longer was he of those who "had never tasted the sweetness of grace."[7] He was firmly convinced that the apostles were "the certain and authoritative amanuenses of the Holy Spirit, and therefore their writings were to be received as the oracles of God."[8]

What reasons could these men give for a confidence so certain that the anathemas of the church and the martyr's stake lost their terrors? Hear Luther first: "The Romanists say, How can we know this or that to be true and God's word? We must learn it from the Pope and the Councils. Very well, let them decree and say what they will, still say I, Thou canst not rest thy confidence thereon nor satisfy thy conscience. Thou must thyself decide. Thy life is at stake. Therefore must God say unto thee in thy heart, This is God's word, else it is still undecided."[9] The experience brought its own validation. God had identified himself. Calvin also in full reliance on this self-authenticating experience developed from it his well-known doctrine of the Witness of the Spirit. The Bible, he teaches, "ought not to be made the subject of demonstration or arguments from reason; but it obtains the credit it deserves with us by the testimony of the Spirit." Its certainty is "equal to an intuitive perception of God himself."[10] "For

3. P. Smith and H. P. Gallinger, *Conversations with Luther* (Boston, 1915), p. 130.

4. Kidd, *op. cit.*, p. 38.

5. P. Smith, *Luther's Correspondence*, I (Philadelphia, 1913), 120.

6. Calvin, *Institutes* (6th ed.; Philadelphia, n.d.), i. 7. 5.

7. *Ibid.*, iii. 13. 5.   9. H. Y. Reyburn, *John Calvin* (New York, 1914), p. 351.

8. *Ibid.*, iv. 8. 9.   10. Calvin, *op. cit.*, i. 7. 5.

the Scripture exhibits as clear evidence of its truth as white and black things do of their color, or sweet and bitter things do of their taste."[11]

It will be difficult for a modern man, for whom heaven is no longer up there or hell just beneath his feet, for whom all spirits have been banished from nature, to enter into this certitude of the reformers. With absolute confidence Luther wrote: "One letter, yea, one tittle of Scripture is of more and greater consequence than heaven or earth."[12] And in the same spirit Calvin said that a man's faith "ought to rest on such firm ground as to be invincible and undismayed in opposition to Satan, to all the machinations of hell, and to all the assaults of the world. This stability we shall find in the Word of God alone."[13] It was because men believed, without the shadow of a doubt, that God, the Lord of life, death, and destiny, had spoken directly to their own souls that the Bible won the central role in the Reformation; all other writings give way before its unique authority as the very Word of God.

This experience of God, considered in its fulness, was identified by the reformers with the faith described by Paul. It was not merely the notion that there was such a Being. Least of all was it the acceptance of theological speculations and definitions concerning the essence of Deity which had engrossed the minds of the Schoolmen. Calvin could even say: "Let us freely leave to God the knowledge of Himself."[14] "For it is not of so much importance to us to know what he is in himself, as what he is willing to be to us."[15] What both of the reformers learned from the Bible was not only that God was *willing* to be gracious; they also believed that the Heavenly Father loved them now; that He who justified sinners had, of his own free grace and not on the basis of any merit of theirs, forgiven their sins—even theirs—and had adopted them into the family of God. Such was their faith.

Thus the Bible had revealed a new way to heaven, one that was diametrically opposed to that of Rome. The papal authorities

11. *Ibid.*, i. 7. 2.

12. F. W. Farrar, *History of Interpretation* (London, 1886), p. 337.

13. *Op. cit.*, iv. 8. 9.   14. *Ibid.*, i. 13. 21.   15. *Ibid.*, iii. 2. 6.

perceived this opposition first, even in the Ninety-five Theses, when it was still hidden from their author. And so it was the Pope who excommunicated Luther and not the latter who broke away from the church. However, at the Leipzig Debate in 1519 Luther discovered that the celebrated Council of Constance had declared heretical certain views of Huss that were "most Christian and evangelical." This left nothing else for Luther to do but appeal to the Bible and assert with Carlstadt that it was to be "preferred not only to one or many doctors of the church, but even to the authority of the whole church."[16]

Calvin took the same stand that Luther had maintained at Worms, for his conscience, too, was taken captive by the Word of God. He would hold valid only those ecclesiastical pronouncements that "contain nothing but the pure and natural interpretation of the Scriptures."[17] Thus it was the Bible that compelled the reformers to deny that the decrees of the church had final authority.

In producing saving faith, not only did the Bible free Protestants from all external ecclesiastical authority, it also produced a sure confidence that they were safe for time and eternity from the fiends of hell. All the protection formerly sought from the church and her ceremonies, from the saints and the sign of the Cross, were thrown aside, for they had been reconciled to God through faith in Christ; and he alone would save them.

> And though this world with devils filled
> should threaten to undo us,
> we will not fear. . . . .
> The Prince of Darkness grim,
> we tremble not for him.[18]

Thus freedom from fear of Satan was in no way born of any skepticism regarding the existence of demons. The tiles on the housetops of Worms were not more real to Luther than the devils he opposed there. In Calvin's treatment of creation he discusses devils as seriously as he does the works of God in this "very beautiful theater of the world." But though of infinite number

16. Kidd, *op. cit.*, p. 44.   17. Calvin, *op. cit.*, iv. 9. 8.
18. *The Hymnal of the Presbyterian Church in the U.S.A.* (Philadelphia, 1933), Hymn 266.

and superhuman strength, skill, and celerity, they "can do nothing without God's will and consent."[19] The man of faith may be assailed grievously, as was Job, but he will never be completely overcome. Faith will always gain the final victory. In liberating men from their fear of the devil and all ecclesiastical curses, the Bible gave to them, as it were, a new Bible—new in extent and with a new central emphasis. Since the doctrine of merit was upheld by certain passages in the Old Testament Apocrypha, these books were no longer given a place among the strictly canonical writings; they could, however, be read for instruction in life and manners, but not for establishing any doctrine.

Luther followed the light of his new faith quite consistently when he placed the books inside the canon on very different levels. For him the Gospel of John and Paul's Epistles held the highest rank, since they taught Christ so plainly and whatever did this was truly apostolic; but in comparison with them the Book of James was a "right strawy epistle." However, as we have seen above, when he argued with the Romanists, he gave absolute authority to every letter and tittle of Scripture.

Though Calvin, too, recognized that faith was not produced by every part of Scripture but rested primarily on the promise of forgiveness in Christ, he held that the entire volume before him was the very Word of God, guaranteed by the testimony of the Spirit. It seems strange that his acute mind never realized that this was a fallacious use of the argument from the Witness of the Spirit. That witness certainly did not guarantee the perfection of the text he used, nor did it ever accompany chronological or merely historical details. This spiritual experience has occurred often with very faulty translations, and Calvin himself emphasized the fact that the Spirit's power attended the preaching of the Word, and no one ever claimed that any sermon was entirely faultless.

But be this as it may, the mental temper of the age was too strong for the purely spiritual use of the Bible as a conveyor of the voice of God, and soon it was handed over primarily to the

19. Calvin, *op. cit.*, i. 14. 17.

mind as an arsenal of proof-texts. Thus, from very early Reformation days on, the Bible played a dual role; it became the generator of faith, and it also served as the source of infallible ideas. Though each of these roles always has overtones from the other, it may be well to examine them separately. Our analysis of each cannot, of course, be exhaustive; yet some important observations must be made.

We inquire, first, what kind of God did the Scriptures present when faith looked into the mirror of the Bible and met God face to face, graciously active in this present world.

All our own reading confirms Koestlin's statement that Luther has far more to say about the love of God than about his righteousness.[20] He even wrote: "We have seen in all the evils we endure naught but the goodness of God."[21] But, since Calvin's view of Deity has been so frequently misrepresented, we shall examine it more fully. God is the "best of fathers," whose "benignity . . . . was displayed in the greatest affluence of all blessings provided for us while we were yet unborn."[22] He is amazed at "the inconceivable goodness of God."[23] Fundamental in his conception is the view that "there is such a close connection between the goodness of God and his deity, that his being God is not more necessary than his being good."[24] Did the Bible and his experience leave any place for arbitrariness in God? At times, he says, "the flesh solicits us to murmur, as though God amused himself with tossing men about like tennis balls," but "the final issue proves the counsels of God to be directed by the best of reasons."[25] We are to "account his will the only rule of righteousness, the most righteous cause of all things. Not, indeed, that absolute will which is the subject of the declamation of the sophists, impiously and profanely separating his justice from his power, but that providence which governs all things, from which originates nothing but what is right, although the rea-

20. *Op. cit.*, II, 284.

21. *Works of Martin Luther*, ed. and trans. H. E. Jacobs *et al.* (Philadelphia, 1915–32), I, 126.

22. Calvin, *op. cit.*, i. 14. 22.

23. Calvin, *Harmony of the Gospels*, III, 329.

24. Calvin, *Institutes*, ii. 3. 5.

25. *Ibid.*, i. 17. 1.

sons of it may be concealed from us."[26] In another place he repudiates arbitrariness in these decisive words: "Yet we espouse not the absolute and arbitrary power of God, which on account of its profaneness deserves our detestation."[27] In the appropriate places Calvin carefully defends the justice of God in all his dealings with sinners, for they "perish through their own iniquity and not through the unjust hatred of God."[28] "Sinners are deprived of the favor of God and chastised with his punishments for their own sin and only for their own."[29] "If all men promiscuously submitted to Christ, election would be common."[30] He speaks of "the incomparable goodness of God, since he deigns to forget all our sins as soon as he sees us earnestly desirous of turning to him."[31] "God rejects no returning sinner, he pardons all without exception."[32] Calvin's constant use of the phrase "secret counsel of God" is his way of saying: The justification of these things is hidden from me, but I still believe the world is governed by a just God. Though his judgments at times are incomprehensible, they are always irreprehensible.[33] Thus both the reformers held tenaciously to the vision of the goodness and love of God which they saw by faith in the mirror of the Word.

In offering Christ as the central object of faith, the Bible presented new aspects of his person and work, one of which we deem worthy of special mention.

Of his early days Luther says: "I shrank back in terror when I saw his picture, closed my eyes and would rather have seen the devil."[34] This medieval concept of the Christ is strikingly portrayed in one of Rubens' paintings. The observer wonders whether the wrathful thunderbolt of an angry Christ can be checked by the intercession even of the Virgin Mary and St. Francis, who interpose themselves between his fury and the world, about which the Old Serpent is coiled. The thought of the reformers was, of

26. *Ibid.*, i. 17. 2. *ad fin.*

27. *Ibid.*, iii. 23. 2.   29. *Ibid.*, ii. 5. 11.

28. *Ibid.*, ii. 8. 20.   30. *Ibid.*, iii. 22. 7.

31. Calvin, *Commentary on Ezekiel*, trans. T. Myers (Edinburgh, 1850), II, 246.

32. *Ibid.*, p. 248.

33. Calvin, *Institutes*, iii. 21. 7. *ad fin.*   34. Koestlin, *op. cit.*, I, 55.

course, largely conditioned by Anselm's theory of the atonement, but a new and characteristic emphasis was put on the indwelling Christ. So great is the similarity of presentation that one cannot help believing that Calvin's mind was colored by Luther's description of the wedding ring of faith, which unites the heavenly Bridegroom to his bride, the soul.[35] Luther says expressly that we are called Christians, "not because He is absent from us, but because He dwells in us."[36] The following question of Calvin implies an exact parallel: "How is faith saving but by ingrafting us into the body of Christ?"[37] Elsewhere he declares: "I attribute, therefore, the highest importance to the connection between the Head and the members; to the inhabitation of Christ in our hearts; in a word to the mystical union."[38] This Christocentric teaching of the reformers' Bible is so rich in suggestiveness and so eminently suited to practical exhortation that it is one of the tragedies of Protestantism that it was so soon neglected and forgotten.

The Bible, which outwardly conveyed the voice of God, compelled attention to the Third Person of the Trinity also, for "nothing," says Calvin, "is effected by the Word without the illumination of the Holy Spirit."[39] Since the days of the Montanist and Macedonian controversies, as the Athanasian Creed abundantly shows, little heed was given to the work of the Spirit, but in the writings of the early Protestants his work is emphasized constantly. In fact, the entire movement receives a flood of light if the Reformation is thought of as a rediscovery of the Spirit's activity. Only by his illumination can the Bible be rightly understood and saving faith produced. By him believers are united to Christ in the unity of the church, and men called into the ministry. Sermons and sacraments become means of grace only through his agency, and, by the Spirit that works holiness the victory over evil is achieved. And, finally, the action by which "the reprobate exclude themselves from salvation" is that of those "who with deliberate impiety have smothered the light

35. Compare *Works of Martin Luther*, II, 320, with Calvin, *Institutes*, iv. 17. 2.

36. *Works of Martin Luther*, II, 339.   38. *Ibid.*, iii. 11. 10.

37. Calvin, *Institutes*, iii. 2. 30.   39. *Ibid.*, iii. 2. 33.

of the Spirit . . . . alienated themselves from the sanctification of the Spirit and trampled on the Word of God."[40]

In the controversy with the Anabaptists, the reformers took the extreme position that only through the Word did the Spirit display his activity at all. Thus the Spirit revealed in the Bible and the Bible used by the Spirit became inseparable. It was their combined activities that determined the role of the Scriptures in the Reformation.

Another major role played by the Bible was as the revealer of what the reformers believed was the true nature of man and of the life that was pleasing to God. For centuries the church had taught that man could become in this life so saintly, so perfectly holy, that he could not only pay the debt due for his own sins but even add to the treasury of merit to aid other sinners still struggling with evil. But if there is one idea absolutely and perpetually rejected by all the early Protestants, it is that of merit. Luther declares: "He that would deserve grace by works going before faith, goeth about to heap sin upon sin, to mock God and provoke his wrath."[41] Chrysostom's words are quoted by Calvin to the same effect: "Every man is not only a sinner, but altogether sin."[42] These judgments are heightened, if possible, by their conviction that the righteousness of God "is so perfect that nothing is acceptable to it but what is absolutely complete and immaculate, such as never was, nor ever will, be possible to find in fallen man."[43] No one can ever win merit, for "sin always exists in the saints till they are divested of the mortal body."[44] Hence their conclusion followed necessarily that "the righteousness of the saints, in this world, consists rather in the remission of their sins, than in the perfection of their virtues."[45] Thus the doctrine of human depravity and inability loomed large in the thought of both Luther and Calvin.

From this "estate of sin and misery" into which man fell, the only release possible was through faith in the Christ revealed in

40. *Ibid.*, iii. 3. 23.
41. H. T. Kerr, Jr., *A Compend of Luther's Theology* (Philadelphia, 1943), p. 104.
42. *Institutes*, ii. 2. 9.   44. *Ibid.*, iii. 3. 10.
43. *Ibid.*, iii. 12. 1.   45. *Ibid.*, iii. 11. 22.

the Word. And so it came about from this time forth, especially among the Calvinists, that great emphasis was placed upon a definite experience of conversion, which became the normal, the indispensable, door of entrance into the Kingdom of God. When, however, Luther, Zwingli, and Calvin agreed in advocating infant baptism, they were bitterly attacked by the Anabaptists, who insisted without compromise that only believers should be baptized.

What, now, is the manner of life produced by converting faith? A full answer, in which all Protestants agreed, is found in this sentence of Calvin: "Thus we see how true it is that we are justified, not without works, yet not by works; since union with Christ, by which we are justified, contains sanctification as well as righteousness."[46] To the same effect Luther says: "I will therefore give myself as a Christ to my neighbor. . . . . I will do nothing in this life except what I see is necessary, profitable and salutary to my neighbor."[47] Thus all actions become sacred if done in faith, even if it be but "picking up a straw." In revealing that faith alone makes a man pleasing to God, the Bible struck a devastating blow at the entire monastic system. And with it went also all glorification of the ascetic view of life. Luther's enjoyment of the good things of this world is well known; Calvin also, and in the strongest language, repudiated all self-imposed austerities, for the good God "intended to provide not only for our necessity, but likewise for our pleasure and delight."[48] He bids us "discard therefore that inhuman philosophy which, allowing us no use of the creatures but what is absolutely necessary, not only malignantly deprives us of lawful enjoyment of the Divine beneficence" but reduces man "to a senseless block."[49]

We come now to the second part of the dual role of the Bible in the Reformation, in which, brushing aside the traditional interpretations of the Church Fathers, the Scriptures offered themselves to the minds of men as the sole, final, and infallible authority.

46. *Ibid.*, iii. 16. 1.   48. *Institutes*, iii. 10. 2.

47. *Works of Martin Luther*, II, 337.   49. *Ibid.*, iii. 10. 3.

We note, first, that an unerring instinct soon produced translations of the Bible into the languages of the common people in order that they, too, might hear the voice of God. Thus Tyndale's oft quoted prophecy to the priest came true, that before many years "a boy that driveth the plow shall know more of Scripture than thou doest." In a day when few scholars knew well the original tongues and many priests, as Erasmus assures us, could scarcely understand the Latin Vulgate, the placing of these translations within the reach of the ordinary man was an event of incalculable cultural, as well as of immense religious, value.

Very early, also, there came from the presses commentaries on various books of the Bible, especially those on the Psalms, the Gospels, and Paul's Epistles. As might have been expected, in those of Luther and Calvin the aim was not merely to shed light upon dark places but also to wean their readers entirely from Rome and to prove that the Scriptures upheld the doctrine of justification by faith. These commentaries and the Bibles with marginal notes circulated widely and had great success in spreading and maintaining Protestantism.

The stimulus given by the Renaissance in the preceding century to the study of the biblical languages led to the printing of the Hebrew Bible and, in 1516, to the publication of Erasmus' Greek New Testament. Luther and Calvin made good use of both of these, not only in their personal development but also in their polemical writings and commentaries. Indeed, the first of Luther's Ninety-five Theses, which furnished a basis for all the rest, is merely the assertion, supported by the original Greek, that Christ said "repent" and not "do penance," as the Vulgate translation read. In Calvin's commentaries we find a surprisingly large number of discussions of the meanings of Hebrew and Greek words. From all this we see that, in Protestant circles at least, it was the Bible in the original languages that was to be the court of final appeal.

Evidence of the beginnings of textual criticism may be seen, for example, when Calvin notes that the texts of I John 5:7 do not agree and admits that he scarcely dares to reach a conclusion. His hesitation in regard to the authorship of II Peter may serve

to illustrate the dawn of historical criticism. Furthermore, the Bible was to be allowed to speak a plain language, free from the ancient allegorical subtleties. Luther put the case bluntly when he wrote: "The Holy Spirit is the plainest and clearest speaker in heaven and earth, and therefore cannot have more than one, and that the very simplest, sense."[50] However, as the plain meanings were studied ever more closely, discrepancies began to manifest themselves. Luther commonly treated them as of little moment— they were not the Gospel. But Calvin constantly tried to reconcile them. In this, as he admits, he was not always successful. Of the difficulty in Acts 7:16 he wrote: "It is manifest that there is a fault [mistake] in the word Abraham . . . . wherefore this place must be amended."[51]

Perhaps this is the place to note that all the early Protestant commentators taught that, according to divine revelation, the world was created in one week about six thousand years ago; plain texts also showed that the sun revolved about the earth, which, less than five thousand years before, had been over-whelmed by a world-destroying flood. Thus what they unhesitatingly affirmed to be the natural and plain sense of Scripture was later found to be erroneous. The zeal for inerrancy manifested in trying to harmonize all discrepancies culminated in the efforts to reconcile the Bible with modern science and in the travail of the theologians to produce a perfect system in which all texts would agree with their classic passages. In these attempts many clear verses underwent deplorable exegetical juggling.

One of the most important roles of the Protestant Bible was the production of a new system of doctrine. The reformers held firmly that, in revealing God to man, the Scriptures also gave true ideas about him; that is, they believed that the Bible contained a revealed theology. Starting with a theory of inspiration that was equated with infallibility, they maintained in good scholastic fashion the transferable infallibility of the Bible; and they unhesitatingly placed the authority of God himself back of their

combinations of verses and deductions from texts which at times were correctly, and at other times capriciously, chosen.

This emphasis on theology produced, on the one hand, works of the highest significance, such as Melanchthon's *Loci communes* and Calvin's *Institutes;* and many creeds and confessions were formulated, in which some of the profoundest insights of recent centuries found classic expression.

On the other hand, it had very sinister aspects. Since Scripture furnished no authoritative list of fundamentals, it was possible for a strong leader, who differed from his group on any doctrine that he deemed essential, to feel that loyalty to God's Word required him to separate from his fellows. One of the most disastrous of the early divisions was that of Zwingli and Luther at Marburg; and, from that day on, Protestantism has been cursed by its unhappy schisms. However, it will be well to remember that these divisions grew out of the illogical continuance of the medieval belief that orthodoxy was essential to salvation. Surely, it was illogical according to their own definition, for the assent of faith that united all believers into the unity of the body of Christ is vastly different from the consent one gives to dogmatic propositions! And historically, in the Reformation era just as in the first centuries, the experience of faith came long before any doctrines were formulated. But the Roman idea that orthodoxy saved and heresy was damnable still surged through most minds —and Anabaptists were drowned at Zurich, and Servetus was condemned to the stake by Roman Catholic and Protestant authorities alike.

Finally, the Reformation Bible compelled new developments in church worship and polity. Luther's theory, that what is not against Scripture, is for Scripture and Scripture for it, allowed him to retain many earlier forms and customs. Far more radical was Calvin, who believed that what was not commanded was forbidden. With this convenient broom a host of medieval practices was swept away, some valuable, many superstitious.

In Geneva an entirely new system of Church government, patterned on the New Testament, was adopted, and elders or pres-

byters became the distinguishing mark of the Calvinistic churches.

Both the reformers saw clearly that their doctrine of salvation by faith was incompatible with any necessity for priestly mediation, and so the primary duties of the minister were to preach the gospel and administer the sacraments, in which, as by visible words, the promised grace of God in Christ was offered to be received by faith.

In our study we have seen that the reformers indubitably believed that through the Bible the Holy Spirit had wrought in them a mystical union with Christ, in which their sins were forgiven and God became a gracious Father. As this union with Christ was created by the Spirit that works holiness, there could be no justification unaccompanied by an active striving against evil; and the life of faith was not one filled with monastic austerities done with the hope of merit, but a normal existence of thankful joy in daily blessings and willing service to one's neighbor.

When it came to the formulation and defense of their beliefs, the scholastically trained minds of the reformers naturally ascribed objective infallibility to the Bible and believed that their deductions were divinely true. Their own divergent conclusions, as well as the errors which the centuries since have disclosed, prove that the doctrine of transferable infallibility must be entirely given up. This abandonment of a revealed theology must not be allowed to minimize in the least the value of the profound insights which they achieved into the heart of man and the righteous rule of God.

Might not our fear-stricken generation do well to uncover afresh the sources of power our forefathers knew when the Bible played its creative role in the Reformation era and guided them into a new age?

A Critique of the Revised Standard Version of the New Testament

ALLEN PAUL WIKGREN

University of Chicago

O N FEBRUARY 11, 1946, the Revised Standard Version of the New Testament was officially and optimistically introduced into the family of English Bibles by the International Council of Religious Education, representing some forty Protestant denominations.[1] The publication constituted the culmination of the New Testament phase of a revision of the entire Bible, which, with the exception of about five years (1932–37), has progressed since 1930 and was aimed at supplying the well-recognized need for a revised English Bible that would be generally acceptable for ecclesiastical usage.[2]

The R.S.V. is a revision of the American Standard Version, a production which, along with its English counterpart, never enjoyed the reception that was eventually accorded to the King James Bible, their common predecessor; for, although possessing much greater accuracy in text, it remained a highly literalistic

1. For details on the members of the committee, rules of procedure, denominational representatives, etc., see the brochure written by the revisers: *An Introduction to the Revised Standard Version of the New Testament* (International Council of Religious Education, 1946), and hereafter referred to as the *Introduction*.

2. While we shall deal with certain of the detailed evidence of this need as we proceed, it must suffice here to refer the reader to the discussion in the *Introduction*, where the data regarding the pertinent points of manuscript discovery; progress in the science of textual criticism; better editions of Greek, versional, and patristic texts; new light from linguistic studies and historical backgrounds; etc., are briefly indicated. An adequate survey of these must necessarily be sought in individual treatments; but the revisers should be commended here for a piece of work which will doubtless, for the first time, bring to the attention of many readers of the Bible some appreciation of the factors involved in its translation and revision.

translation and its diction was artificial for its day. The extravagant reverence which had become attached to the King James Version was also difficult to overcome. One remembers that even the latter was greeted, as the writer of its Preface anticipated, "with suspicion instead of love" and that some fifty or more years elapsed before it was able to displace the popular Geneva Bible in the affections of the English-speaking people. The R.S.V., although not so broadly based as these revisions,[3] aims and claims to be a legitimate descendant of them.

But any estimate of the effectiveness of the work of the revision committee must, of course, be made with full recognition of the general and particular ends which were in view. From various statements in the *Introduction* and elsewhere we may briefly summarize these as follows: (1) an accurate translation of the best available text; (2) a translation into clear, concise, and idiomatic English; (3) a readable and euphonious translation, suitable for public and private worship. Other subsidiary aims will be indicated as we proceed.

In general, we observe from the R.S.V. itself that great progress has been made toward the achievement of the enunciated goals. The attractive format and effective mechanics of the volume are factors contributory to this result. The dropping of antiquated forms of personal pronouns and verbal endings is another.[4] Increased intelligibility comes from less literalistic translation and from greatly modernized English vocabulary and phraseology. The accuracy and force of the translation is enhanced by the appropriation and use of increased knowledge of the Greek text and especially of its meaning as clarified by linguistic study and by new light from research in the historical backgrounds of the New Testament documents.[5] Let us examine this impression in more detail.

3. Cf. Rule 8 of the English revisers' procedure policy. (See *The New Testament . . . . Revised A.D. 1881* [Oxford, 1881], p. xi.)

4. The exception of "language addressed to God" noted in the *Introduction* (p. 56) is not strictly true. Several passages addressed ("prophetically") to Jesus (e.g., in Hebrews, chap. 1) and to cities (Matt. 2:6; Revelation, chap. 18) retain some antique pronouns. In John 12:15 the "daughter of Zion" is so saluted, but not in Matt. 21:5!

5. Improvements are thus to be found on every page in considerable numbers; e.g., Matt. 28:1 ("After the Sabbath"); John 1:5 ("overcome"); Heb. 11:1 ("assurance"); Mark 14:72 ("he broke down"); Rom. 8:4 ("just requirement").

The determination of the "best available text" for translation or guidance in revision is the first and naturally the most fundamental problem which must be faced. Here we learn that the revisers did not base their work on any one Greek text but were guided by the "eclectic principle," modified, supposedly, by the fact that the readings adopted "will, as a rule, be found either in the text or the margin of the new (17th) edition of Nestle (Stuttgart, 1941)."[6] If the revisers' course was charted by the Nestle text, they would be moving in the general direction of the so-called "neutral" form, since Nestle is itself an eclectic production based upon agreements between Hort, Weiss, and Tischendorf, all of whom were disposed to favor this Alexandrian recension. Such a tendency is admitted by Professor F. C. Grant, who offers a list of passages as evidence.[7] It is also confirmed by a study which we made of about two hundred readings, including all the variants marginally noted for Matthew and Mark, where the recent Legg editions provide more evidence for evaluation.

Among the marginal variants, incidentally, our study revealed a goodly number of inexplicable omissions throughout the volume, as, e.g., in Mark 1:34; 7:3; John 1:18; 5:3 f.; etc.[8] The total of those included is, it is true, not large—about 240 all told —but the basis for their choice is not very apparent, since it is not consistently either the kind or amount of evidence or the intrinsic interest of the reading. The formulas used to introduce them may usually be disregarded as meaningless or misleading.[9]

6. F. C. Grant, in *Introduction*, p. 41. The reference to the "margin," if by this the critical apparatus is meant, has no special significance, since many insignificant variants as well as conjectural emendations are there noted. The seventeenth edition of Nestle is generally not available but differs little from the sixteenth.

7. *Introduction*, p. 42. While these support the conclusion, it appears that 13 of the 47 are already read by the A.S.V. and at least 6 others are meaningless because of the large amount of other evidence.

8. Using for an objective criterion the question of whether such a variant was adopted by A. S. V., Goodspeed, or Moffatt, I have noted at least fifty instances where a reference would be desirable.

9. The intended simplification of the A.S.V. system makes them generally only more inconsistent, misleading, or mistaken. The usual formula is "Some" or "Many ancient authorities, etc." (cf. "manuscripts" in Heb. 4–9), but others occur sporadically. "Some" is used repeatedly where "many" or "most" would be correct, and "many" is misleading where almost all authorities are meant (e.g., Mark 7:16).

Some notable variation from the A.S.V. in line with the Hort tradition may be seen in the relegation of Mark 16:9–16 and John 7:53—8:11 to the margin, and in the omissions in Matt. 19:9 and Mark 10:24, of ἐν Ἐφέσῳ in Eph. 1:1, and the so-called "Western non-interpolations" (Hort) in Luke 22:20; 24:3, 6, 12, 36, 40, 51–52. Others may be found in Grant's list. Examples of adoptions on the basis of non-Alexandrian evidence occur in the omission of Matt. 21:44, the reading "of God" in Matt. 21:12 and "broken" in I Cor. 11:24, and in the Lucan omissions just cited. Probable improvements of the text may be seen at Matt. 12:47; Mark 6:14; 15:44; Rom. 8:28; II Cor. 3:2; Heb. 9:11. Some dubious readings or readings inconsistent with the R.S.V. policy appear in Matt. 16:2 (retains the weather prophecy); Luke 22:43 f. (retains the bloody-sweat passage); Luke 23:34 (retains the forgiveness saying); Mark 7:3 (πυγμῇ seems to be omitted entirely, or is without an explanation of its translation or proposed meanings); Mark 7:4 ("when they come"); I Cor. 13:3 ("burned"); Matt. 15:6 (ἐντολήν). Some of these obviously reflect ecclesiastical preferment.

An impersonal judgment of how the committee functioned in the matter of readings where the external evidence was inconclusive may be gained by noting the difference of opinion in such instances as illustrated by the text adopted in the Goodspeed and Moffatt versions respectively, since both these translators were among the revisers. A survey in Matthew and Mark reveals a total of 49 such disagreements (Goodspeed and Moffatt, 11;[10] Goodspeed only, 10; Moffatt only, 28). The high incidence in Moffatt is due to his text (Von Soden) and to his frequent adoption of meagerly attested readings and conjectural emendations on the basis of internal evidence. Goodspeed, on the other hand, is translating the Hort text quite closely.

While there is evidence here as well as in the illustrations already cited that the revisers have not consistently followed the "neutral" or any other text but have given some attention, as Grant claimed and indicated,[11] to internal evidence for readings,

10. This list may be of special interest: Matt. 11:15; 16:2, 12; 21:44; 23:4, 38; Mark 1: 29; 4:40; 7:3, 4; 10:7.

11. *Introduction*, p. 40.

they have been, in reality, rather conservative in departing from the traditional text on this basis. Meagerly supported variants are rarely adopted; one conjectural emendation only is admitted (in Jude, vs. 5) according to Grant, though there are a few other passages which amount to the same thing (e.g., in Matt. 2:6; 25:42; I Cor. 16:12; Philemon, vs. 9). While there may be a legitimate difference of opinion on whether such emendations should appear in the text, it appears to us that many are worth recording in the margin, especially when they elucidate difficult readings. But the R.S.V., by the traditional exclusion, must arbitrarily dismiss the labors of many a scholar who has expended much effort to solve textual problems by just the sort of internal criticism which Grant extols and rightly prognosticates as necessary to future progress in this area.[12]

The R.S.V., then, may be said textually to have made a cautious advance in the direction of the Hort text. Generally speaking, this also represents an improved text, not because the oldest text is necessarily to be defined as Alexandrian but because rational criticism was also to some extent a determining factor in the choice of readings.

When we turn to questions of the accuracy of translation of the text, we are similarly met with the necessity of somewhat modifying our impression of progress. Perhaps we should be prepared for this by Professor Cadbury's observation that the modern translator "is willing to deal less meticulously with the data of a simple style that was naturally not too particular about modes of expression or conscious of some of the subtleties which some later interpreters read into it."[13] There is much truth in this observation; yet the writers of our documents certainly intended to convey definite meanings and impressions, which it would seem to be the obligation of the translator to discover, if possible. Furthermore, differences of opinion may exist as to what should deserve discriminating treatment and what should not. So, for example, among the present revisers, Professor Cadbury felt with regard to the R.S.V.'s identical translation of

12. *Ibid.* This means, of course, that the translator must also be an interpreter of first rank!

13. *Ibid.*, p. 52.

the different verbs for "love" in John 21:15–17: "It seems impossible to differentiate them and hence unnecessary to mention in a note that they are different words."[14] But Professor Goodspeed, in his recently published *Problems of New Testament Translation*, feels strongly that such treatment would "reduce the conversation to mere iteration," and that it "loses the point of the story"![15]

That there is, however, much increased precision in the revision is undeniable and is illustrated by Cadbury himself.[16] It is only regrettable that the revisers have not consistently followed the excellent standards proclaimed by the *Introduction*. An indiscriminate rendering, for example, of Greek imperfects, aorists, and perfects is common; and a disregard for tense-action also results here and there in a loss of exactness and vividness. So, although Cadbury criticizes the previous version for not distinguishing the effective force found in the aorist of $\check{\epsilon}\chi\omega$,[17] this is certainly missed by the revision in Matt. 21:38, where $\sigma\chi\hat{\omega}\mu\epsilon\nu$ is translated "have" instead of "obtain," or the like! Similarly, the treatment of $\check{\epsilon}\gamma\nu\omega\sigma\alpha\nu$ in Matt. 24:39 ("and they did not know until the flood came") is weak and ambiguous for the same reason. Other examples occur in Acts 9:30 ($\check{\epsilon}\pi\iota\gamma\nu\acute{o}\nu\tau\epsilon\varsigma$), John 10:38 ($\gamma\nu\hat{\omega}\tau\epsilon$), Matt. 26:10 ($\gamma\nu\upsilon\acute{v}\varsigma$), Matt. 12:3 ($\check{\epsilon}\pi\epsilon\acute{\iota}\nu\alpha\sigma\epsilon\nu$), Mark 9:26; 14:17; Luke 8:24 ($\check{\epsilon}\gamma\acute{\epsilon}\nu\epsilon\tau o$).[18] The unfortunate lack of this distinction between linear and punctiliar action is probably responsible for the reading of the traditional and less well-supported $\check{\epsilon}\chi o\mu\epsilon\nu$ in Rom. 5:1 instead of the subjunctive $\check{\epsilon}\chi\omega\mu\epsilon\nu$.[19] Disregard for other kinds of tense usage may be exemplified by the iterative imperfect (Mark 11:19; Luke 5:15), the conative imperfect

14. *Ibid.*, p. 49.

15. (Chicago, 1946), p. 118.

16. *Introduction*, p. 51.

17. *Ibid.*

18. Other examples will be found in Matt. 5:1; John 11:35; Acts 28:21; Matt. 20:20; Rom. 6:13 (the present and aorist translated alike in "yield"); Jude, vs. 3 (the different force of present and aorist not represented in "to write").

19. See J. H. Moulton, *A Grammar of the Greek New Testament*, Vol. I: *Prolegomena* (Edinburgh, 1908), p. 110: "Misapprehension of the action-form of $\check{\epsilon}\chi\omega$ is responsible for most of the pother about $\check{\epsilon}\chi\omega\mu\epsilon\nu$ in Rom. 5:1." Cf. I Cor. 13:12, where the linear $\gamma\iota\nu\acute{\omega}\sigma\kappa\omega$ is really "I am acquiring knowledge" (as Moulton suggests, p. 113), in contrast to the perfective compound $\check{\epsilon}\pi\iota\gamma\iota\nu\acute{\omega}\sigma\kappa\omega$ in the same verse.

(Mark 9:38; Luke 9:49) and present (John 10:32), the progressive imperfect (Luke 4:30), the "stative" perfect (Luke 19:10) and pluperfect (John 7:37). In I Cor. 12:2 the phrase "however you may have been moved" seems partly the result of reading ἄν with ὡς, instead of recognizing its iterative force with the imperfect.[20]

The related use of the perfective compound verb is another phenomenon not always given careful attention. So, in Mark 1:36, κατεδίωξεν is translated "followed," although something like Goodspeed's "sought him out" is required. On the other hand, a compound would probably be used for "escape" (Matt. 23:33), the aorist being merely constative, as the revisers, indeed, render it in a parallel context in Matt. 3:7 ("flee from"). Similarly, the verb ἀπέχω retains its traditional, weak translation in the Gospel passages of Matt. 6:5 and parallels, notwithstanding the fact that Cadbury's excellent observation, "At Phil. 4:18 the verb is hardly represented in English by the simple present tense 'I have,' "[21] is as applicable here as in the Pauline citation, where it is given with its full papyrus-revealed flavor.[22]

Only a few other miscellaneous examples of questionable treatment of Greek syntax can be given here. In Matt. 7:4 (= Luke 6:42), ἄφες ἐκβάλω is simply and correctly "let me take . . . . out"; but in Matt 27:49 (Mark 15:36) the same construction (ἄφες ἴδωμεν) becomes "Wait, let us see," the revision thus maintaining a traditional, not logical, distinction.[23] Likewise in Heb. 3:1 the old rendering is retained, "Consider Jesus, etc.," through a failure, shared by most translators, to recognize the indirect-discourse construction of the participle ὄντα. And the same may perhaps be said of ὑπομεμενηκότα in Heb. 12:3. The middle voice causes some difficulty, e.g., in Rom. 3:9 (προεχόμεθα), where the marginal reading is more likely. It must be conceded that the translation "is washed" for λουσαμένη (II Pet. 2:22) is ambiguous

20. Cf. Moulton, *op. cit.*, p. 167.   21. *Introduction*, p. 48.

22. Other weak treatments of compounds will be found in Luke 4:10 (διαφυλάξαι), Luke 2:16 (ἀνεῦραν; cf. Acts 21:4, where the same verb is almost overtranslated), Acts 23:35 (διακούω), Mark 10:42 (κατακυριόω), Luke 2:19 (συντηρέω), Luke 20:14 (διαλογίζομαι).

23. Cf. Moulton, *op. cit.*, p. 175; cf. also John 12:7 and Mark 11:16.

enough to preclude any commitments regarding the pig's ablutions.[24] The forms ἐγήγερται and ἠγέρθη are translated as passives except in the post-Resurrection Gospel narrative and II Tim. 2:8. The distinction between the use in the latter and in such a passage as John 2:22 is not too clear, since the reference here is also to the post-Resurrection period.[25]

From a list of other readings which leave something to be desired for a variety of reasons, lexicographical as well as grammatical, we choose a few for special mention.

Matt. 26:25, 64, and parallels (σὺ εἶπας).—The noncommittal "You have said so," without a footnote hardly does justice to the widely held view of this as an affirmative response. Why the phrase σὺ λέγεις in 27:11 (cf. Mark 15:2) should be identically translated, when such pains are here taken to be literal, is one of the many minor mysteries of the version.

Luke 17:21 (ἐντὸς ὑμῶν).—One wonders what arguments—outside the school of "realized eschatology"—caused the adoption of a reading which is apparently contrary to all Greek usage, for it would be naturally understood as equivalent to "among you" (cf. Moffatt).

Acts 1:18 (πρηνὴς γενόμενος).—The translation "falling headlong" appears less likely than "swelling up," convincingly supported by Goodspeed in *Problems of Translation, ad loc.*, and read by himself and Moffatt in their respective versions.

Acts 6:2 (διακονεῖν τραπέζαις).—For "to serve tables" Field long ago pointed out the more plausible meaning, " to keep accounts," a rendering which well fits the context and is adopted again by both Moffatt and Goodspeed. In the R.S.V. it does not rate a footnote.

Acts 18:22 (ἀναβὰς καὶ ἀσπασάμενος τὴν ἐκκλησίαν).—Most modern translators have felt that the language implies the Jerusalem church and have added the words "to Jerusalem" in the text. The R.S.V. reading, in the absence of any marginal indication to

24. Cf. Moulton, *op. cit.*, pp. 155 f.

25. Cf. also ὑποταγήσεται, passive in I Cor. 15:28 and middle in Rom. 10:3 (ὑπετάγησαν). This follows the A.S.V. (cf. Col. 3:18, a reflexive middle). In Acts 24:27, R.S.V. has returned to the King James reading against A.S.V., Moffatt, and Goodspeed.

the contrary, must be taken, whether rightly or wrongly, as a reference to Antioch.

Mark 14:26 (ὑμνήσαντες).—Since a definite hymn, the Hallel, would be in mind, "the hymn" (so Moffatt and Goodspeed) rather than "a hymn" is preferable.

Mark 1:10 (σχιζομένους . . . . καταβαῖνον εἰς αὐτόν).—The heavens "opened" is a weak representation of the Marcan text and an inexcusable assimilation to Matthew and Luke, who thus altered Mark's picturesque terminology. Likewise "upon" for εἰς is inaccurate and obscures the difference between Mark and the other Synoptics. Though perhaps christologically unwelcome, the Marcan reading deserves recognition.

Acts 21:37 ('Ελληνιστὶ γινώσκεις).—"Do you speak Greek?" is the actual meaning of this elliptical expression.

Acts 28:6 (προσεδόκων αὐτὸν μέλλειν πίμπρασθαι).—There seems no justification for the treatment of the normal Greek indirect discourse as "They waited, expecting him to swell up, etc." It appears to be a conflation of Moffatt ("waited") and A.S.V. ("expected").

II Cor. 2:14 (θριαμβεύοντι).—The revisers' "in triumph" loses the original figure of the victor's triumphal procession.

Heb. 12:23 (πνεύμασι δικαίων τετελειωμένων).—Field pointed out the ambiguity of the traditional phraseology used here, "the spirits of just men made perfect," and cited examples from writings of his day where erroneous interpretations of the English occurred.[26]

Other dubious or weak items appear in Acts 26:28 ("you think to make me"), Mark 14:19 ("Is it I?"), Matt. 18:22 ("seventy times seven"), Luke 3:14 (the two statements are separate), Matt. 26:61 ("in three days"), Gal. 1:18 ("visit"), I Cor. 3:17 ("and that temple you are"), Rom. 12:1 ("spiritual worship"), Phil. 2:5 (vague), I Pet. 1:6, 8 (indicatives?), Matt. 2:1 ("wise men"), Matt. 8:20 ("nests"), III John 6 ("You will do well"), Luke 24:5 ("the living"), Acts 11:29 ("determined").[27]

26. F. Field, *Notes on Translation Problems of the New Testament* (Cambridge, England, 1899), pp. 233 f.

27. Others may be detected in Matt. 16:18; 21:32; Mark 1:23; 3:21; 4:40; 8:33; 13:14; Luke 1:3, 72; 10:31; 11:53; 13:1; 16:1; 18:7, 23; 22:6; John 3:10, 15, 25; 5:39; 8:25; 18:1,

In several of these passages we can readily observe that an explanatory footnote would have been a valuable adjunct to the text, both for its adequate comprehension and for some indication of legitimate and significant differences of interpretation and translation where such exist. The revisers do furnish about a hundred marginal notations indicating the literal Greek meaning where they depart from it, but these are obviously limited to a fraction of such instances and mostly to those involving the vocabulary of names, measurements, and the like.[28] Aside from these and the textual notes already described, there are practically no explanatory marginalia, for the revisers, in accordance with what is now established tradition, have considered these to be the business of the commentator.

Where, of course, a translation succeeds in conveying the real force of the original in clear and idiomatic language, the need for comment naturally decreases. Graphic illustration of genuine progress in this respect on the part of the R.S.V. may be seen by comparing it with its predecessors, on the one hand, and with modern speech translations, on the other. Using Goodspeed and Moffatt to represent the latter, we give two examples of this:

MATT. 20:15

K.J.   Is thine eye evil because I am good?
A.S.V.   or is thine eye evil because I am good?
R.S.V.   Or do you begrudge my generosity?
G.   Or do you begrudge my generosity?
M.   Have you a grudge because I am generous?

I COR. 7:21

K.J.   Art thou called being a servant? care not for it:
A.S.V.   Wast thou called being a bondservant? care not for it:
R.S.V.   Were you a slave when called? Never mind.
G.   If you were a slave when you were called, never mind.
M.   You were a slave when you were called? Never mind.

27; 21:5; Acts 3:22; 11:12; 13:34; 17:17; 19:15; 25:11, 16; Rom. 4:6; 7:14, 25; 8:3; 9:6, 30; I Cor. 4:6; 6:11; 10:33; 13:7; 16:2; Gal. 5:1; Tit. 3:8; Heb. 10:35.

28. Why the paronomasia in Philemon (Onesimus) and John 3:3 ($\pi\nu\epsilon\hat{\nu}\mu\alpha$) is explained but not ἄνωθεν, in the last passage, is not clear. There are some debatable instances of punctuation, as in Mark 1:27, I Cor. 16:3, and Heb. 3:15, where legitimate alternatives might be noted.

K.J.   But if thou mayest be made free, use it rather.

A.S.V.   nay, even if thou canst become free, use it rather.

R.S.V. But if you can gain your freedom, avail yourself of the opportunity.

M.   Of course, if you do find it possible to get free, you had better avail yourself of the opportunity.

G.   Even if you can gain your freedom, make the most of your present condition instead.

Here and elsewhere the improvement resulting from English in modern idiom is apparent. The latter half of the Corinthian passage also illustrates how divergent interpretations of the same Greek may be introduced into the English translation when attempts are made to remove rather than to reproduce its ambiguity. It is in just such instances that marginal comment would be useful.

As might well be expected, the influence of the Goodspeed and Moffatt versions are (happily) apparent in the revision and may be clearly seen in the use of unusual vocabulary and phraseology, especially where complete verses or sentences represent a rather free rendering of the Greek.[29] Available time has not permitted more than a very limited check with other versions which, as Professor Goodspeed implies in the *Introduction*,[30] have also made their contribution.

Further comparative study of this sort quickly shows that the R.S.V. has much more in common with the modern speech translations and with the A.S.V. than it does with the King James. This must be said only because of common allegations to the contrary. Something might be said for the retention of the *ancient* idiom and flavor of the text if it could be recaptured in English and if the mental outlook of the modern reader were the same as that of his first-century predecessors. Since these could never be generally or completely attained, however, it would seem preferable to move in the direction of contemporary, idiomatic speech. This the R.S.V. actually claims to do; and, in fact,

29. E.g., for Goodspeed: Luke 19:48; John 8:44; Rom. 2:11; II Cor. 1:14 ff.; 4:2; II Thess. 3:11; Heb. 9:16. For Moffatt: Acts 17:14; Rom. 16:17; I Cor. 1:26; 6:5; Heb. 10:24; II Pet. 2:4.

30. P. 35.

we may say that it is generally better than the A.S.V. in direct proportion to its departure from the errors, obscurities, and archaisms of the King James. This does not preclude the occasional adoption of some of the readings of the latter.

Here, again, not all was unmitigated advance. The revisers often appear to be moved to strike some sort of balance between the old and the new; and the partial modernization of vocabulary and idiom, especially in the pronominal and verbal forms, creates the immediate impression that revision is more in the direction of modern speech than it actually turns out to be. Detailed study and analysis of a few sections seem to indicate that it remains very close to the A.S.V. In Mark, chapter 1 and Rom. 1:1-17, for example, changes average only two to three per verse, the greater variation coming in the epistolary literature; and, if modernized spelling is not counted, the alteration is even less. In comparison, the English Revised Version averaged about four and a half differences per verse from the King James. All changes in word order amount only to eleven in Mark 1 and to ten in the Romans selection, a surprisingly small number in view of the repeated strictures on the literalism of the word order of the English and American Revised Versions by Dean Weigle and others. The very possibility of making statistical comparisons indicates the closeness of the two versions to each other.

This proximity of the two texts is unfortunately reflected in the considerable number of traditional, semi-obsolete, and sometimes unidiomatic and obscure expressions which, as we have already somewhat illustrated, impair its clarity and accuracy. A brief sampling reveals words like the following: *raiment, asunder, works, householder, behold, lo, brethren, begone, whence* and *hence, wont, render* (for "pay"), *walking* (for "living"), *vessels, smote;* or phrases such as: *made a feast, such a one* (for "a certain one"), *make haste, took his journey,* etc. The attempt is apparently also made to retain certain expressions felt to have traditional theological significance or association, as, e.g., *justify, justification, grace, righteousness, redemption.* But "expiation" is substituted for "propitiation" and "consecration" for "sanctification." "Dispensation" is introduced for διακονία in II Cor. 3:7–9.

Some antique phraseology, such as "Move hence to yonder place" (Matt. 17:21), is intelligible enough without explanation. Other expressions, like "cast up a bank" (Luke 19:43), must be understood from their context. But often the language may become highly obscure, as in "You are true . . . . and care for no man" (Matt. 22:16 = Mark 12:14), or in the many periphrastic Semitic idioms retained in the text, such as "horn of salvation" (Luke 1:69), "son of perdition" (John 17:12; II Thess. 2:3—a rendering which goes back to Wycliffe!), "poor in spirit" (Matt. 5:3), "children of wrath" (Eph. 2:3), etc.,[31] and literally reproduced physiological nomenclature.[32] Incidentally, the R.S.V. preserves the Semitic idiom ("his countenance fell") imported into the text of Mark 10:22.

Literalism of one sort or another is usually a contributory factor when questionable English is encountered. Some of this is traditional, such as the grammatical ambiguity in John 15:4 f. But inadequate translation of a Greek participle contributes one of the two ambiguities in Matt. 26:9. The nadir is probably reached in II Thess. 2:6 f., which really requires a note, since it is obscure in the Greek. Examples, also, of long and rather awkward sentences, which must be read to be depreciated, occur in Acts 26:16–18 and I Pet. 3:18–20.[33]

Thus the revisers, in spite of their declarations to the contrary, have often failed to avoid the traditional forms. This failure extends to sentence structure and word order also, although they have here made considerable progress by such expedients as varying the translation of καί to avoid excessive parataxis, and of intermittently altering or excluding such usages as καὶ ἐγένετο, καὶ ἀποκριθεὶς εἶπεν, the pleonastic λέγων, and the like. Yet they often continue literalisms like "Then went out to him all Jeru-

---

31. Others occur in Rom. 11:8; I Thess. 5:5; Luke 10:6; 20:36; Eph. 5:6.

32. This is inconsistently treated, as Professor Burrows explains (*Introduction*, p. 29). Cf. II Cor. 6:11–13.

33. Other unidiomatic or confusing terminology may be seen in Mark 2:23 ("ears of grain"!), Matt. 6:26 ("gather into barns"), Matt. 10:8 ("received without pay"), Eph. 1:4–13 (pronouns), Mark 6:48 ("distressed in rowing"), Matt. 14:7 ("with an oath"), Acts 25:2 ("urged . . . . asking . . . . planning"), Luke 20:11 (second "him" redundant), etc.

salem" (Matt. 3:5), "Consider the lilies of the field, how they grow" (Matt. 6:28), etc.[34] That this is sometimes due not to the Greek but to traditional English becomes apparent from examples like the *pendens* constructions in Luke 12:20 ("the things you have prepared, whose will they be?") or in Luke 3:11 ("He who has two coats, let him share, etc.").[35] In English there is an idiomatic order for certain commonly associated words forming couplets like "ham and eggs," "land and sea," "great and small," "good and bad." The last three occur in the R.S.V. in the reverse, Greek order (e.g., Matt. 22:10; 23:15; Acts 26:22; Rev. 13:16), a form which irritates one's stylistic susceptibilities and contributes nothing to euphony.

Again, the proposed mitigation of parataxis is not consistently carried out, the phenomenon appearing here and there in a painful, pristine state. For good (or "bad") examples one may consult Matt. 2:14 f.; 17:1–4; Mark 1:16–24; 6:3–7; 8:1–10; 10:32–34; 15:16–29; Luke 2:3–13; etc. In the last passage nine sentences in succession are introduced by *and;* while in Luke 15:16–29 sixteen successive sentences and in Mark 1:16–24 nine successive verses are likewise initiated. Since no attempt was being made to reproduce the flavor of the Greek in general, the recurrence of these unalleviated καί sequences is a bit puzzling.[36] There are still places, also, where variation is really required by the context, as in Matt. 17:16 and Heb. 3:9 (reflecting that poverty of Semitic conjunctions about which the *Introduction* tells us), or where it would have clarified the meaning, as in Luke 24:26, I Cor. 10:8 ff., and John 5:39. In instances like Luke 7:12 a relative pronoun would suffice.

The perennial problem of what to do with such things as coinage, weights, measurements, etc., the revisers have met with an attempt to retain the ancient nomenclature, together with an explanatory footnote. But here again discrepancies may be found. The English "pounds" is retained in Luke 19:13 ff. and "pounds"

34. Cf. Mark 14:3; Acts 7:23; Luke 22:12; Matt. 2:3.

35. Cf. Mark 1:7; John 1:11; Matt. 7:27.

36. In Luke-Acts and a few other places the revisers become almost overpartial to the use of a resumptive "Now," especially in beginning paragraphs (but cf. I Cor. 15:20).

(weight) in John 19:39. In Rev. 6:6 ("A quart of wheat for a denarius") the *choinix* measure is modernized but not the money. Matt. 22:19, however, reads "a coin" for "a denarius," an expedient which would hardly be welcome to interpreters for whom it is important that this particular coin had the emperor's image on it. In Luke 21:2 "copper coins" occurs for *lepta*, without a note. Some Jewish terms are retained from the A.S.V.: "shekel" for *stater* in Matt. 17:27, but without the note; "half-shekel" for *didrachma* in Matt. 17:24. In Luke 12:25 "cubit" is undefined. Luke 24:13 and John 6:19 employ "miles" for the Greek *stadia*, but Rev. 14:20 and 21:16 read "stadia." Time indications are usually in the ancient form, but in Acts 19:9 a textual variant giving Paul's hours for discussion is translated as "from eleven o'clock to four" in the footnotes. Some modernizing of names and customs appears, such as "Malta" in Acts 28:1 and "sitting" for "reclining" at the table.

In attempting to characterize the revision so far, we find ourselves thus often alluding to a quality of inconsistency. We should recall, however, that the revisers definitely proposed to vary translations of the same Greek word or words in accordance with the legitimate demands of the context. To this laudable procedure there can be no objection, and the R.S.V. furnishes some notable exemplifications of it, as, e.g., in six different renderings of διαλογίζομαι in eleven occurrences. While due allowance must, therefore, be made for personal judgment in the matter, it appears that the actual results must often be described as vacillation rather than variation, especially as between traditional and modern idiom. So, for example, δικαίωσις is "justification" in Rom. 4:25, but "acquittal" in 5:18; and δικαιόω is "acquitted" in I Cor. 4:4 (the only time), but "justified" in 6:11 and elsewhere in the volume.[37] Yet variation from "justified" would not be amiss in places like Luke 7:29 and 35 (=

---

37. Of 15 occurrences of δικαιόω in Romans, all but one (6:7, "freed") are rendered "justified," its usual translation. "Freed" also is found in Acts 13:39 twice, and "vindicated" in I Tim. 3:16. The term δικαιοσύνη is rendered "righteousness" or equivalent in all but 11 of 89 uses. The exceptions are "justice" (Rom. 3:5; Heb. 11:33; Acts 24:25), "right" (Eph. 5:9; I John 2:29; 3:7, 10; Rev. 22:11; Acts 10:35), "justification" (Gal. 2:21), and "piety" (Matt. 6:1).

Matt. 11:19). Apropos of this last, it may be pointed out that the revision does fairly well in preserving Synoptic parallelism. I Cor. 5:6 and Gal. 5:9 may be compared for needless variation in rendering the same Greek. The translation "He who through faith is righteous shall live," adopted in Rom. 1:17 and Gal. 3:11, is not used in Heb. 10:38, although the context seems to refer the quotation here also to the Christian. The troublesome ἰδού is generally translated "behold," sometimes "lo" (an outbreak of these occurs in Matthew, chap. 24, and some spots in Revelation). Sometimes it is untranslated. But "look," which usually translates ἴδε, occurs for ἰδού in Luke 22:38, and "behold" for ἴδε in Mark 15:35. The epistolary plural alternates with the singular in bewildering fashion in II Corinthians, both occurring sometimes in the same verse (e.g., 1:13; 5:11; 7:12; 10:2, 8). The plurals supposedly are meant sometimes to reflect Paul's inclusion of fellow-workers in his thought; yet chapter 10 would seem to be highly personal throughout. The variety exhibited in the treatment of μὴ γένοιτο would appear to have its origin in the preference of particular translators, as doubtless others of these phenomena do. It is always translated "By no means" in Romans (eight times), but "Certainly not" in Galatians (2:17 and 3:21), "Never" in I Cor. 6:15, and by the traditional "God forbid" in Luke 20:16.[38] A final example may be cited from the rendering of δοῦλος, where the R.S.V. policy is apparently to retain "servant" unless the context makes "slave" necessary. Yet Luke 2:29 loses the figure of the original text with its traditional "Lord, now lettest thou thy servant depart in peace," a survival from Tyndale. Professor Goodspeed's emphasis in the *Introduction*[39] on the importance of correctly translating this "unmistakable Greek word for slave" seems to have gone unheeded in many instances. "The second word in Romans is 'slave,'" he writes; but when we turn to the R.S.V. the second word in Romans is "servant"!

---

38. In Gal. 6:14 the construction is not independent and requires some other rendering. It is translated "far be it. . . . ."

39. Pp. 33 f.

The various observations which we have been making about the revision all bear in one way or another, of course, upon the question of the readability and euphony of its English. Since we have tended to overemphasize the defects of the work, one might be moved to false conclusions on these points. Actually, the translation reads very well, for the increased clarity of the English more than counterbalances the traditional obscurities which still remain. One other quality may be mentioned which bears upon the achievement of these desiderata and militates somewhat against it, namely, an overconciseness of style, which often produces a staccato effect in the English. While preferable to the unintelligible and soporific cadences which have frequently stifled the religious message of the New Testament in the past, it could easily have been overcome by the use of more words.[40]

Again, in conclusion, we may repeat that the general merits of the work before us considerably outweigh the types of deficiencies upon which we have concentrated our attention. These merits have been sufficiently indicated, however, and may be conveniently summarized by saying that the revision has made notable progress in the attainment of its stated aims. That it has retained much from its predecessors is a characteristic naturally inherent in revisions. In the R.S.V. some of this is due to incomplete application of its own methodology; some may be aptly inferred from the frank confession of Professor Burrows ". . . . again tradition and associations were too strong for us."[41]

Thus, while the R.S.V. of the New Testament faces, Janus-like, in two directions at once, it nevertheless represents a significant step in the achievement of the most accurate English text and in the emancipation of the English Bible from the fetters of archaism. For this all will be grateful to the revisers,[42] who

40. Cf. *Introduction*, p. 57, where Dean Weigle illustrates that the revision is shorter than the A.S.V., which, in turn, was shorter than the King James. The R.S.V. has been estimated at 20,000 words less than the A.S.V.

41. *Introduction*, p. 24.

42. The major part of the work was done among the following nine members of the New Testament committee: Dean Luther A. Weigle, Yale University Divinity School, *chairman;* Professor Henry J. Cadbury, Harvard University; Professor Emeritus Edgar J.

have labored sacrificially in the execution of an exacting task and to the International Council of Religious Education, which sponsored the undertaking.

Goodspeed, University of Chicago; The late Professor James Moffatt, Union Theological Seminary; the Rev. Walter Russell Bowie, Grace Church, New York; Professor Frederick C. Grant, Union Theological Seminary; Professor Millar Burrows, Yale University; Professor Clarence T. Craig, Oberlin Graduate School of Theology; President Abdel R. Wentz, Lutheran Theological Seminary, Gettysburg. Service was also rendered temporarily by the late Professors W. P. Armstrong, Princeton Theological Seminary; James Hardy Ropes, Harvard University; and Andrew Sledd, Emory University.

Old Testament Theology: Its Possibility and Methodology

OTTO J. BAAB

Garrett Biblical Institute, Evanston, Illinois

SINCE the Renaissance and the Reformation, remarkable progress has been made in the study of the Bible. The revival of classical learning was characterized by a new interest in the languages in which the ancient classics and the Scriptures were written. The breakdown of medieval authoritarianism permitted the mind of the individual biblical scholar to examine freely and critically the documents which were the foundation of his faith. Criticism came into its own, with the result that its basic assumptions and method are now firmly established.

The results of the wholehearted acceptance of the canons of literary-historical criticism are impressive. The discovery and study of manuscripts, various editions, and collations of the ancient versions, such as the Septuagint text; the development of research in Hebrew, Aramaic, and Greek grammar; and the discovery and translation of new texts, notably the Ugaritic inscriptions, have provided valuable material for the preparation of critical editions of the Hebrew Old Testament and the Greek New Testament. It is this textual research which has made necessary the preparation of various modern translations and versions of the English Bible. Through the labors of scholars in this field a steady flow of new material is made available for the reconstruction and emendation of the biblical text. Thus no commentary can remain up to date. The widely used "International Critical Commentary," some volumes of which were written half a century ago, illustrates this point.

401

Biblical criticism has also achieved notable success since the time of Wellhausen in identifying the sources of the Pentateuch and in throwing a flood of light upon questions of date, authorship, religious ideas, and social-political background in connection with the individual books of the Old Testament. The cultural history of the ancient Near East has been dramatized with striking vividness through the work of such scholars as Olmstead[1] and Albright.[2] Historical discoveries in the biblical world have required the re-writing of the history of the Hebrews and a re-examination of the development of their religion. Consequently, a detailed knowledge of the Hebrew text, of the nature of the individual books of the Old Testament, of the history of Israel's social, political, and economic institutions, and of the origin and growth of her religious ideas has been made available through the technical skill and research of modern Old Testament scholarship.

Apparently, it simply remains, then, for this scholarship to continue its good work in order that the full literary beauty, moral grandeur, and religious appeal of the Old Testament may be comprehended by an increasing number of persons. If this is the case, the obligation imposed upon Old Testament scholars is easily defined: continued scientific research brought to bear upon textual, literary, and historical problems—a research which involves inductive analysis and objective description. While this assumption as to the present and future task of Old Testament scholarship is evidently generally accepted by American scholars in particular, this acceptance is by no means unanimous. For example, on the occasion of the celebration of the fiftieth anniversary of the founding of the Chicago Society for Biblical Research a few years ago, the theme selected by the program committee was "The Minister and the Biblical Critic." The principal speaker attempted to analyze the value of the critic's work to the preacher and pastor. Whatever else the selection of this theme signified, it certainly indicated the anxiety of the members of the Society regarding the religious consequences of their biblical re-

1. A. T. Olmstead, *The History of Palestine and Syria* (New York, 1931).
2. W. F. Albright, *Archaeology and the Religion of Israel* (Baltimore, 1942).

search. A number of volumes recently published betray this same concern.[3]

It is a disturbing fact that at the very time when biblical criticism has become thoroughly established as a discipline and when its conclusions and viewpoints have been widely disseminated through both popular and technical publications, general biblical illiteracy prevails. Still more serious is the general indifference to biblical teachings and beliefs. Both the liberal Protestant and the liberal Jew are inclined to minimize or to ignore the Bible as the authoritative basis for faith and conduct. The religious liberal thoroughly subscribes to the approach of the biblical critic—and is untouched by the biblical truths which the latter finds. Modern man's dilemma is created by this failure to find a source of authority possessing ultimate validity and capable of giving him lasting peace in his personal and collective life. If he is an educated churchman, he finds it impossible to follow the ultra-conservatives, to whom the unquestioned Bible is the very word of life. However wistfully he regards the simple biblical faith of his conservative contemporary, he is unable to enter into that faith.

For the creation of this dilemma, disregarding general cultural and sociological factors, the biblical scholar of the modern school must accept a large measure of responsibility. The very vigor and thoroughness of his analysis have served to emphasize to the modern mind the variety of the facts assembled rather than any single religious meaning which these facts may have. Authority comes to religion when that which is of supreme worth is found. Such an object of absolute devotion, when found, cannot be the subject of analysis and criticism with respect to its fundamental nature and value. If, therefore, the Old Testament is determined to be primarily the record of a historical culture—the Israelite—whose ingredients were drawn from the ancient civilization arising in the Fertile Crescent, the values in this literature would appear to be only conditional and relative. If the reader of the Old Testament follows his critical guides, he

3. G. E. Wright, *The Challenge of Israel's Faith* (Chicago, 1944); R. B. Y. Scott, *The Relevance of the Prophets* (New York, 1944); W. C. Bower, *The Living Bible* (New York, 1936).

encounters a series of documents recording the various stages through which the Hebrew idea of God developed as men searched for this Being with varying degrees of success and wrote down what they had found. This historical viewpoint acts as a substitute for the religious viewpoint and produces the end-result of obscuring the final Word of God which conceivably lies within the Old Testament.

We do well, then, to inquire whether the work of the Old Testament critic, fruitful as it is in the accumulation of information, leads to a dead-end street, as far as religious faith is concerned. Is the very nature of the historical-critical method inimical to a religious use of the Bible? This is the crucial question which is really involved in recent inquiries as to the possibility and method of formulating an Old Testament theology.[4] Perhaps the debate on this question betrays an uneasy conscience, produced by the religious barrenness characterizing the results of biblical criticism. This debate may mark the beginning of a new period in Old Testament scholarship in America. Yesterday the critic was completely absorbed in textual, literary, and historical research. Tomorrow this same critic and the new generation of scholars now arising will continue inductive study along conventional lines, but they will also face the task of integrating their materials into a pattern of living religious experience intelligible and communicable to their own age. This integration will take a form which may best be described as "biblical theology" or, for the purposes of this particular essay, "Old Testament theology." Up to the present, titles of books by biblical specialists reveal a preoccupation with the history of biblical literature, institutions, and ideas. It is impossible to find a single book written in English since World War I which can be called a survey of Old Testament theology, unless a history of religious ideas can be so designated.

With the recent awakening of interest in this area of research the appearance of volumes on biblical theology may be expected.

4. J. D. Smart, "The Death and Rebirth of Old Testament Theology," *Journal of Religion*, Vol. XXIII, Nos. 1 and 2 (1943); W. A. Irwin, "The Reviving Theology of the Old Testament," *Journal of Religion*, Vol. XXIV, No. 4 (1945).

However, such work may not be undertaken by the Old Testament scholar unless he can justify his purpose and his method by the standards of rigorous scientific research. It is the major task of this essay to examine various approaches to the writing of Old Testament theology in order to test their validity and to arrive at an approach which appears to the writer to be both tenable and workable.

Old Testament theology has usually been written either dogmatically or historically. In the first instance the presuppositions of the author determine a priori what is found in the biblical sources. By logical deduction from these premises the data are systematized into a coherent pattern whose unifying principle is not the living experience of the men of the Bible but rather the creed of the so-called "critic" who conceives his task as confirmation instead of investigation. The earliest Christian attempts to use the Old Testament theologically probably took the form of a collection of prophetic passages suggesting the presence of a messianic teaching. The messianic element in this literature was ascertained not by objective study of the documents but by looking for evidence in support of early Christian views of the life and character of Jesus. More formally and logically, the Church Fathers applied the same criterion to the Old Testament and found therein ideas of judgment, sacrifice, and salvation which they themselves held before undertaking their study. Consequently, Old Testament theology was Christian theology of one kind or another, not only because it was written by Christian scholars but also because its aim was to validate doctrines of the New Testament by reference to the Old.

This Christian dogmatism dominating Old Testament interpretation until the modern period may not be dismissed or treated too lightly. It is true that it was not scientific or inductive in its approach to biblical truth. It is also true that proof-text exegesis frequently provided a distorted view of the teachings of the Old Testament, with the result that its authors were made to say what they never intended to say. Nonetheless, dogmatism, in its insistence upon the continuity of historical revelation, rendered a valuable service by affirming an important truth. Even though

dogmatism's zeal for documenting its Christian faith by drawing upon Hebrew sources caused it to overlook the historical situations conditioning the biblical text, this zeal was motivated by a true insight that history cannot be atomistically conceived. Rather, its events, appearing in time and space, possess a relationship of meaning which derives from a cosmic reality, whose name is God. This is particularly true of that portion of human history recording the appearance of the Hebrew-Christian religion in Palestine. The first man, Adam, and the last man, Christ, the Son of God, stand at the ends of a historical movement in which a complete and unique revelation of the nature of God and man has been made. Over against this may be placed the approach of the undogmatic interpreter, who patiently, book by book, author by author, period by period, explores his material until he has amassed data in encyclopedic quantities. Absorbed in this heroic task, he may either miss its central significance or declare that the problem of meaning is not his responsibility.

The inadequacy of the dogmatic method of writing Old Testament theology is, however, apparent in a fairly consistent disregard for the historical method and for its intellectual demands. Unless all the ground gained by the human mind and spirit since the Renaissance is to be surrendered, the dogmatic emphasis cannot be tolerated. Freedom of inquiry, tolerance of ideas which are not approved, factual observation, classification and evaluation of data, comparative analysis of sources, continuous verification of conclusions, and the unremitting search for new knowledge have achieved priceless results in emancipating the mind of men from ignorance and gross superstition. For this reason the liberal biblical critic must cherish his heritage of intellectual freedom and use it with increasing diligence in furthering his research.

It is the "liberal" biblical scholar who has produced the type of Old Testament theology which may be called "historical" in comparison with the dogmatic emphasis just discussed. By this is meant theology which is written with a full use of the scientific principles subscribed to by the critic. Here the biblical documents are identified and compared, the historical background is

determined, the authorship examined, and the relationship of their particular teachings to their contemporary culture is considered. With these and similar questions the historical student occupies himself. If he tries to write a theology of the Old Testament—provided he admits the possibility of such a venture— these are the questions which he will ask. An examination of Davidson's work[5] or that of Sellin[6] reveals that these theologies of the Old Testament are written from this historical standpoint. Each is conscious of the development of religious ideas in the various periods of Israel's history; each treats the Old Testament books critically; and each is inductive rather than deductive in his treatment of the biblical text. Sellin's outline gives the impression of an emphasis upon ideas and thus suggests an outline of doctrine, but his treatment is actually a textual and literary study of relevant sections of the Old Testament in their relationship to the concepts of God, man, sin, the future life, the Messiah, and the like. Köhler,[7] Eichrodt,[8] and others have written in a similar manner, although they differ in details with respect to emphasis and viewpoint. An author may choose to develop his thesis upon the basis of historical periods, such as the Mosaic, the Conquest, the early monarchy, and so forth; or he may utilize a topical outline based on religious concepts, such as the nature of God, the ideas of sin and salvation. In either case he conceives as his task an accurate description of the religious teachings of Israel in the light of the appropriate historical setting.

Publications of this type are similar to other Old Testament works which make no reference to theology in their titles.[9] Volumes in this category deal admittedly with the historical study of Israel's religious ideas and practices, whether the emphasis is upon chronological development or upon the description of specific concepts, with a minimization of the chronological prin-

5. A. B. Davidson, *The Theology of the Old Testament* (Edinburgh, 1904).

6. E. Sellin, *Theologie des Alten Testaments* (Leipzig, 1933).

7. L. H. Köhler, *Theologie des Alten Testaments* (Tübingen, 1936).

8. W. Eichrodt, *Theologie des Alten Testaments* (3 vols.; Leipzig, 1933–39).

9. A. C. Knudson, *Religious Teachings of the Old Testament* (New York, 1918); H. W. Robinson, *Religious Ideas of the Old Testament* (New York, 1913); W. O. E. Oesterley and T. H. Robinson, *Hebrew Religion* (2d. ed.; New York, 1937).

ciple. The Old Testament, for these writers, is regarded as the record of a definite, historical, religious culture, whose main features may be identified through the use of the critic's tools with the same precision as that involved in the excavation of an ancient artifact by an expert archeologist. Israel's religion is the product of a historical culture; and an exact description of that culture and the religion which it produced is the task of the writer of Old Testament theology as it is of the scholar who wishes to compose a history of the religion of Israel.

If such literary efforts may be called "Old Testament theology," their value lies in their lack of bias or dogmatism, it would appear. Presumably, any critical biblical scholar, skilled in the use of the tools of his craft, whether he be conservative or liberal, Protestant or Catholic or Jew, could formulate a historical theology of the Old Testament which would be essentially the same as that produced by others using the same methods and source materials. Fundamental differences would be the measure of failure to use fully the critical methodology and resources. Such must be the case, for the conclusions of scientists are presumed to be uniform or harmonious with one another when finally verified and accepted. Ideally, therefore, there can be only one theology of the Old Testament, critically determined, as there can be only one biology or astronomy, when all is said and done. Such a theology could theoretically win the acceptance of all scholars, no matter what their religious connections, provided that all subscribed to the tenets and premises of a historical-critical methodology. Here would be, in truth, a scientific theology of the Old Testament, verifiable, communicable, and universal in its appeal to intelligent human beings.

Old Testament theology, formulated scientifically and historically, also has the value of social concreteness and vitality, for such theology is the theistic ideology of a particular community of people, the Hebrews, living with other communities in a time and a world whose tensions and temper can be discovered and described with dramatic vividness by the competent scholar. While the Old Testament theologian—if such there be—extracts from their social-historical context the characteristic re-

ligious ideas of the Hebrew scriptures and attempts to present them according to a systematic pattern, he is constantly able to consult historical records for verifying and clarifying his conclusions. He is able to test his results pragmatically by reference to the historical experience of a people whose faith was hammered out upon the anvil of adversity and social conflict. The result is a "grass-roots" theology, capable of empirical confirmation and social application. Originating in the market place of Bethel, the village of Moresheth-Gath, the city of Jerusalem, and the foreign land of Babylonia and in a time of economic conflict, international struggle, and social upheaval, this theology—the product of human struggle as well as of revelation—as voiced by Israel's religious leaders, was the verbal expression of spiritual realities the acceptance of which was deemed to be essential to national security and peace.

Hebrew history may be viewed as a demonstration of Hebrew faith, a demonstration which is both positive and negative. Hebrew historians consciously interpreted the history of their people in terms of the creative and ethical activity of the living God. In national disaster they saw his judgment, in victory his loving kindness and mercy. At all times events confirmed his nature and will for men. Thus historical biblical study brings to light the very circumstances and situations which had theological significance to the writers of the Old Testament. It is not difficult, therefore, assuming the continuity of the historical process, to find stimulus in this literature for the study of the theological meaning of world events in our own time, a period in which conflict, social cleavages, and religious confusion provide points of resemblance to the ancient biblical world.

Another great value may be found in the historical approach to the writing of Old Testament theology. It has already been indicated that theology, when written descriptively and with scientific objectivity, becomes communicable to representatives of all faiths and cultures, provided that the principle of objectivity in the study of religion is recognized. This opens the way to a general knowledge and possible acceptance of the truths contained in the Old Testament. If the secret of the atomic bomb is

no secret at all because scientists in many lands know the principles governing the fission of the atom and have the skill to master the engineering difficulties, so the knowledge of the nature of the God of Israel cannot be confined to one race or one people; any group admitting the validity of scientific research may have this knowledge—learned Moslems, intelligent Hindus, scholarly Buddhists, and university-bred Christians. While none of these may be persuaded to follow the way of life which the religion of the Old Testament identifies, they may, nonetheless, become informed as to its principal tenets through theological research, which is as unbiased as the work of the physicist or chemist.

In spite of these values inhering in the historical-critical technique as applied to the problems of Old Testament theology, one pronounced weakness should be noted. The reader of histories of Hebrew religion or of Old Testament theologies of the *Religionsgeschichte* school is impressed by evidence which points toward the existence in the biblical writings of not one but several theologies. He learns that Israel's religion unfolded through definite stages, such as animatism, animism, polydemonism, polytheism, henotheism, and monotheism, according to a developmental principle that is consistently illustrated in all religions. The Bible's chronological strata show a variety of religious patterns, each one of which is relative and conditioned upon the culture producing and sustaining it. There is not only variety but disparity between these religious patterns. The task of presenting a single theology of the Old Testament appears to be a hopeless one. While some scholars seemingly continue the effort, they actually are compelled to devote themselves to historical description rather than to theological formulation and evaluation. This certainly is the emphasis among English-speaking scholars, as cited works amply attest.

Such an emphasis may still result in a biblical theology, according to D. S. Adam's definition.[10] "Of itself it [biblical theology] is a purely historic discipline, aiming at the accurate presentation of historic fact and recorded thought in an impartial ob-

10. In his article "Theology," *Encyclopedia of Religion and Ethics*, XII, 297.

jective way without meantime taking into account the bearing of that on permanent normative religious truth." Obviously, this must be the aim of the biblical theologian if the Old Testament is regarded as mainly a depository of interesting but loosely related ideas and customs. When he has given an accurate account of these, his work is done. Yet the question remains, Can the term "theology" be applied to this type of research? The answer is an affirmative one only if Adam's definition is held to be valid. What if the "accurate presentation of historic fact" produces a miscellaneous assortment of religious data whose chief relationship is provided by the accident of preservation in a common literature? Can such a collection of facts be called a "theology"? We are back where we started—with the historian of religion whose work is exciting to the student or scientist but relatively meaningless for meeting the issues of life. A theology of the Old Testament must be one, not many. The historical emphasis as commonly interpreted in terms of analysis and objective description appears to be incompatible with this requirement of unity.

Adam's definition, as well as that of many writers adhering to the critical school, reveals a serious inadequacy at another point also. This definition declares that biblical theology cannot take into account "the bearing of that [historic fact] on permanent normative religious truth." So it would appear that the theology of the Old Testament must remain neutral as far as ultimate validity and meaning are concerned. Yet it cannot be denied that theology—when it is not confused with biblical criticism—is the systematic formulation of religious ideas held to be true representations of ultimate reality as that reality affects the life and destiny of men. Theology always claims to be unique, exclusive, and final in its pronouncements. It may do this without dogmatism; still its claims imply finality and completeness for the truths which it affirms. It cannot be content to state propositions which are tentatively offered as being possibly true. On the contrary, it asserts vigorously and confidently what it believes to be true regarding the spiritual realities which are considered indispensable to man's salvation. This sense of certainty does not pre-

vent utilization by the theologian of the discoveries of natural science, philosophy, and history in order to give belief a rational basis. Unless Old Testament theology has relevance for an understanding of religious realities which are inherent in the structure of the universe, it had better be called by another name.

Lest it be said that this requirement of ultimate truth for Old Testament theology precludes scientific objectivity, in that the philosophical and religious presuppositions of the biblical scholar are involved, it should be added that such presuppositions, when rigorously scrutinized and consciously controlled, are more appropriate than the typical presuppositions of a goodly number of critics who write histories of Israel's religion. We may note, for example, the common fallacy of asserting the superior value of beliefs which represent a later, rather than an earlier, stage of culture. This time fallacy has affected many of the books written about biblical religion in recent years. Various forms of naturalistic philosophy also influence and color the work of biblical scientists. For example, the preoccupation of scientific naturalism with the phenomenal world of sense-experience and its inclination to reduce everything to empirical terms have been carried over into biblical research. The result may be the modernization of biblical writers and ideas to the point of distortion.

These constitute but two of a number of examples of uncritical modernization which makes true scientific detachment impossible. It may be granted that presuppositions of some sort are unavoidable. The question is: Shall they be those of some contemporary philosophy, or attitudes which are engendered by a thorough absorption in the spirit and viewpoint of the biblical records themselves? The suitability of an attempt to prepare an Old Testament theology which is valid because purporting to represent universal truth lies both in the need of modern men and in the fact that such validity is continuously claimed by the Old Testament itself for the major beliefs which it records. When Old Testament research is pushed to the limit and not restricted by assumptions derived from the scholar's philosophical position, such a claim and the religious experiences from which it

grew will be given at least as much weight as is attached to matters of text and historical event.

The methodology for Old Testament theology requires a full and unhesitating use of the scientific techniques peculiar to objective research. The biblical documents must be read in the light of extra-biblical inscriptions of Canaanite, Babylonian, and Assyrian origin, as these exhibit the homogeneous culture of the Near East in biblical times. Every aspect and facet of the life which gave rise to the Old Testament requires intensive investigation. The history of the Israelites, their religious and political leaders, their moral standards, social customs, and religious beliefs, merit diligent study. And beyond all these and other recognized subjects of biblical research there lies a relatively unexplored area of experience which is of supreme importance in creating an Old Testament theology—the religious consciousness of the writers who were responsible for this literature. A quest for all the facts relative to the Old Testament cannot ignore this conspicuous fact standing out in every book and page of Scripture, that its authors were poignantly aware of an influence from without, which they acknowledged to be the power and activity of God.

The Old Testament's "Thus saith the Lord" or "The Word of the Lord is like a burning fire in my bones" and scores of similar statements demonstrate conclusively the orientation of its prophets and saints toward the God who spoke to and through them. The critic may declare that these men were mistaken and confused a personal ethical urge with divine revelation, but he must acknowledge the existence of these passages and offer an explanation of their prominence. This is a substantial datum with which he is compelled to reckon. The literary evidence of this religious consciousness cannot be lightly dismissed as scribal glosses or corruption of the text—a device not unknown to scholars into whose theories the biblical text does not fit—since such evidence permeates the language and thought of the entire Old Testament.

Apart from this fact of the Old Testament's religious consciousness, any real understanding of this literature is impossible. The expert may exercise his skill in extricating from the records

of the life of biblical man information respecting social customs and economic and political institutions. Yet the dead past which the historian thus reconstructs remains dead, because the quickening power of religious faith which once animated it eludes him. Thus Amos may be envisioned as a social reformer rather than as a man of God called from following his flock. Or the priestly writer of Genesis, chapter 1, may be viewed as the literary craftsman who skilfully revised an old Babylonian myth and not as a man caught in the grip of a mighty truth regarding God and the world. The key to the understanding of biblical religion and history is the biblical faith by which biblical men lived.

Any effort to explain away this experience of God or the supernatural in the Old Testament betrays an unscientific bias which is unfriendly both to biblical religion and to truth. For example, an interpretation of the familiar phrase, "The Word of the Lord came to . . . ." as signifying simply the figurative language of the Hebrew prophets or editors, whereby they indicated the importance of what they had to say, reveals a serious misunderstanding of prophetic psychology and religion. Such an interpretation is a polite way of reducing God to a figure of speech. Surely, the language which the prophets themselves used nowhere justifies this attitude. Their words and their deeds reveal their intense realization of the divine will working in and through them. Their courageous defiance of the status quo and stern criticism of powerful rulers in the name of God would be inexplicable apart from their personal experience of a living God who was far more than the verbal symbols used to describe him.

Critical and constructive theological research begins, then, with the central and controlling experience of the men of the Old Testament—the experience of God—and goes on from that point to identify the major concepts of religious experience to the extent that these are amenable to formulation and systematization. This process will necessitate the establishment of certain criteria which can both guide our research and validate its results. First, we may note the criterion of logical consistency by the operation of which the elements within any one religious concept and the several concepts in their relation to one another are made to fit

together as parts of a whole. The second criterion is that of empirical verification. Do the basic concepts of Old Testament religion correspond with experience so meaningfully that their truth may be validated thereby? While other criteria could be set forth the two mentioned are of primary importance and will serve the purpose of this discussion.

To illustrate the application of the first-named principle, that of logical consistency, reference will be made to the idea of God in the Old Testament. Here the difficulty of our task is apparently insurmountable. How can logical consistency be found when the reader is confronted by many gods and by contradictory traits of the one God? In the Old Testament, God appears to be a strange being, wrathful and vindictive, merciful and benevolent, righteous and vengeful, creative and destructive, a fierce fighter, a loving father, concerned for but one people, ruling over all men. The books of the Old Testament contain allusions to demons, gods of fertility, the God of Israel, and the God of the universe. How can the student of biblical theology find God among these gods? Is there a unitary Being which the Old Testament writings present with convincing unanimity? Examination reveals that there is, even though various characteristics of the divine nature may be overemphasized to the point of distortion in certain books or sources.

The Hebrew Scriptures are in fundamental agreement as to the power, holiness, righteousness, and redemptive love of God, notwithstanding that his rule is nationalistic in some writings and universal in others, or creative and constructive in some and righteously destructive in others. Even such books as Leviticus show how the good and holy God of Israel may be approached. He is central in the elaborate Temple ritual. The Book of Judges, containing considerable evidence of crude religious feeling and practice, as a book is a remarkable documentation of the moral majesty of a God who rules the history of men or, in particular, the men of Israel. As soon as the critic abandons his insistence upon the progressive development of the religion of the Old Testament through gradual stages, each of which is higher than that which preceded it, and permits the text to speak for itself, he

may be in a position to discern a logically self-consistent ethical monotheism in much of the Old Testament.

It is true that this consistency is by no means perfect, for the Hebrew writers were more interested in the drama of life than in the nature and relationship of ideas. They reported those personal and national experiences which seemed to them significant in revealing the nature and purposes of God. Further, Old Testament books, particularly Genesis, contain legendary source material, the contradictory portions of which were frequently left undisturbed by compilers. When an entire biblical book is surveyed, however, the undeveloped religious ideas which it contains may possibly be viewed as archaisms or unexpurgated survivals from a primitive cultural period. These compilers and editors were zealous both to defend or propagate a particular viewpoint and to preserve traditions handed down from the past.

It is significant that no Old Testament author or editor is conscious of being an innovator in his presentation of truth. All assume the continuity with the past of the message which they record. Israel's greatest creative thinkers—the prophets—constantly assume and maintain that their messages carry the weight of historical experience. They exhort and condemn in the light of past revelation, going back even to the days of the Exodus to support their contentions. Prophets, priests, poets, and sages alike insist upon the special character of the religious themes to which they all address themselves and whose time-tested validity they never question.

In the very variety of approach and interpretation evident in their work, the unity of their teachings becomes all the more apparent. In the prophet's vision, the priest's sacrifice, the poet's hymn of praise, and the sage's sayings, the God of righteousness and redemptive love is made manifest, sometimes dimly, sometimes with awe-inspiring vividness. There is but one basic theistic position in the Old Testament, and its principal elements fit into a general logical pattern.

The criterion of empirical verification is used to test the correspondence between what is believed to be true about God and

man and what is actually experienced by the community and the individual in relation to these beliefs. Such a correspondence is an outstanding characteristic of Old Testament theology. The God of the Hebrews is a living God, revealing his righteousness and mercy in the continuing historical process. Political events and social conflicts are always viewed by the biblical writers in terms of the nature and will of God. History is never regarded as the result of natural forces operating automatically; instead, it is the account of man's obedience to, or defiance of, the divine will. The character of God is demonstrated by the events of history, never by pure reason alone. It is a striking fact that Israel's monotheism came to its full glory and maturity after the nation had fallen and the righteousness of God had been tragically verified. In national defeat was seen convincing proof of the reality of the God of history.

The national tragedy, which such prophets as the Second Isaiah turned into spiritual triumph, rested upon the fact of man's rebellious will. His collective sin lay in flaunting the will of God and in worshiping the gods which he had made with his own hands but which actually were the projections of his own unregenerate desires. Herein the nature of man as set forth in the Old Testament is clearly described. Man through his creation has a spiritual nature, a capacity for worship and moral commitment, and the power to deny his divine sonship in sinfulness and self-centered living. He is therefore capable of sinning not because he is naturally depraved but because he is free to choose whom he will serve. Here also the experience of the community and of its individual members serves to authenticate this conception of man. Man is made for God and goodness. When he wilfully sets his face against God, he brings ruin upon himself and upon his fellows. This realistic view of human nature receives abundant confirmation in the pages of the Old Testament. The candid portrayal found there is supported by the events of Hebrew history. What the Old Testament teaches us about man it makes convincing by showing us man in action.

What has been written relative to the ideas of God and man to illustrate the principles of logical consistency and empirical veri-

fication could be expanded to include other major conceptions appropriate in a complete theology. For these ideas this essay might attempt the use of a third criterion—that of conformity with the discoveries of the scientists—and might seek to show how what is scientifically known about man and the social order is not necessarily in contradiction to biblical views. If these views can be shown to meet the pragmatic test of experience, as argued above, they might also be capable of meeting the test of natural science. However, enough has been presented, it is hoped, to support this writer's position with respect to the possibility of a genuine Old Testament theology and the method to be used in determining its nature.

Upon the basis of a thoroughly critical approach to the Old Testament, whereby the literature, its setting, history, and text are rigorously scrutinized and its awareness of a supernatural order is given as much weight as its record of sociological and historical data, a true Old Testament theology may be formulated. This theology will be both descriptive of a particular culture and normative for a religious faith which transcends all cultures. Here is an area of research in which biblical scholarship of today must apply itself with increasing diligence and passion, lest the religion of tomorrow be severed completely from the biblical revelation which gave it birth.

New Testament Theology in Transition

AMOS N. WILDER

University of Chicago

T HE predicament of New Testament theology and of biblical theology generally is now widely recognized. These disciplines fell upon evil days at the end of the last century; and, though a strong bid for survival continued to be made, especially in the Old Testament section, the continued use of the traditional terms for the changed subject matter had become problematical. Much of the dilemma can be recognized in the very name of the science; for we now see that it is an anachronism to seek a "theology" in the Bible and an error to distinguish an intellectual element in it from other elements. For what concerns the first term, "biblical," we now recognize how wholly artificial is any treatment of the content of the Scripture in either or both testaments in any kind of isolation from the nonbiblical background. For these and other reasons there has been a strong case for the abandonment of the discipline in favor of the less ambiguous undertaking indicated by the topic "the religion of the Bible" or "the religion of the New Testament."

I

Historians of the vicissitudes of biblical theology customarily point to the monograph of J. P. Gabler, published in 1787, on the proper distinction between biblical and dogmatic theology as the decisive landmark in the whole story, for with it began the pursuit of the task as a historical discipline in the modern sense. Its development and achievements in the intervening period have been very remarkable. All the tools and resources of modern

philology and historical studies have been brought to bear upon the religious conceptions of the Bible in a cumulative way. As a result, in many important respects our day has an understanding of the subject totally concealed from earlier periods.

It is a question, however, as to whether we should allow our conception of biblical theology and of its definition and content to be decided or largely determined by the interests of this period. From the vantage point of the middle of the twentieth century it is possible to see the period after Gabler —the period of such great scientific accomplishments—as only one among a number of periods of concern with this subject matter, whatever the nomenclature. Not only were there earlier periods in which an effort was made to set forth the theology of the Bible, by whatever name, but we now can recognize that the discipline has entered into a new phase in this last generation, a phase characterized by somewhat different interests in what concerns the content of the Bible and by different conditions in the larger outlook of all historical study.

Thus the period between the express formulation of the discipline by Gabler and the formulation, let us say, by W. Wrede in 1897,[1] may well in retrospect count as only one among a number of notable periods in the history of biblical theology—a period, like all others before and after, addicted to the presentation of the content of the Bible under particular presuppositions. This modern period, roughly identical with the rise and heyday of rationalism and historicism, will be seen to have had its peculiar virtues and to have made its unique contribution in much the same way that the period of the Reformation, for example, had its virtues and made its contribution. Present new orientations and curiosities give promise of making a new period in the discipline with new values, no doubt indebted to the earlier periods both as to content and as to method.

The period inaugurated by Gabler in biblical theology, which can be defined in terms of classical historical method, may be said to have come to an end in two senses. For one thing, his-

---

1. *Über Aufgabe und Methode der sogenannten neutestamentlichen Theologie* (Göttingen, 1897).

torical method is itself undergoing modification through its own logic and self-criticism. The character and limits of its task are better understood in the light of modern investigation into the philosophy of history and the philosophy of knowledge. But, concurrently with these trends, a subtle change is at work in modern man's interests, the kind of change which, whether for good or for evil, carries with it a displacement of all the cultural and intellectual activities of men. "If the interest is limited, so is the understanding" (Dilthey). But the interests that have underlain the rise and development of modern historical science have had their special limitations. New interests are emerging. No doubt we confront a period both of opportunity and of danger.

What we are fundamentally concerned with is the conception and exposition of the content of the Scriptures in what concerns their message and teaching, both religious and moral, together with the presuppositions that underlie these. The use of the term "biblical theology," which first appears in 1708 (with Haymann) and more clearly in 1757 (with Busching), and is defined in terms of historical method in 1787 (with Gabler), is less important than the task itself, which, in a true sense, is as old as the earliest canon. Various approaches to the task succeed one another; particular tools and resources are brought to bear upon it; but there persists, throughout, the constant operation of the understanding upon the content of the testaments.

The primitive church gave us no biblical theology by title; but, *pari passu* with the establishment of the canon, successive pre-Nicene spokesmen defended their views of it against what was thought to be false teaching within or without the faith by the presentation, according to their lights, of the content of revelation. It is true that we do not find here systematic statements. We must piece together the "biblical theology" of particular Fathers, gathering it up from separate and fragmentary evidence. But, nonetheless, we may gain a view of their various formulations of the substance of Scripture. The Apostolic Fathers, the apologists, and their successors, indeed, were not conscious of a distinction between the teaching of Scripture (as they

understood Scripture and canon in their respective cases) and doctrine as such.

Now this naïveté with regard to the Scripture, not to mention the defects, as we see it, of their methods of interpretation, constituted a grave liability. But there were compensating factors, in the light of which we shall be wise to reckon seriously with their understanding of the content of the canon and not to think that biblical theology begins with the eighteenth century. Indeed, their handicaps were, no doubt, compensated by the fact that the total world view of the age was more like that out of which at least the New Testament writings came; by the fact that the church was passing through experiences of persecution like those that conditioned the writing of many of the biblical books; even by the fact that their methods of interpretation, however defective in modern eyes, often resembled those used in certain of the biblical writings themselves.

We may cite one illustration of an insight safeguarded in the primitive period, though overlooked in large part throughout the modern period—an insight of which we are now again becoming aware as a result of the contemporary biblical theological revival. We refer to the *heilsgeschichtlich* understanding of the Bible, and we present it in the setting that Ethelbert Stauffer gives it in his recent *Theologie des Neuen Testaments*.[2]

The theological thinking of the primitive church is an ordering procedure. What is undertaken here is not an edifice of metaphysical concepts nor a constructive system, but an ordering activity of thought, exploring the theological interconnections of the various elements of our experience. And this is the answer they found to their inquiry: God has ordered all reality *historically*. It is in this sense that *Geschichtstheologie* is the canonical *Urform* of Christian thinking and of all systematic theology.[3]

But this is a datum which they found in Scripture, a datum with which they combated heresy and on the basis of which they elaborated their theology. We see "biblical theology" at work, though without the name; and we see the important recognition of the historical character of biblical religion and revelation.

2. Geneva, 1945.   3. *Ibid.*, p. 153.

To pass to the reformers: the circumstances of the Reformation called for a theology specifically biblical in character, and this imposed an intense effort to set forth the content of the Bible as they understood it. The reformers were more aware than the Fathers of the issues raised by the tasks of exegesis and interpretation; but, of course, they labored under immense handicaps here whether with regard to textual or to higher criticism, as we have come to understand them. It is our wont to say that they were led into error by their principle of the *perspicuitas* of Scripture and by the test of the analogy of faith which they applied to it. We have here, however, both liability and asset. The principle of *perspicuitas* of Scripture at least left open that recognition of a faculty in man as man capable of discerning meaning in the writings which some modern canons of interpretation have undervalued. As for the *analogia fidei*, while this meant an unwarranted systematizing of the diversity of Scripture, it at least had the merit of giving a prominent place to a crucial motif of the New Testament itself and one far more worthy of such emphasis than various conceptual doctrines underlined by systems of biblical theology in the later period. What was said above as to the favorable conditions for proper grasp of the Bible by the early Fathers applies also to the reformers. Such important aspects in the biblical experience and thought-world as church-state conflict, social pressures, eschatology, and the demonic were also present in the conditions of the sixteenth century. Moreover, the general cultural vitality and stature of the period constituted a favorable circumstance for significant interpretation.

When we pass to the period which saw the first appearance of an actually so-designated "biblical theology," is this not the chief point of difference, that the presentation of the content of the Bible is now motivated by different protagonists? Where the reformers had set forth their understanding of it and of its interpretation against the Roman view, now this understanding, whether of pietist or of rationalist, is set forth as the true "biblical" theology against Protestant scholastic and dogmatic formulations grounded on biblical proof-texts. When at the end of the eighteenth century Gabler invokes a strictly historical procedure,

he is likewise engaged in excluding a formulation viewed as dogmatic, though his own supposedly nondogmatic approach was qualified by presuppositions which characterized all the historical work of the new period which was to follow.

Rudolf Bultmann has drawn attention to presuppositions of the modern period of which many scholars down to the present day fail to take due account:

> Our traditional understanding of existence has been affected by that of more recent developments—namely, by rationalism, classicism and romanticism, by modern natural science and psychology, and by motifs of the Greek understanding of being and reality. The urgent question must therefore be raised with regard to our own understanding of existence and its accompanying concepts, as to how far they are relevant for the exegesis of the New Testament.

Bultmann illustrates the point by referring to the conceptions underlying the Pauline anthropology, pointing out that we interpret these on the basis of a quite different view of life from that in which they arose.[4]

Thus the work of any period will have its own advantages and disadvantages. Indeed, the faculties of human understanding are never mobilized in their totality in a given situation or period or by a given individual or school. The grasp of religious literature may be remarkably furthered by certain specially conditioned procedures at the same time that it is handicapped in respect to others. It is with such considerations in mind that we should approach the present predicament of biblical theology. For the modern spirit throughout has had its particular limitations in historical and theological study which need to be supplemented both by a return to the early Fathers and by new contemporary insights.

II

It is not our intention to retrace here the familiar story of the advance of New Testament theology in its context of biblical theology throughout the modern period.[5] In the most recent period,

4. "Die Bedeutung der 'dialektischen Theologie' für die neutestamentliche Wissenschaft," in his *Glauben und Verstehen* (Tübingen, 1933), p. 129.

5. See Martin Dibelius, "Biblische Theologie und biblische Religionsgeschichte. II. Des Neuen Testaments," in *Die Religion in Geschichte und Gegenwart* (2d. ed. 1927–32), I,

which particularly interests us, the issues and fortunes of the subject can be most adequately grasped by the reading of the Prefaces to the most notable works on the subject in which the successive writers criticize the methods of their predecessors and formulate their own views: thus, Bernard Weiss (1868), W. Beyschlag (1891), H. J. Holtzmann (1897), Heinrich Weinel (1913). After 1897, discussion has largely taken its departure from the monograph of Wrede, *Über Aufgabe und Methode der sogenannten neutestamentlichen Theologie*.[6] Throughout the whole period labors in this field developed in close relation with the advance of general New Testament studies. The drift of the whole movement was toward a presentation of New Testament theology as a particular arrangement of the religion of Jesus and of the early community.

Certain aspects of the later stages may be shown by turning to the Prefaces of Holtzmann and Weinel. The former criticizes Bernard Weiss's work on the ground that he artificially harmonizes the individual differences of the New Testament writings and figures. It is partly on dogmatic grounds that Weiss is confident that James and Paul are not in contradiction and that John and Revelation have their place "in the same head." Moreover, says Holtzmann, "forwards and backwards, all valid threads of connection with other conceptions are ignored or broken."[7] And in the New Testament itself the disconnections and varieties disappear, so that we have an artificial unity, a "well-ordered herbarium."

Beyschlag also, according to Holtzmann, conceals the difficulties of the task under a harmonizing method and an edifying aim. He mixes practical and scientific ends. His purpose is to present not just the raw materials in the sources but a constructive, even an artistic, interpretation, "in great living forms," by the aid of insight and divination. But this involves him, according to Holtzmann, in "a considerable display of the diviner's

---

1091–94. Also Clarence T. Craig, "Biblical Theology and the Rise of Historicism," *Journal of Biblical Literature*, LXII (December, 1943), 281–94.

6. Göttingen, 1897.

7. *Lehrbuch der neutestamentlichen Theologie* (Tübingen, 1897), p. 13.

426 SPECIAL STUDIES OF SALIENT PROBLEMS

phantasy." Instead of what we actually have in the New Testament—namely, unevennesses, rifts, and crevices—"here we have a smoothly polished surface in which the civilized theology of the time can see itself reflected."[8] In short, Beyschlag combines orthodoxy with historical science. But such science, Holtzmann objects, is properly untroubled over the distance, as wide as that between heaven and earth, which separates our present-day thinking and experience from that of the New Testament period. "That it is much more a problem of finding points of connection and antecedents in the thinking of post-exilic Judaism—any comprehension of this is altogether lacking in the case of Beyschlag."[9]

But those who followed Holtzmann found in him some of the same defects that characterized his predecessors. Though he took seriously the context of his subject matter in Judaism and in Hellenistic life, yet, like all the followers of F. C. Baur, he still thought in terms of separate systems of doctrine. And he was still the "liberal" interpreter in ways that the work of Wrede, Schweitzer, and others was to disallow. In the opening section of his *Biblische Theologie des Neuen Testaments*,[10] Weinel points this out. Benefiting by Wrede's monograph, he himself fixes attention on an exposition of the religion of the New Testament. The discipline should be entirely free of dogmatics. "Thus biblical theology passes no judgments on the value and truth of Christianity, but rather on its nature in comparison with other religions." On this view it can still serve dogmatics, he urges. Weinel is primarily concerned here, to use his own term, with the "morphology" of religion, and with that of the religion of the New Testament.

It is to the point to note that Feine, in the introductory chapter to his more conservative work,[11] insists on conceiving of his task as that of a Christian theologian "in the conviction of faith that the content of the New Testament is unique and still today normative for us." He justifies his pre-eminent concern with the canon and argues that Wrede's approach "would not bring us

8. *Op. cit.*, p. 16.   9. *Ibid.*   10. 4th ed.; Tübingen, 1928.
11. *Theologie des Neuen Testaments* (Leipzig, 1909; 7th ed., 1936).

necessarily to Christianity as it really was because one might fail to recognize in the witnesses (so analyzed) the authoritative expression of the pulsing life in those primitive Christian individuals and circles."[12] The religious-historical approach, he adds, has the effect of blinding men so that the full uniqueness of the Christian religion does not come into its own.

This brief review of the outstanding works up to the first World War is sufficient to indicate certain recurring issues, many of which have taken on an even sharper form in the period since then. These issues include the following: (1) Unity versus variety in the New Testament, an issue that carries with it the question as to whether there was or was not a marked cleavage between given figures and phases in the period. (2) Topical presentation (*Lehrbegriffen*) versus chronological presentation of the material, which had largely been settled in favor of the latter alternative, only later to be unsettled by the *geschichtstheologisch* pattern which combines the two. (3) A canonical emphasis versus a *religionsgeschichtlich* approach—a choice rather closely related to that between a normative and an objective appraisal of the New Testament. The second alternative here has widely prevailed but became so vulnerable to charges of antiquarianism and relativism that it has called forth a powerful reaction even among those lacking a dogmatic motive. (4) "Liberal" versus "postliberal" presuppositions and procedures. In one aspect the shift to the latter course here was a mere matter of the advance of scholarship. In another respect such scientific advance was combined with changes in the climate of thought to produce one or another of the new reactions against liberal biblical views now widely manifested.

III

We may turn now to the factors that have brought about a revival of New Testament theology. We have to do here particularly with the modern critique of historicism and of its operation within the discipline with which we are concerned. The rigorously historical approach is attacked, not because it is not devout but because it is said not to be truly historical.

12. *Ibid.* (7th ed.), p. 1.

The aspect of historicism with which we are here concerned may be called "empirical historicism," and here we borrow from an analysis by Dr. Richard Kroner:

Empirical historicism originates in the ambition of historical science to increase the objectivity of historical knowledge in competing with the natural sciences; it is the naturalistic trend of thought which is still at work in this type. . . . . The empirical historicist would like to resign all synthetic attempts, and to restrict his relations to those facts which can be ascertained by absolutely objective and exact methods. The final end of this tendency would reduce historical knowledge to a quasi-photographic reproduction of relics of whatever kind. . . . . It is utterly opposed to systematization and synopsis; it is in this sense utterly unphilosophic. Finally it arrives at bits of bits of life.[13]

Dr. Kroner illustrates by reference to the decomposition of Homer, of Goethe's *Faust*, of the *Critique of Pure Reason* and of the *Corpus juris*, and continues:

Analytical historicism kills the soul and retains the corpse. Even if we assume that the results of its endeavors are historically correct, still the procedure does not do justice to the real value and meaning of the victimized works.

It is true that modern historiography has sought to define itself in ways that would escape the limitations indicated above. Especially has this been true of religious historians. Ernst Troeltsch, for instance, sought to do this by underlining the differences between historical science and the natural sciences. Different subject matters dictate different methods. Nevertheless, Troeltsch's three laws of historical method, which include that of the essential uniformity of all occurrences and the relativity of all events, limit very strictly the kind of significance that can be assigned to particular historical events or experiences. In commenting on them, H. R. Mackintosh writes: "Christianity can no more be put in a universe like this than lightning in a match-box."[14]

13. "History and Historicism," *Journal of Bible and Religion*, Vol. XIV, No. 3 (August, 1946); see also the article in the same number by President George N. Shuster, "Historicism: The Approach of the Student of Literature and the Classics."

14. "Does the Historical Study of the Bible Yield a Dogmatic Theology?" *American Journal of Theology*, XIII, No. 4 (October, 1909), 511.

The commonest charge made against the treatment of the New Testament in the works under attack is that the end results are so disappointing. In these *disjecta membra* of early Christian life, these facts without interpretation, in this alleged antiquarianism and relativism, there is, it is claimed, a self-evident inadequacy to the reality and a lack of verisimilitude in the picture. The most formidable expression of these charges came in the Preface to the second edition of Karl Barth's *Epistle to the Romans*. This bore particularly upon the standard commentaries on the New Testament, but the implications involved New Testament theology. Dibelius in his article in the second edition of *Religion in Geschichte und Gegenwart*, referred to above, includes the task of *Zusammenfassung* of the material among those left over by the recent history of the discipline. In his lecture, "The Present Task of New Testament Studies," in 1936, C. H. Dodd called for a centripetal movement to succeed the centrifugal one that had prevailed, and for "a study of the unity of the process which created the parts, an effort to interpret the deeper meanings of the dominant themes and translate them into contemporary terms."

Yet the charges of irrelevancy and antiquarianism do not furnish a fully cogent or decisive case against the prevailing historical methodology. After all, we wish to know what the demonstrable facts are; and, if the number of these facts is limited, it is of the first importance that we know this, too. We may demur at the reticence of such scholarship, but we should be grateful for its scruples and its exactness.

A more serious and more technical charge against historicism has to do with the inadequacy of the genetic and evolutionary assumptions involved in its work and its view of causal relations. Illustration of these matters can be offered from recent discussion in the biblical and particularly the New Testament fields. Dr. W. F. Albright in his *From the Stone Age to Christianity*[15] gives particular attention to these topics in modern biblical historiography, basing his critique on a canvass of recent work in the philosophy of history. One theme to which he recurs is the false unilinear interpretations of the development of biblical religion,

15. Baltimore, 1940.

interpretations which thereupon become "beds of Procrustes" into which the facts are forced.[16] Overly simple schemes, which block out the evolution of history in general (Hegel) or of religion and culture (Comte) or of Old Testament history (Vatke, Wellhausen) or (we can add) New Testament history (the Tübingen School or, indeed, the more recent liberal school identified with Harnack)—all these break down under the test of the facts. Dr. Albright and others find justification for this revolt in the replacement today of older rationalist or positivist views of history by organismic conceptions.

The relevance of this for New Testament theology lies in the fact that vindication is thus found in contemporary social philosophy for its efforts to read the historical phenomena of its period in dramatic and organismic ways. This impulse to go beyond historicism's "wie es eigentlich gewesen" and even its "wie es eigentlich geworden" to synoptic interpretation is not an arbitrary impulse of the historian, says Albright. It is rather justified by the fact that human life moves in patterns and configurations, whether we consider the life of an individual or a nation, whether we describe the movement of a culture or the development of thought. It is the inner compulsion of the underlying drama of history which has led nearly every great historian of the past to write history in essentially dramatic terms.[17] But C. H. Dodd, working with Arnold Toynbee's conceptions of the history of cultures, has made very suggestive proposals along these lines, looking toward unifying conceptions for the New Testament subject matter.[18] The point here is that synoptic efforts toward a New Testament theology can be grounded in the work of social science, whatever recourse may ultimately be made to dogmatic considerations.

Other aspects of the critique of historicism can best be illustrated in the work of Rudolf Bultmann. As against a naïve evolutionism, which exaggerates the significance of the later stages of a cultural or religious development, Bultmann writes: "In-

---

16. *Ibid.*, p. 50.   17. *Ibid.*, p. 48.

18. *The Apostolic Preaching* (Chicago, 1937), Appendix, "Eschatology and History," pp. 135–67.

sight into man's existence can be more genuine at a 'primitive' stage of culture and science than at a highly developed one."[19] Thus he points out that the idea of *mana* is depreciated as primitive and its New Testament manifestations are judged in these terms. We ought rather to ask ourselves, he says, what view of existence comes to expression in the *mana* conception. Evidently, it is a conception of man as one standing amid the enigmatic and the mysterious:

May it not be that a much more correct insight into the existence of men voices itself in the belief in *mana* than in the world-picture of the Stoa or of modern natural science, even though this last be much more highly developed scientifically than the "primitive" world-picture.[20]

Bultmann illustrates further by the contrast between the oriental conception of the "word" or speech of the deity—a view which brings into high relief the fact that the course of existence is not at our disposal—as against the Stoic or modern concept of the Logos.

Another pertinent theme appears in Bultmann's essays,[21] one, indeed, immediately related to existential philosophy but whose validity can be more widely based. Whatever higher meanings may work themselves out in the development of religion or culture, there is, nonetheless, a vast area in the most significant experience of man which does not greatly change. Man as a creature is always "open" to the perpendicular dimension, whatever his place in the horizontal nexus of historical and social process. This opens up a wide field of possible comment. Martin Dibelius in different terms fixes attention upon this oversight of historicism in pointing to one of the unsolved issues in contemporary New Testament theology. The historian, he says, cannot neglect the sphere of the *übergeschichtlich*. "The scholar will guard the seriousness and purity of historical research the more surely, the more he safeguards the freedom and opportunity that is his to present the *übergeschichtlich* content of the New Testament.[22]

The revival of a synoptic emphasis in the presentation of the

19. *Op. cit.*, p. 121.
20. *Ibid.*, pp. 121, 122.   21. *Ibid.*, *passim.*
22. *Die Religion in Geschichte und Gegenwart* (2d ed.), I, 1094.

content of the New Testament justifies itself from these considerations. No doubt other motives have been at work. The recent period has been one of renewed interest in theology and in the history of Christian thought, and this has focused attention upon the New Testament as offering the first chapter in the development of Christian theology. Meanwhile, interest in the history of religions seems unfortunately to have declined somewhat. To a certain extent the emergency situation of many of the churches has placed a premium upon study of the New Testament outlook and insights and even led to confessional presentations of this subject matter built on insecure critical foundations. More generally, there has arisen a new desire to make available to Christian workers and laymen the results of modern scholarship as they bear on the teaching and religion of the the canon.[23] But a more significant factor still is the incentive drawn from new insights into New Testament religion, resulting in large part from critical study itself.

IV

This paper with its necessary limitations of space cannot present the content of New Testament theology today as illuminated by recent work. Our aim has been to define the dilemma in which the discipline stands and to call attention to the issues involved. There are, however, three matters that call for brief treatment as we conclude.

1. *Unity and variety in the New Testament.*—The very conception of a New Testament theology presupposes a likeness of the writings and a real distinction between them and other writings. These assumptions collide with the fact that the books of the New Testament exhibit sharp variations and dissonances, if not contradictions, and with the fact that there are important continuities between canonical and noncanonical documents. Yet the unity of the canon can be maintained. This unity has been sought unsatisfactorily in various ways: (*a*) Orthodoxy and

23. Stauffer, *op. cit.*, Foreword; see also Millar Burrows, "The Task of Biblical Theology," *Journal of Bible and Religion*, XIV, No. 1 (February, 1946), 13; and R. C. Dentan, "The Nature and Function of Old Testament Theology," *Journal of Bible and Religion*, XIV, No. 1 (February, 1946), 20, 21.

traditionalism find this unity (together with that of the whole Bible) in terms of a common special inspiration or in terms of "the plan of salvation" or in the recognition of Christ as the "center" of the Bible. But these views resort to harmonization and allegory to reach their end. (*b*) Liberalism, which was obliged to recognize an anticlimax in the New Testament after Jesus, could never make more than a halfhearted claim for its unity. (*c*) The back-to-tradition movement (B. W. Bacon *et al.*) saw the unity in the evangelical message of the Cross but took this in individualistic terms. (*d*) Certain writers make a too simple distinction between the common underlying message and its various "forms of expression,"[24] as though the latter were not of the essence of the writers' doctrines. The most satisfactory presentation of this unity is in terms of *Heilsgeschichte*.[25] This takes up the ancient conception of the plan of salvation but corrects it by a better understanding of the biblical view of history, of the people of God, and of eschatology.

As to the canon, the distinctiveness of the New Testament writings can be maintained without denying the close relation to them of many of the noncanonical writings. These twenty-seven writings were born out of an intense and incomparable experience of the confrontation of creature with creator, of sin with holiness, and of time with eternity. These writings have both a high voltage and a high amperage, to use a figure. Ignatius' letters have the voltage but not the amperage. We thus have abundant justification for turning our attention particularly to the canon. The *Heilsgeschichte* criterion corroborates this. Outside the New Testament in one or another of the writings we pass from eschatology to martyrology, from resurrection to immortality, from redemption from sin to redemption from ignorance, from faith to gnosis, from God both Creator and Redeemer to God the Redeemer alone. At some point we shall recognize

24. Cf. E. F. Scott, *The Varieties of New Testament Religion* (New York, 1943).

25. Stauffer, *op. cit.*; A. M. Hunter, *The Unity of the New Testament* (London, 1943), esp. pp. 9, 10; cf. C. H. Dodd, *The Apostolic Preaching* (Chicago, 1937); F. V. Filson, *One Lord, One Faith* (Philadelphia, 1943); Oscar Cullmann, *Christus und die Zeit: Die urchristliche Zeit- und Geschichtsauffassung* (Zurich, 1946).

the attenuation of the realism of the biblical theology of history.[26] The canon of the New Testament is the literary deposit of the catastrophic cultural and religious break between Judaism and Christianity.[27] The profound elements of distinctiveness and unity far outweigh the important divergencies.

2. *Objectivity and Christian presuppositions in the exposition.*— One can distinguish three different levels at which the theology of the New Testament can be presented.

a) The matter can be set forth according to the strictest requirements of scientific method. This is, in any case, an absolutely essential foundation for treatment at any other level. The historian should not, however, imply in any way that the limited results so attained either exhaust the evidence (since there is much evidence at hand not amenable to his method) or dictate the general conclusions.

b) The matter can be set forth as above but with the addition of a judicious element of synthesis, *Zusammenfassung*, or synoptic endeavor. The boundary line between the two levels should remain clear. But all truly significant writing of history, as distinguished from the ordering of data, requires of the writer that he takes the risks of some venture into interpretation and synthesis.[28] The term "empathy" is frequently used to describe the qualification most needed for this role. It is here, too, that the important elements in the subject matter not amenable to scientific method proper call for incorporation into the total picture. Moreover, the fact that life and process manifest themselves in patterns and in organic forms makes it the responsibility of the historian to identify and bring to light such patterns and organic relationships in his material. It is at this level also that a recourse to symbolic and mytho-poetic presentation of aspects of the matter—a form of presentation not permitted at the first level—becomes essential if its full reality is to be conveyed.

26. See Th. Preiss, "Le Mystique de l'imitation du Christ et de l'unité chez Ignace d'Antioche," *Revue d'histoire et de philosophie religieuses*, XVIII (1938), 197–241.

27. Albright, *op. cit.*, p. 85.

28. John Knox, *Christ the Lord* (Chicago, 1945), pp. 3–5.

c) The matter can be set forth in a third way, if not at a still higher level, utilizing the results of the two previous ones, in specifically confessional terms by the Christian scholar. In this case again, there should be no confusion: the writer of such a New Testament theology candidly states his purpose and his presuppositions. He approaches the records from within the community of faith. His claim will be that this is the most advantageous *locus* for the interpretation of writings produced by that community. In much of the task there will or should be no difference between the Christian scholar and the non-Christian scholar or the scholar who in this task seeks to make abstraction of his Christian connection. But the Christian scholar will not be persuaded that, other things being equal, his viewpoint from within the tradition will not immensely illuminate his grasp of the material.[29] Warning, however, should here be voiced against all uncontrolled "pneumatic" exegesis or other forms of arbitrary interpretation. All biblical theology that offers itself as avowedly confessional must run a double gauntlet and is subject to a double correction, that of rigorous historical science, first of all, but also that of other Christian biblical interpreters. It is subject to the test of both reason and the Holy Spirit.

3. *The most promising contemporary approach to the task.*—This lies along the lines denoted by *Heilsgeschichte* and *Geschichtstheologie*.[30] These terms indicate the fundamental conception of the subject and suggest the proper manner of presentation. So viewed, the theology of the New Testament presents the divine plan and the course of divine action from a point before time, through history, to a point beyond time in a history of salvation which is also a history of the totality of existence. The writings of the New Testament taken together present this world picture, some documenting certain aspects of the whole process, others documenting others, but all the writings in their conceptions belonging within the common world view. This historical realism of the Bible, this sense of the creative and redemptive process, in

---

29. *Ibid.*, p. 6; cf., however, W. A. Irwin, "The Reviving Theology of the Old Testament," *Journal of Religion*, XXV, No. 4 (October, 1945), 241, 242.

30. For a recent work organized throughout upon these lines see Stauffer, *op. cit.*

which providence, history, community, conflict with evil powers, and eschatology have so large a place, forbids a presentation in terms of static or conceptual doctrines or phases of religious experience or piecemeal documents. And this view corrects the approach of the dialectical theology; for here revelation is embodied in a thoroughgoing and inextricable way in the process of history—indeed, it is hidden, for the superficial observer, in the context of the relative—and not imposed upon it or abstracted from it. This approach also corrects the method of historicism, which fails to give full recognition to the dramatic and organic unity of the canon and which, in its concern for the morphology of religion and the morphology of the religion of the separate writings and figures, loses sight of the over-all picture of the world process. Such an approach renews the insights of the premodern period, while benefiting by the contributions of modern scholarship, and has the further merit of reading the New Testament more fully in the light of its own presuppositions.

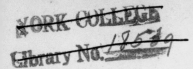